The Family in Bahia, Brazil, 1870-1945

The Family
in Bahia, Brazil
1870-1945

Dain Borges

Stanford University Press
Stanford, California
1992

Stanford University Press
Stanford, California
© 1992 by the Board of Trustees of the
Leland Stanford Junior University
Printed in the United States of America

CIP data appear at the end of the book

Published with the assistance of a special grant from the
Stanford University Faculty Publication Fund to help support
nonfaculty work originating at Stanford

Acknowledgments

EVERY WORK of historical scholarship is in some part a collaboration; many people and institutions contributed to making this book possible. I am grateful to the principal patrons of this project, the Henry L. and Grace Doherty Foundation, which supported research in Brazil in 1981, and the University of Pennsylvania Research Foundation, which supported summer research in Brazil in 1987.

A number of institutions also contributed materially to my research by giving me access to their collections and facilities. They include, in Bahia, the Instituto Geográfico e Histórico da Bahia, the Arquivo Público do Estado da Bahia, the Centro de Estudos Bahianos and its Frederico Edelweiss library, the Arquivo Municipal da Cidade de Salvador, the Biblioteca da Faculdade de Medicina da Bahia, the Arquivo da Cúria Metropolitana de Salvador, and the Instituto Feminino da Bahia; in Rio de Janeiro, the Arquivo do Instituto Histórico e Geográfico Brasileiro, the Casa de Rui Barbosa, and the Biblioteca Nacional; and in the United States, the Stanford-Berkeley Center for Latin American Studies, and the libraries of Stanford University and the University of Pennsylvania.

The generous help of Maria Amélia Ferreira de Almeida, Johildo Athayde, Thales de Azevedo, Eliane de Azevedo, James Goodyear, Anna Amália Vieira Nascimento, José Gabriel Costa Pinto, João Reis, Consuelo Pondé de Sena, Luis Henrique Dias Tavares, Hildegardes Vianna, Fayette Wimberley, and many others made possible my research in Brazil. Amy Iwata, Jorge Antonio do Espíritu Santo Batista, Shannon Clark, and Julia Scott provided patient collaboration in the collection and analysis of archival and demographic data.

As the ideas for this research developed over time, I have had the help of many teachers. Before I had envisioned this project, John Womack's lectures showed me how a history of family structure could speak about classes and culture. I am indebted to him for many questions and categories that I have used. John Wirth's example and guidance turned me toward Brazil and the Old Republic, and Harry Makler introduced me to Bahia. Richard Morse posed many questions that I have explored here and offered many insights into Brazilian society. I am most grateful for his subtle guidance and criticism.

I am grateful as well to Thales de Azevedo, Sheila Borges, Renato Boschi, Nancy Farriss, Efraín Kristal, Joseph Love, Maria Lúcia Afonso Medeiros, Jeffrey Needell, Scott Mainwaring, Rodolfo Pastor, Paul Robinson, Thom Whigham, John Wirth, Michael Zuckerman, and others for reading and criticizing portions of this work, in this and earlier versions.

Many scholars shared unpublished research with me, and theses and dissertations are cited in the bibliography. But I am particularly indebted to Harry Makler, Kátia Mattoso, Johildo Athayde, Bert Barickman, and Julyan Peard for generously furnishing portions of their research.

D. B.

Contents

Maps, Chart, and Tables

Note on Orthography, Naming Conventions, and Currency

PORTUGUESE and Brazilian orthography has changed several times. Not all Brazilian authors and publishers have chosen to follow official conventions. To offer only one example, some authors now differentiate the spelling of "Bahia," with "Baia" designating the state and "Bahia" designating the city, but not all Bahian authors have accepted this usage. Not all Brazilian families accept the modernized spelling of their personal names. I have preferred Gilberto Freyre to Gilberto Freire, Juracy Magalhães to Juraci Magalhães, and Goes Calmon to Góis Calmon. However, the text generally follows contemporary usage, and the notes and bibliography follow original spellings.

Brazilian naming conventions are also inconsistent. The text generally follows conventional Brazilian usage, which may refer to individuals by their first names ("Rui," for Rui Barbosa), by their titles ("Cotegipe," for João Maurício Wanderley, barão de Cotegipe), or by some portion of their surnames ("Machado," for Joaquim Maria Machado de Assis). The bibliography and footnotes alphabetize surnames by the last surname. Thus "João da Costa Pinto" would be ordered alphabetically under "Pinto." Pseudonyms or shortened names are treated as surnames. Thus, Antônio Cândido [de Mello e Souza] is ordered under "Cândido."

Brazilian currency changed in 1942, when the government converted units of milreis, 1,000 reis (expressed as 1$000 or 1$), and contos, 1,000 milreis (1:000$000 or 1:), into units of cruzeiros ($1 or CR$1,00). At that time, one cruzeiro equaled one milreis. In the late nineteenth century, a conto exchanged for approximately U.S.$550. In the early twentieth century, the exchange rate fluctuated in the range of U.S.$135–$330; after World War I, it generally fell below $130. For the exchange rate series, 1880–1937, see Joseph Love, *São Paulo in the Brazilian Federation.*

The Family in Bahia, Brazil, 1870-1945

Introduction

THE FAMILIES of the Bahian upper class offer a vantage point from which to examine the changes in Brazilian culture around the turn of the twentieth century. Slow, yet palpable, shifts in mentalities, in customs, and in the informal organization of Brazilian society manifested themselves partly as changes in the family. Bahian families also provide a touchstone by which to measure the effects of official social reforms. The government, the Catholic church, the medical profession, and free-lance social movements such as feminism all tried to reform the Bahian family. But their leverage was feeble, and the outcomes they achieved were sometimes unexpected. Between 1870 and 1945 Bahian families changed, partly in response to exhortations, fads, new laws, and new ideologies. But they transformed themselves largely in response to an insecure and urbanizing economy. The shifts were subtle, and to a great extent they left intact the traditional structures.

The primary change in Bahian families was a shift from a more patriarchal model of the family toward one that was more "companionate" in marriage, and more "conjugal" or "nuclear" in its definition of kinship. This sort of change was not unique to Brazil. A similar shift occurred in many parts of the world in the nineteenth and twentieth centuries. But Brazilian culture seems to have resisted this change, perhaps more than was the case in Europe. Brazilian families preserved many of their traditional features, such as extended kinship affiliation. On the one hand, the Brazilian family became deceptively similar to the family in France or the United States; on the other hand, it retained customs and roles that seemed exotic to outsiders, such as the preference for endogamous marriage or the routines of *a vida em família,* "life in the family circle."[1]

The ambivalent transformation of Bahian families reflected the ambivalent way in which Brazilians built a civil society in the nineteenth and twen-

tieth centuries. The history of the upper-class family in this period inter-
sects with the general history of state-building. Brazilian state-building
included the deliberate establishment of formal institutions, both govern-
mental and private, that attempted to regulate or guide the family. But "the
family" itself was an informally organized institution, not planned by any
central policy; it was formed instead through the results of myriad separate
decisions by thousands of families. In fact, focusing on the Bahian family
highlights the special nature of official state-building efforts in Brazil.

The family is obviously a unique "institution," and to speak of it in the
same terms as the Catholic church or the medical profession requires a
broad definition. In Brazil the colloquial sense of *instituição*, or "institution," is that of a large, organized public establishment, such as a school,
a hospital, a factory, a museum. To some extent, it is the antithesis of a
family. Within this definition there is also a more focused use of the word
as a euphemism for "insane asylum." There is also a secondary and figura-
tive sense in which an institution is an embodiment of authority, especially
long-established authority: an old street vendor can be an "institution"
in her neighborhood. As Raymond Williams points out for the English
language, the root of the word in the active verb "to institute," meaning
to found or establish, has turned nearly into its opposite, to mean something that is permanent and traditional.[2] However, in worldwide scholarly
usage, and particularly in anthropology, the definition of "institution" has
been extended to cover virtually any sort of patterned behavior, and it is
in this sense that I speak of both "the family" and "the Catholic church"
as institutions.

To clarify how the family and formal institutions are different, it is useful
to distinguish between an institution and an organization. An institution
is a set of roles that authorizes or encourages people to act in certain ways
at certain times. An organization is an attempt to embody and fulfill these
roles. For example, "the university" is an institution; the Universidade
Federal da Bahia is an organization. The family is an institution; the Prado
family of São Paulo was an organization. Institutions are not Platonic
ideals; they must be organized to exist. A single institution can be organized in two, or three, or more quite different ways.[3] Consequently, the
distinction between formal institutions and informal institutions can turn
on the way in which these institutions are organized. Formal institutions
usually develop charters, bylaws, constitutions, or guidelines. Because of
this, their values are often made explicit and easily accessible. Informal
institutions such as families do not always have, or need, an explicit organization. They may in fact be intangible, or invisible as "institutions" in
the colloquial sense of the word. Usually, formal and informal institutions
are studied in different ways. Anthropology, with its interest in primitive

and nonliterate societies, has developed the study of informal institutions most thoroughly.

Conflicts over building the state in nineteenth- and twentieth-century Brazil included many attempts at reform of the upper-class family through formal institutions. Examination of these formal institutions makes most sense in reference to the upper-class family. It would be a mistake to assume that Brazilian elites thought primarily of transforming the families and the lives of the masses. Nineteenth-century Brazil was a slave society, and the paternalistic or crudely exploitative attitude that the upper classes held toward the people made it quite plausible to ignore them, to leave them alone. Twentieth-century Brazilian elites generally continued to neglect the lives of the poor. After 1930 the state became more concerned with the people, but in the 1990's authentic social citizenship is still at issue in Brazil.[4]

Sometimes inappropriately, institutional strategies with regard to family aligned with political positions. At least two major positions on the family aligned easily with political programs. Both were fairly well agreed on the significance of the actually existing customs and laws regarding the family. One was the liberal position, which in the early nineteenth century saw its goal as creating a society stripped of privileges and "feudal" statuses. It supported laws with egalitarian implications. For example, laws defining the emancipation of young men from parental authority were all of a piece with emancipation from slavery and from Portuguese colonialism. The other was the conservative position. It supported traditional authorities within and over the family, and it resisted attempts to reduce the prerogatives of fathers over other family members. In the early decades of independence it was associated with an aristocratic political project; but from the late nineteenth century onward it was usually associated with a generalized social conservatism and the defense of "order."

These articulate "elite" positions on the family and its place in society confronted an inarticulate traditional Brazilian model of the family. In colonial Brazil, popular norms of the family had developed differently than in Western Europe. In a slave-owning plantation society established on an open frontier, many of the old tensions and checks and balances on Portuguese families simply did not apply. In the sixteenth and seventeenth centuries, powerful families, particularly the owners of large plantation estates and sugar mills, had been able to arrange their affairs in near-baronial independence of government rule. Private power really was great when measured against a feeble, indifferent, royal administration and a weak church. The private power of great families in the countryside was not challenged by urbanizing, centralizing pressures such as existed in France and Portugal.[5]

In Brazil, the combination of a frontier society's lack of supervisory institutions and the power relationships cultivated in slave societies probably did create a model of the family that was exaggeratedly "patriarchal." Gilberto Freyre did not invent the label "patriarchal family" in *The Masters and the Slaves* (1933); it had been used by Brazilian historians and legislators at least as far back as the 1890's and revived by Oliveira Vianna in the 1920's. But Freyre popularized it in connection with a flattering and aesthetically intriguing argument about Brazilian national culture. It is fair to say that all subsequent discussion of "patriarchalism" in Brazilian society and culture has derived from Freyre.[6]

His definition of patriarchy, like those of most social thinkers, mixed together several definitions or elements of patriarchy.[7] At times Freyre seemed to identify it with an economic system of production in which the self-sufficient extended household produced and distributed most goods and services. His model of the Big House of the plantation was that of a near-autarchic emporium, "at one and the same time a fortress, a bank, a cemetery, a hospital, a school, and a house of charity giving shelter to the aged, the widow, and the orphan."[8] For Freyre the identification between the house and the family was overwhelming. Houses shaped and formed the lives lived in them. Thus the household economy of patriarchalism ought to accompany the patriarchal authority of masterly men.

At other times, Freyre identified patriarchy simply with the power of the father over others in the family: wife, daughters, and all women; sons, sons-in-law, and all younger men; servants, slaves, and dependents. As such, patriarchy was a power relationship identified with masculinity, fatherhood, and mastery, but one that could at times be embodied in persons who were not slave-owning sugar mill lords.

Women, too, could act patriarchally, could take on the patriarchal role. Of course, prepotent men filled out the contours of the garment best. In this definition of patriarchalism, Freyre showed the influence of Freud and the European psychologists. Patriarchy was a sort of power, or authority, that had emanated historically from the slave-owning Brazilian household, but that had become so deeply imprinted in Brazilian collective memory (only a generation back, in Freyre's childhood) that he believed it was a major component of the contemporary propensity for political authoritarianism.

Freyre's definition of patriarchy was above all part of a positive, affirming definition of national identity. He argued that familiarity and racial confraternization were the happy by-products of the rape of Indian and African women by Portuguese men. In his psychodrama of Brazilian national origins, the Portuguese father established a sort of harem in the Big House, begetting children with Indian, African, and Portuguese mothers and so mixing and combining their original cultures. From this promiscuity (in all the meanings of the word) emerged a racial democracy, a recognition of mutual descent and mutual influence. The son who was heir to the three streams of culture, of course, was the upper-class Brazilian male, psychologically even when not biologically mulatto.[9]

Freyre's model of the Brazilian family in the colonial period and the early nineteenth century prevailed partly because of the appeal of this portrait of national character, and partly because of its scholarly merits. Influenced by the emerging cultural anthropology of Boas and the Columbia anthropologists, it emphasized nurture and nutrition, rather than race, as the determining factors in national development.

It displaced previous discussions of the family by Brazilian scholars, which had centered on categories of race: either as physical type, as genealogical lineage and heredity, or as national spirit.[10] The thesis on "race" that was the most direct antecedent of Gilberto Freyre's, and that Freyre answered in *The Masters and the Slaves*, was the argument of Oliveira Vianna in *Populações meridionais do Brasil* (1920) and *Evolução do povo brasileiro* (1922). In these works Vianna discussed the formation of the Brazilian population in ethnic terms, combining racial and environmental factors. His racist thesis, that Brazil was enjoying progressive "Aryanization" through immigration and natural selection, prevented many people, then and now, from giving him a serious hearing. But before Freyre he did center a political history on the role of the "patriarchal" family and its monopoly of power in the formation of Brazilian society.[11]

Since the publication of *The Masters and the Slaves* in 1933 and its companion volume, *The Mansions and the Shanties*, in 1936, most progress in understanding the Brazilian family has taken the form of revisionist studies pointing out that the patriarchal family was not the single and universal form of the family in Brazil.[12] The most pertinent critics of Freyre, almost from the moment of the publication of *The Masters and the Slaves*, but certainly after 1950, pointed out that most Brazilians were not the children of sugar mill lords, but rather of slaves, squatters, dirt farmers, and city folk. Of course, emphasis on the diversity of forms of the Brazilian family was not entirely new; it had been anticipated by the trailblazer of Brazilian sociology, the positivist philosopher and folklorist Sylvio Romero, whose essay *O Brasil social* (1907) had tried to apply Frederic Le Play's monographic method to understanding the family types pertaining to climatic zones in Brazil.[13]

The best early criticism of Freyre's work came from the São Paulo sociologist Antônio Cândido, who generally agreed with Freyre's vision of the patriarchal family, and who like Freyre saw it in decline. However, Cândido also saw other sorts of families. His essay "The Brazilian Family" (1951) reinterpreted Freyre's thesis by conceiving of differences in family

types as distances from the patriarchal family and its clientele. He distinguished between the legitimate "nucleus" and the bastard "periphery" of
the patriarchal family, arguing that the nucleus had influenced the periphery: "Anchored in the midst of a genuine sexual chaos, it served, on the
one hand, as a stabilizing force, and created not merely a tradition of disciplined life but penetrated with its regulatory power into the chaos and
formed Christian and monogamous families in the midst of slavery." Entirely outside this familial part of society was a nonfamilial mass of social
castoffs, who "reproduced themselves haphazardly and lived without regular norms of conduct." In the nineteenth and twentieth centuries, both the
periphery and the nonfamilial mass had become autonomous and had con-
verged to form monogamous families.[14] If there was any form of the family
other than the patriarchal family, it did not constitute a model, or paradigm, for Cândido. His interpretation of Brazilian society, at least in his
reading of the nineteenth-century picaresque novel *Memoirs of a Sergeant
in the Militia*, was that a realm of order (represented by the patriarchal
household) ruled over a society composed of ever-widening rings of disorder.[15] The nonpatriarchal family did not have an order of its own; it was
not an institution; it was rather a lack of order and a lack of institutions.

In the 1960's and 1970's most research in Brazilian family history
adopted its agenda from European and North American historiography
rather than from the debate over the theses of Freyre. In the 1970's both
Brazilian historians and North American Brazilianists shifted their attention toward the styles and preoccupations of French social history.
Demographic evidence contributed to works of all sorts, but it was a central theme of research on Bahian populations and economies, on the early
social structure of São Paulo, and on the development of Minas Gerais
during and after its gold rush.[16] Sometimes directly, often indirectly, this
demographic research threw new light on the organization of families.
Similarly, research in the social history of colonial institutions, such as
the charitable Santa Casa da Misericórdia or the High Court of Appeals,
illuminated the workings of families.[17] Important insights into the family
have emerged from studies of slavery, plantations, and political bossism.[18]
But historians have not to date arrived at a synthesis that can contend with
Freyre's tale of the disintegration of the patriarchal family. The closest
approach to a contemporary countersynthesis is Eni Mesquita Samara's
A família brasileira (1985), a short essay that centers largely around a
rebuttal of the thesis of the universality of the patriarchal family.[19]

One possible outcome of the maturation of the field of Brazilian family
studies may be an overturning of its perspective that will regard the family
of the people, the *povo*, as "normal" and the patriarchal family of the
elite as a "deviant" variant. In her study of slave, freed, and free families

in nineteenth-century Bahia, Kátia Mattoso has laid the groundwork for study of the differentiated, but overlapping, forms of family in Brazil that decenters each of the types, not privileging any of them.[20] Another possible outcome of the growth of the field may be its fragmentation. Families in different ecological niches, different classes, or different milieus may come to be studied individually and in response to their precise circumstances, much as Sylvio Romero would have wished. Either of these outcomes of the directions Brazilian family studies are taking would necessarily develop alternatives to the hegemony of Freyre's patriarchal family thesis.

This study argues that we need to see the many forms of the family in Brazil as they existed as recognizable options or alternatives. People of different classes had a general, if sometimes caricatured, sense of what one another's families were like. Not only did the lower classes, who rarely married, have a vision of the model of the patriarchal family, but the upper classes had some perception of the typical family lives of other classes. For example, rich Brazilians knew of consensual unions. Probably most upper-class men had mistresses from the lower class during the long years between puberty and the customary age of marriage at thirty. Everyone understood that it was common for men to father illegitimate children before establishing a legal family. Upper-class Brazilians lamented "immorality," and in their formal writings could not acknowledge these norms, but in practice they lived with illegitimate families as an ever-present and important model of behavior. There was a tacitly recognized, informal institution of the illegitimate family that had more weight in Brazil than in many other societies.

This study deals primarily with the families of the upper classes, partly because the sources available for the study of upper-class Brazilians are much more varied than those on the lives of the poor. Many sources afford glimpses into the imagination and ideas of the poor, but they cannot compare with what we can learn of the mental lives and values of prosperous Brazilians. For example, this study makes extensive use of memoirs and private correspondence, and virtually all the extant documents of this kind are by upper- and middle-class individuals. It uses the newspapers, which were written by and for the literate upper ranks of society. And it uses Brazilian fiction, primarily realist and satirical novels, which were written for a cultivated audience and often from an upper-class stance. For similar reasons, this study focuses on the capital city of Salvador and the traditional heart of the province, the Recôncavo plantation counties around the Bay of All Saints. This region was the center of population and of the economic and political life of Bahia during the Empire. The identification of city and province was so strong that the city of Salvador was often called "Bahia" by Brazilians inside and outside the province. Although the scope of this study extends occasionally to other regions, such as the backlands fringes and the southern cacao frontier, the official archival sources and the literature of memoirs, biographies, and genealogies are richest for the Recôncavo. The scope of its conclusions should thus be carefully surveyed. There is much to learn of the Brazilian people from the study of the upper class; there is much to learn of Rio Grande do Sul from the study of the Bahian Recôncavo; but we should keep the boundaries in mind as we develop contrasts and generalizations.

This book examines families and cultural change from the point of view of institutions and their often conflictive relations. It focuses on the shifts in Brazilian mentalities in the period from 1870 to 1945—that is, from just before the abolition of slavery to the end of World War II. Chapter 1 describes the general background of Bahian society between 1870 and 1945. Chapter 2 studies the daily life of households and the organization of families among landlords, the elite, and the middle classes. It compares three forms of the upper-class family to emphasize the contrasts shaped by their contexts and the rank of their members. It ends with a comparison between the families of the upper classes and those of the populace. Chapters 3, 4, and 5 consider the influence of formal institutions on the families of the upper class. They look at the history of crucial social institutions in the nineteenth and early twentieth centuries, such as the medical profession, family law, and the Catholic church, and assess how the purposes of these institutions led them to try to reform families. They argue that attempts by both modernizing and reactionary vanguards to mobilize Bahian families failed. Chapter 6 explores changes and continuities in the informal ideas of Bahians about their families. It deals with attitudes toward courtship, honor, and the place of women, as well as the ways in which families projected a familial ethic onto social relations outside the home, particularly in the construction of political clienteles. And Chapter 7 argues that many families individually determined to change their organization, and with it their values, in order to move out of declining agricultural sectors and into the professions. Many families became smaller, more mobile conjugal units. It locates those changes in the generation from 1890 to 1910 and examines the persistence of some aspects of older family organization.

At first glance, the study of past forms of the Bahian family seems relevant to contemporary Bahian life, perhaps more so than study of the past would be in other regions of Brazil. The city of Salvador today shows strong characteristics of supposedly "old-fashioned" familism. Life in the state feels traditional in comparison with that in the dynamic southern states. Other parts of Brazil also have a reputation for traditionalism. Neighboring Minas Gerais boasts ambivalently about its "traditional Mineiro family," famed for the domination of women by patriarchal men.

But Bahia's legacy is more tolerant and roguish, less resolutely proper, than that of Minas.

Salvador's present-day traditionalism may stem from its underdevelopment. It is the capital of one of the poorer states of Brazil. Today, regional differences in poverty in Brazil largely reflect incomes and conditions in the countryside. The capital cities of rich and poor regions alike hum with prosperity and even opulence. But Salvador's poverty shows in the streets of the center and in the shantytowns on its outskirts. It is a city of people crowding in lines: to catch the buses for a two-hour ride from the center to their homes, for oil, fish, and manioc meal at the subsidized state markets, for free medical visits at the public hospital.[21]

The real difference of Salvador shows in its people, not in the poverty of its infrastructure. The creole style of its people reminds one of the Caribbean. There is the same appreciation of wit, flirting, and clever swindles; the volatile affection and eagerness to make exceptions for a good person; the strong tastes in cooking, music, and dance; the vehement devotion to festivals, holidays, and freedom.

The upper classes, mostly white, appear to embody Salvador's backwardness in their family style. The family, like other institutions, did modernize—or disintegrate, depending on one's perspective—in the growth of the city after World War II. Younger women, even mothers, now routinely work and have some role outside the home. Couples now divorce without disgrace, and divorced persons can now legally remarry. Young people have adopted the norms of the cosmopolitan sexual revolution of the 1960's, and some have rejected the virginity complex surrounding women's sexual honor. These modern styles have created a cleavage between younger and older generations. But despite the novelties, many families still subordinate conjugal families to larger family circles in traditional ways. Life in the family circle entails ritual weekend entertainments that always include family, ritual weekly dinners at the table of an older relative, and residence in family compounds around an old mansion or in several apartments of a single building. Cooperation within family circles entails nepotism in public bureaucracies and the management of both small and large businesses largely by families and their relatives. This study traces the survival and transformation of such patterns of family life, and of the beliefs supporting them, from the mid-nineteenth century through the period before World War II.

1

Bahian Society, 1870-1945

UPPER-CLASS families in Bahia in this period formed a small fraction of a heterogeneous society divided by differences of status and race. Describing Salvador in the 1930's, the U.S. anthropologist Donald Pierson fancied it as a "medieval city surrounded by African villages," with the *ricos* living along its ridges and the *pobres* living in its valleys.[1] And indeed, "rich" upper-class families lived quite differently from the "poor" mass of the population. But the ways in which Bahian society as a whole changed and did not change between 1870 and 1945 conditioned the special culture of upper-class families. As the politicians, as the capitalists, as the slave-owners and landlords, as the teachers, priests, and doctors, members of the upper classes were vitally engaged with any shift in political and institutional power. At least four structural changes of state or society in Brazil set the context for changes in the shape of Bahian upper-class families.

The first big change was the abolition of Brazilian slavery between 1870 and 1888.[2] As a step in nation-building, this can be said to represent the end of a traditional society and potentially the beginning of a liberal one.[3] Bahians' sense of power and autonomy, of patronage, of justice, of human solidarity and difference had been strongly formed by three centuries of slavery. As a transition from unpaid to paid labor in the economy, the abolition of slavery may have contributed to ending the supremacy of the sugar sector and to the development of a more mobile economy.[4] As a transition to paid domestic service in upper-class households, it may have had a direct effect on family customs and budgets.[5]

Yet abolition did not bring about a revolution of racial relations, nor was it meant to.[6] The Bahian racial systems remained complex and subtle. The ethnic classifications of African blacks (*africanos*), Brazilian-born blacks (*crioulos*), Brazilian mulattoes (*mulatos* and *pardos*), Brazilian "Indians" and mestizos (*caboclos*), Bahian near-whites (*brancos da Bahia*), Brazilian whites (*brancos* and *brancos finos*), and Portuguese whites (*portugueses*), were only the beginning of a quite variegated vocabulary of concepts.[7] After abolition, the fundamental mid-nineteenth-century hierarchical ranking of colors along a spectrum from white to nonwhite to black prevailed, but as before, there were so many individual exceptions and contradictions that it may be wrong to conceive of the existence of a system.[8] If Bahia were the United States, one might expect to call its upper-class family type the "white" family. But racial lines in the society were so blurred that a distinction by class—equally globalizing, equally hard to define—will better avoid confusion.

A second big change in Bahia was its political decline following the overthrow of the Empire and the establishment of the federated Old Republic in 1889. Like the abolition of slavery, this transition was ambiguous. Bahian politicians had been powerful incumbents of the inner circles of the Empire. They must have anticipated retaining a major voice during the Republic. Yet during the Old Republic (1889–1930), the politicians of São Paulo, Minas Gerais, and Rio Grande do Sul gradually displaced the Bahian bloc. It is important to note that the establishment of the Republic was not a democratic transition. Though democracy threatened, as it had before in the 1830's, the Bahian oligarchy was able to preserve its power within the state. But it became internally fragmented, divided, and unable to present a common front to other states in the federal system.[9] Bahian upper-class families operated in a declining oligarchy that was losing its direct political leverage.

The third big change was the gradual social urbanization that accompanied the rise of metropolitan society in Salvador and better communications between the capital and the countryside. Economic growth and the demographic growth that accompanied it brought about similar changes throughout Brazil. Bahia remained an overwhelmingly rural state (it was about 13 percent urban in 1940). But Salvador changed in character as it grew from a "giant village" of 130,000 in 1872 to a city of 290,000 in 1940, on its way to becoming a city of 415,000 in 1950.[10]

Formal institutions grew in importance throughout the late nineteenth and early twentieth centuries in Salvador. The rise of the medical profession and the organization of formal health care were just two of many components of a process of state-building. The organizational reform and growth of the Catholic church was another. Alongside such semipublic institutions, the market of the city progressed in sophistication with improvements in transportation and infrastructure. And the state government grew modestly in size: the provincial budget in the 1870's amounted to about U.S.$1 per capita; it had increased to at most U.S.$1.50 per capita in the early 1920's.[11] Although the growth of institutions was concentrated in the capital, it did spread into the countryside and small towns.

The fourth change was the transformation of the "liberal" oligarchical republic into an industrial welfare state that was, in these initial stages, authoritarian and corporativist. There were hints of this change in the 1920's, but it clearly took shape in the 1930's, with Getúlio Vargas's Estado Novo dictatorship of 1937–45. The government abolished elections and centralized laws and powers by weakening state governments. It took control of strategic sectors of the economy, including the most advanced heavy industry, steel, and the most important agricultural sectors, such as coffee and sugar.[12] It expanded bureaucratic control and bureaucratic employment. Only in the 1950's and 1960's did its social-security and labor reforms bear full fruit and significantly change the horizons of families. But the Estado Novo marked the end of an era for Brazil, and for Bahia.

It is important to note that a fifth change did not take place. The Bahian economy did not become industrial during this period, and its industrialization was precarious even in the 1980's.[13] Bahia remained for four hundred years (from 1549 to 1949) primarily an agrarian and extractive economy, based on plantations, ranches, peasant farms, and small-scale mines. During the period from 1870 to 1945, its "backwardness," its failure to develop its economy as some other regions of Brazil were doing, slowed the pace and influenced the nature of social changes.

Bahian Rural Society

Bahia was not always a "traditional" or a "backward" region. In the early colonial period, Salvador was the capital of the Brazils and a prosperous sugar and tobacco plantation colony.[14] The first Bahian decline began in the late seventeenth century, when Caribbean sugar plantations, exploiting new soil and virgin forests, captured much of the market for sugar, and the gold rush in Minas Gerais drew away settlers and markets from the established northeast. In the eighteenth century, Salvador lost its primacy as the capital city. Spanish and Indian military threats in the south turned strategic attention to those regions, and the Crown transferred the title of capital to Rio in 1763. By 1808 it was a foregone conclusion that the refugee Portuguese monarch and his courtiers would reestablish their court in exile in Rio rather than Bahia.

But in the early nineteenth century, Bahia experienced a new boom. The Haitian Revolution of 1791 to 1825, first against slavery and then for independence as a peasant republic, marked a path that Bahia did not take.[15] At times it seemed that Bahia might go the way of Haiti. The first half of the nineteenth century was marked by regional rebellions, slave revolts, secessionist movements, urban riots, and coup attempts and assassinations. Various groups among the plebeian people of Bahia—from mulatto artisans to African slaves to white petty officials—attempted to organize revolutionary movements. The national government was not particularly strong, and the local government relied heavily on militias of planters in the countryside to keep order. More than once during the early nineteenth century, militias led by Recôncavo planters took the city from other forces.[16] Instead, for Bahia, and perhaps for all of Brazil, independence became a "conservative revolution" that incorporated the Portuguese ruling family as emperors and set up a political establishment of great planters, merchants, officers, and officials. This coalition favored building the Brazilian nation, protecting Brazilian agriculture, and preserving its mainstay, slavery. Members of this national establishment dedicated themselves individually to building fortunes in agricultural development and in trade. They controlled legislatures and the parliament, and they pushed for reforms that would improve transportation and trade.

In Bahia the "aristocratic" sugar mill owners (*senhores de engenho*) of the Recôncavo prospered in the early nineteenth century, becoming the leading class of the province. They imported African slaves, cleared land for firewood and to plant sugar, and amassed considerable fortunes. By contrast, the other agricultural sectors—cattle ranchers and the small and medium planters of manioc, tobacco, and cotton—were neglected in provincial policy. Mercantile and trade interests centered around the Recôncavo sugar sector. After a slow time in the 1820's and 1830's, the sugar markets boomed again in the 1840's and 1850's. But around mid-century the Bahian sugar sector stagnated. Bahians had invested late and slowly in the sort of technical improvements that revolutionized productivity on Cuban plantations in the early nineteenth century. Prices fell in world markets, and costs grew in Brazil. Planters continued to invest in sugar land and in slaves, but their voices began a chorus of complaints about the death of sugar that has lasted for more than a century. Elsewhere in Brazil, coffee emerged as the preeminent export commodity in the 1840's and 1850's, eclipsing cotton and sugar. But Recôncavo planters in Bahia did not transfer their interests into coffee planting. By 1870 the sugar sector, and the "aristocracy" of Recôncavo families that had established their fortunes on sugar, entered a crisis.[17]

By 1870 the major regional identities of modern Bahia had taken shape (see Map 1).[18] Farthest from the capital, the São Francisco River valley was a vast region of cattle ranching, manioc farming, and petty mining, whose internal and interprovincial trade with other backlands districts made it almost another state within Bahia. Its informal capitals were the

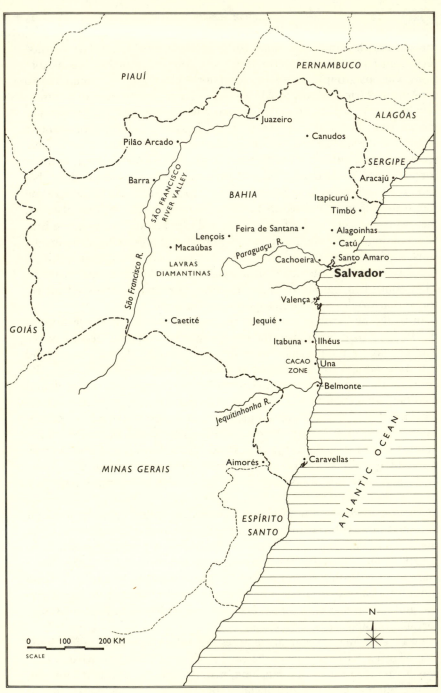

PIAUÍ

PERNAMBUCO

ALAGÔAS

Juazeiro

Canudos

Pilão Arcado

SERGIPE

Aracajú

Barra

SÃO FRANCISCO RIVER VALLEY

BAHIA

Itapicurú

Timbó

Feira de Santana

Alagoinhas

Lençois

Catú

Macaúbas

Paraguaçu R.

Santo Amaro

LAVRAS DIAMANTINAS

Cachoeira

Salvador

São Francisco R.

Valença

GOIÁS

Caetité

Jequié

Itabuna

Ilhéus

CACAO ZONE

Una

Belmonte

Jequitinhonha R.

MINAS GERAIS

Aimorés

Caravellas

ATLANTIC OCEAN

ESPÍRITO SANTO

N

0   100   200 KM
SCALE

Map 1. The State of Bahia

town of Juazeiro in the far north, an entrepôt for the river trade of many provinces, and in its upriver stretches, near the Minas Gerais border, the town of Barra. In the central-west hills, the Lavras Diamantinas was a diversified region of small farming and diamond prospecting. Its towns, such as Lençois, were closer to the markets of the São Francisco than to those of the coast. The northeast of Bahia and the adjacent minor province of Sergipe comprised thickly settled sugar districts along the coast and sparsely populated scrublands inland. The southeastern coastal zone was just beginning to develop as a region defined by cacao plantations in 1870. It was still primarily a forest district of Indian villages and fishing hamlets. The future cities of Ilhéus, Belmonte, and Itabuna were as yet scarcely villages.

The heart of Bahia, the center of its population and trade, was the Recôncavo (the "basin" or "outskirts") around the Bay of Todos os Santos (see Map 2). The capital, Salvador, was its major center, with a population of 139,000, but the tobacco- and manioc-trading city of Cachoeira competed with it in size at 88,000, and the sugar capital of Santo Amaro also held a significant population of 58,000. At the northwestern edge of the Recôncavo, Feira de Santana was the center of interior cattle trade and transport to the market in the capital.[19]

In 1800 almost all of the population of the province had been clustered in the Recôncavo. Over the mid nineteenth century, the diamond rush in the Lavras, the movement of small farmers toward the *sertão*, and the expansion of sugar planters inland to new fields had shifted the center of Bahia's population toward the west. In 1872 most of the provincial population was still concentrated in the Recôncavo, the original nucleus of the colony; but the trend was toward dispersal. The cacao boom in the southeast would, in the 1890's, further shift the weight of population away from Salvador.

The population of Bahia lived primarily from farming, ranching, and mining. The census of 1872 found 90 percent of the population in the countryside and described most of the occupied free population as living from *lavoura*, or farming. A much lower proportion of the population (about 12 percent) were slaves in 1872 than had been in 1819 (about 31 percent). This reflected two phenomena. First, the free colored population had increased and had migrated inland to squatters' frontiers. Second, the supply of slaves for plantations declined after the abolition of the slave trade, because slaveowners sold many of their slaves south to Rio de Janeiro and São Paulo in the 1860's.[20] Plantations found themselves forced to turn to hired workers or sharecroppers for some of their labor supply.

Bahia's rural economies developed a wide range of occupational and social types. The bulk of the population of Bahia were free small farmers.

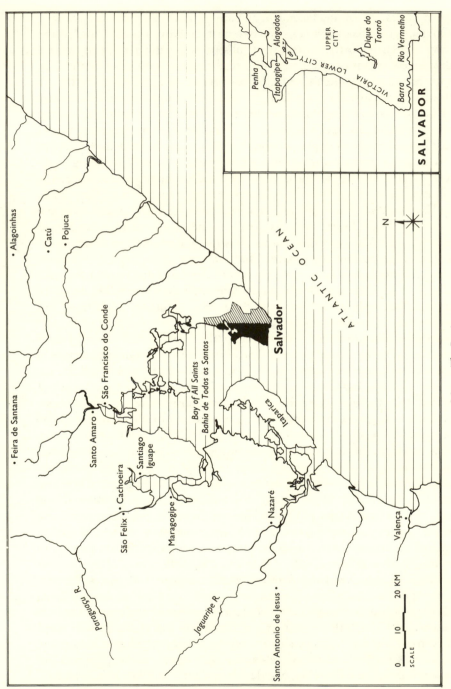

Map 2. The Recôncavo

Many were informal tenants, resident *agregados* or *moradores* on plantations. But most people lived from their own resources: they might run cattle for shares with a rancher; they might grow some cotton or pan for diamonds; they might farm manioc and hope to produce a surplus for sale. Bahia's farmers were not obviously approaching any economic revolution in land use, even though demographic pressure on land use must have increased. Over the course of the nineteenth century, land ownership in settled districts of Bahia became fragmented when properties were subdivided. As populations grew, they dispersed to the frontiers.[21]

The rural population was lumped together by others simply as the people, *o povo*. In the far sertão of the São Francisco River valley and the northeastern regions, the rural way of life produced picturesque types. In 1896 the Carioca engineer and journalist Euclides da Cunha encountered the *sertanejo*, the cowboy-squatter of the dry backlands. Da Cunha thought he could explain the sertanejo as the offspring of the racial fusion of Indian, Portuguese, and African stocks, and of the official neglect of religious education and schooling, but particularly as the product of a harsh and oscillating climate, which had produced an unsettled race with a medieval mentality.[22]

The major formal distinction within the povo was between those who were free and those who worked and lived as slaves. Many slaves lived on small farms, working under—and perhaps alongside—masters who owned only three to five of them. We do not have figures for the late nineteenth century, but two generations earlier, in the early nineteenth century, it had been unusual for a slaveowner of the Recôncavo to have more than seven slaves. Only a large tobacco plantation had more than twenty slaves, and only a handful of sugar mill owners and cane planters owned more than sixty-five slaves. Yet in the late nineteenth century a few sugar mills still had contingents of hundreds of slaves.[23] The experience of most slaves was probably that of living within the confines of an enormous plantation community. It seems that on both large farms and small, slaves wanted, and got, time off and land to plant some crops for themselves, raising manioc and vegetables, and perhaps some chickens, for food or petty cash.[24]

By 1870 the African slave trade had been stopped for twenty years, and even the African-born slaves of Bahia were creolized, speaking some Portuguese and adopting Brazilian ways. Many slaves still thought of repatriation to Africa. But most of the Bahian slave population were native-born creoles. In the countryside, slaves seem to have adopted the customs of the free poor around them and the routines of the plantation or the rural district. They had festivals of their own and tastes of their own, but they also adopted the Catholic festivals and saints that saturated the folk life around them. In the richest country towns, such as Cachoeira and Santo

Amaro, slaves and free blacks formed religious brotherhoods and paid for chapels, processions, masses, funerals, and costumes.[25]

By 1870 the proportion of the population that was enslaved had declined sharply, and between 1870 and 1888 Brazilian slavery was abolished completely. The first compromise of 1871 was the "free womb" law, giving freedom to children of slave mothers. Other halfway measures accumulated in the 1880's in a heated political struggle that ended with total abolition in 1888.

The difference between slavery and freedom could be subtle. The 1886 Law of the Sexagenarians, freeing all slaves older than sixty, seemed like a masterpiece of cynicism to some abolitionists. Even before abolition, as the slave population of the state declined, many plantations had begun to supplement or replace slave labor with sharecroppers or wage laborers. If Bahia was like Pernambuco, the wages of free labor earned little more than the simple subsistence—food, clothing, and barracks—that slaves had gotten from their masters.[26]

One indication that wages in Bahia were low is that, unlike the south of Brazil, Bahia attracted few European immigrant workers after abolition. In the 1890's Bahia's agriculture was in depression, and there seems to have been a sufficient pool of local labor for plantations. But even when the cacao zone boomed later in the 1900's and 1910's, the stories of wealth and opportunity attracted squatters, sharecroppers, and workers from Sergipe, Bahia, and the drought areas of the northeast, rather than Italians and Spaniards.[27]

Before and after abolition, the major social distinction within the free povo in the countryside was that between levels of property ownership. Did a family claim enough land to farm a cash crop, or even to ensure their subsistence? Did they own a horse, oxen, perhaps a grinding mill for manioc?[28] Was their land near water? The hierarchy of status in the countryside ranged from destitute tenant farmers and workers up through propertied, ambitious medium cane or tobacco farmers who aspired to rise into the ranks of sugar mill owners.[29] In the early nineteenth century the *lavrador de cana*, the farmer who grew cane under contract to a sugar mill, often on rented land, was a characteristic middle-rank social type in the countryside. Throughout the nineteenth century the medium tobacco planters of Cachoeira and other parts of the Recôncavo constituted another middle group among the povo. One indication of the great number of middling farmers is the voting lists. Though they were often forged, these lists and the registries of land ownership undertaken on an irregular basis in the 1850's counted many medium and small farmers whose property supposedly qualified them as second-class voters.[30]

Bahian rural society was bound together by a traditional folk culture.

The institutions of the rural povo were informal and simple. Most country households lived apart from their neighbors, with their dogs, their hut, and their pig. Their entertainments were usually what they could provide themselves: music, singing, dancing, drinking rum, fighting. Their rituals were those of the Catholic holy calendar, the days of Santo Antônio and São João, and perhaps the patron saint of the parish. But the church was absent from people's lives on a daily basis. If a walk took them past a chapel or shrine, it would almost invariably be closed and empty. Once a year, if not more often, a circuit-riding priest would open the chapel to baptize infants, marry couples, and hold masses for the dead. Franciscan or Capuchin missionaries occasionally held revivals, collecting big crowds.[31] But if the church was absent, folk Catholicism was omnipresent in the small courtesies of daily life, and the few decorations of a hut would have included a cross and perhaps in later times a carved or plaster saint or a lithograph.

There was little or no education in the countryside. In Bahia's 1872 census, sixty-four slaves claimed they could read. Among free adult men, one in four claimed to be literate, and only one in seven of the women could read.[32] People who lived near enough to a town might hope to place their children with the schoolmaster, to have them beaten and trace their ABCs on a slate. Yet once out of school, people had few opportunities, and little need, to read. A proud man might continue to read tracts and ballad sheets, might insist on scratching his own name on deeds and lists. But many prosperous farmers were content to have another man sign in their places. It could be more important to learn to count, but few men needed to know more than was necessary to barter their goods. Money circulated, but coins were always scarce, often out-of-date silver and copper from the time of the Empire.[33] Country people bartered, borrowed, exchanged gifts, and made what they needed themselves.

The ignorance of the rural people meant that traditional culture was the major counterweight to personal fancy and fantasy. People knew what their parents had known. Their folklore was a repertoire of Portuguese ballads and proverbs and tales of werewolves and of cannibal river maidens who seduced travelers. Yet in 1870 the country people of Bahia had rather broad cultural horizons. A fair number of them had been born in Africa and could tell tales and bring to life saints from their childhood and adolescence in Angola or Guinea. In every town some of the men were veterans of the Paraguayan War's long marches into the swamps of the south.[34] People had often moved to the frontier from the coast, and they continued to get news and stories of the wider world from drought refugees, sailors, and traveling salesmen.

Generally, official politics meant little or nothing to the rural povo. They were loyal to the emperor, to the church, and to their patrons. In every part of the countryside, the povo were solicited as clients by political parties. It was likely that powerful landlords of their parish would call on them to register to vote and then appear at the polls on election day. And it was also likely that they would enlist in the parish's National Guard unit, in which the big landlords made up the officer corps and they the ranks. If only to escape recruitment into the army or a call for jury duty, cultivating the protection of some local notable was essential. Election day was a feast day, the occasion for pitched battles with sticks and guns between rival factions. But on any day the rural povo would have reasons to seek the friendship of powerful godfathers who could influence the courts, settle inheritance feuds, and shift land boundaries.[35]

The period between 1880 and 1900 was one of the most tumultuous in Brazilian political history, but the great political movements seem not to have mobilized the Bahian povo. After the Paraguayan War (1865–70) the abolitionist and republican movements challenged an establishment whose military officers and bishops were at odds with its civilian mandarins. All over Brazil abolitionism developed in the mid 1880's from an upper-class salon movement into a popular movement of civic resistance. Bahia had a weaker abolitionist movement than other provinces, such as Ceará, where the stevedores blockaded the port and abolitionists went from house to house taking slaves away from their masters, or São Paulo, where abolitionists and runaways fought pitched battles with the police. But in the hot last years of 1887 and 1888, slaves on big Recôncavo plantations began to run away, threaten their overseers, and refuse orders to work. By contrast, the declaration of the Republic in 1889 was an anticlimax. The army's coup against Emperor Pedro II began and ended in Rio de Janeiro, and news of the Republic arrived in Salvador by telegram. After brief confusion, the major political groups of the Empire reasserted their domination of local office.[36]

Yet ironically, the major political repercussion of the republican revolution of 1889 in Bahia came from the people. Country people throughout the backlands, many of them former slaves, began to flock to the new town of Canudos, the seat of a prophetic lay preacher, Antônio Conselheiro. By 1896 Canudos had grown to a population of perhaps 15,000; it was certainly close to being the second largest city in the state. Conselheiro had become an important figure, sought after as a godfather and a political ally. Some claimed that he began to preach against the "impious" republic that had overthrown the good emperor, disestablished the church, and instituted the scandalous requirement of civil marriage. Certainly he had gotten on the wrong side of local politics. In 1896 the state police attacked people from Canudos cutting lumber but were driven off. Soon afterward, a federal army unit came to put down the "rebellion of fanatics," and it, too, was routed. Only in 1897 was the third federal army expedition sent into the backlands able to bombard and massacre the defenders of Canudos.[37]

The incident confirmed to its most sensitive interpreter, Euclides da Cunha, the depth of the gulf between the cultures, or races, of city and country in Brazil. Brazil was not a unity or even a harmonious organism composed of complementary parts, but rather an unbalanced, degenerating accumulation of antagonisms and opposites. The man of the backlands, long ignored by the man of the city, was millennia apart from the latter in mentality and development, but his primitivity and fanaticism were the opposite side of the coin of mob rule in republican Rio de Janeiro.[38]

After the massacre at Canudos, the politics of the backlands changed little during the Old Republic. Sporadic banditry occasionally turned into a major threat to rule by *coronéis* (literally, "colonels," but in usage, political bosses, mostly landlords and merchants).[39] More often, the coronéis themselves led armies of cowboys and gunmen in feuds and political battles with rival chieftains. Not even the "Prestes Column" of radical military rebels that shook the nation in 1926 could unseat them. When the Prestes Column passed through the Bahian sertão on its long march across Brazil, local coronéis organized their private armies into "patriotic battalions" to combat the guerrillas. But all of these activities implied enlistment in traditional forms motivated by traditional loyalties, not the political mobilization of the povo.[40]

Difficult conditions or unusual opportunities in the countryside could impel the cautious, conservative families of the Bahian povo to adventures. Bahians left dried-out farms in the backlands to try their luck as rubber tappers in the Amazon in the 1880's. Bahians and Sergipeans flocked to the southeastern coast, whose forests were free land for the taking, even before anyone learned its value for the new crop of cacao in the 1890's.

But over the course of the period from 1870 to 1945, there was rarely any abrupt change in the culture and work of the Bahian rural povo. In the São Francisco valley towns, men followed in the occupations of their fathers: the sons of leatherworkers became leatherworkers; the sons of boatmen became boatmen; the sons of traders became traders.[41] Their institutions changed only subtly. Gradually they became more mobile. And gradually the government and private institutions spread into the backlands.

Transportation facilities multiplied in the second half of the nineteenth century. Water transportation was traditionally the most efficient means within the Recôncavo and along the São Francisco River; in fact, the Bay of All Saints and the river constituted the two great, separate market zones of the province.[42] Service around the Bay of All Saints began in earnest in

1853, in what became the Companhia Navegação a Vapor Bahiana, the major steamboat line that passed back and forth between private concessions and direct administration by the state. Steamboat service along the inland São Francisco River began in 1865 and continued, with interruptions and bankruptcies, through the twentieth century. In 1871 a third steamboat line connected the capital with Una and Belmonte in what would become the cacao region, and in 1904 a fourth transport line, Transportes Marítimos, opened coastal service.[43]

The breakthrough in overland communications came in 1863, when the E.F. Bahia–São Francisco rail line reached Alagoinhas, 123 kilometers north of the capital, on the fringe of the sertão.[44] By 1887 another line linked Alagoinhas to Timbó, and by 1896 the railroad had reached Juazeiro, connecting the capital to the São Francisco River. In 1882 the E.F. Bahia e Minas line began to carry passengers to Aimorés, though the Minas Gerais end was not completed. By 1913 the E.F. Aracajú e Própria line linked Bahia and the lower São Francisco River region. Other lines built routes between Salvador and the Recôncavo. In 1875 the E.F. Central Bahia was carrying passengers to Feira, and in 1880 the E.F. Nazareth began to carry them to Santo Antônio de Jesus. In 1883 the E.F. Santo Amaro began to carry passengers and freight to the Recôncavo, and in 1906 the line connected to the others. Overall, there were 37 kilometers of railroad in 1860, 123 in 1870, 312 in 1880, 1,056 in 1890, 1,434 in 1910, and 1,751 in 1920.[45] The railroads opened up markets, but they also made possible other kinds of urban communications and oversight that had not been feasible before.

Motor road construction began to take over from railways in importance in the 1910's and 1920's. Construction of the Avenida Sete de Setembro in 1916 opened Salvador to automobile traffic, though there were only 1,000 automobiles by 1935. The first significant highway was the road built between Salvador and Feira de Santana in 1921, on the route of the old cattle drive road from the interior to the capital. The Goes Calmon administration of 1924–28 was the first governorship to boast of its highway construction priority. From the 1920's forward, politicians and bishops were able to tour the backlands by automobile rather than by mule train. Governor Goes Calmon was one of the first governors to tour the backlands of the state by car.[46]

Better communications and transportation made possible the extension of urban institutions to the countryside. The state government always promised to attend to the social needs of the backlands, and governments during the Old Republic and the Vargas dictatorships gradually did. The state built rural schools and established rural infirmaries and hospitals.[47] The federal government set up post offices and telegraph stations.[48] The Catholic church also moved into the backlands after the separation of church and state in 1891. Dom Jerônimo Thomé da Silva (1894–1924) was the first Bahian archbishop to visit many backlands dioceses and parishes, touring along the railroad lines in 1894 and in 1906–7.[49]

The period between 1870 and 1890 was a period of contraction in export markets for Bahia, and probably in domestic markets as well. But from 1890 through 1907 exports slowly recovered, and after 1907 there were dramatic booms such as the 1919 high and the 1920's cacao boom. Markets expanded in backland districts, bringing commercial transactions and new products. In many places, booms were transitory. Coffee exports from the Jequié region outshone the depressed exports of tobacco and sugar for a while in the 1890's; a rubber boom briefly brought expansion in certain districts of the sertão around the turn of the century; and during World War I demand for industrial carbonate diamonds flooded the diamond district with prospectors, traders, and the mule trains of traveling salesmen, but a lull in the market emptied the region almost as quickly.[50]

The most dynamic boom in the countryside was the creation of the cacao zone along the southeastern coast of the state. In 1870 the population of the region was small and still characterized by Indian reservation villages. By 1890 squatters were turning their subsistence *buraras* of manioc root into cacao orchards. Families from Sergipe, the backlands of Bahia, and even the Recôncavo began to flock to the area and burn out claims in the forest. Between 1890 and 1910 a violent land grab, punctuated by big and small land wars, established a number of giant plantations. Cacao production, mostly for export, flooded the region with quick cash. The hamlets of the region became villages, and then cities. The Ilhéus area grew as an enclave within the state, connected to Salvador mainly by steamboat and raft until roads began to reach the capital.[51]

The highly mobile population of the cacao zone, many of them wage workers on big plantations, seemed to take on a different spirit from those of the long-established Recôncavo and the traditional rural communities of the dry sertão. Unquestionably, the fast growth of Ilhéus represented the most tangible economic progress in Bahia, and the *grapiunas* felt immense pride in their land and its dynamism. By the 1920's their millionaire planters were beginning to set up town mansions in Salvador, and their sons and daughters were filling the boarding schools and academies of the capital. Their politicians became leaders of the last generation of politics under the Old Republic, and their coronéis were among the top contenders for power in the state.[52] Anyone who wanted to get ahead knew there were chances and risks in Ilhéus.

Less dramatically, populations almost tripled throughout the Bahian countryside between 1872 and 1940. A traditional rural district of manioc farms and tobacco plantations in the Recôncavo such as Maragogipe had about seven acres of land per inhabitant in 1872, and about three acres per inhabitant in 1940.[53] As frontiers filled and magnates fenced the land, rural communities could not support all their children. The cacao zone offered work to some. But the cities offered a chance for employment also. In great numbers on the occasion of drought in the backlands, and in small numbers steadily, year after year, people moved from declining Cachoeira, Santo Amaro, Valença, and Itaparica into the capital and its outskirts. Young women may have been especially likely to leave behind the family plot or the plantation for nearby towns or the city.[54] But married men would also go to Bahia or to São Paulo or Rio, promising to return to their villages. In São Paulo, natives began to call any brown-skinned migrant from the north a *bahiano*.[55] In Salvador in the 1920's, local authorities began to notice the accumulation of new huts in the wastelands at the edge of the town. In the absence of construction of "popular housing," the poor crowded into tenements in the old center of the city.[56] By 1950 the new shantytown of Alagados, shacks built on pilings over the mudflats of a lagoon, had a reputation as the most shocking slum in Brazil.

The Landlords

A few powerful patrons in the countryside—landlords and merchants—stood at the top of Bahia's rural society. In 1870 they formed a dynamic, politically mobilized group. Among them the richest and most powerful were the sugar mill owners and planters of the Recôncavo.

Throughout the nineteenth century, their best energies went into politics. Planters of the Recôncavo, leading the militias and then the National Guard units of Bahia, were several times able to take Salvador away from their enemies, among them Portuguese armies, rebelling slaves, and the Sabinada rebellion of the plebeians of Salvador. The electoral laws of the Empire gave disproportionate weight to rural districts, and planters controlled the provincial assembly. They observed a division of labor in politics. Their educated sons, or other educated men, served as their agents in the national Chamber of Deputies and in the Empire's political service. They themselves dominated local affairs: they controlled juries and judges, led the National Guard, organized the vote, and harassed the opposition.[57] A fairly stable party system made the 1850's and 1860's peaceful.

By 1870 the Recôncavo planters had begun to recognize the difficulties presented by their markets and to respond with public initiatives, such as the foundation of the Imperial School of Agriculture in 1877. Other projects seemed clearly to stem from planter interests, or the interests of agriculture generally. They included a provincial mortgage bank to allow agricultural loans, schemes to promote immigration of European colonists, and the construction of railroads. In doing this they acted with the co-operation of merchants. Examining the political programs of planters and merchants, it seems that the two groups concurred in favoring policies that would modernize agriculture without threatening any vested interests.[58]

They also responded with the semipublic, semiprivate initiative of building central sugar refineries. One of the most enterprising families, the Costa Pintos, pooled their capital to build a central refinery in 1880.[59] Other groups soon followed. But these measures could not rescue the sugar sector. Efficient milling could not compensate for the high cost and lower yield of Bahian cane growing. By the time of abolition, in 1888, many of the great cane-growing and mill-owning families were eager to sell out and put their remaining fortunes into bonds, urban property, and investments. Land-holdings in sugar counties such as Santiago Iguape were already relatively fragmented in the 1860's. In the second half of the nineteenth century, mill owners were among the rich Bahians, but rarely among the richest. Merchants and other capitalists had the largest estates.[60]

After 1870 Bahian planters and urban politicians divided sharply on the issue of slavery. The Bahian mill owner João Maurício Wanderley, baron of Cotegipe, was instrumental in putting together the Conservative party's pro-slavery strategy of concessions to delay and divide the abolitionist campaign. The planter bosses of the Bahian Liberal party split between pro-slavery and abolitionist wings. The final years of the abolitionist campaign deeply shook the political class of Bahia. Planters complained of indiscipline on plantations and feared insurrection like that which was taking shape in São Paulo in the first months of 1888. As a fellow Conservative put it to Cotegipe in 1888: "God grant that the elements of combustion that are accumulating do not break, within a few years, through the thin crust in which they are hidden and consume in the fire the very ones who out of frivolity or womanly fear are blowing on them. I don't know what will become of our institutions within a few years." If not quite a volcanic eruption, abolition did prove to compound the hard times that cane diseases and drought in 1887, 1888, and 1889 brought to the Recôncavo.[61]

Abolition thus marked a breaking point around 1890 in the life-styles of the "traditional" planter families of the Recôncavo. Many lost slaves and, with their slaves, their will to continue in the business of planting. Some converted sugar plantations, at least temporarily, to the low-overhead, low-yield occupation of cattle ranching.[62] Some sold out their estates to others and put their capital into urban real estate. Central mills operated, but under the management of a series of corporations, which profited during exceptional times in world sugar markets, such as the brief boom years of the 1920's, but generally got mediocre returns from vastly increased production.[63]

Progress was the slogan of the republican movement of 1889. The nation had just abolished slavery, and it was easy, in a moment of uncertainty about old institutions, for the army to overthrow the Empire. An early military dictatorship gave way to government by civilian oligarchies, but both had in common the pursuit of progress: European immigration to meet the labor needs of agriculture and to whiten the population; railroads to open up the land to commerce; credit and laws to permit firms to start and banks to open.

Unfortunately, the Bahian political chieftains lost out in the reshuffling of national power at the foundation of the Republic. Other states, such as São Paulo and Minas Gerais, came to hold a controlling interest in federal politics. For São Paulo, federalism was an ideal, mostly because it assured the Paulistas that they could control the revenues of their state and out-flank the concentration of credit and public investments in Rio de Janeiro. Federalism did not do the Bahians or the small states of the north much good. Unable to put together a stable state oligarchy, the Bahians could not bargain effectively for a turn at the presidency or a larger role in Congress. Their best hopes, Rui Barbosa, J. J. Seabra, and Miguel Calmon, were never nominated by the official parties. Internally divided, their federal election returns were subject to nullification by the powerful states that controlled the Credentials Committee in the federal Congress in Rio de Janeiro. Domestic control of export revenues and finances gave them only limited room to maneuver, since the state's financial base was weak.[64]

The weakness of the Bahian party system meant that the Recôncavo politicans with a base in the countryside also lost political power, because they were leveled with backcountry bosses. Although the incumbent party had the strong leverage of being able to decertify county returns, the political leaders in the capital depended on backcountry coronéis to deliver solidly rigged election returns at the county level. As long as the old establishment of Recôncavo state leaders maintained a strong incumbent *situação* with a common front, they could control individual coronéis and promote themselves. But they failed in every attempt to build a stable single-party machine in Bahia. Every *coronel* knew he was in jeopardy of losing his support from the capital, and no coronel could afford to be loyal. Coronéis might be in varying degrees ostracized by, or in alliance with, the incumbent factions. They might suffer outright harassment and enmity, with hostile court decisions and hostile appointments to the state police, prosecutor's bench, and local telegraph office. They might be regarded as "compatible adversaries," allowed control of their county but granted little patronage or share in the spoils of state government. They could switch allegiances and attempt to join the governing clique. Coronéis were thus forced to act independently of their traditional leaders.[65]

Furthermore, while Recôncavo planters lost money, planters in other parts of the state prospered. The difficulties of Recôncavo sugar production did not mean uniformly hard times for Bahian landlords after 1890. The medium-scale tobacco planters continued to enjoy a modest, but steadier, prosperity during this period. Centered in Cachoeira and São Felix, they sold their bales of leaf to German and Swiss merchants, who established first simple processing plants and then cigar factories.[66] Ranchers produced hides in backlands counties. Cotton planters exported their crop to local and world markets. Cacao planters prospered on an almost unheard-of scale.

During the Republic some coronéis in the Lavras and São Francisco regions seemed unconscionably powerful. Electorally, they represented a significant force. If ever put together, their blocs of votes weighed significantly in state returns. Militarily, they were beyond the reach of the state government. Most coronéis, but particularly those in districts where land claims or grazing rights were in dispute, had armed retinues of *jagunços* to ride with them whenever they left their plantation houses, and they could raise bigger bands of rowdies for election days or local feuds.[67] Several times during the republic, coronéis in the backlands precipitated factional falling-out in Salvador. In 1920 the state government faced the march of an army of coronéis from the interior, bent on toppling the governor and installing a faction favorable to them. The federal government settled the war by treaty, informally recognizing the coronéis as warlords.[68]

The power of coronéis was finally limited by Getúlio Vargas's revolution in 1930. At first Vargas's "interventor," Juracy Magalhães, marshaled a new constellation of landlord coronéis as a pro-government political bloc. But under Vargas's Estado Novo, no national elections were held from 1937 to 1945. Coronéis could not barter their votes for patronage from the state government, and they lost the incentive to maintain their clienteles. The federal army and the state police began to campaign determinedly against "bandits" and private armies of all stripes, and by the 1940's they had demonstrated their effective military control of the countryside. At the same time, many of the richest coronéis from the cacao region lost their wealth in the crash of the 1930's. The prestige of landlords did not disappear entirely, and their political power revived with the institution of mass democracy in 1945. But the period from 1937 to 1945 represented a virtual suspension of the power of the backcountry bosses of Bahia.[69]

Public recognition of the "decadence" of Brazilian landlord families, including both the aristocracy of the Recôncavo and the backlands coronéis, dated from the 1930's. For example, the 1930's literature of northeastern regionalist realism, represented by such authors as José Lins do Rêgo, implied that the epic story of Brazil was the decline of the sugar plantations. The outcast sons of this class made its "tragedy" the central story of Brazilian social change.[70] Even where families continued to control districts that their grandfathers had dominated in the mid-nineteenth century, the landlords seemed to decline in status. They had nothing like the lordly command that their grandfathers had had. A few landlord families, notably Santo Amaro families such as the Calmons, Sodrés, Costa Pintos, and Araujo Pinhos, had dominated the inner circles of the state oligarchy through the 1920's.[71] But in general Recôncavo landlords either transferred their connections to the capital or became *coronéis do interior*, back-country bosses, still patrons in their bailiwicks but with little projection outside them.

There was no significant challenge to the landlords' patronal power from other social types in the countryside itself. Over the course of the Old Republic, small town life grew, and in many counties there was a diversification of social types. Even a remote county seat might have its postmistress, its telegraph operator, a public schoolmistress, clerks, shopkeepers, saloonkeepers, and other nonmanual workers. There were also hints that the civic life of the towns could provide a counterweight to the domination of coronéis. Yet every description of country town life through World War II, and even some afterward, stresses the political dominion of coronéis over factionalized, clientelistic small towns. A second-rank political crony made mayor in the town of Santo Amaro had to swallow his pride when, around 1900, the chieftain of Santo Amaro, Dr. Francisco Jerônimo Sodré Pereira, came back from Rio and scolded him, telling him not to repeat expenses like the five contos spent on improvement of the city: "Santo Amaro isn't the capital of France."[72]

In the towns, factionalism was reflected in institutions: each town had two brass bands for its two recreational societies, and two panels ready for civic ceremonies. Epitomizing a small town in the cacao region, Jorge Amado describes it as possessing two doctors (and two pharmacies), two dentists, two weekly newssheets, and many lawyers. Over time, this factionalism could lead to the definition of a party of the "plebeians," or the povo, against the party of the "patricians." And by the 1950's class appeals in politics were being made in the countryside. In the 1950's sugar mill workers went on strike throughout the Recôncavo, supposedly under communist influence. In one county of the Recôncavo the decisive break came in 1967, when a member of the local leading family lost the mayoral election to a "people's candidate," a former clerk of the mill.[73]

Salvador in the Twentieth Century

Perhaps only Salvador—the second or third largest city in Brazil—developed a society complementary to the traditional agrarian matrix of

Bahian society and independent of the patronal powers of landlords and coronéis. But Salvador did not develop a project of modernization that was antagonistic to agrarian interests.

In Bahia, as in most of nineteenth-century Latin America, economies were revitalized by capitalist reforms and by export production to meet the expansion of European demand. Trade grew, export profits brought capital accumulation, and export production had linkages that led to internal economic growth and development. But unlike the Rio–São Paulo axis in the south of Brazil, Bahia did not industrialize. Bahia's economy did not change notably in type during the entire period from 1870 to 1945. It remained, during all this time, an export-oriented plantation economy.

Bahia did experience some industrialization of its economy in the nineteenth and twentieth centuries. In the early nineteenth century, waterfalls in the Recôncavo powered cotton-textile mills, and in the 1870's, a few sugar planters modernized their mills into central refineries. The speculative Encilhamento boomlet of the 1890's capitalized banks, hat factories, and cigar factories in Salvador, and some of them survived the subsequent bust. As the city grew in population, large-scale industrial production competed with imported consumer goods and small-scale artisan production, not always successfully. The great industrial establishments of Salvador, such as the Empório Industrial do Norte textile mills or the naval shipyard, were exceptions rather than the rule.[74] By one estimate, the industries of Salvador may have shrunk in scale in the period from 1930 to 1950, rather than consolidating like those of São Paulo.[75]

Even without industrialization, there was perceptible modernization of the agro-commercial economy of Bahia between 1870 and 1945. Some of its changes were mandated by national reforms. The government reformed Brazil's land laws in 1850, making it easier for planters to survey and claim "public" frontier lands. It reformed commercial law in 1850 and 1890, making it easier and less risky to form companies. And between 1871 and 1888, it gradually and painfully abolished slavery, theoretically "freeing" labor and making it more mobile.[76] The legal and institutional superstructure of the economy became more efficient for doing business.

Yet Bahia never thoroughly modernized its transport infrastructure. In Rio de Janeiro and São Paulo, coffee zones in the hinterland provided overwhelming justification for the construction of railroads opening up the interior to trade. But in Bahia, the provincial and state governments were slow at integrating the Recôncavo and the deeper backlands with railroad lines. Modernization of port works and docks continued apace, but efficiencies in the capital did not necessarily radiate out into the interior.

During this period, the contrast between the facilities of the capital city and of the rural interior grew sharper than before. Salvador had mule-drawn trolleys by 1864 and a network of electrified trolleys by 1900.[77] The city had paved roads, bridges, and a passenger elevator leading from the port up to the ridges of the Upper City. Still, most goods were carried on people's shoulders and heads: in the business district, most cargo in the 1880's was carried by African carriers. Salvador got a system of piped water and some sewerage beginning in 1906, supplementing the public fountains and the open streams and basins. The transoceanic cable connected Salvador to national and worldwide telegraphic communications in 1874. In inland towns, markets were sometimes periodic fairs; Salvador had permanent produce markets and slaughterhouses. While in inland parishes, priests traveled a circuit, arriving in some villages only once a year, in Salvador scores of priests maintained chapels and churches as well as the cathedral. Salvador had more hospitals and clinics; more schools and faculties; more police; more theater.[78]

In spite of this modernization, and in spite of its dominance over its region, Salvador was economically "dependent" in a classic way: it grew, as it had always grown, in the context of an international division of labor, exporting new and traditional tropical crops, importing consumer goods, tools, and capital goods.[79] It was also dependent in the sense that the critics of the 1960's cared about: something in its social structure and traditions seemed to hold back industrialization, to foster poverty.

From the 1890's through 1960, upper-class Bahians faced the issue by declaring their "vocation for agriculture" or bemoaning their lack of a commercial spirit. They could point to the inexplicable success of wave after wave of Portuguese or German merchants: "The small nucleus of immigrants quickly rises to the top of the social pyramid, in the form of an economic elite, something that is characteristic of colonies and not of independent nations."[80] They could complain that the African blood of the populace made it lazy and unsuited to dynamic endeavors.[81] Or they could criticize their own traditions, complaining that they were obsessed with politics, arguing that their families turned out youths who were coddled and too comfortable for the struggle for life.[82] In discussing politics, Bahians were likely to compare their own "low level" to politics abroad, or to shame each other by invoking the gaze of outsiders: "We must remember that outside here there are those who judge us, and our civilization, our patriotism."[83] In the 1950's criticism of Salvador's backwardness by native sons turned to focused economic monographs.[84]

In the early twentieth century, "dependency" was not a term Bahians themselves would have used to identify their situation; they were more likely to talk of "provincialism." Primarily, they felt provincial in the light of Civilization. The opposition of the cosmopolitan and the national was patent in everyday life, in the symbolism of the commodities people consumed. An 1897 newspaper ad for matches offered two brands. One,

"Cosmopolitanos," showed a white woman in a dress with square-cut décolletage and short, lacy sleeves—flanked by neoclassical medallions of bearded, Roman-nosed men in profile—fanning herself and looking coquettishly at the customer. The other, "Nacionaes," showed an Indian man with bow and arrow and a feather cape and headdress, a caricatured Aztec. One brand was "imported exclusively" by the merchant, the other "manufactured expressly." The Empório Industrial do Norte sold cloth under the trademark of a draped, angel-winged white woman between 1902 and 1915; it adopted a new trademark of an Indian princess sitting on a factory wall in the more nationalistic 1920's. Cosmopolitan styles were especially obvious in fashions, which arrived quickly in Brazil: "We . . . unconditionally adopt anything that carries on it the notice, 'product of civilization.'"[85]

Upper-class Bahians also felt a provincialism within Brazil, which they would ambivalently present as regionalism.[86] When Bahian politicians gave a banquet for themselves, the menu was French food: "Poulet à la financière, Filet à Richelieu." When they hosted a banquet for an outsider, the menu included "vatapá, carurú, frigideira de carangueijos" and other Afro-Bahian dishes.[87] And Bahians used an idiom of race even to distinguish themselves from other Brazilians. Among the Brazilian states, Bahia was *a Mulata Velha*, the Old Black Mammy, whose titanic breasts had suckled hundreds of sons. Most of them were loyal white sons of this mother. But some of them were "ashamed to have a colored mother, and pretended to be of aristocratic descent because they found some bluish tones in their veins. . . . In truth, who doesn't have some of that in the family?" Sister states had acquired the "foreign nuance," their sons ate with knife and fork, and had progress and science.[88]

The social hierarchy of Salvador in 1870 still resembled that of the city in 1800.[89] The largest rank in number was the urban povo. At its lowest levels there was a large plebeian rabble, including slaves, vagabonds, and the destitute poor, who might be seen as being beneath or outside the povo itself.[90] Above these was the povo par excellence: the petty clerks, poor shopkeepers, and prosperous street peddlers who carried on the bulk of retail trade; sailors, mule drivers, fishermen and truck farmers; artisans, seamstresses, and workers; soldiers and low-level government employees. If they are to be defined by their incomes, that is to say by their poverty, they were the rank of society with incomes under 500$ a year.[91]

Above the povo in income and social prestige were the middle ranks of the city: retail merchants, bookkeepers in big firms, and moneylenders; ship captains and workshop master artisans; the lower clergy and middle-rank officers, and medium functionaries in the state officialdom or the customshouse; small landowners and urban landlords; and some liberal professionals. If ranked by income alone, they might be defined as those earning between 500$ and 1:000$ a year.[92] And at the top of the social pyramid, few in numbers, were the highest ranks: the upper fringe of the middle class and the elite. Most of them earned incomes of over 1:000$ yearly, but their membership in this group could also derive from their prestige and power. This group included the most prominent physicians, lawyers, and judges; the bishops and canons of the cathedral chapter; high officers in the armed forces and the police, and the high functionaries of the state government; and of course it included retired landowners living in the city, rentier *capitalistas*, and the great wholesale merchants and businessmen of the seaport. This study addresses primarily the families and the lives of these two upper groups, but their many relations with the povo of the city make it important to understand the makeup of the povo.

The "Pobres": Povo and Workers

The urban povo were largely black and mulatto; to foreign visitors they gave the city the appearance of an African seaport. In 1872 12 percent of the population of the city were still slaves. Elements of African culture suffused Salvador, in jewelry and striped cloth, in the smell of palm oil frying in the streets, in the language, in the sound of drumming in the suburbs. Old Africans still preferred to associate with each other and marry each other. Conspicuous "nations" of Africans formed gangs of stevedores and carriers at the docks in the Lower City. But by this time, the distinction between African-born and creole blacks was declining in importance with the diminishing numbers of Africans. African parents apparently did not integrate their Brazilian-born creole children into their groups. And patterns of work served to mix the workers of Salvador into a relatively homogeneous group, as slaves worked with free women and men in all manner of occupations. Slaves in the city frequently worked as domestic servants, and they also staffed some small businesses for their masters. But many slaves were rented out daily as construction workers, stevedores, artisans, and prostitutes. Still others worked for their masters on small truck and dairy farms inside the city limits, working the farm and then peddling the produce from door to door in the center of town. The destruction of slavery in 1888 made clearer how small the difference between the work lives of slaves and the work of the free poor had been.[93]

The opportunities in Salvador were not large enough to attract a significant immigration of laborers from Europe. The povo were largely employed in the myriad of small service activities and artisan production that a commercial city required. Wages for laborers and earnings for small traders were close to subsistence; many people were listed as "without defined occupation" in the censuses of 1872 and 1920. While 18 percent of the total population of São Paulo were foreign-born by 1920, only 2.3 percent of the adults of Salvador were foreign-born.[94]

However, there was a continuing migratory current from Portugal into the povo that had continued nearly unstopped from colonial times. Portuguese merchants in the Lower City sent for young men, often their nephews, from their home provinces and from Lisbon. These boys, whose age was often between ten and fourteen, came to work as *caixeiros* (shop clerks), hoping for a chance to marry the master's daughter or strike out on their own with a little capital. They were miserably paid and commonly slept on sacks of onions in the store in the Lower City. In the mid and late nineteenth century these young men formed a distinct white group in the city's povo. Bahians considered them curious and conservative. At the theater, caixeiros formed claques for certain actresses, enemies of the claques of the upper-class students. In twentieth-century political campaigns, they seem to have been a conservative force. Many students supported Rui Barbosa in 1910, while the caixeiros supported the machine candidate, General Hermes.[95]

By the 1890's, or the 1900's at the latest, a special group of workers in Salvador took shape within the ranks of the povo who might be called a *proletariado*, though they were more often called *operários* or *artistas* (artisans). Among these were the women, children, and men who worked in the textile mills; the scattered employees of small workshops; stonemasons and stevedores; cart, trolley, and taxi drivers; typesetters; and waiters in restaurants. Only a few of them had the experience of work in a factory with a division of labor. Most of them still worked in labor-intensive routine ways, next to their bosses, going through steps like those of all the other workers on their crew or in their shop. Poorly paid and little committed to one job rather than another, they eventually developed a sense of grievance and exploitation.[96]

Around the time of World War I, the shortages and inflation brought on by the trade crisis of wartime pushed them into action beyond the limits of the paternalistic mutual aid associations and political party offshoots that they had available to them. Exports boomed, but as Bahian produce flowed outward and supplies of imported basic foodstuffs such as salt cod were unavailable, domestic markets were disrupted. The rural povo endured days of hunger, eating little but fruit, fish, and coconuts. Without even a subsistence economy to fall back upon, workers in Salvador in all categories went on a general strike in 1919.[97] But the results were inconclusive, and strike organizations were transitory.

Wages were low enough that the concerns of the povo and workers often centered around survival. Housing was expensive, but fortunately many could afford to build themselves a hut in one of the hollows of the city, or to rent a cubicle in one of the "beehive" tenements established around the old Pelourinho Square.[98] Their families were small and weak; both men and women worked outside the home, and children worked as soon as they were able.[99] While parents sent their young children to a year or so of elementary school classes if they were available, few households were so extravagant as to send children to school who could work and contribute to the family budget.[100] The formal institutions of Salvador's workers and povo were also relatively weak. The traditional formal associations of the city included religious brotherhoods, artisans' brotherhoods, and later mutual aid associations, masonic lodges, and unions.[101] The most notably Bahian institutions of the workers derived from the Afro-Brazilian slave culture: musical groups, carnival clubs, and the organized but semisecret *candomblé* cults.[102]

The "Ricos": A Middle Class in Salvador

The failure to industrialize did not prevent the emergence of a "middle class" in Salvador around the turn of the century. That is to say, the irregularly expanding economy of an export-oriented seaport certainly created nonmanual occupations. As a commercial city, Salvador required many clerks and specialists, and as the capital of the state, it was the center of the liberal professions. Between 1872 and 1920 the number of persons working in commercial occupations grew in pace with the total population; the number of public employees grew much faster than the population.[103]

While income and property certainly mattered in the definition of middle-class status, the middle class of Salvador was perhaps only marginally better off than the working poor. In many ways the line between the upper ranks of the working povo of Salvador and the lower ranks of the middle class was hard to define by money alone. Kátia Mattoso has proposed that, in the late nineteenth century, earning an income of more than 500$ separated the lower middle class from the povo. Property of 2:000 to 10:000$ represented a medium fortune: couples who left such an estate owned a townhouse *sobrado*, perhaps another property, and some slaves.[104] It was not income alone, but also criteria of "nobility" or "dignity" that determined status. The differences between the wages of workers and the wages of public employees might be small, but a clerk had the crucial distinction of not working with his hands. The wages of store clerks might be higher than those of petty officials, but officials did not serve customers from behind a counter. However, money elevated certain artisan occupations to noble status. Some of the richer skilled artisans, many of whom also maintained shops for their wares, were considered members of the middle class. Certainly, the son of a goldsmith, educated as a doctor, might marry the daughter of a well-to-do Portuguese merchant.[105]

To mark these subtle distinctions, Bahians developed outward symbols of status. Men at the fringe of the lower class would grow at least one long fingernail to demonstrate that they never did manual labor. Poor public employees would make sacrifices in order to go to work respectably dressed in a coat and tie.[106] And one of the most important attributes of respectable status in this brown city was whiteness. A black or mulatto person might be able to overcome racial discrimination to arrive at middle-class status, but his achievement was individual and precarious. As Kátia Mattoso has put it, whiteness was more important than wealth, because money can be lost, but whiteness lasts. Families and individuals trying to secure their claim to respectability would try to make marriages to lighter people, thus stamping on their descendants the mark of their social rise.[107]

How, then, can we estimate the size of this middle class? If we are to take literacy as an indication of status, no more than 26 percent of the free men in the province could read and write in 1872; but in Salvador, 39 percent of the free men could read. Newspaper circulation might also serve as an indicator of the number of literate households. In 1893 the combined circulation of four of the five major newspapers was 11,000 for the entire state, suggesting perhaps 6,000 or 7,000 newspaper-reading households; at this time, the total population of Salvador was about 180,000, and the number of households in Salvador about 31,000. This suggests that perhaps one in five households in the capital were significantly literate.[108]

The number of public employees in the province, which might also be taken as a rough indicator of the number of middle-class households, was 1,059 in 1872, not including schoolmasters, priests, or legal professionals such as judges and notaries, most of whom were located in the capital. Categories such as merchants and capitalists in the 1872 census cannot be interpreted in this way, as they comprised both street peddlers and bankers. These occupational categories do not overlap in ways that permit of control, and at most offer suggestions, but they imply that 5 to 10 percent of the families in Salvador could have been considered "middle-class," or "elite," in 1872, and that nine out of ten people in Bahia would be classified as "povo." Taking similar occupations as an indicator for 1920, the number of "public employees" in the state had increased by five times, to 5,734, while the state population doubled. The 1920 occupational categories suggest that perhaps 7 to 14 percent of men employed in Salvador had "middle-class" occupations. Perhaps 10 to 20 percent of the families could by then have been considered "middle-class." Between 1872 and 1920 the population had grown, but the number of nonmanual occupations seems to have expanded faster.[109]

Bahians rarely used the term "middle class." Rather, they preferred the adjective *burguês*, or they would speak about the social sphere of *as famílias*, "the families." While implicitly this contrasted them to an aristocracy, that contrast was rarely made explicit. Far sharper was the contrast between their honorable dignity and the lack of identity of the povo. They stood out through their attributes of "decency": wearing decent clothes in public, behaving with a certain respect and decorum toward each other, showing refinement of manners. A refined family, in city or country, was a *família de trato*, which thus demonstrated its prestige.[110]

Both upward and downward social mobility were common in the unstable and insecure Bahian economy. Some members of the middle ranks of Bahian society, particularly the mulattoes and Portuguese, had risen into this position through education or enrichment in trade. But most of the Bahian-born members belonged to extended family and patronage networks that helped to secure their social positions.[111] Middle-class people might be considered the "poor relations" of the baronial landlords of the Recôncavo. But they were above all *relations*.[112] They belonged to upper-class kin networks by birth or marriage. They actively participated in exchanges of patronage and clientelism. Thus, they needed to have someone to patronize: a beggar who ate in the family's kitchen once a week, a spinster aunt or distant cousin living as an *agregada* in the home, a neighbor who needed access to one of their relatives. One did not need much money to be a minor patron in Bahian society. It was enough to have good connections. Some members of the middle class were born with their good connections. Others cultivated them with the talents of good friendship, prudence, and cunning.[113]

Some institutions in Salvador pertained especially to the middle class. By 1870 religious brotherhood membership continued to be a social duty for the Bahian-born. But it was primarily Portuguese merchants and their clerks, who sometimes lacked family connections and needed the mutual aid benefits of the brotherhoods, who still maintained their memberships with vigor.[114] They also led the way in the 1860's and 1870's, when a great many mutual aid societies formed in Salvador. Recreational clubs became more important around the turn of the century. Dancing and carnival clubs such as Cruz Vermelha and Euterpe provided a wholesome atmosphere for public balls and dances on a modest scale. Over time, the number and nature of associations proliferated. By the 1920's the city had scores of philharmonic societies, recreational clubs, and mutual benefit and charitable associations.[115]

Many of the public facilities created as Salvador modernized between 1870 and 1920 benefited members of the middle class more than anybody else. Public libraries and reading rooms made reading accessible to "poor students" and to modest families. The streetcar lines that opened up the city in the 1870's and 1880's followed routes that were useful to its prosperous families, connecting the traditional center to the garden and beach suburbs of Rio Vermelho and to the low peninsula of Itapagipe, one of the more solidly middle-class suburbs. The streetcar greatly extended the mobility of middle-class people, especially women, who were not rich enough to take a carriage or a sedan chair but would have found it demeaning to walk on the muddy avenues of the city.[116]

The most important formal institution for middle-class families was the school. As capital of the province, Salvador had had the majority of its educational establishments for young men since colonial times. In the late nineteenth and early twentieth centuries, the government, the Catholic church, and private schoolmasters greatly expanded the range of educational services, providing high school and normal school education for girls as well as boys. In 1916 there were 1,800 secondary school students in Salvador. Between 1912 and 1922, at the state-sponsored, official Ginásio da Bahia, 215 students completed the six-year course and were graduated with the degree of *bacharel*.[117]

And the academies of higher education offered an opportunity for a few young men of the middle class to be certified as "doctors," fit for any sort of public career. Through 1889 the medical school, the seminary, and the normal school were the only opportunities for higher studies in Bahia itself. Many students went to São Paulo or Recife in order to get a law degree. But following the federal decentralization of education in 1889, Bahian legal scholars founded a law academy, the Faculdade Livre de Direito, in 1891, and engineers and mathematicians from the secondary school founded the Polytechnical Academy in 1900. Enrollments in institutions of higher education had grown significantly by 1922, and more of the students in Bahia's academies were from Bahia rather than neighboring states. In 1943 a group of Catholic intellectuals under the leadership of Isaías Alves opened the Faculdade de Filosofia da Bahia, which became the nucleus of the Universidade Federal da Bahia.[118]

The "students" of Salvador formed a social group of their own and stood in some ways apart from their origins. The Bohemian light-heartedness or debauchery of student residences (*repúblicas*), as well as the shared rigors of the academies, forged enduring friendships within *turmas*, the graduating classes of the academies. The general tone of student life was frivolous, but students also formed political associations in the academies. The law schools had long been launching grounds for radical movements such as the republican and abolitionist movements. After their support of Rui Barbosa's failed *civilista* candidacies in 1910 and 1919, Bahian students became more seriously ideological. In 1920, for example, students brawled with military officers and recruits, whom they had taunted during a parade. The incident revolved fairly simply around honor. But in 1932 students in the medical school fought a siege with guns against the state police, in solidarity with the São Paulo rebellion against Getúlio Vargas's dictatorship.[119] In the 1940's and 1950's Brazilian university politics became a major arena for political competition. Whether serious or frivolous, the figure of the student, formed as a gentleman, possessing powers of rhetoric and science, was vital to the middle-class sense of identity and of the possibility of social mobility.

Two linked political issues for the Bahian middle class were thus the maintenance of public education and the expansion of public employment. Families expected a diploma to qualify their sons and daughters for public posts. Many of the jobs that the state offered paid poorly; yet they offered the compensation of security, tenure, and pensions. In pursuit of government careers, the middle class wavered between publicly affirming the liberal ideals of fairness and open opportunity, and privately pursuing advantage through favor and patronage. State government employment and opportunities in the federal bureaucracy also expanded. During the dictatorship of Vargas in the 1930's, federal revenues and federal employment ballooned, defining what one critic called the "Paper-Shuffling State," the *Estado Cartorial.*[120]

Like workers, middle-class Brazilians also mobilized against inflation, or as they put it in the 1890's, against "scarcity" (*carestia*). Prices rose in Brazil throughout the nineteenth century, the most mobilizing episode of inflation being a state-induced speculative bubble, the Encilhamento of 1890–91. In Rio de Janeiro prices may have doubled between 1889 and 1892. In Salvador the housing crisis was the most prominent feature of inflation in the 1890's. Newspaper columnists complained that couples could not afford to marry because they could not find rooms for rent.[121] Increases in the cost of living became routine in Bahia. The most notable crisis came during World War I, when the state government was in arrears in paying its employees.[122] Public employees went on strike along with workers in 1919, with the sympathy of much of the middle class.[123]

World War I itself marked a division between generations, and a turning point in the mentalities of middle-class Bahians. Though the war was distant, Bahians could participate in it with vicarious enthusiasm, obsessively mapping the battlefronts.[124] Following the war and the Russian Revolution, the crisis of cosmopolitan values was particularly acute in political ideas. Brazilian political thinkers responded quickly to the proliferation of antiliberal ideologies, and the middle classes became notably more mobilized than they had been. The year 1922, symbolic because of the centennial of independence, saw the foundation of the Communist party of Brazil, the

Federation for Women's Progress, the modern art movement, the conservative Catholic Centro Dom Vital, and the first *Tenente* revolt of junior officers in Rio against the "insults" of the oligarchical politicians. Nationalism, rather than "civilization," became the common denominator of a wide variety of movements: monarchist, socialist, fascist, militarist. A few of the politicians of Bahia developed concerns about the social questions of labor and poverty.[125]

But the middle class of Bahia was still, in the 1940's, largely understandable as an appendage to the "aristocracy" of the Recôncavo and the coronéis of the backlands, a collection of second sons and poor relations of the "noble" families of Bahia. It was a way station in the downward mobility of "decadent traditional" families of the Recôncavo that had lost their place in agriculture and were forced to switch their strategies, finding toeholds for social survival in the professions and in the small and large offices of the public payroll.[126]

The "Ricos": The Elite of Bahia

Politics in Salvador was largely a matter for the upper class, the elite. Between 1870 and 1900, the Bahian establishment was still a coalition of the great vote-swaying landlords in the Recôncavo, barons of the Empire who controlled the Liberal and Conservative parties of the province. Bahian figures such as Cotegipe formed a permanent part of the national establishment of big-time political figures in Rio de Janeiro. By the mid-1890's, the demotion of the Bahians could be measured by the contrasting rise to national prominence of Rio Grande do Sul politicians.[127] During the Republic a few Bahian figures functioned as federal power-brokers and federal ministers: J. J. Seabra was a minister, a strong state boss, and often considered a presidential candidate; Senator Rui Barbosa was a leading architect of the first republican military dictatorship of 1890–92, and henceforth a leading presidential contender; Miguel Calmon was a minister and potentially the focus of a Bahia–Minas Gerais alliance. But the symptom of Bahia's decline was that one of the most successful political cliques, the three Calmon brothers, prospered in the 1920's on the suffrance of the Minas Gerais boss, Artur Bernardes.[128] By 1930 the Bahian elite had declined into a provincial oligarchy.

The elite of Salvador were in some ways as diverse as the middle classes. Loosely defined as the "refined people," *a gente fina* (or even as *a gente finíssima* to distinguish them from the middle class), the elite included all the families of sufficient wealth and background to be included in the semipublic balls, theatrical receptions, and political and philanthropic banquets of society or in the semiprivate salons, weddings, baptisms, and funerals of the "traditional families." Money could ease even a newly arrived family into the elite. Anyone with an estate above 10 contos in the nineteenth century could be considered well-off, owning houses, slaves, and other property. But at the pinnacle of the scale of wealth, no more than 2 percent of those whose estates were probated (already a select group) left more than 200 contos; almost all of these were merchants or capitalists, with a few sugar mill owners and professionals.[129]

As defined by the occupations of its men, the elite included at least three major sections. First, it included the "aristocratic" or "traditional" families of the Recôncavo, whose sugar mills were a declining economic force even in the 1870's, but who maintained a firm hold in the inner circles of politics, banking, and the professions in Salvador. Many of them were also landlords. Second, it included the Portuguese and Brazilian capitalists who controlled wholesale trade in the city and portions of international commerce. And third, it loosely attracted the less-rooted north European and North American capitalists, most of them merchants, bankers, and shippers, who dominated certain lucrative lines of business such as the export of cacao and the import of coal. But there were men in the elite who came from outside these groups: archbishops such as Dom Jerônimo, prelate from 1894 to 1924; army commanders, some of them from families of Bahian origins; and backlands politicians such as Luís Vianna, who rose in the Conservative party and came to control state politics in the 1890's and 1900's.[130]

From 1870 through 1889 the Bahian elite always included some career public servants of the Empire. Most of these men followed career paths beginning in the official law academies at São Paulo and Recife and continuing through public service as magistrates, election as deputies, and a rotation of electoral and appointive posts in the service of the emperor. At any given time Bahia might be headed by a provincial president from another province.[131] But the rapidly shifting ministries tended to keep provincial presidents traveling from province to province, so that administrative continuity and effective power usually lay in the hands of the imperially appointed chief of police, the interim vice president of the province, or the inner circle of incumbents in the provincial assembly.

By 1890, if not earlier, Brazilians in Bahia and other states referred to the elite as the *classes conservadoras*, which literally means the "conservative classes" but can perhaps be best translated as "the business interests."[132] Bahia's merchants found a forum and a voice in the Commercial Association of Bahia. Like planters, they believed that measures for the promotion of agriculture and commerce were in the interests of all Bahians and of the state's "agricultural vocation." They believed in railroad construction, improvement of the docks, improvements in public works infrastructure for the capital city and some towns of the interior, and, generally, in policies to promote economic stability and attract foreign capital. They opposed whatever might be considered "social" measures or pandering to the rabble of Salvador. And they were lukewarm to any measures that might be considered aggressively modernizing or "industrializing": European immigration, yes, but abolition of slavery, no; import duties for revenues, yes, but export taxes that burdened agriculture, no; railroad subsidies, yes, but guarantees of profit for factories, no.[133] In their policies, however, the upper classes of Bahia were not extraordinarily different from the classes conservadoras of São Paulo. Even there, it was not until the 1920's that what might be described as an "industrialists' social project" emerged.[134]

Although the classes conservadoras of Bahia developed a commanding consensus on the policies of government, they were not able to form a solid political machine during the Old Republic. The merchants, particularly the foreign-born merchants, were prone to stay "neutral" in politics. At times they formed a sort of "peace party" that protested through the Commercial Association when rioting or police repression threatened business, as in 1899. Their abstention may have contributed to the failure of the Bahian political bosses to assemble a stable coalition. The relative immunity of many backlands coronéis from central military force may also have frustrated the formation of a disciplined single party in Bahia. But the infighting within established factions of state politicians probably had the greatest effect. Every Bahian party that consolidated a solid incumbent position fell apart internally within a few elections. The two epochs of relatively stable incumbency, the Partido Republicano da Bahia coalition of 1900 to 1912 and the Seabrista machine of 1912 to 1920, fell apart under the pressures of internal war and federal intervention.[135]

In 1870 the Salvador elite still had the ideal of aristocracy to hold them together. As the provincial wing of the national establishment of the "best" and most "traditional" families of the Empire, they could easily bind together rural landlords and urban politicians through a common system of honors from the Empire: medals of membership in the Order of the Rose and other honorific orders; commissions in the National Guard; letters of commendation from the emperor for notable accomplishments; and even lifetime, nonhereditary titles ranging from baron to duke. Even Portuguese merchants were rather easily integrated into this system. Through charitable contributions or public service, they could obtain the honorary title *comendador* (commander of a philanthropic or honorific society) or a barony from the emperor. The great slave-trading fortune of the Pereira Marinhos, for instance, earned titles of nobility from both the Portuguese and the Brazilian monarchies.[136]

The ingredients of the elite coalition changed under the Republic. First, some of the establishment families of the Empire, such as the Rui Barbosa family, transferred their associations and their base of operations to Rio de Janeiro. While they cultivated a few Bahian ties and conveniently protested provincial nostalgia, in the second generation these families belonged to the Carioca elite rather than the Bahian. This process continued during the Republic, as many members of some families, such as the Moniz de Aragão, moved to the federal capital.[137] Second, some of the great sugar mill families dropped out of power with the decline of their rural fortunes and the turbulent "revolutionary" transition from empire to republic in 1889. And third, the surviving Bahian politicians found themselves much more dependent on alliances with coalitions of backland coronéis. In the 1920's politicians with academic credentials (*doutores*) were an uneasy projection of the coronéis, supposedly leaders, but often dismissed as "phonographs" of the real bosses.[138]

In the course of the Old Republic, the system managed to survive reshufflings of power with essentially the same complex of ingredients. In Bahia an oligarchy ruled; the republican system there was antidemocratic, as it was throughout Brazil. But that oligarchy was fairly responsive to the claims of organized clienteles of all sorts (particularly those of political allies). And it rested on the fairly comfortable base of consensus in favor of "civilization" and capitalism that prevailed in most of the private and public institutions.

The 1930 Depression and the Estado Novo

After World War I the elites of Bahia apparently shifted their politics to accommodate the participation of new ideologies and new "popular" forces. The Partido Republicano Demócrata of Seabra operated an urban machine in the capital based partly on Seabra's personal popularity, and in alliance with coronéis it dominated state politics from 1912 through 1920. The merchants of Bahia and the elite opposition temporarily made common cause with workers and unpaid state employees, on strike in 1919, against the incumbent governor, Antônio Moniz. The banker Goes Calmon, governor from 1924 to 1928, gave the veneer of an enlightened, "modernizing" movement to the Bahian incumbents by appointing university men to major posts and championing infrastructure development and education. The Calmon coalition nominated Vital Soares, another banker, to succeed him as governor, thus apparently consolidating the leadership of doutores representing the classes conservadoras. Yet counterpointing this apparent "bourgeois" ascendancy was an increase in political fragmentation from 1920 through 1930, when the federal government concluded direct treaties with Bahia's interior warlord coronéis, bypassing the state government in Salvador. If anything, the trend was toward entrenchment of *coronelismo*.[139]

The Getúlio Vargas revolution of 1930 shook all Brazilian state oligarchies. Vargas's revolution proceeded partly because of the national fiscal crisis that followed the 1929 crash, and partly because of a conventional political impasse when the major states split in the caucus to select an "official" presidential candidate. It also stemmed partly from traditional discontents within each state throughout Brazil. Every political machine had accumulated a backlog of opposition enemies and resentful "allies." But it also appealed to the new, radical politics that was challenging the rule of oligarchies. In São Paulo and Minas Gerais, democracy movements of the middle class (similar to that which had opened up suffrage in Argentina in 1912) had called for a secret ballot and an end to electoral fraud. Throughout Brazil, students and professionals in the middle class had been mobilized by Rui Barbosa's two civilista, antimilitary, and anti-bossist presidential campaigns of 1910 and 1919. Some civilians had cheered the challenge to oligarchical "corruption" when *tenentes* (junior army officers) had rebelled in 1922 and again in 1924, and the tenente-led Prestes Column had marched up and down Brazil throughout 1926.[140]

At first, the 1930 revolution suggested the possibility of a political opening in Bahia. As usual, the incumbent faction of the Bahian oligarchy got caught on the wrong side of the fence. The old guard of Bahian politicians would not conciliate with Vargas's 1931 appointed governor, or "interventor," Tenente Juracy Magalhães. They ran "nativist" slates against the "foreign" interventor in 1933, but Juracy was able to put together the Partido Social Demócrata, with enough disaffected coronéis to carry the state elections. Juracy's incongruous new grouping tied the coronéis's electoral power to the "middle-class" reformist coalition of Vargas. It seemed possible that either this party or new ideological movements, such as the fascist Integralista party, might drastically reshape the bases of political power in the state. But both the old guard and the new forces were cut short when the Vargas Estado Novo dictatorship from 1937 to 1945 suspended elections and installed an authoritarian, centralized dictatorship. The Bahian oligarchy was spared a decisive test of its power.

And gradually the old Bahian elites made their peace with the "conquering" federal elite. Both new and old groups survived into the postwar democratic republic. Juracy Magalhães, who had resigned as governor in 1937, returned to Bahia after the Estado Novo to revive the political alliances that he had forged there. In the 1940's and 1950's he and his family used Bahia as a platform for launching themselves into national politics. Other political families of the Old Republic, such as the Mangabeiras, who had formed alliances with Varguista groups, formed the nucleus of another major political grouping in the populist democratic politics of the late 1940's.[141]

Not only the political intervention but also the economic crisis and recovery of the 1930's brought about a leveling and unification of the segments of the state elite. The Bahian economy, particularly the economy of the cacao zone, boomed in the late 1920's and crashed disastrously in 1929. Exports had jumped dramatically during the war; 1919 was the strongest year of exports Bahia had ever had, at £13 million sterling. After the war, they again rose to high levels, peaking at about £8 million in 1927. The crisis began in 1929, when the value of exports fell to £4.4 million, then sank to £2.7 million in 1930, and to £1 million in 1931. The price of cacao had been sixteen cents in 1926; it bottomed at four cents in 1932. Thus, the economic system that had sustained the classes conservadoras coalition of foreign and local capitalists fell apart. In Salvador, where much employment revolved around the commercial activities of the seaport, the crisis was fast and acute. The import-export merchants who had been the biggest capitalists on the Bahian scene were badly hit by the collapse of prices. Importers found themselves stuck with unsaleable inventories and cut off from credit by bankrupt European partners. In Ilhéus, Itabuna, and Belmonte, cacao planters who had borrowed in the boom years were bankrupted, and the merchant houses foreclosed on them. The foreign cacao exporters were also paralyzed. Major firms such as Wildberger and Stevenson, after foreclosing, found themselves turned into plantation owners almost overnight.[142]

The recovery from the Great Depression also changed the Bahian economic elite by making them dependent partners of the federal government. The Bahian Cacao Institute, created in 1931, tried to regulate debts, to control prices and marketing, and, briefly, to monopolize exporting. The Institute of Sugar and Alcohol, created by the federal government to keep sugar mills running during the crisis, set quotas and regulations for sugar markets.[143] These Vargas programs for recovery from the crisis transferred control of the Brazilian economy from private capitalists to state bureaucrats. Initially the government concentrated its efforts on the defense of export commodities such as coffee and cacao. But gradually, and perhaps unintentionally, these and other government measures, such as the devaluation of the currency and the control of labor, had the effect of encouraging an industrial boom. In São Paulo this gave an important boost to established industrial capitalists. Bahia's industrial production also grew, but some measures indicate that it remained structurally stagnant at the small workshop level. Most Bahian businessmen were not prepared to take advantage of state protections and become a subsidized industrial bourgeoisie.[144]

During the Great Depression and World War II, the combination of isolation from foreign ties and growing dependence on the state meant that the Bahian upper classes became both socially and economically more homogeneous and more "Brazilian." Many of the fortunes of Bahian merchant houses became "naturalized" as Brazilian fortunes when branch firms were forced to cut ties with their European parent firms.[145] In the 1940's Bahian capital became more Brazilian, less foreign, than it had been in the 1920's. And socially, the upper classes of Bahia became more unified. Many of the surviving European merchant families intermarried with "traditional" Recôncavo families. This process, which had been going on since the assimilation of Portuguese merchants by Recôncavo planters in the colonial period, blurred the boundaries within the classes conservadoras.[146]

At the end of World War II and of the Vargas dictatorship, Bahia stood on the verge of tremendous modernization and social change. Salvador had grown in population from 129,000 in 1870 to 348,000 in 1945. Fifteen years later, in 1960, its population would be 650,000; in 1980 it would be 1.5 million.[147] Although the economy remained largely commercial in 1945, the city had begun some industrialization, and the Brazilian push for development in the 1950's would force Bahia, like every region of Brazil, to attempt industrial expansion and modernization. Its society would change with the growth of a bureaucratic welfare state determined to regulate and oversee the population to an extent barely imagined beforehand. Its families would transform as well, though they would retain much of their old character. The strategies of families between 1870 and 1945 set a pattern of conservative adaptation to pressures for change.

2

Home Life

THE FAMILY based on formal marriage was the exception, not the rule, in Bahia. Counts suggest that in the 1850's and 1860's at least 30–45 percent of Salvador's population never married.[1] In a partial household survey done in Salvador in 1855, 52 percent of households were found to be informal unions.[2] In a central parish of Salvador in the 1860's, only 30 percent of the free infants born were legitimate. Four out of six white infants were legitimate, but fewer than one out of six nonwhite infants. Taking slave births into account—and virtually all of them were illegitimate—only 25 percent of the births in Salvador were legitimate.[3] The 1872 census of the province of Bahia found that 25 percent of all women and 24 percent of men had married. In 1920, 26 percent of all women had married. The proportion of marriages had increased slightly by 1940: 30 percent of all women had married. A study conducted during the census of 1940 found that 15 percent of all women over 50 were spinsters who had never married; yet half of these "single" women had borne one or more children.[4] Even among the upper classes, marriage was not universal during the colonial period and in the nineteenth century. Virtually every Brazilian of the upper classes must have had an uncle who lived with his mistress, or a great-aunt who went to live with a priest. Everyone had spinster aunts and bachelor uncles who never married.

How, then, could the most influential interpreters of Brazilian history in the 1920's and 1930's, Oliveira Vianna and Gilberto Freyre, have persuaded their fellow Brazilians that the patriarchal family was the representative colonial institution and the most significant colonial legacy to contemporary character?[5] In addition to the common tendency to assume that olden days were stricter and more ordered than the present, the convention of silence among Brazilians concerning the informal norms of the family lives of the mass of the population perhaps contributed to this.

Possibly, too, their more critical readers understood Freyre and Oliveira Vianna in a limited sense as sketching a psychological portrait of the upper classes, as speaking of the masters, not the slaves. Within the upper classes, although there was a broad range of practice, there was indeed a "patriarchal family."

The Bahian upper-class "patriarchal" family was not necessarily a family based on a self-sufficient household economy, but rather a model of a set of social relations. Any codification of the complex and flexible norms of this family is necessarily arbitrary, yet a few general principles were common features of the patriarchal model. It held that men should have authority over women inside the family. Husbands had authority over their wives, fathers over their daughters, brothers over their sisters. It held that elders should have authority over junior members of the family. Fathers ruled their sons as long as the sons lived under the same roof, often into adulthood. It held that the members of the core of the family, usually a couple and their children, but perhaps including a parent or sibling of the couple, should have authority over dependents and servants at the fringes. The Bahian patriarchal family took shape in the context of plantation slavery, and even after abolition it assumed the presence of servants within the household.

The Brazilian model of kinship was more or less similar to west European kinship systems, with some significant local variations that complemented the patriarchal family. Although fathers had authority in their families, Brazilians did not define family relations simply along male lines. Brazilians reckoned their kinship by bilateral descent rules. Every person recognized kinship to both mother's and father's kin. The inconsistency of Brazilian naming patterns, which usually had married women retaining their maiden names, and which might assign surnames from the mother's lineage to sons or daughters, encouraged greater flexibility in identifying kinship with both paternal and maternal lines.[6] Brazilians did not, in practice, recognize kinship farther back than their grandparents and further out than collateral kin descended from their grandparents, first cousins. Theoretically, kinship could be extended nearly infinitely, and Brazilian law recognized collaterals at the second-cousin range for certain purposes, but in practice a principle of "shallow descent" limited the circle of kin. To compensate for the ambiguity of their kinship system, Brazilian families developed preferential patterns of cousin marriage that created better defined in-groups of kin, usually emphasizing male lines. Fathers frequently married their children off to the children of their brothers; these parallel cousin marriages defined a group of kin, all descended from a single grandfather, with a stronger group identity.[7] One consequence of the indeterminacy of the kinship system was that the kin group living in the same household was the effective family. Extended kin ties were important, but they could be lost if not reinforced by familiarity, by inmarriage, or by some other device.

The patriarchal family developed in the context of the Brazilian law on inheritance and property, which also provided some checks on the patriarchal model. The law required that all property in marriage be community property, unless it was specifically excluded by dowry or prenuptial contract. It required the consent of both wife and husband for sale of community property. In a similar vein, inheritance law required that all children receive equal shares of a parent's estate, allowing parents to will at most a third of their estate. To some extent, this limited the power of men to coerce their wives or their children; the claims of family members on property were legally set and sacrosanct. Although families could bend the law in order to endow certain children at the expense of others, they were pressured to endow children evenly. Yet another consequence of the forced division of estates was that siblings of landed families often lived near one another, on their shares of the parents' land.[8]

The patriarchal model of family relations was the predominant ideal for Brazilian upper-class families. But they had access to at least three other models of belonging and authority. One was a model of egalitarian, companionate relations in marriage, and of limited authority of parents over their children. It held that husbands and wives should be bound by affection and companionship, rather than respect and distance, and that children, at least adult children, should have autonomy from their parents. This model had a traditional base of authority in church doctrine on marriage. It became more prominent after 1870, and it fit better with the organization of families in the city.

Another model of the family was a traditional counterpoint to the power of men in the patriarchal family that traced the continuity of the family through its women. It divided authority in the family into spheres pertaining to the husband and the wife respectively. Women had more authority inside the home than did men. This model encouraged sons to break away from their families of origin to escape their fathers' authority. By contrast, it encouraged daughters and their husbands to remain affiliated with the parents' household. Men often had closer connections with their fathers-in-law than with their fathers. As a consequence, family and kinship ties tended to be defined through women.

Finally, yet another model of the family had a long tradition in Brazil. This was the informal, illegitimate family composed primarily of a mother and her children. The mother was the center of this family, though the father might visit, or even live with them in the household. While official culture tended to identify this as lack of a family, rather than as a form of family, in practice Brazilian law recognized it as a common law family. Paternity was a tenuous affiliation in Brazil. A woman could not deny maternity, but a man could formally claim paternity only through marriage or through a notarial act of recognition. Portuguese law codified in the sixteenth century had established two sets of family regulations: laws of marital property pertaining to notables (*nobres*) who married in the church and transmitted significant property; and laws pertaining to the property of the country folk (*peões*), who did not necessarily marry. After a reform in 1847, Brazilian family law in the nineteenth and twentieth centuries continued to define two roads to family formation: marriage and the father's notarial act of legitimation.

Between 1870 and 1945, the major trend in the families of the Bahian upper class was the decline of the hierarchical structure of the patriarchal family and of customs that symbolized patriarchal authority. More companionate forms of marriage, now legitimated as "modern" and "civilized," became the norm. Much of the literature on the family in Brazil assumes that the patriarchal form of the family was simply rural and antique, a phenomenon of the colonial era, whereas by contrast the companionate family was a product of its breakdown in nineteenth-century urbanization. The persistence of old features in twentieth-century families might signify that urban families became "semipatriarchal," or that they constituted a "residual patriarchal" type from the mid nineteenth century onward.[9]

It could also be that there was a common core of roles, or visions of the household and its membership, and a fairly standard repertoire of routines and rituals of family life. They were put into practice in somewhat different ways in the country and in the city. Patriarchal and semipatriarchal forms of the family were not successive stages of social development, but rather coexisting and alternative forms of legitimating and organizing the family.

One Family's Pilgrimages

Perhaps the simplest way to dissolve the dichotomies between rural and urban families is to describe the trajectory of one prominent Bahian family. The story of three generations of the family of Anna Ribeiro de Goes Bittencourt illustrates the close ties between kin in country and city and the frequent passage of families back and forth between rural and urban modes. Born in 1843, Anna was raised on her father's sugar plantation, Fazenda Apí, 50 miles northwest of Salvador. This distance was far enough that she did not see the capital until she was twelve years old. And then her family had to ride for two days, stopping overnight at plantations along the way, in order to take her to consult an eye specialist. Years later, she still remembered the drama of her arrival at night in the lamp-lit, sloping Pelourinho plaza, the bustle of the slaves carrying barrels and boxes up the hilly streets, and the Holy Week processions.[10]

After that, she rarely visited Salvador, but on the *fazenda* the family's relations came from a wide circle. For companions she had her slave chambermaid and neighboring cousins, and staying in her house, the daughters of a priest who was a deputy in Rio de Janeiro. Relatives and other planters from the district crowded in at festivals, some of them young men returning from the academies in Recife and Salvador. Indeed, her first suitor was a cousin studying medicine in Salvador, who died of tuberculosis. In 1865 Anna married another distant cousin, Sócrates de Araujo Bittencourt, who also studied medicine. Yet the fazenda had contacts with remoter backlands as well as with the city. One day in her childhood her grandfather had appeared unannounced, a blind, white-bearded patriarch, leading an entourage of slaves and cowboys from his plantation in Itapicurú.

In 1868 her husband Sócrates took over Apí, and the family settled in the countryside, making occasional visits to the capital. Anna bore her children there on the fazenda. When her son Pedro Ribeiro de Araujo needed to go to secondary school in 1878, her own mother moved to Salvador with him for three years. Later, when he went to law school in Recife, her mother again accompanied him and some other Bahian boys, living there with them for the duration of his studies.

Pedro Ribeiro, born in 1866, became a judge and followed the peripatetic career of most young magistrates, crossing the backlands. In 1900 he settled permanently in Salvador in one of the choice posts as district judge. He eventually rose to be *desembargador*, judge of the appeals court.[11] While his political career prospered, his parents' fazenda had declined. Sócrates and Anna had owned over a hundred slaves, and with abolition they were ruined. The sugar industry slumped, and Sócrates turned the plantation from sugar cane to cattle grazing. For a while they traveled with Pedro to his judgeships. In 1895 they retired to Apí. Pedro's children would remember Sócrates as a quiet, white-haired man who sat on the porch whittling rosewood logs into bundles of toothpicks, which he would send to the family in town. With easier transportation by automobile, Apí became the summer home for the family. After Sócrates died in 1907, Anna and her spinster daughter moved to a house next to her son's in Salvador, and only the boys used the fazenda as an occasional hunting lodge.

Many years later, Pedro's son Clemente Mariani bought Apí. He restored the old Big House, furnishing it with eighteenth-century antiques and plates from the China trade, and stocked the ranch with pure-bred cattle. In 1980, at the end of his life, descendants of slaves of the fazenda still lived in shanties on the estate, some still serving in the Big House when guests came from the city. Behind the hills of pasture stood the derricks of the state oil company, now the major business in the district. Clemente had become an industrialist, apprenticing in the Magalhães sugar company as a young lawyer in the 1920's, moving into politics and banking later, and finally living in Rio and directing banks and a petrochemical refinery in Bahia. His tie to Apí was more than casual, for his parents had sent him as a boy to live with Anna and Sócrates on the fazenda for several years.[12] Having heard stories of the exploits of her grandfather Pedro Ribeiro in the war of independence from Anna, Clemente perpetuated the memory by having his bank reprint the old epic poem *Paraguassú*, which celebrated Pedro Ribeiro's heroism.[13]

More than just a sense of lineage linked urban and rural families in Bahia. As the Ribeiro de Goes family story shows, families of the Recôncavo changed their setting fairly often, while their customs changed less drastically. By the late nineteenth century, with steamboats, roads, and railroads, families could move back and forth from town to country seasonally. They did not necessarily transform themselves in these changes in context. They would bring house slaves from the fazenda to the town house, and women would copy dress patterns from Paris out on the land.[14]

Gilberto Freyre understood the difference between urban and rural families as an antagonism between plantation patriarchy and the city. In the early nineteenth century, he argued, the cities triumphed, succeeding to the mantle that fell from the plantation. But an urban elite culture had always existed in Salvador, which had been the capital of the Brazils under the Portuguese.[15] The change in families was a shift in emphasis between options that already existed, rather than the rise of a novel way of life. In Bahia, by the turn of the twentieth century, the patriarchal family had been transformed in both city and country, but families in the countryside preserved more vestiges of its old customs. The descriptions of types of families that follow suggest the ways in which the organization and the function of the family in three different social classes—landlords, urban elites, and middle classes—inflected routines, definitions of familial roles for adults, attitudes toward children and socialization, and tolerance for deviation.[16]

The Country Family

In the late nineteenth century, the family of large rural landlords was still the family of the Big House, if not quite Freyre's patriarchal family. In Bahia, the sugar planters of the Recôncavo, more than the tobacco growers or ranchers, embodied the grandeur and opulence that Freyre evokes. The Big House, next to its sugar mill and slave quarters, loomed largest and grandest in the rural landscape, dominating an establishment "about the size of a large village."[17] The portrait that follows will speak most often of the Recôncavo families of the sugar plantations.

At times the "families" of the landlords stretched to include all the plantation and its clientele—that is, all the tenants, slaves, and squatters who owed allegiance to the house. As the son of a slave woman remembered it, "the contract farmers and his followers, sharecroppers in cane farming, were in this semi-feudal milieu the peasants [*peões*], the contractors for work on the *engenho*, the voters for electoral campaigns, the companions at cards on the long, tedious nights of that agrarian retreat. In those times, every *senhor de engenho* surrounded himself with a small court in his own fashion."[18]

Rather than residing in a separate barracoon or in cabins, the slaves on Bahian plantations lived in a *senzala*, barracks attached or immediately adjacent to the Big House.[19] But proximity to the master's roof was not necessary. Nearly every free man was informally attached to, or identified with, a fazenda and a patron. Tenants owed obedience to landlords, and the landlords in return owed them protection and toleration of their residence on the land. From the point of view of the Big House, the Christian charity of the lady who took medicine to the huts of the poor ideally manifested the family's protection of its farthest-flung members. Even in punishing slaves, masters would orchestrate poses of forgiveness. They tolerated slaves running away to beg sanctuary on a neighbor's plantation, and a master might collude with the overseer to have him threaten a beating, "so that the delinquent, terrified, would run to seek godfatherly protection from his own master."[20]

If the gravitational field of the "family" sometimes radiated to all the population of the plantation, in a strict sense it included only the core of the master and mistress, their parents and their children. Often this core contained factions, such as a division between the man and his favorites and the wife and hers. Both legal definitions of property rights and custom stressed that the ties between a woman and her children were stronger than those between her and her husband; at the same time they recognized that the center of the family was the man and his lineage of heirs.[21]

Residence in the Big House usually pulled others into the orbit of the family. Dependents of all sorts formed part of the family, among them relatives such as young bachelors, spinsters, and widows, who because of their age ranked higher than the children of the core in daily life. Farther from the center might be illegitimate children of the master, whose position in a family could vary enormously: some were brought up like legitimate heirs, and others were merely pampered servants. Farther still was the sphere of unrelated dependents, or *agregados* (literally, "added on" people). In comparison with the family core, the outer rings of the household were unstable, their membership changing. Dependents were half guests, and hospitality often enlarged the household with guests and travelers.[22]

Beyond the dependents were employees and servants, some of whom might rank higher: a big plantation would have a chapel, with a priest in at least occasional attendance, and in remote areas, a family might hire a tutor or a schoolmaster for the children. Finally, lowest in rank but close to the core were the house slaves, later the servants. The vocabulary for servants differentiated the *mãe preta*, or mammy; *ama*, or dry nurse; *mucama*, or chambermaid; *moleque*, or boy; *cozinheira*, or cook; *doceira*, or candymaker; *rendeira*, or lacemaker; *mordomo*, or butler. The complexity of ranking among the servants was complicated by special attachments. Ideally every lady had her own mucama as chambermaid and every girl her own mucama as playmate. Dependent or visiting kin might own some of the slaves in the house. Yet the servants could be referred to collectively as "the kitchen," *a cozinha*. Slavery bound masters and servants together at the beginning of this period. Probably more house slaves belonged to the family by birth than were conscripted by purchase. Even after emancipation in 1888, the relations between masters and servants, particularly those who had been slaves, preserved the exploitative intimacy of slave paternalism.[23]

The routines that set these complex households in motion were determined by the self-sufficiency and isolation of residence on the plantation: "A trip to Salvador was like a trip to China."[24] A letter saying that a daughter in Salvador was ill might arrive in the Recôncavo only after she was dead. Domestic production or purchases from the small farmers of the neighborhood met most of the austere needs of the plantation. Indeed, in the nineteenth century the thriving of the plantations may have stifled the growth of local market towns.[25] A plantation would buy salt beef, meal, slave cloth, some artisan ware and furniture, blades, machinery, and fuel. Only in the twentieth century was the self-sufficiency of the countryside broken by the railroad, regular mails, and traveling salesmen.

Nevertheless, even in the early nineteenth century, conspicuous luxury spending was the pride of successful planters.[26] In 1854, before the decline of the sugar sector, the British consul James Wetherell observed: "The Senhors d'Engenho, the Lords of Estates, are the great people, and spend with an unsparing hand. Anything they see novel, anything exciting to their tastes or luxury must be had 'coute qui coute.' Shopkeepers in the city are but too ready to satisfy this craving, at the risk of a long payment, or even at a loss."[27] In their pursuit of luxury, planters necessarily looked to urban standards and commercial networks.

Country routines followed natural and agricultural cycles. The division between an active day and a silent, omen-filled night remained marked, even after the Big Houses could light themselves with kerosene lamps and electric lights. In the evenings, families retired to play cards or backgammon among themselves or with their dependents. For most of the nineteenth century, the rainy season bogged families down behind impassable roads. Certain months—May and June particularly—were the season for visits, which might entail extending hospitality for days or weeks at a time. With rail lines and better roads, entire families shifted with the seasons, living in Salvador or Santo Amaro during the slack times, and moving back to the fazenda only for the harvest months.[28]

Women's domestic work or idleness varied relatively little with the seasons. Indoors, ladies supervised the kitchen or made jellies and sweets; they sewed clothes or made lace. Women's education, accomplishment, and manners were one of the major factors distinguishing the gentility of the customs of rural landlords from the rustic folkways of their neighbors, whose wives would come to mass nursing their babies, and with their breasts exposed.[29]

To the extent that the master occupied himself with administration, and most did while they were resident, his days followed the rhythm of tasks of farming and harvest. Men's daily routines took place largely outside the house, in the fields, the mill, or on the veranda. Sugar milling was the business that most regimented the time of the Recôncavo and its families, for the need for close timing and intense work at the harvest sharply marked a different tempo. As central mills came to dominate sugar production after 1880, the rhythms of a factory in the fields, with whistles and work shifts, took over the most prosperous plantations.[30]

If farming established the routines of these families, religious tradition determined their rituals. The cycles of religious festivities and observances, rather than calendar time, marked off their weeks and years. The harvest festival, or *botada*, for the sugar crop, which at its most complete included a mass with a blessing of the mill and fields, a banquet, and dancing, brought the agricultural year and sacred rituals together. It sanctified and celebrated the community of the plantation family with the master at its head. The liturgical cycle and folk festivals intersected in other rituals, too. Saints' days formed a major part of religious practice in rural Brazil, and chief among them was São João, Midsummer's Day. Not only sugar plantations but also smaller households in Bahia celebrated São João with a bonfire, special sweets and genipap wine, and a table that sat the entire clan together.[31]

Every family had domestic, private rituals that also took on religious forms. Each plantation had a festival on the day of its own patron saint, usually the birthday of the master. The great occasions—births, marriages, and deaths—were also sacred occasions—baptisms, weddings, and funerals. But plantations seldom found it convenient to celebrate Sunday mass, either at the parish church or with a priest visiting their own chapel. Some families improvised their own religious rituals, such as Sunday prayers, scripture readings, or hymns in their chapel or oratory. Others led novenas, with each day dedicated to a category of worker on the plantation: cowboys, cart drivers, and so on, until the last day would be a novena for the *senhor*, with a mass said by a padre from the city. Others did without worship, though none did without the saints.[32]

Until the end of the nineteenth century, the absolute, patriarchal authority of the head of the family was prescribed by the military functions of the clan, and by slavery. In the colonial period, the royal government virtually abdicated power in the countryside to landlord families organized in kin groups—clans. It entrusted them with defense against Indians and each other.[33] All expected the head of a family to command his children, kin, and tenants like a chieftain. When a landlord rode out, he would go in white drill, a broad-brimmed hat, and spit-polished boots, with silver trappings on his horse and an entourage of tenants who always accompanied him.[34] During the nineteenth century the state gradually centralized control over the clan-based militias. Yet until the 1930's, the threat of banditry in the backlands required that families and neighborhoods be prepared to adopt military organization.[35]

If military self-sufficiency reinforced patriarchal roles, slaveholding also created an internal structure that encouraged patriarchalism. The great gap in status between masters and their dishonored, "captive" slaves enhanced the personal authority of the masters within the family. The slave-owner could better claim the authority of the patriarch than could the mere landlord after abolition. By 1890 centralization and abolition had eroded both these functions of patriarchal authority. Still, the ideal role of the father in rural families was that of the lord. Under the Empire, Bahian landlords sought the title of baron. After the Republic abolished titles of nobility, Bahian landlords emphasized the military title of coronel in the National Guard.[36]

With the decline of the Brazilian sugar market in the latter half of the nineteenth century, the status of the rural aristocracy of the Recôncavo declined. Fazendas that might have been reserved for inheritance or sold privately now came up for public auction, as noted members of the elite such as the baron of Cotegipe sold off their estates. The abolition of slavery in 1888 hurt many of the most active planters, bankrupting them or forcing them to sink into relatively primitive activities such as cattle ranching. With the decline of traditional fortunes, receptions and balls on plantations and in the cities became less brilliant. But the planter families still projected the solidity of an "aristocracy." The rise of the cacao zone around Ilhéus in the 1890's and 1900's revived a planter class, this time with a new contingent of self-made colonels with obscure origins. But by the 1910's and 1920's, Bahians were far more impressed with the bankruptcies and decline of the Recôncavo aristocracy than with the quick rise of the new cacao coronéis.[37]

Ideally, the lordly roles for men in Bahian families demanded arrogant, virile prowess. Within the family, the lord was supposed to assume command and expect obedience. In the special institution of the feud, he commanded the entire clan to defend their collective honor against other clans. But in daily life as well, the role called on the father to act out his authority by making decisions for his sons and secluding his wife and daughters as thoroughly as possible from the public realm. It expected him to manifest his virility by siring as many children as possible by his legitimate consort, and as many as he pleased by the slaves and servants on the plantation. In practice, of course, Bahian fathers never exercised power in the family unquestioned. And as coronéis, working as the local electoral bosses of the state political oligarchy, their authority over their following depended on recognition from the capital.[38]

Ideally, the lady filled out the role of the baroness, echoing the patriarchal role in a diminished mode. Inside the house, she had more control than the man. It was she who organized the domestic routines of the household and oversaw the kitchen. European travelers of the nineteenth century consistently remarked that Brazilian ladies had loud, rasping voices trained by their incessant yelling at the slaves.[39] To the extent that the role of the patriarch was identical to the role of the master, Gilberto Freyre's overlooked observation that women could also become patriarchs is perfectly understandable. Women, commanding slaves, would assume the manners—and the claims—of the patriarch. Furthermore, every woman could expect to be widowed and to have to act as head of the family sooner or later. On the average, a woman outlived her husband by about six years; as a widow she administered her property and that of the children.[40] The autonomy that went with the role of baroness showed, perhaps, in women who maintained allegiance to their families of origin after marriage. A household might be divided between the loyalties of the mistress and the loyalties of the master, and so decisions about the children's marriage alliances could provoke open conflict.[41]

But another ideal role for the wife in landlord families was that of the saint. Christian religion, and especially the Catholic cult of the Virgin, afforded women a justification for identification with servants, weakness, and suffering resignation. Women often used this role to define an area of subordinate autonomy. Anna Ribeiro in later life always dressed in black and shunned "luxury." She wrote a moralizing novel, *The Angel of Pardon*, counseling a young wife to tolerate her husband's infidelities. In her family's recollections and her own memoirs, she embodied her childhood nickname, "Santinha."[42] While this role deprived women of authority for direct challenges to their husbands' decisions, it opened opportunities for indirect influence through the authority of dreams and visions. Furthermore, the role of the *santa* cemented the family: it emphasized self-denial and altruism in the service of the family and softened conflicts.

The question of what children's roles should be in Bahian families was a difficult one. In *The Mansions and the Shanties*, Gilberto Freyre argued that like every patriarchy, Brazilian families suppressed the personality of the boy. After they idealized the infant and the innocent child, parents rejected the older boy. The ceremony of cutting off a boy's curls symbolized his passage into an ambiguous status. He turned from a little angel into a little devil.[43] If boys as boys had no place in patriarchal families, one solution was to convert them immediately into little men. In the mid nineteenth century, the travelers James Fletcher and Daniel Kidder noted with amusement the gravity of little boys at receptions in their miniature versions of men's formal dress. Yet forcing maturity was the exception. As a rule, Bahian families abandoned their boys to the supervision of mammies, who spoiled them, and to the ruinous companionship of pickaninnies (or so the medical reformers complained). When the German schoolmistress Ina von Binzer arrived in Brazil in 1881 to become governess to a country family, she was appalled by the anarchy. The boys and girls alike ran free and unsupervised through the noise of the house, neglected their lessons, and received no discipline from their parents.[44]

Upbringing in Bahian landlord families rarely aimed to instill "character," in the Puritan style.[45] Parents did not sermonize and indoctrinate as they might have. In early childhood, children were often with nurses and chambermaids. Fletcher and Kidder observed that the home made children difficult for schoolteachers to handle: "Accustomed to control their black nurses, and to unlimited indulgence from their parents, they set their minds to work to contrive every method of baffling the efforts made to reduce them to order. This does not result from malice, but from want of parental discipline."[46]

Still, childhood did teach certain roles of authority. Freyre argued in 1933 that the sadism that pervaded the relations of Brazilian masters toward slaves and Indians formed a character inclined to idealize authoritarian political regimes and acts. And indeed it is true that in Bahia little boys learned to act out roles of domination at an early age. They would be given a slave *moleque* and in games ride him like a horse, or bring him to school with instructions to take any beatings that his young master earned.

They also learned subversive strategies of resistance from slaves, as many moralists affirmed that contact with slaves taught children to lie.[47]

Clearly, in such a family the passage from childhood to maturity presented problems. On the one hand, the customs of the Bahian family could ease the passage by saturating childhood with precocious symbols of maturity. Boys early on wore adult clothes and were called "youths." The idealization of precocious virility, games of bestiality, and the teasing approval given to the first dose of venereal disease all encouraged boys to adopt an identity of manhood in early adolescence. But within the core of the family, an adolescent boy presented a problem in the transition from being ordered around to giving orders.[48]

By law, a boy could become an adult by earning a diploma at one of the professional academies, joining the military, entering a position in public service, or marrying. Property law, at least, held that these changes of status marked a point at which a *filhofamílias*, a dependent boy, could begin to have income and property of his own, separate from the patrimony. And, of course, a boy could become an adult by the death of his father. The early death of his father could mean the difference between dependence and independence in his early twenties. Especially in the countryside, where young men needed an inheritance or a gift of property to assume the adult role of the lord, men waited until their late twenties or early thirties, long after the age of majority, to marry.[49]

Young women in Bahia's country families had an easier trajectory to follow. They could identify with their mothers by imitating them, without rebelling against them. At the age of 15, a girl was considered a *moça*, a marriageable young woman, and by the age of 30, a *senhora de idade*, a matron.[50] Customs of secluding girls may have demarcated the identity of the unmarried virgin more sharply from that of the adult matron. But after the middle of the nineteenth century, the seclusion of women declined, and parents rarely sequestered their daughters even when strangers visited. Country girls grew up with a relatively broad freedom of movement: "[In early adolescence] I continued as I had up to then, playing with dolls in the company of the little black girls my age, and running in the yard to pick fruit, the overeating which later would give me a bellyache."[51] Grown women and girls would go out to a designated spot in the river to bathe. Furthermore, the formal requirements of the upbringing of girls were lighter than in city families. Since the marriage market in country parishes was often restricted to the circle of relatives and neighbors, families felt less pressure to endow their girls with accomplishments. Each family was a known quantity and could bargain with more than its girls' appearance and manners. Around the age of seven, planters and better-off tenant farmers would find a schoolmaster to give their daughters lessons. But if a girl showed no particular aptitude for reading, her parents would instead emphasize teaching her to sew.[52] Still, no country family could assure its daughters' marriages. The wider marriage market of the city enticed families to look beyond their parishes.

The self-sufficient landlord families of Bahia had socialized both their boys and their girls more through apprenticeships and initiations than through school. Not only parents but also elders and servants brought up children, and so children learned a rural tradition from before and beyond the horizons of their parents. Yet during the nineteenth century, the balance between the influence of family and school tipped toward the school. Remote families had to exert special efforts to obtain good schooling for their children, and so the degree of their education varied widely when compared to that of the city elite. Rich planters often preferred to hire tutors or subsidize the establishment of a rural schoolhouse in the neighborhood, thus bringing the school into the family. In the Recôncavo, children would often be sent to boarding or day schools in the entrepôt towns of Santo Amaro and Cachoeira.[53]

After the late nineteenth century, a new emphasis on professional education, or at least secondary education, forced the partial urbanization of some landlord families. For many families the alternatives were to send their children to boarding school, appointing a merchant in Salvador as guardian, or for the mother to move to Salvador with the children for the duration of their education.[54] Boarding academies had a reputation for unhealthy atmospheres and inhuman severity. Naturalist novelists denounced their stifling discipline and subversive homosexual undercurrents; even worse, the Jesuits might encourage one's son to become a priest.[55] Rather than delegate responsibility for their children to boarding schools, many families from plantations near the railroad lines preferred to set up a branch household in Salvador. The mother and children would return by train every season or every week. This allowed families to bring their children up in their own traditions, in the warmth of the home, and still give them a proper, modern education.[56]

Despite the subordination of patriarchal power under the system of coronelismo and the intrusion of the school into childhood by the late nineteenth century, country families remained more independent than elite or middle-class urban families. This autonomy provided individuals with fewer guarantees of being able to resist arbitrary decisions by more powerful family members. Fewer institutions offered an alternative to the family. But as a consequence of rural isolation, each family could improvise its own roles and routines more freely, with less attention to public opinion. Landlord families tolerated escapes from their roles and their routines more easily.

The members of the outer orbits of the Big House, the dependents, governesses, and servants, had no legal ties to the family and its authority. They could theoretically leave for another life or try to attach themselves to another family. Until abolition in 1888, most servants were slaves, permanent members of these families against their will. In the five years before abolition, mass escapes from Recôncavo plantations had demonstrated the desire of many slaves to be rid of their masters. Yet after abolition many former slaves resumed their servitude, though now paid a token wage. The old styles of relations between masters and slaves persisted; though punishments changed and leaving was easier, servants evaded the hardships of servitude by manipulation and passive apathy.[57]

But even a patriarch might want to escape his family. Life outdoors on their horses, or sexual relations with a slave or servant mistress indoors, allowed men to express themselves free of their obligations to the women in the Big House. Other men tried to escape becoming patriarchs. The legal definitions of maturity identified it with marriage. But the sons of landowning families could evade some of the responsibility of maturity by setting up an illegitimate family.[58] We have no descriptions of home life in the illegitimate households of Bahian landlords, such as Jeronimo Sodré. He held a noble entail and was an officer in the militia, yet never married. Until his death in 1881, he lived on his family's plantation with slave mistresses and their children, whom he recognized legally as his own. Such a family did not simply mimic the patriarchal family, because the mistress was kept more secluded than the wife. Families of the backlands reluctantly acknowledged that a daughter could form a union, a sort of quasi-marriage, with a priest. But they preferred that the woman in such a union should never appear in public, or even sit at table with her husband's guests.[59]

An unmarried woman found it much more difficult to escape these families. Unmarried daughters could not move out to an illegitimate family as easily as their brothers could. A young woman's elopement, whether or not it ended in marriage, was a far more drastic step than a young man's taking a mistress.[60] For most daughters, marriage therefore offered the only feasible escape from the family, and the lore of spinsters, matchmaker saints, and love charms reflected its importance. Traditionally, the church had provided a few women with another respectable alternative to their family of origin. From the middle of the nineteenth century until 1891, entry to the nunhood was closed by law, though women could still move into religious retreats without taking vows. After 1891 the novitiates reopened, but women from country families did not move into them in significant numbers.[61]

Married women also could escape from their worldly role into religious obsession. The role of the saint was already an alternative to the role of the baroness, and the preoccupations of the saint could shade into those of the fanatic. Yet religiously legitimated retreat was not the only possible reaction a married woman could have to an unsatisfactory marriage. When conflict between a woman and her husband grew severe enough, she could return to her parents' household.[62] This response was traditional. Legal separation on the woman's initiative was nearly impossible in the colonial period, but became more common in the nineteenth and twentieth centuries.

The Urban Elite and Its Families

With the decline of agriculture, the decline of local military power, and the rise of powerful merchant capitalist firms, social power also shifted from the country to the city. By the late nineteenth century, the urban elite, or *gente fina*, had become the new paradigm of the Bahian upper classes. Even landlord families in the countryside imitated its fashions. On the one hand, this elite, composed of merchants, bankers, politicians, and even a few industrialists, represented the power of cosmopolitan capital in a provincial backwater. The few dozen families at the pinnacle of Bahian society belonged to a class whose center was Europe. They dominated a city that could never see them glorified in the proper institutions: a stock exchange, a racetrack and Jockey Club, a truly opulent opera house. Even in Rio de Janeiro those institutions flourished only as imitations of Paris and London. On the other hand, the Bahian gente fina (the "fine people") and the gente finíssima (the "finest") did shape Salvador in their image. In the first two decades of the twentieth century, they attempted to civilize the public face of the city by building port works, laying water and sewer networks, and ploughing a Parisian boulevard from the center to their beach suburb, straight through monasteries and the old cathedral. With greater success, they created a provincial society based on the private connections of their families with one another and with rural landlords and the middle class.[63]

The typical family of the city elite was smaller than that of the Big House of the countryside, in large part because the latter occasionally included the entire plantation or rural neighborhood under the aegis of the "family." A few urban slaveowners had large slave quarters attached to their townhouses in the early nineteenth century, but after abolition there were no more such establishments. By the late nineteenth century, the separation of merchants from their store clerks also became greater, as the bigger merchants, those with the most clerks, moved uphill from the Lower City to the Victória district, leaving behind the custom of having the boys sleep on the counter or up in the rafters of the warehouse.[64]

The homes and neighborhoods of the urban elite changed simultaneously. Up to the early nineteenth century, city magnates had built *sobrados*, townhouses that filled a city block, with shops rented on the ground floor facing the street. By the late nineteenth century, the elite preferred to build detached *palacetes* or *chalets* that did not extend to the street. Foreign merchants had pioneered the style in the early nineteenth century, when they congregated along the outskirts of the city in Victória, which became an elegant neighborhood. Wealth was displayed in facades resembling Swiss chalets or Tudor farmhouses, in Art Nouveau revivals of Portuguese architecture with gingerbread and wrought-iron decorations. When streetcar lines extended from the center of the city through Victória to seashore suburbs in the 1870's, they transformed fishing hamlets into seaside residential districts. Upper-class families gradually left their old sobrados, which had been scattered among all the parishes of the city, and built mansions in these new districts. By the 1930's most of the sobrados in the old center of Salvador had been subdivided into tenements, and the police designated one a zone of prostitution.[65]

Though more private than plantation houses, the households of the city elite were nevertheless large and complexly ranked. Their ideal was the *casa cheia*, the full and noisy house.[66] The core of the parents and their children was often complemented by kin and dependents. Families in Salvador lodged country cousins on visits and country godchildren studying at the academies. Bachelor uncles who lived alone would have their meals with the family. Along with kin, the elite household also included a circle of dependents. Almost all wealthy households would keep an *agregada*, an old woman living on the charity of the family and performing small services: sewing and praying with the mistress, chaperoning the young ladies, watching the children. Like the Big House, the city mansion often took in informally adopted children, *filhos de criação*, whose status lay somewhere between servants and adopted children.[67]

The "kitchen" of servants was more diverse in elite than in landlord families. Toward the end of the nineteenth century, having white servants became fashionable. After abolition, with increased immigration from Europe, Bahian families could more easily staff their households with Portuguese gardeners and menservants, French cooks, and German governesses.[68] People expressed concern at the possibilities for indiscipline among free black servants, "slaves without the restraints of slavery."[69] Despite the fashion for white servants, black native-born Bahians still formed part of the staff of most households, as wet nurses, stableboys, or bodyguards.[70] A mansion might have a foreign cook, but all needed Bahian cooks occasionally to prepare the local specialties.

The tutor or governess ranked higher than the other servants, and was often recruited abroad rather than in Brazil. The Goes Calmon family set themselves apart by hiring a German governess in the 1910's, who taught all their many children German and took exclusive care of the education of the younger ones. She was adopted into her Bahian family, remaining with them until her retirement to a home for elderly Germans in São Paulo.[71]

One important difference between the households of the urban elite and of rural landlords was that, in the city, close and daily personal ties among relatives easily extended beyond the home. Country houses were not entirely isolated, but they were set back from their neighbors; women would keep up contact with their sisters and cousins through the circulation of notes, letters, and gifts, but visits were special occasions.[72] In Salvador, the architecture of the new bourgeois neighborhoods separated the gente fina from the plebeian street and from their clienteles. But often families tried to have their relatives for neighbors. Brothers would build mansions facing each other on their portions of the father's land. Neighboring families would marry off their children to each other, becoming in-laws. Parents would retire to a smaller chalet behind the mansion, still sharing a yard, kitchen, and water pipe, as well as servants, with their adult children. Overlapping of membership between households, sharing of children among households, and participation in family compounds increased the complexity of the kinship relations of city households.[73]

The routines of the families of the elite meshed with the urban routines of business and society. These routines originated in the cosmopolitan nineteenth-century "civilization" centered on Europe. For instance, the day for both men and women changed in this period from the traditional tropical hours to European ones. Families had been early to rise through the 1850's, but by the end of the nineteenth century they had adopted the customs of the foreign merchants. Instead of rising at four in the morning, in the cool of the dawn, families would rise at six, when the sun had already warmed the city.[74] In general, the Bahian elite sought a way of life that maintained their relations with each other, as a close-knit oligarchy. They had at hand the example of Rio and the civilized capitals, and they followed the shifting conventions of European civilization as far as they could in the port city of a backward plantation zone.

Most men of the elite spent their days outside the home. They traveled by streetcar, elevator, carriage, or automobile from the residential Upper City downhill to the commercial Lower City, or over to the administrative district in the old center of the Upper City. There, cafés, shops, the lounge of the Commercial Association, and the lobbies of certain law offices and newspapers, provided the setting for the city's men of affairs. As Salvador became more urbane, men might spend their evening outside the home as well. Receptions, the opera and theater, and evenings at social clubs or brothels all took place outside the mansion.[75] If the family entertained or kept a salon, then the home itself was transformed temporarily into a public place.[76]

In comparison with those of men, women's lives centered on the home. Indoors their activities did not differ notably from those of ladies in the countryside. Their work involved incessant supervision and scolding of servants, hiring and firing seamstresses, cooks, and nursemaids.[77] Their free time was divided between leisure chores such as embroidery and lace-making, and practice of the lady's accomplishments: singing, playing the piano, drawing. But women of the city elite could also participate in the entertainments and intrigues of a society beyond the household. City ladies could visit far more easily, and probably left the house far more often, than rural women.[78]

Around the turn of the twentieth century, perhaps the greatest change in the routines of city women was the new fashion of shopping on the street. The old system of provisioning a house was to lay in a pantry of staples: barrels of wine, sides of salt cod, and sacks of flour. For perishables, vendors passed under the windows, market stalls stood at the corners, and urchins loitered to be sent on errands. Even luxury goods came to the home. Old African ladies, Syrian peddlers, and pomaded clerks with boards of swatches and samples would bring what these families did not have sent from Europe. Only in the twentieth century did ladies of the gente fina tentatively turn to the new system of shopping in public (always accompanied, of course). Shortages during World War I supposedly forced middle-class families to leave their homes to shop aggressively in stores. Earlier, at the turn of the century, the Rua Chile next to the government palace had developed from a politicians' alley into a fashionable promenade of teashops and stores, with display windows that enticed a female clientele. Like Rio's Rua do Ouvidor, it was a tiny space, a few short blocks. Under the pretext of shopping, everyone could see and be seen, exchange greetings and flirt. But the routines of elite women in Salvador were still centered on the home rather than around public consumerist entertainments such as shopping.[79]

The rituals of the gente fina were also less traditional than those of the landlords. The crop seasons meant little to them. But the Catholic calendar also marked time for the city. The great festivals of the church were celebrated with more elaborate spectacle in town: costumed Christmas pageants, the massive pilgrimage on the day of the patron Senhor do Bomfim, processions by lay brotherhoods on their saints' days, and widespread festivities for Carnival and Easter. By the end of the nineteenth century, elite families usually avoided the "popular" street festivals, unless they participated as dignitaries. They held parallel celebrations indoors: children's costume parties and dances during Carnival, receptions at Christmastime. For a traditional festival such as São João, they would go to a country estate to celebrate with friends or relatives.[80]

Although the gente fina held back from public folk festivals, their family celebrations were often semipublic ceremonies for the whole of high society. Like the country landlords, they preferred to celebrate their weddings in a home oratory, rather than in a public cathedral. But a wedding in the governor's palace was as much an occasion of state as a private ceremony.[81] The funerals of their men were more civic than religious events, with streetcars hired to take mourners to the cemetery, crowds following the coffin, oratory at the tomb, and wreaths from masonic lodges and political clubs. Their tombs themselves had the style of civic statuary. Even more private sacred and secular rituals, such as baptisms, First Communions, and birthday parties, were in the public domain. Meeting a family member arriving by ship could turn into a political rally.[82]

The elite modified familiar family rituals as they overlaid them with displays of wealth and civilization. They made meals into displays of correct European table manners, tinned European delicacies, and elegant dishes prepared by a Portuguese cook that contrasted with the salt beef, manioc flour, and peppers of the everyday Bahian diet. They built new chalets in the city, with gigantic banquet rooms taking the place of the traditional empty reception room lined with rows of straightbacked wicker chairs. When Francisco Marques de Goes Calmon, a lawyer and leader of society, remodeled his old mansion in 1919, he enlarged the ground floor to include a ballroom with cherubs painted on the ceiling and a grand dining room.[83]

As elite entertainments became more public, social clubs, rather than family mansions, increasingly provided their setting. After the mid nineteenth century, both native-born and Portuguese elite families abandoned the traditional religious brotherhoods to middling Portuguese immigrants. Instead, the upper classes chartered new social clubs as recreational associations. Carnival balls and sporting matches, rather than religious processions, became the pretext for association. The club Euterpe, at the turn of the century, and, after World War I, the Clube Bahiano de Tênis and the Iate Clube da Bahia, both located near Victória, became the principal social clubs of the gente fina. The clubs did sponsor sporting activities: the yacht club had its regattas and the tennis club its matches. But the families who joined them could also participate in their annual cycle of dances and banquets.[84]

Some rituals of elite families were private. The most characteristic of these was the trip to Europe. If they expressed their differences from other families largely by their European manners and European origins, then they could best live out that ideal by leaving Bahia. Men left on official commissions and business trips, sons left to study, and whole families embarked with their trunks and nursemaids for tours. In São Paulo the Prado family considered the trip to Europe a necessary seasoning of the character, a "bath in civilization." It gave them a fresh perspective on Brazilian society. In Bahia a grand merchant such as Emil Wildberger, born in a small town in Switzerland, would revisit it, returning from Brazil a millionaire. A lawyer for the French business community such as Goes Calmon would take business trips to France, or go there for medical treatment. When they could not leave Bahia, many elite families affirmed their ties to Europe by attending the theater and the receptions of foreign consulates in Salvador.[85]

While roles in the families of rural landlords could be improvised and negotiated, roles in the families of the urban elite were dictated more uniformly and publicly. Married women in these families had only the role of the lady. A lady was an accomplished hostess, a loyal wife, and a devoted mother. The eulogistic biographies and memoirs of the Bahian elite present women exclusively in this light, as angels of the home.[86] The definition of these roles came from Victorian Europe. It assumed a separation of the sexes between public and private spheres: the domestic, private sphere was the proper domain of the lady. In Europe definitions of the public roles of women were in question in the late nineteenth century. But Bahian elite families drew from the conservative mainstream of European culture, which provided an "aristocratic" definition of civilization and the public role of the lady. Her role entailed deferent obedience to her husband in public matters. In return, by conventions of chivalry, he deferred symbolically to her and to other ladies. The comparative lack of education of most Brazilian women until the 1900's probably contributed to their deference in public and in society. In the early nineteenth century, women in Salvador would talk of "dress, children, and diseases." Mid-nineteenth-century observers found that women at public gatherings stayed away from men's conversations, possibly because of lack of knowledge. By the twentieth century, women more often had education, but habits of deference remained.[87]

The role of the man in these families illuminates the roles of the wife. The ideal man was not a lord—whether autonomous baron or subordinate coronel—but a man of affairs, a counselor. His power derived not from military chieftainship but from control of political influence or financial capital. Cosmopolitan urbanity was the ideal of the man's manner in public. His honor was not measured by military prowess but rather by polish and "education," education understood also to mean good manners. Philanthropy, the largesse of an enlightened benefactor of the community, was one means by which he translated his money into honor. But these men were also authoritative and commanding. A big merchant was expected to exercise paternal authority over his clerks; the director of an establishment became the patron of his employees.[88]

Within the "private sphere" of the family itself, the role of the counselor was more ambiguous. The rough despotism of many rural patriarchs was out of place, or at least out of fashion, in a civilized household. Chivalry prescribed that men treat their wives with tender deference and their children with stern respect, but it did not prescribe any specific functions for men in the house. The emphasis on the public sphere of affairs for men made it difficult for them to insist on authority in the private sphere. Women controlled the household budget, tried to make matches for their children, and influenced decisions about the education and careers of the children. In many Brazilian families of the elite, the old custom of wearing a light shirt or dressing gown and slippers indoors contrasted sharply with men's serious, authoritative dress out of doors.[89]

The roles of children in elite families were potentially better codified than they were in rural families, not so much because roles were different (boys still turned from little angels into little devils), but because these families tried to organize childhood more. Schooling—which was universal among the city elite, unlike among the rural lords—set off a distinct realm of childhood. Putting a white governess rather than a slave in charge of the children multiplied the levels of command in the family and increased the social distance between parents and children. But in fact, children in families of the gente fina were as unruly and loud as children on plantations. The children of large families remembered ebullient, noisy houses. As one Bahian described her home in the 1910s, "It was never calm, there was always a child crying, another who didn't want to study, always some problem . . . it was noisy but always lively and happy."[90]

Like the rural landlords, the urban elite tried to bring up their children in the private traditions of the family. In more than one mansion in Salvador, parents or a grandmother required children to speak French inside the home, constantly reminding them of the difference between home life and the street. Most parents tried to keep children from playing with urchins in the street; unlike their cousins on the plantations, children of the elite did not have moleques or chambermaids for playmates. Particularly after the 1890's, tutoring was the ideal, though it was expensive and cumbersome; eventually most families relied on the private academies of the priests or the pedagogues. Eventually, for most boys, some kind of higher education outside the home became inevitable. Only a few Portuguese merchant families could afford the luxury of turning their sons into idle sportsmen rather than licentiates.[91]

Elite families, like the gentry, increasingly entrusted their children to schools with missionary ideologies. The Catholic secondary schools that had been founded by teaching orders after the 1890's, such as the Jesuit Colégio Antônio Vieira, represented a new attempt to build character and instill Christian militance. Their ascetic regime shocked city boys almost as much as those coming from lax landlord households; their religious fervor put off parents whose Catholicism was largely formal. Private academies that adopted a military tone in the 1910's, such as Isaías Alves's Ginásio Ypiranga, preached a new rhetoric of nationalism and discipline. They, too, seemed at odds with the indulgent urbanity of elite families.[92]

Getting a legal or medical diploma initiated a young man into adulthood in elite families as well as in landlord families. Young men from rural families were far from home, and often established their own households, "republics" of students. The "republican" regime was defined by contrast with the Victorian "monarchy" that prevailed in boarding houses, where the word of the mistress was law.[93] But young men from elite families lived at home and missed the experience of Bohemian liberty in the republics. After a law school was established in Salvador in 1892, and a polytechnic school in 1900, fewer Bahian students left the state for education and few students from other provinces came to Bahia. Education became less of an odyssey in the lives of urban boys.[94]

Young and old, children of the elite had more contact with their peers than did children in the countryside. In crowds formed in school, through neighborhood and family, and through membership in clubs, children of the upper class formed each other's identities and habits. In the mid nineteenth century, Freyre suggests, the types of the tubercular poet and the *amarelinho*, the anemic pipsqueak, had represented the ascendancy of urban civilization over the countryside. But by the beginning of the twentieth century, the figure of the sportsman, and above all, of the rower, combined elegance and health in an urban, bourgeois ideal. Sports, with their emphasis on youth, provided urban Bahians with a new identity that was hardly relevant to their country cousins. Gentlemanly team sports were in a sense a metaphor for urbanism, just as prowess on horseback represented rural lordliness.[95]

The roles of members of elite families were perhaps not decided as arbitrarily as those in landlord families. But because families were more public, these roles were more obligatory. Individuals found it harder to escape their elite families.

It was far easier for men to escape these families, because their roles were specified much less in the private sphere than in the public sphere. Married men of the elite could maintain a clandestine parallel household with a mistress, and sometimes even with her children. In a letter to his mistress before his divorce, one man pointed out that he had been better off when he had lived with his family, as "society didn't see anything wrong in it because I had not ABANDONED my home." They could travel abroad to Europe, or to the plantation in the countryside. Old bachelors could openly maintain unorthodox establishments. In Salvador, a confirmed bachelor could preserve a respectable social facade, have a career as a hospital director, and live alone in a libertine's den decorated with monumental paintings of nudes. Young bachelors could escape into Salvador's Bohemia or into the disorder of a student republic.[96]

Women, by contrast, were far more bound to the official household of the legitimate family. Married women could escape into devotions in the home or into the charitable and pious activities of religious sisterhoods outside the home. But the role of a lady—with its conventions of genteel deference to the man—was far harder to abdicate than the aggressive role of a baroness. Wives could hardly become more self-denying than their conventional roles required of them. Single women in some families pressed against the limits of the role of the young lady by becoming active in the public sphere of schooling and work. After the reopening of the convents in 1891, they could elect a respectable identity as nuns entirely outside the family. But married women in Bahia could rarely accomplish an open rejection of the home, such as Veridiana Prado's sojourn in Europe. Despite the appearance of greater opportunities in the city, urban women were probably more restricted to life with their husbands than were the women of landlord families, who had the pretext of moving to the capital to supervise their children's schooling. Divorce, or rather legal separation, offered an exit for a few women in the city after the mid nineteenth century. Women generally initiated the few suits that were filed in Salvador, but the disgrace of divorce and the difficulty of winning a contested suit made it an unpleasant alternative.[97]

Families of the Middle Class

Differences between the organization of landlord and elite families turned upon the difference in their contexts and functions. Landlord families conducted their daily life in the isolation of individual plantations; elite families carried on their affairs in close-knit provincial social and business circles. Landlord families needed to maintain solidarity with their clan and control over their followings; elite families worked to keep up connections with others in the Bahian elite and with their European associates. Landlord families often stretched their organization to educate their children; for elite families, accommodation with the schools was relatively easy.

Yet both landlords and the elites were grand patrons. Other families shared their standards and prejudices, indeed were their close kin, but were not powerful in the same way. The discussion of the organization of what

I call middle-class families that follows will throw light on the extent to which shifts in the customs of Bahian families can be traced to changes in the organization of these families.

Kinship with the landlords and the elite blurred the identification of members of the middle class with one another. The largest part were off-shoots of landlord lineages, "traditional families." By identifying with the grandeur of some notable in their clan, their families could consider themselves part of the elite of the city.[98] Very few members of the middle class in Salvador and the towns could remark that all the men in their family had been professionals, and nothing else, for two generations. The part of this class that was formed by the rise of immigrant Portuguese traders or poor native sons was probably relatively small.[99]

Family ties stretched across class lines, integrating quite diverse social ranks into social groups. The middle class of Bahia was not different in kind, but in rank, from the elite. It included small merchants, local politicians, professionals, and many government employees. At its upper fringe it would include families such as that of João Barbosa, Rui Barbosa's father. Descended from a clan of urban functionaries, João was a leading politician, a sometime doctor, and a failed brickyard entrepreneur. Solidly in its center the middle class would include families such as that of Alfredo Ferreira Bandeira, Rui's father-in-law. He was a public functionary in the customshouse at Salvador, and a poor cousin of the sugar baron Bandeiras. At its lower horizon it would include José Viana Bandeira, Rui's brother-in-law. He was an underpaid clerk at the lowest level of Bahian officialdom. The middle class was not a caste, and individuals passed back and forth from the middle class to the elite, as they could pass from the class of landlords to the elite. Rui himself was launched by his education from the provincial middle class into the antechamber of the national elite, and eventually he reached the pinnacle of national politics as senator and presidential candidate.[100]

The decisive difference between the elite and the middle class in Bahia was patronage. Middle-class family heads were less patrons than they were brokers, situated in the middle ranks of clienteles. Associations that seemed autonomous, such as the associations of clerks, were reputed to be dominated by their patrons among the elite. The intermediate rank of men could be expressed explicitly in the symbolism of titles and honors. If rural bosses might be called "Coronel" whether or not they actually had a commission in the National Guard, men in the middle class and the upper ranks of the populace might be granted the honorary—though sometimes ironically pretentious—title of "Major."[101]

The middle class concentrated in Salvador, the capital and seaport, but every small town had a few professionals and storekeepers. Outside of

Salvador, the bigger entrepôt towns of the Recôncavo and the cacao zone, such as Feira de Santana, Cachoeira, Santo Amaro, and Ilhéus, had the largest numbers of "middle-class" town dwellers. In small towns of the backlands, the middle class was more conspicuous by its difference both from the rustics and from the local "nobility," the landlords, though in some towns the "social distance between them didn't have the density of a rigid protocol of class." In Santo Amaro in the 1900's, the aged viscount of Ferreira Bandeira would ride into town every day with a servant dressed in livery to gamble with people of all classes, whereas the viscount of Oliveira, more the gentleman, rarely came in to his town house. The doctor, the merchant, the schoolmistress, and the telegrapher all stood out as isolated exemplars of propriety and civilization. If a schoolmistress was popular, many children in the county would be named after her. When an event such as the outbreak of World War I occurred, people crowded around to hear the pharmacist read from the newspaper he subscribed to.[102]

The differences in wealth and power between the elites and middle class changed roles and customs within families. One could belong to both the group of the landlords and the elites; in the same way, one could feel both part of the elite and part of the middle class. The households of the urban middle class were smaller, if not always in numbers, then in grandeur. Rent was a crucial institution for many who were employees in irregularly paid state sinecures. In periods of inflation, such as the 1890's and during World War I, the erosion of real salaries threatened their status. If any political issue in Brazil became a "middle-class" issue during the Republic, it was the cost of living in the cities.[103]

Their households differed in another way. Unlike the elite, whose mansions and chalets increasingly concentrated in Victória after 1870, the middle class spread among many districts when they moved out of the old center of the city. Paying rent, they might even share a hall or an entrance with a family of workers. Hildegardes Vianna has neatly ranked the scale of status as reflected in lodgings: to occupy an entire house was best; if sharing, to live on the upper floor was better; if living in a small house, to have a vestibule rather than a front door opening into the parlor; finally, not to live in an alley or a basement apartment. "The first sign of the decline of a family was their move into a ground floor apartment." By the time of World War I, when the elite had concentrated in Victória, Hermes Lima could feel that as a student he had inhabited the "city of the bourgeoisie": the business district, the Cidade Alta from the governor's palace to Victória, the seaside suburbs of Barra and Rio Vermelho, and that he had missed the other neighborhoods, the "city of the lower middle class and the little people."[104]

Household goods, decorations, and luxuries had always been a sign of status in Bahia. But after 1870 imported consumer goods became increasingly important as a mark of familial, patriarchal solidity. In all memoirs, and in satire, the indispensable central icon of the home was the *prateleira*, the china cabinet, with its display of luxury dishes. There were other important commodities. Pianos became widespread in the 1850's and remained an important symbol of bourgeois solidity and prosperity. In the 1920's the radio set emerged, perhaps replacing the piano as the musical center of the household. One man remembered most vividly of his childhood the Belgian kerosene or gas ceiling lamp, hung by chains, that all middle-class homes had in the 1910's.[105] Both foreigners and Bahians who went abroad noted a general austerity to furnishings in many homes. But in the late nineteenth century, stuffed furniture in foreign models replaced (or displaced) the wicker and jacaranda-wood sofas and chairs of the traditional reception room.

The membership of the middle-class household was usually not as large or complex as that of elite households. It included the family core, and perhaps some kin. If it included dependents, they were often relatives of one sort or another. The big difference was the size of the staff, the cozinha. While one servant was indispensable as a mark of status, the middle-class family could not hold a large group of followers. Often a filha de criação was desirable specifically because she could perform the small, symbolic sweeping tasks and supplement the work of the cook.[106] If the household did not have a servant, or only had a cook, then it might have a regular washerwoman.

Since marriage could only be contemplated if the couple could afford to establish a household of their own, these questions of paying rent and affording servants were more than vanities. Some commercial firms were reluctant to admit married clerks, as they feared that family money problems were likely to tempt them into stealing. Many clerks never married, but only had a mistress or lived alone.[107] Rui Barbosa's sister-in-law, Adelaide, wrote often to her mother in the 1880's, describing the plight of her brother Cazuza, who could barely afford the suit and shoes he needed as a public employee. Cazuza eventually set up house with a "hussy" and her mother, Adelaide implied. Rui himself, when planning his marriage in 1876, at first determined that he would not marry until he had worked off his father's debts and established himself. For a variety of reasons, he decided to compromise those principles, marry on a loan from their friend Salustiano Souto, and live for a few months under the roof of his brother-in-law, Dobbert.[108] It may not be possible to establish a salary line below which marriage was unthinkable, but the rate of marriage of clerks seems to have coincided with the prosperity of the economy. During the years of

World War I, and during the commercial crash of 1928–30, there was a great drop in the number of marriages of clerks.[109]

This principle of autonomy, expressed in the punning proverb "Quem casa, quer casa" ("He who marries needs a house"), was often compromised. Among middle-class Bahians it was common to share a house with relatives at any point in a marriage. There was an old Portuguese tradition of a "society among brothers," usually a partnership to work a farm. But in modern city households usually only expenses, and not income from salaries outside the home, were shared, in what was still called a "joint economy." Although there was a strong tendency to establish senior and junior partners, so that one family became in a sense the dependent of the other, households with multiple or double heads did exist.[110]

As in families of the landlords and elite, fathers tried to keep their married children close to home, and siblings liked to stay together. A father might build adjoining houses for his children, providing them with ostensibly separate households, but in fact keeping them within the orbit of a family compound. One Bahian woman who married in the 1920's recalled that they continued to share meals with her father-in-law in the old mansion even though their new, adjoining house had its own kitchen. Not until an illness required that they prepare separate meals in the new house did she become the mistress of her own kitchen. Long after that time, the households shared a garden, a private water tank, and the services of servants. Beggars that the family supported would visit each of the households for meals in turn. When apartment houses became respectable in the 1940's and 1950's, families would buy a block of apartments in the same building, or even buy all of a small apartment building. Though middle-class households may have been less complex, families could recreate patriarchal compounds by combining households.[111]

The routines of middle-class families resembled those of the elite: they followed the rhythms of urban work and separated the outdoor *praça* (marketplace) sphere of men's activity from the indoor *casa* (home) sphere of women's activity. One difference was that more often than not, middle-class men were employees. The adjective *pacato*, perhaps best translated as "mild-mannered," applied to the public servant who rode a streetcar to the Lower City every morning, signed in the logbook, and when possible returned home for lunch with the family.

The image of the pacato bourgeois also implied evenings at home, or in the neighborhood, rather than involvement in the ceremonial nightlife of the gente fina. In one of the oldest middle-class neighborhoods of Bahia, the street of townhouses descending from the monastery of São Bento, chairs were brought out from the houses into the little iron-fenced front yards in the evening. Families would visit one another or gossip up and down the street. Although Salvador was surrounded by water, swimming remained a therapeutic as much as recreational routine of respectable families, who took their "seawater bath" discreetly, early in the morning. Not until the 1950's did manners change to make beach days and the display of bodies part of their routines.[112]

Just as the adjective *pacato* implied humbler habits for men, the term *dona de casa* ("housewife") hinted at the more mundane routines of middle-class women. Their routines involved less supervision, and more work of their own, than those of elite women. Some women did all their own housework, lifting the cast-iron cauldrons and coaxing the charcoal fire to life every morning. Others worked to earn money for the family. Most women sewed or embroidered for pin money; a few would also work in the back of the family shop or the bakery, or run a small business of their own making sweets; a few became schoolteachers.[113] If any portion of the upper classes in Bahia came close to conforming to the image of domesticity and routines centered on the home and hearth, it was the women of the middle class.

The rituals of the middle class came closer to those of the people in the annual folkloric cycle of festivals. Portuguese shopkeepers who still belonged to the white religious brotherhoods marched in processions. But the tone of middle-class celebrations in Salvador was often an extension of the usual quiet evenings on small streets, with the small talk of neighbors and men smoking. On the night of São João, the same groups gathered to drink genipap wine in front of a bonfire and launch hot air balloons that floated like Chinese lanterns over the silent city. For these families, the Mês de Maio observations were the perfect vehicle for conviviality. Held in the home, with neighboring families invited, a solemn hymn and candle hour at the home altar would be followed by fiddle music, homemade cordials, and dancing.[114]

Middle-class families often observed civic ceremonies. Descriptions of the Independence Day celebrations were always pleased to note the presence of families: the paterfamilias, *pacato* and proper, his lady and his children. In smaller cities, such as Santo Amaro, the middle class and local notables could project their cosmopolitan fantasies onto the entire ceremony, erecting a model of the Eiffel Tower above the bandstand in the square. And the middle class formed explicitly recreational social clubs, such as Euterpe, to organize their participation in Carnival.[115]

In the middle class, preoccupation with European fashions did not conflict so deeply with Bahian folk traditions as in elite families. Birthdays, baptisms, weddings, funerals, Christmas and Holy Saturday dinners, and not the public festivals, were the true family occasions. Their rituals for such occasions often preserved what seemed antique or folk customs by cosmopolitan standards. Writing in 1945, a young man recalled that as a boy in the 1920's, he had snuck in to pay a forbidden visit to a woman lying in after childbirth and tasted her special infusion of herbs in wine and broth. He wrote about these customs as though they belonged to a forgotten age.[116]

In their entertainments and ceremonies, then, the middle-class family exhibited more domesticity. Yet in many respects, these families followed the patterns of the elite on a diminished scale. Rather than retreat to the fazenda, the middle-class family might summer on the island of Itaparica in the bay. Rather than tour Europe to bathe in civilization, they might make a pilgrimage to fashionable Rio and see the Paris Opera scaled down by a third. Like the elite, they were educated, and they could keep up with currents of fashion and opinion. Reading the evening newspaper was an important ritual for bourgeois fathers, and after the 1920's gathering around the radio set became emblematic of middle-class evenings at home.[117]

The conventional roles in the family of the middle class resembled those of the elite. The ideals were, if not the counselor and the lady, then at least the gentleman and the lady. Civilized manners were supposed to guide the behavior of the couple in every respect. He owed courtesy and protection, she deference and obedience. If among the elite the logic of cosmopolitan bourgeois roles overshadowed the appeal of homegrown patriarchal ones, in the middle-class family the pull of the traditional roles was strong. Many of Salvador's civil servants had, after all, been brought up on plantations themselves. When men in the urban middle class tried to live by the code of the patriarchal lord, what their sons remembered was typically a distant father, who never spoke, who silenced the entire house when he returned in the evening: "The atmosphere in our house was one of solemn respect when he entered, despite his capacity for tenderness. One glance was enough, and we all shut up." One man said his father never seemed alive except once, when raising the Brazilian flag on the 2d of July. The illogicality of the exercise of patriarchal manners was increased in many of these families by the fact that the wife was no baroness, but rather a "useful" housewife, teaching school or sewing to earn pin money.[118]

In the lower ranks of the middle class, these roles might seem caricatured. Inside the family the father might try to exert lordly power and command that he lacked elsewhere. This is one of the consistent themes of Jorge Amado's satires of Bahian middle-class life. In *Gabriela, Clove and Cinnamon*, for example, the pompous men of the small-town middle class of Ilhéus in the 1920's waver between the models of the urbane businessman and the imperious coronel. In his novels, Amado symbolizes the greater power and authenticity of women through their command of the folk art of cooking: Gabriela's fritters make Nacib's restaurant successful; Dona Flor runs a cooking school.[119]

Middle-class children were both more and less closely controlled by their parents than were the children of the elite. On the one hand, mothers less often had governesses between them and the children. They would usually hire a mammy for the youngest child, but the mother took direct charge of older children. On the other hand, children were less controlled sometimes because they had the run of the city: a point of pride of some men is that they had played outdoors with urchins like plantation boys. They had streetcars; friends who read Sherlock Holmes and Jules Verne and owned chemistry sets; and, from the 1910's on, movie houses.[120] But Bahians still noticed a push for precocious maturity in boys. Writing in 1939, the educator Isaías Alves said that Bahians called a boy a *criança* (child) only up to the age of three. From the age of eight or nine, boys had the demeanor of men and resented being called crianças. By the age of eleven or twelve, families put long pants on their boys, whereas in the south of Brazil, they wore short pants until they were thirteen or fourteen.[121]

The ways in which these families socialized their children presented another paradox. There was more apprenticeship, and at the same time more reliance upon education. A few fathers—mostly unlettered Portuguese shopkeepers and artisans—opposed formal education because they despised the pretensions of doutores and their public sinecures. They punished their sons if they caught them reading books and tried to force them into the family business.[122] But, more commonly, families tried both to initiate sons into the secrets of their trades and to encourage education. In their memoirs, many sons of these families remember their childhood as learning by watching. One recalls his father, newly appointed police chief, haughtily returning all the presents that had arrived the day before. He also remembers looking on as cronies of his father joked cynically while forging an election roll. Another recalls lessons learned running errands for his father, a manioc trader in the upriver town of Pojuca. A third remembers sitting for afternoons in front of the glass cases in his father's pharmacy, listening to the gossip of doctors.[123]

For much of the middle class, of course, the school was the institution that prepared sons to follow their fathers or rise above them. Elite boys would be teased: "If you don't study, we'll put you in a shop."[124] But for middle-class boys, the threat was real: at adolescence a middle-class boy generally became either a student (*académico*) or a shop boy (*caixeiro*). Experience in commerce, "the school of work," only rarely led to higher positions in the merchant houses.[125] Earning a diploma conferred the quasi-noble status of "doctor" and promised a professional career or at least a respectable sinecure as a public employee. Once a "doctor," a man could never go back to working with his hands without shame. When a young engineering graduate, the son of a clockmaker, tried to help his widowed mother run their store, he was jeered at as "the doctor of clockmaking," disgraced, and eventually left Bahia. When a schoolmistress married a carpenter, people gossiped about her as "the schoolmarm in the workshop."[126]

Consequently, most middle-class families tried to promote their sons up the rungs of the academic ladder. There was no question for most of keeping the children home to be tutored by English governesses. They sent their children to public or private neighborhood classes held in the homes of the teacher.[127] The content of lessons in one school or another probably differed little. In memoirs, Bahians almost proudly affirmed that they were terrible students. They justified their paradoxical pride through description of the stupefying rote repetition and bizarre hornbooks that were supposed to teach the alphabet.[128] Although in every generation adults hoped that school would be transformed from "the slaughterhouse of children" into "a nest of canaries singing happily in the morn of the renewed nation," what virtually every child remembered were brutal punishments, fierce exercises in penmanship, and humiliating public quizzes.[129] One or another elementary schoolmistress might be remembered as tender, but in the 1910's schoolmasters were still known as being "of the old school in the matter of rigor" or "the terror of the boys of that time."[130]

After families had made the momentous decision to set a boy to study rather than trade, some could obtain free secondary education at the Ginásio da Bahia, the distinguished (and the only) public secondary school, whose professors were prominent intellectuals. Just as cohorts of the elite met at the Colégio Antônio Vieira and formed cliques that lasted lifetimes, cohorts of middle-class youths met at the Ginásio.[131] Medical school, law school, and the polytechnic, the last steps toward forming a professional, were expensive. Professional academies required not only tuition but also wardrobes of an elegance befitting their students' status. It was a matter of pride for a man to have paid for the education of sons, nephews, or godsons. He could point and say, "I graduated him." Or a man might arrange patronage to give a student a comfortable public sinecure, such as a job as proofreader on the *Diário Oficial*. Some families could not afford to finance a diploma for more than one son or daughter, and had to decide which, if any, was to be put through school.[132]

Like landlord families, middle-class families also had a crisis in youth. But the issue was less the assertion of the son's adulthood in the face of a patriarch's overwhelming power than the testing of the father's influence to place his son respectably in the face of limited opportunity. Middle-class fathers and sons did not compete for control of the land and patrimony; the entire family collaborated to win sons a place in the government or commerce. Education only certified eligibility for certain positions. Young men and their families needed to cultivate patrons in order to maneuver the crucial first placement, the *colocação*.[133]

Girls' roles grew more problematic in these families than they were in rural or elite families. Girls still identified with their mothers. But in the city the roles of women changed more rapidly than in the countryside. The model of the marriageable girl was that she be discreet and withdrawn. For older people, especially, the most damning characterization of a girl was that she was *namoradeira*, flirtatious, or *saida*, forward. Yet as the styles of urban courtship changed, girls had to take more initiative in making their own marriages, and fathers could recruit or impose a suitor less easily. Already by 1870, girls needed more education in social graces. Furthermore, people agreed that a degree qualifying her for a job would insure a girl against the fear of a destitute spinsterhood. By the beginning of the twentieth century, families gave girls an education as a sort of dowry.[134]

But issues of education paled in comparison with quandaries over how girls should participate in public entertainments and dances. The *melindrosa* of the Belle Epoque and the flapper of the Jazz Age, new and glamorous roles, were legitimated by the illustrated magazines and the movies. They suggested manners and a display of bare arms and legs that conflicted with traditions and with the demeanor of the lady. Even more directly than the ideal of the lady, the ideal of glamour contradicted the utilitarian values of dignity in housework, education, or careers for women. A cautionary skit written by Amélia Rodrigues for schoolgirls around 1910 dramatizes this conflict in the outburst of a spoiled, frivolous girl whose mother has finally resolved to send her to school: "A person like me, twelve years old, almost a grown woman [*mulher feita*], going to school for the first time!" Over time, in all the upper classes, women won access to new activities. In the 1950's, it seemed like an achieved, emancipated way of life that upper-class girls should "flirt, swim, dance," travel to Rio and São Paulo, and take holidays at the beach.[135]

Roles were more vulnerable in middle-class families, in part because individuals could escape them more easily than in the families of the elite. The sexual repression that was so feeble in all of these families was weak among the mild-mannered bourgeois as well. Men usually could not afford to set up a mistress in a second household, but they would find a mistress who could support herself, the maid, or a prostitute. For example, a divorce case in 1911 turned on the accusation of a woman who, accompanied by a manservant, followed her husband to rooms in the back of his brother's shop, "The X-Ray." She found what she had been told: that her husband was keeping "a former seamstress" there. Men's memoirs nostalgically idealize the libertinism of the student republics, when a medical student could meet a girl during Carnival and then share her time with a dockworker for the rest of his student days. To explain these revelations as deviance would be to misjudge the extent of even lip service to propriety in Salvador, and to underestimate the tolerance—or hypocrisy—of families toward occasional escapes.[136]

In the middle class, it was even conceivable that men and women might abandon their families. Social pressure to behave as a model, set standards, and honor the coat of arms was not as strong as among the elite. Children also escaped the family more often by simply running away. Bahian families of all classes routinely shared children. Children could usually take a long leave from home if they had an aunt or grandmother to take them in. But middle-class children could leave against the will of their parents. One Bahian woman described how, at the turn of the century, her young uncle, tired of his mother's beatings, ran away at the age of nine and went to live with a widowed aunt. He never returned to the family, and in time his brothers and sisters lost touch with him. When one of the brothers died, her father spent an evening walking up and down the neighborhood where he thought his brother lived, calling out his name, to tell him the news. At a more benign level, it was customary for unmarried girls to spend time with their friends, sometimes living in another house for weeks or months at a time. Spinsterhood did not condemn women to living in their father's house.[137]

The Families and the Populace

Bahians had an offhand way of classifying crowds that suggests what the word *family* meant to them. Journalists or writers describing a crowd would speak of *as famílias e o povo*: "the families and the people." "Families" meant not just any family, but rather a properly organized establishment. Outside of the "families," the rest of Bahian society was disorganized, anonymous, the "populace." The realm of the "families" was the house, that of the "povo," the street. Repeatedly, decent Bahians complained that an honorable head of a family could not take his wife and children out into any part of the city without being assaulted by bad language.[138] This idiom reinforced the assumption that legally constituted, patriarchal families, despite significant variations by rank or between city and country, belonged to one general type. It implied that moral respectability was attained only in the upper classes.

There was certainly a basis in practice for this snobbish distinction. In the mid nineteenth century, white infants brought to baptism in Salvador were much less often illegitimate than brown or black infants.[139] To the extent that color served as a proxy for social rank in Bahia, these differences confirm what every Bahian observed: the poor, and especially blacks, rarely made use of formal marriage, rarely constituted a legal "family." In marriage registers, men who were professionals were noticeably overrepresented.[140]

The dichotomy between "families" and "populace" handled at least one social group poorly: the artisans, petty peddlers, and skilled workers of Salvador, and the small farmers of the Recôncavo and sertão, almost all of them colored Brazilians or recent Portuguese and Spanish immigrants. They often formed families that enforced roles like those of the upper-class family. They often married, secluded and supervised their women, and insisted on the authority of fathers over children, like the upper classes. They wished to protect and marry off their daughters.[141] These families could not claim the kinship ties, education, or wealth that defined the middle class. In addition, their men often worked with their hands. But some form of the patriarchal family was within their grasp. Consider Luiz Tarquínio's factory housing, the Vila Operária:

It wasn't just any worker who could live in the Vila. The main condition: you had to be *gente de família*, that is, a married woman or a *serious* widow, a family girl, and an upright man. A *mulher dama* [loose woman] couldn't enter a Section of the Vila even as a visitor. A drunken man was called to order. Courtships were regulated: you couldn't court at the gates of the Sections, because the watchmen had orders not to allow it. The gates were closed at nine, so that visitors, even boyfriends, had to leave as soon as the curfew whistle blew.[142]

Few records illuminate their family history. In early-twentieth-century São Paulo, Florestan Fernandes discerned a group of "proper Negroes" among the anomic mass of freedmen who descended on the city after abolition. These proper Negroes attempted to observe the standards of the legitimate families of the upper class, but found it difficult to guarantee the future of their sons and prevent the ruin of their daughters. For these freedmen and the poor European immigrants who filled the city after 1890, criminal complaints of defloration indicate that female chastity and legal marriage was at least formally their ideal.[143]

In Bahia, it seems likely that the many complaints of defloration in the city came from parents of this class, trying to force the marriage of their daughters. But even formal marriage was not an absolute requirement for the status of a "family" in Bahia. Among the upper class as well as the lower class, tacit recognition of a stable union by the couple's peers was enough and was widely, if begrudgingly, granted. What seems to have been the minimum definition of a *casa de família* was the presence of a man as head of the household.[144]

Many households among the populace (and many among the upper class, for that matter) consisted only of a mother and her children. In nineteenth-century Bahia, Kátia Mattoso has argued, the families of freedmen and slaves were most often tentative and fragile coalitions for the survival of the very poor. Marriage might be more important to an old couple pooling their small property than to the parents of children.[145] Some backlands communities of Bahia strongly sanctioned unformalized unions, requiring a religious marriage. Yet in general, lower-class families remained outside the church and the law. In Salvador the norm of the families of the populace was not to marry. Indifference to marriage and customs positively legitimating a woman's headship in the family made it far easier for men and women to break up, and for children to run away. That, and desperate poverty, made it easier for parents to abandon their children.[146]

One significant result of the weakness of mating ties in the lower class was that women became much more independent. Women had more claim on children because paternity was established only through the mother's relation to the father. Outside the family as well, lower-class Bahian women worked independently. They marketed much of the city's produce. Certainly the classification *famílias e povo* connotes a division of women into the escorted and the unescorted. "Families" escorted their women in a crowd, whereas among the populace, men and women mixed.[147]

Cultures and Integration

In his essay on the family in Brazil, Antônio Cândido relates patriarchal and nonpatriarchal families in a way that recapitulates the relations of order and disorder in his "dialectic of roguery."[148] His analysis of Manuel Antônio de Almeida's picaresque novel *Memoirs of a Sergeant of the Militia* proposes that its sketches of manners were unified by the author's unspoken vision of society. In Almeida's vision, Brazilians had no internalized conscience, but rather only a habit of obeying figures who paradigmatically represent order. Some zones of the society were governed in strict order. Others were disorganized and anarchic. Yet a dialectic of mutual tolerance and connivance united the continuum of order and disorder. Each pole occasionally needed the other: through lust, a feared disciplinarian might fall to the level of the rogues that he policed. Similarly, when Cândido describes Brazilian families, he sees their structure as a symbiotic relationship between a patriarchal, hierarchical core and a disorganized periphery. At the edges of the patriarchal sphere of influence were dependents, servants, and illegitimate by-blows, whom it organized weakly.

Cândido's hypothesis helps us to understand and describe the organi-

zation of the family in Bahia from the perspective of the upper class, and
at their level. His image of a paradigm of lordliness or order explains the
relations of the elite to the landlords and the middle class. The families
of the elite stood at the apex of a pyramid of civilized manners. Downward and outward, in many gradations, spread the families of the middle
class, toward the limits of decency. Yet Bahian families did not maintain an irreconcilable boundary between decency and disorder. They were
able to accommodate deviant behavior, and, particularly through kinship
and domestic service, they maintained constant contact with the realm of
"disorder."

Cândido's vision is not as plausible from the perspective of lower-class
families. It confessedly leaves aside the families of independent peasants,
which he studied in another work, and does not recognize other fractions
of the lower class as such.[149] It sees their families and their identities as
incomplete, being completed by their attachment to the clienteles of patriarchal families. However, clientelism was only one aspect of the allegiances
and associations of the people and their families. The lower classes in fact
had allegiances and institutions of their own: candomblés, religious fra-
ternities, colored Carnival associations, militia regiments, and *favela* and
saloon neighborhood life.

Another approach may be helpful in regard to Bahia. Sidney Mintz and
Richard Price, surveying the culture of the Caribbean, suggest that the
culture of enslaved Africans and their descendants everywhere developed
two faces. One part of it developed in order to bridge the gap between
the slaves and their masters. It emphasized smooth, clientelistic relations.
But another, internal part of the culture of the slaves remained exotic
and independent. In some institutions, such as religious cults, it explicitly valued secrecy and duplicity. In other institutions, such as the family,
it may merely have encouraged indifference and passive resistance to the
white culture.[150] Whites and Africans married within their separate groups
in Bahia; the brown mass of the population married out to all groups.
In the late nineteenth century, Bahia's African freedmen increasingly rejected Catholic marriage and sought out African women of their "nation"
for free unions, forming a notably endogamic, but "unofficial," type of
family. Mattoso has interpreted this as "a break with the dominant culture in an attempt to assert their own cultural identity," and connected it
to the rejection by Africans of Catholic brotherhoods and the growth of
candomblé.[151] This may be an optimistic interpretation. Or, it may be that
from the perspective of one segment of the lower class in Bahia, the culture
looked less like a continuum from order to disorder than the combination
of two alien hemispheres into a single globe.

The writings of Jorge Amado, Bahia's most dedicated social novelist of the generation from 1930 to 1960, seem to support this interpretation. From an upper-class perspective—or at least for the literate reading public—he romanticizes the duality in Bahian society, presenting it as an endless wrangle between a repressive, Victorian upper class and a tolerant, eroticized lower class. In *Quincas Wateryell*, for example, Amado's lower class is Bohemia. The heroine is not the mother, but the good prostitute. In fact, Bohemia becomes a utopia where reconciliation of the antipodes is possible in festive disorder for Amado, as it did for some European writers. He implies that Bohemia can be the new zone of community, replacing the old bridge of clientelism.[152]

All of these analyses support one speculation with regard to the upper-class family. It may be that the sort of dual culture that existed in Bahia was not amenable to rationalization in the mold of liberal universalism. Liberal institutions that stressed equality before the law, for instance, ran counter to the reality of at least two classes of citizenship, and to the overriding loyalties of chieftains and followers that cut across them. Any reform program that assumed some degree of cultural integration was certain to founder. The church's crusade against divorce in the 1920's, for instance, rang hollow in a state where the bulk of the population never married at all.

The disjunction in society was largely the legacy of slavery, which had formed a society out of Portuguese and African segments. But it may also have derived from a Portuguese culture that never abandoned its medieval, Iberian worldview.[153] Modernization of the formal and public institutions of the society from without found very weak traction between its ideologies and most people's experience. The culture had most potential for finding wholeness and solidarity in its creole folk culture.

There was "modernization" of some informal norms of Bahian family life, especially those having to do with clientelism and the place of women in courtship and honor. The three types of family were likely to react in different ways to changes in norms. During the period from 1880 to 1930, the families of rural landlords still relied largely on their own authority, rather than on the expertise of others. With increasing self-doubt, they referred to folk traditions or improvised their roles themselves. Elite families embraced the agenda of European civilization wholeheartedly, at least until the Jazz Age after World War I. They were linked personally to European fashions and fads, and read expert advisors on fashion, hygiene, and morality. Middle-class families were linked by their origins and by ties of clientelism to the landlords and the elite. The middle class did not choose roles with entire autonomy, but, like the elite, listened to the dictates of experts more than to the voice of tradition. Unlike the elite, middle-class families could not afford the consumerist styles of European fashion.

They combined old ways and new fads in an eclectic fashion that became characteristic of the half-modern, half-patriarchal style of Bahian families between the wars. To better understand how and why Bahian families changed their ways of life, it may help to explore their responses to direct pressures from formal institutions: the medical profession, the law, and the Catholic church.

3

Medicine and Families

DISEASE wove through the lives of all families in Bahia. Illness and health were a constant concern of their conversations and correspondence. This was certainly not unique to Bahia. But nearly everyone agreed that the tropics were more "unhealthy," less salubrious environments than northern climates, and that within Brazil, Salvador, like Rio de Janeiro and Recife, was an unhealthy city. Yellow fever, malaria, and other tropical diseases gave Brazil a reputation as the grave of white men.[1]

Speaking to one another, Bahians took note of the dangers, and the disruption of families, in epidemics. During the great cholera epidemic of 1855, one great landlord lamented his destiny: "God wished to punish my sins, taking away from me the Angel who sweetened my days." Another commented cynically on the price of life for a man suspected of killing his wife during the epidemic: "The baron of Cajaíba is also widowed because my cousin died on the 24th, they say from the cholera. . . . Well, in the final account, she was the one who died. He has also lost many Slaves!!" During a smallpox epidemic in 1882, a Salvador broker wrote to reassure his brother-in-law that the family had chosen vaccination, despite its risks. In the great smallpox epidemic of 1919, most members of one modest middle-class Bahian family chose not to be vaccinated; the epidemic ran through the family, left widows and orphans, and forced kin to move in together for survival.[2]

Bahians gossiped not only about the acute epidemic diseases of cholera, yellow fever, and smallpox, and the major endemic diseases, such as tuberculosis, malaria, and beri-beri, but also about the minor daily concerns of health: children with runny noses or weak chests, a heavy cold brought on by "a chill upon going up in the Elevator," aches and nervousness. Families anxiously watched over the health of children, with good reason. Infant mortality in Salvador can only be estimated roughly, but it was almost certainly in the range of 30 percent for the population as a whole and not much lower for the upper classes. Many families must have lost an infant or a child, preserving as a remembrance the funeral bill for an "angel." After the childhood diseases, they feared most urgently the routine dangers to women in pregnancy and childbirth. Childbirth meant at best a time of suffering and fever, and especially in the countryside, a brush with death for mother and child.[3]

Diagnosing each other's complaints and recommending treatments may have been a general pastime, but healing was particularly a family matter. Some families thought of themselves as unhealthier than others, with notorious common problems: "weak eyes," or, most feared, "weak chests."[4] The family also took basic responsibility for the medical care of its members. Medical consultations seem to have been expensive, as do medicines. For a child's illness in 1881, the costs were 20$, about half a month's rent, for medicines that had to be bought at the pharmacy, a chicken for broth, "and finally you know very well what treating a sick person costs." The medicines may not have been complicated, but treatment could be all-absorbing: "He is taking sea baths and the tincture of cod-liver oil and the mint tea, as well as the port wine that Doctor Couto said be given two times a day with water." Medical care was provided not only to the immediate family but to the entire household. Masters might spend as much on the treatment of a slave as on the treatment of a child. Brites Barbosa, Rui's sister, consulted two prominent doctors over the illness of Eva, a slave left her by her father, first thinking the problem was her liver, then swelling owing to pregnancy, then dropsy. Finally, she asked her brother to take Eva to be examined by a third physician.[5]

In the end no family could evade the sufferings that came from inevitable, incurable diseases. They might speak lightheartedly and hopefully of health compensating for poverty, saying, "Happily the only thing that they catch at that house is poverty, which is always worsening." But virtually every home, rich or poor, was eventually struck by tragedy. Hospitals did not remove the scene of suffering from the home. As Brites wrote her brother in 1867, she was glad he had not been home during their mother's illness. He had not suffered as much as she had, had not seen their mother's agonized gaze in her last days or heard her yell out, " 'My daughter of Heaven,' with a pained voice that won't leave my ears; after that I went downstairs, because Father thought that she was dying, and I only saw her again two days later, already expiring."[6]

The medical profession in Bahia became the formal, public institution most directly concerned with family life and most closely involved in private households. Families avidly sought advice from physicians on how to understand and control the mysterious matters of health, life, and death.

Over the course of the nineteenth and twentieth centuries, the medical profession proposed increasingly active remedies that implied significant reform of traditional family customs and of social life outside the family. Medical social thought became the most prominent formal statement of models for family life.

Medical Education and Ideas

The organization of the medical profession in Brazil, and particularly the nature of medical practice and medical education, influenced the social models of Brazilian medical thought. Until 1808 the Crown did little to organize the profession. Trained and licensed physicians, *físicos*, and surgeon-barbers came from Portugal, many of them sent to fill official posts in the army, the city sanitary administration, or the hospitals of the Santa Casa da Misericórdia. Some religious orders, particularly the Jesuits, sent missionaries trained or experienced in medicine. But the practice of medicine fell chiefly to barbers, bonesetters, apothecaries, and folk healers. The status of the profession remained relatively low, even suspect because of the tradition that it was a career for New Christians (Jewish converts). Initiatives for sanitary measures in the cities and for public responses to epidemics came principally from civil officials rather than from their medical advisors.[7]

In the year 1808, King João VI of Portugal fled from Napoleon's armies to Brazil, where he began to establish the cultural institutions of a complete nation in a colony that had hitherto not even had a printing press. This marked the turning point for the Brazilian medical profession. The Crown convoked commissions and immediately established surgical courses. It chartered the Medical and Surgical Society of Rio de Janeiro in 1829, and in 1832 it established two medical academies in Rio and Salvador. These two academies, the counterparts in prestige of the law academies founded in Recife and São Paulo, became the centers of Brazilian medical debate and thought (though not always of medical research) for at least the next century. They graduated and certified all the doctors of official medicine under the Empire, and retained their prominence after the founding of other medical schools during the Republic. The medical school of Rio drew influence from its location in the court, close to imperial concern and favor. But in the smaller milieu of Salvador, the Bahian Medical Faculty was one of the few national institutions with no competitor for local prestige. It was the intellectual center of the province, and as such assumed responsibilities far beyond a narrow definition of medical education.[8]

The Brazilian medical faculties existed to transmit ideas more than to invent them. Formally, medical education at the Faculdade de Medicina da

Bahia followed the model of European academies and provided a setting for science. Professors competed for chairs by defending original theses at public disputations. Students entered by passing oral and written exams before boards of examiners in a variety of subjects. They followed a course of instruction that included lectures, laboratory practical sessions, dissections, and, for some, internships in hospitals and clinics. After completing their studies by writing a thesis addressed to one of the chairs of the faculty, accompanied by a list of propositions for oral defense before other chairs, they emerged full-fledged to practice medicine. Informally, the students' medical education required supplementing mediocre, haphazard instruction with the personal patronage of professors. For internships, favor weighed as heavily as merit. Although standards for graduation had relaxed by the end of the nineteenth century, without favor even an exceptional student felt hard put to advance. The quality of instruction suffered from the absence and indifference of some professors and the helplessness of the best ones in the face of inadequate facilities for teaching, much less research.[9]

Although it provided homeopathic doses of practical experience in anatomy and microbiology, medical instruction in Bahia gave students a bounty of experience in the scholastic mode. Professors cited, confronted, and reconciled the pronouncements of foreign authorities; students memorized and repeated what they had heard from the professors (or from the beadles in the courses whose professor appeared only on the first and last days of the term). When José Silveira was a student in the 1920's, the best representative of this tradition was the fierce anatomy professor Eduardo Diniz Gonçalves. His fame rested on his having memorized Testut's *Descriptive Anatomy*, which he delivered in lectures year after year without emendation, down to the typographical errors.[10]

Empirical and experimental medical research took place mainly outside the medical schools, in private laboratories such as that of the Tropicalista group in Salvador, who carried on empirical investigations into tropical diseases in the 1860's and divulged them through the *Gazeta Médica da Bahia*, which they founded in 1866 somewhat at the margin of the medical schools. Scientific research in Bahia declined after the Tropicalistas, probably because the new paradigm of experimental medicine required financing and equipment that were not assembled successfully in Brazil until the establishment of the Oswaldo Cruz Institute. The next significant movement in Bahian medical research, Nina Rodrigues's investigations in legal medicine and criminological anthropology in the 1890's, also took place largely outside his faculty position, in hospitals and morgues.[11]

The medical schools served to interpret and transmit the authoritative body of medical doctrine. Students graduated having been brought up to date on the medical orthodoxy of their times. That orthodoxy, of course, was European. All realms of Brazilian intellectual life took ideas and agendas from the European center of civilization, and especially from France. The first Brazilian professors of medicine had studied in Coimbra and Montpellier; they had at hand the developed tradition of medical thought on hygiene that provided them with a general framework, occasional scientific validation, and even specific prescriptions for medical intervention in the family and in society.[12]

It is legitimate and important to ask why Brazilian medicine only imported science and ideas, for by the turn of the twentieth century, Brazilians had begun to produce their own science. But in respect to the nineteenth century, it is more pertinent to ask what Brazilians chose from European medical debate and how they adapted it. For instance, it took some time for germ theory to be accepted, and it always coexisted with hereditarian theories of disease. In 1885 one influential professor at the Rio medical school continued to reject Kock's finding of a bacillus that caused tuberculosis, deducing instead from the inconsistent patterns of contagion that a hereditary disposition to pulmonary lesions was the cause. Brazilian physicians, like physicians anywhere in Europe, had to select a position among competing theories.[13]

And in their medical social thought, Brazilians also borrowed and adapted. In the first two decades after establishment of the medical schools, Brazilian physicians used a series of arguments about hygiene, public health, and the state that had emerged in Germany and France in the late eighteenth century. They established a tradition of argument from French authority, and throughout the nineteenth century, through communications with French and European medical schools and journals, they remained in touch with that tradition.[14]

Linking social theory to scientific discovery in the nineteenth century was a risky strategy. The trajectory of scientific inquiry could introduce a random element into the working out of social theory. For example, in positivist social thought, the common metaphorical comparison of a nation to an organism or a body invited careless reasoning by analogy. But the consequences for provincial or dependent areas such as Brazil were doubly arbitrary, because they harnessed themselves to a tradition whose adjustments reflected alien needs, responded to European conditions.

Brazilian medical thought did not move in unison with French medical thinking (nor, of course, did novelties stated in Paris diffuse to the French provinces instantaneously), but it did generally follow the agenda of European debates.[15] Brazilians might abridge, amend, or distort, but they always cited European precedents and authorities. The range of European medical theory was broad and contested enough to provide room for local adaptations. For one example, Brazilian social medicine did not enunciate a stance against slavery, or rather, did not think its condemnation of the moral and medical consequences of familiarity with slaves through to a call for abolition. For another, the lag in accepting materialist philosophical foundations for medical science indicates local adaptation in medical thought. All but a few theses at the Faculdade de Medicina da Bahia up to the end of the Empire subscribed to vitalist theories of life, holding that life was the soul or that there was some life force separate from the soul and the body. The first positivist and materialist theses presented in the 1870's were rejected by the faculty or approved only after delay, supposedly because the faculty found them "offensive to religion." [16] Brazilian doctors hesitated for some time, then, before shifting to the mechanistic or materialistic premises of positivism.

Yet the scope of these theses indicates how widely the concerns of "derivative" medical theory could range. One student began with a consideration of the nature and functions of the brain, arguing that all thought is merely cellular activity. He moved on to many of the themes of positivism, to an attack on metaphysics, on priests, and clericalism, as well as an attack on vitalist theories of life. In an aside he explained and reduced poetry; the poet was "a great apparatus of condensation." [17] Brazilian medical thought, like the contemporary European medicine from which it drew its inspiration, was hardly modest in its presumption to make relevant comment on all areas of life.

Imbedding Hygiene in the Family

Hygiene was the discipline through which Bahian medical thinking most often addressed the family. Hygiene, understood as the field of preventive medicine, potentially turned medical inquiry toward all of society and nature, to any phenomenon that could be identified as a cause of disease. In the late eighteenth and early nineteenth centuries, European medical theorists extended their interest to all sorts of phenomena that they could group under their concept of "policing": city streets, ventilation of houses, sewers and water, markets and vendors, paupers and criminals and lunatics. Brazilian physicians borrowed these concerns while emphasizing some that seemed particularly appropriate to local medical problems, such as yellow fever, which could be traced to the hot climate. Jurandir Freire Costa lists just a few of the practices and objects that they brought into the "field of medical knowing" by their concern with salubrity, *salubriedade*: "Wilds [*matas*], marshes, rivers, foodstuffs, sewers, water, air, cemeteries, barracks, schools, brothels, factories, slaughterhouses, and homes." Others can easily be added to the list: ships, churches and images, furnishings, clothes.[18]

A great many of these public concerns impinged on the family and private behavior. Concern with houses, for instance, turned to a criticism of dark, damp, and stuffy quarters, to concern with the proper placement of rooms, and with proper maintenance of the kitchen and latrine. It embraced issues such as proper lighting and the dangers of green wallpaper tinted with arsenic. And it extended to the custom of secluding women. Thus, early-nineteenth-century hygienists created an image of the woman confined to the inner chambers of the house, the *alcova*, whose obesity and pallor from lack of exercise and sunlight demonstrated her bad health.[19] As a young man argued to his fiancée in the 1870's, "I think it is indispensable to your health that you not shut yourself up in the house; because that sort of life is ordinarily one of the main causes of chronic and incurable illnesses among Brazilian ladies."[20] What began, or was most easily presented, as a denunciation of bad architecture, thus became a denunciation of bad family customs. This is not to say that medicine addressed only indirect criticism to the family. Doctors often said frankly and bluntly what they thought of different forms of family organization and specified in detail what they wanted.

In extending its scope to include the family and the home, Brazilian medicine aspired to become an institution imbedded in the family, controlling it.[21] The authority of physicians in Bahian families grew significantly over the nineteenth century. Freyre argues in *Sobrados e mucambos* that the replacement of the figure of the priest-confessor by that of the doctor-counselor as the man admitted to the intimacy of women occurred during the first half of the nineteenth century, and that it accompanied a shift in Brazilian culture from an emphasis on death and the other world to an acceptance of life and this world: "The figure of the family doctor, becoming larger than that of the confessor, inside the mansions and later in the plantation houses themselves, little by little finished off such anti-social idealizations [as that of the dead baby and the dead virgin]."

Freyre's discussion of the rising influence of doctors over women during the nineteenth century develops into a consideration of the decline of patriarchal power, through the metaphor of a transition from absolute to constitutional monarchy, and of "the extent to which other institutions grew up around the Big House, diminishing it, belittling it [*desprestigiando-a*], opposing counterweights to its influence." Women and children, Freyre says, were elevated as they submitted to the new influences of the doctor, of the school, of the theater, and of secular literature.[22]

The pronunciamentos of doctors testify to their ambition to take over authority for the family. One aspect of their strategy was to discredit the competence of lay people as parents and spouses. A new image appeared in Brazilian medical writing of the 1830's, that of the harmful family, incapable of bringing up its children in proper health. This image contradicted the secure self-confidence and self-sufficiency of the rural patriarchal family. Throughout works on childbearing, nursing, and pediatrics, doctors warned against the ignorance and carelessness of families. They sometimes called for the state to protect children against the errors or abandonment of parents, "for the law to shelter [*abrigar*] these innocents in its paternal and benevolent mantle." But more often they implied that the law had nothing to do with the relation of the doctor to the family, a relation that one student compared to creation: "In the face of the newborn, the doctor can be considered as an architect and the newborn as the edifice that he tries to raise."[23]

Rural Bahian families were indeed self-sufficient in their healing, but their isolation forced it on them. On plantations, the master was often obliged to attempt healing. In the 1860's, the head of the Pinheiro Canguçu family treated virtually every ailment of family members and moradores on his plantation, consulting a medical handbook and traditional family recipes, leaving only amputations to the doctor from Caetité. With the habit of self-reliance came skepticism of the special knowledge of doctors. Anna Ribeiro's family did not get her eyes treated in the 1850's because they did not trust doctors. One treatment to decrease her eye inflammation had left the scars of abscesses on her upper arms.[24]

As doctors asserted authority over parents, they confronted, not the patriarch, but rather other figures who could claim expertise. The medical literature on childbearing and childrearing abounds in attacks on wet nurses, midwives, and old wives who might presume to speak with authority or to interpret tradition. Theses and treatises on childbirth typically mention with contempt the baths in wine given to newborns by superstitious midwives. Wet nurses, besides being "mercenary," were to be condemned because they were "[in our country] ordinarily Africans, stupid, immoral, without education," and they were stigmatized as bearers of syphilis. But the generalized attack on customs, on *usos*, commonly identified no specific culprit. It implied that women's lore was superstition. Significantly, a guide addressed to a general public, rather than a thesis directed principally to other doctors, made this most explicit, saying that pregnancy is usually simple if the woman follows good sense and hygiene, not popular tales and the advice of "matrons."[25]

The touch of misogyny in doctors' arguments about the incompetence of women was echoed in the resistance by some doctors to women entering the medical school, which graduated no women before 1887. That resistance faced the strong argument that women would be superior attendants upon each other because of their natural sympathy and the greater modesty of the relationship. An article reprinted in the *Gazeta Médica da Bahia* in 1868 refused this logic in an aggressive tone rare in the journal, insisting that women were created to be wives and mothers, and that if they were to be "elevated," it should be by educating them to be good wives, mothers, and teachers. Woman doctors would not be proper to attend decent wives and daughters because only *mulheres fortes*, strong women, "perhaps not unfamiliar with vices," would become doctors. It mocked the temerity of women wishing to become medical students in a satire with scatological overtones. Could one imagine a girl, "leaving the house of her parents, honest and timid, with the modesty of her twenty years, to approach cadavers, and scalpel in hand, ask of Nature all its secrets!"[26]

The writings of doctors only prove that medicine intended to imbed itself in the family. But accounts of Bahian home life in the nineteenth and twentieth centuries do show thorough infiltration by doctors and medical ideas. To take one prominent example, in 1876 Rui Barbosa was a young lawyer trying to earn enough in Rio to return and marry his fiancée, Maria Augusta Viana Bandeira. He wrote to her in Bahia urging her to follow the advice of her family physician and friend, Counselor Salustiano Ferreira Souto. Souto was particularly close to Maria Augusta's married sister, Adelaide Dobbert. He accompanied Adelaide and her husband to a spa near Rio to treat her for weakness and paralysis. Writing daily, Rui described their idyllic stay at the cool spa, where from her wheelchair Adelaide courted Rui, her new brother, and Souto, her "second father." In one letter Rui urged Maria Augusta, who was melancholy herself, to go on "hygienic outings" accompanied by her brother, though he agreed that outings of a betrothed girl in the company of some persons would be "inconvenient." A few days later he asked Maria Augusta to stop working at her sewing machine: "Statistics demonstrate that sort of work is a frequent cause of ailments [*incômodos*] like yours. . . . The person who says this is our Conselheiro Souto, who joins to the voice of a fiancé, that of a father, for he is yours in his heart."[27]

And soon after, he sent yet another list of prescriptions from Souto, including cod-liver oil and sea baths in the early morning. Rui's family and circle of friends were very close to the medical profession, as his father had been a doctor. The bachelor Souto was so close a friend of the Dobberts that he left much of his property to their daughters. But in Bahia, where a great many upper-class families had more than one relative in the profession, and where the medical school dominated provincial intellectual life, such familiarity may not have been uncommon. The tone of his correspondence takes for granted that medical authority is accepted common sense and that everyone is familiar with the routine diagnoses and prescriptions.[28]

Doctors spread their influence through other means than direct contact with families. Throughout the nineteenth and twentieth centuries, columns and didactic articles appeared in Brazilian newspapers and magazines giving advice on hygiene in diet, clothing, and so forth. Such legitimations of medical authority in the family were widely disseminated among the Bahian and Brazilian publics. Medical or hygienic advice was a major part of the "domestic interest" portions of the Bahian Catholic press, which was otherwise full of moral tales. For example, the October 1910 issue of *Paladina*, a Catholic women's journal, had articles on the instincts giving way to will in early childhood development, on eating slowly being important for health, and on the uses of cabbage water in treating fever.[29]

Yet medicine had no monopoly of influence on the family. To begin with, most of the population were too poor or too isolated to see doctors and continued to treat their health in other ways. All classes had access to curers, to homeopathic physicians, to spiritualist mediums, to druggists, to miracles of Nosso Senhor do Bomfim, and, most important, to domestic remedies. Most families consulted doctors, not for routine matters, but for serious illnesses. Within their "allopathic" discipline, doctors had to compete with pharmacists and the home medical dictionary of Dr. Chernoviz.[30]

Two memoirs of the small-town childhoods of storekeeper's sons provide an example of the practical counterweights to medical authority. José Lemos de Sant'Ana recalled that in the 1920's, doctors' prescriptions of whatever sort were tested for compatibility with the habitual home remedies, and that infusions and castor oil remained the most common treatment for simple illnesses, prayer the most effective treatment for major ones. Similarly, Gilberto Amado described the many strategies his parents used to heal his inflamed knee in the 1890's. After home remedies and apothecary's brews did no good, the family bypassed the incompetent town doctor to request prescriptions by mail from city doctors in Aracajú and Bahia. As a last resort, and against their better judgment, his parents called in an old black woman, whose prayer cured him overnight. Families were not hostile to the advice of official medicine, but they were just as receptive to advice from any quarter.[31]

So, as medical ideas diffused to the upper- and middle-class public through journalism, schools, and visits to families, they were diluted or distorted by their confrontation with other medical systems and with the unsystematic inventories of commonsense ideas about health. The analysis of medical theories that follows shows how medicine tried to legitimate its authority as it proposed reforming the family.

Maternity and the Protection of Children

The framing premise that medical social thought brought to its theories of the family was that children needed protection. High infant mortality provided the occasion for the earliest Brazilian medical condemnations of the family.[32] They blamed the deaths of children on the ignorance or negligence of incompetent or immoral parents. In Bahia, medical works rarely addressed infant mortality until the end of the nineteenth century. However, they often took the care of early childhood as their topic.

In the first half of the nineteenth century, the medical literature focused its reforming zeal on schools, and particularly on boarding schools. It apparently assumed that efforts to remold children could not possibly succeed unless they could be removed from pernicious home influences. In the heyday of their pedagogical emphasis, doctors proposed ideal curriculums and entire educational programs. The keynote of these programs was austerity and morality. Children were to be separated from demoralizing contacts with servants and old customs at home; they were even to be discouraged from home visits and vacations if at all possible.[33]

In the later nineteenth century, medical interest in boarding schools, their construction, their curriculum, and their routines declined; doctors shifted their emphasis to reform of the family and the household. The austere ethic of the boarding school also characterized most medical ideas on home education. Doctors argued that Brazilian children ran the risk either of being hopelessly spoiled by an indulgent upbringing or of having their spirits crushed by an unnecessarily harsh family regime. One medical student in 1853 approved Locke's teaching that disciplining children from the cradle would tame their passions, but also disapproved vehemently of excessive authority: "Servile treatment turns the character vile and low." In 1913 another sounded the same themes, this time linking them to the differences in character of the Saxon and Latin races. He defined the correct path in childrearing as a mean between the extremes: "The abuse of authoritarianism yields men of meek heart, afraid of greater responsibility; its opposite, an upbringing all of tenderness, of endearment, laden with caresses, a permanence for many years in maternal warmth, just as it increases love, sympathy, between parents and children, so it diminishes their energy, makes them effeminate, incapable of great enterprises." The tendency toward spoiling among Latins, he added, led to a "sublime backwardness" in character.[34]

Criticism of undue harshness was always directed at fathers, while criticism of indulgence was pointed toward mothers. Thus, it may be that the trend among some medical thinkers to idealize a Spartan boarding school as an antidote to family defects translated into the project of reforming, or spartanizing, the primitively overindulgent mother in order to be able to leave children at home safely in her care.

The emphasis on the child as having paramount importance, rather than on the adult, may have marked a new cultural emphasis in Brazil, a new recognition of childhood. But doctors did not devote much thought to sentimental praise of the child. In their analysis, children had value primarily because they would increase the future population of healthy adults. Brazilian hygienists probably picked up this populationist theme from European sources. Local circumstances did not warrant much concern about population growth, with the exception of the growth of the African population. Brazilians, particularly Brazilians of the upper classes, did not begin to show a decline in their birthrate, or in the fertility of women, until the very end of the nineteenth century, and even then the decline was not as alarming as in France.[35] The birthrate in Brazil remained high, as did infant mortality. This relatively late shift toward limiting family size may explain the evasiveness of Brazilian doctors on the perennial French topic of birth control and contraceptive techniques, though they did discuss abortion and infanticide.

The emphasis on the role of adults as being first and foremost procreators may have led to a novel celebration of sexuality within marriage in a culture previously overshadowed by religious denial of the flesh. The medical praise of sexual pleasure is rare in Brazilian formal discourse of the nineteenth century for its frankness. Earthy or naughty affirmations of sexuality existed in folklore. But in high literature and in public discourse, medical theories legitimated sexual pleasure, or at least sexual pleasure in marriage. The naturalist literary movement that flourished in the 1880's and set the tone for writing about sexuality through 1920 relied heavily on medical diagnoses of the sexual needs and sexual excesses of its characters, particularly its female characters. Influence went the other way as well, as Bahian physicians imported clichés from naturalist literature.[36]

Brazilian hygienists devoted less attention to sexuality than to maternity, perhaps because the latter proved more tractable to reform. More inaugural theses at the Bahian medical school discussed infant feeding than any other issue in family life.[37] Orthodoxy—which had changed little in substance from French and Portuguese advice of the eighteenth century—held that mothers should nurse their own infants. Mother's milk was the best food for infants. Nursing increased affection for the mother and passed on the "germ of constitutional similarity" between mother and child. A syphilitic mother's milk might even inoculate her child against syphilis. The next best alternative was to choose a nursemaid, and while medical writings offered advice on scheduling and methods of maternal feeding, they had most to say about the choice of a proper wet nurse. Though they gave rules of thumb for parents to follow in selecting a wet nurse, rules that seem to have held throughout the nineteenth century (that she be elegant, strong, have a good chest, clear skin, fresh breath, good teeth, no swollen glands, good nipples, blue veins on her breasts, and good habits), they always recommended that parents have a doctor examine her. They often suggested that municipal regulations require that wet nurses obtain a medical certificate. They proposed elaborate procedures for the examination, observing that wet nurses often resisted it. Finally, if maternal nursing and "mercenary nursing" were impossible, doctors recommended "artificial nursing" as a last alternative. Here again, they had a standard series of prescriptions, often recommending goat's milk straight from the teat, warning against the adulteration of urban dairies' milk, and describing various techniques for cleaning bottles and sterilizing milk.[38]

The stereotyped alarmism of this propaganda for maternal nursing raises the question of whether there was a practical reason for this choice of topics. Giving infants wet nurses was a common custom in the well-to-do families that were doctors' principal clientele. During and after slavery, Bahia was a culture of mammies, and the *mãe preta* was a standard figure in the Brazilian repertoire of social types. In the early nineteenth century, Bahian families took for granted that infants would have wet nurses. A bejewelled wet nurse was a symbol of status.[39] From 1870 onward, families seem to have taken more pride in mothers who nursed their own infants. Rui Barbosa's daughter Dedélia was left for a while with her maternal grandmother in 1879, and perhaps reluctantly given a wet nurse: "The Doctor doesn't want Dedelhe to give up nursing because her chest is a bit weak, so let her keep on nursing every day this month." Upon the birth of Rui's daughter Francisca in 1880, her mother, Cota [Maria Augusta], was ill, and Rui wrote that "my newborn daughter is doing poorly, and I am forced to take on a nurse here." But in 1911 his son Ruizinho thought it worth mentioning that his wife was nursing her baby herself.[40]

But the repetition of injunctions against the custom, and their uniformity, suggests that some other motive shaped them. A strong reason for the theme of maternal nursing in Brazilian medical treatises was simply the example of French hygienic reformers. In France, the theme of supporting maternal nursing went back further than Rousseau's *Emile*, and in France it typically included condemnation of the practice of putting out city infants to a wet nurse in the countryside. Whatever the reasons for this preoccupation in French medical thought, in Brazilian medical thought it responded to the rationality of scholastic accommodation to metropolitan science, as well as to the rationality of empirical observation. One thesis went so far as to admonish Brazilian parents solemnly never to choose a red-headed wet nurse, and to avoid a blonde one. Another insisted that the custom of putting out children to nurse was to be condemned, before conceding that bringing the wet nurse, and often her own child, into the employer's home was thankfully almost universal in Brazil. However, Brazilian doctors did observe practices of nursing. They noted that more mothers nursed in the countryside than in the city, and in 1909 one doctor hypothesized that the lower reported rates of infant mortality in backward Salvador than in industrial São Paulo might reflect more mothers nursing in Salvador.[41]

Thus, in the 1920's and 1930's, medical theses continued to emphasize wet-nursing, but their works begin to show the effect of observation that even middle-class mothers were turning away from wet nurses to bottle feeding. Though working mothers had moved to bottle feeding before the end of the nineteenth century, it was apparently only as the upper classes shifted their habits that doctors noted the "predominance" of bottle feeding. However, during these years, official medicine began to extend its scope further to all of society. Brazilian medical writing became a hybrid of conclusions drawn from global statistics that reflected the social conditions of the masses, and prescriptions aimed at their traditional upper- and middle-class clientele: that mothers should use litmus paper and a density meter to inspect milk from dairies, or that they should weigh the infant every day. As progressive physicians such as Alfredo Ferreira Magalhães established clinics "for the protection of children" and "of assistance to infancy" in Salvador in the early twentieth century, more doctors began to bifurcate their prescriptions, developing programs for poor mothers as well as for rich ones.[42]

Whether or not the ideas about wet-nursing were based on empirical observations, the medical admonitions to mothers to nurse carried an important symbolic message. They defined new terms for the intimacy between mother and child, urging mothers to take care of their children directly in order to raise them hygienically. They urged the Brazilian woman to change her role from that of a feudal lady, secluded in the inner chambers, to that of bourgeois housewife and mother, who went on outings but generally kept to the home. Some medical treatises portrayed the mother who nursed idyllically: nursing was the "glad offering of the pure snow of her breasts."[43] But most often they defended nursing as a duty, something mothers did for the benefit of their children, and as something *natural*, and hence to be recommended. One thesis described it as a duty imposed by God through nature.[44] They preferred to define the virtue of the nursing mother by contrast with the vices of the mother who gave her child to a nurse, who was at once artificial and the accomplice of barbarism. Wet-nursing, or *aleitamento mercenário*, was barbarous because of the bad influence of the slave nurses, "ordinarily Africans, stupid, immoral, lacking in education, without beauty, without religion, barren of affectionate sentiments, badly fashioned, irascible, poorly groomed, hateful, careless, coarse-skinned, often carrying those sorts of complaints that can be transmitted by means of nursing. Among us I believe that the free nurse should always be preferred."[45]

The barbarism of nurses, documented with anecdotes about their drugging infants in order to abandon themselves to libertinism, or transmitting nicotine through their milk, was most often presented as the danger of contagion. The nurse "could be the door through which contagious diseases penetrate into families." Most often, the danger was syphilis, the most dreaded symbol of contagion. Doctors told anecdotes of "a nurse who, introduced into the bosom of a family, syphilizes the child, which child in turn syphilizes the mother, and she the husband and two children."[46]

But the main purpose of exaggerating the barbarism of nurses was to castigate the artificiality of mothers who did not nurse.[47] When one doctor raised his voice in favor of the "astonishing generosity" of nurses, it was only in order to condemn the mother, to say that a "healthy peasant" might be better than an "opulent city dweller." Similarly, in an impassive tone, one doctor suggested that a dull mother might prefer to give her child to a bright nurse, as there was evidence that children might inherit the characteristics of their nurse. Or, more melodramatically, "the child that sucks [*suga*] the 'white blood' of that nurse as it would that of its own mother is deceived."[48]

The artificial, worldly mother who abandoned her duty to her child was the most ornately drawn character of this symbolic trio. Given over to luxury, to receptions, the theater and opera, to "the convulsions of the waltz," she strayed from her natural path.[49] Doctors scolded her for evading her duty, for putting up "futile pretexts" such as wishing to preserve her figure, for giving in to a fashion. They warned her that even though she might wish to nurse later, "some become incapable of lactation from inheritance, from constant residence in the large capitals, from abuse of worldly pleasures and from the fatigues that accompany them, from an intensive intellectual and artistic cultivation."[50]

Thus, doctors presented the identities of the natural mother, the barbarous wet nurse, and the artificial woman to Brazilian women. I believe that among the motivations sustaining this consistent, century-long propagandizing lay an intention to reform the family, to divide women from the "world" while reshaping the traditional household to a more restricted and intimate conjugal family. The definition of ideal hygienic maternity also promoted an ideal of domesticity.[51]

Eugenic Marriage, Domesticity, and Pollution

Just as hygiene addressed womanhood from the premise that maternity was part of reproduction, so it also extended its domain to the family life cycle from the perspective of reproduction. Hygiene concerned itself with schools and education, as mentioned above, advising families on the handling of youth. It also addressed adults through the theme of marriage.

The medical understanding of marriage embraced several aspects. First, it disapproved sexuality outside of marriage. While physicians legitimated sexual pleasure in marriage, they condemned "gratuitous" sexuality.[52] For the urban upper and middle classes, most male sexuality outside of the institution of marriage was handled by the complementary institution of prostitution. Doctors attacked prostitution because the prostitute was a bad mother to her children, because sexual indulgence with prostitutes was bad, like any overindulged passion, and because prostitution infected boys and men with syphilis: "It is from there, from this great concentration [foco] of contamination, that syphilis wins its way to the bosom of the family and has its repercussions in the descendants in a disconcerting gamut of consequences, each more disastrous, each more grim than the next." It left youths useless for marriage and procreation, "ruined by orgies, spoiled and perverted." They would see marriage only as a place to recuperate, their wife only as a nurse for their last moments or as a moneybag to finance more depravity.[53]

Prostitution, then, was bad chiefly because it contributed to the destruction of marriage, but in its turn it was a consequence of bad social organization. Within the framework of legal medicine, doctors therefore generally proposed regulation of prostitution as an intermediate measure until such time as a reformed society no longer produced prostitutes. While they approved only of marriage, they could conceive of no way to restrain male sexuality, which, one social critic noted with ambivalence, seemed to be exceptional among Brazilians: "Any superficial observer notes immediately that the Brazilian character has a propensity to sensuality and to love. . . . Is there, however, merely an exuberance of the sexual instinct or are we already in degeneration?"[54]

Doctors linked the recourse to prostitution to irresponsible "celibacy," or bachelorhood, among men. Hygienists took for granted that celibacy was an excuse for libertinism in most cases. For many Bahian hygienists, openly or tacitly embracing positivism, the attack on celibacy became their occasion for criticism of priests, the rivals of doctors for counsel of the family: fasts and penitences were morbid, monastic life was "an insult to natural laws, to society and to hygiene, . . . social death." The priesthood should marry honestly. Doctors were more tolerant of female

celibacy. Though they concurred with popular opinion that sexual abstention was a major cause of hysteria in young women, they tended not to
criticize the older spinster.[55] However, all celibates, whether priests or laymen, bachelors or spinsters, were to be condemned because their status
was unhealthy in comparison with hygienic marriage. Borrowing one of
the statistical commonplaces of European populationist demography, that
the death rate was higher among unmarried adults, they concluded that
celibacy was therefore morbid.[56]

Second, after urging adults to marry, hygienists also aspired to direct
eugenic choices in marriage that would improve the national stock. They
condemned marriage between partners of disparate ages, for example, satirizing it mercilessly as well as warning "that there remains no doubt that
the sons born of old men are bad" and often showed senility. And they
borrowed heavily from romantic and naturalist literary clichés to condemn
marriages of interest, satirizing fathers "who insure their daughters with
a few *contos*, so that men will frequent the markets of love more assidu-
ously." Proper love, however, had nothing to do with romantic passion,
but rather was founded on friendship. It was also founded with an eye to
"the procreation of the child, who represents the family and continues the
race, and not toward the satisfaction of mutual desires, an egoism without
limits, or of the generative instincts exacerbated by the imagination or the
sight of the coveted object." Choices in marriage were to be rationalized
by the logic of hygiene and eugenics.[57]

Between 1870 and 1930, medical thought on marriage and heredity centered on fears of degeneration and hopes of eugenic improvement of the
"race," whether it be the family or the nation. Many physicians believed
that sickly or defective parents, perhaps poisoned by alcohol or ridden
with syphilis, produced even more sickly children, whose "degenerated"
descent would eventually turn out imbecile and sterile. These degenerate
families destroyed themselves, and their multiplication could also reverse
the progressive evolution of the national social organism. Though Brazilians often contested this, many European theories of degeneration held
that race mixture was a major cause of degeneration. Eugenics (a term
coined by Francis Galton in 1880 and soon used by Brazilian physicians)
was the policy of encouraging progress of the race by encouraging the
breeding of healthy people and discouraging the unfit from reproducing.
By 1917 Brazilian eugenicists had begun to organize associations. *Puericultura*, the branch of eugenics most represented in Brazil, sought to improve
racial strength through public health, such as the protection of infants,
more than through measures related to breeding.[58]

Quite understandably, Bahian medical writings became preoccupied
with the issue of consanguineous marriage. The preference for cousin mar-

riages among Brazilian families attracted the notice of foreign travelers. Brazilian folk medical tradition, and a few physicians, held that the practice was dangerous because it led to degeneration of the descent.[59] And some European medical statistics, such as the famous observation that an unusual proportion of children in a French hospital for deaf-mutes were the offspring of consanguineous marriages, could be cited in support of this belief. But most of the Bahian doctors and students who considered consanguinity found it innocuous in itself.

The most thorough confrontation with the topic was Gonçalo Moniz's *A consanguineidade e o código civil brasileiro* (1925), whose main point was that consanguinity is merely a relationship, not a force or an agent. Citing examples of healthy endogamous aristocracies, reviewing the statistics on defects associated with consanguinity, and explicating Mendelian genetics, Moniz concluded that only the defects of abnormal parents were transmitted by consanguinity, and that rather than regulate the degrees of kinship in marriages of healthy persons, perhaps the state should prohibit the marriages of people with transmittable diseases in general. While there would be practical problems in enforcing a prenuptial exam, the advantages outweighed the disadvantages. Rather than being sterilized, misfits could be left to form free unions: "There would be formed, in this way, with the legitimate families, a sort of aristocracy of hygienic types [*tipos hygidos*], biologically superior, in the physical as well as the mental realm, and continually preserved from the degradation that would result from any infra-alliance with these abnormals belonging to the spurious race." Natural selection would eventually extinguish the "bastard lineages." Members of talented families might indeed be *encouraged* to inbreed in order to preserve their characteristics. He continued to support prohibitions against incestuous marriage for the same reasons that he believed religious codes imposed them: to defend the "honesty of domestic habits." Thus, he concluded that biology did not support the 1916 civil code, for instance, in its innovative prohibition of marriages between uncles and nieces, but that morality did when there had been common residence.[60]

At one level, the question underlying this preoccupation with consanguinity was exogamy.[61] Most doctors concluded that consanguineous marriage was permissible, but few could endorse it. One of the best reasoned and most original theses written at the Bahia medical school, Francisco Cavalcante Mangabeira's *Impedimentos do casamento relativos ao parentesco* (1900), attacked consanguineous marriage through an analysis of the incest taboo. After skillfully rejecting the current anthropological explanations of the incest taboo, including those of Spencer, Morgan, and Durkheim, he concluded that no theory as yet could explain the universal and instinctual horror of incest. He argued that the fact that everyone had some genetic defect, or *tara*, suggested that consanguineous marriages should be avoided. But the young poet linked this conclusion with regard to consanguineous marriage in general to the loathing inspired by incest, in one of the best naturalist set pieces of medical prose against consanguineous relations:

For the good of morality these [incestuous] unions should be hampered as much as possible, so that the home and the family remain forever shrouded in a veil of chastity and of love, a veil that would be entirely withdrawn [*se rasgaria inteiro*] the moment that there disappeared from the human spirit that respect that makes a brother kiss a sister as one embraces and kisses a child or a part of one's own body.

Mangabeira implied more forcefully than Moniz that consanguineous marriages were morally incompatible with living in the same household.[62]

But use of literary conventions was all of a piece with using the statistical evidence of European medical research in Brazilian medical social thought. Without attempting to segregate the elements that ring false to a contemporary ear from those that seem scientifically authentic, I would argue that a principal implication of medical theory was to redefine or highlight social boundaries around the conjugal family rather than the extended family or the clan. The colloquial meaning of *hygiene* is cleanliness. And it is by defining cleanliness, by establishing an ideology of purity and pollution concepts, that Brazilian hygienists addressed the family.[63]

Medical advice on childrearing and marriage defined the servants of the household as a threat, a "door" through which contamination might "penetrate" the family. Similarly, it fiercely resisted sexuality outside of marriage by condemning prostitution as another potential source of contamination. At the same time, it proposed new rituals that might help mediate the contradiction between the rigidity of the boundaries it proposed to draw around the conjugal family and the incest taboo that forbade sexual relations or marriage between family members. Hygiene proposed, to use Mangabeira's words, that a brother see one flesh in himself and his sister, but at the same time forbade him to seek "in the perfume of her girlish and unconfined flesh the pleasure that is found in the arms of lost women."[64] Many hygienists extended the interdiction beyond siblings, to cousins as well. They proposed, in the institution of the prenuptial exam, a hygienic rite of passage to sanction the opening and mingling of family boundaries for an exogamous marriage.

Through such symbols, hygiene provided authoritative validation of a reformation of Brazilian families into a model of bourgeois domesticity.[65] Rural families and their traditional customs contrasted most with that model; urban families were more similar to it. But it remained only one of many models for the family. Other institutions, including the "patri-

archal" extended family itself, repudiated exogamy and declined domesticity. The resistance of tradition, of common sense, held fast against hygienic "progress" and "improvement." For example, one traditional realm
of the household, the kitchen, utterly resisted attempts to modernize it
and make it hygienic and domestic. It remained filthy, uncomfortable, and
symbolically invisible to the formal realm of the house.[66] Even among its
upper-class clientele, medicine met opposition. It tried to regulate their
sexuality, apparently with little more success than other Victorian institutions. It tried to change cherished practices such as wet-nursing, and
to judge by its persistent jeremiads, had no greater success in changing
those habits. The common sense of Brazilian society that tolerated parallel
illegitimate families, prescribed wet-nursing for young mothers, and encouraged marriage between close kin was probably the strongest source of
resistance to medicine's authority over the family. The medical campaign
of reform of the Brazilian family was, like most cultural struggles, inconclusive. But by the end of the nineteenth century, medicine had inextricably
imbedded itself in the Brazilian family, and its cues were acknowledged, if
often ignored, influences on family behavior.

Doctors, the State, and Legal Medicine

Medical reformers addressed upper-class families directly, through private visits or publications. They addressed the populace indirectly, through
appeals to the government for action. Understanding the relation of doctors to the state can throw light on the difference between the two models
of influence.

Graduation from medical school did not launch young doctors into independent careers. Establishing a private medical practice in the cities was
prohibitively difficult without patrons; indeed, winning an appointment
to the medical faculty was considered a prerequisite for a good practice
in Bahia. The alternative, for those without patrons, was practice in the
small country towns, in which case the doctor inevitably entered into the
political arena, either as a contestant or as an auxiliary. The alternative for
those with a reasonable amount of "protection" but no taste for private
practice was a position in an institution or the government bureaucracies. For example, in Bahia, a declining province that sent many sons to
its medical school, almost every elite family had relatives who emigrated
into the army medical corps, probably because the local institutions were
saturated with equally well-connected place-seekers.[67]

This importance of patronage and sinecure-seeking will seem obvious
to anyone familiar with Brazilian career patterns in the nineteenth and
early twentieth centuries, and it was not peculiar to the medical profes-

sion.[68] What is relevant about this to a consideration of medical ideas is that some Brazilian doctors, especially professors of medicine, thus constituted another Brazilian clerisy, another category of state intellectuals, like magistrates and army officers. The state sponsored the creation of the medical profession and continued to finance and supervise medical education. Yet those doctors' dependence upon the state, like that of military officers, mobilized rather than demobilized them. From the logic of their position emerged a persistent tendency to lobby the government to extend its activities in the area of health, to delegate authority to them that they might turn to their own ends.

The number of medical graduates seeking positions apparently exceeded the resources of the state and patrons. In a parallel to the arguments that have asserted that the pressure of an excess of law graduates upon the system of career advancement contributed to dissatisfaction with the monarchy, I would argue that the structure of medical careers built a drive into medical thinking to perpetually extend the scope of the doctor's responsibilities, and to encourage the state to establish institutions that would enable doctors to make careers in new areas. In other words, because medical graduates with diplomas were there, they pushed to expand their authority and the demand for their functions. Because of specific traditions of attention to persons and populations, the medical profession turned its interests to private life and the family, and then to public health.[69]

Brazilian doctors often proposed legislation or volunteered the counsel of the medical profession on matters of state. Theses commented on codes of law, or suggested that doctors be consulted before drafting laws. Roberto Machado defines the discontinuity between colonial and nineteenth-century medicine precisely by the appearance of this impulse to orient the state, though he argues that it was not necessarily expressed in relation to legislation. Jurandir Freire Costa extends this, implying that medicine and the "State," by which he apparently means the highest government officials, colluded to invent a strategy of social control of the Brazilian population that would strengthen the hand of the government in its dealings with the dangerous city mob and the intractable seigneurial patriarchs who dominated society.[70] While both exaggerate the power of medicine, not least by taking doctors' words for an accomplished ideological conversion of society, and while they ignore the importance of other institutions and elites, such as the priests and magistrates, in building a nation, they convincingly demonstrate that some medical thought offered rationales and programs for organizing society, for controlling institutions such as hospitals, cemeteries, and factories. Another large part of those programs had to do with prescriptions for individuals and households in the name of hygiene.

The area in which the practice of medicine plainly supported the coercive functions of the state was the field of legal medicine. This specialization offered expert advice to the police and courts on questions such as autopsies to discover the cause of death, investigations of sanity to determine the criminal or civil responsibility of people for their actions, identification of criminals, regulation of prostitution, and defloration. Many of these issues extended to concerns that seemed to go beyond their initial scope. For example, the issue of criminal responsibility, addressed by Raimundo Nina Rodrigues in Salvador through Cesare Lombroso's psychology of the "born criminal," led him to a study of the degeneration of the Brazilian race that seemed to contribute most to criminality, the mulattoes. And from there it led him to a study of the conditions and religion of the Bahian people. Issues of legal responsibility led to definitions of the political and civil natures of women and children. The issue of the regulation of prostitution led to opinions on sexuality in Brazil.[71]

And likewise, to the extent that the state imposed limits and sanctions on the sexual behavior of underage women, it enlisted the techniques of doctors in aid of its enforcement. The issue of legal medical thought that bore most directly on the family was defloration. The writings on the crime of defloration show how consistently Brazilian medical thought moved from physiological to social issues.

The crime of defloration, as opposed to rape, had existed in colonial and Brazilian law since the Philippine Code. The Brazilian criminal code of 1830 defined the crime of *defloramento* as deflowering (without violence) a virgin under the age of seventeen. Legal commentators distinguished ordinary defloration, accomplished by presents, tender words, and other means of seduction, from criminal defloration, accomplished by means of a fraudulent formal promise of marriage.[72]

The procedures of the law called for the offended girl and her family to lodge a complaint before the police, followed by a medical examination. The examining doctor had to answer a fixed series of questions: Was there defloration? By what means? Was there copulation? Was violence employed? Were drugs or hypnosis employed?[73] The difficulty of evaluating the condition of the membrane of the hymen, on which the exam hinged, made the function of doctors in this police routine unpleasant. One scandalous private case, the Braga Affair of 1878, developed into a polemic that pitted distinguished professors from Rio, Portugal, and Salvador against each other in years of debate over the description of the membrane in the first clinical report. Afterward, physicians, especially in Bahia, complained of the uncertainties of the legal procedure, in which "an ofttimes incomplete examination can imperil the honor of an entire family," frequently referring to the Braga Affair.[74] This dissatisfaction with the demands made on the examination for virginity led some doctors to criticize the law against defloration itself. The prominent professor Afrânio Peixoto, in his textbook *Medicina legal* (1931), referred ambiguously to cases as late as 1913 of husbands killing or accusing their brides on their wedding nights because of doubts about the hymen.[75] In his lectures he frankly criticized the "anatomical concept" of virginity, calling its definition by intactness of the hymen an "oriental" notion. He introduced the figure of the *demi-vierge* as an anomaly that revealed the hypocrisy and inadequacy of the legal definition: "We commonly observe brazen girls, unabashed, without reserve nor a shred of modesty, giving themselves up to petting [*a bolina*], to anal coitus, and who, notwithstanding, retain physical virginity, the integrity of the membrane."[76]

Peixoto and other critics of the test for virginity retained the stance of supporters of the dominant sexual morality and the virginity taboo. But one medical student in 1935 based his attack on the entire sexual double standard, and his utopian call for free love, upon his reflections on the penal code. He argued that its imposition of a fine for the deflowered girl's dowry implied that honor is a commodity to be bought and sold. He cited the much lower rate of complaints of defloration in Rio than in Salvador in the 1920's as evidence that when a milieu becomes more socially advanced, the law protecting virginity becomes a dead letter.[77]

While some Brazilian doctors were not shy about calling for legislation to enforce their precepts (as I shall show below), the debate about defloration indicates how uncomfortable direct involvement in enforcement through the law could make physicians, not only because it embroiled them in sordid controversies, but also because they preferred the voluntary cooperation of individuals. It is important to note that doctors appealed to a rational individual who would yield before the invincible demonstrations of scientific truth, who would overturn traditions voluntarily (and virtually automatically). Where they recognized opposition to their prescriptions, they identified it with obscurantism. The most important prescriptions of medical teaching for family life, then, fell outside the domain of legal medicine, and were usually categorized under chairs of hygiene and obstetrics.[78]

The Immense Hospital: Public Health, Race, and Nation

During most of the nineteenth century, medicine offered its elaborate models of reform mainly to the upper and middle classes. The whole debate over wet-nursing, for instance, could be reduced to the issue of how to handle the servants.[79] Individual doctors cared for the poor, but the medical profession usually ignored the conditions of the mass of the population, except in drafting municipal sanitary regulations, collecting the ritual vital statistics, and filing away the Bertillon measurements of the dangerous classes.

The issue of who the "people" were and what they did grew more important to the Brazilian government during the nineteenth century. Until 1850, policy on increase of the working population had simply focused on the African slave trade. After the abolition of the trade, planters and the government needed a policy on how to form a national population. Issues of labor and population, not only of whether to maintain slavery, but also of how to promote free immigration, came to dominate Brazilian politics in the 1870's and 1880's. The preferred solution was European immigration, and planters in the most dynamic regions marshaled their state governments behind successful immigration programs as soon as it was clear that slavery would be abolished.[80]

But the issue was not merely economic. It had political and social dimensions. Addressing the dilemma of building the nation, of putting together a people after abolition, many Brazilian intellectuals used categories of race and some version of the medical theories of degeneration or eugenics. Around the turn of the century, most of them aligned themselves around the project of "whitening" the Brazilian race by encouraging European immigration and leaving the degenerated native and African stock to be absorbed or pulverized in the struggle for life.[81] Medical science contributed to this debate by lending scientific validation to pessimistic evaluations of the dangers of degeneration. However, immigration was not the only solution. Mass education attracted enthusiastic support after World War I as a panacea for national backwardness. But some political leaders saw more of a threat than an advantage in having an enlightened and perhaps restless population. They almost universally endorsed another, more paternalistic solution: public health measures that would directly heal the national race.

Brazilian doctors shaped the debate on building a Brazilian people chiefly by stressing the need—and the possibility—of public health. Public health was first and foremost the campaign to sanitize the cities. Long traditions of medical concern with overcrowding, water supply, drainage, and burial grounds existed. But they were hampered by the gap between their empirical observations and their theories. Doctors could connect swamps and fevers, but they were able to explain that connection only with the unsatisfactory concept of miasmas. After the acceptance of germ theory in the 1870's, and the mosquito vector in the 1900's, doctors felt powerfully assured that they knew how to reform tropical cities. Led by Oswaldo Cruz and other physicians with bacteriological and parasitological orientations, the 1904 campaigns of mosquito eradication and vaccination in Rio de Janeiro dramatically demonstrated the possibility of conquering yellow fever and smallpox. The turn of the twentieth century in Brazil was an era of the cleansing and remodeling of cities that were also being whitened by immigration. Programs of vaccination and insect control, of building water and sewer systems, were all of a piece with other civilizing improvements, such as the opening of boulevards. Doctors could demonstrate that the facts themselves demanded and authorized huge campaigns to remake the cities.[82]

After World War I, physicians urged the government to carry the campaign for public health from the cities to the countryside. The observation of Miguel Pereira in 1916 to the effect that "outside of Rio and São Paulo, capitals that are more or less sanitized, and of a few other cities where Providence oversees the hygiene, Brazil is still an immense hospital" struck the Brazilian intellectual conscience hard. Belisário Penna's *Saneamento do Brasil* (1918), intended as a "red-hot iron to apply to the festering sores that are spreading through the limbs of the nation," warned that fundamental political reforms were necessary to restore health to the race. Intellectuals who were not doctors took up the issue. The nationalist writer Monteiro Lobato caused a stir in 1919 by addressing an apology to his character Jeca Tatú, the lazy hillbilly who had symbolized the racial defects of the Brazilian people: "I didn't know that you were that way, my dear Jeca, because of tremendous diseases. It is proven that you have got the worst kind of zoo in your blood and your guts." Starting in the 1920's, with support from the Rockefeller Foundation, the federal and state governments established rural health posts and began limited programs of rural health education to eradicate diseases such as hookworm, malaria, and Chagas disease.[83]

Yet targeting the health of the entire population as the critical problem of nationality did not necessarily entail mobilizing the people to reform their own health. The campaign for public health spoke about the Brazilian populace more than it spoke to them. At its worst, it combined legal medicine and hygiene in the theme of eugenics. To ensure that only the best races multiplied, hygiene demanded that the inferior breeds cease to have children. Some doctors favored a program of voluntary appeal to the consciences of their clients. In their prescriptions for hygienic marriage, they suggested that couples should not follow their passions or interest, but rather consult their doctors. They should submit to a prenuptial exam rather than run the risk of passing on the myriad defects and hereditary complaints that were endemic in society: tuberculosis, syphilis, alcoholism, insanity, arthritis, and so forth. Other doctors recommended that the law require a prenuptial examination, as the civil marriage law of 1891 had allowed.[84] Praising the United States as a "great laboratory of sociology," one medical thesis recommended that the laws should intervene in the marriages of carriers of contagious diseases, citing the law of North Dakota that forbade marriage by madmen, tuberculars, and alcoholics. Doctors should not be limited by the ethic of medical confidentiality, because they had a duty to care for the descendants as well as the couple. As the "representative of science and priest of Charity," that was the role of the doctor in the family. Another student recommended that every family should keep a book in which it would log all the diseases that had occurred in it. A "medical marriage," in which the family doctors of each spouse would give their opinions, should precede both civil and religious marriage.[85]

The group within Brazilian medicine that became the strongest advocate of eugenic legislation, the Liga Brasileira de Higiene Mental, fell under the influence of German psychiatric eugenicists in 1931, and some of its members called for the sterilization of degenerates and the prohibition of Jewish and Asiatic immigration as measures to purify the Brazilian race. It moved from an initial position, in the 1920's, of addressing individual mental hygiene, to a militant strategy of calling for state intervention in the formation of the race. But most Brazilian eugenicists opposed coercive measures, and favored policies for protection of maternal and infant health.[86]

At its best, the campaign for public health called for paternalistic state intervention in social welfare. Joining the national question to the social question, doctors formed leagues for the protection of infancy and lobbied hard for the government to take over the welfare functions of charities. These movements were strongest in São Paulo, but in the first decade of the twentieth century spread to Bahia, where Alfredo Ferreira Magalhães established his model maternity clinic, the Instituto de Proteção e Assistência à Infância, in 1904 and called for the establishment of a free milk program. Until the coming of the Vargas dictatorship and the establishment of the Ministry of Health in 1931, government support was limited to token subsidies of charitable organizations. Margatão Gesteira founded the Liga Contra a Mortalidade Infantil in 1924, but it foundered after he left Bahia in 1935. Even afterward, the resources of the government simply did not allow the maintenance of anything like the philanthropic program of intervention in the family that France developed in the nineteenth century.[87] For better or worse, the Brazilian government was not powerful enough to organize a "tutelary state."

In the twentieth century, the program of medicine for the Brazilian family divided into two main parts. One continued to advise decent, literate families. The other lobbied the state to adopt an official ideology of public health, either to carry out a benevolent paternalism of sanitation, vaccination, and the protection of minors, or a harsh paternalism of social control and eugenics. Neither ideology seriously attempted to enlist the sympathy of the Brazilian masses. If it addressed them, it was to tell them that their identity was a negative one. The people of Rio realized that the rhetoric of progress and civilization justifying urban renovation criticized their barbarous customs. And exploiting their alienation, opponents of the government were able to use Oswaldo Cruz's campaign for compulsory vaccination as a pretext to goad them into rioting in 1904. In Bahia, the intellectual most dedicated to studying the life of the people, Raimundo Nina Rodrigues, wavered between sympathetic interest and the foregone conclusion that the religious practices he described were symptoms of a degenerate collective psychology.[88] Medicine did not have an ideology that could integrate the Brazilian nation; there was no single model of the family with versions that were relevant and appealing to all classes. Perhaps, considering the sharp differences between classes and the differences in their cultures, it would be too much to ask that it could have one.

4

The Law, Political Reforms, and the Family

In BRAZIL both church and civil law defined families, their formation, their honor, and their rights to property. The legal structure surrounding families changed very little from 1870 to 1945. Indeed, it had changed only in minor details since at least the early seventeenth century, when the Philippine Code was written in Portugal, and after the Council of Trent had unified Catholic doctrine and practice. Over the course of the nineteenth century, Brazilian family law and judicial practice subtly shifted in accordance with trends of liberalization and secularization. In 1888 the abolition of slavery, and in 1889 the separation of church and state, dramatically confirmed this. And in the mid twentieth century, from 1920 through the 1940's, the rise of social legislation tentatively set the cornerstone of a welfare state and changed the relation of families to work and property. But we must remember that most people lived at the margin of the laws and institutions. It was not only the anonymous poor whose kinship and family relations largely avoided formal institutions, but also the notable rich, whose customs and interests often went against the grain of the law, and who consequently maneuvered to evade it.

It is conventional to contrast the rigidity of law to the fluidity of people's relations. And certainly it is true that the family laws of Brazil changed very little in the nineteenth and twentieth centuries, while real social relations outgrew their assumptions. For example, the changes in women's public roles from the 1870's forward, as women moved into conventionally "male" professions and occupations, and as married women began to assert their rights against their husbands, most obviously conflicted with the inflexibility of Brazilian laws that presumed and reinforced women's subordination in traditional ways.[1]

But it is just as pertinent to confront the rigidity of the law with the rigidity of people's customs. For instance, over centuries many Brazilians (and perhaps most Bahians) formed familial unions without formal marriage. And for centuries, Brazilian law persisted in recognizing only the legal form of the family. *Mancebia* or *amasia* common-law marriage was recognized only at the margin of the laws, to the detriment of the property rights of a large portion of the population. Similarly, for centuries Brazilians attached great customary weight to the godparent and co-parent relations formed through church rituals such as baptism, confirmation, and marriage. Yet Brazilian civil law never regulated the rights and obligations attaching to this vital relationship.[2] It was not simply that conservative Brazilian law declined to "catch up" with the rapid social change of the twentieth century, but also that Brazilian law had, from its origins, persistently defined formal and informal zones of family and kinship relations.

Brazilian family law did change between 1870 and 1945. Great social reforms such as the abolition of slavery in 1888 or the institution of a welfare state in the 1930s had an immense impact on individuals' opportunities to organize their private and family lives. And the great near-revolution of 1889, establishing a republic, separating church and state, and decreeing civil marriage, did effect an enormous formal change in the theoretical bases and authorities on Brazilian family law. If nothing else, it established a potential for change that had seemed unlikely under dogmatic church authority, and it brought regulation of the family into question. Eventually, in the 1960's and 1970's this potential for change was partially manifested in the laws enlarging married women's rights against their husbands' authority and liberalizing divorce.

The Traditional Legal Matrix

Since the colonial period, regulation of the family had fallen mainly to the lot of the church in the division of labor among agencies of the Crown. The church and its law controlled certain crucial rites of passage, such as marriage, that allowed persons to define their status and define the membership of legitimate families. The secular magistracy and civil law controlled other aspects of the family, such as the rights and duties of family members and the transmission of property through inheritance, dowry, or gift.

The structure and the tensions of family law in Brazil resembled contemporary law—and tensions—in Europe. Portuguese civil law had developed from Roman and customary traditions parallel to those of other European kingdoms. In Portugal, as in the rest of Europe, church regulation of marriage had grown in the Middle Ages, when the church gradually assumed authority over the conventions of mating and marriage. It encouraged the acceptance of priestly celebration of the sacrament of marriage, and then required it after the Council of Trent (1545–63). In Brazil, a missionary frontier, the church gradually attempted to impose a single, Christian model of marriage on a diverse population that included many Indians and African slaves. Only in 1707, after two centuries of colonization, did the *Constituições primeiras do Arcebispado da Bahia* consolidate Brazil's canon law on marriage, establishing the preferred form for marriage.[3]

Brazilian canon law on the family concerned itself principally with marriage, annulment, and separation, and its provisions were fundamentally the same as European ones. By establishing the conditions under which a couple could qualify to receive the sacrament of marriage, and thus legitimate their children, the church held a potentially powerful sanction. Canon law, while not absolutely prescribing age limits on marriage, set them at the presumed ages of puberty, twelve for women and fourteen for men.[4] It defined impediments to marriage between certain persons. These canonical impediments included difference in religion, certain civil crimes, previous fornication with close kin of the prospective partner, spiritual kinship from godparenthood, or kinship by birth or marriage within the fourth degree of consanguinity (third cousins).[5] The impediment of consanguinity was an onerous one for Bahian families, for its insistence on exogamy conflicted squarely with the widespread custom of endogamous marriage, particularly cousin marriage. Church doctrine held that a valid marriage could not be dissolved except by death; consequently, canon law determined grounds for perpetual separation rather than divorce: apostasy or heresy by a spouse, extreme cruelty, adultery, abandonment. Even when it decreed a separation, the church admonished couples to attempt reconciliation. However, the church did allow that some flawed unions, in which impediments had been hidden or ignored, had never become valid marriages, and it permitted annulment on grounds including incest, impotence, ignorance as to the "essential nature" of the spouse (such as lack of virginity or contagious disease), and inability to consent. Unlike a separation, after an annulment an individual could remarry.

Of course, the authority of the church to regulate marriages did not mean everything in Brazil, for a great many families formed entirely outside of marriage. In support of consensual unions, civil law supplemented canon law. Portuguese civil law on the family had been collected in the Philippine Code, or *Ordenações do Reino*, in 1603, decades after the Council of Trent set the regulations for mandatory public celebration of marriage. Nonetheless, it retained contradictory vestiges of customary law on marriage, such as a provision stating that publicly acknowledged consensual unions would have civil effects like those of marriage. Another provision, though not recognizing the status of wives in common-law unions, said that the children of plebeians (*peões*) could inherit as if legitimate.[6]

But in general, the balance between church and civil authority over marriage in Brazil had reached an equilibrium by the early nineteenth century. This was possible because, as I shall discuss below, church officials generously granted families dispensations from the stated impediments to marriage, and because the church tolerated the widespread practice of consensual union.

Instead, most controversy arose, in public debate and in family circles, over property laws. Families found it more difficult to live with the rules established by civil law for the transmission of familial property through marriage, dowry, and inheritance. In the early nineteenth century, liberal politicians who were committed to equality before the law, and to equality of children within the family, abolished some of the special types of property that had allowed upper-class families to preserve their estates.

The seventeenth-century Philippine Code, which remained the basis of Brazilian property law until 1917, was an anachronistic mixture of absolutist and feudal provisions. Brazilian legal practice simply ignored dead letters such as incentives to ransom captives from the Moors. But nineteenth-century Brazilian legislation and decrees modified or abolished many special property arrangements, such as perpetual claims, *prazos*, that could be passed on through a line of primogeniture or in trust. The Philippine Code had authorized the Crown to charter entails, *morgados*, that were usually settled on the line of primogeniture; though few had been chartered in Brazil, the Brazilian government abolished them in 1835.

The Philippine Code, and Brazilian practice, preferred the marital property regime of absolute community of property (*comunhão universal* or *casamento por carta de ametade*). All property of the spouses was joined in one estate, which was divided evenly upon death or dissolution of the marriage. In the European world, contemporary family law has tended toward the establishment of community property as the sole or default property arrangement in marriage, but in the sixteenth through early twentieth centuries, the Luso-Brazilian legal tradition was unusual in this respect.[7]

It seems that most marriages in Bahia in the colonial period involved some payment by the wife's family to the husband. Though they could take the form of "dowry property," a sort of gift in trust, they usually took the form of gifts that entered a couple's community property. Marriages through the mid and late nineteenth century continued to include gifts and payments on the occasion of the wedding, but they, too, were rarely formalized as dotal property. Usually, they went into the joint property of the new couple. Some of the prenuptial contracts surviving from the first decades of the nineteenth century hint at cautious negotiations that included specific provisions on how and when property was to change hands between the notarization of the marriage contract and the celebration of the wedding.[8] But after the 1850's, when prenuptial contracts seem to have enjoyed a last surge of popularity, the transfer of property seems to have taken the form of a wedding gift.

The property transferred included cash, bonds, or houses, and, until abolition, often slaves. Slaves had the advantage of being a sizeable and relatively portable gift that did not bind the new couple to a certain location, as the gift of a house might. But, of course, sentiment also intervened in these gifts. Gifts to brides were often of female slaves, sometimes a mother and child, sometimes a young woman. Probably she was often the girl's *mucama* from her parents' household.[9]

But Brazilian law allowed a couple and their families to establish special regimes of marital property by written, notarized prenuptial contract. Though rarely used after the 1850's, in nineteenth- and twentieth-century practice, prenuptial contracts usually established some form of separate property. The law allowed absolute separation of property, partial separation, and the so-called *regime dotal*, dowry property. In the dowry regime, parents or the future husband settled property in trust on the woman. Her husband administered the property and received its income "to support the expenses of the couple," but on her death it returned to her family or to the donor. In other contracted regimes of separate property, all or part of the property of both husband and wife might be designated as separate property that did not enter the marital community.[10]

At times, one or all of the parties to a marriage wanted to establish separate property. When a woman's family instituted a separate piece of dowry property for their daughters or nieces, they often indicated a desire to safeguard that property from the man and his heirs, reiterating the law's stipulations that the property should return to the woman's kin if she had no children to inherit. The nature of the property itself, family slaves or land near family holdings, might emphasize the ties of the woman to her family of origin. In one case in 1873, parents gave a half-interest in a large townhouse that was next to another property that the parents owned. They also gave three slaves and three contos in cash.[11]

When men instituted a separate piece of dowry property for their future wives, it seems to have been with the intention of insulating their estates from the claims of their wives' relatives. The contracts usually stipulated a marital regime of separate property, and simultaneously the man would give his wife a sum to constitute her separate stake outright. This was not, I should emphasize again, a common practice. Often, the husband was a foreigner, Portuguese or Italian, and the woman a Brazilian. When these men were marrying their mistresses and legitimating previously born children, the prenuptial contract seems to have been aimed at defending the man's property from the woman and her kin, while recognizing the children and instituting them as heirs.[12]

Sometimes an older couple established separate property upon their marriage, without mention of or authorization by the woman's parents. Then, it seems, the couple preferred not to merge their property, or perhaps the woman, a widow or an older spinster, wanted to preserve her control of her property. After 1900, and particularly after promulgation of the civil code of 1916, many prenuptial contracts seem to have established separate property in order to protect the property of the wife against the claims of her husband's creditors, as debts did not communicate in a regime of separate property.[13]

Whatever the regime of marital property, after setting aside the property of the surviving spouse (usually one half of the estate), the remainder of the estate was divided in equal shares among all the children (male and female, elder and younger, married or single) of the marriage, deducting any advance gifts of property made during the lifetime of the parent. If there were no descendants, the estate passed to the parents of the deceased spouse, and only if there were no living ascendants did it pass to the spouse. Provided there was a will, the deceased spouse could dispose freely of one third of his or her half of the community property. That third, the *terça*, could be willed to anyone: wife, child, stranger, or charity.[14]

In all regimes, the inheritance law emphasized the norm of passing property on to children or keeping it within the family of origin rather than delivering it to the surviving spouse from another lineage. It prescribed equal shares among children as the ideal, an ideal that Bahian families usually followed. It left the property relationship between spouses to their decision at the beginning of the marriage, but it required that each parent's property pass in part or in whole to the children. In a number of provisions, the law expressed concern that parents share the expenses of the children fairly, and required that widows and widowers who remarried— especially widows, who passed into the power of another man—put the two-thirds of their own property that represented the mandatory portion of the children into trust for their children from the first marriage.[15]

In other regions of Brazil many families frustrated the egalitarian intent of the law by settling huge dowries on the first daughter to marry, exceeding her equal share of the estate.[16] Though the law prescribed returning the value of dowry property to the estate in order to calculate shares among siblings, in practice families in São Paulo did evade its intent. By declining to enter the inheritance division, a daughter and her husband could avoid returning property.[17] In nineteenth- and twentieth-century Bahia, it seems that dowry payments were in fact deducted from the forced share at inheritance, and that favored daughters sometimes paid back dowries that exceeded a mandatory share.[18]

Liberal Reform in the Nineteenth Century

The eighteenth-century Pombal ministry in Portugal set a precedent for the revision of traditional laws and customs, and the conflict between church and civil authority that nineteenth-century Brazilian liberalism would later pursue for its own reasons. Pombal's near-dictatorship relied heavily on the Lei da Boa Razão (Law of Good Reason) of 1769, which virtually revoked all existing legislation, authorizing judges to follow their rational judgment or the example of civilized nations in remaking the law. The government expelled the Jesuit order and diminished church powers in many ways.

With regard to the family, conflict broke out most openly over the issue of consent for marriage, which mattered more to the upper classes. The church's insistence on freedom to choose a marriage partner clashed sharply with patriarchal customs of parental authority over children and with family strategies of arranged marriages of convenience. In the eighteenth century, Portuguese civil law, like that of many European countries, tried to restrict the freedom of couples to take the sacrament of marriage. While not explicitly contradicting canon law, the Philippine Code allowed parents to disinherit children under the age of twenty-five who married without consent. It allowed that if a disobedient daughter married "better and more honorably than her father and mother could have married her," her parents could only disinherit her from half of her share. In the era of feverish reforms surrounding Pombal's ministry in Portugal, the Crown experimented erratically with family law, decreeing and then rescinding radical changes in the period from 1761 to 1784. The Law of June 19, 1775, tried to penalize rascals who seduced girls in order to blackmail their parents into consenting to a marriage and paying a dowry. It prohibited priests from celebrating a marriage without paternal consent. But the Law of November 29, just months later, stated that experience with the law requiring priests not to celebrate marriages without parental consent had shown that some fathers forgot themselves and denied consent even for useful marriages, "elevating their private and domestic power into a despotism to prevent marriages . . . to the notorious detriment of families and of the population on which the principal force of these states depends." As the "common Father of my vassals," the monarch took upon himself the power to authorize marriages. Later, the Law of October 6, 1784, tried to require that betrothals be registered publicly, that minors obtain parental or judicial consent, and that adults over 25 *ask* for parental consent, to "comply with the important, and religious duty of obedience, and respect, that is owed to these heads of families." [19]

At independence, the Brazilian assemblies and parliaments were filled with men influenced by the romantic and republican ideologies of liberation sweeping Europe. The Brazilian political elite, and especially the Bahians, had significant contingents of men trained at Coimbra in Portugal, or in the Brazilian law faculties, who were acquainted with contemporary debates. In nineteenth-century Europe, perhaps one could define a liberal project for the family: the abolition of "aristocratic" preferences such as primogeniture, and an ideology of equal, partible inheritance, or of complete freedom of parents to will their property as they chose. While complete freedom of testation was far from the civil law tradition, equally partible inheritance, as in France, was compatible with an understanding of fairness, and of the familial, rather than solely individual, stake in property. Other elements included a rejection of the authority of established churches over the consciences and marriages of citizens, affirmation of the individual rights of individuals, even minors, to choose a spouse without the interference of parents, and an affirmation of the primacy of romantic love in courtship, and hence a rejection of arranged marriage and dowry. In Latin Europe, the defense of the equality of status extended to defense of the rights of bastard children to inherit from their fathers. In France, the nation whose legal codes and legal commentators influenced Brazilians most heavily after those of Portugal, the eighteenth-century absolutist conflicts between Crown and church, the radical egalitarianism of the early days of the Revolution, the Napoleonic Code, and then law under restoration governments, more or less spanned the gamut of alternatives to which Brazilians referred when they defined positions of policy on family law.[20]

After independence, Brazilian liberals extended the patterns of Portuguese inheritance law, eliminating "feudal" provisions and emphasizing its egalitarian aspects. One early, and mostly symbolic, measure was the abolition of entails in 1835. The types of entails that previous decrees allowed included endowments for saying masses (*capellas*) and estates entailed upon the lines of primogeniture in a variety of arrangements (*morgados*). The Law of October 6, 1835, decreed that all Brazilian entails would be extinguished in the person of the current heir, and that upon his death they would pass to his heirs according to the regular laws of succession. In Bahia, very few entails—perhaps no more than a dozen—had ever been chartered by the Portuguese Crown. Small capellas were common, but there were few significant morgados. Some contemporaries attributed this to the "jealousy" of the Portuguese toward Brazilian colonists, because of which "the increase of capitalists and large proprietors was systematically prevented."[21]

Brazilian statesmen of the 1830's debated the abolition of entails in terms similar to those of their European contemporaries. The creation of titles of nobility by Pedro I had dismayed liberal deputies, and after they forced his abdication in 1831, they argued for the abolition of entails in order to prevent the consolidation of hereditary privileges. Arguing for the preservation of morgados, conservative senators pleaded that strong families would be good for the nation.[22]

The debate over the abolition of entails and the recognition of illegitimate sons was apparently linked to the pressing constitutional issues of the Regency period and early Second Empire of Pedro II. The votes over morgados were closely linked to the debates on whether the Empire should issue hereditary or lifetime titles of nobility (the deputies chose lifetime titles), and whether the emperor should be allowed to issue medals and honors in honorary orders (as Pedro I had done, with apparent success in winning adherents). It was also linked to constitutional debates over the nature and function of a senate. Although the Brazilian deputies decided against a hereditary senate, a sort of House of Lords, they did establish a lifetime senate, whose members were nominated by ministers but selected by the emperor, whose purpose would be to impose a "conservative" counterweight to the passions of the directly elected, frequently renewed, lower Chamber of Deputies. As in the young United States, rejection of favored statuses among brothers was symbolic of a rejection of aristocracy.[23]

As well as abolishing entails, Brazilian legislators affirmed the transmission of property from upper-class, "noble" men to their illegitimate children outside of marriage. Even earlier, in 1831, a law had recognized the right of men to give legacies to illegitimate children of any sort, as long as their parents had no obligatory heirs—that is, no legitimate children, parents, or spouse. A law of 1847 greatly extended the rights of illegitimate children. It allowed men, including "nobles," to recognize children by public deed, and provided that recognized children would then share equally in the paternal inheritance with any legitimate children from a subsequent marriage.[24]

Brazilian legislation thus revised the legal tradition of the Philippine Code, which already provided for equal shares for all legitimate children in most cases, in order to suppress favoritism and admit even illegitimate heirs to a share of inheritance. It began to duplicate the church's authority to determine (through marriage) what children could have legitimate property rights. But the civil law held back from contradicting the canon law's standards as to who could marry. Men could only recognize their natural children if no impediment had existed between the parents that would have prevented them from marrying. They could not recognize children of illicit or adulterous unions as heirs.[25]

The practice of recognition of illegitimate children gave rise to special forms of the Bahian family. In strict legality, a man could have two successive families: first, he could have one or more families of mistresses and "natural" children. If he recognized those children by deed, they became his heirs. Second, upon marriage, he founded a single legal family, and after marriage he could no longer legitimate his previous "natural" children without his wife's consent, as to do so would be retroactively to dilute the inheritance shares of her children. Nor could he legitimate any children born after his marriage; these were not "natural" children, but "adulterine" children, who could never be willed an inheritance that diluted the shares of the legitimate or legitimated heirs. But this charter for a serial polygamy, with a lesser and then a higher form of union, was probably most prevalent among the upper classes. The records of deeds of legitimation in nineteenth- and twentieth-century Salvador suggest that most legitimations were undertaken by never-married men of the lower middle class and povo who were simply ensuring the inheritance rights of illegitimate children from a single consensual union.[26]

Men of all classes legitimated bastard children. The names of men and women who legitimated children suggest that the common impression is correct, that the conventional pattern of a consensual union with legitimated children was one in which a lighter-skinned man legitimated his children by a darker-skinned woman or women. The fathers' names were often traditional Portuguese or European surnames (e.g., Magalhães, Bandeira, Bittencourt) without religious connotations, which suggest Portuguese ancestry, while the mothers were given only first names ("Maria de Tal") or religious surnames (Maria da Conceição, Maria do Amor Divino) that suggest African ancestry.[27] Occasionally, but not consistently, the deeds described the mother, often as a *creoula* or a *cabra*.

Furthermore, the proportion of Portuguese immigrants among the men legitimating children in Salvador was notable. This also confirms the tradition that Portuguese shopkeepers and artisans often never married, but formed consensual unions with black Bahian women.[28] While this pattern strongly suggests the existence of a conventional pattern of sexual exploitation of browner women by paler men, it also suggests that men in such situations often felt responsibility of some sort to their children. They did not reject them, but rather acknowledged kinship and property rights.[29] But men of upper-class families also legitimated their natural children. These men hewed more often to the pattern of a young-adult affair, or relationship with a mistress, followed by a marriage in their late twenties or early thirties. The illegitimate sons and daughters of their youth, then, might be the older siblings of their "legitimate" children.[30]

Families also would discriminate against legitimated natural children. Legitimation by a notarial deed did not guarantee inheritance, as heirs might attempt to swindle their cousins or half-siblings out of their shares. At least two notorious cases of discrimination are documented. In 1809, Cristovão da Rocha Pita, the owner of the rich Engenho Freguesia, died unmarried. He had legitimated bastard sons, and in accord with the provisions of the law of 1831, should have been able to will them property. However, when his bastard sons applied for their inheritance, relatives of Rocha Pita challenged them, declaring that the sons had not lived according to the standards of "*nobreza*," and hence could not be contemplated as heirs to the noble estate of a sugar mill owner. The lawsuit continued for 36 years and was finally settled in 1843 in favor of the illegitimate sons.[31] In another case, the legitimate siblings and nephews of Jerônimo Sodré, who had died on his plantation and had willed all his property to his illegitimate children, contested the rights to one part of the estate, that which derived from a morgado entail. Acknowledging that the morgado had ended in the person of the last administrator, they nonetheless argued successfully that the morgado property should be distributed only to legitimate successors to the person of the final administrator.[32]

In permitting the option of recognition of natural children, the laws of 1831 and 1847 struck a blow against the traditional relationship between religious and civil legislation. In that relationship, the church blessed certain unions, and their offspring, as legitimate and honorable. Fornication out of wedlock was sinful and dishonorable. The civil legislation had reaffirmed this by mandating that property pass (if the man died intestate) only to children honorably linked to him through wedlock. But the egalitarian legislation of Brazil in the nineteenth century leveled the inheritance rights of legitimate and bastard children, removing one of the tangible privileges and dimensions of the honor of legitimacy.[33]

Certainly, though, not all civil legislation was liberalizing. The criminal code of 1830, perhaps the most ambitious work of Brazilian legislation during the Empire, defended the traditional customs and roles of families. It meshed support of the honor of families with enforcement of the control of marriage by the church. Its primary "liberal" innovation was abolition of cruel and unusual punishments in the Código Philippino.[34]

The code made the patriarchal relationship between parent and child, or, to be more precise, father and son, the model for most relationships of authority and obedience. It considered some acts justifiable, "when the damage consists of the moderate punishment that parents [*pais*] give their children [*filhos*], masters their slaves, and guardians their wards." It considered that aggravating circumstances in a crime included lack of respect due to a person old enough to be the father of the criminal, or the offended person having the quality of ascendant, teacher, or superior, "or any other that constitutes him in the condition of the father" with respect to the criminal. The assumption of paternal power as a fundamental relationship, on which other social relations could be modeled, reflected the patriarchal model of authority. Still, as legislated and limited authority, it was different in nature from the patriarchal customary justice that Freyre imagined existed in colonial times, which permitted a father to kill his own son in punishment.[35]

The criminal code contained provisions that provided civil sanctions to reinforce or supplement the canon law regulation of marriage. For example, it punished the priest who married a couple not qualified by the laws, and any couple who contracted a clandestine marriage.[36] Still, the contrast between Christian morality embodied in canon law and its secular norms based on honor showed in a number of its measures. One was the definition of a double standard for adultery. Husbands could only be charged with adultery if they openly kept a mistress. Wives could be charged with adultery for any sexual transgression.[37] Another such measure, though perhaps a dead letter, was the crime of "feigned pregnancy," which consisted of pretending to be pregnant and claiming another's child as one's own. It reflected a culture predisposed to melodramas of honor. It only made sense in the context of the sort of society that maintained a foundling wheel at the public orphanage in which mothers could secretly deposit their illegitimate and shameful infants.[38]

The preoccupation with honor showed also in the definitions of abduction and rape, which distinguished precisely between deflowering a virgin who was kept secluded in "the house of her father, guardian, *curador*, or other person in whose power or custody she may be" and simply deflowering a virgin. It punished the former offense far more severely, not only with banishment from the district and payment of a dowry, but also with prison. In any case, these penalties for abduction were meant mainly to coerce the man to take the customary escape: in the case of both statutory rape and abduction, the man could avoid the penalty by marrying the girl. As they worked in the late nineteenth century, perhaps the laws on defloration were intended to enforce sincerity in the customary bride-capture ritual of elopement, giving families a last resort to sanctions in law to bring against men who seduced daughters out of their houses and then did not do the expected and proper thing. By the twentieth century, if not earlier, most "abductions" were elopements staged by the couple. After a night in another house supervised by respectable matrons, the couple hoped to return to the father to go through a drama of repudiation, followed by a reconciliation. Through the mid nineteenth century, if the woman's father would not accept the abduction, honor obliged him to declare a feud against the offender and his kin. However, these blood feuds, chronicled prominently in Bahian folklore, were probably the exception rather than the rule.[39]

Within the assumption that the code of honor guided the action of society, the criminal code of 1830 nonetheless protected women from some of its abuses. If it defined a double standard in cases of adultery, nevertheless it also insisted that the adulterers be tried and sentenced jointly. If it legitimated the virginity and shame complex underlying the definitions of abduction, still it assured girls of having their disgraceful status regularized as much as it guaranteed families would have their honor repaired. By putting customary rights into law, the code in effect limited them, just as it ratified the right of fathers and masters to punish, but to punish moderately.

So, during the Empire, as in the colonial period, the regulation of the Brazilian family was divided between canon and civil law. The church controlled the regulation of marriage and the preservation of records of births, marriages, and deaths. The civil and criminal laws regulated the transmission of property and the enforcement of norms of honor. There was apparently no great tension in Brazil, as Verena Martínez Alier has found in the case of Cuba, between ideologies of marriage based on hierarchical and on egalitarian principles. The contradiction between the formal ecclesiastical prohibition of consanguineous marriage and the informal custom of arranging cousin marriages apparently was resolved simply by a convention of excusing violations of that portion of canon law. That tension between powerful families' aims and the law of the church is not sufficient to explain the separation of church and state, which responded to other struggles, many of them beginning outside Brazil.

The Practice of Family Law Under Mixed Authority

In the second half of the nineteenth century, families seem to have found regulation by the church relatively easy and accommodating. Certainly there was an inherent conflict with the church's ideology of exogamous marriage, just as there was a contradiction between families' customs and strategies and the medical hygienists' definitions of hygienic or eugenic marriage. Doctors could advise against and promote anxiety about cousin marriage; priests and bishops could theoretically prohibit such marriages.

The impediment to consanguineous marriage with close kin was, as a practical matter, the most onerous one for Bahian families. Insistence on exogamy conflicted squarely with the widespread custom of endogamous marriage, particularly cousin marriage. Nearly a fifth of all marriages in some regions of Brazil were marriages between first cousins or uncles and nieces. Half of the marriages among some Bahian upper-class clans in the late eighteenth century, and at least a fifth of the marriages for most of the nineteenth century, were between close kin. In parishes of the city of Salvador in the nineteenth century, between 5 and 10 percent of marriages were consanguineous unions requiring dispensations.[40] Fortunately, church policy distinguished between absolute (*dirimente*) impediments such as incestuous consanguinity and dispensable impediments such as consanguinity between cousins.[41] By petitioning and stating a motive for dispensation from the impediment, couples could obtain permission to marry. One convenient motive for dispensing a couple from the impediment of consanguinity, for example, was the lack of other suitable marriage partners of the same station in life in the locality. By instruction from the pope in 1790, Brazilian bishops could delegate power to dispense couples from certain impediments to parish priests, rather than require that petitions for dispensation go to Rome for consideration.[42] Dispensation from the impediment of marrying a cousin or more distant relative could apparently be granted at the discretion of the parish priest in Bahia, for the records of petitions to central ecclesiastical authorities pertain almost entirely to impediments between uncles and nieces or brothers and sisters-in-law. At the parish level, families could pay, coerce, or cajole priests to grant them dispensations. Consequently, the effective limits on marriage for the upper-class families of Bahia were probably those of the absolute impediments rather than the dispensable impediments.

Couples could even get dispensations from very close degrees of relationship (uncle and niece, brother and sister-in-law, double cousinship, etc.) by petitioning the ecclesiastical court in Salvador. A review of the petitions for dispensations from impediments of consanguinity in the Arquivo da Cúria suggests that the regulations took into account considerations such as the love a couple had for each other; the need women had for support and protection; the need a man had for a woman to look after his household, especially if it included orphaned children; and the danger of a couple falling into the sin of a consensual union (*mancebia*) or the possibility of rescuing a couple from the disgrace and sin of such union.[43] While the petitions for dispensations were apparently careful to demonstrate that the motive of the marriage was not pursuit of property, they also went to pains to demonstrate that the man could indeed support the woman. In the rural districts, a parish priest would know the assets and reputation of his parishioners, and the reports of priests on the applications often discussed them in blunt language: "Her mother has five more children besides her, all of them minors, and so it is to her advantage to shelter [*amparar*] this daughter of hers with the petitioner, who by his excellent conduct and good qualities can serve and protect her well. The two of them possess three contos."[44]

In their arguments in favor of the couples petitioning for the lifting of impediments, priests generally displayed a practical view of marriage. Whereas the petitions themselves would often speak of "mutual affection," the priests would comment on the claim that in an isolated district, there was nobody else of equal social stature, and that it was unlikely that the woman would marry if she did not marry this man, be he kinsman or Protestant. In one case in 1870, a priest noted that the man was a widower of the woman's aunt, and "was left with children." Since the woman was "poor and destitute [*miserável*]" and lived with her grandmother, "chastely and without any dowry whatsoever," he said, "she won't easily find anybody else with whom to marry."[45]

Not only the rich got dispensations from impediments of consanguinity. The royal families of Europe may have had to pay huge indemnities to the papacy for marriage dispensations, but the donations imposed on Bahian rural couples were relatively modest. The cost of getting a dispensation from the archdiocese, which involved significant paperwork and judgment, was about equivalent to the price of a horse. Poor couples could compensate the church with acts of piety, doing public penance as an example to their community, while better-off couples paid in cash, with symbolic gifts of wax for the parish church, and by donations to charities.[46]

Counting on the leniency of the church, Bahian families certainly developed customs and patterns of marriage that went against the grain of Catholic ideals. The combination of rural isolation and the codes of honor that kept women confined to the household encouraged romantic and sexual relations among members of the same family. Case after case alluded to the necessity of a hasty marriage without the customary banns, or the need to accomplish the marriage because an engagement within a household was giving rise to scandal, or simply to the desire of a couple who had begun a sexual relationship to legalize it.[47] The level of guilt and tension within families can be surmised. In one petition, the man confessed that, not only were he and his intended wife cousins, but also that "at some time, unhappily, he the petitioner committed illicit copulation with a sister of hers."[48] In another petition, the couple had between them not only the fact of their kinship as cousins, and his marriage to her deceased sister, but also that she had served as godmother to two of his six children.[49]

It also legitimated the custom of a brother or sister marrying a deceased sibling's spouse. In the most common pattern, a widower might marry one of his wife's sisters. Although this may have stemmed from a desire to renew or maintain the ties of kinship with his wife's family, the dispensations never alleged such abstract and self-interested motives. Instead, they typically claimed that the man needed the sister to take over the role of the deceased wife as mother, and in many cases that she already had, before any desire to marry developed. Petitions cited "the care that she has had in the upbringing of her nieces and nephews," or the man avowed "that having children of a tender age, he does not wish to give these children any stepmother except a lady who can best take the place of a loving mother." [50]

Although the church had developed an accommodation with marriage customs, no satisfactory accommodation with the problem of marital breakdown and separation had evolved. The church did not, of course, offer divorce with remarriage, but only perpetual separation of bodies and of property, which it called *divórcio*. Over the course of the nineteenth century, there seems to have been a shift in the nature of separation proceedings that favored women slightly more than before. Through the late eighteenth century, a woman who initiated divorce proceedings might be confined and cloistered by her husband, who could effectively frustrate his wife's maneuvers for a separation, but by the turn of the nineteenth century that practice changed. Though the church did not officially allow *divórcio* by mutual consent, a woman would often initiate the action and the husband would decline to appear when cited, allowing the action to proceed by default. [51]

In sum, the Catholic church ruled rather lightly over Bahian society. It did not excessively curtail the endogamous marriage customs of rich or poor. And it did not push the issue of marriage for the poor with excessive zeal. The priest himself often offered the most prominent example of an irregular union in his parish. The laws were out of tune with society. But the relation of the society to canon law under the Empire provides an example of legal *jeito*, of the Brazilian preference for side-stepping rules, rather than either enforcing or changing them. [52]

In its practical effects, nineteenth-century Brazilian family law formed two models of marriage. One required a legal church marriage and allowed a variety of options for property arrangements within the couple's estate: absolute community property, separate property, partial separation of dotal property, and other devices. It also permitted a gamut of inheritance strategies, ranging from preferred equal shares for all children to entails for favored male heirs and dowries for favored daughters. The other model of marriage, theoretically reserved in civil law for the lower orders, "peões," acknowledged customary consensual unions, even those that had not been blessed by the church. It did not recognize any status or claims to property for the woman in these common-law unions, but it did protect the inheritance rights of children, who if formally recognized could inherit from their father, by equal shares, as if legitimate.

Conflicts of Church and State

The conflict over the relations of church and state in Brazil, as in most of Latin Europe and Latin America, served as a substantive and symbolic issue that divided "liberals" and "conservatives" and defined antagonistic postures. This was not simply a matter of rival elites, as in the case of doctors taking over the counseling roles of priests, but a case in which one faction of laymen attached themselves to the church, and another faction was anticlerical. Yet the Brazilian anticlerical liberals were not particularly fanatical, at least not the Bahians. The issue was primarily debated by laymen. Whereas many clergymen had served in early governments, priests were rare in the Chamber of Deputies by the late Empire.

Two issues relating to the family formed part of the "Religious Question" in the middle and later years of the Empire. One was the closing of novitiates in monastic orders in 1855. This was primarily a response to the reputed immorality of many of the male religious orders, and in fact, it was not presented as a family issue at all. But indirectly it affected the strategies of upper-class families, which had placed some of their daughters in convents since colonial times.[53]

The question of civil marriage, on the other hand, was directly related to family matters. Throughout the Empire the regalist civil government had occasionally asserted its authority over the church in marriage law. An 1830 administrative law on public functionaries included penalties for priests who placed illegal impediments in the way of couples requesting marriage. The Ecclesiastical Commission of the legislature proposed establishing civil jurisdiction over divorce and other marital cases in 1831. A bishop brought the question of how canon law was to be applied in attempting the reconciliation of the parties in divorce cases before the Ministry of the Empire for an opinion in 1850.[54]

From the 1850's on, the parliament debated the manner in which Brazilian marriage law, among other laws, should be changed to encourage Protestant immigration. The precipitating event was a petition by a German Protestant woman for a ruling on the jurisdiction to which she should apply for a divorce from the Portuguese Catholic man who had abandoned her. The bishop of Rio de Janeiro said that the ecclesiastical courts had jurisdiction only to annul the Catholic spouse's "clandestine marriage." In 1854, the justice section of the Council of State upheld him and determined that neither Brazilian nor foreign civil courts could grant her a divorce for a Brazilian marriage.

Unsatisfied by the opinion, the minister of justice, José Tomas Nabuco de Araujo, drew up a complex bill that left marriage of Catholics in the hands of the church but made the marriages of Protestants subject only to civil jurisdiction and required that they marry by civil ceremony before any later religious celebration. It compromised on mixed marriages: they would be valid after a civil ceremony without any religious celebration, but if the spouses wanted a divorce, it remitted the Catholic spouse to religious courts, and the non-Catholic spouse to the civil courts.[55]

This solution to the problem of mixed marriages did not meet the approval of the Council of State, which held to Emperor Pedro II's opinion that the easiest solution would be to negotiate with the papacy to delegate to Brazilian bishops the authority to grant plentiful dispensations from the impediment of religious difference. Fearing that tinkering with the customs of Catholics would outrage the public, the emperor persuaded most of the council that it would be impractical to require civil marriage for all, as in France. The council agreed that creating the institution of civil marriage for Protestants would be a lesser evil and would not seriously inflame public opinion.[56]

The law that the parliament finally passed in 1861 allowed non-Catholics and mixed couples to marry by civil ceremony and gave the government authority to regulate the manner in which permanent separation would be judged. The regulation that made the law effective provided for the establishment of a civil registry in which non-Catholics could record their births, deaths, and marriages. But the situation of immigrants remained difficult. An 1865 court decision annulled a mixed marriage because of the Protestant husband's refusal to let his wife raise their children as Catholics. An 1867 opinion of the Ministry of the Empire required a Catholic celebrant for mixed marriages. In the 1870's Brazilian priests in the province of Rio Grande do Sul still harassed German women in mixed marriages, requiring them to annul their Protestant marriages and remarry in the Catholic church. The general civil registry of births, deaths, and marriages authorized in 1871 and given regulations in 1874 had still not been effectively organized by 1879. In Salvador, the first civil marriages were registered in 1877.[57]

The issue of marriage for Protestants had relatively little resonance in Bahia, as the province experienced much smaller European immigration than Rio Grande do Sul or other southern provinces. The most notable group of Protestants were the members of the merchant community, which was mostly composed of single men. Marriages within the Protestant community did not concern the church. And, in at least a few cases, the church in Bahia granted dispensations from the impediment of differing religions, *cultus disparatus*, permitting Bahian women to marry Protestant men, usually upon the promise that the couple would raise their children as Catholics. The parish priests advocating mixed marriages apparently felt it useful to adduce the necessity of the match, to demonstrate the need on the part of the woman for it. In one marriage of a Protestant man to a daughter of the Bahian nobility, the parish priest pointed out that great affection existed between them, that the man lacked a woman of his sect to marry, and that the woman demonstrated a firm resolution to remain Catholic. It appears that the church did not always grant dispensations for mixed marriages, and the extant records are not complete, but it did grant some.[58]

The whole tenor of debate on civil marriage issues changed in the 1870's because of the Question of the Bishops, an incident of principle regarding ultramontanist church authority over religious brotherhoods that ended in the imprisonment of two bishops. Before the Question of the Bishops, the liberal proponents of different forms of civil marriage almost always framed their bills as an aid to valuable German immigration, which would dwindle if Germans could not be sure of the rights of their families. Nabuco de Araujo, introducing another bill regulating mixed marriages in 1866, argued that the civil marriage he was proposing was "not a general institution for the State, but an institution for those who do not have any other way to constitute the family; so the question will be situated between concubinage and marriage."[59]

After the Question of the Bishops (and after the Paraguayan War had generally sharpened partisan and ideological cleavages in the political class), Brazilian liberals linked the issue of civil marriage with the question of freedom of religion. Factions of the Liberal party included freedom of religion and civil marriage in their platform. The 1879 session of the Chamber of Deputies, swept up in the turmoil of a possible constitutional reform to allow direct elections, also considered revising the constitution to remove the requirement of a religious oath for legislators. Anticlerical deputies, including the young Joaquim Nabuco, Rui Barbosa, and Joaquim Saldanha Marinho, argued for compulsory civil marriage, which Saldanha Marinho said, "has to do with a contract, and when one is dealing with a contract, the church has nothing to do with it."[60] They presented a civil marriage law that required that no religious marriage ceremony be celebrated without the presentation of a certificate of previous civil marriage.

The defense of religious marriage virtually conceded the liberals' arguments of principle. The minister of the Empire, Leôncio de Carvalho, would not argue against the merits of the proposals, but only asked the deputies to recognize that secularization was a "delicate task," in which the government needed to move discreetly. He warned that in pursuit of the ideal of separation of temporal and spiritual orders, the government should be careful not to give up any of its means of controlling the church. Here he struck a note that the anticlerical deputies rebutted. Silveira Martins argued that it was precisely by enfranchising the church that the constitution had "put the citizen into constant conflict with the religious duties that are imposed on him by a power that resides outside the country." [61]

The bill introduced by Saldanha Marinho got no further than these debates, and none of the other bills for civil marriage introduced between 1879 and 1889 survived the rapid ministerial shuffles and crises of those years. The Ouro Preto cabinet, which was organizing to assume the government just as the military coup of November 1889 overthrew the emperor, also included civil marriage in its platform. [62]

What none of the parliaments had been able to resolve, the provisional government that came to power with the military coup of 1889 immediately imposed by fiat. The republican leadership, which included positivists and anticlerical liberals such as Rui Barbosa, put the conflict between civil and religious authority on a new footing by separating church and state. The measures that they eventually settled upon in the 1891 constitution, after abandoning their more anticlerical provisional decrees, effectively disestablished the Catholic church without punitive confiscations or restrictions. The constitution omitted mention of God in the preamble, then went on to declare the separation of state and church. It gave all religions the right of open worship. It forbade religious education in public schools. It secularized jurisdiction over cemeteries. It abstained from the persecution of the church that some wanted, allowing religious corporations to own property. However, it forbade members of the clergy who were bound by a vow of obedience to vote.

Most important from the perspective of families, it established mandatory civil marriage, to be performed before a justice of the peace and recorded in a civil register, and it denied the civil validity of religious marriages. While a couple could choose to celebrate a second time with a religious ceremony, any religious marriage taking place before the civil marriage was declared invalid. [63] Religious marriage was thus made optional and redundant; the state did not vest authority to perform civil marriage in recognized clergymen as well as civil officials.

Family law issues became rallying points for a "Catholic" resistance to the republican regime. Of course, Brazilian responses were influenced by the writings on both sides generated in the disputes in Europe and other parts of the Americas in the course of secularization in the nineteenth century. [64] Apparently, some priests resisted the declaration of civil marriage from the beginning, for the January decree declaring civil marriage was followed fast by the June decree making celebration of a religious ceremony prior to the civil ceremony illegal, and referring to acts of defiance by priests who were urging couples to marry only by the religious ceremony. Throughout the Republic, and in Bahia, the press contained debates on the requirement of civil marriage and the government's refusal to acknowledge religious marriage for civil purposes.[65]

The anxieties seem to have been strongest in the remote sertão districts of the countryside, where priests and missionaries, some of them refugees from anticlerical persecutions in Europe, gathered crowds in rousing revival missions. Priests, on their side, had little to lose by fanning fears that civil marriage would cost couples their salvation and their property.[66] In the religious pilgrimage city of Canudos in the 1890's, the largest center of population in the backlands, the apocalyptic prophet Antônio Conselheiro allegedly preached against civil marriage as the "law of the Hound" of the satanic republican government, whose paper money should be rejected and whose laws should be ignored. In a less inflammatory, but persistent, way, country priests seem to have counseled their parishioners to ignore civil marriage requirements and marry only in the church.[67]

In the cities, however, the church came to obey the order requiring prior registration of civil marriage before celebration of Catholic marriage. The liberal newspapers criticized the Catholic press for occasionally printing a subversive essay against civil marriage. Certainly, urban Catholic writers often denounced it, but the church seems begrudgingly to have acceded to the institution.

Devout families—or, better put, respectable families—satisfied both authorities by celebrating marriages twice, first with a civil ceremony, and then, later in the day or on the following day, with an elaborate religious ceremony. Marrying only by civil ceremony was the cut-rate alternative for workers who were relatively indifferent to the church, but among the upper classes it represented an aggressive, symbolic repudiation of the church.[68]

In 1908 Archbishop Dom Jerônimo issued a pastoral letter clarifying the Bahian church's policy on civil marriage, an addendum to the Third Collective Pastoral of Bahian bishops. The essay was a masterpiece of temporization, simultaneously seeking to order priests and laity to obey the hated requirement and encouraging them to despise civil marriage in principle. It began by assuring them that "the civil contract is not a true marriage between Christians, and it would be gravely sinful and suspect of heresy to consider it so." It said that those who had only married by the civil registry were in a state of concubinage, and listed the grave consequences for the couple and their children. But in many ways it capitulated to the power of the state. It counseled priests not to marry those too young to marry by civil law without consulting the bishop, and it encouraged priests "out of charity" to tell their parishioners about the dangers of not marrying by civil ceremony. It recommended that, when people were "simple and ignorant," or when the groom "does not inspire confidence," the priest should insist that the civil ceremony be held first. If a priest was under pressure to grant a couple dispensation from impediments in order to avoid their marrying only by civil ceremony, he should always add a note to the effect that "peril of civil marriage" was one reason for the dispensation.[69]

Whether that settled matters to the satisfaction of the central powers or not, the lower clergy still virtually monopolized marrying in the countryside. It seems that they made no effort whatsoever to recommend or require civil marriage. A state survey of marriages in 1923 found almost twice as many religious marriages celebrated as there were civil marriages registered, except in the capital city of Salvador. In the backlands of Bahia, marriage by religious ceremony alone, without recourse to the more cumbersome and expensive civil ritual, was common until the 1950's.[70]

Now that family law fell under the authority of the government, Brazilian legal commentators and legislators assumed greater importance than Catholic moralists and priests in defining the legal limits of family organization. Lawyers and judges had a secondary place in the Brazilian legal system, in which laws changed, not with case-by-case jurisprudence, but rather through changes of codes and through commentaries. *Bacharelismo*, the lawyerly, legalistic approach to social problems that Brazilians were beginning to condemn in the late nineteenth century, gave great authority to legal scholars and commentators.

Salvador was not a major center of Brazilian legal thought and debate. Bahian legislators and legal scholars had figured prominently in legal circles throughout the Empire, but they had studied at Coimbra, Recife, or São Paulo. Individual Bahians, such as the great compiler Teixeira de Freitas, whose authoritative *Consolidação das leis* of 1850 approached the weight of a code, made their careers in Rio de Janeiro.[71] As members of a Bahian delegation, gifted liberal politicians such as Rui Barbosa left a mark on laws and constitutions. But there was no identifiable Bahian position on family law or family policy.

The establishment of the Faculdade Livre de Direito da Bahia in 1891 did little to change this. The decentralized federalist constitution of 1891 had given the states freedom to charter their own academies, so that Bahia opened a law faculty in 1892, Rio de Janeiro in 1891, Belo Horizonte in 1898, Rio Grande do Sul in 1900, Ceará in 1903, Pará in 1905. The Bahian faculty, like the others, provided diplomas and credentials for the growing crowd of candidates for higher education. It also gave a base to Bahian intellectuals from which they could pursue both state and national careers.

But aside from works in the discipline of criminology, which could build on the nucleus of Nina Rodrigues's tradition in legal medicine, it did not develop a marked identity or tendency.[72]

Throughout the Old Republic, Brazilian jurists and legislators continued in the positivist and comparative law traditions established in the Recife and São Paulo faculties during the Empire. Clovis Beviláqua, the author of the final, successful draft of the civil code, the illegitimate son of a priest from Sergipe, became the leading jurist and proponent of the comparative law approach. His treatise on family law, *Direito da família* (1896), emphasized the universal progress of human law on the family, from barbarian through Roman institutions, to the contemporary law of civilized nations. Civil marriage in Brazil, for instance, became necessary because of immigration, as it was "broader and more compatible with the demands of civilization." Yet his "progressive" vision of legal change was conservative and evolutionist. His draft of the civil code, submitted in 1899 and passed in 1916, quite deliberately made only minor changes in the laws of civil marriage and of inheritance that had prevailed since the Philippine Code.[73]

After the declaration of the Republic, the long-pending reform of the ancient Philippine Code seemed more urgent, and governments reappointed commissions to draft a civil code. Compilation of a civil code had been a stated objective of the Brazilian government since the constitution of 1824. Through a combination of rivalries and happenstance, Brazilian legislators had failed to act on any of the drafts written in 1865, 1882, or 1893. The new code drafted by Beviláqua in 1899 almost ran aground on a debate over grammar among Rui Barbosa, Beviláqua, and Carneiro Ribeiro. But the commissions that revised its drafts made relatively few changes with regard to marriage, and the code finally passed in 1916. Despite the excitement surrounding the accomplishment, the civil code did very little to change family law from the law of 1890, or even from the Philippine Code of 1603. With the exception of the issue of divorce, there was what approached a conservative consensus on family law in most of the Old Republic.[74]

Family Law After Secularization

Indeed, despite the great symbolic shift represented by the requirement of civil ceremonies for marriage, the substance of family law changed very little from church marriage regulations. The 1890 law of civil marriage that the provisional government decreed soon after taking power reproduced most of the canon law on marriage, even though it formed part of the republican measures to strip the Catholic church of its temporal authority. Perhaps the very haste of the transition encouraged the republicans to use, conservatively, what traditions they had at hand. In any case, the range of marriage law in contemporary civil codes was not very large, for European nations also drew on common traditions of canon, Roman, and German law. For example, with regard to the role of religious marriage, there were more or less two options: either empower clergymen to perform civil marriage, as in states of the United States, or require that couples go to a civil official for their official marriage. Brazilian republican law was only slightly more anticlerical than that of other reforming nations. It did not authorize clergymen as well as registry officials to perform civil marriages. It remained within the tradition of southern European and Latin American liberalism in actively excluding the Catholic church from civil roles.[75]

The 1916 civil code did innovate to some extent in its definition of the roles and rights of spouses. While it was far from fulfilling Beviláqua's boast that it gave "complete juridical equality" to women, it did recast traditional Portuguese laws, such as those requiring the woman's consent to any sale of community property, in the context of a modernized law of contracts and property.[76] In some ways it defined women's status lower. It said explicitly that the husband was the head (*chefe*) of the couple, that he administered both common and separate property, and that he must authorize his wife to take a profession or establish residence outside his house. However, once authorized, a working woman could "dispose freely of the product of her labor." The code also defined the rights of parents over children more explicitly than legislation had before.[77] It made small changes in the rules of marriage, discussed below, but the law of 1890 had been a much larger break with the past.

In the laws of 1890 and 1916, the procedure for marriage remained similar to that of the canon law. Prospective spouses had to appear before an official with documents to demonstrate their qualification, wait while their banns were published—now on a government bureau's bulletin board or in a newspaper—and swear an oath at a ceremony. The ceremony of civil marriage substituted the banality of notarial procedure for the mystique of the nuptial mass. The custom of holding dual marriage ceremonies and even dual receptions caught on quickly in the upper classes. The ambiguous interval between civil and religious marriages was, of course, immediately exploited by Bahians for various purposes. Some upper-class couples petitioned the church to exempt them from banns for their religious marriage so that they could "free themselves [*livrar-se*] from civil marriage." Almost as quickly, men in the lower classes devised the strategy of marrying for the first time by a religious ceremony alone, in order subsequently to be able to abandon their wives and remarry by civil law.[78]

Like canon law before it, the chief secondary effect of marriage under the civil law was that it established rights of property. It linked parents, particularly men, to their children. Brazilian civil law took great care to assure that marriages, even ones that were later annulled, or took place after the birth of children, established legitimate paternity. In both the nineteenth and twentieth centuries, some Bahians used deathbed marriage as a substitute for making a will.[79] In 1855, the year of the great cholera epidemic, marriage increased, probably because many couples decided finally to regularize their unions. In the years of the optional civil register from 1877 to 1889, several elderly African-born black couples married so as retroactively to legitimate their common children.[80] Civil marriage also set up property relations between the spouses. The 1890 law preserved the patterns of the Philippine Code, which assumed absolute community of property unless a prenuptial contract specified some other regime. Though morgados had been abolished and property arrangements such as dower (*arrhas*) were obsolete, the law of 1890 retained the alternatives of dowry, complete separation of property, and partial separation of property.[81]

Civil regulation of eligibility for marriage continued to conflict with the interests of families. Like canon law before it, the civil law was preoccupied with ensuring that marriages were voluntary and not coerced. Now, of course, the liberal principle of freedom of contract, rather than the Christian principle of freedom of conscience, lent its vocabulary to the law. The most concrete, if somewhat oblique, provision to guarantee freedom of contract was the requirement that doors be kept open during the celebration of the wedding. The article perhaps prevented some fathers from forcing their children into marriages of interest, but it was probably meant to block abductions, for elsewhere the law made abduction an impediment to marriage until the woman was out of the man's power. Where the nature of the relationship between the spouses raised the suspicion that the marriage was not sincere, but a fiction based on money interests, the law forbade the establishment of community of property. If a woman married over the age of 50, or if she married an uncle, a nephew, or a double cousin, the law required that her property remain separate as a dowry.[82]

The principle of mutual, voluntary consent also underlay the rules for marriage annulment, roughly as it had in canon law. Either coercion or evidence of having given consent under fraudulent premises justified annulment. In the civil law, the existence of an "essential error" with regard to the physical condition (impotence), status (loss of virginity, other marriage), or character (a serious crime) of the spouse permitted the innocent party to request an annulment. Some marriages, by their nature, could not be consented to. Such was the case of incestuous or bigamous marriages, which were simply void.[83]

Civil law was able to give parents power over the marriage of children with fewer contortions than canon law. It required that children under 21 and dependent adult children living at home (*filhosfamílias*) obtain the consent of their parents. Or to be precise, obtain the consent of their fathers, for if the parents disagreed, the paternal will was to prevail. If the child could prove that consent was being withheld unreasonably, consent would be furnished by a judge. The 1890 law innovated in specifying that parents could demand a medical certificate of freedom from contagious diseases from the prospective spouse, and they could demand of the groom that he furnish a certificate of good character from his last places of residence. This provision of the law merely enacted the customary procedure of inquiring into the character of a suitor.[84]

The civil law also returned power to families by eliminating the practice of granting dispensations from the impediment of consanguinity. Perhaps the liberal principle of individual free will to enter into a contract was less compatible with the institution of dispensations than was the Catholic vision of a conscience guided by priestly experts. In any case, impediments under the law of 1890 were either absolute, such as the impediment against marrying one's accomplice in adultery, or else they were a function of coercion and could be remedied by the actions of the parties themselves. Civil law drew the boundaries of permissible marriage distinctly, eliminating the gray areas within which the canon law had allowed priests to judge individual cases. The law of 1890 chose to pare the impediment of consanguinity back to a prohibition only against marrying siblings and parents, but the civil code of 1916 later amended the rules to forbid marriages between persons related in the third degree: uncles and nieces, aunts and nephews.[85]

In some articles, the law recognized that marriage was not entirely a transaction between individuals, but also involved their families. It did so, for example, by requiring parental consent for the marriages of minors. In practice this meant consent for daughters, because the median age of marriage for men was 27. Very few upper-class Bahians married as minors. The median age of marriage for women was 22, and given the typically long courtships and engagements, this meant that many girls were under paternal power when they became engaged. The most common situation, then, was one in which an adult man would ask the family of a minor woman for consent to marry her. Persons in other statuses could not contract marriage as freely. A widow or widower was not allowed to remarry until an inventory of the estate of the couple had been concluded if there were children whose interests should be protected. Persons whose disinterested freedom of consent was suspect, because of property considerations or vulnerability to coercion, as in the case of marriage between wards and members of the family of their guardians, might have their marriages impeded. But the impediments could only be invoked by members of the immediate families of the principals.[86]

A shadow of the structure of dispensable impediments remained here, but rather than obtain a relaxation of the rule through appeal to a priest, the couple marrying had to obtain it from the family. To say that the secularization of family law in Brazil gave power to families would be to ignore the fact that laws—or failure to legislate on a question—redistributed authority to some families, or some persons within families, at the expense of others.

Family Policy and Ideological Polarization

In the 1880's, legislators had used civil marriage as a pretext for debating issues of church and state. After the secularization of family law, Brazilian legislators and judges had to confront cosmopolitan trends toward "modernity" in family law directly. The pressure for changes was mild in Brazil, as even the anticlerical "liberal" political elite avowed respect for the traditional form of the family, but the church intransigently determined to make a stand on the issue of divorce. It brought fierce pressure against any hint of change, and even against marginal opposition such as the incipient feminist movement. The conservatism of divorce law demonstrated the rooted resistance of legislators in the early twentieth century to the idea of legislating social change in the family. But the very fact of the debate indicated the growth of competing ideologies. The liberal-positivist near-consensus of the turn of the century was less solid by the 1920's and 1930's.

The question of divorce, for example, cannot easily be explained simply as a transfer of power away from the conservative, inflexible church, and toward individualistic liberal secular values. Brazilian divorce legislation under the Republic was not significantly different from practice under church jurisdiction, and few, even of the radical republicans, favored the institution of divorce followed by remarriage. It is not clear what families, or what individuals, wanted divorce in Brazil; certainly no organized movement formed to lobby for it. It was primarily the development in divorce jurisprudence in the courts that hinted at a gradual trend in favor of more liberal divorce laws.

Yet the fantasy was powerful that republicanism and the separation of church and state had opened the door to the institution of divorce, and consequently to the destruction of the sanctity and authority of the family. In 1919 the Bahian conservative novelist Xavier Marques recreated the Bahian perception of the "revolution" of 1889:

A new society. . . . In matters of business it was enterprising in the "Yankee" manner. In religion it fluctuated between tolerance and indifference. In points of love, it banished certain social rules that modesty had invented. In education it loosened discipline and put sports ahead of the cultivation of intelligence. Finally, in family life, it made concessions to exotic feminism and daringly aspired to divorce.[87]

Brazilian feminists were, in fact, divided on the issue of divorce. At the Second National Feminist Congress, held in Bahia in 1934, the feminists were looking for an agenda after winning the suffrage. They privately considered pushing for divorce, only to find themselves divided on the issue. But when feminists said openly that the home, "where there often reigns the absolutism of a negligent and despotic chief," could be bad for women, men heard that as a call for divorce.[88]

The various revivals of the long-standing project of revision of the civil code between 1890 and 1917 also raised the specter of divorce. The pro-divorce politicians, such as Leopoldo de Bulhões, were often quite timid in their proposals. Responding to a draft bill for divorce in 1894, Bulhões wrote a committee report that proposed dissolution of a marriage only for the innocent spouse in a separation, and only when circumstances suggested that reconciliation was impossible. But in the 1910's and 1920's, during and following the creation of the civil code of 1916, opposition to divorce became a major symbolic issue in the Catholic church's attempt to regain political influence and to block changes in private morality and social relations. The Minas Gerais bishops were the leaders in this campaign. In Bahia, it seems to have been a small, yet perennial, part of the activities of the church.[89]

In fact, Brazilian civil law on divorce diverged slowly and cautiously from canon law. The civil marriage law of 1890 followed canon law closely. First, it affirmed the principle of indissolubility of marriage. Death was the only way that the bond of marriage, once legitimately joined, could be dissolved. Annulment was a judgment that the bond of marriage had never existed between a couple, even though legitimate children might have been born of the union. As the law put it, "divorce does not dissolve the conjugal bond, but authorizes the indefinite separation of bodies and makes the regime of property cease, as though the marriage were dissolved." *Desquite*, as it came to be called, was not divorce allowing remarriage but rather only perpetual separation. Second, the law of 1890 gave essentially the same grounds for separation as canon law. It pared away archaic grounds for separation such as apostasy or contagious disease (i.e., leprosy), and kept the three principal grounds: adultery, grave cruelty (*sevícias e injúrias graves*), and desertion (abandonment of the home for more than two years).[90]

The principal innovation of the 1890 law was separation by mutual con-

sent. This recognition of the existence of mutual consent to separate legitimated a trend in Brazilian practice that perhaps signified increasing power
of wives in relation to husbands. In seventeenth- and eighteenth-century
Bahia, it was women who usually sued for ecclesiastical separation. Their
husbands could, and usually did, obstruct the process by sequestering their
wives in convents to prevent them from being able to press their cases. By
the beginning of the nineteenth century, Bahian women were able to resist
this imposition. Around the same time, in São Paulo, ecclesiastical courts
began to ignore the requirement that divorces be adversary proceedings
and to allow the "guilty" spouse to accede to the allegations. That trend
continued throughout the nineteenth century, and some ecclesiastical divorces in late-nineteenth-century Bahia seem to have proceeded by mutual
connivance of the spouses, as one of them would fail to answer the charges.
Legalization of separation by mutual consent in the 1890 law allowed men
to accept the court judgment without the dishonor of admitting guilt, and
may have made it possible for some women to get a divorce peacefully.[91]

Judging from the small sample of divorce records remaining, perhaps
as many as a third of divorcing couples in Bahia filed formally for divorce
by mutual consent after 1890. Relatively friendly couples may have preferred it, for it allowed the couple to appear privately before the judge,
and to decline to specify the motives for the divorce. Most of the formally
"contested" divorces filed in Salvador in fact proceeded as if by mutual
consent, for in most cases the accused spouse failed to appear or defend
the suit, and the accuser won by default.[92]

For the remaining women, divorce could be difficult as well as unpleasant. Almost all men, and most women, who brought suits for divorce
accused a spouse who had already left home. But a few resolute women
tried to dissolve existing households against the opposition of their husbands. Typically such a woman endured petty harassment during the proceedings from a husband who felt shamed by the suit and who denied her
support or stole the couple's joint property. During appeals after a woman
had lost her first hearing, one particularly eloquent lawyer described his
client as starving for lack of the support payments her husband was obliged
to pay during the proceedings, "with the expectation of living shackled to
her tormentor—quite a model conjugal society!"[93]

A typical case, then, was that of a woman who filed for divorce on the
grounds of severe cruelty, often including an accusation of adultery. Her
strategy included getting the court to confirm her "deposit" in the home
of a respectable family and then proceeding to the divorce suit, which
would take at least two or three months. In such a case, a woman who
succeeded against the opposition of her husband was one who proved, by
medical testimony and the witness of neighbors, that her husband beat her

and behaved abominably in general. The woman who failed was the one who continued to live with an abusive husband after beatings or evidence of adultery, or who could be depicted as the puppet of some malevolent enemy of the husband (usually a kinsman or the mother-in-law).[94]

When men sought a divorce, it was almost exclusively in order to separate themselves and their property from a wife who had left their home years ago. Most of the accusations affected an air of stoical or bitter indifference to the woman's behavior: "She left the path of honor"; "She has prostituted herself, and she had a child after she was no longer in the company of the plaintiff."[95] In a society that condoned murder in flagrante delicto, for men to admit their cuckolding must have been difficult. Yet many of these plaintiffs were poor men, who described themselves as artisans or food vendors; others are referred to by the documents as mulattoes or destitute. They were situated in a milieu in which consensual unions, easily broken by abandonment, were normal, and in which marriage was exceptional. They sometimes indicated indirectly that they had resorted to the legal separation, not only to satisfy their honor, but also in order to shield some small property from their wives. In one case, the plaintiff implied that he had come forward to recognize a long-past desertion in order to gain custody of his son and to protect a small inheritance, two houses from his mother to be divided among three brothers.[96]

While the opponents of divorce often condemned it as a harbinger of the breakdown of social ties, ironically the cases of divorce themselves often implicated the parties in complex kin and neighborhood networks of relations. Like many Brazilian legal disputes, the divorce scenario was not simply a conflict between individuals, but rather pitted two sets of relations against each other. At one level, a case might involve an impressive array of character witnesses, and in order for a woman to contest a divorce, she needed to find another household in which to take refuge.[97] At another level, in contested divorces, the stereotypes that lawyers and witnesses employed characterized the parties by their social relations. Two interesting cases involved the second marriages of well-to-do widows to younger men. Theoretically, the women might be considered at an advantage here. Their husbands could easily be portrayed as indolent, less than masculine, gold diggers who had traded on their youth to deceive vulnerable, foolish widows. But the husband's defense lawyer in each of these cases tried the tactic of demonstrating that the woman was indeed weak, and that she was not acting by her own will alone in pursuing the divorce. After all, a true wife would share her husband's will and interests. The lawyer portrayed her as the dupe of a dominating mother or a scheming nephew who hated the husband and wished to control his wife: "The *devil* in that house was the mother-in-law." This defense of the husband did not attack the wife directly (for after all, he was pleading to preserve the marriage), but rather indirectly, through impugning the motives of her witness and her protectors.[98]

While divorces in Bahia seem often to have reflected cleavages and collective enmities in a densely interconnected society, as much as a trend toward individualism, the trends in divorce did indicate a weakening of the traditional model of the marriage bond. It would be difficult to draw any conclusions from the divorce rate in any case, but the existing statistics do not allow estimates of the divorce rate in Bahia.[99] Census counts of the number of divorced persons in Brazil indicate that the rate of legal separations declined between 1920 and 1950.[100] But this does not seem to accord with the perceptions of members of the upper class in Bahia, who recall a rise in divorce beginning in the 1920's. Divorce was an exceptional resort, and it is perhaps significant that among the few divorce files in the archives, several concerned foreign women who had married Brazilian men: a British or North American woman, a Frenchwoman, an Italian, a German Protestant. Whether or not divorces became more frequent, they became more accepted among Bahian upper-class families, and these families sought other measures to allow remarriage.

Innovations at the margin of the law showed that some families wanted divorce with remarriage. In the 1910's and 1920's, couples began to seek out judges who would grant them annulments, rather than separations. They claimed grounds such as coercion by parents to enter into the first marriage or belated discovery of an essential error about a contagious disease such as syphilis. Clovis Beviláqua, author of the civil code, lamented that "the letter and the spirit of the law has been forced abusively, creating, under the pretext of annulment of marriage, a sort of *judicial divorce* that I abstain from judging." He went on to appeal to the judiciary not to bend the law, arguing that "divorce is a mistake and a regression. Let us not be deluded by the practice of other nations, that consider themselves more cultivated."[101]

Though separated women often found themselves forced into near-seclusion if they wanted to maintain their reputations, separated men could contemplate a second union, though never an entirely respectable one. In the 1940's, legally separated individuals, most of them men, developed a number of subterfuges to substitute for a second marriage. In the contract of "commercial marriage," a divorced person would form a partnership of property with another person that replicated the property arrangements of marriage. In "marriage in Uruguay," a separated Brazilian would divorce again in Uruguay and enter into a second marriage there, both by proxy arranged by agencies in Brazil. Both these practices were illegal by Brazilian law, but they provided remarriages with some semblance of legitimacy.[102]

The proliferation of hypocritical judicial fictions and improvised legalistic institutions demonstrated that there was significant support in private for divorce followed by remarriage. But in public no movement could shamelessly oppose the organized and committed stand of the church and conservative laymen. Not until 1977 did the law change to allow persons who had obtained a separation (*desquite*) to file later for a divorce (*divórcio*).

From the Social Question to Protection of the Family

The rise of social legislation had greater impact on Bahian families than the obviously "modern" and controversial issues of divorce and women's rights. With the growth of metropolitan industrial cities and under the influence of contemporary political programs and social legislation in Europe and the United States, Brazilian authorities turned toward legislation in protection of the social "rights" of workers and the poor in the 1910's and 1920's. In doing so, they naturally imported European ideas and slogans. Positivist, Catholic, and socialist ideologies displaced liberal, laissez-faire indifference to labor issues. For example, the use of the expression "social question" to refer to the problems of, and the challenges from, workers derived from European Catholic social thought of the 1870's through 1890's, from pronouncements such as Leo XIII's *Rerum novarum* encyclical of 1890.[103]

From the financial bubble of 1891 through the depression of 1929, both the growth of Brazilian business and its periodic crises created new forms of misery for urban working families. Opportunities in some regions of Brazil were good enough to attract European immigration. But urban social conditions were bad enough to attract the notice of the press and the government. In a 1920 survey of São Paulo, women were found to account for perhaps a third of the work force, while half of the workers were under eighteen, and almost 8 percent under fourteen. Representatives of the textile industry claimed that approximately 60 percent of their workers were children. Women's and children's labor was not in itself shocking. That whole families should work together was taken for granted in the Brazilian countryside; that women and small children should be employed full-time may have seemed congruent with the traditions of slavery and apprenticeship. But the sustained, exhausting pace of factory labor for whole families, with children sometimes working alongside their parents in a mill, may indeed have been something new. In Bahia, urban poverty and child labor were not only related to industrial work. Unemployment, not industrial employment, was the great fear of urban workers, and child labor flourished in commercial businesses, which employed scores of adolescent shop clerks.[104]

Some Brazilian industrialists developed paternalistic workers' villages as a way of yoking employment to the maintenance of family life.[105] One of the largest textile mills in Bahia, the Empório Industrial do Norte, which Luiz Tarquínio founded in 1891, had a model village for married workers that offered housing, a school, a bandstand, a company store, and a nursery. (Children might begin work at the ages of eight to ten under the supervision of the company doctor, who regularly visited the factory floor.) Like many other factory villages, the Empório Industrial complex insisted on decorum, decency, and discipline among its wards. It required legal marriage of couples among its workers, imposed a 9 P.M. curfew, and forbade drinking inside or outside the walls. In 1901 Tarquínio published a book titled *Moral and Civil Precepts* for his workers, and the company newspaper printed testimonials to his godlike creativity and Christlike benevolence.[106]

The choice of paternalism may have been rational for employers in Brazil, limiting employee turnover and guaranteeing a dependent work force.[107] It also fit the patronal complex well; employers in Salvador expected to control the votes of their men.[108] And it fit the Catholic ideology of harmony between classes and the need to moralize industrial conditions. To many poor people in Salvador, the combination of discipline and security in a company village must have been attractive. It perhaps also fit the Comtian positivist ideal of incorporating the proletariat into a cooperative order.[109]

The labor movement, and particularly the anarchists within it, proposed a very different solution to the crisis in workers' lives and families. Early Brazilian unions had developed out of mutual-aid associations and Catholic brotherhoods, and they retained a strong concern with survivors' and burial benefits. The leading labor organizations in Bahia, the Associação Tipográfica da Bahia and the Centro Operário, were accommodationist unions, the latter particularly close to J. J. Seabra. But from 1900 forward, the militant anarchist movement proposed a very different attitude toward the family and workers' goals. If the anarchists recognized influence by any positivist doctrine, it was the libertarian message of Herbert Spencer, his goal of a minimum state, and his belief in social cooperation without central supervision.[110] Their workplace and revolutionary goals disdained paternalistic measures to "succor the family," such as pension funds. Instead, they wanted a millennial revolutionary upheaval that would liberate individuals and reconstitute families as voluntary associations based on free love.

There were contradictions between the theory and practice of anarchist cultural politics. Though they theoretically favored free love and birth control, in practice most anarchist militants in Rio de Janeiro and São Paulo were ascetic, puritanical, and monogamous. They were obsessed with respectability and scatologically fascinated with the perversions of priests and bourgeois. They opposed drunkenness and the uncomradely sexual aggression of dance halls in language that coincided ironically with that of the authoritarian eugenicist medical reformers of the 1920's. Anarchists opposed political involvement, yet indirectly their militancy greatly influenced the growth of paternalist social legislation.[111]

During World War I, elite opinion began to focus on the labor question as a "social question." Waves of general strikes from 1917 to 1919, including the 1919 general strike in Salvador and much larger strikes in São Paulo and Rio de Janeiro, forced an abrupt change in the political agenda. The undeniable wartime cost-of-living crisis mobilized clerks and white-collar employees in addition to workers. In Salvador, shop clerks who had been organized by merchants into subservient associations formed the autonomous União Caixeiral in 1919.[112] This "middle class" protest suggested to politicians that the strikes were a function, not simply of agitation and subversion, but also of basic questions of family survival and decency. And international trends, from the Russian Revolution to the Versailles Conference on the postwar world, emphasized labor issues.

Increased competition within the political oligarchy also encouraged politicians to court labor support. Bahia's political leadership had since the 1880's included men with an electoral base among workers in Salvador: Manuel Victorino Pereira, J. J. Seabra, Rui Barbosa, Antônio Calmon, Octávio Mangabeira.[113] None of these was primarily a "labor" politician, but workers' votes became important in political machines. At the national level, the first contested presidential election of 1910 had led to a government-sponsored labor congress in 1912. In 1911 and 1912 two radical deputies, Maurício Lacerda and Nicanor Nascimento, were elected from Rio de Janeiro, and in 1917 they led the Congress in proposing a full-fledged package of labor legislation. From 1917 on, labor questions confronted every government, however much people might joke that "the social question is a question for the police." After World War I, veteran politicians who had formerly ignored labor issues included labor planks in their campaign platforms: Rodrigues Alves in 1918 and Rui Barbosa in 1919. In the final, contested presidential campaign of 1929 before the Vargas revolution of 1930, the silence of the official candidate, Júlio Prestes, contrasted starkly with the labor platform of the opposition candidate, Getúlio Vargas, which promised everything to labor.[114]

Yet in the 1920's governments handled labor issues largely with repression and obfuscation. Under the threat of military coups and regional rebellions, they dealt harshly with strikes as well. They responded to the anarchist challenge with a series of deportation laws (in 1907, 1913, and 1921) aimed at subversive aliens. Congress, led by the intransigent Rio Grande do Sul delegation, tabled the major labor packages of 1918. Prodded and counseled by businessmen's associations, legislators hesitated to pass laws that seemed "inappropriate to Brazilian circumstances." The government declined to implement or enforce the labor laws that did pass. As a consequence, the only major social measure to emerge from the wartime agitation was a workers' accident compensation law of 1919. In the 1920's, however, governments passed a series of unimplemented, yet symbolic, measures: the creation of a national labor commission in 1923, the chartering of pension funds in 1923 and 1926, the paid vacation law of 1925, and the minors' code of 1926 (which included child labor regulations).[115]

Public debate over the social question repeatedly addressed the regulation of women's and children's work conditions. Business spokesmen rarely opposed labor legislation on principle, but they were more likely to oppose recognition of unions and less likely to oppose the protection of women and children, a respectably neutral and charitable concern that they could frame in terms of public health. In São Paulo, executive regulations of the Sanitary Service had established norms for the employment of children in 1911, and on paper at least, the state sanitary law of 1917 had laid down conditions for women and children. Bahian administrations also regulated work conditions. In Salvador, a municipal act of 1911 forbade work under the age of fourteen to both Brazilians and foreigners. Industrialists were capable of casuistical defenses of children's labor, noting that it kept them off the street between the age of eleven or twelve, when virtually all left school, and the age of fourteen, when it was generally agreed that some work should be permitted. But their lobbying focused on the details of the minimum age for work and the workday of the minor: should children work at ten or at fourteen? should the minor's workday be six, eight, or ten hours? Legislation in the late 1920's and in the early 1930's, and finally the social democratic constitution of 1934, repeatedly restricted the employment of women and children. The most important symbolic measure was the minors' code in 1926, though it was repeatedly modified and its labor provisions were not enforced.[116] Until the creation of labor courts with workplace inspectors in the 1940's, governments did not enforce these laws in most of Brazil.

The federal social legislation that had the most practical impact on middle-class families was probably the establishment of mandatory pension funds in certain occupations. In Bahia, mutual-aid associations and private subscriber pension funds had proliferated since the 1870's, though their existence was often precarious. The pension fund for public employees, the Montepio, was a well-established institution. Families sought to place their sons in public service partly because of the security that a functionary enjoyed. And some private companies offered pensions to their workers. But the Eloi Chaves Law of 1923 mandating the establishment of a privately run pension fund for all railway workers was the first state-sponsored pension plan for private employees. It provided medical, retirement, and survivors' benefits. Other laws followed, extending pension funds to dockworkers, maritime workers, telegraphers, and others.[117]

Under the Vargas regimes of 1930 to 1945, the government extended the coverage of sectoral pension plans to more categories of workers and encouraged the formation of public bodies that would consolidate the many autonomously administered funds. Though there was inequality among funds, and benefits were not standardized but rather proportional to workers' contributions from their salaries, the pension funds did provide a small proportion of the Brazilian people with significant social insurance from the state. By 1950, perhaps 20 percent of the working population had some coverage.[118]

The government-organized pension funds had the effect of insuring families and perhaps created different perspectives and opportunities for family strategies. On the one hand, they may have emancipated individuals (and couples) from reliance on a network of relatives, and especially from dependence on the generosity of patrons. On the other hand, they may have reinforced the tendency of patrons in Bahia to jettison their clienteles after 1930. And they may have reinforced the model of the legal, nuclear family, by encouraging working-class couples to marry in order to qualify for survivor's benefits. The proliferation of the social-service bureaucracy also directly benefited the middle class by creating office jobs: by the 1950's one in seven federal jobs was related to the social security administrations.[119]

With the rise of Getúlio Vargas's "revolutionary," quasi-electoral dictatorships of the early 1930's, and his authoritarian, quasi-fascist Estado Novo dictatorship of 1937 to 1945, social legislation became an integral part of the program of the Brazilian state. Vargas began his regimes in uneasy alliance with radical junior officers and other reformers. His labor policies in 1931 and 1932, including establishment of a Department of Labor and passage of nearly the full package of labor reforms proposed in the 1910's, seemed like an overwhelming change of course in national policy. But the protectionist and welfare measures that Vargas decreed went hand in hand with corporatist union regulations that attempted to subordinate the labor unions to the state.

There was no single doctrine or movement behind the growing state regulation and "protection" of the family. The doctrine of hygienic intervention in family affairs, which had grown into a small eugenics movement by the 1920's, provided a major buttress for government authority over abandoned, delinquent, abused, or exploited minors. The reactionary mobilization of the Catholic church had led to calls for government activism in the amelioration of poverty and misery, as well as the reinstatement of the church in education and official charity work. Nationalist schemes to regenerate the people through immigration, public health measures, military service, or education proliferated. Contemporary fascist and corporatist thought emphasized the solidarity of members of the nation, envisioning a different sort of citizenship (and much more state intervention in mobilizing citizens) than the liberal model that had prevailed. And contemporary social democratic legislation in Europe, Argentina, and elsewhere certainly influenced Brazilian opinion. Combined, these amounted to a change in the climate of public opinion that favored an interventionist and bureaucratic approach to the uplifting and reform of the *povo*, and the strengthening of familial security.[120]

If any central expression of that consensus emerged, it was in the constitutions of 1934 and 1937. The first, written by an elective convention, was nonetheless highly influenced by Vargas's deputies. The Bahian deputation, for instance, was dominated by pro-Vargas deputies.[121] The 1934 constitution, a contemporary observer said, reflected the "sociodemocratic consciousness of the period. A pronounced collectivism permeates its provisions, with the emphasis on the people as a whole and on the forgotten man."[122] It also expressed the influence of the Catholic lobby, which had gotten commitments from delegates and managed to pass its minimum demands: symbolic concessions, such as mention of God in the preamble; material changes, such as religious education in public schools; and substantive family measures, such as prohibition of divorce.[123] The 1937 constitution, written by Vargas's ideologist Francisco Campos, was much closer to a fascist model. Neither was ever fully in effect; Vargas governed as a dictator under a series of states of siege. But they expressed the idealized aims of the corporatist project.

The constitution of 1937 distinctly mapped out an interventionist policy for the family immediately following its highly contradictory provisions on individual rights.[124] Article 124 declared that "the family, constituted by indissoluble marriage, is under special protection of the state. Large families will be granted compensation in proportion to their necessities." Article 125 proclaimed the joint responsibility of parents and the state for the education (and upbringing) of children, asserting that "childhood and youth must be the object of special care and guarantees on the part of the state, which will grant them physical and moral conditions of healthy life and harmonious development of their faculties." Article 127 indicated that the state would take responsibility for the maintenance of indigent or abandoned children.[125]

Bahian state governments participated in the social-welfare movements of the 1930's by expanding the traditional social-welfare infrastructure: schools and hospitals. Part of that expansion continued the policy of distributing state subsidies to private social-welfare agencies and establishments, now tying them to an earmarked municipal tax. Establishments run by the church or by Catholic societies, such as Saint Vincent de Paul orphanages and maternity clinics, got operating funds from the government, and the state itself built hospitals, institutes, and schools. The third Vargas-appointed interventor, Juracy Magalhães, completed urban waterworks, built more schools (especially in the countryside), expanded teacher training and the Ginásio da Bahia, and began hospital construction. He created the Conselho de Assistência Social and the Departamento Estadual da Criança. Later administrations further expanded the school network and the hospital and rural clinic system.[126]

Perhaps the leading Bahian ideologue of this state-led expansion of social services was Isaías Alves, a schoolmaster and psychologist who served as secretary of education under Landulpho Alves. Alves epitomized the concerns of the Estado Novo: he was obsessed with forming, disciplining, and uplifting the people, imbuing them with "a syndicalist spirit in which the individuals are integrated like cells in a greater organism." A practicing Catholic, he favored alliances between the government and church social agencies such as orphanages and hospitals. He organized the reintroduction of optional religious instruction in the schools. God, he said, was "a divine Being who orders, who decides, who systematizes, who organizes, who directs, who orients, and guides." He supported scouting organizations, women's charity drives, and rural 4-H clubs. His view of contemporary customs was critical: the "excessive liberty" of modernity made youth too precocious, too disobedient. Above all, he was an educator. His most lasting accomplishment was the foundation of the Faculdade de Filosofia in 1941, which became the nucleus of the Universidade Federal da Bahia.[127]

Alves's spiritualized authoritarianism was not the only tendency in Bahia. On the left, a generation of young Bahians—among them Jorge Amado, whose early "proletarian" novels of the 1930's denounced the poverty of the cacao workers of Ilhéus and the tenements of Salvador, and Anísio Teixeira, whose Catholic educational ideal was liberal democratic—represented a less authoritarian approach to the social question. But both Alves and the left operated in a political arena that was still populated with leftover politicians of the oligarchy, and whose electoral coalitions always had to enlist small-town coronéis in the interior. The Bahian oligarchy had shattered in the 1920's, and so the federal interventorships rebuilt politics along basically bossist lines.[128]

The effort to expand education received most attention from Bahian governments. The renewal of the state's school system began in the late 1920's, under the Goes Calmon government, which pointed out that the Bahian primary school system, whose budget had been one-third that of São Paulo in 1895, had fallen to one-tenth that of São Paulo by 1923. Goes Calmon himself was an elitist, who feared that the expansion of primary education would simply produce dangerous, half-educated men susceptible to Bolshevik doctrine. Nonetheless, under his young education secretary Anísio Teixeira, the state built schools in the backlands and laid the basis for an increase in enrollment in the late 1920's. Primary school enrollment grew from 18 percent of the school-age population in 1924 to 25 percent in 1929. Enrollment figures are difficult to interpret, as at times they may have missed the large numbers enrolled in religious and secular private schools, and as few children finished primary school. In 1926, five times as many children were enrolled in the first grade as in the third. But by 1943, total enrollment in primary education had risen to 116,000, by any standard much higher than the enrollment of 25,000 in 1924.[129]

Conclusion

Brazilian family law was conservative. It preserved the fundamental outlines of seventeenth-century family law through the republican revolution of 1889 and through the rise of an authoritarian, quasi-welfare state. Its primary innovations were the changes in the early nineteenth century that reinforced its bias toward simplified rules for transmission of property in inheritance and definition of the rights of common-law unions as a secondary form of marriage.

Bahians, like many people in Europe, believed that changes in family law could radically shift the shape of families. The Catholic church, in its opposition to civil marriage and to divorce, encouraged that belief. Radical movements such as feminism focused some of their oppositional energy on proposing legislation that would remedy social oppression. But the posturing of Catholic spokesmen and of legislators usually ignored the long-standing tradition of manipulation of laws and legality by Bahians of all ranks. Marriage, the institutional vertex of legal regulation of family relations, was barely the norm in nineteenth- and early twentieth-century Bahia. For the poor, it was the exception rather than the rule, and even for the rich, it was desirable but not necessary.

For better or for worse, social relations in Bahia took place in the context of intricately intermingled "formal" and "informal" sectors of kinship. This was not unique to family relations, of course. Brazilian society was far from universalistic and integrated in most of its sectors; the grounds of national common identity and dialogue were personal rather than institutional. At first glance, we might assume that slavery, which produced deep and lasting cleavages among people, or simply rural isolation, which discouraged the continuous contact, communication, and coercion that can build social citizenship, might account for this. But perhaps the informal structure of upper-class Brazilian culture itself may have inhibited the legal rationalization of family relations.

5

Church and Family

*F*ROM THE mid nineteenth century on, the Catholic church became a stronghold of traditionalist projects for the family. Physicians' dreams of hygienic reform might spiral up into fantasies of eugenic breeding, and liberals' programs for equality and personal freedom might progress to projects for divorce, but the church cultivated an image and a message of stability and permanence. In Brazil, of course, traditionalism with regard to family roles could not simply be complacent. The widespread indifference to, or lack of observance of, norms of marriage and parenthood made it difficult for Brazilian Catholics to pretend that modern times had fallen away from some better age of morality and innocence. Any determined moralizing campaign by the church had to mobilize against custom as much as in defense of it.

The colonial roles of the Catholic church and its agencies guaranteed the church a large, diffuse influence in contemporary society. Catholicism was the established religion of Brazil from the foundation of the colonies until 1889; but the Catholic church in Bahia was less an autonomous monolith than a collection of organizations dependent on public and private patronage. In the countryside, parish priests and chaplains became household clients of individual planter magnates around the Recôncavo.[1] In Salvador, the regular clergy found that their functions were determined by the rich lay brotherhoods and associations, such as the Santa Casa da Misericórdia, as much as by any international strategy of their orders. Even where its efforts might have been centralized, the church found that royal control over the collection of tithes and financing of the clergy tended to limit its activity; ecclesiastical institutions were fewer and poorer than in Spanish America.

The church was not a single organization, but rather an estate, or category, to which a number of similar and competing organizations pertained.

Its functions were similarly dispersed. Church agencies held a monopoly, often an explicit one, over a variety of social services. Health services were provided by private practitioners, public health officers on city councils, and religious charities such as the Santa Casa da Misericórdia, which had a royal charter to bury slaves, maintain a foundling wheel and orphanage, and keep open a hospital for travelers and indigents.[2] Welfare for the poor, mostly in the form of alms, was provided by a number of orders and brotherhoods. Education was a primary function of the Jesuits, whose academies were the foundation of Brazilian intellectual life. Religious organizations concerned themselves with both social services and social control. In the bluntest manifestation, representatives of the Inquisition on intermittent visits repressed petty crimes as well as heresy. Besides regulating marriage, canon law was also important in the internal policing of the affairs and the personnel of the religious estate.[3]

In the late eighteenth century, the Portuguese Crown had increased its control over the organization of the church. For reasons partly of political expediency, the reformist prime minister Pombal expelled the Jesuit order from Portugal and its territories in 1759, and reformed the seminary at Coimbra to install a curriculum and faculty that followed regalism, the ideology of royal control over territorial churches. At independence, therefore, Brazil inherited a clergy trained in regalist ideas.

After independence, the Brazilian constitution of 1824 perpetuated Crown control of the church (the Portuguese Padroado). Despite an early crisis over the refusal of the Vatican to recognize the Padroado in a concordat, the Brazilian government soon extracted a tacit agreement from the papacy for its retention. The emperor kept the power to make ecclesiastical appointments, control church revenues, and determine whether papal letters were to receive the *placet* allowing their publication in Brazil. In return, the constitution of the Empire recognized Catholicism as the state religion, although it permitted the discreet practice of other religions. Under the Empire, the church was at once a weak branch of the Brazilian bureaucracy and the local representative of an international organization with traditions and interests of its own. Parish priests were burdened with functions as public employees. They kept land registers, recorded vital statistics, and ran elections.[4]

Catholic Practices and Daily Life

Unlike the disciplines of medicine and of law, whose elites spoke mainly to each other, using a specialized vocabulary referring to specialized knowledge and a private consensus, the church shared a language and a popular set of symbols with the people. For centuries the church had

had a grass-roots engagement with the people and a mission to speak to everyone. However crudely, it baptized and catechized African slaves and forest Indians. Whereas physicians and bacharels did at times approach the insularity of what Ortega y Gasset calls "watertight compartments,"[5] the clergy always communicated at some level with rich and poor alike.

This did not mean that the doctrines and beliefs of the clergy and educated Christians were identical to those of the povo. On the contrary, recent self-critical scholarship by Brazilian church historians has preferred to chastise the church for misunderstanding the people.[6] Yet there was a fairly fluid meshing of the formal doctrine of the church and the informal, unauthorized practices of folk Catholicism. For example, the church presided over unorthodox practices such as the annual washing of the chapel of Nosso Senhor do Bomfim in Salvador, occasionally banning the most egregiously pagan or bacchanalian parts of the ritual, but not refusing to shepherd the laity.[7]

In 1870 Catholic observances still saturated the great and the small practices of daily life in Bahia. Salvador was a city where bells tolled the time of day, pacing lives to sacred hours. Bells tolled for funerals, rang in jubilation, and called for processions. On no day was one ever more than a short walk from an open chapel, with beggars congregating outside and women praying or gossiping inside. Every night pious old women in hooded cloaks walked the streets on missions of charity. Holiday processions united blocks of the faithful behind the excursion of a saint's image.

Before the separation of church and state, the church had obviously shaped the family directly by controlling the institution of marriage. It disallowed certain unions—sometimes cousin marriages, which seemed convenient to Bahian families—and permitted others. But the church, and Catholic religion, also provided much of the ritual and many of the symbols that pervaded daily life. Marriage was only one ritual of passage among many that the church offered to families to mark their changes in status.

Consider baptism, for example. It gave newborn infants status in the community by bringing them into the church. Until the creation of the civil register in 1877, the certificate of baptism established every person's legal and social status, giving his or her age, legitimate or illegitimate filiation, and the godparents' names. Baptism provided the ritual context for the important secular custom of godparenthood. By appearing in place of the parents to perform the ceremony initiating an infant into the church, the godparents entered into a relation of spiritual kinship whose roles were extensively defined by custom, though they were ignored by law.[8]

Bahian families used church ceremonies to mark other important passages in their lives. They marked the passage from infancy to the age of reason by celebrating the child's first communion with white costumes and spinsters' gifts of lace trimming, ribbons, candles, and, almost invariably by the late nineteenth century, a photograph. They marked young maturity in the rite of confirmation; they went to church for weddings.

They managed deaths in the family by reliance on a church funeral to follow the secular customs of the wake and burial meals. A death itself was best when a deathbed scene with confession and administration of the last rites could be arranged.[9] After a funeral, commemorative masses at increasing intervals, like the customary degrees of mourning and half-mourning clothes, helped to combine a cult of the family dead with symbolic representation of their removal from the company of the living.

Religious ritual served not only to dramatize the meaning of the universal transitions in the life cycle, but also to solemnize special occasions. A family would commission a mass of thanksgiving to celebrate recovery from illness, graduation from an academy, or the annual cracking out of the first pan of molasses sugar from the harvest of their cane. The government commissioned masses of observance and commemoration.

Religious observances filled the daily life of families and communities. Well-brought-up children asked their elders for a blessing in the morning. Slaves showed their respect for their masters by greeting them with a mumbled "Praise be Our Lord Jesus Christ," to which the master replied, "Praised be." In pious households, the evening ended with prayers. When attendance at Sunday mass was impossible, families might hold special prayer meetings.[10] The religious calendar gave meaning to the year; time was measured not only by days and months, but also by festivals and saints' days. Some times of the year were different because of the concentration of festivals: June for the Santo Antônio and São João days; Advent through Christmas and Epiphany; Carnival, Lent, and Easter. All Saints' and All Souls' Days were sacred in the midst of trivial worries:

I went to Santo Amaro, eager to end the homesickness of a long absence and spend with my kids those first two days of November that represent the alternation of life:—joy and sadness, celebration and mourning.
    The harvest is meager and the price of sugar ridiculous.[11]

Many religious festivals centered on communal processions of a whole parish, brotherhood, or town, but others centered on the house and its neighbors. The fire lighted on Midsummer's Day, the day of São João, might be the bonfire of a plantation Big House and its dependents or just the backyard fire of a town family and relatives.[12] Most of these festivities for favorite saints incorporated such a hodgepodge of folklore and profane custom that their religious core became almost irrelevant. The fact that they were private social gatherings made them family rituals by default, as much as any specific "familial" symbolism in their content did.

In every community there was some "religious" festival that was regarded as licentious and improper for families. Carnival was the strongest bit of profane folk ritual attached to religious ritual. The custom of
license and mirth before Lent's Ash Wednesday existed throughout Catholic Europe and Latin America. In slave societies, it seems to have fulfilled
an important compensatory function as a holiday of misrule. Officially,
the church combated Carnival because it was irreligious, frivolous, and
libertine. Pious Catholics were always involved in campaigns to stop it.
Carnival was antifamilial because it was nonhierarchical and libertine, the
antithesis of decency and honor. Other festivals could offend honor too.
In Santo Amaro around 1900, for instance, the Mês de Maria mass in the
Rosário church was rowdy; men went just to stare at the girls, and the
police had to be called in. In the sertão in the early twentieth century,
the Christmas festival was a drunken celebration of the flesh that ended in
fights and rapes.[13]

The Church and Women

Religion and the church were specially influential in women's lives. "A
woman should only leave her house three times: to be baptized, to be
married, and to be buried," went the saying. And by defining women's activities as being in a separate sphere, the church reinforced the hierarchy
of the sexes and the ideal of the seclusion of women, which was crucial
to the concept of honor. It obeyed the ideal of seclusion by seeing to it
that women's escape from the family could lead only to an even more rig-
orously separate setting: to the cloister of a convent or the sanctuary of
church buildings. Women's religiosity hewed more to private spaces and
domestic themes. The sphere it defined was also characterized by resignation—that is, by denial of this world and affirmation of the other world.
European travelers in the early nineteenth century observed mothers of
dead babies laughing and accepting congratulations from their friends as
they dressed the little *anjo* in white for its reception into heaven.[14]

Within its separate, "unworldly" sphere, the church authorized some
active roles for women. The ideal of charitable works allowed women a
pretext, if they wanted it, to take an active public role. Sisterhoods such
as the Associação das Senhoras de Caridade da Bahia, founded in 1854
by ladies of high society to support the Sisters of Charity and provide an
orphanage and day school for poor girls, afforded women the opportunity
to do good works in public, while emphasizing the virtue of self-denial in
charity.[15] In the twentieth century, there was a great increase in the activity
of groups such as the Women's Catholic Social Action.

The caricatured social type of the *beata*—a word connoting a stubborn fanaticism that cannot be translated by the English "churchmouse"—was ever present in Brazilian society, representing the woman whose religiosity went beyond the role of "saint" and became unseemly. In a self-deprecating way, Brites Barbosa conceded to her free-thinking brother that religion was women's business more than men's: "No, God has to come through for us. . . . I don't say this because I am a woman, who they say always drags God into it, no. I'm not a foolish woman. God exists and He will not abandon you."[16]

In Bahia, the epitome of the beata was the *mulher de capona*, the cloaked woman. The capona was still associated with beatas as late as 1900, when caponas were no longer seen on the streets. For most of the nineteenth century, caponas were the only women who could decently be abroad in the streets at night, out on errands of midwifery or asking alms for the church. During the rebellion of the religious center at Canudos in 1896–97, the image of the beata was transfigured into a demonic negation of femininity: a newspaper report spoke of an officer being shot in the back by a woman fanatic whose life he had spared. In Canudos one found "women with a pistol in one hand, a cross in the other."[17]

Probably drawing on his own experience, Gilberto Freyre argues that in patriarchal Brazil, confessors provided a therapeutic outlet for the tensions of women who were otherwise confined and isolated. Evidence of the counsel of priests as confessors in the late nineteenth century comes largely from novelists who were critical of priests, though memoirs mention or suggest the influence of confessors. In some families, as an extension of their role in the cure of souls, priests gave advice and counsel in secular family affairs.[18]

The convent and the *recolhimento*, an informal cloister that women could join without taking vows, offered Bahian women a physical escape from the family. Even in their heyday, however, convents were kept too small to offer an alternative to most women. At their high point in 1853, the three traditional Bahian convents held only about 73 nuns, although recolhimentos contained many more women. Moreover, convents were not simply places of refuge. In colonial times husbands were able to use them as private prisons for rebellious wives, and well into the nineteenth century, recolhimentos served as a means of confinement. They also sheltered "fallen" women: the Recolhimento São Raymundo was founded as a lodge for prostitutes and unwed mothers.[19]

In the nineteenth century, the tyrannical cloistering of beautiful maidens was the stuff of ballads, but many young women may have preferred convent life to spinsterhood, because in effect it emancipated them from the tutelage of their fathers. Nuns in the prestigious Convento do Desterro in Salvador lived in a sort of perpetual women's club, making candies and practicing their lutes, served by the slave chambermaids they had brought from home. Many of the residents were not nuns but girl pupils and ladies who were staying temporarily. In the mid nineteenth century, country families that had connections with the convent used it as a hostel for women who had to stay alone in Salvador. Though the government banned new admissions into the orders in 1855, convents remained important as temporary retreats.[20]

The convent was always a crucial symbol, representative in the clearest way of the fact that the church was the one place women could go to escape their homes. When Salvador was a city paved in mud, with shops only for men, the public space of convents, the buildings of the charitable sisterhoods, and the foyers of churches were notoriously the places in the city where old gossips gathered, and where women spent their leisure time decorating altars and dispensing charity. Even after there were trolleys, tearooms, clubs, and shopping, the church remained a focus of women's leisure. The preponderance of women in the public activities of the church reinforced—as it reflected—the attitude that religion was women's business.[21]

Brazilian Catholicism provided spiritual and emotional solace for subordinates of all sorts. Symbols such as the figure of the Virgin Mary defined women's roles and thus helped to define roles in the family. The nineteenth-century church promoted devotion to Mary as a merciful intercessor with her increasingly remote Son. Proclamation of the Dogma of the Immaculate Conception in 1854 symbolized the aggressive differentiation of Catholicism from Protestant practice. The figure of the Virgin became crucial to the definition of women's roles as resigned, suffering, chaste mothers, who achieved glory through the men they served. No figure was as important as Mary—Virgin, Madonna, bereaved mother, and Queen of the Heavens—for defining the tone of women's religiosity and the essence of their roles. Virgins and martyrs engraved on bookmarks, stamped on medals, molded in porcelain, or carved in wood were everywhere among the possessions of Bahian women of all classes. In the home oratories that were the center of religious practice in most Brazilian families, statues of Our Lady were sure to figure prominently. May, the month of Mary, was a joyful festival of flowers, novenas, and family dances.[22]

Other saints might be invoked because they were women or because they had special attributes for women. Devotion to Nossa Senhora de Santana, Saint Anne, the grandmother of Jesus, was widespread in Brazil and often mentioned among the Bahian upper classes. Widows could appeal specially to the widowed Santa Rita de Cássia, knowing she would take pity on their affliction. Single women would ask matchmaking favors of Saint Anthony; on his day a girl could learn the name of the man she would marry. On a daily basis, women could call on Saint Anthony to find lost objects; turning his statue would find the object. The cult of São Gonçalo, described by Gilberto Freyre as a sort of fertility cult, included lighthearted legends of his pulling a deceitful suitor out of the sleeve of his robe.[23]

Christianity's ethic of resignation to the tyrannies of this world and to personal sacrifice—in sum, the virtues of the meek and humble in the Beatitudes—made even elite women something akin to slaves, identifying them with service and servants. Nonetheless, even the most devout of them could on occasion find it hard to forgive:

Two ladies whom I knew well . . . told me that they did not go to confession because they could not forgive the complaints they had of their husbands. My daughter, who was present, observed: "Then what good is it to say you are Christians, to pray, to go to mass, if you don't follow the example of Jesus Christ who died forgiving his tormentors?"[24]

In candid moments, religious writers acknowledged that the duties of women as wives were difficult and often painful. Yet they insisted that the sacrifice of self was ennobling and spiritualizing. They identified the wife as "the queen of the home and the angel of sacrifice." In some households, women took this message seriously as bonding them to the servants and led the kitchen in household prayers and worship. But there is no indication that the Christian message made women treat their slaves better than men did. If anything, the critical writers portray women as crueler, more sadistic slaveowners.[25]

The church did rise above Brazilian society in preaching a single morality of marriage to men and women. Ideally, Christian marriage was based on love, on the mutual affection and spiritual consecration of the couple to each other. Marriage was modeled on the church's marriage to Christ; it represented a sacred union. But within the marriage, the church recognized the authority of husband over wife, and the Bible authorized prescriptions that women should be silent and submissive. As Dom Macedo Costa put it in 1875, she should "love her husband, respect him as her chief, obey him with affectionate promptness, admonish him with discretion and prudence, answer him with all gentleness, serve him with devotion, keep silent when he is irritated, tolerate his defects with patience, have no eyes nor heart for another." In a girls' textbook of 1898, the lay Catholic writer Amélia Rodrigues said a wife's credo should be: "I dedicate myself entirely to the happiness and the honor of my husband. My life must be all abnegation, all obedience, all work."[26]

Only in marriage was sexuality divine and sanctioned. The church defined marriage as a remedy for lust. But the sexual repression of the church centered particularly on women's behavior. "In the streets you find nothing but sensuality and excesses of all stripes," priests preached in the sertão in 1900. They told horrible cautionary tales of adulterous women. However, the church was perhaps unsure in its condemnation of sexuality. Like everyone else, Catholics found medical metaphors irresistible (Mary was a "moral disinfectant"; divorce was a "plague" or a "virulent contagious disease"), and priests were correspondingly impressed by medical arguments that associated celibacy with ill health.[27] In one dispensation of the marriage impediments of an uncle and his niece, the petitioners pleaded "the unavoidable need of the bride to take on her new estate for the good of her health, as she is constantly affected by hysterical attacks, for which the physicians have prescribed marriage as the only specific remedy." The priest commenting on the case noted both their mutual affection and "the need for immediate marriage recognized by professionals." Ultimately, however, the clergy resisted medical arguments that sexual satisfaction was demanded in the interests of health. Dr. Alfredo Ferreira Magalhães lectured in 1912 at the Nossa Senhora da Victória secondary school on "eugenics," condemning tobacco and alcohol and assuring his audience that "no disease was caused by continence."[28]

From the church's point of view, its family morality was eternal, notwithstanding that the form of Christian marriage had changed significantly over the course of the Middle Ages and Catholic ritual for the celebration of marriage had only been solidly codified by the sixteenth-century Council of Trent. In two major encyclicals in 1880 and 1930, the church stated its doctrine on marriage and family in opposition to the secularization implied in civil marriage. Pope Leo XIII's *Arcanum* (1880) defended the spiritual nature of marriage, and opposed civil marriage and divorce. Pius XI's *Casti connubii* (1930) restated these themes, but attacked the legitimacy of erotic satisfaction, rejected birth control, and emphasized the "natural" roles of spouses and parents. Both these statements of doctrines counterposed the stability of Catholic doctrine to supposed false "progress" in sexual liberation or liberation from marriage.

The Church and Men

Like women's lives, men's activities often entailed some Christian symbolism or church affiliation. But while women's religiosity was commonly expressed in the private space of the home or the cloister, men's piety expanded into public spaces. Whereas women sometimes participated in street processions, the procession was the typical form of men's religiosity. Men accompanied the coffin on its *sahimento* to the burial ground, while the women stayed behind to sweep the house.[29] And it was mostly men who carried the images and banners of saints in processions. The procession itself may have enacted a symbolism of resignation and Christian humility in the face of the sacred, but men abased themselves in the street, women in the home.[30] Outside of the family, a religious brotherhood was still the most important affiliation for most men in the 1870's. The numerous brotherhoods, Third Orders of laymen associated with monastic orders, and charitable associations functioned as social clubs as well as mutual benefit associations and religious congregations.

But the decline of the irmandades after 1870 indicated the secularization of men's lives. An 1860 law authorized the chartering of associations, particularly mutual aid societies, along lines that closely resembled the organization of the brotherhoods. By the end of the nineteenth century, only 15 percent of those leaving estates mentioned that they belonged to irmandades, whereas 85 percent had claimed membership at the beginning of the century.[31] Even such prestigious associations as the Santa Casa da Misericórdia ceased to be centers of the elite of Bahia. Elite men who maintained membership as benefactors would no longer have considered it the vital symbol of status. In the early nineteenth century, the strongly Catholic matrix of social life may have inhibited the integration of Protestant British or German or North American merchants into Salvador society. By the turn of the twentieth century, however, many institutions and associations had become secular, allowing Protestant merchants to associate with Catholics without disadvantage. Some brotherhoods, such as the Conceição da Praia at the port, had always been primarily Portuguese. But now many of the traditional brotherhoods came to have a reputedly Portuguese membership. Prominent men turned to masonic lodges, to recreational clubs, to sports clubs, and to interest associations, not necessarily rejecting membership in a religious brotherhood, but no longer considering it central. In some Brazilian cities, masonic lodges organized within the shell of Catholic brotherhoods; in Bahia, the Udo Schloessner lodge organized openly.[32]

With the coming of the Republic, the linking of religion and civic life waned. Religious blessings, and masses of thanksgiving had marked many of the civic celebrations under the Empire. Elections themselves had typically been held in the parish church, the most useful public building. Even under the Republic, however, the civil authorities commissioned masses to celebrate important events. On the Bahian independence holiday of July 2d, following a mass of thanksgiving, a secular procession carried the symbolic statue of two Indian scouts who had aided the patriotic forces.

The Church and the Povo

The church had a mission to serve not only the upper classes but all of society. Its accommodations with slavery were notorious, but in however hypocritical and limited a way, it was the church of slaves as well as of free men.

The Brazilian church did not lead the abolitionist movement, but members of some of the orders, notably the Benedictines, did voluntarily free their slaves just before abolition. Tacitly the church's position amounted to support of slavery. Nonetheless, although accepting slavery, the church often criticized the treatment of slaves by their masters. The Bahian church's charter admonished masters who prevented their slaves from resting on Sunday, receiving religious instruction, or marrying. In a famous sermon to both masters and slaves in the chapel of the black brotherhood of Rosário in the seventeenth century, Padre Antônio Vieira warned masters that they were very likely enslaving their souls while obedient slaves were freeing theirs. In however perfunctory a way, the Catholic church did provide religious services to Bahian slaves, and did attempt the religious conversion (or at least the formal baptism) of the great numbers of African captives brought to Brazil before 1850.[33]

As a consequence of the openness and pervasiveness of the church, African religion in Bahia organized within the margins of Catholic practice. Originally established by small groups of slaves, African religions had spread throughout society by the late nineteenth century. Though a small clique of Africans had maintained a clandestine Muslim church, most attended the semisecret candomblé cult shrines, which held most of their public ceremonies in conjunction with Catholic saints' days and festivals. The less determinedly purist Afro-Bahians probably considered their additional devotions to the saints to be Christian practices; at the festival of Saint Lazarus, Bahians offered popcorn to the African saint Omolú, patron of smallpox.[34]

In a negative way, the entrance requirements of the Bahian Baptists for their working-class converts in the 1880's and 1890's give a sense of how ingrained "Catholic" observances were in daily life. Converts were refused baptism or expelled for going to séances or candomblés, for working on the Sabbath, even for associating with Presbyterians. But they were also excluded for wearing a rosary, being godparent in a Catholic baptism or allowing their children to be baptized, accompanying processions in the street, kissing images, working in a shop that made niches for saints' images, and the "idolatry" of making devotions to saints. Trying to keep their members apart from Catholic festivities, the Baptists encouraged them to celebrate Christmas on some day other than the worldly festival of December 25th.[35]

Despite its lack of priests to visit and practice in the countryside, the church's reach extended there indirectly. Most Bahians, particularly those in the countryside, observed a homemade set of folk religious practices, a little tradition that bound them loosely to the great tradition of Catholic Christianity. The folk Catholicism of Bahians consisted primarily of traditional personal rituals and symbols that had little to do with the clergy. Though virtually every family took their children to a chapel to be baptized, country folk would not necessarily have any further connection with church life-cycle rituals such as communion and confirmation, marriage, extreme unction, or burial. Instead, rural laymen would honor a saint's image in the home, pray at roadside shrines, walk in pilgrimages, and bury their own dead. Their Jesus was perhaps above all a cross of suffering. The most dynamic intrusion of the church into their routines came when, once every few years, they would hear a mission preacher on circuit. Then, the Franciscan or Capuchin preachers would spread an apocalyptic version of Christian fear and exaltation, emphasizing the burning horrors of divine punishment and the narrow hope of divine reward. Franciscans on missions to the sertão, around 1880–1900, would speak in the language of the povo against civil marriage: "Girl, if your daddy wants to marry you to some boy only by the civil, tell him No Sir, but don't fall into that sin!"[36]

In the eighteenth and nineteenth centuries, the church promoted a set of religious observances and symbols of its own that slowly gained acceptance among the Brazilian population. The cult of the Virgin Mary, which built upon familiar practices, did spread easily among the masses of laity. The cult of the Sacred Heart of Jesus gradually became part of the symbolism of the folk, and the church actively promoted it by authorizing prints, images, and medallions. The stations of the cross, observances especially tied to entering the church and attendance at mass, were also promoted. These might have encouraged a turn in the religious mood toward more focus on Jesus and his acts, but there is little indication that religious instruction or sophistication grew. The church may have discouraged festivals with "pagan" aspects after 1860, but the people continued to practice them.[37]

The church's criticism of folk practice was cautious and discreet, because there was always the possibility that superstition might give access to the supernatural. Everyone in Bahia knew of miraculous cures obtained through Our Lord of Bomfim or other saints, and priests encouraged grateful petitioners to contribute ex-votos to shrines in chapels. When miraculous gifts seemed to come from new places, the church was more wary. In Juazeiro de Ceará, north of Bahia, the church declined to authenticate the miraculous bleeding of the Host in Padre Cícero's congregation in 1889. Despite this, Juazeiro became a popular pilgrimage center. At all times, priests had to confront cures and benefits that people believed had followed consultation with quasi-Catholic *rezadeira* praying rituals, or with heterodox sorcerers and *curandeiro* healers. Judging the line between pious folk ritual and witchcraft required either vigilance and understanding, or else apathy and indifference, from priests.[38]

The Church and Forms of Patronage

Christianity provided an ethic for many facets of social relations, but one of the most notable areas in which Catholic symbolism reinforced social relations was in its modeling for patron-client relations. On the one hand, both the Christian ethic of universal love and the sense of God's omnipotence were antihierarchical. The latter, in particular, encouraged a sense of the common and leveled abasement of all mortals as sinners before God's judgment. On the other hand, the cult of the saints as accessible intermediaries between a remote God in Heaven and his faithful on Earth, or as powerful spirits in their own right, conditioned a vision of social power as something hierarchical, personified, many-layered, and manipulable by subordinates.[39]

In particular, devotion to the saints may have authorized active social roles for women, because the compact of worshipper and saint modeled for the relation of client and patron better than any other characteristic activity of women, except perhaps their relations with servants. The supplicant directed a petition to the saint, who could dispatch some matters and would intercede in others with a distant deity who was not directly approachable. In return for the favor, the petitioner usually offered the saint a *promessa*, a promise to perform some act of penance, devotion, or charity. The model of the promessa and bargaining that Catholic religiosity offered Brazilians taught them, and reinforced for them, the processes of patronage and favor that emanated from extended family relations and permeated daily life. Religious devotions themselves may have isolated women in a private sphere, but the range of religious practice embraced most roles in society.[40]

Turn-of-the-century Brazil did not develop any profound theologians or Catholic social thinkers. But it did foster the novelist Machado de Assis, a profound Catholic skeptic. Machado analyzed the Catholic conscience and the Brazilian Catholic ethic in many works. In his novel *Dom Casmurro* (1900), for example, he satirized the contradictory sacredness and worldliness of the promessa. At the outset of the novel, Dona Carmo, Bento's mother, grateful for his delivery from a childhood illness, has promised

God to deliver him to the church, to make him a priest. Now an adolescent seminarian and deeply in love with Capitú, Bento would like to ask his mother to let him leave the seminary, but knows that she could hardly dare to break her bargain. Enlisting the intercession of a family dependent, and finally even the cooperation of the priest who is his mother's spiritual counselor, Bento gets everyone together in a scheme to edge out of the bargain with God: just as Abraham could substitute a lamb for the sacrifice of Isaac, so Bento's mother can pay to prepare another boy for the priesthood in place of Bento, and thus still satisfy her *promessa*. In this novel, as in many of his works, Machado de Assis plotted out the debasement of charity and the destruction of individual character that resulted from the manipulation of other people as tokens of power, whether as slaves or masters, patrons or clients.

In the gateway of the Passeio, a beggar extended his hand toward us. José Dias went on, but I thought of Capitú and of the seminary. I took two pennies out of my pocket and gave them to the beggar. He kissed the coins. I asked him to pray for me, that I might satisfy all my desires.
"Yes, my devout one."
"My name is Bento," I added to enlighten him.[41]

Through the ritual of baptism, the church supervised godparenthood, the most fundamental relationship of patronage in Bahian society.[42] From the point of view of church doctrine on baptism, the *padrinho* or *madrinha*, the godparent, assumed the spiritual responsibility of bringing their infant *afilhado* into the church and educating her or him in Christian doctrine. This was the purpose of the ritual. But the church also recognized that sacred kinship joined the parents, the godparents, the infant, and even the officiating priest. Priests recorded the names of godparents and parents. And the church retained some small power to disqualify individuals as godparents. Marriage was secularized by the state after 1890, but baptism was not. The government required the civil registry, but civil law did not or could not endow the witnesses to the civil register with the status of godparents.[43]

Finally, Bahian priests operated directly as patrons and political bosses, and the church was a major agency for social organization and social control. Religious brotherhoods and priests were involved in many of the riots and disturbances of the turbulent early nineteenth century, sometimes because their interests were directly involved. Priests intervened directly in the affairs of irmandades, counseled their members, and oversaw their spiritual development. In the late Empire and under the Republic, individual priests continued to be influential as politicians and bosses. Monsenhor Hermelino Leão of Macaúbas was a major force in the boss politics of the Lavras diamond district, and one of the senior incumbents of the state senate during the Old Republic. But as a boss, Leão represented his family's interests as much as he did any institutional church presence.[44]

Nation-Building, Ecclesiastical Reforms, and Secularization

From the 1850's on, the Brazilian church reformed and Romanized itself in order to overcome its inertial stagnation, to remedy its lack of influence in society, and to forge a more active social role. The Catholic church occupied an ambiguous position in the nineteenth-century Brazilian Empire. It was at once the "official religion" and one of the stepchildren of the Brazilian bureaucracy, less cherished than the regional militias. For all that it held a monopoly in so many realms, the church was commonly thought to have little influence. Within the church hierarchy, tensions and competition over power were endemic, showing up as murders within religious orders and riots in religious retreats, slave rebellions on plantations, and lawsuits over convent debts. Many priests were the sons of aristocratic landlord families of independent means, and many priests were patronized by plantation or religious brotherhood chaplaincies that were not controlled by the hierarchy.[45]

Lack of priests and money made it almost impossible for the clergy to serve the peasant and slave masses of the nation. Emperor Pedro II, ruling from 1840 to 1889, created very few new dioceses and parishes, and those that he did open often lay vacant for lack of candidates to fill them. In 1872 there were 282 religious in Bahia, and not all of them parish priests, to serve a dispersed population of 1,400,000. Over the course of the early and mid nineteenth century, the province's population had shifted westward, inland, into huge, sparsely populated frontier parishes. Even devout barons and coronéis in the countryside might not see a priest for months at a time.[46]

Even where priests were present in towns and cities, they had little moral authority. Attempting to explain the lack of clerical influence, most scholars have followed contemporary observers and blamed the moral laxity of the clergy, which manifested itself in gambling and the wearing of ordinary clothes rather than the clerical habit. In Salvador, the monastic orders were wracked with scandals, such as accusations of embezzlement and murder among the Calced Carmelites.[47]

"Moral laxity" showed clearest in the almost universal violation of the vow of chastity by both lower and upper clergy. The North American missionaries James Fletcher and Daniel Kidder reported in 1866 that the "priests, to some extent, owe the loss of their power to their shameful immorality" and commented that a Bahian, looking for a chaplain for the female workers at his factory, had found all five candidates immoral, the last being "in open concubinage." The English consul James Wetherell concluded in 1860 that religion in Bahia had declined because of the bad character of priests: "The men in most instances, are, I fear, Deists, and the confessional has driven numerous families from the practices of the church." The senhores de engenho, he believed, had less interest in religion than before.[48]

These comments were accurate about the facts of clerical concubinage. In the country parishes most priests openly kept mistresses and families. In the urban chapters they were usually only slightly more discreet. About half of the priests in Salvador had children in the late nineteenth century. But it may have been mistaken of the foreign observers to assume that lack of celibacy among the Brazilian clergy greatly alienated their parishioners. On the contrary, a great many of the devout laity regarded the requirement of celibacy as a pointless rigor that the papacy should relax; they saw priests as its "victims." Indeed, the priest Diogo Antônio Feijó, when minister of justice in 1831, had support for his proposals to have the government lift the discipline of celibacy for Brazilian priests. But entering consensual unions was among the most flagrant violations of clerical discipline.[49]

Pedro II apparently used his power of appointment as much as possible to promote celibate and morally impeccable bishops, and to urge them to reform the church. He encouraged the education of dynamic young priests abroad at the special Pio Nono seminary for Latin American priests established in Rome in 1858. He and his ministers authorized what were apparently anticlerical measures on these grounds. Most notably, his minister Nabuco de Araujo justified the 1855 suppression of novitiates in all monastic orders by the need to extinguish their "immorality."[50]

Among the bishops who also determined to reform the clergy was Dom Romualdo Seixas, archbishop of Bahia from 1828 to 1860. He campaigned to reform the priesthood of the province, building up the seminary, requiring priests to wear their habits, and organizing regular religious instruction. Under his administration, the seminaries were reformed. The upper seminary reopened in 1834 with a much more antiregalist, pro-Roman ideology, teaching an orthodox, antimodern curriculum. The upper seminary usually had between 25 and 50 students in the late nineteenth century, though it produced only five to ten ordinations a year.[51]

In promoting the education of an elite of Brazilian clergy, Pedro II unintentionally spread the ultramontanism of Pius IX's Catholic revival and led to the polarization of political and ecclesiastical elites. The combative dogmatism of the Vatican in the late nineteenth century under Pius IX was the opposite of the relaxed, tolerant modus vivendi between the church and its society in Brazil. Brazilian priests educated abroad and foreign priests sent to Brazil brought this ideology and spirit of intransigent Catholic militancy to a society that was little prepared for it.

Dom Romualdo and the other reformist bishops that Pedro II appointed failed at reining in the licentious parish priests. Concubinage remained the norm for the lower clergy in rural Bahian parishes through the 1920's. Even then, Bahia's Cardinal Dom Augusto, who had been a bishop in the backlands and knew the situation firsthand, was at best able to get priests to agree to live apart from their children. However, the nineteenth-century reformers successfully pressured the upper clergy by blocking promotions to cathedral chapters of priests who led notoriously immoral lives. And reformers were also able to reshape the curriculum of seminaries to train a more militant generation of priests. By the end of the nineteenth century, Bahian priests were more discreet about celibacy, and better educated, than they had been before. As the church controlled their activities, and as landlords and religious brotherhoods reduced autonomous chaplaincies, they became more dependent on the meager salaries of parishes or on other posts within the hierarchy.[52]

If the Romanizing Brazilian bishops failed in their internal reform of the clergy, they did succeed in provoking the Question of the Bishops, a dispute with the Freemasons that exposed the contradictions between the increasingly Romanizing church and a political elite that was regalist when it was not actively anticlerical. It began in 1872, when the young bishop Dom Vital of Olinda, who had studied in Rome, ordered Catholic brotherhoods to expel Masons. The Trindade brotherhood refused and appealed to the government, which ordered Dom Vital to lift his interdict. He refused, as did another bishop, Dom Macedo of Pará. For their disobedience to the Crown, they were tried and sentenced to four years at hard labor in 1874. The emperor commuted the sentence to one year, and in 1875 a new ministry gave the bishops amnesty.[53]

The affair caused no profound religious division within the upper-class laity. In Salvador a petition circulated in favor of the bishops got 2,501 signatures from women, but only 71 from men. Few laymen spoke up in favor of the church on this issue. The devout Manuel Victorino Pereira, brother of a priest, was one of the few politicians to support Dom Macedo. But the affair exposed the magnitude of the split between the government and the church. The Question of the Bishops was interpreted by many contemporaries as the beginning of a split between church and monarchy that contributed to the overthrow of the Empire in 1889.[54]

For other reasons, the radical decade of the 1880's saw Brazil move into a near-revolutionary mode, as abolitionists turned to direct action against slavery, slaves mutinied on plantations, army officers resisted civilian control, and republican radicals called for an end to the monarchy. This was a bad decade for the church, as the abolition issue was out of its control. The church showed no inclination to challenge or anticipate government policy on slavery.[55] The Masonic movement and secularized sects such as positivism attracted many men in the upper class. Petty disputes between the church and Masons, and the church and the government, continued until the end of the Empire. Priests and bishops were stoned and jeered in the pulpit or attacked on the street. At the time of one such incident in Rio in 1876, the young Bahian lawyer Rui Barbosa fled home to marry his fiancée, for he expected that after the forthcoming publication of his translation of the Masons' anticlerical tract *O Papa e o Concílio*, no priest would consent to perform a wedding for him.[56] On its side, the church resisted the emperor by postponing the competitions for lifetime sinecures as parish priests (*vigários collados*). Rather than let the emperor fill the posts, taking the influence of political patrons into account, the bishops declined to open nominations and instead appointed their own candidates as temporary parish priests (*vigários encomendados*). By 1887, out of 190 parishes in Bahia, 124 were filled by encomendados or other interim appointments.[57]

The republican coup of 1889 separated church and state. The 1891 constitution omitted mention of God in the preamble, then went on to declare the separation of state and church. It gave all religions the right to open worship, and it forbade religious education in public schools. It secularized jurisdiction over cemeteries. But it relented at the expropriation of church property that characterized disestablishment in other Catholic nations in Latin America. Its most punitive anticlerical measure was primarily symbolic: it forbade members of the clergy bound by a vow of obedience to vote.

Though they believed in the principle of the establishment of Catholicism, and although they missed privileges such as authority over marriage, Brazilian bishops begrudgingly welcomed the republican separation of church and state because it lifted the imperial government's restrictions on their expansion. The most farseeing strategist of the church, Padre Júlio Maria, drafted a collective pastoral of the Brazilian bishops in 1890 that deplored the secularization of the nation but recognized new opportunities for the church. In an essay written in 1900, he reinterpreted the Empire as a period of Babylonian captivity, in which, under the guise of state patronage, the church had declined. Though its laws were impious, the Republic had emancipated the church. Júlio Maria pointed to the example of the United States, where the Catholic church had grown, while it was stunted in Brazil. He reviewed the regrowth of the church since 1889 and saw promise for religious revival. In subsequent pastoral letters during the

Old Republic, the bishops reversed the tone of their collective pastoral. But the clergy in general profited from the opportunities that the separation allowed them to build and reorganize the church, to create new dioceses and revive the monastic orders.[58]

In 1889 the most eloquent sign of the plight of the church in Bahia was the emptiness of the monasteries. The 1855 reforms had forbidden the regular orders to admit novices; the last Franciscan had professed in 1846. By the end of the Empire, attrition had so reduced their numbers that only three elderly monks occupied the huge Franciscan monastery opposite the cathedral. Only six Carmelites lived in their monastery, and a handful of Benedictines in theirs. In 1853 there had been thirty-three nuns in the convent of the Poor Clares; in 1890 there were only six.[59]

After 1889 the rescue of the religious orders from extinction spearheaded the rapid organizational revitalization of the church. The immediate importation of a wave of foreign clergy saved old orders and established new ones. Six German Franciscans arrived in 1892, two Belgian Benedictines in 1894, four French Ursulines in 1895, a Salesian brother in 1897, two Spanish Carmelites and two more Salesians in 1899. These new foreign religious quickly—and not always gently—took control of the orders from the aging Brazilian abbots and abbesses. They reopened novitiates, founded charities and workshops, and started publishing houses.[60]

The revitalization of Catholic education by foreign teaching orders had a great impact on the upper classes. Ursulines and Marists expelled from France in 1904 and Jesuits expelled from Portugal in 1910 founded schools that soon became the best in Bahia: Colégio Nossa Senhora das Mercês, Colégio Nossa Senhora da Victória, and Colégio Antônio Vieira. Students were drilled in a new "high" Catholicism, in which they were indoctrinated in a stricter morality and participated in ceremonies such as the jubilee of the proclamation of the dogma of the Immaculate Conception, 1854–1904. Most notably, the elite Colégio Antônio Vieira, founded by exiled Jesuits in 1911, became one of the intellectual centers of the state. It became a powerful formative influence on subsequent generations of the Bahian elite.[61]

The number of both regular and secular clergy in the state of Bahia more than doubled, from 288 in 1872 to 698 in 1920. Much of the increase was in foreign religious, who were 2 percent in 1872 and 30 percent in 1920. In the city of Salvador, where the teaching orders concentrated, over half of the male religious were foreigners. The growth and Europeanization of the Bahian church mirrored what was happening throughout Brazil. Foreign clergy constituted 45 percent of all religious in Brazil by 1920.[62]

Another dynamic archbishop, Dom Jerônimo Thomé da Silva (1894–1924), led the revival of the Bahian church. While most Bahian archbishops had never left Salvador, Dom Jerônimo traveled extensively through the backlands of the state, visiting remote parishes. He once again emphasized the reform of the parish clergy. He convened them at congresses, organized classes and lectures for priests in the capital, established scholarships for study in Rome, and raised funds for parish church ornaments. Yet there were limits to the numbers of priests who could be recruited, and limits to the hierarchy's ability to take priests out of familial roles, whether as fathers of families or simply as the heads of the families of widowed sisters.[63]

The increase in the church's attention to the rechristianization of country folk was dramatic, but the emphasis on orthodox practice for the "decent" families in the cities was just as important. If the masses were attracted by Protestantism, the elite were seduced by spiritism and positivism. From the 1890's forward, religious associations designed to increase devotions and religious participation in the liturgical church proliferated. The old religious brotherhoods might have declined, but new female-led associations, such as the Daughters of Mary, and parents' associations supporting Catholic schools emerged.[64]

The change showed, perhaps, in the shift in the symbols of women's devotions. The favorite images families left to their heirs in the backlands county of Itapicurú in the nineteenth century were of traditional objects of devotion: Santo Antônio, N.S. da Piedade, Santa Ana, the crucifix, and N.S. da Conceição. In Rui Barbosa's urban family in the early twentieth century, the souvenirs were of newer cults, particularly French ones: "N.D. de Lourdes Priez Pour Nous," dated 1891, lace-trimmed, on the back of a print of a girl kneeling, looking up at the apparition of the Virgin; Mary praying in front of a chalice engraved with French script; Mary guided by a boy Jesus through thornbushes, with a French dedication on the back; N.S. do Bom Conselho, with mother and child inside about to nurse; a French card showing a boy Jesus pointing out a word to a kneeling boy, dedicated on the back, "souvenir for grandma"; Jesus feeding doves, with the motto "La Nourriture Celeste"; a French child kneeling in front of Jesus holding tablets, with the motto, "Gravez, O Jesus, Votre Loi sur Mon Coeur," with white rays passing between the child's flat heart and Jesus's exposed Sacred Heart in flames, dated 1910.[65]

It was not only elite women who were shown new cults: priests tried to spread the cult of Saint Joseph as worker and as the chief of the Holy Family to the working middle class and the povo; they tried to encourage the Mês de Maria and Coronation of the Virgin; and to discourage shepherds' pageants (*bailes pastoris*) and other "folkloric" festivals.[66]

By the 1920's, if not sooner, middle-class Bahian women were practicing the new devotions along with the traditional ones. For example, in

1926, a spinster in Salvador left small legacies for the Church of Nossa Senhora do Rosário (600$), to Nossa Senhora das Dôres (100$), and to her godchildren. She divided among them her images: N.S. da Conceição, Santa Amélia, Sacred Heart of Jesus, Santa Luzia, "Deus Menino," Heart of Mary, N.S. do Rosário, Jesus, "His Mother," Joseph, N.S. de Lourdes in silver, and, in wood, a small Santo Antônio.[67]

Women's Duties, Amélia Rodrigues, and Catholic Social Action

As the Brazilian church reorganized and expanded its ambit, it seemed to the church's moralists that one of the major obstacles to religion's penetration of the upper classes was "modernity." The secular mentality of modernity took many forms, but it was most obviously manifested in daily life by the changes in the behavior of decent ladies. For example, criticism of "immodesty" in dress, as a symbol of sexual immodesty, occupied the attention of both church and secular moralists. In Dom Macedo's instructions to young girls in 1875, he had counseled "much modesty in all her actions" in first place. Modesty meant primarily seclusion in the home, but also the "abhorrence of vanities in dress and adornments." By the twentieth century, if not earlier, church criticism of women's fashion addressed not only its luxury, but also its erotic incitement. Fashions, but particularly the fashion of short hair in women, became the demonic symbol of sexual liberation for religious writers after World War I. Bathing suits became the focus of criticism in the 1930's and 1940's.[68]

The nineteenth-century Brazilian church had been so intimately tied to families as they were—Freyre has said that Brazilian Catholicism became almost a domestic religion—that almost any change in family roles would affect it. Probably the change in the family in the first decades of the Old Republic that seemed most threatening to the church was the emergence of women in public life, which contradicted much of the traditional message of the church about their roles. In Bahia more women of the upper and middle class worked as schoolteachers and clerks; women attended the medical school and even the law school. Family customs also changed: seclusion in the home lightened; new patterns of courtship put girls out in society. These changes in work, private life, and public life could be seen either as the disintegration of a patriarchal order or, as some feminists did, as progress that rescued Brazilian women from a medieval oppression.[69]

Whether degeneration or progress, the changes had in common that they increased women's presence in the public sphere, outside the family circle. By putting women out in public, they decreased the difference of women. They put women in the same activities as men. This juxtaposition threatened the sense that men's power was a function of natural differences between the sexes, and weakened the legitimacy of any claim that the "duties" of men and women were dictated by nature rather than by social convention.

From 1890 through 1930 the Brazilian church responded to the unsettling of the natural order of the sexes by adopting the European church's agenda of reaction against modernity. To some extent that agenda was inappropriate to Brazil. The reaction against divorce, for instance, seems in retrospect to have been out of proportion to the threat. Although divorce had been made slightly easier by civil law after 1890, it was still not as common as in Europe or the United States. Yet the Brazilian church adopted criticism of divorce as part of its program as enthusiastically as it took up defense against the equally insignificant Protestant and communist threats.[70]

The principal concrete measure of the Bahian church was to restate the proper duties of women more emphatically. Alarmed by the great increase in the influence of "impious" newspapers and magazines, Brazilian bishops began to call for an expansion of the Catholic press. They usually envisioned Catholic daily newspapers and journals of opinion. But they also understood that "only the saints read our newspapers" and tried to establish a popular Catholic press and, later, a Catholic cinema. In Bahia, a shower of tracts, circulars, series of readings, and almanacs aimed at the middle-class reading public, especially the female public, addressed the question of women and the family in the 1910's and 1920's. Probably the most important publication was the weekly newspaper *Mensageiro da Fé*, founded in 1903 by Bahian Franciscans.[71]

Its annual almanac, the *Almanach do Mensageiro da Fé*, circulated to as wide a public as any Catholic publication in the state. The almanac was a potpourri of genre lithographs, photographic views of local landmarks, stories, cartoons, and essays. It attempted to integrate the activities of the church with the activities of polite society: a typical edition included an article on how to interpret the crimps in the corners of calling cards correctly, an ode to the aviator Alberto Santos-Dumont, and an article publicizing a new secondary school, in whose boarding section, "the Marista Brothers make an effort to substitute for the Family, forming their students in the politesse of demeanor and in the decorum with which they should behave, not forgetting that their important mission is to make them love Religion and country, developing, fortifying, and perfecting all the faculties of the soul." The *Almanach* generally presented a genteel, rather than flagellant or apocalyptic, religiosity. It had little of the melodramatic iconography of sacred hearts in flames and pietàs so widespread at the time, and almost nothing of Bahian folk Catholic practices, with their symbolism of the cross of suffering.[72]

Among the generally uplifting pieces in the *Almanach*, there were a number that presented a model for the family and women's place in it. Perhaps most obvious was the lithographic frontispiece of the 1917 edition, "The Holy Family," which showed Mary sitting and sewing, looking at a robust ten-year-old Jesus handing an angle to the carpenter Joseph standing at his workbench. Different from their readers only because of the auras around their heads and their biblical costume, they exemplified the ideal of industrious and cooperative domesticity. Typical of the almanac was a poem in which a poet chided his youthful romantic stereotypes of love and said it was enough that his muse be

> a good woman, of serene soul,
> that she understand people, and as well as sew,
> know how to arrange the comfortable scene
> of a good lunch, and a better supper.

Yet rising above the general tone of philistine good humor, one essay addressed "Counsel of a Father" to a daughter on the eve of her wedding and painted a more somber picture of family life. He implied that she would have to live at her husband's parents' house and accommodate herself to them, warned that the honeymoon would soon end, and told her to be obedient above all. If she ever wished to scold her husband, she should do so in private; if she suspected infidelity, she should hold it back, continue to woo him, and not be demanding.[73]

Such satirical or serious affirmation of the subordination of wives was not the characteristic theme of the Catholic press. Its major theme was the mother's formative influence on children. Like medical literature, the Catholic popular literature urged mothers to care for their children directly, dispensing with the possibly dangerous mediation of nursemaids. An essay in *Lar Cathólico* in 1923 argued that mothers cannot be substituted for, leaving children to "mercenary nursemaids"; if they are, the children may grow hard and flinty-hearted, like the men of Plato's Republic or the women of Tolstoy's "Kreutzer Sonata." In the opinion of this author, what threatened to make women abandon their children was going into politics. Women in politics debased the image of motherhood and sacrifice offered by the Virgin. Other examples of this theme abounded in Catholic writings. In many voices and tones, the Catholic press argued that the role of mother was an active and adequate sphere for engaging the talents of women, and some offered it explicitly as the Christian alternative to feminism.[74]

Another important response of the church to the changes in women was to endorse the establishment of a Women's Catholic Social Action movement. Modeled after the French Women's Catholic Social Action, which was founded in 1890 and had inspired similar organizations throughout Europe, the Liga das Senhoras Cathólicas Bahianas (later the Liga Cathó-lica das Senhoras Brasileiras) was founded in 1909 to provide an explicitly antifeminist organization for women's action in the public sphere. In a 1915 speech, its founder Amélia Rodrigues explained what was different about the league:

> Pious associations act only in the circle of devotion, of individual sanctification. Their statutes do not set them any other task. If some of them, such as, for example, the Daughters of Mary, here or there establish and support small newspapers, schools, or catechism classes, sign petitions against divorce and other things, this is not a widespread movement.

What the league could do, she said, was to have an educational effect on women, "pulling the Brazilian woman out of the intellectual swoon that weakens her and makes her a slave of the indecent dress pattern and the dangerous moviehouse." Like the European nations that had mobilized women to prepare for war, the Brazilian church could tap "the *new force*, the immense force of the heart, the immense force of love" that women possessed.[75]

Yet as Rodrigues acknowledged, it proved difficult for the league to mobilize antifeminist women. Founded in 1909, it did not arouse much interest until World War I. Even then, it never found a style of action that could sustain it, and it suffered from a lack of commitment by its members. At its best moments it could fill the lecture hall of the Benedic-tine monastery with an audience of society ladies and a few men. It never achieved its goals of establishing censorship commissions and controlling Carnival. It did most by circulating its journal among ladies of the Bahian middle class. The organization dwindled, and in 1919 Rodrigues moved on to found another women's association in Rio, the Alliança Feminina.[76]

The writings of Amélia Rodrigues illustrate the contradictions inherent in the reactionary project of mobilizing women against their own mobili-zation. Born in 1861, the daughter of a small farmer in the hinterland of Salvador, she showed talent as a poet and was given a primary school job in the capital in 1891. Her early poems included some abolitionist verses such as the short poem "Verso e reverso" (1886), which counterpoints the lights, smells, and sounds of the birthday party of a planter's daughter with the darkness of the slaves languishing outside in the stocks. But from the time of her transfer to the capital, she wrote only religious poetry, and her career came to be oriented by her religious commitment. This re-mained a constant as the development of her ideas reflected her changing understanding of women's identities and roles.[77]

Her 1898 novel *Mestra e mãe* (Teacher and Mother), adopted in Bahian schools as a sixth-grade reader, was the strongest statement of her ideology. It combines religious and patriotic themes to offer a model for girls' identities. The novel is a series of episodes in the maturing of Euphrosina, the orphaned daughter of a landowner, under the tutelage of a wise schoolmistress, Maria das Mercês. It is set on an estate to which an old priest has retired and where he has gathered landless tenants, "domesticating" them under his benevolent, theocratic reign. The structure of the book is a series of instructive episodes, each concluding with a moralizing dialogue between Maria das Mercês and the girls.[78]

The ideal is the formation of a healthy, practical girl, and a principal symbolic opposition is the contrast of the cities and the healthy countryside. At the level of manners, this is reflected in the contrast between the "anti-hygienic," superficial education of city girls and a solid rural education. The good old priest says of a girl bound for boarding school:

She'll come back from there with her hair curled, corseted, speaking French, singing Italian arias, embroidering little cushions, but not knowing how to darn a sock or salt a soup. . . . I am an enemy of bad schools and china doll girls. I want woman to be a housewife, modest, hardworking. The strong woman that I read of in the Scriptures. Is that going against Progress? Oh well. But I think that to take woman out of the place that God and nature set for her isn't progressing, it's retrogressing.[79]

Thus, Euphrosina grows from a good girl into a healthy young woman and eventually marries well, while her foils, the spoiled daughters of the impious diamond merchant Botelho, grow up useless and make disastrous matches.

The principal concern of the book is to show how women fit into the main task of society, to build a religious and civic order. One model is the elderly, widowed schoolmarm who teaches the girls the virtues such as obedience (above all), order, humility, and forgiveness, and warns of vices such as pride, vanity, lying, gluttony, ignorance, and superstition. The role of the schoolteacher clearly offers women an opportunity to act as missionaries in the spread of religion that will strengthen the country, but outside of that, the question that one girl asks after a civic ceremony is quite pertinent: "Can women be patriots?" Answering the question, Maria das Mercês gives the crucial doctrine of the book for women:

Women cannot, it is true, take up arms to defend their nation, nor go to the assemblies to discuss political and financial questions, to legislate the codes, etc., but from them spring the soldiers, the ministers, the legislators, the government and the governed. It is they who educate and form the character of those who are to be the citizens of the nation . . . and all this is born and grows in the family, and the majority of all this goes, so to speak, from the mother's hands into the midst of society.

As the priest says to Maria das Mercês, mouthing the title of the book, "the teacher who doesn't become a mother and the mother who doesn't become a teacher fail in the duty that God and society impose on them."[80]

The essence of a woman's duty in marriage, just as in motherhood, is to restrain and subordinate herself. Mary is the best model of all virtues and furthermore is a shelter, refuge, and consolation. As Euphrosina matures, she is, to her surprise, sought in marriage by Doctor Guilherme, the son of a neighboring landowner. Her engagement begins in obedience, for she asks the advice of her elders rather than her girlfriends, and she agrees with the opinion of her father, who has already decided in favor of the match. Furthermore, Doctor Guilherme has done the right thing by "observing" Euphrosina for a long time before deciding to ask her father, making sure that her air of docility is not a hypocritical mask. Rejecting the idealization of married life, Maria das Mercês warns her that marriage is not a dance, but often a great disillusionment, that "between the fiancé and the husband there lies the distance between a dream and reality," and that her life must be one of abnegation, obedience, and work. Euphrosina's marriage promises well, of course, because she has already learned her duty as a housewife: to watch over the kitchen and the hygiene of the household, taking care of the life and health of its members, just as the husband's duty is to defend the house.[81]

To contrast with Euphrosina's promise, the novel ends as the Botelho girls provide a grim example of a bad family. Sr. Botelho is murdered by his slaves while taking a hoard of diamonds to the city, and the impoverished widow and daughters bear up poorly under their trial. In the city, the vain Augusta Botelho marries a boy she has met at a dance without her mother's consent, and after two years they separate. Having neglected their studies, the Botelho girls do not have the protection offered by the possibility of becoming schoolteachers, and they are thus reduced to being dependents of their relatives.[82]

The early twentieth century saw some change in Amélia Rodrigues's ideology. She encouraged less domestic, more militant, roles for women. It was only in 1907, more attuned to the social question, that she urged women to come out of their homes. In a speech inaugurating the Association of Ladies of Maria Auxiliadora, she offered the outlines of a new model for women, shaped in reaction to the agenda of feminism. Identifying men and women respectively with the forces of the head and of the heart, she warned that nature had marked that division of forces. The Brazilian woman was still "the queen of the hearth and the angel of sacrifice and tenderness," and she should let the ferment of feminism pass by outside of Brazil. But women could act in two ways. They could be the power behind the thrones of men's achievements in politics, commerce, science, industry, and the arts. Or they could do battle in the field of charity, in which women excelled men. "The beneficial action of the Catholic woman should not be limited to the narrow circle of the family," she said, citing the Salesian countess of San Marco. Like Brazilian men imitating European progress, women should follow the European example.[83]

The decisive differences between the neighborhood good deeds displayed as examples by the characters of *Mestra e mãe* and this new model of charitable action were its form of organization and its scope. Informal and individual charity, like any act of piety, was commendable, but women's action had to take a different form to address the issues that began to interest Rodrigues. In 1909 she founded the Liga das Senhoras Cathólicas Bahianas and became editor of its journals, *Paladina* and *A Voz*. She hoped to forge a missionary movement of women that would join other militant Catholic organizations to restore Catholic predominance in society.

The special kind of social influence that Catholic women should exert was an effort to reverse the changes in customs and morality that were corrupting Brazilian youth. On the one hand, these changes seemed most obviously to derive from foreign examples of a false progress: "Until a certain time childrearing was severe in Brazilian families and it seems also in those of other places. Later came progress to say that the severity was excessive (on some points it really was) and then we opened the way for all the liberties in this regard, without judgment, without selection, blindly."[84] Yet, on the other hand, some of the changes in customs seemed to have developed inside Brazil, and within decent society rather than among the libertine colored populace. In 1915 Amélia Rodrigues spoke out urging Bahian women to join their voices to those of Catholics from around Brazil to condemn the most blatant and concentrated expression of disorder, Carnival. Speaking during Lent, she reminded Catholics of the mourning of European civilization, blackened by war, and contrasted it with the childishness of the dancing Brazilian populace, "suffering from moral rickets." This Carnival had included, not only the populace, but also "genteel señoritas, the angels of the family, the palest lilies of the garden of honor, of virtue, of Bahian decorum," who had left their wings at home, put on costumes, and danced on "the open decorated streetcars where the electric light streamed down," going through the city, some of them "dancing the *maxixe*, the immoral dance of women without pride," and coming back late at night "shouting . . . leveled with those unfortunates of the street with whom they never level themselves on any day." This exhibition led her to ask "how had the old rigid standards of Brazilian families gone so far astray?" and to wonder what would become of the family with such early exposure of children to lewdness. She concluded by urging mothers to organize harmless diversions during Carnival to occupy their children.[85]

During World War I, Amélia Rodrigues changed her position for the third time. She apparently stretched her vision of the proper sphere of action for women. She was clearly impressed by the mobilization of women in Germany and France. "Woman nowadays has ceased to be a machine and become in certain areas capable of thinking and acting on her own." In 1915 she attacked the feminism that turned women into ridiculous, forward suffragettes in the streets. However, by 1918 she had cut herself off from the foundering Catholic Ladies, and in 1919 she announced the formation of the Women's Alliance, Aliança Feminina, based in Rio, which would be modeled on the Ligue Patriotique des Françaises. In an interview she explained that the alliance would be a Catholic institution dedicated to the education of women, the cleansing of the theater and cinema, the purification of customs in the family, the development of patriotism, and the protection of workers. It would also "fight for civil and commercial equality, and for other feminist ideas." The sort of feminism she meant, she hastened to say, was one that would not sidetrack women from their natural mission. Woman would remain in the home, as an enlightened companion of man, able if necessary to work. This feminism sought to open all careers to womankind without "masculinizing her." Rodrigues, formerly opposed to granting the vote to women because she believed that domestic duties were enough, said she had lately been swayed by arguments in favor of votes for women. She believed that most Brazilian women had very little civic sense and would have to be prepared for the vote. The Aliança itself would stay out of politics and work through the schools, lectures, and the press.[86]

By the end of the war Rodrigues was thus eager to coopt the label and some of the agenda of feminism, while continuing to attack other varieties of it. In a late playscript written two years before her death in 1926, she again satirized whatever in feminism exceeded her limits as an absurd inversion of roles. Here she portrayed a "feminist" family in which the husband stays at home, bungling the administration of the servants and finally putting on an apron and trying to cook a meal himself. Meanwhile, his cigar-smoking wife bungles her career as a lawyer. Ironically, the court system is shown to be unsuitable to women mainly because it is thoroughly corrupt. She loses an important case because her antagonist's lawyer knows how to cultivate the favor of the judge.[87]

Other writers for the Catholic press in the early twentieth century used the same strategy as Rodrigues. They criticized any innovation in women's roles as role inversion, while tentatively endorsing activity seemingly related to traditional domestic roles: for example, a medical career could be accepted more easily than a scientific or legal one.[88]

The new identity that the reactionary Catholic feminists began to define for women was not that of grande dame or traditional housewife, but rather that of Catholic missionary. The role they praised in their literature and practiced in the activities of Catholic Action groups went beyond the traditional scope of Bahian women. Whether they participated in public charitable activities or remained in the home as housewives shaping the characters of their children, the new ideology cast these roles in the vocabulary of public militancy.

While the clergy and Catholic intellectuals often spoke of "the crisis of the family" and the need to reevangelize society after 1890, in practice their pastoral efforts and propaganda focused on women, not men. This was probably mostly because women were the traditional constituency of the clergy and were accessible to persuasion. As one Catholic author observed of men in 1914: "When Sunday mass is heard in any church whatsoever, one sees immediately that women are more conscientious in carrying out their duties to God than men. Because of all those present, 90 percent or more are of the female sex."[89]

It was the deathbed scenes of men of the elite that Bahian memorialists dramatized as demonstrating either dramatic returns to the church and the crucifix or else stoic refusal to believe in an afterlife.[90] At times the Bahian church did attempt to evangelize men. Within the Catholic secondary schools, organizations such as the Congregação Mariana Académica tried to encourage young men to keep sexually pure and to develop their religious understanding. Padre Luiz Gonzaga Cabral organized a Círculo Católico de Estudos da Mocidade Académica, and briefly published the *Arquivo Mariano Académico.* Students at the Colégio Antônio Vieira and Colégio N.S. da Victória founded the Liga para a Restauração dos Ideaes in 1926. Members pledged love of study, frequent communion, and avoidance of dirty words, bad company, unseemly reading, degrading entertainments, quarrels and fights. Many Bahian gentlemen cooperated with the charities of the Salesian brothers, and the traditional religious brotherhoods continued to be active as devotional and social organizations. Alfredo Ferreira Magalhães, of the Institute for the Protection of Infancy, founded Catholic charities and led Catholic laymen. Some pious associations encouraged devotions by the whole family. But by and large, the Catholic press and literature assumed a predominantly female audience.[91]

After the decline of the League of Catholic Ladies, women's charitable action continued in Bahia without the benefit of an organization urging that it be linked to a militant missionary agenda. Amélia Rodrigues, though an important figure among the Bahian Catholic laity, was exceptional in her dynamic faith, as well as in her talents. The majority of Bahian Catholics merely avoided the league rather than joining or confronting it. The foundation of the Instituto Feminino da Bahia in 1923 by the pious philanthropist Henriqueta Martins Catharino, who had been active in the Association of Ladies of Charity and a friend of members of the league, represented a major step toward establishing permanent and continuing facilities for women's social action. As well as providing an employment agency, a secretarial school, and basic charity, the institute established a voter registration station in 1933, after women won the vote. Whereas the propagandizing and mobilizing league, with its independent female leader, had met some opposition among the clergy, the charitable institute, always closely guided by Monsignor Flávio Osório Pimentel, apparently enjoyed full support.[92]

The Militant Church

After World War I, the Brazilian Catholic church proceeded from policies of internal revitalization and alliances with "pious" politicians toward active leadership of reactionary politics. Rio de Janeiro's Cardinal Sebastião Leme led the movement with a 1916 pastoral letter laying out a strategy for the rechristianization of Brazil. It was necessary, Leme argued, for the church to regain control of education and ideas as a first step in restoring Catholic Christianity in Brazil. In carrying out this strategy, Leme followed two paths. He lent church support to friendly presidents and lobbied them for religious education in the schools and for official recognition of the social agencies of the church. And he patronized the right-wing Catholic intellectuals who were mapping out a reactionary authoritarian politics.[93]

The Centro Dom Vital and its journal *Ordem*, founded in 1922 by Jackson de Figuereido, and including Alceu Amoroso Lima, Gustavo Corção, and other Catholic intellectuals, became the vanguard of Catholic social thought in Brazil. Influenced by the French traditionalists, the Centro Dom Vital called for restoration of authority and hierarchy in Brazilian society. Writings in *Ordem* tend to use the family as a metaphor for their primary concern with order in political and aesthetic movements. This metaphor was common property of the Brazilian right. The family, as an image of harmony and cooperation, as opposed to social conflict, is also often mentioned in the authoritarian propaganda of the 1930's and 1940's. The family symbolized order and consecrated, organic hierarchy. Class struggle and selfish individualism were metaphorically like the rebellion of children against parents, or of wives and husbands against each other. Differences of racial or national identity within the nation, as represented by the tightly knit, "cystlike" Japanese and German immigrant colonies, were metaphorically like a willful abandonment of family.[94]

Typical of the Centro's lofty and abstract approach was Alceu Amoroso

Lima's *Idade, sexo, e tempo* (1938), which added little to the practical agenda that preoccupied Catholic writers on the family. His concern was more philosophical than pastoral. He explored the nature of the ages of man, and of the sexes, in order to argue that the only truly "modern man" in any age was one who remained in touch with the "eternal man," whose spiritual nature had been defined by the church. Yet in discussing sex as a dimension of human psychology, he did descend to anecdote. He had been shocked in the countryside by men who sat at table while their wives served, or who rode while their wives walked. He found in this a universal lesson: men had a "complex of superiority," which Christianity had challenged with a single moral standard for both sexes. In discussing women, he commented on the "dangerous confusion of sexes" by contemporary "false feminism," which the Bible could remedy with the model of the "strong woman."[95]

The Jesuit Leonel Franca, spiritual advisor to the Centro Dom Vital, the promoter of University Catholic Action and founder of the Catholic University, contributed to the national debate on the family with *O divórcio*, a treatise on divorce published in 1931. Franca's polemic against the institution of divorce in Brazil was, however, almost entirely a compilation of negative foreign examples: the consequences that divorce had had in the United States and France, such as the dropping of the birthrate and the disorganization of families. Like Lima, and like much of the Catholic thought of the 1920's and 1930's, Franca was emphatic in contrasting the eternal and natural to the human and perishable.[96]

The church's explicit social campaigns on divorce and family morality fit into the political alignment. From a rearguard action against civil marriage in the 1890's and 1900's, church efforts shifted to a fairly aggressive and successful campaign against divorce.[97] Catholic *anti-divorcistas* identified divorce with a long-term progressive libertine agenda of dissolution of morality—and ultimately with war and anarchists. They again and again affirmed the contention of Pope Leo XIII's 1880 *Arcanum* encyclical that the existence of divorce weakened attachments within the family and created mutually suspicious marriages. They could point to the evil consequences of atheism in France—infanticide, juvenile crime, prostitution of minors, suicide of minors, divorce!—and lament the establishment of divorce mills in the United States.[98] The few *divorcistas* who openly advocated reforming the institution of separation in order to allow divorce with remarriage defensively (and perhaps hypocritically) denied or played down the liberating consequences that would follow for individual men and women. Rather, they emphasized the palliation of intolerable mental agony and the gains to social "order" that would result from allowing separated people to remarry rather than obliging them to indulge in concubinage.[99]

The anarchist ideology of free love and liberation of women from slavery in the bourgeois family provided the church with a suitably demonic antagonist. Since the anarchists were the major scapegoat of the Brazilian right in the 1910's and 1920's, the divorce issue gave the Catholic clergy and politicians a claim to front-line status in the defense of Civilization.[100]

National lobbying by Cardinal Leme and the pressure of bishops on state politicians led to near-reestablishment of the Catholic church as an official church. The foremost example of this strategy was the activity of the church in the conservative state of Minas Gerais. There a revitalized clergy, stimulated by the influx of European priests, who spread the idea of Catholic social action, had sponsored a resurgence of lay activity in pious associations and political groups. In 1913 they had collected 210,000 signatures against the legalization of divorce with remarriage, then a remote possibility in the drafting of the new civil code. Failing in their early attempt to challenge the political machine that ran the state, the Minas hierarchy had changed tactics and begun to work within the machine. Their main goal was to restore state government aid to religious education, abolished in 1906. Their success at the state level in 1929 helped push the restoration of religious instruction at the federal constitutional convention of 1933.[101]

In Bahia no dynamic leader mobilized the laity to the extent that the Minas bishop Silvério Pimentel did, but the intense activity by the Bahian clergy and some of the devout middle-class laity strongly contrasted their religiosity with both the tolerant, apathetic secularism of most middle-class nominal Catholics and the unorthodox folk Catholicism of the masses.[102]

When Getúlio Vargas took power in 1930, Cardinal Leme organized demonstrations, such as the mass procession to the dedication of the statue of the Cristo Redentor in 1931, that reminded the recently installed dictator that Catholic support could be powerful. Vargas did choose to cooperate with the church, and by 1934 Leme had accomplished many of his goals. The 1934 constitution was rewritten to include mention of God in the preamble, to allow religious organizations and schools to receive aid from the state when they worked in the collective interest, to allow religious instruction in the public schools, and to allow the clergy in orders to vote. Soon afterward, Vargas passed a law allowing religious marriage ceremonies to include civil registration. As the federal and state governments expanded social programs, they continued to rely on church agencies, which they now subsidized at higher levels. The 1937 constitution that announced Vargas's second dictatorship, the Estado Novo, was less favorable to the church. But the nationalist policies of the Estado Novo included nativist measures discouraging Jewish immigration and dissolving foreign-language schools such as the Protestant German schools in the southern states.[103] Thus, the political offensive by the church and activist laity in the 1920's, which built upon the organizational reconstruction made possible by the separation in 1891, had succeeded in many of its aims by the mid 1930's.

Though the Brazilian church had by the 1930's succeeded in expanding its political influence to a point where it was far greater than under the Empire, its direct social influence on the laity may have declined. The debate in the 1940's and 1950's over the failure of the church to achieve significant social influence was largely provoked by the discovery of the growth of Protestantism, and the hierarchy's response was to blame this on the lack of priests and call for education to combat the "religious ignorance" of the people. Writing in the 1980's, Kátia Mattoso has pointed out that in the long run, religiosity centered on street processions and the traditional saints has proved more durable than the educated religiosity introduced by the mid-nineteenth-century reforms of the church.[104] "Folklore" outlasted prayer circles.

By comparison with the people, the upper classes were orthodox and devout. The educational work of the teaching orders had a great influence, and the Catholic press and devotional associations strongly influenced middle-class Bahian women. Except in extreme need, the middle class rarely used the social services that the church provided in the form of hospitals, orphanages, and workshops, but everyone acknowledged that they were both useful and necessary.[105]

Yet the influence of the church within upper-class Bahian homes decreased. From the turn of the century onward, accounts of family life, even that of practicing Catholics, rarely describe anything like the familiarity with chaplains and priests that is so important in Anna Ribeiro de Goes Bittencourt's memoir of life in the 1860's. Whether because of the scarcity of priests that the church complained of, or because of a secularization of family life, the informal influence and presence of priests in homes was no longer as powerful a means for the church to exert influence in families.

Around the 1910's and 1920's, the rituals and entertainments of upper-class Bahian family life became more secular. Perhaps a fair indication of this may be the rise and decline of the Mês de Maria. These May hymn devotions to Mary illustrate the way in which families traditionally used religious festivities to organize their leisure. In the nineteenth century they had become widespread and popular in Europe and Brazil. During the month of May, women and girls decorated their church's altar with flowers, and groups came to the church in the evening to sing hymns to

Mary. But by the turn of the twentieth century, if not earlier, the festivities had moved into urban homes, where families hosted a hymn meeting and decoration of the home altar, followed by a party that lasted until late in the night, with dancing, music, and refreshments. In the staid middle orders of Bahian society, this celebration was an unusual opportunity for courting. Yet mention of social evenings organized around the Mês de Maria wanes after the 1920's. By the 1950's, memorialists and folklorists were speaking of it as something that had disappeared in the cities and was dwindling in the towns. Courtship went on in movie theaters, promenades in parks, and social clubs. The church continued to be the only public institution that could hold a central place in the lives of Bahian families, but other institutions gradually crowded it out of certain spheres of daily life.[106]

Like the medical reformers with their plans for hygienic insulation of families and eugenic regeneration of the race, religious reformers found no simple organizational mechanism for inculcating their traditionalist family agenda. Under the ambivalent protection of the Empire, the church had established a relaxed accommodation with upper-class families, tolerating their marriage customs and accepting the primacy of domestic religion over public worship. With its disestablishment under the Republic, the church aggressively expanded its organization, importing foreign clergy and founding new schools and associations. It tried to confront the change in women's roles by propagandizing in favor of domesticity and missionary activity. Nonetheless, Bahian families remained remarkably impermeable to advice from the church, just as they had resisted the counsel of hygienists. Bahian families were loyal to their domestic Catholicism, but mostly indifferent to the new evangelization.

The failure of medical and religious zealots and of the law to significantly change family practices suggests that there were both an informal set of norms and a relatively unrecognized rationale for them. To understand how families ignored or resisted well-meant advice, we may look at their "common sense," the informal norms that they sustained without formal institutional endorsement. These could change, but not necessarily for the reasons that reformers wanted or in the direction that reformers hoped for. The changing strategies of families for maintaining their status eventually had more to do with changes in familial norms than with the exhortations of professional elites.

6

Common Sense

ALL CULTURES allow some inconsistencies among their norms. Perhaps in good times a society can tolerate incompatible beliefs more easily than in times of crisis.[1] Whatever the case may be, between 1870 and 1945 the culture of the Bahian families accumulated more and more disparate beliefs and symbols, and these overlaid the existing contrasts between the model of the patriarchal family and the free unions of the people. Modernizing European ideologies and manners crucially influenced changes in Bahian norms. The impact of medical ideologies of hygiene and liberal ideologies of the separation of church and state might suggest that Brazilian institutions had become transmission belts of cosmopolitan civilization. However, formal institutions had far less traction on individuals and on families than their spokesmen had hoped. The reformist movements and institutions succeeded mainly in multiplying the contradictory reference points for Bahian families.

Around the time of World War I, Bahian families apparently did begin to "modernize." The political and social crisis of the 1920's and 1930's led to social legislation that began to change the environment in which families operated. After World War II, changes throughout Brazilian society led individuals to reject many of the customs and authorities that seemed most antique and patriarchal. Though Bahian culture hardly became consistent or uniform, the increasing urbanization of "traditional" families with rural backgrounds led them to abandon old ways and ideas.

We may measure this change by examining the informally held beliefs of Bahian families, ideas that were usually tacit and rarely expressed in writing. In comparison with the body of medical prescriptions or the legal codes, they were unsystematic and often unexamined. To call them tradition might imply that they constituted another code that sat unchanging over generations. It may be better to call them common sense.[2] Using both changes in people's statements and changes in their customs and practices for clues, this chapter looks at the shift in the center of gravity of common sense from 1870 to 1945, recognizing the persistence of residues of old traditions and the emergence of tentative innovations.

In particular, this chapter examines the relation between informal ethics of behavior inside and outside the family. It begins by reviewing the range of ideas about the place and roles of women, expanding upon the treatment of those roles in Chapter 5. It first considers patterns of courtship, then codes of honor, and then the roles of women in the public sphere. The public roles of women changed dramatically, and household roles and ideas about the place of women changed along with them. Ideas about women in the family continually overlapped with issues of the status of the family, especially issues of the honor of its men. One of the requirements of manhood in Bahia was that one be able to protect and control one's women.

Another important set of Bahian ideas about the family was the series of ideas about solidarity and reciprocity. The customs and norms of patronage built on a vocabulary of kinship, out from the small group of kin into the wider society. Bahian society was to a large extent organized by clientelism, and hence the familial dimension of clientelism is an important theme in its own right.

Courtship and the Place of Women

Courtship customs—the symbolism of the ritual for allowing a man to join the family—reveal the attitudes of families to outsiders. Courtship and the regulation of romantic love outlined the place of women in high relief. At one extreme the sense of the place of women was that they should be subordinate to the interests and the will of the patriarch. They had no legitimate claims to identity as individuals; they existed in order to complement the figure of the patriarch, and their roles were dictated by his indulgence. Beneath this caricature of the "traditional" or "patriarchal" family lies a good deal of truth. Marriage and courtship practices in colonial Brazil made sense in terms of the assumption that women were tokens in marriage exchanges between men.[3]

Much of what we know about the patterns and forms of dowry in colonial and early-nineteenth-century Brazil suggests that fathers directed the marriages of daughters in their own interest. There was little room for love or sentiment. First, many women in Bahian upper-class families did not marry. From the mid eighteenth century to the early nineteenth century, perhaps one-third to one-half of the upper-class women who lived to maturity never married.[4] As most marriages were arranged by parents, and those who married needed a dowry provided by their parents, it seems likely that parents rather than daughters made the decision against marriage. Second, parents used marriages to establish alliances with sons-in-law. The dowry was an advance on the daughter's share of the inheritance. If it was informally given to the couple as a gift upon marriage, it helped to establish the young couple immediately. If it was legally donated as dowral property, it constituted a sort of loan made to the husband on the condition that the couple have children: if the wife died childless, the dowry capital reverted to the parents. If she died with children, the dowry property passed to them and was subtracted from whatever share they might later be entitled to from their grandparents' estate.[5] Because dowry property would pass into another male line, it seems that parents made every effort possible both to choose a husband whom they could bring into their orbit and to maintain good relations with the son-in-law and dowered daughter. This is, after all, one resonance of the proverb "Quem casa filha, ganha filho; quem casa filho, perde filho" ("Marry off a daughter, gain a son; marry off a son, lose a son").[6] Thus, continuity of status from a patriarch to his successor might be transmitted through a daughter to his chosen son-in-law as often as directly to his sons.[7]

In Bahia, the marriages of women also mattered to men because they guaranteed the legal continuity of men's lineages. Many men had two "families" at the same time, one legal and the other with an unofficial concubine. That is, though they arranged their marriages for policy, men could have unions determined by sentiment, whether love or lust. Only the legal relationship of a man to their mother—whether marriage or consensual union—could establish legitimate, legal relations between him and his children. A man needed a legitimate wife in order to have legitimate heirs, and only his children through his wife could inherit his status and property. Undoubtedly, a man generally took it for granted that he owed primary loyalty to his legitimate family. The law of 1847 that allowed men voluntarily to claim paternity and recognize illegitimate children, and gave the latter inheritance rights, somewhat modified the difference between the consequences of legal and of consensual unions, but it set limits on men's right to recognize children. Such recognition of paternity was always taken to be less certain than paternity in marriage.[8]

Yet if the commonsense view of marriage emphasized the primacy of the father's interests and wishes, other institutions challenged this assumption. Church doctrine always held that the marriage contract was an individual decision. It was consent of the couple to be married that constituted a marriage. The priest was only the celebrant who oversaw a sacrament that the parties administered to each other.[9]

Of course, paternal control of marriage involved the questions both of whether a father could impose a husband on his daughter and of whether he could refuse a suitor a daughter had chosen. In the late eighteenth century, European governments had enacted paternal consent into law, or else required it in practice. Parliament passed the Matrimonial Act requiring parental consent to marriage in 1753 in England. One topic of the regalist conflict in France between the Crown and the church was the authority of the Crown to require that priests inform themselves of paternal consent before celebrating a marriage. A series of contradictory decrees and regulations from 1775 to 1784 in Portugal first required, and then dispensed with, paternal consent to marriage.[10]

In Brazil, the assumption that daughters—and sons living under the father's roof—must subordinate their feelings to the will of their parents, that "women were almost slaves," apparently changed in the early nineteenth century. The new European ideal of romantic love and new customs of courtship had a strong impact on Brazilian ideas about marriage. However inappropriately, Brazilian novels mimicked the themes of marriage and the independence of youth developed in the European sentimental novel.[11] In 1823, after commenting on a society wedding in Rio, Maria Graham analyzed marriage, love, and independence in Brazil in much the same terms:

I hope we shall have more such free matches in our free Brazil, where, hitherto, the course of true love is apt not to run smooth. . . . Seriously, perhaps there has not hitherto been refinement enough for the delicate metaphysical love of Europe. . . . Grandison or Clarissa could not have been written here; but I think ere long we may look for the polish and prudent morals of Belinda.

In the decades when romanticism and political liberalism seemed all of a piece, a measure such as the lowering of the age of majority from 25 to 21 in the constitution of 1831 could symbolize the diminution of paternal power over the marriages of children, could appear to be putting the new ideas into practice.[12]

Practice around the middle of the nineteenth century indicates that the norm had changed from the assumption that parents should arrange marriages to the assumption that couples should choose themselves. Around 1850 there was an increase in cases of elopement and abduction in Bahia and throughout Brazil, which Gilberto Freyre takes as a sign of the conflict between the individualistic norms of a younger generation and the patriarchal traditions of their parents.[13] Though courtship and elopement had both gone on in Bahia for centuries, they now became the primary means of bringing about marriages. At some time around mid-century, customs of supervised courtship became established as the norm.

The last blind matches and child marriages mentioned took place before

1870 and were reported as curiosities. Albino José Barbosa de Oliveira, a Bahian magistrate, had eluded some matches thrown his way during his studies. But in 1846, at the age of 37, he accepted a marriage to an orphaned São Paulo heiress arranged by his father. In the tradition of dynastic matches, he had a portrait made to send to her, but in his modern day he had to hide it from the teasing of his friends on board ship. Even at that time, arranged marriages seemed more likely to involve orphaned girls. In 1855 the count of Sergimirim arranged the marriage of his 17-year-old son, Antônio, later viscount of Oliveira, to an orphaned niece, who was then 12. By 1895 these customs seemed quaintly antique to the young. The grandfather of Helena Morley, a lucky Minas Gerais diamond prospector, had married off his daughters two at a time in the 1860's. Each year he chose educated city suitors by mail himself; his daughters could only peer through a keyhole for glimpses of their future husbands arriving to complete the negotiations. The dramas of her aunts' matches fascinated the adolescent Helen as stories from another age.[14]

Anna Ribeiro de Goes Bittencourt's life illustrates the overlap of conventions of arranged marriage and courtship in planter families in nineteenth-century Bahia. Her parents' marriage in 1836 was apparently arranged and turned out badly. Her father had mistresses among the slaves, and her mother and father kept apart as much as they could. But she herself, born in 1843, assumed that she would marry for love. She first fell in love with Pedro da Trindade, a cousin and a tubercular student. Secretly, they pledged to marry. In 1861 Pedro spoke to her father, who without consulting Anna objected to her marrying before she was 20, imposing a postponement of two years. Pedro died in 1862, before the marriage could take place. After Pedro's death, she swore she would never marry and rejected reasonable proposals that her father received. Finally, however, when her father was discussing a questionable prospect with relatives, they suggested a match with Sócrates Araujo Bittencourt, another cousin. Sócrates had said he was interested, and her father mentioned his name to Anna. At first she refused, "but out of pure formality," her father later said. "I knew she would marry that one." Sócrates initiated a courtship, and Anna consented to marry him in 1865. But in fact, this second courtship was not a private, individualistic contract. It was debated among the parents and relatives of the couple. Explaining this in the 1920's, she wrote: "We were no longer in the times when two strangers would marry, as happened with my mother. I knew Sócrates because he had come to our house in the company of Manoel Saturnino."[15]

In Anna's memoirs, her own happiness in courtship and marriage—for she was happily married to Sócrates—contrasted with the misfortunes of two daughters of a *monsenhor* who had been left in their home under her father's guardianship. One died tubercular in a convent in Salvador. A stranger insinuated himself into their social circle and courted the other. Taking the responsibilities of a guardian seriously, Anna's father tried to make the customary inquiries into the character and circumstances of the young man before consenting. Soon after the wedding, he got back reports that the young man was a gambler, and indeed, the marriage turned out unhappily.[16]

Brazilian customs of courtship and marriage varied for most of the late nineteenth century and into the early twentieth century. Families were arranging matches, or at least proposing candidates to their children, well into the twentieth century. Recalling his plantation childhood in Paraíba around 1910, José Lins do Rêgo describes the lengthy negotiations and debates over the marriage of his favorite aunt. His grandfather, the Coronel, felt guilty that he had delivered two of his daughters to bad husbands, who mistreated them, and agonized over this decision. His grandmother favored marrying the daughter off to someone on her side of the family. Some sets of in-laws tried to promote candidates in order to double the Lins family's ties to their families. Yet once the decision about the match was made, and José's aunt had been consulted, the couple began a courtship in romantic style, getting to know each other as if the matter had not been settled beforehand. Spoiled little José, who had slept in his aunt's bed for years, was disgusted to spy her kissing her fiancé passionately in the shadows of the veranda.[17]

Courtships could be arranged by middle-class families with fewer dynastic pretensions than the Lins clan. Recalling his days as a poor medical student around 1930, José Silveira tells how he fell into courting the daughter of good friends. He stayed with his family in Santo Amaro over two vacations, and saw the girl often. His aunts and grandmother pushed him into courting her because they liked the match, but he did so without great enthusiasm. The girl's father, out of friendship for the family, paid for his graduation ring, leaving him with a feeling of obligation. But his engagement was an accident. Returning from studies in Germany, he absentmindedly kissed her in greeting: "I had sealed my engagement, so my friends proclaimed, in the very presence of her father."[18]

The intricacy of the customs of urban courtship that prevailed from 1870 through 1945 defined the restrictions on romantic love. These customs probably began well before mid-century and evolved in parallel with the customs of courtship in southern Europe. In the nineteenth century, Bahians credited the change in customs to the influence of Europe, and especially of European sentimental literature. Thales de Azevedo calls the old ways *namoro à antiga*, old-fashioned courting, to distinguish them from the newer forms of *flirt* and *paquera*, superficial relations not leading to marriage. In the twentieth century, Bahians began to call the older customs *namoro português*, Portuguese courtship, to distinguish them from the scandalous *namoro americano*, American courtship.[19]

Bahian *namoro* had at least two different forms: courtship begun in family circles and conducted under the sponsorship of elders was *namoro de casa*, house courting; courtship begun without sponsorship, in public places, was *namoro de rua*, street courting. House courtship and street courtship ideally both led to an engagement within the house, but the street courtship might lead to an elopement, or to disgrace.

The first two steps of a courtship resembled flirting. First came the *cumprimento*, the greeting, forcing the girl—and perhaps her chaperone—to take notice of the young man. Then there was a vigil on the street outside her house that might be either furtive or semipublic, designed to attract notice. In Bahian slang, the young men who hung around on corners at night or strutted back and forth up the streets where their *namoradas* resided were "turkeys" or "nightwatchmen." "Keeping the nightwatch" had its counterpart in the girls' custom of lingering at the window, *janelando*. Gazing from a window was simultaneously an assertion of seclusion and of accessibility. It emphasized both the protection of the woman within the walls of her home and, at the same time, her willingness to stand at the margin of that protection. Too much looking out the window was considered forward, improper, or even immoral.[20] In the twentieth century, the telephone short-circuited these early, tentative stages of courtship. Admission into the home ordinarily signified an expression of confidence, and the protocol of answering and opening the door was elaborate, but the telephone allowed anyone to penetrate the family sanctum: pranksters, the impertinent, suitors.[21]

The third step in a courtship decisively opened it to family concern: the young man sent a secret note to the girl, like one a little brother observed, "embossed with flowers and with a dove holding a letter in its beak."[22] However furtive it might be, this was an unambiguous move. It made the courtship official, whereas the earlier stages of courtship, albeit aboveboard, were noncommittal. Brazilian folklore made this challenge to the honor and discretion of the household the salient feature of courtship. The figure of the go-between, the *alcoviteira*, excited the imagination. Bahians often accused the hooded caponas, who until the 1880's went from door to door asking for alms, of carrying love notes.[23] Other accounts accused house slaves, servants, or urchins.

The disreputable love note could be dispensed with if the young man moved directly to the fourth step, which was to speak with the brothers of the girl. Her father was unapproachable, for he was formally the adversary. But the brothers could be impartial. They were equally concerned about the honor of their sister, but did not bear the responsibility for consenting to her marriage. Whereas speaking to a girl's father implied a commitment, speaking to her brothers might indicate only tentative interest. Accidental features of the families of some girls thus made courtship difficult: if it was handicapping to have a house too far from the street for window-gazing, it was devastating not to have brothers.[24]

Once the man established a public courtship in this indirect and face-saving fashion, the couple moved into the fifth step, a long phase marked by increasing intimacy. Families and suitors marked the progress of intimacy by degrees of physical approximation to the house. Even after passing notes and speaking with the brothers, a man might have to linger in purgatory outside the house, walking back and forth or taking the same streetcar ride ten times a day. In modest middle-class neighborhoods, a couple might have conversations at the parlor window or at the door for some time before the suitor was admitted to the house, ending the namoro de rua.[25]

Of course, it was far more comfortable for a suitor never to have to endure the many awkward steps of the namoro de rua. It was ideal to be invited into the home before beginning a courtship and to meet the girl under less formal circumstances. A young man who had once been admitted to the home was harder to turn away than one who had never gotten his foot in the door. Under the pretext of continuing attendance upon the family, a young man could court the girl more effectively and secure a stronger understanding with her than he could with notes, nightwatches, and serenades. Most courtships had no street phase, at least among the upper classes.[26] Planter families had no public places adjacent to their homes. Instead, young people associated at masses, birthdays, and feasts. One young man wrote of a party that was splendid "and well attended by friends of ours . . . they brought their families, such as the Martins, Sancho Bittencourt, etc., with 25 Ladies, and among these the Nunes from Bahia . . . who enchanted and swept away everyone!!!"[27] In the city, elite and middle-class families associated street courtships with the rakish impudence of students' compliments, and certainly felt they were out of place for an older girl.

The sixth step moved out of courtship proper and into the engagement, which led inevitably either to marriage or to a scandal. The ritual of the *pedido*, the formal request for the hand of the girl, epitomized the indirect ceremoniousness of the entire courtship. Once again, it could avoid a direct confrontation between the father and the suitor. The man could send a delegate (better his uncle or godfather than his father) to visit the girl's father and request her hand in marriage. The discussion was supposed to be a frank assessment of the merits of the young man, the qualities of the woman, and the prospects of the match.[28] The father might refuse flatly, and even rudely, but the intermediary buffered the refusal for both. However, it was more polite of the father to ask for some time to consider. This prolonged the process and sometimes involved another round of embassies and delegations. In the nineteenth century, when dowries were still common, they would also negotiate the amount and terms of the dowry.[29] This request for more time was part of the ritual even when the decision had been made beforehand: it was almost as rude to accept immediately as it was to refuse directly. But the relief was immense when a request was granted:

> On that day I brought up my marriage to the daughter of our good Friend Martins, we were all well pleased to see the way in which my proposal was accepted, and decided in less than two minutes, and even more so to see the assent and contentment of my Father. I would hope that this meets your approval, as only affection, friendship and consideration for Dona Maria obliged me from my Heart to take this step. I know that many people . . . will become my enemies! What do I care!!![30]

The father rarely decided the girl's future alone, even in the nineteenth century, when vestiges of "patriarchal" autocracy still existed. After 1890 the civil law required that he be consulted.[31] Custom recommended that he consult with the kin, beginning with senior members of the immediate family and the girl's brothers. For example, in 1885 the baron of Cotegipe, then living in Rio, wrote to his estranged son João in Bahia informing him with strained courtesy of a request for his sister's hand, but pointedly saying that he had already given his consent. Most commonly a drawn-out series of family councils began before an anticipated request appeared. Particularly if the young man came from outside the family and the locality, a father had to "make inquiries" and try to locate character references from the man's home town. The civil marriage law of 1890 enacted this custom by authorizing parents to demand a certificate of freedom from communicable diseases.[32] Although the fact was rarely documented, many fathers must have opposed suitors as furiously as the man who complained in 1927 that he was not able to disinherit his daughter "even though it would be just that [I] disinherit her for the obstinacy and disobedience with which she carried out her marriage."[33]

The issue of whether or not the girl was consulted might seem to be the most important question in a discussion of changes in Brazilian courtship around mid-century. Freyre, with overtones of melodrama, invokes the nightmare of a sentimental girl of noble family being traded off to a fat, thick-fingered Portuguese merchant. But it seems that the norm in Bahia was that fathers sincerely consulted their daughters and did not actively initiate negotiations to promote a match unless the girl was agreeable.

Certainly by the twentieth century, elders assumed that girls chose their husbands, albeit often for frivolous reasons. But in the 1850's adults might speak of having "married off" women in the family, as though they were responsible for contriving the marriage.[34]

If the parents, the relatives, and the girl approved, then the courtship moved into the phase of engagement, in which the lovers became betrothed (*prometidos*). Marriage by no means followed soon after. Instead, a further stage of approximation brought the young man closer into the family circle. His visits became routine and respectable, and the family's relations with him took on a new formality, maintaining vigilance while increasing intimacy. The iron finality of the betrothal made the wedding less urgent. The young woman sewed, preparing her trousseau, a clear sign to gossips that a wedding was in the works. Unreasonably protracted engagements were suspect, but some delay was taken for granted. An etiquette book in 1942 decreed that an engagement should not exceed three months, but many were longer.[35] Rui Barbosa's engagement lasted for six anxious months, which he spent in Rio de Janeiro trying to make enough money to pay his debts and set up a household.[36] Other engagements went on for years, and the suitor would become the "official candidate" for the girl's hand, a fixture in the parlor and at Sunday luncheon. Only setting a date for the wedding could rid the father of the expense and inconvenience of supporting him.

This pattern of courtship was not unique to Brazil. William Goode's continuum of the place of romantic love in courtships throughout the world would accommodate "namoro à antiga" under the broad category of supervised courtship: between arranged child marriages in India, which virtually exclude romantic love from marriage decisions, and the dating and courtship system of the modern United States, which idealizes love and stigmatizes parental meddling. And it may be that Brazilian customs never diverged far from European patterns of courtship; since most contemporary European societies fell within the supervised courtship range, Goode's model is not particularly useful for mapping fine distinctions. In the mid nineteenth century, when arranged marriages and child marriages were still occurring, both Bahians and travelers could, for instance, see the changing Brazilian custom of secluding women as lagging merely a generation or a decade behind the practice of the most "enlightened" parts of Europe.[37]

But the ritual of courtship and the strategies of marital choice among upper-class Bahians revealed characteristic, if not unique, visions of the roles and functions of women in the family. These included the delicacy of marriage alliances, the strong norm of endogamy, and the implication that daughters were an inconvenience or a threat to their families.

The earnest seriousness of courtship, its brittle delicacy, reflected the dangers families found in undertaking marriage alliances. The description of the steps to a courtship outlined above resembles a flowchart. It implies that the suitor could always proceed to the next step or merely exit and return to zero. In fact, there was a great difference between recognition and nonrecognition of the courtship. Once the family had acknowledged the courtship and brought it indoors, they exerted pressure on the suitor to go through with it to the end: "Emília's [wedding] is also spoken of as very certain; they say that the trousseau is ready, and the groom is Bacellar, who was being talked of for some time."[38] To court openly, with the knowledge of the family, incurred a tacit obligation to proceed to engagement and marriage. To break an engagement stained the honor of the family and invited reprisals from the woman's father and brothers. It was perhaps more difficult for a young man to escape a courtship once inside the house than it was to penetrate a family from outside its walls. Part of the purpose of the labyrinthine progress of courtship in Bahia was to prevent misunderstandings by requiring deliberate passage across well-understood boundaries. Despite this, because of the restriction of opportunities for contacts between young men and women, any coincidence throwing them together could make a young man fall into the role of a suitor in the family's eyes. Well before the engagement, it was difficult for him to extricate himself without implying some dishonor of the girl and her family.[39]

A second peculiar aspect of the transitional mixture of romantic love and arranged marriage in Bahian courtship was that it probably reinforced the norm of inmarriage among relatives. Probably many endogamous marriages were marriages of policy designed to keep property in the family or maintain alliances. But the combination of customs of seclusion of young women and of courtship beginning in the home may have kept up the high rate (almost one in five) of marriages to cousins and brothers-in-law in the late nineteenth century, past the time when it had a significant impact on property holdings. The structure of courtship, with its hostility to a suitor from outside the family circle, yet its reluctance to release a suitor who had once stuck his hand into the ratchet, favored kinsmen. The way in which any man made himself acceptable was to be adopted by the entire family. The patterns of visiting and entertainment of these families also made it more likely that young people would meet the sons and daughters of their parents' relatives, usually also neighbors.[40] Stiff formality prevailed at dances; except for cousins, young men and girls stayed in separate groups. Within the home, too, single men and girls could only converse guardedly unless they were cousins. Cousins thus had greater opportunities both to fall in love and to overstep the bounds of courtship: "It's cousins and pigeons that dirty our houses," went the proverb.[41]

The endogamous clannishness of Bahian families may have been a significant expression of their racial prejudices and racial anxieties. Many prominent Bahian families were colored, and even more families in the middling orders of society had peers who were colored or black. Other families derived pride and a sense of distinctiveness from their fancying themselves whiter than their neighbors, counting their "Portuguese" grandparents, noting people in the family who had blue eyes, and delighting in children who "looked like Germans."[42] Clothes, manners, and conspicuous consumption could override the stigma of color, but could not make people forget it. In every marriage match in Bahia, gossips compared not only the fortunes, talents, beauty, and origins of the couple, but also their color:

"All I know about him is that he is a ship pilot, and that he is *paler* than she is."

"So dear old Tonico has just crowned the sufferings of poverty, marrying a primary school teacher from Caravelas, a mulata, daughter of Marcelino, sister of Emília from the Boarding Section—an older woman, without any attractions."

In public and in contemptuous doggerel, a dark-skinned schoolteacher might be warned against courting a white girl:

And tell me what's your reason
For courting a white wench?
Don't be a fool, my lad,
Go spend your time at the bench.[43]

Families that wished to present themselves as pure whites intermarried to prevent the suspicion of tainted blood entering the family. These suspicions fell more on rural landlords' families than on city families. Possibly this is what was meant when in 1856 the young heir to a sugar mill fortune, who thought his courtship was favored by another landlord family, joked with a colored friend, soon to become his brother-in-law, that he would soon arrange the business, unless there was some impediment from the other side, "since I am from the bush."[44]

A third feature of the Bahian attitude toward romantic love in marriage was that it reflected a paternalistic concern for daughters: "Nobody can read the future; but obviously that of a man worries a father less."[45] Fathers may have wanted to use girls as pawns in marriage exchanges, but they also hoped to secure the futures of their daughters, whether in marriage or in spinsterhood. In wills and deeds of gift, rich families endowed women with rental houses and government bonds that were thought to provide a secure income.[46] Women also used what property and power they had to take care of each other. For example, in an 1870 deed of gift, a widow gave the use of a townhouse to another widow and her four spinster sisters, saying they could use it for a residence and school as long as they were unmarried, on condition that they teach six poor girls a year free for as long as they could. Upon their death, the house was to revert to her heirs.[47]

Marriage threatened to deliver a girl into the power of a man who would tyrannize over her, disrespect her, and humiliate her family. In the colonial period, particularly in the early eighteenth century, some upper-class families preferred the convent to marriage so vehemently that Crown officials had to restrict admissions to the convents.[48] Courtship, by taking the decision about the man out of the father's hands, and putting it in the hands of an adolescent girl, unsettled parents' peace of mind. Marriage alliances that were cemented principally by love, rather than by links of friendship or kinship between the two families, seemed risky to fathers. In the twentieth century, moralist literature addressed to girls frequently and sternly warned them of the disillusionments of married life. Etiquette books on marriage criticized the Brazilian customs of men's domination and mistreatment of their wives. The day after the wedding was "like waking from a dream," one said in 1914.[49]

Between 1900 and 1910, a modern pattern of courtship, "namoro à americana," developed in Salvador. It went on outside the home, like the namoro de rua, but it did not aim exclusively at marriage. Couples kissed, and more, enjoying intimacy without obligations. Obviously, it stemmed from an increasing freedom of young women from supervision, from the presence of girls in places outside the home. At mid nineteenth century, Salvador had "no exhibitions, no paintings, concerts, lectures—no shopping, museums, raree-shows, or sights—no show places, or ruins—no drives or promenades, except the public gardens on Sundays, which are but poorly attended. The one theater is only partially filled."[50] By the turn of the century, however, with the increase in street shopping, and the opening of teahouses, accompanied women could visit the center of Salvador, especially the Rua Chile. Here grew the promenades that had never flourished in the public garden. Here Salvador had a center for the *flirt*, an English word that was adopted just as *mademoiselle* and *señorita* were being adopted. Here one could not always tell a demimondaine, dressed up and doused in scents from the Sloper variety store, from a señorita of one of the traditional families.[51]

The glitter of metropolitan anonymity in the Rua Chile promenade did not quite extend to the promenades established in neighborhoods around the city, and eventually, by the 1930's, in country towns. Another English word, *footing*, was adopted for neighborhood promenades, which became highly stylized, with separation of the sexes. In the middle-class neighborhood of Itapagipe in the 1920's, bands of girls escorted by their younger brothers circled in opposite directions around the park from groups of young men. The evening footing was not anonymous, but a congregation of neighborhood acquaintances.[52] It substituted a new clannishness of the neighborhood for that of the family circle. What the footing had in common with the flirt of the Rua Chile was that it was not a commitment, like *namoro*. It was not always a ratchet pulling the couple toward engagement and marriage, but rather a casual, experimental relationship.

But the adoption of looser forms of association stopped at that ambivalent point before 1945. It did not continue toward toleration of an engaged couple being alone together before their marriage, for instance. Writing in the 1920's of the manners of her childhood in the 1860's, Anna Ribeiro said that "those times, if not like olden times, in which the *noivos* seemed almost like enemies, were not like these times in which there is such broad familiarity between them that they seem already to be married."[53] Yet writing in the 1970's of his youth in the 1920's, José Silveira recalled that manners prescribed exaggerated respect and reverence toward his official *namorada*, when at the same time he walked arm in arm around the city with girls he would never think of marrying.[54] Similarly, with the opening of opportunities to initiate courtships around 1900, girls did not obtain the right to marry at will. Parents continued to propose or veto suitors. The "opening" of courtship and the institutions of flirting and footing probably only increased the pressure on girls to attract suitors, without giving them complete freedom to choose one.

Honor

The elaborate stages of courtship in the nineteenth and twentieth centuries highlighted the boundaries of families and the position of young women in families. The ideas of Bahians about honor, implicit in their norms of courtship, organized much of their commonsense vision of the family and the relations of its members. In realms other than courtship, honor defined the proper position of women within the family and in public. The standards and symbols of honor in Bahian society showed implicitly in the custom of secluding women; their functions came closest to explicit and articulate expression in scandals such as the Questão Braga and in realist novels such as those of the Bahian satirist Jorge Amado.

Honor in Bahia, understood as the public standard of pride or shame, had many dimensions. In Bahia, as in other Latin European and Latin American societies, the word *honor* referred principally to one sort of pride, pride in manliness. It retained or transformed the medieval martial sense of honor as a hierarchy of male power, a distinction gained at another's expense, through another's defeat. In southern Europe and Latin America this vision of honor has accompanied a contrary value of pride in Christian virtue. The incongruence of the two scales of value perhaps helped to reinforce the sense that male honor was detached from morality and guilt and might include bullying and lying, if they were performed correctly.[55]

The work of Maria Sylvia de Carvalho Franco on rural São Paulo in the late nineteenth century suggests one "function" (if there need be any) of the ethos of male honor in Brazil. Studying the free peasantry, she implies that the many outbreaks of violence between neighbors, brothers, and spouses stemmed from a culture that periodically promoted contests, rather than hierarchy and certainty, in people's relations. Revising earlier interpretations of the collective barn-raising or harvesting bee, the *mutirão*, that saw it as an emblem of the communal solidarity of the folk, she suggests that it embodied a competitive ethic. Testimony in murder trials shows that the mutirão often began with challenges between groups of men to see who could outwork the others, and it often ended in blood.[56]

Honor in Bahia was an institution that allowed competition within an equilibrium. In the hierarchical, formalized social relations of Salvador, points of honor occasionally provided open arenas in which the outcome was unpredictable. They thrust identity momentarily into the crucible in a society that expected persons to be stable and solid. It was not that violent conflict could decide precedence at any moment. First of all, not every occasion was a dispute over pecking order. Codes of honor made it improper to compete with people too far beneath or above one in station. Rather it was simply that Brazilian social conventions and institutions did not at all times guarantee social statuses. At certain times, they allowed competition to define precedence. And secondly, in Salvador, the conflict was not necessarily murderously violent. In most instances it was merely playful and mischievous, a jibe or a practical joke rather than a duel.[57]

Competition over honor affected the rank of entire families. Within the family, the honor of one was the honor of all. The individual absorbed honor from, and radiated it to, his kin. Thus it may be that the collective pursuit of honor limited other solidarities. If the culture sporadically channeled its tensions into risky competition, everyone except a kinsman was a potential antagonist.

A man could inherit pride or shame from his father and even his remote ancestors. In colonial Brazil, European notions of nobility, combined with the distinction between Old Christians and converted Jews in terms of "purity of blood," and complicated by the distinctions of race in a slave society, encouraged an obsession with lineage. In this immigrant society, newly risen traders or cane planters could fabricate noble origins, "so that they themselves believe that a duke is nothing compared to them," as the satirists charged. The exploration of a man's family tree in the newspapers became a standard tactic of polemics in nineteenth- and twentieth-century Bahia: "Some not very pleasing episodes are brought to light—men's ancestors are not allowed to 'lie quiet in their graves.'"[58]

Through the twentieth century, prejudices associated with slavery further complicated the issue of ancestry, mobility, and honor. Ideas about color in Bahia had much to do with the shame of descent from some slave concubine. In an attempt at a general theory of slavery, Orlando Patterson has argued that its universal, and hence fundamental, trait is the assumption of "social death" and "natal alienation." These are the master's real or symbolic right to kill the slave, and the slave's consequent identity as a person socially dead, unable to transmit any honor or identity to children. The slave is in every sense the antithesis of the honorable person. One need not agree that there is an essence to the master-slave relationship to observe, as Verena Martínez Alier does, that in all the New World slave societies, the slave, and particularly the slave woman, had no honor, or what is the same thing, could not claim any.[59] Furthermore, in the scheme of honor, the mulatto as well as the black slave and freedman was degraded: he descended from a black woman and a white man. Bahians quoted a telling refrain:

Of his white father, whom he never saw,
He has a picture in the parlor;
But of the Negro woman who gave him birth
He has no picture, nor does he even speak of her.[60]

Not only slavery, but the additional stigma of illegitimacy, besmirched the fame of mulattoes. In defense against a newspaper libel in 1897, one man published a reply whose telling ambivalence and unconscious self-contradiction demonstrate the internalization of these prejudices:

I'm not a *creoulo* [nigger], as was said to lower me in a certain organ of the Bahian press, which raises questions of races and colors, under a regime in which men are valued by their behavior, character, and virtues, and not by the differences of colors and races. If I were a *creoulo* I would not feel lowered; on the contrary, I would be very proud, because there are blacks with greater sentiments than many aristocrats of the time of the Empire and many puffed-up whites who, by the way, don't know their own origins.[61]

But the family dimension of an individual's honor did not only extend up and down the lineage. The honor of sisters, brothers, in-laws, cousins, and nephews affected any individual's claim to public pride in Bahia. However, the disgrace or fame of remote kin cast a weaker aura on the individual's honor. Bahians drew their only indivisible lines of solidarity around the immediate family: spouse and children or parents and siblings. Questions of honor involving elopements, land grabs, and political precedence in the nineteenth-century backlands led to family feuds that clearly defined the breaks between families within kin groups.[62]

Among the upper classes, the standards of honor for women were relatively uniform in comparison with the differing standards for men. Because men's public roles differed more, honor for men was more differentiated by class. The roles of baron, counselor, and gentleman emphasized physical force, wealth, cunning, political influence, and respectable demeanor in different proportions. Someone like Rui Barbosa, the epitome of the elite counselor, would recognize the respect due someone like Horácio de Matos, the epitome of the warlord coronel.[63] A man's honor derived from his position in public, in "the world," on some hierarchical scale. An archaic knightly ethic underlay everyone's sense of honor, but it counted for less—even in the countryside—by the end of the nineteenth century. Landlord coronéis of the twentieth century acknowledged that they relied more on institutional power than had the landlord barons of the nineteenth century, or than had the rough-hewn, self-reliant patriarchs of the eighteenth century, who would despise a man for going to mass without a sword. In the city, lordliness had been transformed into the "chivalry" of good manners.[64]

Largesse in patronage was one common denominator of masculine honor in Bahia in the nineteenth and twentieth centuries. One demonstrated one's claim to pride by the ability to exercise benevolent paternalism: to treat one's slaves well, grant their infants liberty, and protect them in old age even after abolition; to take care of one's tenants and shield them from the law; to place godsons in public employment. A powerful and brutal man could demand deference in Bahia, but only a powerful and generous man could command unmixed respect. Being a patron measured wealth, for it cost money to dispense favors and gifts. It measured political power, for much of the currency of patronage was intangible favors such as exemption from criminal prosecution.[65] And it measured social skill and "prestige," for a clever man could become a patron simply by trading in others' favors.

And regardless of his position in the world, every married man in Bahia also derived some honor, some minimum and commonplace dignity, from his role as head of his household. In ironic recognition of this, the epitome of faint praise was "at least he is a good father": "é bom pai de família."[66] And it was in relation to this lowest common denominator of their honor that men needed to control the place and roles of family women. Unconventional behavior and demeanor on the part of the wife could easily diminish the honor of the husband. Here again the Bahian pattern resembled that of the Mediterranean cultures. She had to have "shame," *vergonha*. Adultery was the ultimate humiliation, and custom required that a man "wash out the dishonor with blood" by murdering his wife and her lover. Although the law could not openly condone the ritual of murder, it allowed legal separation on the grounds of a woman's single act of adultery.[67]

Yet a woman's role in determining a man's honor was not all negative. The man and the woman conferred honor on each other. Within the family, the solidarity and mutual pride of honorable family members was condensed in the concept of *respeito*, "respect." Respect was honor turned into manners. It expressed, often through symbols of deference, the complementarity of their pride and the warmth that bound families together.

Still, honor required that women's roles be restricted. The Brazilian ideology of women's honor stressed that a woman's only essential characteristic in the ideal marriage bargain was *pureza*, purity: "She is as pure a girl as you are, and as virtuous as the most virtuous in this world. My Mother was not any more pure."[68] Impurity was the only way that a girl could be unquestionably disqualified as a marriage partner. The spatial symbolism of house and street, which corresponded to realms of purity and pollution, probably contributed to the notion that women's purity corresponded to their physical seclusion within the home. Bahians called a forward girl *saída*—that is, "gone [or going] out"—and said that a girl who had been seduced and had lost her virginity *saiu de casa*, "left home." Inwardness symbolized virtue, and outwardness perdition. Like the hymen of the virgin's body, which allowed no gradation between virtue and vice, rupture or integrity, the threshold of the home was a symbolic boundary line that women could cross only in one direction.[69] In courtship, the man was allowed by degrees into the woman's home and then took her out of it only to marry. A girl risked disgrace merely by lingering too long at the window.

Thus changes in the customs of seclusion palpably marked the pace of relaxation in the standards for honorable behavior by women. In the early nineteenth century, European travelers, and Bahians from the capital visiting the backlands, reported that in patriarchal homes women were kept inaccessible: sent behind doors when a traveler appeared, they peered at strangers through the lattices of a balcony. Freyre makes use of this harem atmosphere to buttress his theory of an "oriental" tone to Brazilian culture. Yet memoirs of rural life after the mid nineteenth century indicate that seclusion was rare; daughters might be sent upstairs or out of the way when a stranger arrived, but in their daily life and in the familiar social circle, they were impeded only by friendly scolding. By the 1870's, the severity of Coronel Exupério Pinheiro Cangaçu, who kept his daughters upstairs sewing with the slaves when men arrived, seemed eccentric.[70]

The exotic symbol of the seclusion of upper-class women in Salvador was the sedan chair, borne by Angolan slaves clad in yellow, red, and green, if it was a public chair for hire, or else in the livery of their house. In 1857 the Englishman James Wetherell had a wry comment:

The ladies here seldom go out, except in full dress to pay formal visits, and to mass. Young ladies are *smuggled* to church in cadeiras, the curtains of which are carefully drawn, and held by both hands, to preserve them from the eyes of the profane sight-seeing portion of the world. When the wind happens to overpower the curtain-holder, the recluse . . . often disappoints the gazer. The mothers having been taught this seclusion, endeavour to instil it into their daughters, but the *pretty girls* are becoming tired of this maternal despotism, and I do not think cadeiras *close so tightly* as they did a few years ago.

An 1878 engraving by the German traveler Julius Naeher depicts the sedan chair, enclosed with multi-folded curtains, as a symbol of femininity against a field of phallic imagery: the breeches of soldiers, a running cat, tall palm trees, and boys' kites rising stiff against the wind.[71]

The seclusion of women was a corollary of the power of heads of households to control associations in a city without much of a civic sphere or much public space. Not only women, but some classes of men were under heavy supervision in the city. In 1840, young shop clerks, caixeiros, often lived in the warehouses of their masters, sleeping on the counter, and not going much further than they were sent on errands. To grow a mustache was audacity; to smoke in public, effrontery. Bahian ladies never ventured past the dingy, cod-smelling shops of the Lower City except in sedan chairs. When a foreign lady disembarked and actually set her feet on the mud of the port, the clerks would sometimes "jump over the counter, so that they could see these rarities from the door." When a young man got to a dance, he had to contend with the hostility of some of the older generation, who detested the idea of any upstart being able to request a dance and balked at the new dances in which the couple touched each other: the schottische, the polka.[72]

By the turn of the twentieth century, the seclusion of women in Salvador lifted. The city's facilities for extrafamilial association became more plentiful for both women and men, and women of decent families asserted themselves more often in public: shopping, going to work, and collecting money for charity. The changes in courtship at the turn of the century with the innovation of footing promenades were part of the disintegration of the custom of seclusion. Yet even in 1980 in Salvador, a man in his sixties could comment defensively: "I am certain that your mother doesn't go out of the house more often than she has to; it doesn't look nice."

The Questão Braga

The Braga Affair, or Questão Braga, a scandal of honor that began in 1878, revealed with rare publicity the themes of the code of familial honor in Salvador: seclusion and seduction, enmity and trickery, ancestry and effrontery.[73] It involved a young obstetrician, José Braga, who married the daughter of a Portuguese merchant, Cândida Ferreira. On the day after the wedding, he sent her back to her parents, complaining that he had examined her on their wedding night and found her not to be a virgin. Her father called in medical experts, and they contradicted Braga. Braga claimed that he had found an old defloration, but he admitted that he had proceeded to have intercourse with the girl, partly in order to confirm his hypothesis. The experts concluded that the condition of the hymen reflected a recent trauma to the membrane rather than any older one.

In the first skirmish of the dispute between the Bragas and the Ferreiras, scientific expertise was the ostensible issue. The father's champions published their report and conclusions in a special issue of the *Gazeta Médica da Bahia*, which sold out on the first day. Braga fled to Rio and obtained opinions from prominent physicians there, then went on to Lisbon, where he obtained further endorsements of his diagnosis. At this point in the dispute, both sides framed the issue in terms of the law on annulment, which allowed a husband to seek annulment of a marriage if there was some "essential error" as to the person of the spouse.

As the medical-legal front of the affair slowed to a war of attrition, the families shifted their tactics to the traditional style of polemic defaming the characters, reputations, and motives of the others. Manuel Alves Ferreira, the father, took the offensive, defending the honor of his family by impugning the motives of Braga. Ferreira claimed that Braga (incited by his father, the mastermind behind the scheme) had plotted to marry an heiress with a delicate heart condition. He had planned either to kill her with the shame of his denunciation or to extort a dowry from her father. Ferreira's case was strong. On the three days before the wedding, Braga had transferred assets from his bank account and deeded property to his parents. On the wedding night, instead of behaving as a man of honor should and rejecting a bride who was not a virgin, he consummated the marriage. The next morning, he calmly invited her parents over for the wedding dinner. It was not until that evening that, spurred on by his father, he wrote a note to Ferreira repudiating Cândida and asking to send her back. After her father had arranged medical and police examinations that threatened to expose his scheme, he had tried to get hold of vital evidence: the nightshirt and bedsheets. The purity of Cândida, her family concluded, had been "reborn like the phoenix."[74]

These accusations in the paid announcement columns were answered by accusations from supporters of Braga. They dared not attack the girl directly. But they accused the father implicitly of exerting insufficient vigilance over his daughter, and of obtaining his fortune through ignoble means, in commerce. Braga's version of events was that he had confronted Cândida on their wedding night, and that she had confessed. She had been deflowered as a schoolgirl while picking fruit with her Uncle José in the woods, and later she had been raped by a Portuguese who was staying in her father's house, waiting to find a job in commerce. She had continued to have sexual relations with her Uncle José from time to time. In his confusion, Braga claimed, he had consummated the marriage but had not slept that night. However, when her parents arrived the next day, he had not toasted their health. It would have been hypocritical. Cândida's honor concerned him, but as one defense of his cause put it: "What is honor? Is it an exclusive possession of woman? Is there not an honor for the husband? And what else did the husband in this matter do but defend his honor? . . . Is this fact with which we concern ourselves an act of violence, as some say, or an example of high courage and morality?"[75]

Besides shocking and titillating the staid population of the city, some of whom began to write threats on the walls with charcoal, the "monstrous nuptial drama" ramified as each side chose its champions. The Ferreira family had immediately brought in expert outside assistance to counter the medical authority of Braga. On the panel for the police medical-legal exam, these doctors were joined by two others who were "relatives of a person with whom the wife has spiritual kinship" and were thus "suspect of partiality."[76] Braga, when he left Bahia for Rio, tried to get medical opinions from doctors there. In addition, the Ferreiras later charged, he got Antônio Tavares da Silva Godinho, who had been convicted of deflowering a minor in Bahia six years earlier, to publish an article praising him in a Lisbon newspaper.[77]

From this point forward, the feud between the two families latched on to previously existing factional divisions. The *Diário da Bahia*, which belonged to one faction of the Liberal party, defended the Ferreiras. *O Monitor*, the newspaper of the dissident Liberals, became the forum for the Bragas.[78] Other newspapers published notices about the affair, and indeed, one of Cândida's uncles complained that two small papers had tried to extort money from him. All parties saw involvement in the matter as a declaration of allegiance. When Braga had tried to find a lawyer, so the Ferreiras claimed, some had refused saying, "I am not married, but I have nieces, and I don't want them to suffer because of me." Finding a lawyer, Braga could not sell bank shares to pay him, because no one would buy them. Later, another lawyer complained that Ferreira had circulated a pamphlet warning him that he should be concerned for his own daughters, "for his good deed cannot fail to be remunerated on him and on his, by the very hands of GOD!"[79]

The conclusion of the affair was anticlimactic. After exile in Europe, Braga returned to Bahia, where in 1884 he was refused the courtesy of a seat on the examining boards of the medical school. A later pamphlet published by the Ferreira family said: "Let him and the world know that we are going to follow him step by step, and point him out everywhere— in the streets as well as the sacred temples—we are going to point him out as the *damned one*, as the *reprobate* of society."[80] Yet Braga remained on the medical faculty until his retirement. One version of the affair reports a tradition that Manuel Alves Ferreira distributed two thousand porcelain chamberpots and spittoons with Braga's portrait on the bottom, thus ending the battle with the last laugh.[81]

The Braga Affair was only unusual in that it became a public scandal. In most cases fathers of daughters were vulnerable to blackmail. For instance, they customarily consented to the marriage of eloping daughters. Most such tussles over honor and virginity probably stayed indoors: parents wanted to silence them, and few bridegrooms had the cold nerve of José Braga, who exposed himself, as well as his bride, to ridicule. When families did bring a complaint of defloration to the police or to the church, they usually did so as a last resort and preserved some bit of privacy. The unrepresentative case of the Ferreira family does illustrate the themes of honor, and how honor was able to mobilize two families and eventually whole factions.[82]

The Braga Affair also stood out in singular relief against an informal Bahian counterethic of moral tolerance, or cynicism, in which women's dishonor was ultimately discounted or begrudgingly accepted. Some Bahians defended the enlightened view that virginity was irrelevant. A satirical poem, supposedly written in the 1830's by a man to his future wife, mocked the superstition that the leaves of the sensitive plant will wither at the touch of a girl who is not a virgin: "Your reason is sufficient / to make you realize / that there's nothing a little plant / can know about our lives."[83] But others, while affirming the importance of female virginity, denied that it was relevant to every woman. The sexual double standard honored men for sexual conquests and encouraged them to seduce their *namoradas* with promises of love and marriage. However, once they had obtained sexual favors from a girl, they could no longer trust her honor and were wary of marrying such a woman. If the defloration became public knowledge, and particularly if the girl became pregnant, a struggle over the definition of the relationship might develop. The family would try to excuse the slip and maintain that the man had promised marriage. The man would claim that there had been no talk of marriage, and that he had simply taken a woman as a mistress. His responsibility to her was simply that of the father of an illegitimate child.[84]

Consider a much more obscure case than the Braga Affair, but one that also became public to some degree. In August of 1869, a father in Salvador petitioned the church to impede the marriage to another woman of Benício, a ship's machinist who had deflowered his daughter Dazinha and fathered a daughter by her. For almost two years, until the ecclesiastical court gave its decision in favor of Benício's freedom to marry, the family was able to delay his wedding. The testimony and love letters that they submitted as evidence documented Benício's shift in tone from fervent, supplicating suitor to cool and impatient lover. Before anyone else could have known about the pregnancy, Benício warned Dazinha that they didn't have enough money to marry happily: "At first we might get along well . . . but later everything would turn distasteful from so much suffering. . . . If it weren't for my Mother, to whom I owe all due decorum, and meeting my obligations, we would long since have been united forever." Through the birth at least, he had supported her, calling a midwife himself. At first, the family had tried to cover up the pregnancy, even concealing it from Dazinha's father. A spinster seamstress who had been their neighbor said that when "the veil that covered all these facts had been broken," they had moved to her Uncle José's house in another neighborhood, where it wouldn't be "common knowledge up and down the street." After a year, the family's hostility gave Benício an excuse to break off the relationship out of injured pride: "Now hear what José said to me the other day here on board, that no man will set foot in his house except himself, so think over whether I should go there." When Dazinha returned money that he had sent, he cursed his mother's neighbors, who had maliciously sent him wedding presents, and told Dazinha she could gaze out the window any time she wanted, "as I don't have anything to do with that, and if milady has her whims, I also know where you are selling yourself." With palpable hypocrisy, Benício pretended concern for the honor of José's household while implying that he had paid for Dazinha.[85]

On the one hand, this was simply a case of aggressive, antisocial sexual exploitation. On the other hand, the norm toward which Benício's actions referred was that of the consensual union so common in Bahia and in Brazil. In Salvador, more than half of all infants born were illegitimate, and many stable unions were consensual. The best documents of consensual unions are the deeds of paternal recognition of illegitimate children.

Fathers could not recognize certain illegitimate children (essentially those born after the father's marriage to another woman), and not all fathers chose to recognize their children, but enough did so that deeds of recognition probably outnumbered marriages in Salvador, at least in the nineteenth century.

The deeds show a concern with female sexual honor even in informal unions. Men would claim confidence in the paternity of their children because the mother had been "in his company for the term of her pregnancy," or because she and his daughter lived "under his roof and exclusive and immediate protection." [86] However, the relationship between the man and woman was not marriage, but rather *amizade* (friendship) or *amasio* (consensual union). As a cobbler put it in 1870, he was recognizing his infant daughter, because he "maintained relations of amizade with the second party [her mother] . . . and there resulted from these relations having had a daughter by her." [87] The impersonal unsentimentality of the notarial formula is even more convincing in cases when men recognized children by two or three women. [88] Some men in Salvador eventually married their amásias, including couples among the traditional families. Priests could not marry their mistresses, and so could only compensate by recognizing their daughters and sons. [89] But most deeds give little indication of a sense of responsibility, solidarity, or *respeito* between the men and their mistresses. [90]

From the Braga Affair in 1878 to the year 1925 is almost half a century, yet the Bahian novelist Jorge Amado grounds his analysis of Bahian small-town culture in similar dramas—mostly farces—of honor. *Gabriela, Clove and Cinnamon* (1958), set in the cacao town of Ilhéus in 1925, during Amado's childhood, addresses the elusive quality of cultural change. The nativity scene built with cut-out magazine illustrations that is the pride of the town symbolizes the piecemeal assimilation of modern times:

The tableau represented, of course, the birth of Christ in a rude manger in distant Palestine. But this basic element had become little more than a detail in the center of a kaleidoscopic, growing world in which the most diverse scenes and figures, from the most divergent periods of history, mingled democratically with one another. Statesmen, scientists, military men, artists, famous writers, domesticated wild animals, and saints with drawn faces—all side by side with the radiant fleshiness of semi-nude movie stars.

Morals are similarly eclectic. The novel frames its tableau of provincial manners within a courtroom drama: a coronel has murdered his wife and her dentist paramour, and it is expected that the jury, heeding traditional norms, will absolve him. But at the end of the novel, the jury renders an unprecedented guilty verdict, which fuses symbolically with the electoral victory of the "progressive" boss and the modernization of the port works that will energize the town. It deceptively parallels the central plot as well: the barkeeper Nacib decides not to murder his wife Gabriela in revenge for her cuckolding him. But this happens in a less straightforward way. Nacib spares Gabriela and yet salvages his honor through a legalistic maneuver, a *jeito*. His friends annul their marriage, based on a falsified birth certificate. Therefore, since he never possessed her in marriage, her infidelity did not compromise his honor. He can keep her (as a cook) and love her (though only as his mistress) without being a cuckold. This plot does not show urbane tolerance replacing old prejudices, but rather how Nacib's conscience balances ambivalence in order to deceive himself and others. He is celebrated by some as a fine rogue who defended his honor with quick wits and by others as "the most civilized man in Ilhéus." Gabriela, an innocent who is indifferent to conventions of honor and had fretted at the role of married woman, is grateful to be freed from the confinements of respectability.[91]

This vision of honor in Bahian society consistently criticizes the repression implicit in family respectability. In *The Two Deaths of Quincas Wateryell* (1961), set out of time, but probably in the 1920's or 1930's, Amado's criticism of the hypocrisy turns to a satire of the stifling conventions of the lower middle class. On the day of his retirement, the good, *pacato* civil servant Joaquim Soares da Cunha curses his wife, abandons his family, and enters Bohemia. There, among prostitutes, sailors, and drunks, his nickname becomes Quincas Wateryell. Years later, he dies, and his family come to claim him, but they are indecently concerned to balance their accounts between the price of a pair of new shoes and the cost of a respectable funeral. Left alone at the wake, Quincas's underworld friends give his corpse a last swallow of rum. It revives, and their wake turns into a last night on the town, until he finally dances off a sailboat into the sea. In this fable, as in his novels, Amado uses the figure of the good prostitute to epitomize the contrast between the deadening hypocrisy of bourgeois manners and the resurrecting promiscuity of Bohemia. In most of his works, the contrast is one between the old and the new: old conventions and the new cosmopolitan ethic of sexual liberation. In *Quincas Wateryell*, as in *Gabriela, Clove and Cinnamon*, the sophistication of the Jazz Age converges with the timeless permissiveness of the Bahian poor. Although Amado sees the 1920's in Ilhéus as a transition from the provincial to the cosmopolitan, Quincas's adventure takes place outside of time.

Amado's analysis of honor and its workings in Bahia is more subtle than a simple scheme of modernization, in which the bourgeoisie from above and the people from below erode the excessively rigid sexual morality of the petty bourgeoisie. Rather, what his novels portray is a society in which the old standards of respectability are not challenged, but continually subverted. In *Tent of Miracles* (1969), set in Salvador around 1907, the exposure of a slave great-grandmother in the family tree of a "white" coronel discredits his opposition to his daughter marrying a mulatto medical student. The racial dimension of the honor of the family dissolves in Bahia's universal "dishonor." In *Dona Flor and Her Two Husbands* (1966), Dona Flor manages to have both the security of conformity and the pleasure of irresponsible sexuality: she lives with her kind, but dull, second husband, and receives visits from the ghost of her sexually exciting but good-for-nothing first husband. Her vacillation between two heroes is typical of the resolutions in these novels. The pretexts on which goodwill and good sense prevail over cruel punctiliousness or racism in *Gabriela* and *Tent of Miracles* indicate a vision of people whose relation to their rules and norms is extremely flexible—and insecure. When impulse or love require that they violate their rules, they dodge around them as deftly as possible. Amado's vision of social change and modernization sees conflicts dissolving in tolerance and the permissive side of the patriarchal ethic.

The Public Roles of Women

The dimensions of honor and courtship took women in Bahia not as individuals, existing for themselves, but as limited to setting off the individuality of men in a family. The way in which women of the upper classes entered the professions—as tokens in the 1880's, rapidly after 1930—showed that women themselves began to redefine their place in the society, claiming an identity outside the home.

Although it was only a conventional figure of speech, the frequency with which Bahian women identified themselves with slaves or with prisoners in the home indicates how frustrating their roles as ladies were. As an example of parents' power in the mid nineteenth century, Anna Ribeiro cited a woman she knew who forced her daughters into a convent. "Women were almost slaves," she said. Condemning the sexual license of Carnival in 1916, Amélia Rodrigues unconvincingly echoed the Catholic argument that Christianity had elevated women from their enslavement in Roman society: "In place of the Bacchantes and the servitors of Venus, there arose in the world a legion of chaste virgins, of wives and mothers who were dignified by the true love, which is completely of the soul and completely heavenly." Much more common was the observation that married women were "more the slaves than the companions of their husbands." Such subordination was especially difficult for women who had known other places, or who were accustomed to excursions with their husbands. Adelaide Dobbert compared their frustration to "really living like Nuns, we are alone in the house all day." Even with her husband at hand, she could describe her house as a "prison."[92]

Women's separation from the world was underlined by the customs of mourning. The old Portuguese custom of *nojo* decreed that an entire family shut itself up in the house for mourning after a death; in Brazil, particularly in the countryside, nojo was sometimes carried to extreme lengths. In the late nineteenth and early twentieth centuries, women vacillated between criticizing each other for mourning too long, and reveling in the material symbols of their suffering: "We ordered some mourning outfits from the house of Mme. Guion, and when you pass through Rio please do us the favor of going by there and ask her if she sent earrings, bracelets, and necklaces; and if not, will you do the favor of bringing some good ones; that will always do for us and also [hair]pins."[93]

It was scandalous when women abbreviated their mourning, particularly when girls married soon after a parent's death, or when a widow remarried quickly: "It really is too soon; however, those who have money soon forget their sorrows [*desgostos moraes*]."[94] Etiquette manuals carefully discussed the timing of full and half mourning, and the degrees of kinship that demanded mourning. This emphasis on women's segregation from the world suggests that formal employment, especially work outside the home, would have forced disruptions in the routines and customs of Bahian families.

It seems that fewer Brazilian women overall worked in the early twentieth century than had worked in the late nineteenth century. The census of 1872 counted about half of all women in the labor force, while the census of 1920 counted only a tenth. Although the sharp drop probably reflects a narrower definition of employment in 1920, it is possible that ex-slaves and other lower-class women worked less after abolition in 1888. Between 1920 and 1940, women reentered the labor force, but at a slower rate than men. On the other hand, women worked more than they had before in some industrial and clerical occupations. From 1872 to 1920, women's education had increased, qualifying them for more occupations. In Salvador, about a quarter of women of all ages knew how to read and write in 1872; this declined to a fifth in 1890; then it rose to over half in 1920. Whereas in 1872 there had been a large gap between the literacy of men and women, by 1920 almost as many women as men could read and write. Still, in 1920, as in 1872, the most common occupations for women in Salvador were as textile workers, peddlers, seamstresses, and house servants. The only skilled occupations with a significant number of women were midwife and schoolteacher.[95]

Bahian women in the upper classes got more and more education during this period. This showed partly as a generational difference: by the 1880's, there was a palpable difference between the capricious handwriting and grammar of unschooled grandmothers and the neat hands of their accomplished granddaughters. And by the late nineteenth century, the schooling of middle-class and elite women often went past the primary level. The revival of religious orders in the 1890's brought teaching orders of nuns who founded primary and secondary schools for girls. From its establishment in 1836, the Normal School for schoolteachers took in some female students, and in the 1860's the students of the boarding section were almost entirely women. By 1895, more than nine-tenths of the external and boarding graduates were female.[96] The Normal School thus became identified as the principal female institution of higher education, but the 1879 educational reform also opened the Bahian Medical School to women. The first woman doctor graduated in 1887. By 1930, eighteen had graduated, and by 1945, sixty-one more. The Bahian Law School, established in 1891, had fewer female graduates. The first woman graduated in 1911. By 1923, only two women had graduated, but in 1929 there were eleven women studying law.[97]

Bahian women moved into the professions in the same patterns. In 1856 women held 15 percent of public school teaching jobs, but by 1872 they occupied 34 percent. The proportion of female teachers increased steadily; more than 56 percent of teachers were women by the 1890's, 76 percent by 1920, and 90 percent or more after 1924.[98] Women's entrance into the teaching profession matched its demotion in prestige. After 1910 men virtually ceased to become teachers. In 1923 Egas Moniz lamented that the salaries of teachers were so low that men would no longer enter the profession:

The public school teachers of Bahia in fact constitute a class worthy of compassion and support.

Earning much less than a stonemason, carpenter, stevedore, or foreman, this class of public employees constitutes a legitimate proletariat, especially in the interior of the state, where they live in the most complete isolation, without even means of subsistence when their meager pay is delayed.

It is very rare that young men dare to study at the Normal School, because it would certainly be absurd to embark on a career without a future, when any shop boy or public office clerk manages to get a better salary.

The female sex alone represents an overwhelming majority on the list of enrollments.[99]

However, women also entered less markedly "feminine" professions in small numbers. Female dentists and doctors were practicing in Salvador by the 1890's, and after 1917, when federal laws changed to give women access to positions in the civil service, women found places throughout the bureaucracy. By the 1920's and 1930's, women began to take white-collar clerical jobs in commercial and financial firms.[100]

Women associated change in their work roles with their assertion of other public roles in the city. In 1878, before many middle-class women actually were working outside the home, a critic said:

I always found that there were two things that the girls of this land fancied more than anything else: freedom and their money. By freedom, they mean the ability to go out where and when they please. By their money, they mean an income they can dispose of without giving satisfaction to anybody. It is because of this that many girls sew, make flowers, or crochet, or anything else, even when they don't need to: it's a matter of *their* money. . . . What seems outlandish to me, however, is that they should turn to the masculine professions.[101]

To be more accurate, what was outlandish and scandalous was that "decent" ladies should take these freedoms. Colored women had always worked on the streets of Salvador. Bahianas dressed in picturesque layered skirts carried on much of the city's retail marketing, and they had long represented women out in the city. Forced by circumstances to work, some women who usually wore hats and dresses would put on the turban and calico skirt of the bahiana. Similarly, midwives in the nineteenth century had gone abroad dressed in long, hooded cloaks. Therefore, when "family" women began to work in offices and schools in the 1920's and 1930's, they put on suitably severe uniforms that identified their profession as their excuse for being outside the home.[102]

But it was not work alone that expanded conventions of women's "place" in the 1910's and 1920's. As shopping became more acceptable, respectable ladies would routinely go out in public. The streetcar replaced the sedan chair as the genteel means of getting from the residential districts to the Rua Chile, the shopping street in the center of the Upper City: "During the journey, it is no longer the custom that we keep quiet, with our eyes lowered and our cheeks blushing, no."[103] Being escorted, if only by another woman, was still essential, but the presence of women on certain streets was now taken for granted.

As Bahian women moved into new public spheres, they forced a change in standards of common sense. Seclusion remained the ideal for "family" women, but more activities became permissibly modest. Bahian women could argue that they were merely catching up with civilized places. By an inexorable process of evolution, Paris and New York moved in the forefront, followed closely by Rio de Janeiro, and with a judicious lag, by Salvador. The first woman in Bahia to raise her hemline, bare her arms, wear a bathing suit, graduate from the medical school, or run for Congress could appeal to the example of civilized Europe.[104]

The cinema and other improved means of communication brought cosmopolitan and exotic examples concretely into the view of Bahian families: in 1906, the old patrician Teatro São João was presenting "The Indiscretions of the Servant," "The Russo-Japanese War," "A Voyage over Lake Geneva," "The Strike (A Present-Day Social Drama in 5 Colored Scenes)," "Coronation Festival for the King of England in India," and other shorts, synchronized to a gramophone sound track.[105] In 1910 Amélia Rodrigues listed among contaminants of the Brazilian mail novels, poetry, engravings, polychromes, almanacs, and advertising, which Brazilians received "like children accepting pretty things that daddy sends them," but above all, indecent postcards, which many collected in albums. Just five years later, in 1915, she emphasized the danger of fashion pattern magazines and the cinema.[106]

The result was perhaps a greater spread in norms between the habits of a few up-to-date, emancipated women and the cloistered majority: Bahian and Brazilian common sense tolerated greater pluralism, or a greater incoherence, than other cultures. Thus, the North American suffragist leader Carrie Chapman Catt, visiting Brazil in 1923, could puzzle at the

curious contrasts in its women's movement. Very many women are held in almost harem restrictions, never going on the street alone and shopping only when escorted by their husbands. On the other hand Brazil has many practicing women physicians, dentists, and lawyers, many able women writers, sculptors, poets and painters, a famous young aviatrix, six civil engineers, several women engaged in the chemical service of the department of Agriculture and several very notable in science.[107]

And young women with minds of their own, but under parental tutelage, probably suffered the restrictions most. Reminiscing about her frustrations in the 1930's, one woman who became a feminist said: "I think that resentment at seeing the doors of the university open to my brothers and closed to me showed me the clear profile of female inferiority, throwing me into the arms of the struggle for women's rights." The daughter of a well-to-do middle-class family, educated in a nuns' school but forbidden the university by her father, she studied commercial courses and began to work in a commercial firm, "at a time when only four girls took the cable car down to the business district."[108]

Could any social force or social movement account for this? Arguably incipient industrialization and the ascendancy of an ethic of bourgeois consumerism pulled European women, and perhaps even those of São Paulo, out of their traditional roles as domestic producers into modern roles as consumers, but these conditions operated less evenly on women in Salvador. Women in Salvador shifted, perhaps as early as the 1870's, from making up dresses by eye, as their grandmothers had, to paying tailors to copy Parisian dress patterns. They enjoyed window-shopping and could read definitions of their role as defenders of the home economy.[109] But in Salvador no profound economic and social transformation promoted broad changes in the roles of women.

The Brazilian feminist movement tried to elevate the issue of women's status to national dimensions. Though feminist groups had existed before, the foundation in 1922 of the Federação Brasileira pelo Progresso Feminino (the Brazilian Federation for the Progress of Women) marked the turning point.[110] The federation lobbied steadily through the 1920's, until Getúlio Vargas's government gave women suffrage in 1932. In emphasizing the vote, Brazilian feminists followed the North American example. As a symbolic issue, the vote for women required that legislators pass explicit judgment on the right of women to a public role. If suffragette victories in other nations seemed to assure the outcome in Brazil, still the campaign required that Brazilian women test and overcome the formal forces against their entry into the public sphere.

The branch of the federation founded in 1931 in Bahia rapidly showed success. It got support from prominent male politicians from the day of its inauguration with a solemn ceremony in the Instituto Geográfico e Histórico. Antônio Moniz Sodré encouraged its formation, and Juracy Magalhães became its patron. Edith Mendes de Gama Abreu, its leader, later described the Bahian movement as "a superior thing, of women from noble families, of the elite, of Christian morals." Perhaps its high point as a movement came in 1934, when the Bahian branch hosted the Second National Feminist Convention at the Bahia Tennis Club. A woman, Maria Luiza Bittencourt, was elected to the Bahian Assembly in 1934. But in 1935, after women had obtained the vote, its agenda floundered. Internal conflicts developed between its incumbent senior leadership and its youth wing, and concerns of communist infiltration troubled the leaders. Active participation dwindled to a hard core of ten to twenty members. From then through its dissolution in 1948, the Bahian branch turned to social and educational work, training more than 300 women in its vocational classes for "ladies and girls of good moral conduct." It sponsored lectures, organized classes and job placement agencies, and did charity work.[111]

The truncated incumbency of the first female state deputy, who was elected shortly before the 1937 Estado Novo dictatorship shut down elections for several years, demonstrated the insignificance of women's suffrage as a practical measure. Those antifeminists who had argued against women's participation in electoral politics had argued partly on those grounds. During the Old Republic, political machines were so tightly organized that the polls often never bothered to open. In this context, the vote was little more than a symbolic victory. Opponents could sincerely oppose it as a symbol of pure femininity's implication in corruption.[112]

Women's participation in the boss politics of the Old Republic, in coronelismo, had been limited to appearing at civic solemnities and to brokering favors behind the scenes. There were no famous female coronéis in Bahia, though the small-town postmistress who intercepted the letters and telegrams of the opposition was a stock figure in political intrigues. During campaigns, women might actively marshal support, but on election day they stayed behind: "There goes Felipe and here stay the skirts." [113] After the 1934 constitution ensured women the right to vote, there was no easy way for women to define their own platform. No other issue beyond the vote—except perhaps the issue of opposition to divorce—had the symbolic simplicity to unite and mobilize women. The feminist leaders tried to rally the movement around reform of measures subordinating wives to husbands in the civil code of 1916, but they had little success. [114]

The feminist movement, just as much as the medical profession, attempted to exert leverage on the family, to shift norms and change customs. Feminists saw the link between confinement to the private sphere and subservient roles within the family: "I felt subjugated by the family. One had to ask permission to do things, even though one was already an adult . . . and I didn't like that. It was a matter of questioning why my brother could do things and I couldn't. . . . I couldn't understand why I couldn't. And the struggle was to get out of that!" [115] Yet unlike the medical profession and the church, the movement was never chartered by the state. And although it developed its own intellectuals, its own press, and its own set of prescriptions, it never attempted to institute a permanent authority over the family. It remained a movement, rather than a public institution.

The career of one Bahian feminist, Francisca Praguer Frões, shows how she used her position of authority within the medical profession as the fulcrum from which to press a feminist argument. Although the implications of most medical ideology were hostile to feminism, she was able to turn the themes of eugenics into a criticism of marriage and men's despotic authority. Born in 1872, she graduated from the Bahian medical school (in the same class as her brother) in 1893, and married another physician, João Américo Garcez Frões, in 1899. She practiced obstetrics in a Bahian maternity clinic for twenty years.

Speaking as a doctor, Praguer Frões consistently defended women's rights in articles and interviews in the Bahian press. In addresses such as "Hygiene and Maternity," presented at the 1931 Second Feminist Congress in Rio de Janeiro, she was able to twist the arguments of medical hygiene and eugenics, which usually defended women's obedience to nature and natural hierarchies, in order to defend women's rights in the family. Maternity, she argued, was a sacrifice that women made, and they deserved to be protected by the state against venereal disease. The optional prenuptial examination in the 1890 law of civil marriage, omitted from the 1916 civil code, should be restored in order to protect women. It would be an insurance policy to protect women against fraud by their husbands. Although she pointed out that this would have implications desirable to conservatives, such as preventing applications for annulments later, she saw it as part of a move against men's tyranny and adultery, which would implant "the *true monogamous regime* . . . in the social milieu."[116] Hygiene and eugenic supervision by the state, then, would in her vision become part of a strategy to increase the power of women in relation to husbands who often abused them. It was of a piece with instituting equal education and a female police corps to combat the white slave trade.

Yet her organized feminism was as unrepresentative of common sense as Amélia Rodrigues's Catholic antifeminism was. Both were unrepresentative not so much because their programs stood at the extremes, as because their ideological and organizational mobilization was alien to most Bahian women. Amélia Rodrigues appealed vainly to the Catholic ladies to administer their organization. In 1931 Praguer Frões had to argue that "women's participation in public life is a natural consequence of world progress."[117]

In Bahian common sense, new institutions such as "a woman's profession" and "shopping," as well as new roles and places for a woman of family, lay like a new layer on top of the old bedrock of patriarchal norms. They were quintessentially urban themes; there was no way to realize them, except vicariously, in the country. And they were upper-class themes; they related to literate, privileged women. Some ideologues tried to connect them to old values, to justify women's education in the name of strengthening motherhood, or justify mobilizing and organizing women in the name of tradition. But it seems that common sense sorted these competing ethics into some evolutionary order. Traditions of seclusion and domesticity were perpetually giving way to novelties of emancipation and public participation. The differences tended to be cast in terms of generations and of country and city: grandparents were always scandalized, grandchildren always audacious; the country always lagged behind the city. This way of neutralizing the contradictions among their norms for the position of women led to the "curious contrasts" that the North American visitor Carrie Chapman Catt observed in 1923. It also gave Bahians less purchase on their culture, less ability to rationalize it and create reformist social projects. As long as the change in the position of women was interpreted passively as "a natural consequence of world progress," it was difficult for Bahians actively to evaluate or change their lives.[118]

Change in values occurred partly because of the growth of the middle class and the facilities of the city. The growth increased both opportunities and families' demands for women's presence in the public sphere. In some middle-class families, men encouraged their daughters and wives to find a profession. Gossips and moralists delighted in the figure of the Felipe, the man supported in part (or entirely!) by his schoolteacher wife.[119] Some men apparently were willing to reconcile their honor to the advantages of having a woman work.

Patronage and Kinship

The ideas that Bahians held about the relations of family and kin modeled for their ideas about patronage in particular, and about social relations in general. Common sense about obligations within the family and the roles of family members gave Bahians a personalistic ethic that resisted the organizational rationalization of political and institutional life.[120] The ethic of reciprocity that governed the extension of family solidarity to the society at large structured the novels of Cardoso de Oliveira and Xavier Marques. And it linked familism and patronage, in institutions for extending kinship such as godparenthood, and in the ways in which family ethics affected political alliances, from the Empire through the breakdown of familistic clienteles at the end of the Old Republic.

One ideal of behavior within the family was mutual assistance, solidarity and reciprocity, all summed up in the concept of *respeito*, respect. As the ethic of honor tended to divide society into competing individuals or groups, it reinforced the family internally. Roberto Da Matta, elaborating a distinction suggested by Gilberto Freyre, has argued that in the vernacular and in rituals, Brazilian culture symbolizes the world, especially the city, by contrast between the house and the street. The house is a personalized realm of warmth, security, and authority, in which relations and places are known and given. The street is a cold, competitive, impersonal realm such as the marketplace, in which each person is an individual, and every situation can be defined in its own terms. The distinction does not so much mark the separation between the private and the public realms— there are elements of house and street within homes and outside them— as it does the difference between the personal and the impersonal.[121]

And so, to understand how family ties organized politics, one should begin with the question of ethics for family behavior, and the relations between kin. The predominant ethic of roles within the family was that of the house—that is, an ethic of authority and solidarity. Relations within the family were supposed to be generous, warm, and fraternal. While it was important that everyone know their place, at the same time fraternity diminished distances within the family, even between a patriarch and his son, a mistress and her slaves, the family and its dependents. Bahians thought of their social relations in the same way, as being ideally as generous as those within the family.

The outstanding Bahian novel of manners and customs, Cardoso de Oliveira's *Dois metros e cinco* (1905), analyzes the ethic of the family by counterpointing the characters of two law students making a grand tour of Bahia in 1889, on the eve of the Republic.[122] The hero, the respectful Ricardo Luz, is the type of the gentleman, on his way to acquiring the prestige of the counselor. He elicits all that is generous and engulfing in the ethos of familiarity. His companion, the rogue Marcos Parreira, provokes its retaliation. From the opening of the novel, set in a student "republic" in Recife, Ricardo shows himself to be sober and hardworking; he has taken jobs while his father's fortunes are reversed. Marcos, on the other hand, having squandered his allowance, lives by cadging drinks, meals, and a sofa to sleep on. Ricardo pays Marcos's way in return for guiding him through Bahia, as he has been absent from the province for years.

On their tour through the province, the Bahians shower Ricardo with hospitality, which he reciprocates. They punish Marcos constantly for his abuses of trust: he is thrown out of his brother's house, chased by a jealous husband with a knife, caned by the ex-slave he mistreated as a boy. As the pair travel through the picturesque backlands by mule train, horse, and riverboat, even nature reaches out with branches, cactuses, and mud puddles to punish Marcos. As Ricardo moves through Bahia, he is immediately adopted into Bahian homes. He is offered meals, shelter, gifts, respect, and, at the end, a wife. By the end of his journey, Marcos has utterly exhausted his resources of parasitism. He finds a new home in the museum of a German naturalist when, in return for a lifetime sinecure, he sells his grotesquely tall body as a specimen.

The moral standard of the novel is reciprocity: Ricardo's favors earn a like reward, Marcos reaps the consequences of the ill will that he has left behind him. Yet in another sense the conclusion of the novel is the inseparability of Ricardo and Marcos, the "dialectic of roguery." [123] Ricardo, whose surname Luz means "light," perfectly recognizes Marcos's character and lies. But out of sentimentality he will not denounce him and keeps him as a companion. And Marcos, whose surname Parreira means "climbing vine," is the inextricable counterpart to Ricardo's uprightness. Though Marcos's brothers finally cut off his allowance, though every old victim in Bahia is eager to get revenge, Ricardo supports him. Such tolerance and generosity are commonplace. When they first arrive in Bahia, Ricardo and Marcos are invited to the home of the merchant Santos. There they witness the train of uninvited houseguests and visitors who descend on this "Noah's ark." The family doctor comments on the scene to Ricardo:

Interesting! What you are seeing in this wealthy house is what happens every day on a lesser scale, depending on each one's abilities, in all our families. Yes indeed!

This plenty, this open hospitality, and let's say it, this squandering. . . . They don't eat a third of what you see here; the rest goes to the kitchen. The servants gorge themselves, their friends supply themselves. . . . And here, my dear Doctor, is one of the reasons, we must say to be practical, why few people can be—I won't say rich, but at least well off. We live in a sort of communism. Interesting! Interesting! if you please; noble and admirable, I do not deny, but you must agree that it is not practical.[124]

Bahian generosity is not confined to the home. Through the spirit of charity, the Santos family extend their generosity to their employees. When a worker is injured in their quarry, the daughter of the family nurses him herself. Every family meal in Bahia is a banquet, and every banquet becomes a neighborhood fiesta, as hangers-on and visitors drop by to fill a plate at the second sitting.

As the Questão Braga demonstrated, family solidarity could also entail sharing enemies. In Xavier Marques's naturalist novel *O feiticeiro* (1922), set in Salvador around 1878, the relations of enmity between two families ripple outward through the city.[125] The Bôto family unite in support of their spinster, the spirited Eulália, who is courted by the heir to a Salvador fortune, the idealistic Amâncio. The neighboring family of Dr. Brasilino has designs on Amâncio as well and cuts off relations with the Bôtos. It is whispered that they employ sorcery. Plates of blood and chicken feathers appear outside the Bôtos' front door. Rather than woo Amâncio directly, the Brasilino family successfully court his father to promote, or demand, his marriage to their daughter. In self-defense, the Bôtos also commission a sorcerer, through dependents of the family, to counter the spells. In an ironic reversal of the apparent order of society, these competing demands reach the same sorcerer, Elesbão, who has also been paid to put a spell on the Bahian Republican Club, led by Amâncio. The sorcerer alone is able to cut through the knot: he manipulates the father to give Amâncio permission to marry Eulália in return for Amâncio's resignation from the Republican Club. Through rivalries that travel along lines of patronage, the decent families of Salvador surrender control of their affairs to a black witch doctor.

Novels such as *Dois metros e cinco* and *O feiticeiro* share a vision of Bahian society immobilized by a moral economy of reciprocity and webs of patronage spun out from family ties. The house, which ideally extends to the entire city, represents not only generous solidarity but also a hierarchy of given places and relations. Within the family, the exaggeration of respect due to the father and elders marks the difference in the status of different members of the household. Furthermore, the inclusion of an outer ring of dependent kin and friends around the core of the legitimate family adds at least another octave to the scale of statuses within the house. The complex

range of statuses and degrees of membership within the household itself
ideally suits the upper-class family as a model for patronage relations outside the family. Xavier Marques and Cardoso de Oliveira portray both
the charms and the defects of the impulse to extend family relations to
clienteles.

Familism, in order to organize society, needed some system of organizing the kinship obligations of the *parentela*, or "clan"—that is, the
extended kin group.[126] Patterns of marriage clarified kinship obligations
and defined the clan. Theoretically, in the European bilateral kinship system, any one person descends from, and belongs to, two different family
lines at birth. Through marriage, one acquires kinship in another family
with two lines. Thus, in the abstract, no rule set the boundaries of Bahian
kin groups in the nineteenth century. Because their extended kin groups
were large (anthropologists in the 1950's found that many upper-class Brazilians could easily name 50 to 200 relatives), in practice most individuals
could form close alliances with only part of their kin.[127]

One way in which Bahian landlord families defined "clans" in the eighteenth and early nineteenth centuries was through traditions of marrying
between certain families, usually cousin marriage. An alliance with one
branch of the kin, rather than another, made clearer the side with which
kinship ties to cousins and more remote kin should be strengthened and
the side toward which they could be ignored. Clans in the countryside,
through the accumulation of generations of intermarriage, were able to
create group identities that their lineage system alone did not.[128]

Marriages, however, happened once in a lifetime: too seldom to provide
the only basis for building alliances by creating kinship. Godparenthood,
rather than marriage, provided the primary institutional framework of
clientelism within the kindred and in society. The ritual of baptism symbolized the extension of the strong ties of blood. Although godparenthood in
baptism was supposed to address the spiritual needs of infants, in Europe
it had long ago taken on the profane meaning of a ritual establishing
fictive kinship. In Brazil, as in other parts of Latin America, godparenthood in baptism took on a broad overload of customary obligations. The
verb "to godparent," *apadrinhar*, became synonymous with "to sponsor"
or "to protect." Any client would be called a godchild, an *afilhado*. In
church doctrine, baptismal godparenthood created spiritual kinship not
only between the godparents and the child, but also among the child, parents, godparents, and the priest officiating at the ceremony. In other parts
of Latin America, the relation between the godparent and the parents of
the child, the co-parenthood or *compadrio*, might even take precedence
over the relation between the godparent and godchild. In their rhetoric,
Brazilians emphasized the relation of protection and obedience between

godparent and godchild. But in practice, they recognized that the stronger relationship was often that between *compadres*.[129]

One suggestion of the relation between godparenthood and clientelism would lie in the custom of landlords becoming godparents of their slaves. Masters in eighteenth-century Bahia would only become the godparents of the slaves of others, never of their own, but in southern Brazil in the nineteenth century, masters became the godparents of slave children from their own plantations. Antônio Cândido, proposing his theory of the relation between the patriarchal core and the illegitimate periphery of the Brazilian family, stressed the function of godparenthood as one of the links joining the two.[130]

But it appears that upper-class families may have practiced dual strategies of godparenthood. Some elite families, it seems, chose godparents for their children only from among their own kin: they preferred grandparents or uncles as godparents. Yet these same families agreed to be godparents to unrelated children of families of other classes. Individuals of the elite were often godparents to a great many children. In 1897 the countess of Pereira Marinho, widow of a millionaire slave trader, left legacies to each of about 26 godchildren she had sponsored over 40 years. It was not unusual when, in 1926, a much less wealthy spinster left legacies to 14 godchildren. In the northern city of Natal, a survey of politicians, industrialists, and philanthropists in the twentieth century found that these men had between 25 and 88 godchildren apiece. In the 1950's, politicians in Brazilian country towns could call on as many as 50 godchildren for support at election time.[131]

The law set no requirements for godparenthood. Yet the sanction of custom was very strong. The norm was that the godparent incurred an obligation like that of parents to protect the godchild, and support him when necessary; the godchild owed filial obedience and respect to the godparent. In canon law spiritual kinship was an impediment to marriage; in popular belief as well, sexual relations between godparent and godchild, or between co-parents, "made people shiver," as they were tantamount to incest. Traditional customs symbolized the relationship of protection and obedience by requiring that the godparents provide the child with gifts on special occasions, and that godchildren go to their godparents' house at Easter to request a blessing.[132]

Since godparents were desirable, and selecting godparents only once in a lifetime was no more flexible a means of building alliances than marriage, Bahians customarily acquired additional godparents at confirmation (*crisma*) and for both civil and religious weddings. In fact, considering the age difference between many children and their baptismal godparents, it would seem that parents used baptismal godparenthood as an occasion to cement their friendships with co-parents rather than to provide their children with lifelong patrons. That is how, in 1880, a woman evaluated her daughter's choice of a godparent: "As far as the choice that you made for the godmother of the [baby] girl I think that you made a very good one, because that way the woman will be your friend." [133] While the roles of godparent and godchild were strongly prescribed by tradition, the roles of co-parenthood were not. They were mutual, yet slightly asymmetrical. The parents of the godchild had yielded some of their authority over the child to the co-parent. It was virtually unthinkable for a parent to seek out someone of lower status as a godparent. [134]

Godparenthood, marriage, and recognition of illegitimate children provided institutions through which kinship could be constructed voluntarily. But it is important to remember that even blood kinship imposed few requirements upon Bahians. Inheritance laws required that most property be kept within the legitimate family and be distributed more or less evenly. Laws about parental authority weakly prohibited disobedience by children. Support laws, apparently little enforced, required kin to feed the destitute. But aside from this, kinship roles were not compulsory. Brothers and sisters, uncles and nephews, cousins and distant kin could not be coerced to favor one another. As William Goode has put it, kin were "ascriptive friends."

Certainly, the cousin marriage patterns of the nineteenth century suggest that families wished to put some limit on the circle of kin whom they would recognize. Linda Lewin has argued persuasively that patterns of cousin marriage in Paraíba probably reflected a strategy by men of building alliances by exchanging women. More often in the twentieth century, they did this by exchanging sisters. [135] But it may be that matches and marriages reflected the strategies of women as well. Men may have tended to break off ties with their families of origin after marriage ("Quem casa filho, perde filho"), while their wives kept up ties with their parents and sisters. [136] It seems that married men found it easier to identify with the families of the sisters of their wives. That is, it may be that there was not an indiscriminate allegiance to the wife's family, but rather to the wife's sisters and the men who had married them. One can find examples of generous patrons refusing special favors to the families of the brothers of their wives, despite pleas, in one case, from a sister-in-law that her indolent brother was "going around in a threadbare coat and needs a better post badly," and, in another, from a shiftless nephew by marriage that he was living off the rent of three oxcarts and without some post, "I will wind up a bum." [137]

Women, everyone agreed, were especially effective at manipulating patronage and in the constant exchanges of small and large favors that kept kinship alive. As Xavier Marques has one of his characters say knowingly,

"O melhor empenho é o de mulher" ("The best advocacy is a woman's advocacy").[138] It may be that women were more "central" in kin networks, passing messages, dress patterns, and gifts of produce among each other so often that passing along a request for a job was simply another part of their routine.[139] But it seems that there were other dimensions to women's special involvement in patronage. Brazilians usually preferred to ask favors indirectly, rather than directly. Involving multiple intermediaries in a request meant that a single favor circulated through a larger circuit of persons, refreshing and renewing many relationships. As Rui Barbosa's sister-in-law wrote to her mother, "Please add your plea to Cota for her to ask Rui in my small name the favor of his pleading on behalf of this young man, the son of the baroness of Rio Vermelho, whose request is enclosed." Women's participation in requests from one man to another may simply have reflected this custom. Or it may have been that men preferred women as buffers to avoid the potential for offending honor in direct contacts between males. Asking through a woman, perhaps, a petitioner could pester her impertinently without fear of retaliation. Passing on a request via her daughter on another occasion, Rui's mother-in-law demurred: "You know very well that I am not a demanding person, but I have been embarrassed with notes for more than a month asking me; finally, I don't have any alternative except to bother you."[140]

However, there is also evidence that women relished the sport of patronage, that they practiced the art of social exchange with enthusiasm that often left men at a loss.[141] In 1844 one Bahian politician writing to another complained about not being able to fill a county magistrate's post easily: "My wife has a commitment with Barreto's wife, and I try to be a happily married man!" Then he proposed a plan to pretend to his wife that he had a previous agreement to fill the post. In 1876 four sisters of the Wanderley family banded together in a collective letter to their politician brother, João Maurício, pressuring him to arrange a nomination to suit them. Most of the favors that women could offer in exchange for those they asked were vicarious; that is, they were able to trade primarily on connections through them to men. Yet some women simply asked in their own right, for example as a nun and an elder in the family, or as a landlord lending her family's clientele to her cousin: "As for the other moradores who know how to read, they are voters and they will give you their votes." Ultimately, most formal power rested with men, and women frustrated by the limits to their actions could fall back on comparing themselves with slaves: "It is incredible that you, being with Ruy, haven't arranged a good position for Cazuza; it makes me say what our slave Tito used to say, only the one what seen it could b'lieve it."[142]

Kinship, or a friendship whose fraternity approached the strength, givenness, and naturalness of kinship, was the principal informal means of organizing political groups and parties in Bahia from 1870 through the 1910's and 1920's. The political model of familial obligation eventually submerged after 1920, inasmuch as a more complex society, a bigger and more bureaucratically organized city, could no longer be organized—or understood—in terms of paternalism.

In the early nineteenth century, the emergence of national political parties created impersonal political allegiances that could conflict with familial and personal loyalties. During the colonial period, when the population of Salvador was never more than 45,000, politics was largely a matter of administration and petition, of lawsuits and intrigues. Bahian families seem not to have mobilized permanent coalitions, but rather to have acted ad hoc to corrupt colonial officials to serve their interests.[143] The institution of elections and parliaments upon independence in the nineteenth century prompted Bahian clans to organize into parties that transcended any one family. That is to say, families were required to form coalitions and develop some norms of loyalty to the larger association.

The ideal model of parties in the Second Empire was that they should be voluntary associations of property-owning yeomen that presented candidates for election by their peers. Another ideal, usually tacit, was that parties should be disciplined associations united by programs and some agreement on how to manage the spoils system.[144] The most covert ideal was that parties should cleanly reflect divisions between families. In each district, one clan should be conservatives and the next liberals, thus preventing confusion of family and party loyalties. Of course, the same ambilateral kinship system that prevented clear definition of any individual's membership in one or another kindred or "clan" made it almost impossible to define pure kin factions in politics. But despite inevitable impurities, Bahians expected the local party structure to follow family lines. They may have found it easier to realize this ideal in rural districts, where families were usually neighbors. Rural family groups were more effective than those in city parishes.

Political parties in Bahia in the late nineteenth and early twentieth centuries organized as clienteles, whose cells were the "clans" and their loyal electors. As the local units of a party pyramided into the leadership, they formed factions, which they spoke of in military terms: subordinates spoke of being "faithful soldiers," referred to their helpers as "lieutenants," and the head of their faction as the "chief." This language of discipline and command counterpointed the pejorative metaphor of treason: those with opposing interests were intriguers and egoists; undisciplined party members were "sharpshooters."[145]

Such language revealed more of a longing for military discipline than any reality. Under the Empire, both the Liberal and Conservative parties were splintered into hostile factions and included maverick "sharpshooters" whose loyalty had to be confirmed at every election or test. The Liberal party was obviously divided between the Souza Dantas abolitionist faction and the Saraiva emancipationist faction, while the Conservative party seemed more united under the slavocrat baron of Cotegipe.[146] But during Cotegipe's final ministry, near the end of the Empire, the Santo Amaro Conservative boss Araujo Pinho wrote to his chieftain and father-in-law Cotegipe that "in my district the Liberal candidate, who was defeated last time, got a very good vote—due to his relatives and friends from the Conservative side who helped him this time. There is no party discipline." [147] Under the Republic, Bahian parties were less cohesive than during the Empire. They split repeatedly; none attained any significant continuity. Because parties were unstable coalitions, the chieftains of parties built personal familial clienteles. Rather than staff their administrations with the heads of factions, they preferred to fill their governments with politicians who were personally loyal to them.[148]

The hardest conflicts of ethics in both imperial and republican politics arose when a family was divided by politics. In making appointments, for example, Bahian politicians constantly had to choose between party and family loyalties, between patronage and nepotism. To occasionally bend party loyalty in order to favor relatives was a peccadillo. The newly elected candidate who gave a choice sinecure to a kinsman from the opposite party might be reminded that he was breaking a trust: "Politics knows no flesh [*não tem entranhas*], Sr. Dr. Assis, and he who needs to place adversary relatives should not accept positions of confidence." A leader of the Conservative party such as Pedro Moniz might complain of the harsh treatment accorded a Liberal, Virgílio Gordilho, who had been stripped of his position as public prosecutor in Salvador, while another Liberal was kept for reasons of kinship: "Family relations should not be above public interest, but in any case, Dr. Virgílio is *my* son-in-law." But to permanently split a family over political loyalties was a cardinal sin. When the Dantas clan in the northeast corner of the province split over the question of who would be the candidate on the party's official slate in 1856, other politicians in the party were unanimous in their protestations that it would be far better to abandon ambitions than to provoke a split in the family. When the Barbosa de Oliveira family divided between the two factions of the Liberal party, Rui's uncle Barbosa de Almeida still huffed years afterward that it was unseemly of Rui to open a polemic between kinsmen in public.[149]

Indeed, the career of Rui Barbosa admirably illustrates the intertwining of the informal familial norms and the official impersonal norms for political behavior during the Empire and Old Republic. In large part because he embodied classical liberal principles for his generation, his nepotism and his exploitation of the spoils system have been unsparingly exposed. João Barbosa, his father, was a physician and a failed entrepreneur, who died with his brickyard bankrupt. João succeeded as a politician, however, helped by his marriage to the sister of his cousin, Luis Antônio Barbosa de Almeida, a leader of the Liberal party. Nonetheless, in 1865, just as Rui was beginning law school in Recife, João Barbosa followed José Antônio Saraiva in founding a new faction of the Liberal party, breaking in the process with his brother-in-law Luis Antônio. This family quarrel never healed, despite occasional truces.[150]

After his father died in 1874, Rui inherited his family's personal connections with the leadership of the Bahian Liberals. He was in effect adopted by his father's friend, Manuel Pinto de Souza Dantas. Young Rodolfo Dantas, Manuel's son, was his close companion. Rui had prestige of his own from his brilliant advocacy of abolition. But he first entered Congress in the Sinimbú ministry of 1878 on the coattails of Dantas's leadership. Indeed, when Rui married a woman from one of the obscure branches of the Bandeira family rather than a Dantas daughter, he showed an independence that presaged his eventual break with the Dantas faction.[151]

Though falling with the Liberals in the Bahian congressional elections in 1885, Rui established his autonomous power base by joining the military conspirators who overthrew the emperor and declared the Republic in 1889. His position as minister of finance in the early stages of the military government gave him immense power, which he might have used to build his own political machine in Bahia. He chose instead to build his career in Rio, among the elite of national politics. He was elected senator from Bahia during much of the Republic, but his ambition was the presidency, and his role as Brazil's foremost statesman removed him from the intrigues of backland coronéis that dominated Bahian elections.[152]

Once installed at the top of Brazilian politics in the 1880's, Rui became a patron in his own right. His correspondence shows how much a political family took it for granted that they should broker favors and keep a few for themselves. He was able to promote the career of his wife's young brother, Carlos Bandeira, whom they had raised after his father-in-law died. He gave his sister-in-law's husband a position on a government commission to Portugal, and in the 1910's and 1920's he built his Bahian political connections around the careers of his sons. But Rui remained estranged from his Barbosa de Almeida kin and apparently did not attempt to protect all of his Bandeira kin. Despite letters from Adelaide, he would not promote their brother Cazuza, a government clerk who was too poor to marry, though he later brought Cazuza into his house during illness. By the ethic of familism, he had shown himself ungenerous toward one of his brothers-in-law, and his sisters-in-law did not hesitate to say so. By the ethic of liberalism, he had perhaps shown himself corrupt in granting favors to Carlos, another of his brothers-in-law. It is easy, then, to find a contradiction between Rui's rhetorical condemnation of favoritism and nepotism, of the "plague of kinfolk" who became "sucklings at the thousand-tipped udders of the state," and his practice of ordinary nepotism.[153]

During the years of Rui Barbosa's active career, the late Empire and early Republic, politicians felt the tension between the ideals of family loyalty and "impersonal" political partisanship. And at the same time, a third ideal, effective democratic suffrage, reemerged in the 1870's to complicate the use of kinship among the elite to organize politics. The issue of party loyalty and family loyalty largely concerned the organization of power within the group of propertied electors, at the top and middle ranks of society. During most of the Empire, the two-tiered system of indirect elections made politics a transaction among local notables. Districting arrangements gave greater weight to rural districts than to the cities. By the late Empire, one wing of the Liberal party voiced the ideal of popular democracy. This challenged the domination of families and the family ethic. In 1881 the Saraiva Law instituted direct elections, albeit with a property requirement that required high cash incomes of urban electors while requiring less landed property of rural electors.[154] In 1891 the republican constitution abolished the property requirement altogether but restricted suffrage to literate males. The electorate of Bahia grew only slightly, if at all, from Empire to Republic, as few people without property could read and write.[155] Still, even a slightly enlarged electorate challenged the oligarchies to invent new techniques of clientelism.

On the one hand, bosses during the Republic met the challenge of political participation with new techniques of fraud and repression. The *política dos governadores* deal among the state oligarchies in 1900 informally gave incumbents at each level of the pyramid of offices—from the Congress to the state to the county—the power, as a last resort, to veto unfavorable election results at the level below them. This tactic of "beheading" opposition politicians who chanced to win an election made it likely that the opposition would capitulate and allow the entrenched parties to rig "penstroke" elections.[156] Even earlier, in the 1890's, Bahians commented on an increase in fraud. "In the old days, we had the stick that resounded in the polls on the backs of the poll watchers and the phantom voters; nowadays, the government . . . [has] created the penstroke, peaceable institution, a poem of wisdom, that does everything without spilling blood, without noise or riot," sneered a newspaper columnist.[157]

On the other hand, Bahia's republican oligarchies tried to meet the challenge of "democracy" by reforging the ethic of paternalism. Principally, they raised the price they paid to some clients. Among the mobile, proletarian workers of the factories, shops, and port of Salvador, the old, given clientelism of landlords and tenants no longer held. Some party leaders at the state level, such as Seabra in the 1880's and Antônio Calmon and Octávio Mangabeira in the 1910's and 1920's, continued to trade on their "popularity" in Salvador—that is, on a multitude of personal friendships with lower-class people—as well as on their "prestige," their ability to deliver favors to their electors.[158] Even in the countryside, it seems, many voters did not have memories of friendship or ties of godparenthood to the political families. They chose, rather, to barter their votes for new shoes or a hat.[159] To control the larger and less submissive electorate, parties became less like "tribal" families and more like bureaucracies, or at least more "collegial," in Eul-Soo Pang's terms. However, they did not establish permanent cores of officials and written bylaws. It seems that instead they grew by increasing the number of intermediate layers of the pyramid of clienteles. More "lieutenants" and "corporals" emerged whose power was brokered from the figure who actually held office.[160]

Coronelismo and election-rigging in Brazil were unwieldy systems. After 1910, splits between the powerful states that held a controlling share of the votes in Congress made the outcome of presidential elections uncertain. At the federal level, the restive army could influence the balance of power unpredictably. The breaks in unanimity at the center encouraged dissident factions in second-rank states such as Bahia to contest elections and then petition for federal recognition to unseat the old incumbents. In Bahia the deals among the elite and landlord coronéis broke down repeatedly. In 1912, ships of the federal navy bombarded Salvador in order to oust an incumbent coalition. In 1920, well-armed private armies from the backlands combined against the state police force in an attempt to oust the incumbent governor. Finally, after the coup of 1930, the federal interventor Juracy Magalhães dismantled the political system: he swept out the politicians in the capital and recognized only obedient coronéis in the countryside; in campaigns against "banditry," federal forces overwhelmed the irregular armies.[161]

But it was not infighting among the oligarchies alone that destroyed the system of coronelismo. A stronger ethic of democracy, or, better said, of participation and autonomy, had emerged among the middle class during Rui Barbosa's Civilista campaign in 1910 and the gubernatorial election of 1919. Middle-class indignation at the humiliations of election-rigging showed in demands for the secret ballot. This demand, eventually incorporated into the constitution of 1934, challenged the politics of clientelism. It implied that a democratic election was the expression of individual decisions more than a public, collective affirmation of support.[162]

The demands of clients in the capital and Recôncavo also seem to have changed as Bahia grew. It is instructive to compare the shop talk within the campaign staff of José Wanderley Pinho, son of a state governor and grandson of the baron of Cotegipe, before and after 1930. In 1919, tactics were divided between the traditional coronelismo of guaranteed votes and newer manipulative bargaining. A campaign lieutenant could warn that "Oliveira is made up of a flock of lambs and they are easily guided to any fold. Without anybody to herd them, the same thing will happen as the first time, I mean, election." [163] In the same year a powerful and jaded kinsman could ask Wanderley Pinho to: "make things clear and tell me whether we must go to the polls with the electors to conduct the Election on the 29th, or if it is enough to do it with a penstroke at home, or even if somebody there in Santo Amaro could make up the election by penstroke." [164]

At the same time, Wanderley Pinho's campaign needed hard-working ward corporals in other districts, negotiating with millworkers to buy their votes. In 1934, campaign workers were already using the secret vote as an alibi for not being able to calculate support in their districts. After the resumption of democratic elections in 1946, there were still coronéis in the countryside who could hand over the votes of their tenants, but Wanderley Pinho's campaigning in the towns had to emphasize general, rather than personal, issues, and to present the candidate in new ways: through flyers, radio, loudspeaker rallies, and automobile caravans. [165]

The primary virtue in the ethic of familial reciprocity was loyalty. For both parties it entailed respecting the obligations and duties accruing to one's roles: as father and child, patron and client. In turn, the primary vice was ingratitude. It consisted of denying reciprocal obligations. In 1888 a bankrupt landlord, ignored by his kinsmen, cast their indifference to his plight as ingratitude in the light of past electoral favors: "The three of them answered promising me, and [gave me] nothing—but when the moment of the election comes, it's Mr. Zinho over here, and Mr. Zinho over there." [166] Betrayal of the obligations assumed in a familial relationship was a grave transgression. Part of the humor of Cardoso de Oliveira's novel *Dois metros e cinco* lies in the contrast between the ferocity with which Marcos's brothers all disown him and the eagerness with which a family of strangers adopt (wealthy) Ricardo. Marcos's brothers expel him, not because he has squandered his allowance and never passed his first-year exams, but rather because he has published an anonymous lampoon about one of them in the newspapers. His ingratitude justifies their inhospitality and indifference to his fate. It may be that in politics as well, the Bahian upper classes perceived moves for autonomy by the middle and lower classes in terms of ingratitude. [167]

In the new, harder game of Bahian politics, clients could understand the reciprocal obligations between themselves and their patrons not as familial paternalism, but rather as friendship, as a contract, or as a bit of each. The self-justification of a Bahian supporter of the revolution of 1930, Raphael de Albuquerque Uchoa's *Odysséa de um revolucionário*, makes explicit both the conventions of patronage and his own hair-splitting distinctions of honesty and honor. After a youth spent in the army and failure as a storekeeper, he had taken a job with the meat-packing firm of Amado Bahia in 1916. Immediately he had been told that "politics here is part of the business of the firm," and pushed into wardheeling for State Senator Alfredo Queiroz Monteiro, Amado Bahia's son-in-law. In 1919, galled by the servility of his position, he asked the mother-in-law of a federal senator to find him a state job. Queiroz Monteiro, who "found it convenient always to keep me enslaved as an employee of his father-in-law," interposed another candidate for the same job. Uchoa's patroness, piqued by this affront, went personally to her kinsman the governor, arranged another position, and said, "Now go find Senator Queiroz and tell him that you are nominated Fourth Clerk of the Treasury, and if he has any prestige, let him try to block your nomination." Uchoa was indeed named to the place, but Queiroz Monteiro claimed credit for it. Later, in March of 1921, Queiroz asked him to enroll voters in the Penha district, in return for a transfer to another division. The election went smoothly, the transfer was granted, "and so, I ask, were there favors from one to another, or simply a deal, or almost a business transaction?"[168]

Uchoa designed this long preamble to clear himself of suspicion of ingratitude, before he proceeded to analyze the failings of Queiroz Monteiro as boss of the district of Penha. "His *prestige* should be great, but he never does the least favor for his partisans, who only get what they can obtain independently of his intervention." In Penha, independent electors were abandoning him, "reducing him to leading a politics of shop clerks, butchers, teamsters, and slaughterers." The failings of Queiroz could be summed up in one word: *stinginess*. Living far from his electorate, he would not receive voters in his mansion for fear they would dirty his rugs, he would not visit voters, and he would do nothing for them as city councilor. "He hasn't even the courtesy to pay a trolley or elevator fare for a friend." Bolting from the Seabra faction in 1924, he had betrayed not only his lieutenants but also Governor Antônio Moniz, "whom Sr. Queiroz had taken as godfather for one of his sons." An employee of Amado Bahia who cast a Seabrista ballot was fired the day after the election. Albuquerque Uchoa himself was eventually jailed during the 1925 declaration of martial law.[169]

Many of the themes and structures of the allegations that Albuquerque Uchoa presented echo those of the Braga Affair polemics and Xavier Marques's novel *O feiticeiro*. Direct antagonisms rapidly ramified along lines of patronage: to medical experts, to a sorcerer, or, in this case, to an Olympian battle between Queiroz Monteiro and a woman adept at maneuvering, the mother-in-law of a federal senator. Uchoa's attack on Queiroz Monteiro shows more clearly than the other cases that an ideology of contract mixed with the ethic of reciprocity. He took pains to demonstrate that his relationship with Queiroz had never been one either of loyal friendship or of "slavery," but rather one of ephemeral contract. Consequently, his disobedience was not ingratitude. At the same time, he wanted to make clear that Queiroz's stinginess (*mesquinheza*) disqualified him as a paternalistic patron. Albuquerque Uchoa's autobiography, the odyssey of his emergence as a masterless man, a "revolutionary" of 1930, carefully avoids challenging the ethic of reciprocity. Instead it portrays his career as straddling the fence between an individualistic and a clientelistic role, each honorable in its own way.

Looking back at the novel *O feiticeiro*, we see that Xavier Marques's fidelity to the nuances of the ethic of reciprocity blurs his idealization of the individualistic rebellion of the hero, Amâncio Neri. At its center, the novel contrasts the honest friendship and open courtship between Amâncio and the Bôto family with the insincere tactics of the Brasilino family: Dr. Brasilino betrays the Conservative party, defecting to the victorious Liberals on the day of the election. Similarly, the entire Brasilino family schemes to promote a marriage between Amâncio and their daughter by manipulating Amâncio's father and resorting to witchcraft. This opposition between good and bad characters at first seems consistent with the development of the character of Amâncio as a romantic rebel. After losing the legislative seat promised by Conservative friends of his father, he becomes disgusted with monarchical politics and joins the idealistic Republicans. He continues to court Eulália, despite hints from his father, and swears to her that he will break with his father if necessary. But rather than proceed to the expected confrontation between father and son, the novel retreats, conciliates, and evades the catharsis. Instead, well-meaning manipulations of the Bôto family rescue Amâncio from that fate: they and their mulatto dependents collude in the sorcerer's plot to have Amâncio resign from the Republican Club in return for his father's consent to marry. Xavier Marques seems to conclude that the duplicity of the black sorcerer, who cynically but evenhandedly accepts commissions to hex both families, is fitting punishment for the fecklessness of the supposedly civilized whites.

In the final analysis, there is no independent will in Salvador. Even the highest potentate of the novel, Amâncio's father, is subject to his passion for Marciana, his black maid. In a decisive vignette, the Bôto family and Amâncio spy the father jealously following her at the pilgrimage of Bomfim:

He hid behind the other passengers, while the adorned Marciana, hanging on to the runningboard of the trolley, spread herself out on one of the seats in the front of the same car. "He does well to guard his cattle," concluded Bôto. Amâncio smiled indulgently, certain that he had been seen by the Comendador. But vexed at the same time by that weakness in which his father had let himself be surprised, he broke off the conversation and shut up.[170]

In Marques's vision, Salvador seems to be a Möbius strip in which there is neither top nor bottom, but rather a twisted circle of manipulations. That vision flaws the conventions of the sentimental love plot; *O feiticeiro* fails esthetically, though perhaps it keeps faith with the creole morality of Bahian families.[171]

The vision of novelists as diverse as Xavier Marques and Jorge Amado suggests that a long-standing ethic of reciprocity, rooted in the respect and honor that members of a family owed to each other and extended through patronage to kin and friends, obstructed liberal democratic politics in Bahia.[172] But criticisms of corruption and familism in Brazilian life, especially in politics, did come to a head in the 1920's and 1930's. Intellectuals from both left and right denounced the inauthenticity of the Old Republic. One set of criticisms urged that the democratic principles that the political system used for its legitimation should be applied authentically, with institutional safeguards such as the secret vote, in order to weed out corrupt leadership. It also focused on the evils of patronage and defended the bureaucratic ideal of advancement through merit. Another set of criticisms took the gap between principles and practice, between the "visible Brazil" and the "real Brazil," as a symptom of the need to revise principles. If political practice in Brazil was not liberal, then perhaps an authentically authoritarian constitution would work.[173]

Some of the reflections on national problems in this period put the family at the center of their analysis. Oliveira Vianna's *Populações meridionais do Brasil* (1920) argues that the "patriarchal clans" that organized country people in the colonial period decisively molded the social psychology of the Brazilian people. Though centralization had broken their local power by 1840, their legacy still shadowed politics. They developed an internal esprit de corps, but built no external solidarities to encourage political integration. The classic studies of national character and the legacy of the colonial period by Gilberto Freyre and Sérgio Buarque de Holanda explore the constitution of families in greater depth. In *The Masters and the Slaves* (1933) and *The Mansions and the Shanties* (1936), Freyre portrays the links between slaveholding and authority within and without the patriarchal family. Like Oliveira Vianna, Freyre argues that the family, and not the Crown, organized colonial society. But he emphasizes that it was racial mixture on slave plantations, not racial purity, that left both good legacies of "hybrid and harmonious" racial fraternization and problematic legacies of sadistic authoritarianism. According to Freyre, Brazilian individualism emerged in the early nineteenth century in the context of rebellions against paternal authority within the patriarchal family. In *Raízes do Brasil* (1936), Sérgio Buarque agrees with Freyre that a paternalistic style of politics derived from the authority of the patriarchal family. But he develops the point further, arguing that the ethic of family was opposed to the impersonal norms of the state, and that Brazilians, particularly the sons of slave-owning patriarchs, were poorly disposed to observe a difference between private and public realms.[174]

By the 1940's the suggestions put forward in these essays inspired many sociological analyses of the link between informal family structure and politics. Most look back retrospectively at the decline of family power. Nestor Duarte's *A ordem privada e a organização política nacional* (1939) argues that throughout Brazilian history, the "private power" of the family and its influence in the rural neighborhood outweighed the public power of the state. Luiz de Aguiar Costa Pinto's *Lutas de famílias no Brasil* (1946) surveys private vengeance in universal history in order to illuminate the feuds of colonial Brazil. It argues that these feuds are clear indicators of the weakness of the state and of the persistence of a rural household economy that supported patriarchalism. Oliveira Vianna's *Instituições políticas brasileiras* (1949), returning to the question of political clans, criticizes the legal formalism of Brazilian politics for impeding adequate reflection on, and adaptation to, the real political institutions of the nation, such as the political clans in the countryside. Victor Nunes Leal's *Coronelismo, enxada e voto* (1949) studies the history of local government in Brazil, concluding that *coronelismo*, rural boss control, was a function of the decline of family patriarchalism and the strengthening of the central state. It was a compromise between family power, which was no longer patriarchal, and state power, which was not yet entirely dominant.[175]

To a much greater extent than hygienic programs, liberal ideologies, or religious moralism, this political sociology of the 1930's and 1940's began to give a name and articulate expression to the informal norms of the upper-class family. Its tone was often misleadingly retrospective, and it generally relied on a simplified version of Freyre's argument that the "patriarchal" family represented "the" Brazilian family.[176] But it opened the way for an informed, nationally grounded public debate on the social dimensions of Brazil and on aims and means for reform. As the Vargas dictatorships of the 1930's and 1940's vastly expanded the scope of government action and social engineering—in public health, "protection of women," "protection of infancy," education, civic and moral propaganda, social welfare, and the like—it became more important that Brazilians understand their social life and their culture.

How, then, did changes in Bahian upper-class families and in their culture happen? Some commonsense norms of family life contradicted each other, as well as the prescriptions of modernizing and integrating formal institutions. By controlling their children in order to make marriages a means of shaping alliances for the whole group, by referring their conduct to codes of honor, and by focusing the ethics of their members on solidarity among kin and pseudo-kin, families impeded the integration of the upper class around loyalty to bureaucratic procedures or liberal rules. The family throughout this period embodied the warmth and rewards of a particularistic ethic and particularistic norms. Unconscious and conscious defense of its traditional organization probably did hinder the political groups and movements that by the twentieth century were trying to build solidarity around modernizing ideologies and institutions.

In the course of the late nineteenth and early twentieth centuries, the collapse of the sugar industry and the rise of the cacao frontier unsettled the economic basis of the families of the old Recôncavo establishment; at the same time, it allowed precarious perpetuation of urban officialdom and the urban commercial class. A great many oligarchical families shifted their activities entirely from the land to the professions and trade. The next chapter examines how the organization of individual families may have shaped the spread in roles and the range of common sense. It explores the change in family organization that conditioned shifts in common sense from the perspective of these families' self-interest.

7

Mobility and Family Strategies

THE LITERATURE on French "family strategies" offers two challenging starting points for the interpretation of Bahian families. One is the suggestion that analysis should replace the concepts of "social codes of behavior" and "rules" with the concept of "strategies." People cannot possibly follow foreordained patterns in their relations with one another; the accidents of life are too varied and diverse. Instead, people compete with one another to achieve their desired ends, exercising socially learned, near-instinctive strategies. The metaphor is that of a game of cards in which luck deals the hand, but skill in following learned strategies for winning determines the outcome. An observer studying social action witnesses the outcomes, the end results, of people playing out these strategies, and can only reconstruct intentions by reference to them. Another insight of this literature is that the strategies of families might be understood in collective, even corporate, context. People live as though the ghosts of their dead were looking over their shoulders, and they plan not only for tomorrow but also for the days of their grandchildren. They are inherently conservative.[1]

Both of these perspectives on family history highlight—by contrast—Bahian peculiarities. For one thing, the institutional context of Brazil was hostile to the conservation of family property through generations. By requiring partition of estates, the Brazilian inheritance laws posed extraordinary difficulties for a strategy aiming at keeping a lineage's land and status intact. Economic instability made consistent planning for any purpose difficult. Second, the deeds and words of Bahians more often imply an impulsive and improvisational outlook on life rather than one based on a consistent, lifelong plan. The model of rational play in a bridge game seems somewhat remote from the spirit of their lives and their "strategies."[2] And finally, Bahians' "plays" in life, their actions, were often self-defeating. That may be the point: Bahian upper-class families were ultimately unsuccessful at reproducing their "patriarchal" institutions and unintentionally changed into something else, something "semipatriarchal" or even "bourgeois." They walked backward into the twentieth century.

To explore these possibilities we may try to reconstruct Bahian family strategies, particularly those regarding marriage, from the eighteenth through the twentieth centuries. The marriage customs that landlord and urban families followed from the late colonial period through the mid nineteenth century, particularly endogamous marriage, may have limited the dispersal of their estates. And the marriage strategies that they used to build alliances, both within clans and with other groups such as merchants and politicians, may have worked to increase their social influence. Around mid-century, changes in courtship customs weakened marriage alliance strategies and inmarriage strategies. Families relied more indiscriminately on general provincial and national marriage pools. By the end of the nineteenth century, parents turned to limiting births in order to limit the dispersal of their estates. Yet limiting the size of the family did not indicate thoroughgoing rationalization and planning. Bahian families continued to extend and expand their kin obligations to illegitimate children and godchildren. They did not all close themselves off from their significant illegitimate wings.

In the twentieth century, the crisis of agriculture turned many families of the Recôncavo toward a new emphasis on building cliques through friendship and kinship. Because of exogamous marriage customs, these supple and mobile alliances could take advantage of opportunities over wider distances than the old clans. Families invested in education and the cultivation of patronage useful in urban occupations. By the end of the Old Republic, there was a marked difference between the style of urban families and the style of those rural families that preserved the traditional patterns.

Inheritance, Traditional Marriage Policy, and Alliances, *1800–1870*

Contemporary European observers of Brazilian customs were well aware that the law of partible inheritance, requiring that every child receive an equal portion of the parents' estate, and allowing the parents to will only one-third of it, put special pressures on landed families. James Wetherell, English consul and amateur botanist in Bahia at mid-century, wrote of the "disastrous" effect of Brazilian laws:

Upon the death of a rich and influential man, with a large family, the division of his property in accordance with the law is disastrous in the extreme. When [he is] alive . . . there is always a home. . . . The father dies: the property instantly becomes divided by law; a portion goes to the widow, smaller portions to each of the children. The estates are sold to make those divisions; the sons sink into small landed proprietors . . . the children have no tie beyond relationship to draw them together, or to keep them in one place, and they become dispersed over the empire. . . . The Brazilians already see the disastrous effects of this law, and of course every generation shows its bad consequences still more. . . . Thus, there are few *families* in Brazil; although some have adopted the dreadful alternative of intermarriages to keep some portions of the large estates amongst them. These marriages are carried to such an extreme that some are even incestuous.[3]

The case imagined by Wetherell illustrates the "ideal" workings of the system of inheritance; in fact, families had at their disposal a variety of devices for favoring one heir. Still, the dispersing pressure of the inheritance laws was among the most important determinants of Brazilian family strategies.

Brazilian law stood at an egalitarian extreme in systems of marital property and inheritance, preferring absolute community of property in marriage and equal division of property at inheritance. Though it allowed families leeway in assigning property, with such devices as freedom to will one-third of the estate, premarital dowry settlements, and entails in the line of primogeniture, it limited them. For example, Brazilian legislation early in the nineteenth century did away with all entails. Brazilian laws could be bent to a "stem family" strategy of establishing one child on the estate to carry on the family name, while sending the cadet sons and daughters off to the cities. But such a maneuver went against the grain of the laws and customs.

Demographic pressure compounded the pressure of inheritance law. The typical family of the Bahian landlords of the Recôncavo was so large that almost no testamentary maneuvers could preserve an estate. In the nineteenth century, a family of four children was the median, and most children were born into families of seven or more children.[4] Considering this, it is no surprise that the structure of rural property in Bahia was fragmented, if not pulverized. In comparison with the huge sugar estates of Jamaica, the typical plantation in Bahia was small, with a handful of slaves. Most planters in the sugar regions were small growers, *lavradores*, who sold their cane crops to the great landowners who owned the sugar mills. Despite the common practice of a group of heirs holding a property in shares until one could buy the rest out, the frequent division of estates upon inheritance must have contributed powerfully to forming a rural landscape of small and medium properties.[5] Wanderley Pinho's nostalgic evocation of the sugar mill lords from whom he descended, *História de um engenho do Recôncavo*, affirms their grandeur and stability, but the chronicle of his own family's sugar mill contradicts this with a Sisyphean tableau of energetic proprietors who raised the property up only to see it ruined by spendthrift sons or pass with daughters into another name. Analyzing similar phenomena in Minas Gerais, John Wirth has suggested that it may be characteristic of the rural culture of Brazil that "an economic elite in flux" created a compensatory myth of family stability.[6]

Taking inheritance division for granted, the rural families of upper and middling status in Bahia used marriage policy to preserve their status and wealth. The involuted marriage patterns of families that based their power on fortunes made in sugar, tobacco, and hides suggest that the concentration of the patrimony was a major aim of marriage. Restricting who could marry and directing marriages toward the children of relatives in a fashion that recombined portions of the divided estates were salient characteristics of their family strategies.

The more patriarchal of the two strategies was to prevent some children from marrying at all. In certain families in the late seventeenth and early eighteenth centuries, as many as 90 percent of the daughters never married. Among a sample of "traditional" upper-class families from 1800 to 1860, about a third of the women never married.[7] They were kept spinsters at home or were placed in convents. While one consideration was possibly the reluctance of upper-class families who fancied themselves pure-blooded to contract alliances in the colony, another was probably the cost of a dowry. Suitors quite reasonably expected that the dowry property be delivered immediately. As dowries could be as large or larger than an inherited share of the estate, a father had to be willing to break off a significant piece of his capital at each marriage. Legally a family could give dowries as deeded "dotal" property in a sort of trust that would revert to the family treasury if the daughter died childless. If she had children, the dotal property would go to them. But it seems that few nineteenth-century Bahian families gave their dowries in this form.[8] The most secure strategy was to prevent a daughter from marrying.

Through the mid nineteenth century, Bahian families placed some women in church careers. Young women may actually have preferred placement in the convivial Bahian convents to spinsterhood at home. Yet in Bahia the nunnery was an option for only a few women of the richest and best-connected families, who monopolized the much-sought-after places. Though it might be smaller than the portion of a marriage dowry, the dowry for the Convento do Desterro was large. Furthermore, Crown policy discouraged both the custom of fathers sending their daughters to convents in Portugal and the establishment of more convents in Brazil, perhaps fearing that too much wealth would fall under the control of the church with an unlimited expansion of the convents.[9] For most daughters, not to marry meant spinsterhood.

Sons also might be discouraged from marriage, and an ecclesiastical career similarly provided them with a dignified "celibate" status. Unlike nuns, who were strongly enjoined to remain chaste, Bahian priests and monks were tacitly expected to form illegitimate families that would not inherit intestate and hence would not multiply the claims upon the family's estate. And priests often returned to the family plantations as chaplains, further diminishing their differences from their brothers.[10] Sons and daughters diverted from the mainstream of succession and reproduction into the church served not only to enlarge the worldly estates of their marrying brothers and sisters but also to reflect divine glory on the family as a whole. The savings of a nun's dowry over a bride's dowry may have been less important in the calculations of parents than the prestige of the offering to God. After all, Bahians with children often willed the free third of their estates to pay for masses, even to endow hundreds of perpetual masses for their souls.[11]

Perhaps Bahian endogamy can also be understood as a patriarchal strategy to preserve family continuity at the cost of sacrificing the freedom of children as individuals. The most exotic tactic in the marriage strategies of Brazilian families was inmarriage. For Wetherell, it belonged among the curiosities of Bahian customs, along with dying French poodles blue and growing mandarin fingernails. For Maria Graham, visiting in 1822, it was reminiscent of clanship in Scotland. Yet it was a mainstay of the marriage policy of virtually all the most powerful families, and of many less powerful ones.[12] Many Bahians assumed it could preserve properties. For example, theoretically, a marriage arranged between first cousins would reunite two shares of the estate of their common grandparents. Suppose that a couple had four children, each of whom married and had two children. Arranging a marriage between two of those eight grandchildren would recombine at least two-eighths of the grandparents' estate.[13] Of course, families were usually larger and the potential gains of inmarriage smaller. A plausible case might be that of a couple that had five children, each of whom had five more. In a family of that size, one cousin marriage between two of the twenty-five grandchildren would clearly be a weak resort against the subdivision of property. Willing all of the third of the estate that could be disposed freely to one child or grandchild would be a much stronger tactic, yet the cultural norm of equal shares was very powerful. Most estates were divided evenly among the obligatory heirs.[14]

The rationalizations that Bahians gave for their strategy of cousin marriage varied widely. Justifying the behavior of their own families, they spoke of the desire to protect the purity of blood or race by not admitting spouses of unknown ancestry. Petitioning the ecclesiastical tribunals to grant dispensations from the impediment of consanguinity, they cited affection, or the lack of anyone of equal station in the neighborhood. Implicitly, they invoked caste rules that forbade marriage with anyone colored. It was only in gossiping about marriages arranged by other families that they would speak of calculation and "interest."[15]

The practice appeared to Maria Graham chiefly as having the effect of defining a family core. She spent an evening in Rio with some handsome ladies, "most of them sisters, or cousins, or nieces of the lady of the house," and later reflected:

The family attachments here are quite beautiful; they are as close and as intimate as those of clanship in Scotland: but they have their inconveniences, in the constant intermarriages between near relations, as uncles with their nieces, aunts with their nephews, &c.; so that marriages, instead of widening connections, diffusing property, and producing more general relations in the country, seems [sic] to narrow all these, to hoard wealth, and to withdraw all the affections into too close and selfish a circle.[16]

Families such as the Gonçalves Tourinhos, merchant-planters who had their country base in Santo Amaro and São Francisco do Conde, illustrated the intensity of endogamy that these strategies could attain. The recorded alliances within the family began in 1836 when a widower, José Vicente Gonçalves Tourinho, remarried to his niece, the daughter of his elder brother, the coconut trader "João dos Cocos." By his first wife, he had had three children. By his niece, Maria Euphrosina, he was to have nineteen, of whom twelve survived to maturity. In 1850 his son by the first marriage Demétrio, a doctor and soon to be the founder of the newspaper of the Liberal party, married another daughter of João dos Cocos, Maria das Mercês. Demétrio was marrying his first cousin, also his stepmother's younger sister. Of Demétrio's six children by Maria das Mercês, three married children of José Vicente and Maria Euphrosina—that is, married their "aunts" and "uncles." The difference in age between Demétrio and his half-brothers and sisters was such that his children and his father's children, whose marriages took place in the 1870's, were more or less the same age. By the time that the patriarchal José Vicente died in 1888, he had seen others of his and Demétrio's children marry their first and second cousins. Inmarriages among the Tourinhos continued into the 1920's. When a North American anthropologist came to study their community in the 1950's, the web of alliances within the family was so tangled that from the perspective of contemporaries the pattern was simply one of a long tradition of marriages between two families of different surnames.[17]

Perhaps variations in the rate of endogamy among families explain something about the motivations or logic of their practices. Comparing the rates of cousin marriage among several Bahian families, Kátia Mattoso notes that the families given to less endogamous marriage had fewer marriages, and that the families with fewer bachelors and spinsters practiced the highest rates of cousin marriage. For example, the more "urban" branches of the Araujo Goes family had many female spinsters, perhaps because the family found it difficult to provide dowries. The rural, land-holding Costa Pinto family, on the other hand, had a very high rate of endogamous marriage, and more men who never married. Perhaps their strategies concentrated on preserving their actively exploited properties. At least one of their marriages, the 1856 marriage of Maria Rita Lopes at the age of thirteen to her cousin Antônio da Costa Pinto, later viscount of Oliveira, was certainly an arranged marriage. She had been orphaned at the age of six, and her guardian married her to his son when the latter was only eighteen.[18]

Celibacy and inmarriage were not the only traditional family strategies in Bahia. Indeed, it seems that they were characteristic of established, especially landed, families. They may have fit goals of keeping land and slaves intact as a family estate, or of preserving ties with kin-neighbors, but they were apparently less appropriate to merchants and those in other urban occupations, whose capital in some cases was more liquid and more comfortably divisible.[19] Other strategies of marriage characterized merchants in Salvador and the sorts of exogamous alliances that took place among families of merchants, planters, and professionals in the upper class.

Although most planters in Bahia belonged to families that had been on the land for at least a generation, and had been born in Bahia, most merchants in the late colonial period, the early nineteenth century, had been born in Portugal. Perhaps as immigrants they pursued more individualistic and less familial strategies. Sometimes merchants made choices that indicated allegiance to a family based in Portugal. Some merchants, especially those in partnership with their brothers, remained unmarried, possibly out of an agreement to ensure the continuity of the capital of a partnership past the death of the bachelor brother. Merchants' strategies of arranging their daughters' marriages could also indicate an identification with Portuguese kin. One pattern of marriage that does seem to have been characteristic of merchants was the cultivation of an immigrant nephew as an apprentice or junior partner who might marry their daughter and succeed to the business. And beyond marriage, their choices about inheritance and legacies indicated transatlantic allegiances. Bahia's merchants, who were mostly Portuguese-born, made their Portuguese brothers, cousins, and nephews, as well as their sons, into junior partners and successors.[20]

In the nineteenth century, the Portuguese merchants in Salvador were of two sorts, and when it came to making marriages with Bahians, they followed two paths. The smaller merchants, who were middlemen and shopkeepers, lived in the shorefront commercial quarter of the Lower City, in apartments above their ground floor shops. They perhaps had fewer chances to meet similarly ranking small planters of the Recôncavo, who participated less in the social life of the capital. When they married in Brazil, they tended to make alliances within the Lower City community, with the daughters of other merchants and urban artisans. Or they tended to form consensual unions and not marry at all. The grander merchants, who were wholesale importers and factors, had relations throughout the Recôncavo. They dealt directly with the sugar mill owners and tobacco growers, establishing associations based on confidence. These rich men sometimes bought plantations and herds themselves. They or their children married into the families of the rich planters and mill owners.[21]

Alliances between urban and landed families had mutual advantages. From the perspective of the larger merchants in the early nineteenth century, both the strategy of establishing one's sons on the land and that of marrying into a landed family oneself probably reflected the recognition that landed wealth had more prestige than the wealth of the businessman, and the calculation that agriculture had more certainty than overseas commerce. Crops were subject to the weather, but ships and their cargoes were vulnerable to storms, and the Bahian trade fluctuated unpredictably according to panics in the market and whims of policy. From the perspective of planter families, these alliances with wealthy merchants would bring capital into the estate and financial connections to all the clan. Whereas endogamous marriage contributed to an essentially conservative strategy for the patrimony, alliances with Portuguese merchants allowed families to annex new capital and lines of business.

The traditional marriage strategies of upper-class families in Bahia from the late colonial period through the nineteenth century thus comprised at least two major variants. One strategy, which seems to have been characteristic of country families (and to a lesser degree of merchants), emphasized endogamy and the restriction of marriage, perhaps seeking conservatively to reduce the division of property through inheritance, while defining a core of closely related kin. A complementary strategy entailed opening alliances outward from the family and the clan toward "strangers," making matches among established planter families, "newcomer" Portuguese merchants, and officials of the capital, each of whom could offer different forms of capital or power. One family might simultaneously pursue both strategies, building an endogamous core or stem, while extending offshoots onto new ground.

The Vicente Viana family, for instance, was established in Bahia by the Portuguese merchant Frutuoso Vicente Viana in 1750 when he married a Portuguese woman in Bahia. Of his three sons, two died unmarried. The third, Francisco Vicente Viana, a Coimbra-trained judge and eventually baron of Rio das Contas, married a woman from the Bandeira family in

1795, thus merging the new mercantile fortune with an "old" planter lineage. Several of their eight children married into aristocratic families of the Recôncavo, such as the Bandeiras and the Monizes, in the early nineteenth century (between 1814 and 1831), building a web of endogamous alliances. But in 1831 one of their daughters, Maria Clara Viana, again married out to an "urban" man: Luiz Paulo de Araujo Bastos, viscount of Fiais, a financier and industrialist from Rio de Janeiro. Of the seven children Maria Clara bore before she died in childbirth in 1842, three died in childhood, one remained a bachelor, and three married into titled, landed families in the 1850's and 1860's, one to a Bandeira cousin.[22]

In the nineteenth century, though, the "renewal" of established fortunes by marriage to rising merchants may have been interrupted. Around independence in 1822, British, French, Swiss, and German merchants supplanted the Portuguese in much of the overseas trade of Bahia, but they did not immediately take their place in the social life of the city. Differences of customs, religion, and nationality separated them from their clients. They built their own churches and their own cemeteries. The English and Germans built villas along the cliff at the outskirts of the Upper City, far from the unhealthy miasmas of the waterfront. They retired to Europe after selling their businesses to other Europeans. They did not sit on the city council or the administration of the Catholic brotherhoods and civic associations. Instead, they associated with the Bahians and the Portuguese merchants in the new and relatively formal setting of the Commercial Association.

Portuguese merchants had buffered Bahians from the Atlantic market during the colonial period. Although they functioned as parasitic middlemen, they had nevertheless connected Bahia socially to the mother country. The foreign merchants brought Bahia into direct contact with the markets of progressive Europe, but deprived it of the old cultural and social connections. In the early and mid nineteenth century, these strangers did not figure in the marriage strategies of Bahians in the way the Portuguese had. Over time, the foreign merchants became acclimatized, and Bahians Europeanized, until by the late nineteenth century they mingled relatively easily on the common ground of a cosmopolitan "civilized" culture.[23]

And in the nineteenth century, the sugar mill lords of the Recôncavo became powerful again, as they had not been since the seventeenth century. The war of independence and the civil disturbances afterward proved that their militias were the strongest force in the province. Their economic power recovered with booms in sugar prices through 1820 and again in the 1840's and 1850's. Along with big tobacco farmers and ranchers, the sugar mill owners formed an establishment of the richest families in the state. Their styles and customs came to represent the elite of Bahia.[24]

Although the families of the sugar mill lords no longer needed to build marriage alliances with Portuguese colonial officials in Salvador as they had in the seventeenth and eighteenth centuries, a new element in the family strategies of the Bahians was to seek marriage alliances with powerful families from other provinces. This first took the form of marriages with the new national political elite that had taken the position formerly occupied by officials of the Portuguese Crown. With the transfer of the Portuguese royal family to Rio in 1808, Bahians were among the many who flocked there to offer their services to the Crown and win favor at court. In the troubled 1830's and 1840's, when secessionist and republican revolts threatened to end the Empire, the Bahians proved themselves strong allies of the central government. Many Bahians joined the political elite of magistrates, deputies, and provincial presidents. The grand families of the Recôncavo developed marriage alliances with powerful families from all over the Empire, promoting marriages that cemented relations built at the court in Rio.[25]

Outside of marriage strategies, Bahian landlord families pursued two roads to preserve their status: expansion of their agricultural production and extension of their influence into politics and the urban professions. The failure of their agriculture and the success of their politics in the mid nineteenth century decisively changed their family strategies and even their family structure.

In the years of the sugar boom at the beginning of the Empire, Bahian planters undertook an expansion into new agricultural frontiers in order to enlarge their patrimonies and maintain family power despite the partition of estates. Roger Colson has argued that families all over the Empire faced the same dilemma of promoting large families, and that a "special demography of wealth" drove the Brazilian landlords who formed the establishment of the 1830's to expand production into new frontiers. The most successful of those frontiers was the Paraíba Valley coffee zone of Rio and São Paulo. In Bahia, the great families of the Recôncavo reequipped mills, bought more slaves, and stretched the cultivation of cane and cutting of firewood inland from the bayshore up the rivers and into the backlands. Production of hides and cotton in the sertão and tobacco in the Recôncavo also increased.[26]

But the drive to build fortunes on traditional crops in Bahia failed; the fortunes of Bahian landlords seem to have declined from 1860 onward. Land seems to have dropped in value in the late nineteenth century; after abolition, many planters complained that it was impossible to sell their estates. And there had always been a preponderance of modest and marginal mill owners. It is indicative that the wealth of seventeen "senhores de engenho" whose estates were inventoried in Salvador in the nineteenth century averaged only 58 contos (about $32,000). Merchants left much larger estates, averaging 85 contos.[27]

New Marriage Strategies and the National Marriage Pool

Although Bahians failed at keeping their state powerful as an economic center in its own right, they did succeed in staying at the center of imperial politics. Many of the leaders of the nineteenth century were Bahians: for example, the baron of Cotegipe and José Antonio Saraiva. In the late Empire, after the economic power of the province had declined, and when the military power of its landlords seemed obsolete, Bahians kept the prominence they had won in the parliament and the council.[28]

The attendance of Bahians and families from other provinces at the court in Rio formed a new national marriage market, and Bahian families merged into it as they had formerly merged families of Bahian landlords, Portuguese merchants, and colonial officials in Salvador. One of the most candid glimpses of this process is the memoir of Albino José Barbosa de Oliveira, the son of an urban family of Salvador that had prospered through educating its sons in the clerical and legal professions in the late eighteenth and early nineteenth centuries. He describes how his father, having seen him through a close scrape with marriage in his student days in Recife, arranged a marriage for him in 1847 with the orphaned daughter of titled São Paulo planters. The transaction, in this case, paired Albino's promising judicial career with his bride's diamonds and land, Bahian talent with a São Paulo fortune. But in other cases, Bahian families formed alliances in Rio with political families without great fortunes, pooling two regional reservoirs of influence. The decline of the prosperity of Bahian agriculture, and the relative success of Bahians in politics and officialdom, encouraged a shift in the strategies of the establishment families.[29]

Conventional Bahian customs of courtship gradually shifted, around the mid nineteenth century, to reject arranged marriages and to recognize supervised courtship, *namoro*, as proper and normal. As I have argued above, this reflected a change in informally held, commonsense ideas about marriage. And this change may have stemmed from a shift in the strategies that families individually were undertaking to advance their interests. The trend in patterns of marriage for upper-class Bahian families had begun in the last colonial generation, 1800–1830, but it took clear shape in mid-century.

One dimension of the change in marriage patterns was an increase in marriage. In the seventeenth century, as few as one-tenth of the women of some powerful families married.[30] The proportion of women from upper-

TABLE 1

Proportion Never Married Among Those Who Survived to Age 35
in Bahian Traditional Families

Year of birth	Men	N	Women	N
1740 to 1769	47%	15	61%	23
1770 to 1799	31	29	27	22
1800 to 1829	12	26	37	19
1830 to 1859	26	38	32	31
1860 to 1889	23	79	28	67

SOURCE: Traditional Families Sample (see Appendix).

TABLE 2

Proportion of Kin Marriages by Males in Bahian Traditional Families

Year of birth	Niece/aunt	First cousin	In-law	Second cousin	All	N
1740 to 1769	0%	30%	0%	20%	50%	10
1770 to 1799	10	25	0	10	45	20
1800 to 1829	0	15	8	0	23	26
1830 to 1859	7	10	7	0	24	29
1860 to 1889	2	11	6	3	22	63
1890 to 1919	0	6	0	1	7	85
1920 to 1949	[a]	5	5	0	10	41

SOURCE: Traditional Families Sample.

[a] Marriage with an uncle or aunt was outlawed after 1917.

class families who married, as recorded in genealogies of the traditional families, increased significantly in the early to mid nineteenth century. In the same generation, the proportion of men who married also rose (see Table 1).

A second major dimension of change in marriage patterns was the decline of intermarriage among close kin (see Table 2). Between 1750 and 1870, about a third of all marriages in the Bahian elite were endogamous marriages of some sort. Between 1870 and 1900, about a quarter of all marriages were endogamous, and between 1900 and 1944, only an eighth.[31] The decline in endogamous marriages suggests that parents were less able, or less inclined, to pick a match for their children. Whether or not it reflected the shift in authority over marriage, it showed that families were finding marriage partners outside the local clan circles of the early nineteenth century.[32]

It is certainly possible that *fathers* had never had much direct control over the marriages of their sons, because a father was usually dead by the time his son was courting a wife. Men married around the age of 28 to 30, and the median difference in age between husbands and wives was six to seven years, so that husbands usually died before their wives. Indeed, they tended to die around the time when their children were reaching marriageable age. Between 1850 and 1900, only 40 percent of Bahian men of upper-class families married while their fathers were still alive. (Because daughters married at younger ages, they were more likely to be married off by their fathers: 65 percent of women married while their fathers were still alive.) Mothers were thus much more likely than fathers to be alive at the weddings (and so during the courtship) of their children, much more likely to be making the decisions and arrangements for a match; 69 percent of men and 71 percent of women married during the lifetimes of their mothers.[33] This gave rise to some charming legends in Bahian families. "On the wedding day of my maternal grandmother [in 1874], my paternal grandmother was already expecting my father," Stella Calmon Wanderley Pinho recalled in 1981. "And she went to prepare the room for the wedding night. And they say that on that day they agreed that the boy who was going to be born would marry the first daughter of the one who was getting married."[34] In light of the preponderance of decisions by women in marriage choices, it would be interesting to have a fuller picture of the contexts and directions of endogamous marriage. If Bahian families preferred to marry their children to cousins on the father's side, could this have been because widows were trying to salvage ties with that set of kin after the father's death?[35]

These changes in patterns of marriage stemmed partly from a change in ideology, from a conscious collective movement of juniors against elders, of sons against fathers, as Freyre argues in *The Mansions and the Shanties*. Young nineteenth-century Brazilians did read European sentimental novels, come to believe in romantic love, and perhaps find a principled ideological justification for rejecting the despotism of patriarchs. They came to believe that marriages entailed companionship based on affection and to ridicule the open admission of "interest" in marriage. This movement was also supported consciously by liberal, egalitarian legislation. In the turbulent decades after independence, legislators lowered the age of majority from 25 to 21, abolished entailed estates, and recognized the inheritance rights of illegitimate children. They defended these measures on a variety of grounds but acknowledged that, added together, the changes had the effect of reducing paternal power.[36]

The nineteenth-century anticlerical attack on the church also clearly affected one dimension of traditional Bahian marriage strategies, the recourse of placing "excess" children in celibate religious careers. For women, the nunnery was in some ways the structural equivalent of marriage, as the metaphor "bride of Christ" implies. But a spinster at home really remained a girl all her life. For a girl to take vows was to "assume an estate" (*tomar estado*), the same words used to describe a girl who married.[37] The only status that an unmarried woman could enter, and then only gradually, without a demarcation or rite, was that of an "auntie," a *tia*, which never quite amounted to adulthood. In the 1850's the situation of the girl forced into the convent became the occasion not only for melancholy ballads and gothic romances but also for political conflict. In 1855 the ministry, led by the anticlerical Nabuco de Araujo, forbade Brazilian monastic orders to admit any more novices, effectively closing off that avenue to families. At about the same time, Alvaro Tibério, president of the province of Bahia, refused a petition from a father to have his daughter admitted to the convent of the Ursulines. In doing so, Tibério challenged contemporary conventions regarding the right of a father to determine the career of his children. In the 35 years during which novitiates were suppressed, Bahian establishment families lost interest in ecclesiastical careers, particularly as other professional careers opened for their sons and daughters. When novitiates in the monastic orders reopened after 1889, a few women from traditional families joined the revived orders, but men never returned to them in significant numbers.[38]

Much later, and in a less significant way, the family law reforms of 1890 and 1916 restricted traditional family strategies of endogamous marriage. Although the church had considered kinship within the sixth degree an impediment to marriage, the impediment could be lifted by a dispensation, and it seems that Bahian families could easily obtain dispensations. The 1890 law required that marriages with an uncle or aunt, as well as marriages with a double cousin, hold to a rule of absolute separation of marital property, rather than community property. Of course, forbidding community property in such marriages did not prevent couples from later willing property to each other or to their common children. The civil code of 1916 went farther, outlawing marriages with kin in the third degree (uncles and aunts), but it omitted any mention of marriages between double cousins.[39]

But the shift in patterns of marriage in the generation between 1860 and 1890 was not necessarily entirely the result of conscious rebellions and legislation against paternal authority. Elders themselves may have decided to abandon the authoritarian control of marriage. The traditional patrimonial strategy of restricting marriage was only one of the strategies that was functional for families, and it was mainly useful to landlord families. Bahian families had long employed strategies of making exogamous marriage alliances with families from other groups, and it could be that in the mid nineteenth century, parents (as much as children) shifted much more heavily to that strategy.

Criticism of endogamous marriage, for example, came from patriarchs as well as hygienists and legislators. Anna Ribeiro's father turned away one cousin's request for her hand, saying that he didn't want her to marry a close relative: "It was already said in those times that the good families of our land were degenerating as a result of the unions between close kin."[40] Bahian medical treatises on consanguineous marriage usually cited the popular argument that inbreeding led to idiocy and degeneration of the race, if only to refute it.[41] The Bahian press and folklore repeated insinuating mock-indignation against cousin marriage, as in this passage from a boulevardier columnist of the 1890's:

The Review is against it, not only because in general it produces bad results, but also because he has seen cousins who are at each other like cats and dogs, and strangers who have nothing to envy the angels. If the Review could, he would change Brazilian law to the Chinese law [forbidding marriage of those with the same surname]. But unable to do anything in this field, he protests that he will only marry a cousin if he sees that she is going to be left an auntie once and for all, because there interest speaks louder. That business of being an auntie, they say, is quite base.[42]

And it is important to emphasize again that parents did not abandon control of marriage entirely after the 1860's. The supervised courtship that they tolerated generally took place between young girls and older men. The median ages of marriage were 22 for women and 28 for men, and courtship of course began earlier. This pattern of courtship provided the fathers of girls with ample power to encourage some suitors and veto others.

For landlord families, the shift in patterns of marriage was part of a general strategy to urbanize their lives that began around 1870. At the same time that they tolerated courtship and loosened the seclusion of their daughters, fathers from the landlord families were cultivating connections in the city and seeking sinecures in public service. The changes in marriage coincided with the improvement of communications in the province after 1870 and the foundation of institutions in the city that allowed even backlands families to enter the regional marriage pool. In the early nineteenth century the seclusion of women and the limited number of "public" institutions restricted the social life of Salvador, but by the mid nineteenth century, it was a city with a theater, social clubs, and graduation dances. At mid-century, opportunities for courtship were still limited enough that young women may have had few opportunities to fall in love with anyone but a cousin or a brother-in-law. But a generalized upper-class marriage pool seems to have emerged by 1880 or 1890. By the end of the century, graduation parties and *festas de asalto*, spontaneous parties, brought young women together with a generalized "society" of young men ranging from medical students to shop clerks.[43]

But Bahian families remained extremely wary of courtship. In the context of these relatively open circles, the figure of the *almofadinha* became notorious. He was the dandy, literally the "pincushion" or "tailor's dummy," whose effeminate concern with his appearance proved his lack of masculine character, and who threatened to infatuate frivolous girls. Though not necessarily a fortune-hunter, his dandyism made him immediately suspect to sober fathers. In a culture preoccupied with the theme of the projection of character, with masks and facades, the almofadinha became the trickster of anecdotes such as the one about the son of a blacksmith who passed himself off as a pianist in the salon of a Victória family. One day, as the family was walking down a cobbled hillside lane to the Lower City, the girl surprised him without his diamond tiepin and white gloves, dressed in a leather apron, hammering an anvil. When he glanced up she said, "Keep on, maestro, I wouldn't want to interrupt your piano practice." Other figures of ridicule embodied the suspicions that surrounded courtship and marriage. The "Felipe," an indolent husband supported by a schoolmistress, or the young man who married a rich widow could both be invoked as evidence that women who chose for themselves in marriage would choose badly and be exploited.[44]

The Small Family and Conjugal Strategies

As it became harder for Bahian parents to shape the futures of their families by directing and restricting the marriages of their children, it may be that their attitudes toward children changed. Rather than force their children's lives into differing courses as components of a collective strategy for the family unit, it may be that Bahian parents began to "invest" more heavily and more evenhandedly in each of a smaller number of offspring. Separately and informally, they brought about a demographic reform of their own.

One indication of this is that around 1890, after they had accepted open forms of courtship, they began to limit the number of children that they raised. In Protestant countries perhaps parents could count on their children having internalized the goals of parents and making marriage choices that would further the collective interests of the family and clan. Bahian parents, who brought up their children to externalize authority, could not rest complacent about their children choosing prudently in marriage.[45] No longer able to determine that a set of their grandchildren would become the principal heirs to the family patrimony, parents still could defend their family's status by planning how many heirs they would have. The shift from marriage strategies to fertility strategies of perpetuating family status took the decisions from the council of parents, uncles, and aunts on the veranda, and withdrew them to the chambers of individual couples making decisions about limiting births.[46]

TABLE 3
Number of Siblings of Bahian-born Members of Traditional Families

Year of birth	Number of siblings	N
Before 1840	6.7	401
Second Empire (1840 to 1864)	7.1	87
Late Empire (1865 to 1889)	7.7	139
Early Republic (1890 to 1914)	6.4	138
Late Republic (1915 to 1945)	4.9	202

SOURCE: Traditional Families Sample.
NOTE: The mean number of siblings including ego.

TABLE 4
Family size, Bahian Traditional Families

	Parents born		
Number of children	1840 to 1864	1865 to 1889	1890 to 1914
0	17%	14%	18%
1–4	37	56	71
5–9	24	26	9
10–14	22	4	2
Total	100%	100%	100%
(N)	(41)	(100)	(131)

SOURCE: Traditional Families Sample.

The decline in fertility was not precipitous. The average number of children in a sample of Bahian "traditional" families may have declined only slightly from the nineteenth-century norm, from 4.14 for parents married between 1750 and 1874 to 3.7 for parents married between 1875 and 1925. The families of those who had migrated to the south of Brazil were slightly smaller.[47] But the number of families so large that they could dismember even an enormous estate declined. The average number of siblings, a measure heavily weighted to reflect the proportion of large families, increased until the generation born in the late Empire, after which it declined dramatically (see Table 3). Though the size of families declined, the proportion of very large families declined even more dramatically. A family such as that of José Vicente Gonçalves Tourinho, with twelve of nineteen children surviving to maturity, grew increasingly rare among the upper class. Bahians born after 1890 rarely established large families of their own; only 11 percent of their families had more than four children (see Table 4). Yet though the median size of families declined, it is important to recall that more upper-class Bahians were born into the larger families. Half of those born between 1915 and 1945 were born into families of more than five children.

TABLE 5
Age at Marriage

Population sample	Years	Median		Mean	
		Women	Men	Women	Men
Salvador, two parishes	1800 to 1889	22	27	24	29
Salvador, Santana district	1894 to 1898	24	28	—	—
Salvador, all marriages	1901	22	25	—	—
Salvador, all marriages	1929	23	27	—	—
Traditional families, all marriages	1830 to 1859	20	27	21	29
	1860 to 1889	20	26	22	29
	1890 to 1919	23	28	25	29
	1920 to 1945	23	28	24	29

SOURCES: Salvador (first marriages, parishes of Conceição da Praia and Paço), 1800–1889: Athayde, "Ville de Salvador," pp. 335–36. Salvador, Santana: Arquivo Municipal, Livros de Casamento Civil, Santana, February 1895–November 1898, livro 18.3–21. Salvador, 1901: Oliveira, "Demografia Santária" (1902), median interpolated. Salvador, 1929: Bahia, Directoria Geral de Estatística, *Anuário estatístico da Bahia, 1929–1930*, p. 246, median interpolated. Traditional families: Traditional Families Sample.

The cause of the decline in family size was probably deliberate limitation of births rather than an increase in infant mortality. Although Bahian genealogies, and even the baptism and birth registers, often omit mention of children who died in infancy, Bahian infant mortality probably went down slightly over the course of the nineteenth and twentieth centuries. Among the upper classes, the spread of medical advice about hygiene and the availability of vaccination probably had significant effects. Infant mortality statistics for the population of Salvador are unreliable, but they hint at a slight decrease in infant mortality rates, which fluctuated in the .200–.300 range after 1910.[48] It seems likely that women in the lower classes had more children, and more infant deaths, than women in the upper classes.[49]

It may be that Bahian couples limited their births by having women postpone marriage to older, less fertile ages. In some regions of Europe through the end of the nineteenth century, peasant villages regulated fertility by the custom of postponing marriage until a relatively advanced age. Average ages at first marriage for women might be 25 to 28.[50] Thus, chaste women would not begin bearing children until an age when the biological potential of fertility was lower. In Brazil, the age of women at marriage was low by European standards in the nineteenth century. Men married at a median age of 27, but the median age at first marriage for women was 22 (see Table 5).

For the Brazilian population, fertility was not as strictly related to marriage as it was in most European countries. Many more women had children outside of marriage. A survey in Bahia during the 1940 census, for instance, suggests that women who had illegitimate children began their unions at younger ages than women who married.[51] And because many girls who had children out of wedlock eventually did marry at a later age, the figures for age at first marriage may imply more postponement of child-bearing than actually went on.[52] This was not simply a pattern among slave families or "black" families, but rather throughout society. In the nineteenth century, white women also bore children out of wedlock in high numbers: disproportionate numbers of white infants were abandoned at the foundling wheel, and a third of all "white" infants were illegitimate.[53]

Among the upper classes, for whom female chastity was mandatory, the low average age at marriage indicates that couples did not limit fertility by postponing marriage, although the high rate of spinsterhood did limit the growth of that population. Upper-class women began to marry at later ages after 1900, but the fertility of upper-class couples had begun to decline even earlier. In Bahian upper-class families, it may be that one cause of the decline in family size was postponement of marriage by women. The median age of marriage for women born in Bahia increased from 20 to 23 in the 1890's.[54] But the fertility within marriage of the Bahian traditional families may also have declined: the fertility rate of married women, when standardized for age, declined in every generation (see Table 6).

It is likely that the decline in fertility was owing in part to use of contraceptive techniques, but Bahians kept silent in public about techniques and strategies of contraception. Despite their strong emphasis on obstetrics, the journals and theses of the Bahian medical academy almost never mentioned contraception. Theses on miscarriages always included at least a mention of induced abortion, and several theses covered the causes of infanticide and means of its detection. But the official medical press dealt with contraception by ignoring it. The influence of French pronatalist medical ideology may have led Brazilian doctors to their denial of contraception. The Franco-Brazilian publisher Garnier's marriage manual *O matrimônio* (ca. 1880–1900) provided a rare, brief discussion of the types of "matrimonial fraud," but it was deliberately unhelpful, as the means were said to be "all too well known and employed." The most

TABLE 6
Index of Fertility of Married Women in Bahian Traditional Families

Cohort married	Fertility rate	Index	N
1800 to 1859	.223	102	52
1860 to 1889	.220	100	42
1890 to 1919	.205	93	59
1920 to 1944	.169	76	17

SOURCE: Traditional Families Sample.
NOTE: The index is 1860 to 1889 = 100. The fertility rate is the ratio of the sum of children born in each cohort to the sum of years women were at risk of pregnancy (from marriage to death or widowhood), weighted by their ages at risk, in each cohort.

popular home medical manual, Chernoviz's dictionary, had no entries on the subject of contraception.[55] One consequence of the lack of public discussion of contraception may have been a heavier resort to abortion. Newspaper ads for patent medicines included products for women's troubles, such as little vials of Apiol to "cure pains, delays, and suppression of menstruation."[56] These advertisements hinted at their efficacy as abortifacients.

Whatever techniques upper-class Bahian couples may have used to limit fertility, the pertinent question is what motivated them to do so. Fertility apparently did not decline among other groups in Bahia until much later. In the census of 1940, married Bahian women who had completed their families reported an average of seven to eight live births—that is, almost double the number of children mentioned in the genealogies of upper-class families. Comparing the fertility of Brazilian populations in 1950 and 1940, the demographer John Saunders concluded that urbanization was the most significant factor in lower fertility.[57] But with respect to the Bahian upper and middle classes, we can speculate more closely as to whether the deliberate decision to bear fewer children was consistent with a change in their family strategies.

In Europe the reduction in family size was consistent with the shift to strategies based on the conjugal family—that is, the unit of parents and children. In England, Lawrence Stone has argued, the structure of upper-class families up to the late eighteenth century is best described as an "open lineage" one; the master's family formed part of an open household, in which its members lived in constant contact with servants, apprentices, and boarders. Affection between parents and children was less important than it became in the next period, in which the "companionate" family centered on the intimacy between spouses and between parents and children.[58] The change in the English family meshed with a great ideological and cultural shift over the centuries in England.

But the change in Bahian family size and patterns of marriage happened over about a century at the most, and it did not accompany a monumental change in the culture of families. Changes in marriage started in the early nineteenth century and had become established by 1860. A trend toward smaller families was noticeable by 1890 and had asserted itself by 1920. And it happened long after the superficial assimilation of the ideas and attitudes of modernizing Europe. Freyre has argued persuasively that even as Brazilian families put on the drapery of bourgeois Europe, they kept the form of the patriarchal Big House. I have argued above that in differing ways, Brazilian formal institutions—the medical profession, the law, and even to some extent the church—promoted models of a companionate family oriented toward domesticity. But powerful informal traditions, customs, and habits of the Bahians resisted this transformation. The diminution of family and household size did not entail discarding old mentalities and old strategies. Scaled down, some of the old features of the family took on different proportions, and others disappeared. Before discussing these changes, it is important to consider some of the evidence of an alternative rationality, or perhaps irrationality, in Bahian family strategies.

Illegitimacy and Kinship

The traditional family strategy of restricting marriages, and hence reducing the number of legitimate claimants on the family estate, implied a policy of favoritism toward some children and exclusion of others. The newer conjugal strategy of limiting the number of children but allowing them to marry relatively freely implied a policy of evenhanded investment in all children. Both marriage "strategies" that can be inferred assume some rationality in planning the future of the family. But marriage was never the whole story of Bahian families.

Some traditional strategies had nothing to do with concentrating the inheritance, and instead aimed at widening the numbers of the family, and of the kin. It may be, as I have argued, that men "escaped" the patriarchal family by taking lovers, by entering into consensual unions or parallel unions, but this was not entirely "outside" the realm of family norms and family strategies.

In biological terms and in informal norms, rather than merely legal ones, Brazilian families included not only the legitimate family "nucleus," as Antônio Cândido christened it, but also the vague "periphery" extending from dependent relatives in the household to mistresses and their illegitimate children, and to slaves and servants. In upper- and middle-class families, it was assumed that all women were chaste and faithful, and the historian will uncover little evidence to the contrary. Even the laws gave women the benefit of the doubt, stating that no legal doubt could be cast on the paternity of a child born to a married woman.[59]

But it was entirely another matter with men of the upper class. Many men had both legitimate children by their wives and other children by mistresses. Laws passed early in the nineteenth century tried to regulate property rights in such families. The law of 1831 allowed men (including parish priests) to make wills leaving their property to illegitimate children of any sort, and the law of 1847 subsequently allowed men to recognize their illegitimate children, if no impediment to marriage to their mother had existed. The law forbade a married man to recognize illegitimate children born after his marriage, but it was quite common for bachelors, widowers, and even married men, with their wives' consent, to recognize children born before their marriages.[60] There is no count of the notarial acts of recognition entered between 1847 and 1890, but they probably compared in number with marriages. A single notary in the 1870's might record a deed of legitimation every other week, but in the entire city there was at most one marriage a day. Posthumous recognition in wills was also common, if perhaps less significant as an indication of the social recognition of kinship between fathers and illegitimate children.[61]

The law of 1847 allowed a father to form a legal link between himself and his natural children without legitimating his union with their mother. It created an initial quasi-marriage, an informal concubinage, for a man before his true, legal marriage. Children born and recognized before the true marriage were "natural" and could inherit; children born after the true marriage were "adulterine" or "spurious" and could not be recognized. Thus all Brazilian family law, from the Philippine Code to the civil code of 1916, outlawed transactions between a married man and his "concubine" and allowed a wife to annul any such sales or gifts for up to two years after the death of her husband. The law forbade fathers to recognize children of adulterous unions. It also discouraged men from leaving legacies to their adulterine children by giving legitimate heirs leverage to challenge any such legacy as being an "indirect transfer" to the concubine. But fathers often gave their spurious as well as their natural illegitimate children capital in the relatively discreet form of schooling.[62] The lore of Bahian families is full of anecdotes of illegitimate children, even the children of slave mothers, being raised in the father's household in a secondary status alongside the legitimate children.

This pattern was established even before the law of 1847. In 1843, Francisco Joaquim, the illegitimate firstborn son of Senator Francisco de Souza Paraiso, was included with the legitimate children as an heir to his father's estate.[63] His paternal grandfather and his uncle were made his guardians. He was sent to Rio to study and given his father's books and decorations in the division of property. There were some differences in his treatment; he was the only one of the children not given a share in his father's house. But most of the evidence suggests that he got favored treatment. Confirmation that this was not an aberration came a generation later, in 1880, when the legitimate secondborn half-brother, Francisco de Souza Paraiso, recognized three natural children (1864, 1869, 1877) by two different mothers, a "crioula" and a "cabra," and also recognized "as his child the fetus or newborn to which the aforementioned Maria Geralda do Patrocínio will give birth."[64]

Of course, the best-documented cases of illegitimate children being added into the legitimate family are those of sons and daughters who demonstrated that they "merited" the confidence that their fathers placed in them. In the Moura family of Santo Amaro, one prominent case was that of the politician João Ferreira de Moura (1830–1912), who married a cousin in 1853, and after her death married her sister, his brother's widow, in 1859. Although he had no children by either of them, he recognized an adulterine son by another woman: Caio Octávio Ferreira de Moura (1878–1930). Caio Moura was born on his father's plantation, the Engenho Jacú, which he later came to own. He graduated from the Bahian medical academy in 1899, and taught at the academy from 1909 onward. With his relatives, he held city and state offices. Perhaps the strongest proof of his acceptance by the family is that he married the daughter of his father's sister and was later remarried to his first wife's niece in 1913. Though he had no children by either marriage, he did become the patron of his nephews. They were interns under his chair of surgery at the medical academy and later joined him and their father in politics.[65]

Though the adoption of a bastard son in the absence of other children created few conflicts, other grand families of the Recôncavo combined both legitimate and illegitimate half-siblings, sometimes in harmony and sometimes not. The Sodré Pereira family, for instance, based its prestige in part on the possession of a morgado entail that was fabled to contain great properties in Portugal as well as Brazil. Francisco Maria Sodré Pereira (1780–ca. 1835), the next to last administrator of the entail, had five children by his wife; he also had an illegitimate son after her death: Francisco Sodré Pereira, later baron of Alagoinhas. Jerônimo, his firstborn legitimate son, became the last administrator of the entail upon his father's death in 1835, just before the law extinguishing all entails took effect. Jerônimo never married, but lived all his life on the plantation, leaving several illegitimate children, whom he had recognized by notarial deed. Others of his brothers and sisters did marry, and when Jerônimo died in 1881, they and their children claimed the property of the morgado. His brother-in-law, Antônio Ferrão Moniz, wrote in his journal:

We are very busy now with lawsuits. Jerônimo Sodré, who was the last administrator of the entail of the Sodrés, died last month (October 24th) and recognized children of his slaves and married one of their daughters to a little Portugee. These characters got it into their heads that they can be heirs of the morgado, and so are creating disturbances so that they can take over the sugar mill that was part of it, and in fact took it by force and are in there armed, so that it will be necessary to throw them out by force.

They did succeed, "with some effort," in taking back the sugar mill. In the subsequent lawsuit, the legitimate nephews argued successfully that the personal property of Jerônimo did indeed belong to his recognized bastards, but that the property of the extinguished entail should be distributed

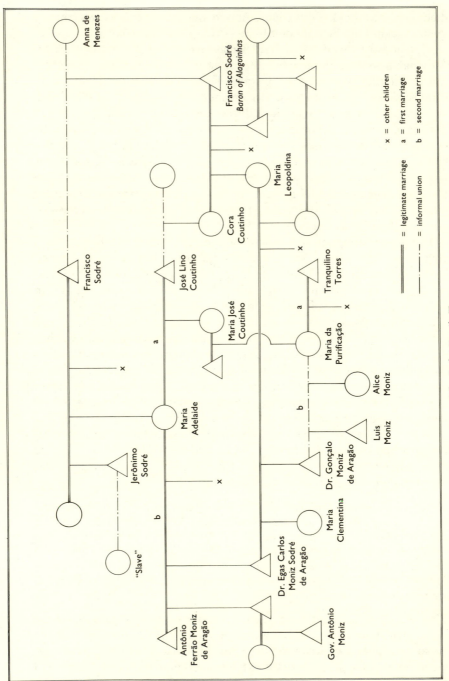

The Sodré Family Tree

x = other children
a = first marriage
b = second marriage

—— = legitimate marriage
—— = informal union
—·—·— = informal union

according to the laws governing morgados, which required that property pass to legitimate collateral kin rather than illegitimate children.[66]

If the issue of inheritance property might divide legitimate and illegitimate members of the family, the supposed dishonor of bastardy apparently did not. In the Sodré Pereira family, marriages repeatedly intertwined legitimate and illegitimate branches (see genealogical chart). The illegitimate youngest brother, Francisco (1818–82), married Cora Coutinho (1819–80), the illegitimate daughter of the great Bahian physician and politician José Lino Coutinho. Around the same time, in 1834, Francisco's legitimate half-sister, Maria Adelaide Sodré Pereira, married Lino Coutinho himself. Lino Coutinho died soon afterward, and Maria Adelaide remarried in 1837 to Antônio Ferrão Moniz de Aragão (1813–87), once secretary of public education in Bahia. Maria and Antônio had six children; Francisco and Cora had ten.

In 1867 Maria's son Egas Carlos Moniz Sodré de Aragão (1842–93), a physician, married Francisco's daughter Maria Leopoldina (1845–1915). This marriage reunited the legitimate and illegitimate lineages of the family and affirmed links between the brothers of Egas, who had provincial political and military careers, and the brothers of Maria Leopoldina, who were chieftains of the Liberal party in Santo Amaro and ministers and councilors of the Empire. One of the nine children of Egas and Maria Leopoldina, Maria Clementina Moniz Sodré de Aragão (1872–1944), married the son of one of Egas's brothers, Antônio Moniz, who became governor of Bahia. Another daughter married the son of one of Maria Leopoldina's brothers.[67] A third, Gonçalo Moniz (1870–1939), was medical professor at the Bahian academy and author of *A consanguineidade e o código civil brasileiro*.[68]

With Gonçalo Moniz, the family once again issued an illegitimate branch. Around 1898, he entered into a consensual union with his widowed cousin Maria da Purificação Coutinho da França (1867), the granddaughter of Maria Adelaide Sodré Pereira.[69] They had two children out of wedlock: Luis (1899–1902), who died in infancy, and Alice (1903), whom he recognized both in the civil register and in notarial deeds.[70] Gonçalo and Maria da Purificação later married, thus legitimating their children.

This thicket of endogamy and illegitimacy may convey how important, or perhaps how ordinary, the question of legitimacy was in Bahia, even in families of the elite. The list of members of these families, which included barons, ministers, and councilors of the Empire and governors and senators of the Republic, would, if extended to the layer of brothers-in-law, include a good many provincial presidents and governors of Bahia, high judges, and presidents of the medical academy. If bastardy could divide the Sodrés on an issue of property, as an issue of propriety it apparently did not, even in the Victorian century. As Kátia Mattoso has put it, there were many hypocrisies in Bahian society, but concubinage was openly admitted.[71]

The many private decisions to bring illegitimate children into the family, and the legal reform requiring that any recognized illegitimate children inherit equally, indicate that reducing the number of heirs was not always the dominant consideration in traditional Bahian family strategies. Indeed, the kinship customs of upper-class Bahian families seem to have been largely designed to broaden the range of dependent kin and children through alliances. Through godparenthood, couples acquired an informal obligation to support and protect the godchild. Through informal adoption of *filhos de criação*, many families brought abandoned or pauper children into their homes and raised them, using them as servants and paying for their upbringing. Families often took their grandchildren and nephews into their homes as well, in effect adopting them.[72]

It may be mistaken to analyze Bahian family strategies, even those of the big landed families, exclusively in terms of a lineage-oriented, stem-family goal of "preserving property." The horizons of Bahian families, especially those of the upper class, were broader than those of French peasants; although anthropologists may explain French peasant families' strategies in terms of an obsession with narrowing claims that might divide the land and obliterate the house, we cannot similarly reduce the motives of upper-class Bahian families, who were concerned with status in a far more mobile and varied milieu.[73] Many of these families saw that it was to their advantage to increase and extend the number of their relations.

Furthermore, if some parents devised farsighted strategies to defend their patrimonies and build up their descendants' interests over generations, others were apparently irrational in economic terms. Ignoring conventions of legitimacy that Europeans employed to create clear-cut family membership and inheritance property rights was only one sign of this. Bahians were not hidebound, self-denying conservators of house and soil, but rather adventurers. The legend of the Recôncavo lingers over accounts of conspicuous consumption and ruin, of the despoiling of estates by shortsighted, profligate heirs. As a Bahian-born business executive put it in 1980, with some irritation:

One constant you will find in the traditional families here is that they lived rich and died poor, because they wouldn't deny themselves anything, they had to have "the best and the better," they laid out a good table, they liked to receive guests. . . . They traveled to Europe, but they died poor. They didn't accumulate. . . . They were no good at saving.

Or as a newspaper column told the joke in 1897, a Jewish merchant offers a deal to his prospective son-in-law: "Promise to close the shop on Saturday, and I will raise my daughter's dowry to 30 contos." Says the groom: "Raise that to 50, sir, and I promise to close it for good." Even the Brazilian civil code recognized the *pródigo*, the spendthrift of Roman law, who could be stripped of his power to dispose of his own property.[74]

The Crisis of Mobility, Emigration, and Families

The new, smaller families of the Bahian upper class after 1890 did not aggregate into clans, as the larger families of the early and mid nineteenth century had. But they did not separate from their kin as streamlined monads either.[75] Instead, they cultivated strategies of making flexible alliances in cliques that offered them opportunities in the new urban careers that took shape after abolition. As they moved off the land and into the professions and business, the Bahian traditional families modified some old career strategies of manipulating urban opportunities in business and the professions and adopted new ones.

In 1883 the abolitionist Joaquim Nabuco wrote that slavery had desolated Brazilian society from top to bottom. The great slave-owning families had strangled the commerce and towns of the interior by bypassing their markets. They had kept their tenant lavradores in a state of precarious dependency. In turn, these families had lost their wealth to their creditors, the foreign merchants of the capitals. Only the state had grown, leeching taxes and credit from the nation in order to feed its swollen corps of functionaries. Public employment became the asylum of the descendants of slave-owning families that had wasted their fortunes. At the same time, it was the incubator of politicians, because the only roads open to an ambitious poor man were to marry money, becoming a "meek client of slavery," or to find shelter in a public post. "This means that the nation is closed off in all directions," Nabuco said. All roads led to public employment: even the independent professions needed public posts in order to survive; even capitalists wanted subsidies and guarantees.[76]

Nabuco's polemic, however overstated, did render the texture of Bahian career strategies. Wetherell had noted in 1860 that when the estates of the great landed families were divided in inheritance, the sons either became small landed proprietors or were "dispersed over the empire, as they are able by means of their father's friends to procure for themselves civil or military employment." Commerce was considered the last resort by native Bahian whites, who relegated it to the avaricious Portuguese and "refuse to place themselves in a similar *degrading* position, namely that of making money." They would rather "accept small underpaid Government positions" or "starve from day to day," he thought.[77]

There were some Bahian families that had long traditions of mobile careers in urban occupations rather than on the land. The family of Rui Barbosa and Albino José Barbosa de Oliveira, the Barbosa de Oliveiras, exemplified some of this pattern. They had been priests, notaries, and officials in Salvador for generations. Rui's father took a medical diploma in 1843, but he preferred politics to medicine and served as director of education at one point. Not averse to trade, he founded a brick factory, but lost it and died in debt. Rui, who had gotten a law degree, started out in 1876 to practice law in Rio. He hoped to earn enough to pay off his father's debts, finance his sister's trousseau, clear the family honor, and marry his fiancée. Writing home to Bahia, he complained that there was money to be made as a henchman in corrupt deals, but that in the honest practice of law he could not get ahead. Finally, he abandoned the practice of law and staked everything on a scheme to publish a Brazilian edition of an anticlerical tract with a subsidy from the Masons. After this failed, he went back to Bahia and worked in politics and journalism. His political career took him back to Rio, where during the speculative bubble of the Encilhamento, he eventually turned his political connections into a living.[78]

Such mobile careers were an obvious choice in an expanding economy such as that of São Paulo or Rio. The economic rise of São Paulo was a mark by which many people measured the stagnation of Bahia. In a sense São Paulo contradicted Nabuco's argument that slavery could bring only ruin. Both before and after Paulista coffee planters replaced slaves with paid immigrants, their trade supplied the foundation of expanding commerce, railroad construction, and eventually industry.[79] Opportunities there seemed unlimited compared with those in Bahia.

Yet it seems that even in São Paulo many avenues were closed. In the 1950's Bertram Hutchinson measured upward mobility between generations in São Paulo. He found that almost all of it resulted from the creation of new occupational positions and almost none of it was balanced by downward mobility into lower-class positions. The higher the class, the more likely that a son's position would be the same as his father's.[80] The illusion of an egalitarian free-for-all in São Paulo was created by a game of musical chairs in which no one ever surrendered a seat, but new chairs were being added.

Bahia presented the opposite image at the turn of the twentieth century. If São Paulo was the Locomotive pulling the empty boxcars of the other states, Bahia was the Old Black Mammy (*a Mulata Velha*), worn out from having suckled so many sons at her breast.[81] If upper-class Bahians blamed anything for their travail, it was not slavery, as Nabuco argued, but rather abolition. The loss of capital at abolition really did ruin some planters, although the crisis of the sugar industry derived more from its failure to modernize at mid-century and preceded abolition. But planters could point to desperate cases, and they believed that abolition had caused their problems. João Ferreira de Araujo Pinho lost 300-odd slaves, but continued his planting with wage labor. However, his wife's cousin, Antônio Rocha Martins Argolo, who had been living off the rent of a team of slaves, was left with worthless land and three oxcarts for hire.[82]

While the expanding economy of São Paulo made room enough for a rising middle class, the collapse of Recôncavo agriculture crowded the middle class of Bahia with fallen landowners. In the cholera epidemic of 1855, the Conservative party boss Pedro Moniz had lost his wife and 110 slaves, but at that time he had determined to stay on his Santo Amaro plantations despite the losses. In 1885 he proposed to retire into a judgeship, leaving his sons with the plantations. But only three years later, in 1888, he completely reversed his plans. He placed his sons in the magistracy instead and retired to the plantation himself. He now was resolved to give up sugar cane, complaining of slaves who ran away and others "whom I always saw happy and submissive, seeing them now with a certain boldness that causes me serious concern."[83] Another Conservative politician, João Ferreira de Araujo Pinho, wrote in 1885: "No one knows what occupation or industry to choose with profit. Whence an irresistible and fatal tendency toward *empregomania* [the craze for government jobs]: the stomach is subject to imperious laws."[84]

Yet following the collapse of the sugar sector in the 1880's and 1890's, the Bahian agro-commercial economy recovered dramatically. The value of exports, the leading sector of the economy, recovered slowly through the 1890's and 1900's, led by coffee exports, and then stabilized in 1907 at a level four times that of 1889. Bahian exports—even sugar—boomed briefly and dramatically during World War I, peaking in 1919 at a value twelve times that of 1889, and they stayed high through most of the 1920's. During most of the period from 1898 to 1930, cacao and tobacco accounted for nearly half of the state's export trade.[85]

So by no means all social mobility was a flight of impoverished slaveowners into officialdom. The urban elite of Salvador that crystallized at the turn of the twentieth century was formed in part by newly arrived European capitalists and newly risen commercial and industrial entrepreneurs. As tobacco and cacao increased in importance as export crops, new figures appeared in their commerce. German and Swiss families dominated the new cigar industry. English and Swiss merchants dominated the new cacao trade. One of them, Emil Wildberger, started in Bahia in 1892 as a clerk in an established French commercial firm and rose to the top as its capital quadrupled between 1903 and 1923. In the 1920's, Wildberger turned its Bahian operations almost exclusively to cacao exports, until in the last boom years of the 1920's, it went from handling perhaps $800,000 worth of cacao to handling $8,000,000 in 1927.[86] Most of the heroes of Bahia's rags-to-riches tales came out of commerce: Luiz Tarquínio, the founder of the dazzling Empório Industrial do Norte textile mill, had been clerk to an English import firm; Manuel Joaquim de Carvalho, the codfish king, had come from Portugal at the age of thirteen to be a clerk.[87]

Bahian planters and foreign entrepreneurs alike tried to exploit the new industrial opportunities. But alongside firms that succeeded, there were prominent failures, such as the central sugar refinery of Bom Jardim, founded in the 1880's, which lurched from one group of creditors to another, and the Chapellaria do Norte hat factory, which floated a popular stock issue during the Encilhamento, and collapsed soon afterward. Commerce was the site of many changes in status, both of those who rose and of those who stayed in trade for some time only to abandon it in defeat. The result may have been an economy whose leaders were talented at speculation.[88]

The most dynamic economic frontier in Bahia was the southeastern corner of the state, where cacao cultivation extended further and further up the rivers and spread out from the first centers around Ilhéus and Belmonte. Yet the nineteenth-century establishment families that had opened sugar frontiers in the Recôncavo apparently did not dominate the cacao frontier. Instead, homesteading small farmers, many of them from Sergipe and the northern counties of Bahia, began the cultivation of cocoa palms on small plots in the 1870's and 1880's. In a violent land grab, the "cacao colonels" accumulated huge orchards. By the time Recôncavo families might have transferred their capital to the cacao orchards, the easy land grab was over. Although the pioneer migrants to the region often settled together as groups of brothers and their families, they did not follow the traditional landlord family strategy of forming endogamous clans. Perhaps the violent and speculative economy did not encourage the establishment of territorial inmarrying clans. Some of the clans of the Recôncavo had tried to delay the gradual fission of huge land grants, but in the cacao region a process of rapid fusion of small plots into large plantations took place. These new families apparently did not identify their fortunes with continuity in a place, but with speculation.[89]

For most Bahians looking for opportunity, the solution was not to trek to the cacao region, but rather to take the steamboat to Rio or São Paulo. Bahians staying behind routinely lamented the loss of talent, speaking of ingrate sons of the Mulata Velha, but they followed in great numbers: "Ah, Bahia! She exports men and cigars!"[90] Up until the end of the Empire, almost all descendants of the traditional families of the Recôncavo were born in Bahia. After 1890, a third were born outside Bahia, and after 1915, half.[91] Most of those who migrated went to Rio and São Paulo, not only to the capitals but also to the towns of the interior.

An elite family like the Mangabeiras demonstrates how Bahians turned to emigration as a strategy for social ascent. The Mangabeira brothers, Carlos, João, Octávio, and Francisco, were the sons of a middle-class pharmacist who kept shop near the cathedral in Salvador. Each brother was sent to a different faculty in the 1890's: pharmacy, law, engineering, and medicine, with each establishing his own set of connections. Though all were talented enough to have floated up through the sargasso of favors and intrigues that constituted an elite political career in Salvador, only Octávio chose that route. João, Francisco, and Carlos headed for frontiers: João to the courtrooms and politics of Ilhéus, Carlos to Rio Grande do Sul, and Francisco to the rebellion against Bolivia in Acre. Francisco, the poet, died in the Acrean war. But his brothers João and Octávio survived to combine their political careers, each built from a separate constituency, into leadership of the Bahian delegation in Congress and a major Bahian faction in the late Republic.[92]

Most Bahian families had less meteoric trajectories. Yet even when their ambitions focused on small sinecures, they had to travel far. The career of a larger and less prominent family, the Rocha Limas, eulogized in a commemorative volume written by a granddaughter, sounds familiar themes of migration from country to city and from agriculture or trade into public employment. In 1881 Veridiana, the matriarch of the family, had married at twelve in order to have a home for herself and her orphaned sisters. For years, she and her husband Chico had kept a general store, where her old slave mammy was the candymaker, on the plaza of an inland town. There she had given birth to her ten children. However, in 1912 she followed her eldest sons to Salvador, where they were clerks. She and her widowed sister brought all their young children to attend school in the capital. As the children graduated, she sent them off to join their brothers, who by now were trading in the interior of Pernambuco. In 1920 one daughter won a chair as a schoolmistress in the backlands of Bahia, and Veridiana and some of the other daughters accompanied her there, where she married the son of a rancher. Several stores and ranches failed, and part of the family began to travel in the wake of a brother who held a series of strategic posts in the army, rising from sergeant to captain. After the coup of 1930, he was able to get one brother-in-law appointed a small-town mayor, another set up supplying the troops on campaigns against bandits, and a brother appointed an inspector on the Salvador vice squad. Eventually, part of the family settled in Rio, where he helped to place his brothers as functionaries in the war ministry.

By the end of the 1930's, all Veridiana's children had left the uncertainties of business and settled into state jobs. Her grandchildren also went into the bureaucracy and the professions. Several of the brothers and sisters struck out on their own at times, but all eventually returned to give and receive help from their siblings. The story of their mobility recalls the strategies of a team of mountain climbers, tied by ropes for security, gratefully taking advantage of the toeholds that the first ones had found, spreading their weight out along a wide face of rock for stability.[93]

As the families of the upper class located in the city or in urban professions, they had fewer children, and they educated those children more intensively. Whereas in the early nineteenth century landlords had felt no compulsion to educate all their sons, by the end of the nineteenth century a diploma was a necessity. Before, a family strategy might have been centered on accumulating slaves, oxen, and land, or on restricting marriage so that the favored heirs would have enough property to maintain themselves, but now it centered on graduating the family's sons, and even the daughters. Financing an education was a transfer of assets before inheritance. Families sacrificed to promote the most likely son, and an impoverished family would concentrate its dwindling resources on getting scholarships or tutoring for its children. Like Veridiana, many mothers of proper families in the countryside moved to Salvador so that the children could get schooling, leaving their husbands to earn money for the family. Boarding schools and private academies proliferated, and the state government expanded public secondary education.[94]

One indication of the new attitudes and plans for children was the increase in the education of women. On the one hand, parents wanted to endow their daughters with the accomplishments that counted in the marriage market: piano, French, dance, and drawing.[95] On the other, many families began to value a diploma as insurance against a daughter being left unprotected. Where the charitable lords of the seventeenth and eighteenth centuries had provided for funds of dowries to enable orphans to marry, the state government now provided jobs as schoolteachers. As one woman wrote to her mother in the 1880's, although she was sorry to send her daughters away to school: "Oh well, schooling is the most necessary thing in the life of the poor person today, because if they learn they can earn their living better with teaching than with a sewing machine that ruins your health and barely anything to show for it."[96] This new strategy for taking care of unmarried women was added to the older recourses of entering a convent, working as a seamstress, or living as a hanger-on, a tia or an agregada, in another household.

As families became smaller, they also relied more on impersonal public institutions for social services than they had before. Under the Empire, as during the colonial era, the church and the autonomous religious brother-hoods had provided families with hospital and burial service.[97] During the nineteenth century, private associations and the state founded other social-service institutions. As many Portuguese immigrants arrived in Salvador without the support of a family, the Portuguese community of merchants established one of the first private hospitals, and the Spanish community was later to build a Spanish hospital. Around the 1870's, guilds, unions, and professional groups began to form mutual-aid societies. Though most were feeble and short-lived, they changed the texture of the city. During the Republic and around the decade of the 1910's, pension plans were established. These secular organizations began to take over the social-service functions of the religious brotherhoods, just as social clubs pro-vided a secular organization for their recreational functions. Recreational associations—carnival associations, theaters, social clubs, philharmonic societies—began to organize leisure outside of the family circle, and to emphasize public feasts, especially Carnival. Eventually, in the 1930's, the gradual extension of social security by the state, absorbing some of the autonomous public employees' pension funds, provided at least the prom-ise of care in old age by the state. Paradoxically, by coercing couples to marry legally in order for the woman to qualify for widow's benefits, social security may have "strengthened" the lower-class family.[98]

In the early twentieth century, there were many families with members belonging both to the class of rural landlords and to the urban elite. The family of Pedro Ribeiro de Araujo Bittencourt, for example, had moved back and forth between country and city in the nineteenth and early twen-tieth centuries.[99] In the 1910's and 1920's, however, many of these families virtually left the land, and in doing so, they came to depend increasingly on patronage and favors.

The family of Antônio de Araujo Aragão Bulcão Sobrinho, the leading genealogist of the Bahian traditional families, provides an example of a landlord family that became decisively urban. Bulcão Sobrinho's parents were cousins. His mother, Maria Isabel, was the daughter of the 3d baron of São Francisco, one of the Liberal bosses of the province and a leading state politician in the Republic. His father, Inácio Bulcão, ran the Engenho de Agua in the county of São Francisco do Conde and supplemented his income by occupying minor public posts. Possibly after living together in a consensual union, they married in 1898.[100] But Inácio died young, aged 47, in 1917, leaving Maria Isabel widowed with eight children, the youngest aged 3. She died eleven years later, aged 51.

All of the Bulcão children followed urban careers. Inácio's oldest son, Antônio, was 23 when his father died (or 19 as he calculated it later) and had been working for five years as a clerk-secretary in the state senate, over which his grandfather was president, while finishing his engineering degree. All of his sisters became schoolteachers; the oldest, Beatriz, had already been preparing before her father's death. In 1945 four of the sisters were spinsters in their thirties and forties, and one had married at the late age of 29, in 1934, to a medical school professor. Two of the brothers married schoolteachers, perhaps having met them through their sisters. None of them had more than two children themselves.

Antônio, the "chief" of the family, was a public servant. In his careers as intellectual, politician, and functionary, he never used his engineering degree directly. He was head stenographer of the Bahian senate, an early supporter of the revolution of 1930 and subsequently secretary to the early interventors, a prefect in Itaparica under Juracy Magalhães, and, on and off, inspector of museums and monuments. He was a leader of the Association of Public Employees, a founder of political parties, a professor of mathematics and school inspector. He was dismissed from public posts several times in apparent political reprisals, and just as many times reinstated or promoted to his offices. A person who followed the multiple, politically sensitive careers that he did needed, not just talent, but also the protection of kinship and friendship.[101]

Alliances After 1890

In the Republic, upper-class families still understood marriages as building kin networks, but the shape and purpose of marriage strategy changed. Rather than picking alliances to bind together a local clan, parents put their children in a marriage pool, or social set, and exercised a veto rather than nominating power in courtship. It was left to young men alone (or perhaps men working with their brothers) to put together networks.[102]

The elite and landlord families cast their net of relations wider than before. By the late nineteenth century, it was apparent that marriages were once again integrating rising foreign merchants into Bahian establishment families, as they seemingly had not done during the mid nineteenth century. The case of the Urpia family, themselves Portuguese immigrants who became prominent Bahian merchants, is illustrative. In 1895 Bahian-born Horácio Urpia, a salt and sisal manufacturer, invited two young Swiss clerks to rent a cottage he was building on the grounds of his family's estate. Within a few years, both young men were engaged to Urpia daughters, and both of them, Karl Neeser and Emil Wildberger, founded families that continued to marry into traditional landlord and elite families.[103] From the 1920's through the 1940's, some of Wildberger's sons married women from traditional families such as the Gomes de Oliveiras, the Pereira Aguiars, the Sodrés, and the Tourinhos. Through these marriages they were also connected to established merchant families such as the Portuguese Costa Pintos and Amado Bahias. And some of Wildberger's daughters married Swiss and Italian businessmen who had come to Bahia in banking or trade and had become established there. These marriages clearly formed a looser elite and middle-class network that wove immigrants into the traditional family circles.

Yet the process of absorbing immigrants required far less openness of Bahian elites than it did of the planter elite of São Paulo, who were confronted by a huge contingent of rising foreign immigrants. As the sons and daughters of Bahia's traditional families moved out of their parish marriage pools into the capital's marriage pool, most simply made alliances with a larger circle of other traditional families, so that by the 1950's, one Bahian anthropologist reported that at almost any public gathering of the upper class, several in the room could trace kinship to her own family.[104]

The new informal unit that typified the strategies of urban families was the clique (*panelinha*) rather than the parentela.[105] One had to be born into, or marry into, a clan, but one could acquire membership in a clique through friendship or sometimes just interest. Clans included at their margins those who married into them, but their practice of local, endogamous marriage helped to limit the number of those eligible to marry in. Loyalties within the clan carried the weight and complexity of obligations incurred over generations; loyalties in a clique were lighter. They were at once easier to establish and easier to break. Whereas a clan might orient itself around the figure of a white-bearded patriarch, a clique oriented itself around brothers and brothers-in-law. Cousin marriage did affirm brotherhood between the cousins who became brothers-in-law, but exogamous marriage clearly stressed the immediate relationship between brothers-in-law over any link to a common ancestor.[106] The primary institution for building social bonds outside the family had long been the school.[107] In the nineteenth and twentieth centuries, schoolmates, particularly the graduating class, became almost a second kin group.

Cliques acted in many realms of public life, in business as well as public institutions. They were most visible in politics, where allegiances are best documented. At the top of Bahian politics, each administration represented the hegemony of one faction among the many that coalesced for elections. In negotiations for a coalition, the place-seeking interests of different factions would be conciliated, but typically a governor would select his "men of confidence" from among his kin, pseudo-kin, and friends. During the Empire, one of the clearest examples came during the 1878 return of the Liberals to power under Sinimbú. Bahia's Liberal chieftain, Manuel Pinto de Souza Dantas, became senator. His son Manuel Júnior, fresh out of law school, was appointed president of the province of Paraná. Among those

Dantas brought with him into the national government were brothers-in-law; cousins; godchildren; the family doctor, Salustiano Souto; and "friends" such as Rui Barbosa. One of his rivals from the other wing of the Liberal party gleefully lampooned the kinship of the new government: "It's a shame, my neighbor, that we don't have the happiness of some such kinship. Even something by marriage, or some poor godparenthood. . . . Devil take me! If I hadn't been baptized, or could get confirmed twice, like our Barreto de Menezes, I could be Dantas's godchild!" [108] Clique patronage prevailed at the upper level of politics, and such blatant nepotism as that of the Souza Dantas sweep was not common.[109] But at the local level of rural politics, through the twentieth century, the clan continued to be most significant.[110]

In the Republic, while upper-level Bahian politics became less familistic, more "collegial" in Eul-Soo Pang's terms, local politics became, if anything, more familistic. The parties were unable to discipline the coronéis. Some of the more famous coronéis commanded armies of hundreds of mounted rowdies. Others had a smaller base. But both large and small coronéis relied on family to staff their local governments, filling all posts, from schoolmistress to postmaster, with loyal dependents. This was not mere graft. Since politics required that almost every public official act with partisan efficiency at some time or another, most coronéis preferred officials who were also bound by family and kin ties. Less fortunate families in the countryside and small towns of the backlands also associated in clans, if only to protect themselves from the petty harassment that came with "ostracism." The factionalization of small towns was expressed most colorfully in the organization of rival brass bands and social clubs. Daily fraternization obscured this factionalization, but any event that implied a public pledge of allegiance or loyalty, such as elections and civic rituals, brought out the divisions. The ethic of reciprocity demanded absolute partisan loyalty to one's patrons in the clan, above any other consideration.[111]

After the revolution of 1930, the intervenor Juracy Magalhães forged a series of direct deals with local coronéis in order to displace the political incumbent groups.[112] But with the authoritarian coup of 1937, political power became more centralized and militarized. The state extended roads into the backlands beginning in the 1920's, diminishing the impunity of local armies. When elections resumed after 1946, the electoral power of country families was reduced.[113] It did not disappear, but gradually the clans of the rural coronéis lost their value to their members, except as country versions of the more supple urban cliques.

When electoral politics became less important after 1930, even some families among the urban elite jettisoned their lower-class political clienteles, perhaps concentrating on developing their "collegial" connections with peers in positions of power. Inocêncio Marques de Goes Calmon, for example, "inherited" the political machine of his father, Francisco Marques de Goes Calmon, and his uncles Miguel and Antônio when they all died between 1930 and 1935. With the headship of the family, however, went the responsibility of taking care of the electors and their requests: for medicine, for jobs, for a recommendation. As Inocêncio's sister put it, "He was left holding the pineapple." [114] One day, he simply packed up his family and left on a boat for São Paulo without saying good-bye. It may be that something like that happened in the countryside, impelling landlord families to abandon their places and move to the capital.[115]

It was during these years, after World War I, and particularly after 1930, that the difference between "patriarchal" landlord families and the smaller urban middle-class families that Freyre calls "semipatriarchal" showed most sharply. Landlord coronéis embodied the autonomy of the old patriarch, and they could believe sincerely that their personal power over the land and the family was lordly. The urban fathers of the bureaucracy, whom Nabuco called "glebe serfs of the Government, living with their families on lands of the State, subject to an eviction without notice, which is the equivalent of starvation," had no such support.[116] The urban paterfamilias of the early twentieth century could still silence the house with his presence, but his multiple ties to bureaucratic favor prevented him, in many cases, from projecting an image of independence. As families came to rely more on public institutions for services and to order their strategies around competition for state patronage, they became amenable to fashions that swept away some of the old symbols of family authority and solidarity. The small urban family was perhaps not "individualistic," inasmuch as it promoted neither the loneliness nor the autonomy of individualism, but it was decidedly less self-sufficient than the traditional family. It built its clique relations in a wider circle than the clan had, but it continued to link its members in relations of patronage, using the cordial customs of the patriarchal family to organize an unofficial structure of power in Salvador.

Conclusion

THE FAMILIES of the Bahian upper classes, through a series of small steps, transformed their patriarchal family values to those of the conjugal family. This change in the institution came slightly later than the equivalent transformation of families in Western Europe and the United States. It was uncoordinated and subtle enough that it was not easily detected at any single moment. And it was also conditioned by the special characteristics of Brazilian and Bahian society.

Perhaps the most salient of these characteristics was the high number of informal families, formed by consensual unions, and the high rate of illegitimate births—high even for Latin America. This pattern was probably a legacy of slave concubinage, Portuguese custom, and the frontier isolation of rural families. Whatever its origins, by 1870 it was profoundly set in Bahian society. In nineteenth-century Salvador, about half of the population came from unions and households not officially recognized as families.

On the one hand, in this context marriage became less the common denominator of social dignity than a badge of social honor. In Bahia it established a distinction between "the families" and "the people." On the other hand, the universality of consensual unions affected the upper-class family in unique ways. Many upper-class Bahians (mostly men but not only men) lived in informal unions before their marriages, maintained parallel families during their marriages, or formed informal unions instead of marrying. The patriarchal family's norms were undermined by a subversive deviance. This set a special creole, picaresque tone for Bahian culture, in which "tolerance" or "laxity" toward sexual deviance coexisted with a severe, traditional code of honor and with a new nineteenth-century Victorianism. Admittedly or not, many upper-class values intermingled with those of informal unions. For example, it may be that the presence of the "mother-centered" informal family model combined with the tendency of patriarchal families to identify lineage through daughters to make children's relations to their mother and her kin stronger than their relations to the most patriarchal father.

Another, less unique, characteristic of Bahian families that affected the transition to conjugal family values was the strong connection between social class and the various styles of organization of the patriarchal family. To build an ideal patriarchal family was costly and demanding. Patriarchal families took shape in complex households centered on a married couple and their children, surrounded by dependents, widely connected through blood kinship, marriage, and godparenthood to other such households, and regularly refreshing their connections through the ritualized social life that constituted "life in the family circle." Their maintenance required hospitality, gift-giving, passing of patronage favors, and retribution of insults. Below the ranks of the great rural landlords and the urban elite, Bahians found it difficult to maintain such an establishment. Among the urban middle class of Salvador, the organization of the patriarchal family took a form that always stretched its institutional values in the direction of the conjugal family. Modest middle-class households could implement the customs, roles, and rituals of the patriarchal family to some extent; but they could not entirely reproduce the practices of either the exemplary elite household or the old-fashioned planter household: surveillance and seclusion of women, rituals of deference and patronage, subordination of children's ambitions to corporate family aims.

Thus, the crisis of the agro-commercial economy of the Bahian Recôncavo between 1880 and 1910 contributed simultaneously to the belated "emergence" of a middle class and to the "modernization" of the family. Many families of the Recôncavo "aristocracy" fell from the planter or merchant class into the urban middle class. Unlike the dynamic southern cities of Rio de Janeiro and São Paulo, northeastern cities such as Salvador had little foreign immigration or upward mobility into the middle class. The fall in status fed a general urbanization of traditional ways of life. Now successful families also urbanized, though virtually every family preserved a token tie to the land. Even the families that remained rooted in the countryside—decadent sugar aristocrats, rising cacao millionaires, rancher or trader coronéis—were affected by a twentieth-century social urbanization of country life: roads, mail, telephones, radio, boarding schools, rural hospitals, police outposts.

One palpable dimension of this shift was the change in family strategies, demography, household organization, and customs that began to take shape from 1870 to 1890, became an obvious trend between 1890 and 1919, and became the new norm after 1919. The full-fledged patriarchal phase of the upper-class family (whose origins may date from the sixteenth century) lasted until the early nineteenth century. Clan political and economic power prevailed in society. Many couples had large families. To conserve property and purity, they restricted many children from marrying, and preferred to marry off their selected heirs to cousins or kin. But between 1810 and 1870, courtship rose and patriarchal marriage patterns declined. Parents no longer arranged blind matches for their children with the approval of public opinion. The government undermined some of the legal props of patriarchal and stem-family marriage policies by lowering the age of majority, abolishing entails, securing the inheritance rights of recognized bastard children, and forbidding monastic careers. Families more often pursued the previously supplementary strategy of exogamous marriage alliance. From 1870 to 1890, urban career opportunities and leisure routines enlarged the public roles of women and further eroded authoritarian patterns of arranged marriage based on the seclusion of women. The turning point of 1890, as much as any, marked the disintegration of the patriarchal family model.

Between 1890 and 1919, the conjugal family emerged as a new norm. It idealized roles that allowed more equality and companionship between husband and wife and more individual freedom for children. Families permitted relatively freer courtship, and the city developed new social clubs and other vehicles for the association of families in a generalized high society. Novelties ranging from the technological (the telephone, which allowed anonymous calls) to the legal (marriage between uncles and nieces became illegal in 1917) frustrated patriarchal strategies. This showed in changed family patterns. Marriages with cousins and close kin became the exception, rather than the rule. Some upper-class Bahian couples limited births deliberately in order to form smaller families. Despite the economic recovery after 1907, Bahians migrated all over Brazil, stretching their kin networks as they moved—inevitably diminishing the givenness of family circles and the direct pressure of clanlike parentelas.

Between 1920 and 1945, the conjugal family became the prevailing form of the Bahian upper-class family, as changes outside families cemented the new model of relations within them. The revolution of 1930 formed a social-welfare, social-control coalition that altered social relations of all kinds—not only among upper-class but also among lower-class families. The granting of suffrage in 1932 symbolically ratified the new status of women as citizens and individuals. Small changes in roles, customs, and the values of families added up to a change in type; the occasional "patriarchal" family came to be seen curiously and nostalgically, as something old-fashioned.

Formal institutions had an ambivalent influence upon these changes.

The transformation of Bahian families after 1870 reflected broader changes in Brazilian society—both in the private sphere and in the public institutional framework of the nation. Early state-building after independence had included a strengthening and regulation by the government of social institutions: a new medical profession, liberalized and modernized legal codes and courts, and a reformed Catholic clergy. Later, the separation of church and state in 1889, following the fall of the Empire, and the rise of a welfare state toward the end of the Old Republic each contributed to the strengthening of the state. Yet the modernized formal institutions rarely had the power—even when they had the will—to intervene heavily in society. Their influence was limited by their meager resources and by the incoherence of Brazilian society, which was sharply divided between city and country, between the upper classes and the povo. The government could barely reach lower-class families, and upper-class families, though close at hand, were too strong; they easily resisted attempts to dilute private power. Consequently, institutions tried to intervene in families by exhorting them to change their culture; they tried to reform the intangible realm of beliefs.

The medical profession, for instance, by presenting a model of the healthy family, tried to reform relations between husbands and wives and parents and children. Doctors writing on the family contrasted the healthy purity of housewifely domesticity to the contamination threatened by wet nurses within the home and prostitutes outside it. Doctors emphasized that women reproduced the race and had a special responsibility to guard the health of the family. To a great extent, doctors simply secularized Catholic moralism on marriage and maternity. But, beginning in the 1880's, physicians moved beyond traditional wisdom and formed a model of rational, "eugenic" marriage choice based on the health and hereditary traits of the partners, rather than on money or passion. Medical social thought used European racial theory to propose a vision of the Brazilian people as a sickly race threatened by degeneration as a result of African barbarism, syphilis, tobacco, and rum; a race in which the upper-class families ought to be a eugenic elite whose superiority would be manifested in their hygienic isolation. This language of race and degeneration became the dominant social ideology of the Old Republic and guided official policies on immigration, urban renewal, and education.

The Catholic church, long before the medical reformers, had enunciated some antipatriarchal principles: freedom of choice in marriage and prohibition of consanguineous marriage. But, since colonial times, the weak Brazilian church had accommodated itself to patriarchal power. For example, it bent to families' wholesale violation of its rules on cousin marriage through the pretext of freely granting piecemeal, "exceptional" dispensations. It supported the general interest of the upper class by justifying slavery and the special interests of some families by providing ecclesiastical places for excess sons and daughters. It furnished symbolic vehicles for patron-client relations in the cult of the saints and the ritual of baptism. The hierarchy held little more influence over the povo than over the families. It exercised only marginal control over the practices and beliefs of a creole folk Catholicism.

When the Catholic church reformed—first under government sponsorship during the Empire, then on its own after the separation of church and state in 1889—activist priests aggressively pushed a reactionary model of the family. Catholic lay and clerical writers celebrated women in idealized, supposedly traditional, domestic roles and attacked them in new public roles of work, politics, or courtship. Bishops and Catholic intellectuals elevated civil marriage and divorce into primary symbolic issues that represented the defense of Catholic tradition against modernity. In its pursuit of social influence, the church aligned itself with an emerging political right in the 1920's and 1930's, promoting the "eternal and unchanging" as a defense against radical change. Catholic social thought portrayed a nation threatened by anarchists, Masons, and libertines, a Brazilian people who were good but religiously ignorant, among whom the women of decent families should be missionary beacons of morality. This vision was not quite as influential a guide for national policy as the metaphor of degeneration. But its claims of a conservative function for the family justified blocking specific changes, such as divorce, and contributed to the paternalist social project after 1919.

The combination of flexible conservatism with reform in Brazilian institutions showed best in family law. The colonial state system of dividing responsibilities between church and state had worked well for the purposes of patriarchal families and not badly for the purposes of the state. After independence, Brazilian legal reformers changed little. Though Bahian families were different in practice from those in most of Europe, Brazilian family law showed very little formal difference. Brazilian liberals reformed family law in the early nineteenth century, notably by abolishing such symbolically aristocratic devices as the entailed estate. But legal reforms embraced contradictory values; they reinforced social values of sexual honor and the subordination of women, while they simultaneously provided for dishonorable informal families by granting inheritance rights to men's recognized illegitimate children.

Ultimately, the government did little through the law to change families. A reform that felt radical at the time, such as the decree of mandatory civil marriage in 1890, generated great heat but introduced little substantive change in marriage or separation. Indeed, at most it probably further alienated the rural povo from formal institutions; through the 1950's, Bahian country people rejected civil marriage, preferring religious marriage even when it did not confer legal rights. A controversial reform such as the civil code of 1916 did little to change rights and powers within families; if anything, it increased the subordination of women to their husbands. The 1934 and 1937 constitutions stepped back toward church control of marriage policy; the prohibition of divorce lasted until 1977.

Around 1914, the Brazilian intellectual and political elite felt widespread frustration at the inability of their institutions to regulate or uplift the people (or even to control their own sort, their cousins and fathers). It became a commonplace criticism that a real, "invisible" Brazil lay smothered beneath the artificial institutions of the "visible" Brazil. Most country people, and many city people, lived beyond the reach of schools, of the law, of public health campaigns, of the parish church, or of real political participation. Theories of racial incapacity furnished a partial exculpation of the elite, but they were cold comfort to Brazilian patriots. Realist intellectuals identified dangers presented by backlands zealots such as the Canudos messianic community, by bandits, by anarchists, and even by middle-class strikers. They argued that it was imperative to discipline and strengthen the national race. The perception of a threat in the "social question" of labor made even conservative members of the elite willing to address what they believed to be the problems of proletarian families.

The outcome of this was a public consensus, between 1920 and 1945, to turn from "liberal" indifference to private life toward intervention to protect children and the family. Symbolic enactments (unenforced child labor laws, limited pension funds) and practical measures (public schools, sanitation, clinics, statistical agencies) both referred to the paternalist utopia of the nation as a family, in which the government would play the role of a father to loyal and dependent children. This semifascist vision of society enlisted the support of public health reformers, eugenicists, and Catholic social workers; all approved of measures that would regenerate the population by improving its health, particularly the health of mothers and children. It transcended many differences of left and right. For example, the Catholic clergy supported universal public education, once the 1934 constitution guaranteed that public schooling would include religious instruction.

The new social project supposedly aimed at families of the urban working class (and at women as mothers in all classes), but it had both direct and indirect effects upon middle-class families in Bahia. The expansion of social-service bureaucracy created white-collar jobs; this consolidated the middle class and fueled a new intensity in the pursuit of patronage. Pension plans and other public social benefits offered a supplement to the traditional support network of extended families. They would eventually define a new privileged sector in twentieth-century Brazil: the minority that had coverage under the benefits of the state. Though Brazil had not become a welfare state by 1945, the trend in that direction certainly encouraged the changes in upper-class families. Perhaps the state had finally become stronger than "the families."

Yet the formal institutional projects of guided modernization of familial mentalities barely touched Bahia's commonsense culture. First, they could hardly discern elements of culture as basic as the beliefs and practices of honor, embodied in courtship customs and restrictions on the place of women. They were extraordinarily obtuse with respect to the practices surrounding consensual unions; Brazilian censuses, for example, were slow to incorporate the category of religious marriage into their counts. In the second place, their alternative visions were extreme and simplistic. It is difficult to imagine that families could have abandoned their subtle and nuanced conventional wisdom for such brittle and idealized visions of the family as those of the medical reformers. Nonetheless, though families were slow to change cherished and convenient customs, they did find the language and symbolism of hygiene appealing as a resort in their private quarrels and conversations over health and proper behavior. Similarly, few Bahians lived lives by the book; yet they found lip service to the moral pieties of Catholicism irresistible when they publicly considered topics such as divorce. Thus, it is fair to say that in early-twentieth-century Bahia, a superficial secularization of upper-class beliefs coincided with an equally superficial flowering of Catholic piety.

New ideologies did add resources to Bahian culture and deepened reflection upon issues such as the relations of individuals and families to clientelism. Liberalism offered Brazilians a critique of patronage that went beyond traditional condemnations of unfair nepotism, to provide new principles of equality under the law and individualistic citizenship. Officially liberal, Brazilian political culture tacitly observed an opposing ideology of linked hierarchical statuses ranked by honor and power. The culture of the family supported it. Respect within the family (like the cult of the saints and many other facets of Brazilian culture) built emotional and practical habits: deference, gratitude, generosity. These habits modeled for the reciprocal obligations of paternalism and loyal dependence that could make a patronal society (even a slave society) more humane. Family allegiances were also the backbone of social networks. The lines between families, kin networks, and factions were thin. As feuds, elections, and cases such as the Questão Braga showed, familial disputes easily rippled outward to factional enmities. Over time, Brazilians assimilated the liberal critique of patronage; yet the linkage of extended family networks to patronage grew in modern Brazil.

Cultural change in the Bahian upper classes happened in interaction with the reception of a ready-made cosmopolitan Belle Epoque repertory of ideal social types, entertainments, and manners. Most scientific, technical, ideological, and economic innovations came from outside Bahia. Consequently, the transformation of turn-of-the-century Bahian culture is a case study of provincialism—that is to say, of conservative accommodation to cosmopolitan leading cues. Most of those cues came from civilized France in the nineteenth century and from the progressive United States in the twentieth century. This accommodation was never simply inertial, however much it suited Bahians to pretend that they were just catching up. With talents perhaps derived from three centuries of colonialism, Bahians creatively chose, embroidered, and adapted. They did so largely by making room for novelties without discarding old customs or beliefs. This perhaps made Bahian culture more baroque and contradictory than cultures elsewhere.

Although Bahia had a distinctive regional culture, there was virtually no mechanism for Bahian voices or institutions to project their minor contributions abroad, or even to other parts of Brazil. The travel literature that had been the chief genre for presenting Brazilian social life to foreigners in the nineteenth century became more superficial in the twentieth century. Mid-twentieth-century Bahian "regionalist" intellectuals such as Jorge Amado (or northeastern regionalists such as Gilberto Freyre) arrived late at styles of sociological realism capable of conveying elements of that culture in a fashion relevant to people outside Brazil. They, and other nationalist historical sociologists of the 1930's and 1940's, began the task of bringing Brazilian common sense into self-awareness and presenting it abroad.

Was there any achievement of Bahian informal culture that was lost? Should foreign contemporaries have looked beyond the mediocrity in formal institutions to the vigor in folk life and practical reason? Perhaps there was no transferable wisdom, but merely local knowledge. Yet from an outsider's perspective, what distinguishes the culture of family in Bahia and perhaps in all Brazil was the extent to which informal compensatory practices complicated the patriarchal main thrust. If there was the tremendous and unjust blockage of mobility in slavery, there were also high rates of manumission from slavery and curious avenues of advancement toward autonomy for slaves. If there was racism and prejudice, they were countered by broad recognition of the humanity of all sorts of people and by a supple ceremonialism in race relations, which buffered indignities. If the family usually denied authority to women, nonetheless widows, spinsters, and even wives devised ways to arrange marriages, manage property, and broker favors. If formal institutions gave little support to illegitimate children, families often integrated them into their homes and their circles of relatives. There was no insurmountable contradiction between the ruthlessly hierarchical and dominating strategies of the patriarchal family system and the host of escapes, small deviations, and exceptions that allowed individual leeway. Such a culture did not offer examples in its system so much as in its style of life and its mentalities.

Appendix

Appendix: Sources and Methods

SOME BRAZILIAN families, like some families everywhere, have kept family papers and records. Two major public collections of documents from prominent Bahian families, the Cotegipe archive in the Instituto Histórico e Geográfico Brasileiro and the Rui Barbosa archive in the Casa de Rui Barbosa, contain correspondence, inventories, and other personal papers that afford many insights into private life. Individuals in Brazil have also left memoirs and biographies. But Brazilians have tended not to leave diaries or write autobiographies. Perhaps because of conventions of discretion and reticence, possibly because of the lack of a Protestant tradition emphasizing private examination of conscience, it has been, and is, rare for Brazilian authors to write from the standpoint of their individual character development. By comparison with western Europe or North America, there is therefore a gap in the documentation available for a study of this kind.

I have accordingly deployed a range of other sources in an effort to triangulate upon Bahian mentalities, including memoirs and travel literature, private correspondence, newspapers, and other social chronicles that bear directly on family life. In addition, I have scrutinized official records that indirectly bear witness to family life because they unintentionally preserve scraps of testimony on daily life: notarial deeds, inventories and testaments, and court cases. I have been guided, too, by interviews with survivors of the period.

Brazilian fiction also provided me with a valuable source of insights into culture and domestic life for this study. In literary genres such as the sketch of manners and the novel, verisimilitude required the author to present concrete details reflecting the daily lives of readers in his city. The line between "a fact" in the traveler's chronicle; the memoir; the newspaper *crônica*, or sketch of manners; and certain descriptive passages in realist novels is a fine one. Where a novelist's or storyteller's intention is documentary, I have treated such a passage skeptically and critically, as one among other sources.

But this study has also found unique arguments in Brazilian literary realism and literary satire, arguments that it takes differently, as analyses rather than details. In "Literatura e cultura de 1900 a 1945," Antônio Cândido argues that, given a "weak division of intellectual labor" and a lack of organized social sciences before the 1930's, Brazilian literature sometimes served to improvise a social vision and present social problems for Brazilian elites. Whether or not Brazilian novelists consciously attempted to furnish an ersatz sociology, they did propose and imply arguments about social life and social relations that can be taken seriously. In stories and in novels, they constructed models of social relations and social dilemmas that often commented on family life. I have read novels and stories for examples of contemporary interpretations of issues such as honor, patronage, and individual conscience, interpretations that sometimes emerge more clearly from fiction than from scientific or sociological literature.

And, additionally, Brazilian literature directly documents the ability of Brazilians to reflect critically, ironically, or humorously on themselves. It demonstrates in a refined form the wit and self-awareness with which Brazilians even today confront painful problems. It manifests the breadth and sophistication of Brazilian culture. As such, literary language—like personal correspondence, like trial testimony, and like words quoted in a variety of other documents—provides an antidote to the arrogance of social history, which sometimes assumes that it has discovered unsuspected truths. This study argues that there were significant limitations along the dimensions of formal ideology in Brazil that frustrated understanding and reform of families. I hope that it has also shown how Bahians formulated creative responses to family questions within the limits of both formal and informal knowledge.

To supplement the demographic data available in censuses and other official sources, some of the analysis of family structure and demography in this book uses the Traditional Families Sample constructed from published genealogies. This sample is a data base of linked records of 2,025 individuals and couples descended from prominent Bahian families (including spouses and spouses' fathers who were not family members by descent, about 3,000 individuals in all), taken from Antonio de Araujo de Aragão Bulcão Sobrinho, *Famílias bahianas* (1945–46), and Arnold Wildberger, "O Marechal de Campo Francisco Pereira de Aguiar" (1954). The genealogies trace descent groups of ancestral couples, all of whom had established themselves by the late eighteenth or early nineteenth centuries, and some by the seventeenth century. They include families who represented both landed (Bandeira) and mercantile (Vicente Viana) wealth. They emphasize families from the Recôncavo region, which dominated Bahian (and to some extent, national) politics in the early to mid nineteenth century, and especially families that won titles of nobility under the Empire. Some of the connections traced back into the sixteenth century may be apocryphal, but others have a plausible base in entailed *morgado* property.

The genealogical movement in Bahia took shape with the foundation of the Instituto Genealógico da Bahia in 1941. Bulcão Sobrinho's *Famílias bahianas* was its most impressive work, though there were quite substantive genealogies by Herman Neeser, Arnold Wildberger, João da Costa Pinto Dantas Júnior, and others. Some of the genealogists were political monarchists; the *Revista do Instituto Genealógico da Bahia* published some essays in praise of the Bragança dynasty and debates concerning succession in that house. But most of the genealogists focused their research on their own pedigrees. They did not always specify their research methods, but they must have found some manuscript family registers such as those that have been preserved in the Frões collection of private papers and in the Coleção Araujo Pinho in the Arquivo do Instituto Histórico e Geográfico Brasileiro. Some of the genealogists documented their studies with reference to parochial records, government documents, bibliographies, and published biographies. In addition, Bulcão Sobrinho sent questionnaires to surviving members of some families to supplement his archival research.

Still, the use of genealogies for collective biography must be treated with caution. For instance, there is an amusing contradiction between two versions of Bulcão Sobrinho's family genealogy, in which he seems to postdate his own birth in order to make it fall after his parents' marriage. Occasionally, genealogies are evasive or euphemistic about illegitimate unions and descent. And some of them are much less complete and careful than others. Recently, a team of genealogists and historians at the Arquivo Nacional revised the genealogy of the Costa Pinto family of Santo Amaro and unraveled discrepancies in an earlier version, publishing the results in Eul-Soo Pang's *O Engenho Central de Bom Jardim* (1979). But other genealogies of the Instituto Genealógico, such as those of Bulcão Sobrinho, are usually both internally consistent and consistent with other sources.

This study uses genealogical data as a sample for the calculation of historical demographic trends. This diminishes concern about the reliability of details in individual entries, but increases concern about distortion deriving from systematic bias toward errors in the genealogical research. For example, it is likely that the genealogies omit some children who died young, which would skew calculations of family size. Completed family size is much smaller than that reported by married white women in the 1940 census. But cautious use of these figures to compare trends over time within Bahia is possible, and the trend of decline in family size counters the likely bias toward underreporting children born in the distant past. Where it has been possible to compare data derived from the genealogies with data derived from official sources, as in the case of age at marriage, these data sometimes confirm the genealogical data, but also, as in the case of the absolute number of children in completed families, sometimes cast doubt on it.

Reference Matter

Glossary

Afilhado, afilhada	Godchild.
Africano	African; African-born black person.
Agregado, agregada	Free dependent in a household or on an estate.
Ama	Nurse, nursemaid.
Amasia, amazia, amasio	Informal, consensual union.
Amásia, amásio	Partner in a consensual union.
Amizade	Informal, consensual union; literally, friendship.
Arrhas	An archaic Portuguese form of marital property not much used in Brazil, either property the husband donated to the wife for a widow's pension, or property that the husband brought to match the woman's dowry; similar to dower.
Bacharel, bacharéis	Law graduate.
Bacharelismo	Legalistic political idealism.
Bahiana	A Bahian woman; primarily, a street vendor in typical Afro-Bahian costume.
Beata	Fanatically religious woman.
Branco	White person.
Branco da Bahia	Someone passing for white. Usually ironic.
Branco fino	Very white person.
Cabra	Mestizo person with some African ancestry; sometimes specifically the child of a mulatto and a black person.
Cadeira	Sedan chair, palanquin.
Caixeiro	Clerk in a shop or commercial firm.
Candomblé	Afro-Brazilian religious sect; also the center (properly *terreiro*) where candomblé ceremonies are held.

Capella	Entailed property committed to maintain a pious endowment.
Capona, mulher de capona	Lay religious woman who wore a hooded cloak in public.
Carioca	Inhabitant of the city of Rio de Janeiro.
Carurú	Shrimp and okra stew, a typical Bahian dish.
Cidade Alta	Upper City, Salvador's traditional administrative and residential districts along cliff ridges overlooking the Bahia de Todos os Santos.
Cidade Baixa	Lower City, Salvador's traditional commercial district, on the waterfront at the base of the cliffs.
Civilista	Follower of Rui Barbosa's 1910 unsuccessful "civilian" presidential campaign against the "military" candidate, General Hermes de Fonseca; afterward, adherent to antioligarchical politics.
Classes conservadoras	Literally, conservative classes; usually, the business interests.
Comendador	Person with the title of commander in a charitable or honorific order.
Compadre, comadre	Co-parent; parent of one's godchild, or godparent of one's child.
Compadrio, compadresco	Godparenthood.
Conto	Unit of Brazilian currency for large transactions; 1,000 milreis, expressed as 1:, 1:000$, or 1:000$000.
Coronel, coronéis	Since the Old Republic, a local-level political boss, named for the title of colonel in the National Guard.
Coronelismo	Political bossism and machine politics.
Cozinha	Kitchen; also staff of servants, or kitchen staff as opposed to above-stairs staff.
Creoulo, crioulo, crioula	Through the nineteenth century, a Brazilian-born, rather than African-born, black person; in the twentieth century, usually impolite.
Curador	Guardian or trustee for a legally incompetent person.
Desembargador	Appeals or high court judge.
Desquite	Legal marital separation.
Divórcio	In the nineteenth century, marital separation; later, divorce as opposed to separation.
Doutor	Graduate of a law or medical school.
Empregomania	Craze for public employment.
Encilhamento	Inflationary speculative bubble of 1889–92.
Engenho	Mill, especially sugar mill.

Estado Novo	"New State," the second authoritarian dictatorship of Getúlio Vargas, 1937–45.
Favela	Shantytown.
Fazenda	A farm, plantation, estate, or ranch.
Felipe, Filipe	Man supported by his wife; especially a schoolteacher's husband.
Filho de criação	Informally adopted child.
Filhofamílias, filho-família	Child under parental authority, including a financially dependent adult residing in the parental household.
Footing	Promenade for courtship in a town square or park.
Frigideira de carangueijo	Crab casserole, a typical Bahian dish.
Gente fina	Refined people, social elite.
Grapiuna	Person from Ilhéus.
Interventor	Especially in the revolution of 1930, a federally appointed state governor, and later occasionally mayor, with emergency powers.
Irmandade	Religious brotherhood.
Jeito	Ruse to outmaneuver official norms.
Lavrador	Farmer.
Lavrador de cana	Contract cane farmer, not a sugar mill owner.
Madrinha	Godmother.
Mãe preta	Black wet nurse or dry nurse, especially a slave mammy.
Mancebia	Informal, consensual union.
Maxixe	Afro-Brazilian dance, precursor of the samba.
Melindrosa	An affected, overdressed girl of the turn of the twentieth century; a Carioca social type congruent to the U.S. Gibson Girl.
Mês de Maria	Month of Mary, May devotions to the Virgin.
Milreis, mil-réis	Unit of Brazilian currency for small transactions; 1,000 reis, expressed as 1$000.
Moleque	Urchin; slave child.
Morador	Dependent tenant farmer.
Morgado	Crown-chartered entailed estate, and its holder.
Mucama	Personal servant, especially lady's chambermaid, almost always a slave.
A Mulata Velha	The Old Black Mammy, nickname for the state of Bahia in the Old Republic.
Mulato	Mulatto; mestizo person of African and European ancestry; in twentieth-century speech often impolite.
Município	County, municipality.
Namorada, namorado	Proper girlfriend or boyfriend; suitor.
Namoro	Courtship.

Negro	Black person.
Nobre, nobreza	Literally, noble and nobility, but in Brazilian law referred to virtually all notables.
Noivos	An engaged couple.
Nojo	Traditional deep mourning.
Old Republic	The oligarchical, usually civilian, governments of 1889–1930; also called the First Republic.
Pacato	Discreet, mild-mannered.
Padrinho	Godfather.
Padroado	Patronage; the authority of the Portuguese or Brazilian Crown over the Catholic church in its domains.
Pardo	Mestizo person, especially in official documents through the nineteenth century; may be of African, European, or Amerindian ancestry.
Parentela	Extended family network including relatives by blood and marriage.
Paulista	Inhabitant of São Paulo.
Peão, peões	Commoners in Luso-Brazilian law (archaic).
Pedido	In courtship, a formal proposal of marriage.
Pelourinho	A central plaza of Salvador, named for its whipping post.
Política dos governadores	Unwritten pact during the Old Republic to share power and patronage between the presidency and state oligarchies.
Povo	The people or populace; the lower classes; the population of a city.
Promessa	Personal religious vow, usually to a saint to perform a penance in return for some grace.
Recolhimento	Religious retreat with semiconventual discipline, usually for lay women and often for fallen women.
Recôncavo	Region surrounding the city of Salvador and the Bahia de Todos os Santos, including other cities such as Santo Amaro and Cachoeira.
República	Student residence without a resident landlady; literally, republic.
Respeito	Respect.
Saída	Forward, immodest.
Santa Casa da Misericórdia	Holy House of Mercy, semiofficial charitable brotherhood.
São João	Saint John the Baptist, or his holiday.
Seabrista	Follower of the popular politician J. J. Seabra.
Senhor de engenho	Sugar mill owner, sugar mill lord.
Senhor do Bomfim	Our Lord of Bomfim, patron of Salvador; also his chapel or his holiday.

Senzala	Slave quarters on a plantation.
Sertanejo	Person from the sertão.
Sertão, sertões	Any backlands region in the northeast of Brazil, but in Bahia usually the dry northern and western parts of the state, particularly the São Francisco river valley.
Situação	Political incumbents or their coalition.
Sobrado	Townhouse or mansion.
Tenente	Lieutenant; especially any of the radical junior officers who rebelled in the 1920's or in 1930.
Terça	The third of one's estate that could be willed freely by a person with obligatory heirs.
Tia	Aunt, but generally any spinster.
Vatapá	Fish-based paste, a typically Bahian dish.

Notes

Complete references for the works cited in short form are given in the Bibliography, pp. 381–412. In identifying and locating Bahian publications that may not be catalogued elsewhere, a starting point is Bahia, Secretaria do Planejamento, Ciência e Tecnologia (SEPLANTEC), Fundação de Pesquisas, CPE, *Bibliografia baiana*. Public archival documents cited include box, sheaf, and document numbers when these exist, with the exception of the Wanderley Pinho collection in the Arquivo Público do Estado da Bahia. This collection was uncatalogued at the time of my research; I worked from photocopies. I have supplied dates to identify documents when possible.

The Bibliography follows Brazilian convention in alphabetizing names by the final surname. For example, "João da Costa Pinto" is ordered alphabetically under "Pinto, João da Costa." To facilitate consultation in the Notes, I have supplied other elements of names in brackets where helpful: "[João da Costa] Pinto."

Abbreviations

ACRB	Arquivo da Casa de Rui Barbosa
APEB	Arquivo Público do Estado da Bahia
APEB, Notas	Arquivo Público do Estado da Bahia, Livros de Notas da Capital
Arquivo Araujo Goes	Arquivo do Instituto Histórico e Geográfico Brasileiro, Coleção Araujo Goes
Arquivo Araujo Pinho	Arquivo do Instituto Histórico e Geográfico Brasileiro, Coleção Araujo Pinho
Arquivo Cotegipe	Arquivo do Instituto Histórico e Geográfico Brasileiro, Arquivo do barão de Cotegipe, João Maurício Wanderley
Arquivo Wanderley Pinho	Arquivo Público do Estado da Bahia, Seção Histórica, Coleção Wanderley Pinho
Casamento Civil	*Casamento civil: Recapitulação em ordem alphabética do Decreto n. 181 de 24 de janeiro de*

	1890 e dos demais que se seguiram, compiled by Manuel André da Rocha
CEPEHIB	Centro para Estudo da História da Igreja no Brasil
Código Civil	Brazil, *Código civil dos Estados Unidos do Brasil*, Law 3071 of January 1, 1916
Código Criminal	Brazil, *Colleção das leis do Império do Brasil*, Law of December 16, 1830
Código Philippino	*Código Philippino ou Ordenações e leis do reino do Portugal*, edited by Candido Mendes de Almeida
Diário Oficial do Centenário	*Diário Oficial do Estado da Bahia: Edição especial do centenário*, July 2, 1923
IBGE	Brazil, Instituto Brasileiro de Geografia e Estatística
Recenseamento de 1872	Brazil, *Recenseamento da população do Imperio do Brazil a que se procedeu no dia 1º de agosto de 1872*
Recenseamento de 1920, instrucção	Brazil, Directoria Geral de Estatística, *Synopse do recenseamento realizado em 1 de setembro 1920 ... segundo o grau de instrucção, a idade, o sexo e a nacionalidade*
Recenseamento de 1920, profissões	Brazil, Directoria Geral de Estatística, *Synopse do recenseamento realizado em 1 de setembro 1920 ... segundo as profissões, a nacionalidade, o sexo e a idade*
SEPLANTEC	Bahia, Secretaria do Planejamento, Ciência e Tecnologia

Introduction

1. Representative attempts to describe this family in the 1950's include [Carmelita] Hutchinson, "Notas preliminares," and Willems, "Structure of the Brazilian Family."

2. Williams, *Keywords*.

3. I owe these definitions to Charles Dreckmeier.

4. For debates on political and social citizenship, see [Wanderley Guilherme dos] Santos, *Cidadania e justiça*; [Murilo de] Carvalho, *Bestializados*; Da Matta, *A casa & a rua*.

5. Morse, "Brazil's Urban Development."

6. Freyre, *Masters and the Slaves*.

7. Lasch, "Freudian Left and Cultural Revolution"; Lerner, *Creation of Patriarchy*; Weber, *Economy and Society*, pp. 231–41, 370–84, 1006–15, 1070.

8. Freyre, *Masters and the Slaves*, p. xxxiii.

9. Ibid., p. 278.

10. For São Paulo, Ellis Júnior, *Primeiros troncos paulistas* (original title *Raça de gigantes*); [Alcântara] Machado, *Vida e morte*. For Bahia, consult the fine anti-

quarian and traditionalist historians or genealogists [Wanderley] Pinho, *Engenho*; Bulcão Sobrinho, *Famílias bahianas.* Miceli, *Intelectuais e classe dirigente*, offers an interpretation of the intellectuals of the 1930's.

11. [Oliveira] Vianna, *Populações meridionais* and *Evolução do povo brasileiro*; the latter reprints "O povo brasileiro e sua evolução," in the 1922 introduction to the results of the 1920 census.

12. Freyre, *Mansions and the Shanties.*

13. Romero, *Brasil social.*

14. Cândido, "Brazilian Family," p. 303; see also Willems, "Structure of the Brazilian Family" and "Portuguese Family Structure"; [Carmelita] Hutchinson, "Notas preliminares"; [Henry] Hutchinson, *Village and Plantation*; some of the findings of anthropological community studies are summed up in Wagley, "Luso-Brazilian Kinship Patterns," pp. 174–89.

15. Cândido, "Dialética da malandragem."

16. Athayde, "Ville de Salvador"; Mattoso and Athayde, "Epidemias e flutuações," and other studies from *Colloque international sur l'histoire quantitative du Brésil*; Marcílio, *Cidade de São Paulo*; Luna and Costa, "Sinopse de alguns trabalhos de demografia histórica"; [Donald] Ramos, "Marriage and the Family in Colonial Vila Rica" and "City and Country"; Kuznesof, *Household Economy.*

17. Russell-Wood, *Fidalgos and Philanthropists*; Schwartz, *Sovereignty and Society* and "Patterns of Slaveholding."

18. Lewin, *Politics and Parentela in Paraíba*; Pang, *Bahia in the First Brazilian Republic*; Schwartz, *Sugar Plantations.* Cf. Balmori, Voss, and Wortman, *Notable Family Networks.*

19. Samara, *Família brasileira.*

20. Mattoso, "Au nouveau monde" and "Slave, Free, and Freed Family Structures in Nineteenth-Century Salvador."

21. Souza and Faria, eds., *Bahia de todos os pobres.*

Chapter 1

1. Pierson, *Negroes in Brazil*, pp. 20, 3–20.

2. There is no specifically Bahian history of abolition; but see Mattoso, *To Be a Slave*; Russell-Wood, *Black Man in Slavery and Freedom*; Schwartz, "Recent Trends"; see also [Viotti da] Costa, *Da monarquia à república*; Toplin, *Abolition*; Conrad, *Destruction*; Galloway, "Last Years"; [Wanderley] Pinho, *Engenho.*

3. [Buarque de] Holanda, *Raízes do Brasil.*

4. Eisenberg, *Sugar Industry*, p. 214; Galloway, "Last Years"; [Wanderley] Pinho, *Engenho.*

5. [Sandra] Graham, *House and Street*, explores a shift in elite perceptions of the functions and threats of domestic servants in Rio de Janeiro.

6. Haberly, "Abolitionism"; cf. Fernandes, *Negro*; [Viotti da] Costa, "Myth of Racial Democracy."

7. See contributions in Wagley, *Race and Class*, esp. pp. 28–33, 93–95.

8. [Thomas] Flory, "Race and Social Control," hints at the sharpening of a three-caste system from the late eighteenth century through the mid nineteenth

century that may have eventually disappeared with the blurring of lines of "mulatto identity."

9. The literature on the "Old Republic" of 1889–1930 is copious. On Bahian politics, see Pang, *Bahia*; [Consuelo Novais] Sampaio, *Partidos políticos*. On other regions, see the strongly comparative coordinated studies of Love, *Rio Grande do Sul*; Wirth, *Minas Gerais*; Levine, *Pernambuco*; Love, *São Paulo*. See also Lewin, *Paraíba*, on kinship and politics; Needell, *Tropical Belle Epoque*, on the national elite arena. On the empire and its fall: [Buarque de] Holanda, *Do Império à República*; Stein, "Historiography"; Boehrer, "Brazilian Republican Revolution"; [Murilo de] Carvalho, *Construção da ordem*; [Viotti da] Costa, *Da monarquia à república*; Colson, "Expectations"; Needell, *Tropical Belle Epoque*. On the threat of democracy in the 1830's, see [João José] Reis, *Rebelião escrava*; Morton, "Conservative Revolution"; [Thomas] Flory, *Judge and Jury*. On democracy in the Old Republic, see [Murilo de] Carvalho, *Bestializados*; [Wanderley Guilherme dos] Santos, "Praxis liberal"; Fausto, *Revolução de 1930*.

10. Salvador had a population of 129,108 (108,138 in urban districts) in 1872; 173,879 (144,959 in urban districts) in 1890; 205,813 in 1900; 283,422 in 1920; 292,574 in 1940; and 417,235 in 1950. Bahia had a population of 1.379 million in 1872; 1.919 million in 1890; 2.117 million in 1900; 3.334 million in 1920; and 3.918 million in 1940. As a rule of thumb, the population of Salvador was around one-tenth that of the state or province; the state of Bahia was usually the third largest in Brazil. Brazil, IBGE, *Características demográficas*, pp. 18, 19; Mattoso, *Bahia*, pp. 130–41, esp. 134–35; Ludwig, *Brazil*, p. 55, table II-3.

11. The revenues of Bahia were 2,041 contos in 1872, when the provincial population was 1.38 million, or 1$478 per capita; at current exchange rates that was approximately U.S.$0.81. The revenues of Bahia were 43,159 contos in 1923, when the state population was approximately 3.33 million, or 12$945 per capita—at current exchange rates, that was approximately U.S.$1.32 ($1.11 in 1872 dollars). Food prices rose by about 215 percent between 1872 and 1923 in Bahia. Food was not the only component of Bahian price inflation, but the growth in revenues standardized in these terms would have been about 178 percent. Calculated from Bahia, Directoria do Serviço de Estatística, *Desenvolvimento progressivo*; and comparing Mattoso, "Au nouveau monde," p. 408, table 1c; food price index computed from price series in Mattoso, pp. 443–60; the rate of Bahia's price inflation in the nineteenth century was much lower than that of Rio de Janeiro, perhaps 2.5 percent per annum, as opposed to 5.1 percent per annum: Leff, *Underdevelopment and Development*, 1: 122–24; cf. Wirth, *Minas Gerais*, pp. 262–63, indicating that Bahia's state revenues were less than half those of Minas Gerais in the 1920's.

12. Wirth, *Politics of Brazilian Development*.

13. [Rômulo] Almeida, *Traços*; Mariani, "Análise"; Tavares, *Involução industrial*.

14. Schwartz, *Sugar Plantations*.

15. Comparisons with Haiti were in the minds of Bahians around the turn of the century; see Maxwell, *Conflicts and Conspiracies*; Morton, "Conservative Revolution"; [João José] Reis, *Rebelião escrava*.

16. Morton, "Conservative Revolution"; [João José] Reis, "Elite baiana."

17. Schwartz, *Sugar Plantations*, pp. 432–34; Morton, "Conservative Revolution," pp. 329–36; Mattoso, "Au nouveau monde," pp. 835, 962; cf. Leff, *Underdevelopment and Development*, 2: 5–40, for regional comparisons.

18. Mattoso, *Bahia*, pp. 5–38; Pang, *Bahia*, pp. 47–55, on "geoeconomic zones" in the republic; Pierson, *Negroes in Brazil*, pp. 3–15, for an introduction to the capital, Recôncavo, and sertão in the 1930's.

19. All figures are for *municípios* (counties), from *Recenseamento de 1872*; the urban parishes of Salvador County had a population of 108,000, and the "urban" portions of the population of Cachoeira and Santo Amaro were probably significantly smaller than their county populations. Poppino, *Feira de Santana*.

20. Schwartz, *Sugar Plantations*, p. 463, table 16-7; Mattoso, "Au nouveau monde," p. 407, table 1b, and pp. 112–19.

21. On subsistence farming, see Azevedo, *Povoamento*; Mattoso, "Au nouveau monde"; [Costa e] Silva, *Roteiro*; [Pondé de] Sena, *Itapicurú*; [Hermes] Lima, *Travessia*, p. 8. See also Mattoso, *Bahia*, pp. 39–46, on Santiago de Iguape land. And cf. APEB, Registros Ecclesiásticos de Terras, 1856–58, São Francisco de Conde and Maragogipe, in a transcription courtesy of Bert Barickman; Wright, "Market, Land and Class"; Garcez, "Mecanismos de formação da propriedade cacaueira." [Francisco Vicente] Vianna, *Memoir*, surveys backlands districts in 1893.

22. [Euclides da] Cunha, *Rebellion*; Lins, *Médio São Francisco*.

23. Schwartz, *Sugar Plantations*, pp. 439–67, esp. 441; Galloway, "Last Years"; [Bittencourt] Cabral, "Prefácio"; [Wanderley] Pinho, *Engenho*. See [Henry] Hutchinson, *Village and Plantation Life*, p. 20, on the persistence of large units through the 1950's.

24. Schwartz, "Resistance and Accommodation"; [Ciro Flamarion de] Cardoso, "Peasant Breach."

25. [Herundino da Costa] Leal, *Santo Amaro*.

26. Eisenberg, *Sugar Industry in Pernambuco*, pp. 180–214, esp. 188–90. Cf. Arquivo Wanderley Pinho, letters, José Pacheco Pereira to José Wanderley [Araujo] Pinho, Engenho Terra Nova, June 20 and 28, 1949, confirming an agricultural day wage of $500 around 1890, similar to that of Pernambuco; Arquivo Cotegipe, 56/126, Araujo Pinho to Cotegipe, Santo Amaro, Jan. 20, 1889, mentioning pay for cowhands of 10$000 a month. Cf. wages for urban occupations in Mattoso, "Au nouveau monde," pp. 418–25.

27. Wright, "Market, Land, and Class"; Garcez, "Mecanismos de formação da propriedade cacaueira." Jorge Amado's novels *Cacau* (1933) and *Terras do sem fim* (1942) dramatize the lure of opportunities and wages.

28. Bert Barickman, work in progress on lavradores and small farmers in manioc-growing districts such as Maragogipe; for example, APEB, Inventários, Maragogipe, 2388/4, Francisco Rodrigues Lima, Mar. 1, 1882; APEB, Inventários, Maragogipe, 2388/8, Manoel João de Sousa Barreto, Sept. 10, 1881.

29. Arquivo da Cúria, Dispensas, 1859–85, includes frank assessments by priests of the property and prospects of a couple; e.g., Oct. 10, 1867, Firmino Dias de Affonseca and Maria Guilhermina de Jesus, Freguesia of Conceição da Feira. Many are described as *pobres*, barely holding enough property to constitute a viable family, having no resource other than being hard-working.

30. Schwartz, "Free Labor in a Slave Economy," "Elite Politics and the Growth of a Peasantry," *Sugar Plantations*, and "Patterns of Slaveholding"; Lugar, "Portuguese Tobacco Trade" (describing the region in the late eighteenth century); Morton, "Conservative Revolution," pp. 37–40, 385–86. For examples of voting *lavradores*, see APEB, Presidência da Província, Governo, Qualificações, maço 2807, "Alistamento eleitoral, Freguesia N.S. da Piedade, Matoim" (1847); maço 2808, "Lista dos cidadãos qualificados pela Junta Municipal, Freguesia de São Sebastião" (ca. 1875); maço 2807, "Acta da Junta de Qualificação da Freguezia de São Domingos de Saubara" (1857); maço 2803, "Lista dos cidadãos qualificados, Freguezia de San'Thiago Iguape" (1878).

31. [Herundino da Costa] Leal, *Santo Amaro*; Diamantino, *Juàzeiro*; [Henry] Hutchinson, *Village and Plantation Life* (for the 1950's); Harris, *Town and Country*; [Costa e] Silva, *Roteiro da vida*.

32. *Recenseamento de 1872*, p. 509. Of the free population, 25.7 percent of the men and 14.9 percent of the women could read; of the entire population (slave and free), 22.5 percent of men and 13.2 percent of women could read. It is implausible, however, that so few slaves in Bahia could read; the figures probably reflect the practices of census reporting. But in any case, the slave population was so small by 1872 (only 12 percent of the total) that variations in its literacy had only a limited effect on the total rate. There were great variations in literacy from parish to parish. In one parish of Nazaré das Farinhas, free male literacy was 30 percent, female 19 percent; in Santiago de Iguape, it was male 18 percent, female 7 percent; in Juazeiro, it was male 6 percent, female 4 percent.

33. Schools were located disproportionately near the capital; see [Dias] Tavares, *Duas reformas*, p. 21, with distribution of appointments to schoolteaching positions in the province in 1886. The signatures on inventories, notarial deeds, and other documents suggest that much literacy as counted by the census was probably marginal. On coins and trading in the backlands, see *Westphalen, Bach*, pp. 36–39, 48–52, 76; Wildberger, *Notícia histórica*, pp. 42–48; cf. [Herundino da Costa] Leal, *Santo Amaro*, p. 51; Harris, *Town and Country*, p. 62.

34. Ott, *Formação étnica*; [Vale] Cabral, *Achegas*, pp. 22, 61–63; [Nina] Rodrigues, *Animismo fetichista*; [Nina] Rodrigues, *Africanos no Brasil*; Querino, *Raça africana*. Bahia had sent 15,000 men to the Paraguayan War, many of them recruited through their National Guard units (Pang, *Bahia*, p. 9).

35. APEB, Presidência da Província, Governo, Qualificações, contains lists by parish officials of exemptions from recruitment in the 1850's, 1860's, and 1870's. See also [Thomas] Flory, *Judge and Jury*, pp. 91–93; Franco, *Homens livres*; Aufderheide, "Order and Violence"; and Santos Filho, *Comunidade rural*, esp. pp. 149–79, on Canguçu family patrons, feuds.

36. See Arquivo Cotegipe, 5/87, Pedro Moniz to Cotegipe, Mar. 16 [1888], on runaways; 56/70, Araujo Pinho to Cotegipe, Nov. 14 [ca. 1887] on "calling slaves to order," and 56/119, Apr. 3, 1888, on strikes on plantations. Earlier slave resistance is documented in Reis, *Rebelião escrava*. On arrival of republic, see Pang, *Bahia*, pp. 42–66.

37. Levine, "Mud-Hut Jerusalem"; [Pondé de] Sena, *Itapicurú*, pp. 154–55;

Della Cava, "Brazilian Messianism"; [Euclides da] Cunha, *Rebellion*; Sampaio Neto et al., *Canudos*.

38. [Euclides da] Cunha, *Rebellion*.

39. On definitions of *coronel* and *coronelismo*, see Pang, *Bahia*, pp. 1–42; [Victor Nunes] Leal, *Coronelismo*; Lewin, *Paraíba*, pp. 17–36.

40. Pang, *Bahia*, pp. 158–59. On elections and the electorate generally, see Love, "Political Participation."

41. Harris, *Town and Country*; and see also Braudel, "In Bahia"; Lins, *Médio São Francisco*, pp. 157–58.

42. See *Westphalen, Bach*, pp. 36–39, 44, 48–58, 65–66, 75, on the intermittent unification of markets (even across state lines) during booms, and fragmentation during slumps; cf. Levine, *Pernambuco*, pp. 130–32; Lewin, *Paraíba*, pp. 55–58, 87–97.

43. As early as 1818 there were attempts to establish boat lines in the Bay of All Saints; the 1853 line had the most continuity; [Wanderley] Pinho, "A viação na Bahia."

44. In 1860 the E.F. Bahia–São Francisco already carried passengers to Aratú (37 km).

45. [Wanderley] Pinho, "A viação na Bahia"; *Westphalen, Bach*, pp. 66–67; Brazil, Directoria Geral, *Annuário estatístico . . . 1908–1912*, pp. 58–59.

46. Pierson, *Negroes in Brazil*, p. 16, cites a figure of 1,028 automobiles in the city in 1935. See also [Wanderley] Pinho, "A viação na Bahia"; *Westphalen, Bach*, pp. 78–79; and cf. Poppino, *Feira de Santana*, pp. 204, 208–9. Roads were, of course, built earlier by the Antônio Moniz and Seabra administrations ([Pedro] Calmon, "Um homem," p. 34, in *Goes Calmon*).

47. The figures are not consistent, but [Goes] Calmon, *Mensagem . . . 1925*, pp. 75–80, reports that 71 percent of the 1,227 schoolmasterships and 77 percent of school enrollment of 47,589 were outside Salvador in 1924; id., *Mensagem . . . 1927*, pp. 41–44, reports that 84 percent of school enrollment of 50,088 was outside the capital in 1926; Renato Pinto Aleixo, *Relatório . . . 1943*, p. 66, reports that 89 percent of 105,185 students were enrolled outside the capital in 1943; Brazil, IBGE, *Educação no Estado da Bahia*, reports that 75 percent of the 3,086 schools were located outside the capital in 1945. In 1862, 67 percent of the 180 places for schoolteachers were outside the capital; Masson, *Almanak* (1862); [Isaías] Alves, *Educação e saude*, passim.

48. [José Antonio] Costa, "Corréios"; Brazil, Directoria Geral, *Annuário estatístico . . . 1908–1912*, pp. 68–71, 80.

49. Müller, *Religião na Bahia*, pp. 39–40, 43; Nóbrega, "Dióceses," pp. 257–58.

50. Mattoso, "Au nouveau monde," pp. 835–36, charting decline, 1860–87; Jancso, "Exportações"; [Goes] Calmon, *Vida econômico-financeira*; *Westphalen, Bach*, pp. 28–31, 42–45, 54, 65–66; [Barretto de] Araujo, *Reminiscências*; [Rômulo] Almeida, *Traços*, p. 10.

51. Ott, *Formação étnica*, pp. 72–73 (on Indian villages); Garcez, "Mecanismos de formação da propiedade cacaueira"; Wright, "Market, Land and Class"; Wildberger, *Notícia histórica* and *Meu pai*.

52. The novels of Jorge Amado both express and describe the expansionist spirit of Ilhéus society: see *Cacau* (1933); *Terras do sem fim* (1942); *Gabriela, Clove and Cinnamon* (1958). See also [Francisco] Mangabeira, *João Mangabeira*; but cf. Pang, *Bahia*, pp. 39–40, on Ilhéus's failure to consolidate bossism.

53. Although the land areas of *municípios* have changed, this is based on comparison of the *Recenseamento de 1872*, pp. 509–13; Mattoso, "Au nouveau monde," pp. 342–43; and takes the land area of 421 km² given in Brazil, IBGE, *Características demográficas*, pp. 18–21 and passim. Schwartz, *Sugar Plantations*, p. 441, points out that Maragogipe property was in smallholdings in 1816.

54. The 1920 census showed a bulge in the age pyramid of Salvador between the ages of 15 and 30, with significantly more females than males in that age rank. This suggests that there was notable female migration to the capital. *Recenseamento de 1920, profissões*, pp. 70, 92–93.

55. In 1940, when the population of the state was close to 4 million, 340,000 Bahians had moved to other states. Azevedo, *Povoamento*, p. 236; Cruz, "Aspectos . . . Rio Rico"; Harris, *Town and Country*, pp. 90–95.

56. The number of buildings in Salvador increased from about 18,000 in 1872 to 40,000 in 1920, 88,000 in 1950, and 300,000 in 1977. See *Recenseamento de 1872*, p. 508; *Recenseamento de 1920, profissões*, p. 205; Gordilho, "Sítio urbano," p. 1. And see Bacelar, *A família da prostituta*, pp. 52–54, on the subdivision of colonial mansions into tenements in the Pelourinho and Maciel districts after 1920. Amado presents a cross-section of contemporary proletarian life through the chronicle of a Pelourinho tenement, *Suor* (1934). See also [Guaraci Adeodato Alves de] Souza, "Urbanização," pp. 103–6.

57. Morton, "Conservative Revolution"; [João José] Reis, *Rebelião escrava*; [Pedro] Calmon, *História da Casa da Torre*. See Mattoso, "Au nouveau monde," pp. 408–10, for the composition of the Provincial Assembly in the nineteenth century; Colson, "Destruction of a Revolution," pp. 41–42, esp. n. 27; [Murilo de] Carvalho, *Construção da ordem*; Mattoso, "Au nouveau monde," pp. 408–10 (of Assambleia Provincial deputies whose origins were identifiable, two-thirds were sons of rural landowners); [Thomas] Flory, *Judge and Jury*. I was not able to consult Richard Graham, *Patronage and Politics in Nineteenth-Century Brazil* (Stanford: Stanford University Press, 1990).

58. Pang, *Engenho Central*; Ridings, "Elite Conflict" and "Merchant Elite."

59. Pang, *Engenho Central*, pp. 36–38, 44, 56–57. The group had failed by 1891, when it reorganized by reselling to a public corporation, at a nominal loss of 300 contos.

60. Mattoso, *Bahia*, pp. 39–46. Mattoso, "Au nouveau monde," pp. 890–95, studying a sample of inventories and testaments from Salvador, found that *senhores de engenho* were likely to leave moderate fortunes (10–50 contos) rather than large fortunes (50–1,000 contos). The value of the land in their estates became a smaller proportion of their worth over the course of the nineteenth century, while the value of slaves increased as a proportion of the value of their estates (pp. 933–39). These Recôncavo estates were still larger than those of landowners and planters in communities such as Itapicurú, in the Agreste, where an estate worth more than 5 contos was exceptional ([Pondé de] Sena, *Itapicurú*, pp. 117–18).

61. Arquivo Cotegipe, 56/117, Araujo Pinho to Cotegipe, Bahia, Mar. 20 [ca. 1888]; 56/126, Araujo Pinho to Cotegipe, Santo Amaro, Jan. 20, 1889.

62. [Bittencourt] Cabral, "Prefácio," pp. 36–37; Arquivo Cotegipe, 6/105, Argolo to Cotegipe, [Engenho] São Paulo, July 29, 1878; 6/113, Bahia, Feb. 19, 1888; 6/114, Cajahiba, June 4, 1888. Arquivo Araujo Pinho, 549/20, Argolo to Mariquinhas [Maria Luiza Wanderley Araujo Pinho], Bahia, July 15, 1897, and Maria Luiza Wanderley Araujo Pinho to Argolo, Santo Amaro, June 18, 1897.

63. Jancso, "Exportações"; Pang, *Engenho Central*; [Henry] Hutchinson, *Village and Plantation Life*. Arquivo Wanderley Pinho, letters, João Ferreira de Araujo Pinho Júnior to José [Wanderley Araujo Pinho], Santo Amaro, Nov. 9 and 24, 1927, exemplifies the tone of complaints about sugar planting.

64. Love, *São Paulo*; Wirth, *Minas Gerais*, pp. 118–39, 169–70; Levine, *Pernambuco*; esp. Love, *Rio Grande do Sul*, pp. 137–38, a comparison with Bahia; Pang, *Bahia*; [Consuelo Novais] Sampaio, *Partidos políticos*; cf. Lewin, *Paraíba*, on the success of a small state in this system.

65. Pang, *Bahia*, pp. 119–21, 139. [Hermes] Lima, *Travessia*, p. 6, sums up his faction's position: "We were the opposition." See also Lewin, *Paraíba*, p. 316.

66. *Westphalen, Bach*, pp. 34, 46. Sant'Ana, *Bambanga*, pp. 16–18, describes tobacco processing in Pojuca.

67. Pang, *Bahia*, pp. 14–15, 208, table 2. Bahia had 144 municípios in 1912, with an average of 753 votes in each. Each município usually had its own coronel, though a powerful coronel might dominate several municípios. Lins, *Médio São Francisco*; Pang, *Bahia*; Moraes, *Jagunços e heróis*.

68. Pang, "Revolt of the Bahian *Coronéis*."

69. Pang, *Bahia*, pp. 189–205; Garcez, *Joaquim Inácio Tosta Filho*; Wildberger, *Notícia histórica*, pp. 56–59, on decline of cacao landlords; [Nelson de Souza] Sampaio, *Diálogo democrático*.

70. Miceli, *Intelectuais e classe dirigente*.

71. [Henry] Hutchinson, *Village and Plantation Life*, pp. 47–51, 61–62, 179–92; Pang, *Bahia*; Pang, *Engenho Central*; [Herundino da Costa] Leal, *Santo Amaro*.

72. [Herundino da Costa] Leal, *Santo Amaro*, p. 15. Five contos would have been about U.S.$1,000. Diamantino, *Juàzeiro*; *Westphalen, Bach*; [Hermes] Lima, *Travessia*, pp. 6–7, but cf. Leal, *Santo Amaro*, pp. 16–17, and Amado, *Terras do sem fim*, pp. 128–39, 162–64, describing the "gestation" and birth of towns out of hamlets and plantations, and ironically showing jagunços trampling the Dia do Arvore civic ceremony in Itabuna.

73. [Herundino da Costa] Leal, *Santo Amaro*, p. 95; Diamantino, *Juàzeiro*, pp. 47–52; Sant'Ana, *Bambanga*, p. 80; Bahia, Directoria do Serviço de Estatística, *Anuário estatístico: 1924*, pp. 188–90, listing associations; Amado, *Terras do sem fim*, pp. 136–39; [Henry] Hutchinson, *Village and Plantation Life*, pp. 184–85; [Mary Garcia] Castro, "Mudança, mobilidade e valores," pp. 84–87.

74. Fletcher and Kidder, *Brazil and the Brazilians*, p. 498; Stein, *Brazilian Cotton Manufacture*; Pang, *Engenho Central*; [José Luis Pamponet] Sampaio, "Evolução de uma empresa"; Lloyd et al., *Impressões do Brasil*; Bahia, Directoria Geral de Estatística, *Anuário estatístico: 1926–1927*, pp. 47–55. Inventories and

property settlements after the 1890's show many estates that included some shares in industrial firms; one estate affected by the Encilhamento crash is described in APEB, Seção Judiciária, Autos Cíveis da Capital, auto 4, maço 6650, 1903, pp. 77–84, 100–114.

75. [José Luis Pamponet] Sampaio, "Evolução de uma empresa"; Bahia, Directoria Geral de Estatística, *Anuário estatístico: 1926–1927*. [José Sérgio Gabrielli de] Azevedo, "Industrialização e incentivos fiscais," points out that Bahia's share of national industrial production fell from 2.8 percent in 1920 to 1.8 percent in 1940. There was an industrial boom in the 1940's in which Bahian industrial production quadrupled, but the average size of industrial establishments declined from 13 workers in 1940 to 8 in 1950. See also Tavares, *Involução*; [Rômulo] Almeida, *Traços*, p. 14.

76. [Viotti da] Costa, *Da monarquia à república*, pp. 127–48; Dean, "Latifundio and Land Policy"; [Goes] Calmon, *Vida econômico-financieira*; Leff, *Underdevelopment and Development*, 1:48–77 (on abolition and immigration).

77. Within the capital, mule-drawn carriage and tram lines were organized in 1851. The first major lines on rails were those of Transportes Urbanos, which connected the Upper City to the elegant Graça suburb in 1864; Companhia Veículos Econômicos, which laid rails from the Lower City to the Itapagipe peninsula in 1865; and Trilhos Centraes, which connected Barroquinha and Rio Vermelho in 1870. Between 1897 and 1907, these lines were all electrified. See [Wanderley] Pinho, "Viação na Bahia."

78. [Goes] Calmon, *Vida econômico-financieira*; Simões Filho, "Evolução urbana," pp. 4–8; *Westphalen, Bach*, p. 36, and p. 40, referring apparently to the 1880's, says that Africans, organized by nation, often spoke little Portuguese. See also Luz, "Bahia renovada"; Gordilho, "O sítio urbano," p. 9; Wetherell, *Stray Notes from Bahia*, p. 89; [José Antonio] Costa, "Corréios"; Wildberger, *Presidentes da província*, p. 627. *Diário Oficial do Centenário* describes the facilities of the city in 1923.

79. Evans, *Dependent Development*, pp. 55–100.

80. [Nelson de Souza] Sampaio, *Diálogo democrático*, pp. 86–87. See also Mariani, "Análise"; [Rômulo] Almeida, *Traços*; interview, Paulo Sérgio Freire de Carvalho, July 1980.

81. [Nina] Rodrigues, *Africanos no Brasil*; cf. Querino, "Africano como colonisador"; Juvenal, "Cavaqueemos," *Diário da Bahia*, Apr. 1, 1897.

82. [Nelson de Souza] Sampaio, *Diálogo democrático*; "Revista dos Jornaes," *Diário da Bahia*, Feb. 6, 1897.

83. "Revista dos Jornaes," *Diário da Bahia*, Feb. 6, 1897.

84. Mariani, "Análise"; [Rômulo] Almeida, *Traços*; Tavares, *Involução*.

85. Tristão de Mattos, "Cavaqueemos," *Diário da Bahia*, Feb. 7, 1897, p. 1. Matches in advertisement for Mello, Pedreira, & Cia., *Diário da Bahia*, Apr. 14, 1897, p. 4. Empório trademarks reproduced in [José Luis Pamponet] Sampaio, "Evolução de uma empresa," pp. 102–5. The Bahian upper classes had no great need for department stores in Salvador, because they ordered from the Bon Marché in Paris (Teixeira et al., "Memória fotográfica," p. xi–5; cf. Needell, *Tropical Belle Epoque*, analyzing fashion in Rio).

86. Morse, "Erecting a Boomstone," has suggested the relevance to Brazil of the distinction between provincialism and regionalism made by Allen Tate in *Limits of Poetry*. For expression of contemporary northeastern regionalism, see Freyre, *Manifesto regionalista*.

87. Instituto Geográfico e Histórico da Bahia, Coleção Gonçalo Moniz, pasta 36, doc. 37, menu of banquet for Balthazar Bruñi, at Hotel Sul-Americano, July 26, 1918, and banquets of Partido Republicano Demócrata, 1916, 1917, 1918. Arquivo Araujo Goes, 556/53, menus of banquets for Miguel Vicente Calmon Vianna, Petrópolis, May 6, 1909; Petrópolis, Feb. 11, 1911; luncheon given by Bahian deputies to Miguel Calmon, Hotel do Globo, Nov. 10, 1903; 556/54, menu of banquet given by Miguel Calmon du Pin e Almeida for Affonso Pena, May 23, 1906. At home and in private, Bahians in Rio pined for real palm oil and dried shrimp for their recipes; ACRB, Maria Luisa Viana Ferreira Bandeira, letter, Bahia, July 3, 1880, Maria Luisa to Cota [Maria Augusta Barbosa]; letter, Rio, Apr. 19, 1882, Maria Augusta Barbosa to Maria Luisa; ACRB, Brites Barbosa de Oliveira Lopes, July 1, 1869, Brites to Rui Barbosa, asking whether he had been able to eat *canjica* corn pudding for the São João fiesta in São Paulo.

88. Tupinambá, "Cavaqueemos," *Diário da Bahia*, Apr. 6, 1897, p. 1.

89. Vilhena, *Bahia*; Mattoso, *Bahia*, pp. 159–70; and Mattoso, "Au nouveau monde," pp. 871–74, emphasize continuities. For a more elaborate scheme, cf. [Mário Augusto da Silva] Santos, *Caixeiros*, pp. 158–60.

90. [Murilo de] Carvalho, *Bestializados*, pp. 114–15.

91. Mattoso, "Au nouveau monde," pp. 871–75, suggests this income ranking. In 1870, 500$ would have been approximately U.S.$275—in the range of the wages of U.S. coal miners and farm laborers in the 1890's, when average annual earnings in the United States were $462 (U.S. Bureau of the Census, *Historical Statistics of the United States from Colonial Times to 1957*, p. 91, Series D 603–17). On income per capita in Brazil (denominated in 1950 dollars), see backward-extrapolated estimates in Coatsworth, "Obstacles to Economic Growth in Nineteenth-Century Mexico," following Leff's 1972 estimate of .4 percent annual growth: $62 in 1800, $83 in 1877, $89 in 1895, $94 in 1910. But cf. Leff, *Underdevelopment and Development*, 1:47, following Claudio Haddad, with revised backward-extrapolated estimates based on .1 percent annual growth: $196 in 1822, $215 in 1911. By Leff's 1982 interpolation, Brazilian income per capita would have been $207 in 1877, almost half of U.S. income per capita.

92. Mattoso, "Au nouveau monde," pp. 871–75.

93. *Recenseamento de 1872*, pp. 509–11, lists 12 percent as slaves, but Mattoso, *Bahia*, p. 123, analyzes a population count of 1870 that listed 20 percent of the population as slaves. Mattoso, "Slave, Free, and Freed," discusses slave marriage, and Arquivo Municipal da Cidade de Salvador, Registro de Casamento Civil, records several marriages of aged Africans, such as Santana parish, livro 18.1, Apr. 1871–Dec. 1883, June 4, 1878, Martinho José Coutinho and Maria Ritta Vieira. Cf. Fry, "Negros e brancos no Carnaval," on Africanisms around the turn of the century, and Mattoso, "Au nouveau monde," pp. 236–45. On occupations, see *Recenseamento de 1872*, p. 515; Mattoso, *To Be a Slave*, pp. 60, 96–97, 160.

94. *Recenseamento de 1920, profissões*, p. 109; Love, *São Paulo*, p. 10.

95. [Mário Augusto da Silva] Santos, *Caixeiros*, esp. pp. 121, 133–38, and *Comércio português*; Ott, *Formação étnica*; Campos, "Crônicas bahianas," pp. 323–33.

96. On factories, see Bahia, Directoria Geral de Estatística, *Anuário estatístico: 1926–1927*, pp. 47–55. Altogether, the largest twelve mills in the state had about 5,000 workers and used 6,700 horsepower of motor energy. See also *Westphalen, Bach*, pp. 59, 75. On labor organization, see Sampaio and [Silva] Santos, "Trabalho urbano na Bahia."

97. Jancso, "Exportações"; cf. [Wanderley] Pinho, *Engenho*, pp. 339, 518–19; Pang, *Bahia*, pp. 116–21; Dulles, *Anarchists and Communists*, pp. 92–95; Sampaio and [Silva] Santos, "Trabalho urbano na Bahia."

98. Mattoso, "Au nouveau monde," pp. 841–45, estimates that the proportion of income that a day laborer spent on food in the late nineteenth century was between 45 and 59 percent. See also Pierson, *Negroes in Brazil*, p. 17. And see Gouvéia, *Puericultura social*, pp. 27–32, on housing and neighborhoods in Salvador.

99. Requião, *Itapagipe*, p. 117. *Recenseamento de 1920, profissões*, pp. 110–11, shows that in Salvador 6 percent of boys and 3 percent of girls under 15 had "defined occupations," as did 74 percent of males and 31 percent of females in the 15–20 age group. Workers aged 15–20 represented 22 percent of all those with occupations, 39 percent of those in textile manufacture, 31 percent of those in domestic service, and 22 percent of those in the garment trades. See also [Mário Augusto da Silva] Santos, *Caixeiros*, pp. 40–41.

100. Requião, *Itapagipe*, pp. 17–20; Tavares, *Duas reformas*, pp. 22–33, 57.

101. APEB, Presidência da Província, Sociedades, maço 1575, cadernos 66–72, on the Sociedade Protectora e Beneficente dos Artífices Carpinteiros e Calafates, 1861–84, shows overlap between the form of religious brotherhoods and mutual aid societies, esp. "Estatutos," caderno 66; *Diário Oficial do Centenário*, p. 475; Bahia, Directoria do Serviço de Estatística, *Anuário estatístico: 1924*, pp. 190–91.

102. After the separation of church and state in 1889, initiates of the candomblé cults perhaps felt freer to reject Catholicism (see Mattoso, "Slave, Free, and Freed," pp. 75, 77). There is some evidence of a resurgence of overtly African styles and practices between 1890 and 1910 ([Nina] Rodrigues, *Africanos no Brasil*; Fry et al., "Negros e brancos").

103. *Recenseamento de 1872*, p. 515; *Recenseamento de 1920, profissões*, pp. 20–21, 110–11. Between 1872 and 1920 the total population of the state grew 142 percent, while the population of Salvador increased 119 percent. The number of commercial employees in the state grew 130 percent, and the number of public employees grew 441 percent. Salvador had 8 percent of the state's population in 1920, but 52 percent of its public employees and schoolteachers and 32 percent of its commercial employees lived in the city.

104. Mattoso, "Au nouveau monde," pp. 888–95.

105. *Questão Braga*; Mattoso, "Au nouveau monde," p. 919, shows that one goldsmith who died in 1883 left an estate of 121:000$ (about U.S.$67,000). The mean estate for all other artisans whose estates were probated (a select group) was 5:600$ (about U.S.$3,000 in the late nineteenth century).

106. Wetherell, *Stray Notes*, p. 18. See also ACRB, Adelaide Dobbert, letter

to Mãe [Maria Luiza Ferreira Bandeira], Bahia, Jan. 4 [n.d., ca. 1884], on cloth-ing. Both [Xavier] Marques, *O feiticeiro* (1922), and [Jorge] Amado, *Two Deaths of Quincas Wateryell* (1962), use holes in shoes as a symbol of the anxieties of lower-middle-class poverty.

107. Mattoso, "Au nouveau monde," pp. 4–5, 234; id., "Slave, Free, and Freed," pp. 69, 82; [Thales de] Azevedo, *Elites de couleur.*

108. *Recenseamento de 1872*, p. 508: 19,731 of 50,519 free men in the eleven urban parishes of Salvador were literate. Newspaper circulation: [Francisco Vicente] Vianna, *Memoir*, pp. 410–14. Population figures: Mattoso, *Bahia*, p. 135. Number of households: estimated by interpolation from figures on households, 1872 and 1920, in *Recenseamento de 1920, profissões*, pp. 204–5. An interpolated estimate of the number of households in the state of Bahia, using rates of growth either between 1872 and the incomplete census of 1900 or between 1872 and 1920, would be either 324,000 or 277,000 households in 1893. Newspaper-reading households were at most 4 percent of the households in the state.

109. *Recenseamento de 1872*, p. 515, "População considerada em relação às profissões." *Recenseamento de 1920, profissões*, pp. 20–21, 110–11. Estimates of nonmanual, professional, and adminstrative occupations for Salvador, and some of those employed in "commerce" suggest that perhaps 8,000 to 17,000 of the male population of Salvador could be counted as middle class, which would have been at most 14 percent of those with occupations in Salvador. If there were 8,000 middle-class male heads of household and 40,615 households, possibly 20 percent of the households in Salvador could be considered middle class.

110. [Bittencourt] Cabral, "Prefácio," p. 15. On use of *as famílias*, see Chapter 2. For a review of the literature on the Brazilian middle class, see Saes, *Classe média.*

111. Schoolmasters, for instance, were often *pardo* and *negro* (Sant'Ana, *Bambanga*, pp. 50–53; Querino, *Raça africana*, p. 161). On fears of loss of status by white families, see Arquivo Wanderley Pinho, letter, Maria [Luiza Wanderley] to Filha [Maria Luiza de Araujo Pinho], Nov. 2, 1923; Sampaio, "Evolução," pp. 124–25.

112. Da Matta, "Ethic of Umbanda" and *A casa & a rua*. In "*Dona Flor*: A Relational Novel," Da Matta calls Brazil a relational society. Cf. Leeds, "Brazilian Careers," pp. 379–404, on "classes" and "masses."

113. Patronage: ACRB, Maria Luisa Viana Ferreira Bandeira, letter, Bahia, Feb. 27, 1882, Maria Luisa to Maria Augusta Barbosa; *Transcripções do "Diário da Bahia*," p. 7; Requião, *Itapagipe*, pp. 45–55; [Raphael de Albuquerque] Uchoa, *Odysséa de um revolucionário.*

114. Portuguese were reputedly the major participants in many *irmandades* ([Mário Augusto da Silva] Santos, *Comércio português*, p. 145; but cf. [Targínio] Martinez, *Ordens terceiras*, pp. 91–93, tables 16–18, showing many members of undetermined nationality). They also led in secular associations: APEB, Presidência da Província, Sociedades, maço 1575, caderno 90, n.d. [ca. 1871], "Mappa de sociedades de socorros mútuos," shows that the Real Sociedade Portuguesa Beneficente 16 de Setembro (founded 1861) had 1,259 members, as many as all others combined in the total of 2,459 members of twelve mutual-aid societies. The next two largest associations, both artisans' mutual-aid societies, had a combined mem-

bership of 509; cf. maço 1575, cadernos 50, 51. Conniff, "Voluntary Associations," says that the Sociedade Portuguesa de Beneficência in Rio de Janeiro had 20,000 members in the 1880's. Clearly, associations in Rio were larger and more numerous. By 1920 the Sociedade 16 de Setembro had apparently disappeared or been consolidated into another (Bahia, Directoria do Serviço de Estatística, *Anuário estatístico: 1924*, pp. 190–91).

115. APEB, Presidência da Província, Sociedades, maço 1571, shows charitable as well as recreational activities in carnival clubs such as Cruz Vermelha and Fantoches da Euterpe during the 1870's and 1880's. Bahia, Directoria do Serviço de Estatística, *Anuário estatístico: 1924*, pp. 190–91, lists twenty associations, with 11,833 members, as *beneficente* in 1924. This apparently included some charitable, rather than simply mutual-aid, associations. See also *Diário Oficial do Centenário*, pp. 319–21, 455–56, 475, 480, 494–96.

116. *Diário Oficial do Centenário*, p. 533; [Wanderley] Pinho, "Viação."

117. Approximately 7,000 students were in private primary and secondary schools in Salvador in 1923, about a quarter of the total school enrollment (*Diário Oficial do Centenário*, pp. 311, 334, 335, 449–53). For example, the Educandário do Sagrado Coração de Jesus added a normal school for girls to its primary school in 1909. By 1923 enrollments had gone from 29 to 279, and of 3,013 students, 604 had earned certificates. At the Ginásio da Bahia, the official secondary school, the proportion of girls enrolled rose from 6–7 percent at the beginning of the century to 20–26 percent in the 1920's. See [Goes] Calmon, *Mensagem . . . 1927*, pp. 85–86; Cássia, *Memórias de Veridiana*; interview, Hilda Noronha, 1981. And see Sant'Ana, *Outros bambangas*, pp. 46–55, 69–77, on student life in the Ginásio da Bahia.

118. Calasans, *Faculdade Livre de Direito*; "Faculdade de Direito da Bahia," *Diário Oficial do Centenário*, p. 360. The Faculdade de Filosofia was founded in 1941 and inaugurated in 1943 (*Faculdade de Filosofia*).

119. [Herman] Lima, *Poeira*, pp. 270–79; Nogueira, *Caminhos*, pp. 18–19, and [Hermes] Lima, *Travessia*, p. 23, on the "Papagaio Louro" affair; Ribeiro, "Estudantes."

120. Hélio Jaguaribe, cited in [Lawrence] Graham, *Civil Service*, pp. 94–100. On the ethics of patronage, see Chapter 6. Possibly the most bitter indictment of the relation between schools, diplomas, and posts is the report of Anísio Teixeira, secretary of education and health, in [Octávio] Mangabeira, *Mensagem do governador . . . 1948*, pp. 2–6.

121. See Chapter 2, n. 103.

122. Inflation in Bahia during the Encilhamento may not have been as severe as in Rio de Janeiro. A price index using Kátia Mattoso's price series for foodstuffs in Salvador, weighted according to Leff, *Underdevelopment and Development*, 1:124 n. 2, gives an increase of only 26 percent between 1889 and 1892, largely because the price of manioc in Salvador actually fell during those years. Other components of the cost of living, such as rent, clothing, or fuel, are not included. Leff's Rio de Janeiro price index increased 58 percent, and Wirth's differently weighted Rio de Janeiro price index increased 97 percent during those years (Leff, *Underdevelop-*

ment and Development, 1:245; Wirth, *Minas Gerais,* pp. 32, 262–63; price series from Mattoso, "Au nouveau monde," pp. 443–61). The weighted Salvador price index increased 53 percent between 1914 and 1919, and 153 percent between 1914 and 1926; the Wirth Rio index increased 186 percent between 1914 and 1919, and 238 percent between 1914 and 1926 (across a splice between two price series).

123. Pang, "Revolt," on the Moniz administration; [Mário Augusto da Silva] Santos, *Caixeiros,* pp. 133–39; and cf. [Octávio] Torres, "Discurso," pp. 98–104.

124. [Antonio] Vianna, "Evocação," pp. 1–21.

125. Fausto, "As crises dos anos Vinte." For testimonies to generational differences in Bahia, see [Hermes] Lima, *Travessia,* pp. 22–25; [Walter da] Silveira, "Discurso"; Todaro, "Pastors, Prophets, and Politicians," pp. 66–70. See also [Francisco] Mangabeira, *João Mangabeira,* pp. 75, 91, 93, on Mangabeira's trajectory from 1910 *civilismo* through World War I to semisocialist rhetoric in 1926.

126. [Carmelita] Hutchinson, "Notas preliminares"; Mattoso, "Au nouveau monde," p. 6.

127. Needell, *Tropical Belle Epoque;* [Buarque de] Holanda, *Do Império à República,* pp. 271–82; Wirth, *Minas Gerais,* pp. 118–39, 169–70; Love, *Rio Grande do Sul,* pp. 111, 137–38, 156–58.

128. Pang, *Bahia,* pp. 137–58, passim.

129. Interview, Arnold Wildberger, November 1981, on *gente fina* and *gente finíssima;* Mattoso, "Au nouveau monde," pp. 888–95; 10 contos was approximately U.S.$5,500; 200 contos, U.S.$110,000.

130. Lloyd et al., *Impressões* (1913), pp. 876–93, lists firms and figures in the upper circles of Bahian commerce; Pang, *Bahia,* pp. 55–59.

131. Wildberger, *Presidentes da província;* [Renato Berbert de] Castro, *Vice-presidentes,* gives a sense of the pace of rotation in office. It was a sign of Bahia's power in the empire that it was often governed by a president from the province, despite the unwritten policy of appointing presidents from outside.

132. [Consuelo Novais] Sampaio, *Partidos políticos,* p. 156; *classes conservadoras* might also be translated as "vested interests."

133. Ridings, "Bahian Commercial Association"; Garcez, *Associação Commercial da Bahia;* [Mário Augusto da Silva] Santos, *Caixeiros,* pp. 42–44, 53–59, and *Comércio português;* Ridings, "Elite Conflict," pp. 87–92, and "Merchant Elite," p. 343.

134. Dean, *Industrialization;* Cardoso, *Empresário industrial.*

135. [Mário Augusto da Silva] Santos, *Caixeiros,* pp. 113–37; Pang, "Revolt."

136. Wetherell, *Stray Notes,* pp. 61–62; Pang, *In Pursuit of Honor and Power;* Bulcão Sobrinho, "Titulares bahianos"; Mattoso, "Au nouveau monde," pp. 269–71; Valladares, *Arte e sociedade nos cemitérios,* pp. 590–96, 940–41; Mattoso, *To Be a Slave,* p. 66; APEB, Seção Judiciária, Inventários da Capital, Francisca de Piedade Marinho, condessa de Pereira Marinho, 1897–98.

137. Needell, *Tropical Belle Epoque;* Bulcão Sobrinho, *Famílias bahianas,* pp. 88–149, passim.

138. [Consuelo Novais] Sampaio, *Partidos políticos,* pp. 160–65.

139. Pang, "Revolt"; Pang, *Bahia,* pp. 25, 90–92, 104, 117–19, 155–58; Arquivo

Wanderley Pinho, letter, José Muniz Souza Sobrinho to Pedro Lago, Valença, Dec. 6, 1919, indicates the paternalist nature of this "alliance" in elections; [Consuelo Novais] Sampaio, *Partidos políticos*, pp. 160–65.

140. Love, *São Paulo*, pp. 116–20; Wirth, *Minas Gerais*, pp. 135–39; Fausto, *1930*; Levi, *Prados*, pp. 177–83 (on elite leadership of the "democratic" movement in São Paulo).

141. [Juracy] Magalhães, *Minhas memórias provisórias*, pp. 102–5, 121, 140; [Nelson de Souza] Sampaio, *Diálogo democrático*.

142. Jancso, "Exportações," pp. 343–44; export prices and values are expressed in pounds sterling and U.S. dollars because milreis values fluctuated widely during these years. Garcez, *Instituto de Cacau*, p. 20; Garcez and Freitas, *Bahia cacaueira*. Amado's documentary novel *Suor* (1934) attempts to convey the individual dimensions of the *"crise"* in Salvador. See also Wildberger, *Meu pai* and *Notícia histórica*.

143. Garcez, *Instituto de Cacau*; Garcez and Freitas, *Bahia cacaueira*; Wildberger, *Meu pai*; [Henry] Hutchinson, *Village and Plantation Life*, pp. 40–44, 179–84; Nunberg, "State Intervention in the Sugar Sector" and "Structural Change and State Policy: The Politics of Sugar," esp. pp. 55–57.

144. [José Sérgio Gabrielli de] Azevedo, "Industrialização e incentivos fiscais."

145. Wildberger, *Meu pai*. This had happened during World War I as well—see *Westphalen, Bach*.

146. See Chapter 7.

147. Ludwig, *Brazil*, p. 55, table II-3. I have interpolated the population for 1945 between the count for 1940, 290,000, and the count for 1950, 417,000. The censuses of 1920 and 1940 show almost no growth in the population of Salvador between 1920 and 1940. As this contradicts evidence of a housing crisis and a construction boom, it suggests that one count was high or the other low.

Chapter 2

1. Athayde found that 45.7 percent of men and 51.5 percent of women in the parish of Sé, 1856–65, never married ("Ville de Salvador," pp. 164–69). Of deceased persons whose property was inventoried in the 1850's, 29.6 percent had never married; of persons counted in the partial census of 1855, 36 percent had never married; of men registered to vote in the São Pedro parish in 1857, 26.7 percent had never married (Mattoso, "Au nouveau monde," pp. 215–20).

2. Mattoso, "Au nouveau monde," p. 220.

3. Athayde, "Ville de Salvador," pp. 164–69. I have excluded foundlings from these figures, because the presence of an orphanage in the parish undoubtedly skewed the total population figures; cf. [Eudóxio de] Oliveira, "Demografia sanitária" (1902), pp. 427–29, suggesting that 55 percent of all births were legitimate in 1901.

4. *Recenseamento de 1872*; *Recenseamento de 1920, profissões*; IBGE, *Características demográficas*, p. 249.

5. [Oliveira] Vianna, *Populações meridionais*; Freyre, *Masters and the Slaves*.

6. Wetherell noted in 1860 that women kept their maiden names, "seemingly a very inconvenient custom, but one of great antiquity, and so consecrated. . . . The

husband's name is, however, now almost invariably added if the final name is not changed" (*Stray Notes*, p. 92). R. Magalhães Júnior, *Como você se chama?*

7. Lewin, *Politics and Parentela in Paraíba.*

8. See Chapter 5.

9. Freyre, *Sobrados e mucambos*; [Carmelita] Hutchinson, "Notas preliminares."

10. Bittencourt, "Memórias," pp. 54–59.

11. Dantas Júnior, "Desembargador Pedro Ribeiro de Araujo Bittencourt."

12. The custom of giving a child to be raised by the maternal grandmother or a maternal aunt was common in Bahia. Cf. Peixoto, "As origens," in *Goes Calmon*, pp. 9–10.

13. Interview, Clemente Mariani, 1980; Mariani, "Análise," esp. pp. 3–5; [Bittencourt] Cabral, "Prefácio"; Bittencourt, "Memórias"; [Thales de] Azevedo, "Introdução," to Bittencourt, "Memórias."

14. [Wanderley] Pinho, *Engenho*, p. 337; Arquivo Araujo Pinho, 549/8, letters and notes from Maria Luiza Wanderley Araujo Pinho to Maria de Carvalho Araujo Pinho, 1895–98.

15. Freyre, *Sobrados e mucambos*, p. 18; Russell-Wood, *Fidalgos and Philanthropists*; Boxer, *Golden Age of Brazil*, pp. 126–61.

16. I owe the model for the categories and organization of this analysis to John Womack.

17. [Teodoro] Sampaio, "O engenho de assucar no recôncavo de Santo Amaro," in Instituto Geográfico e Histórico da Bahia, Arquivo, Seção Theodoro Sampaio, pasta 2, doc. 8. Freyre refers mainly to the early eighteenth century or to an undifferentiated colonial period when he describes patriarchy in *Casa-grande & senzala* (1933); in *Sobrados e mucambos* (1936), he distinguishes three types of families: patriarchal, plantation, and urban. See [Pondé de] Sena, *Itapicurú*, pp. 138–44, on backlands ranchers; [Wanderley] Pinho, *Engenho*; cf. Schwartz, "Free Labor in a Slave Economy" and "Elite Politics"; Lugar, "Portuguese Tobacco Trade."

18. [Teodoro] Sampaio, "Engenho de assucar," p. 17.

19. Freyre, *Mansions and the Shanties*, pp. 107–9; [Wanderley] Pinho, *Engenho*, pp. 296–97; on selling family slaves, see Arquivo Cotegipe, 6/105, Argolo to Cotegipe, July 29, 1878.

20. [Teodoro] Sampaio, "Engenho de assucar," p. 18; landlords might speak of moradores and slaves in the same breath; see discussion of deaths from cholera in 1855, Arquivo Cotegipe, 7/1, Argolo to Cotegipe, Matoim, Dec. 28, 1855. On tenants, see Franco, *Homens livres*; Schwartz, "Free Labor in a Slave Economy"; Aufderheide, "Order and Violence"; Bittencourt, "Memórias," pp. 107, 131.

21. Bittencourt, "Memórias," p. 19; Rêgo, *Meus verdes anos*, p. 35; Lewin, "Historical Implications," pp. 271–72.

22. [Teodoro] Sampaio, "Engenho de assucar"; Pierson, *Negroes in Brazil*, pp. 165–66, 353–61, and see the discussion of illegitimacy in Chapter 7 below; [Wanderley] Pinho, *Engenho*, pp. 103–19, on illegitimate children; Bittencourt, "Memórias," p. 107, on agregados who were compadres, pp. 98–99, on the distinction between the first and second seating at a feast, p. 13 on agregada seamstresses; Cássia, *Memórias de Veridiana*, p. 13, on a "filha de criação."

23. Rêgo, *Meus verdes anos*, pp. 137–56; Santos Filho, *Comunidade*, p. 187; Morley, *Diary*, pp. 35–36, 67, 111, 176, 263; Bittencourt, "Memórias," pp. 13–14; [Teodoro] Sampaio, "Engenho de assucar," pp. 18–23; Cássia, *Memórias de Veridiana*, pp. 14, 16–19; [Sandra] Graham, *House and Street*; [Bittencourt] Cabral, "Prefácio," pp. 5, 34.

24. Bittencourt, "Memórias," p. 14.

25. Bittencourt, "Memórias," p. 11; on the austerity of backlands planters and farmers, see [Pondé de] Sena, *Itapicurú*, pp. 138–44; on towns and plantations, see Morse, "Cities and Society."

26. [Wanderley] Pinho, *Engenho*, pp. 315–27, 485, on luxury; [Hermes] Lima, *Travessia*, p. 5; [Bittencourt] Cabral, "Prefácio," pp. 14–15, mentions family lore of conflict in the 1830's between a spendthrift senhor de engenho, "*fidalgo*" and "*um tanto desperdiçado*," and his thrifty son-in-law, from a family known as "*gente mais parcimoniosa*," to whom he had given administration of the estate.

27. Wetherell, *Stray Notes*, p. 74.

28. [Henry] Hutchinson, *Village and Plantation Life*, pp. 23, 50; Santos Filho, *Comunidade rural*, pp. 61–62; [Teodoro] Sampaio, "Engenho de assucar," p. 24; [Bittencourt] Cabral, "Prefácio," p. 18, describing an old planter "besieged by goddaughters, *mucamas*, and that court of agregados that surrounded the senhores in those days." Arquivo Cotegipe, 75/45, Antonia Teresa Wanderley to Cotegipe, T.G., Mar. 10, 1862; Arquivo Araujo Pinho, 549/8, letter, Maria Luiza Wanderley Araujo Pinho to Enteada [Maria de Carvalho Araujo Pinho], May 21, 1898.

29. Von Binzer, *Meus romanos*; Bittencourt, "Memórias," pp. 13–14, 36, and 86 on the monotony of plantation life; Morley, *Diary*; Arquivo Araujo Pinho, 549/8, letters on exchanges; Araujo, *Vinte anos*, p. 107, describing customs in the sertão in the 1930's and 1940's.

30. [Teodoro] Sampaio, "Engenho de assucar," pp. 24, 27–31; Pang, *Engenho*; Santos Filho, *Comunidade rural*, pp. 62–63; Arquivo Cotegipe, 56/106, Araujo Pinho to Cotegipe, Dec. 8, 1886.

31. [Wanderley] Pinho, *Salões*, p. 48, gives verses describing a *botada* at mid-century; Frões, "Barão de Villa Viçosa"; [Herundino da Costa] Leal, *Santo Amaro*, pp. 89–92.

32. Santos Filho, *Comunidade rural*, pp. 185–90, p. 61; interview, Sr. Maria Teresa [Mariana da Costa Pinto Dantas], 1981; see also Dantas Júnior, "João D'Antas dos Imperiais Itapicurú," pp. 104–15; [Wanderley] Pinho, *Engenho*, p. 337, on festa of Piedade.

33. Schwartz, *Sovereignty*; [Costa] Pinto, *Lutas de famílias*; Santos Filho, *Comunidade rural*, pp. 80, 147–78, on Indians, feuds.

34. [Teodoro] Sampaio, "Engenho de assucar," p. 24; [Bittencourt] Cabral, "Prefácio," pp. 15, 18 (on 1850's), 6–7 (on 1907).

35. Pang, *Bahia*; interview, Luis Raimundo Tourinho Dantas, 1980.

36. Pang, *Engenho*, pp. 47–48; Cunha, *Parlamento e a nobreza*; Stein, *Vassouras*, p. 122; Pang, *In Pursuit of Honor and Power*. In its narrowest construction, *coronel* meant colonel in the state militia, but in the broad construction, it meant a political boss. Like a title of nobility, the attribute *coronel* assumed some relation to central authority: as Victor Nunes Leal puts it in *Coronelismo*, the system of

rural boss politics presumed the decline of rural power, but the inability of the central government to assume full control in the countryside. [Mary Garcia] Castro, "Mudança, mobilidade e valores," pp. 84–87, argues that the paternalism of the plantation lords did not pass to local government until the 1960's.

37. [Wanderley] Pinho, *Engenho*; Arquivo Cotegipe, 56/126, João Ferreira de Araujo Pinho to Cotegipe, Santo Amaro, Jan. 20, 1889; [Wanderley] Pinho, *Salões*, pp. 60–61; and see the description of a graduation party given by Cel. Cerqueira Lima on his Matoim plantation in 1905, "Reunião," *Diário da Bahia*, Jan. 18, 1905; on bankruptcies, Santos Filho, *Comunidade rural*, pp. 70–71, on the loss of 100 contos in an ironworks venture, leaving an estate of 10 contos.

38. [Costa] Pinto, *Lutas de famílias*; Santos Filho, *Comunidade*, pp. 149–78; cf. Chandler, *Feitosas*. [Alencar] Araripe, "Pater-Famílias"; [Wanderley] Pinho, *Engenho*; Pang, *Engenho*, p. 195; Pang, *Bahia*, pp. 13–17.

39. Von Binzer, *Meus romanos*, p. 20; Fletcher and Kidder, *Brazil and the Brazilians*, p. 164. Wetherell observed that ladies at receptions were talkative, slaves on the street vociferous (*Stray Notes*, pp. 135, 15); and a Bahian traveler in Germany noticed the quietness of conversations on the street and in hotels in Berlin (P. Serrano, "Impressões do Berlim," *Diário da Bahia*, March 5, 1897, p. 1).

40. Fletcher and Kidder, *Brazil*, p. 169; Freyre, *Mansions and the Shanties*, pp. 74–76. On widows, see Arquivo Cotegipe, 74/1, Luiza Flora Bulcão Vianna to Cotegipe, Jan. 11, 1888; and Arquivo Cotegipe, 6/113, Argolo to Cotegipe, Feb. 19, 1888 on separate property; also Schwartz, "Patterns of Slaveholding," p. 63. Wives in "traditional" families outlived their husbands by an average of six years in the nineteenth and early twentieth centuries; see Chapter 7 below.

41. In Paraíba, José Lins do Rêgo observed the conflict between his grandfather and grandmother over the direction in which the marriages of his aunts would turn the connections of the family (*Meus verdes anos*, pp. 162–78). See also, on marriage conflicts in the nineteenth century, interview, Sr. Maria Teresa (Mariana da Costa Pinto Dantas), 1981; Morley, *Diary*, p. 213; [Pedro] Calmon, *História da Casa da Torre*, pp. 163–64, and [Wanderley] Pinho, *Engenho*, pp. 103–4. On divisions within patriarchal households between husbands and wives, see Lewin, "Historical Implications"; Bittencourt, "Memórias," p. 19; [Bittencourt] Cabral, "Prefácio," p. 26. On a wife's alliances and kin in politics, see Arquivo Cotegipe, 5/77, Pedro Moniz to Cotegipe, Oct. 30, 1887; [Wanderley] Pinho, *Política e políticos*, pp. 7–8. On feuds dividing spouses, see Santos Filho, *Comunidade rural*, pp. 145–78.

42. [Bittencourt] Cabral, "Prefácio," pp. 39, 44–45; and see Chapter 5 below on the role of the *beata*.

43. Freyre, *Sobrados e mucambos*, pp. 67–69. See also Arquivo Cotegipe, 56/70, Araujo Pinho to Cotegipe [ca. 1887]; on behavior attributed to teething, 56/114, Jan. 13, 1888; 56/122, Nov. 4 [1888]; and 75/44, Antonia Teresa de Sá Pita e Argolo Wanderley to Cotegipe, Mar. 7, 1862.

44. Fletcher and Kidder, *Brazil and the Brazilians*, p. 176; von Binzer, *Meus romanos*, p. 20.

45. Morgan, *Puritan Family*; Fletcher and Kidder, *Brazil and the Brazilians*, p. 163; Carteado, *Cultura d'alma*; Rêgo, *Meus verdes anos*.

46. Fletcher and Kidder, *Brazil and the Brazilians*, p. 163.

47. Freyre, *Masters and the Slaves*, pp. 72–74; [Cardoso de] Oliveira, *Dois metros e cinco*, p. 249; [Abílio Cesar] Borges, *Vinte annos de propaganda*, p. 25. For analysis of the argument that slaves corrupted families, see Haberly, "Abolitionism."

48. [Isaías] Alves, *Educação e brasildade*, pp. 41, 58–61; Rêgo, *Meus verdes anos*; Diamantino, *Juàzeiro*, pp. 271–73. In works such as *Dom Casmurro* and "Rod of Justice," Machado de Assis makes learning to give orders a symbol of loss of innocence. On delayed maturity, see Arquivo Cotegipe, 75/61, João Maurício Wanderley to Cotegipe, Jan. 29, 1881, and 75/63, Dec. 6, 1885.

49. *Código Philippino ou Ordenações e leis do reino do Portugal*, 4: 900–912, livro 4, título 81/3; 4: 928, livro 4, título 88; and 1: 206–10, Law of Oct. 31, 1831; *Código Civil*, art. 379–84. See Viana Filho, *Vida de Rui*, pp. 40–41, 48–59, on the early emancipation of Rui Barbosa. See also Alida Metcalf, "Families of Planters," on property and marriage; for age at marriage, see Chapter 7, Table 5.

50. Bittencourt, "Memórias," pp. 19, 114; Morley, *Diary*. See [Bittencourt] Cabral, "Prefácio," p. 39, on the wisdom of a grandmother's advice to her granddaughter about sex and marriage in the 1920's.

51. Bittencourt, "Memórias," p. 14, and cf. p. 63, describing escorting of women in Salvador. Helena Morley's account of her childhood in a small town of Minas Gerais near the Bahian backlands gives a clear sense of the freedom to play and exercise that girls often had, and of the limits (*Diary*, pp. 197, 256). See, too, [Bittencourt] Cabral, "Prefácio," p. 4, "a liberdade de correr pelos pastos." Santos Filho, *Comunidade rural*, p. 61, describes a relatively sequestered rural family.

52. Bittencourt, "Memórias," pp. 13, 19; Sant'Ana, *Bambanga*, pp. 74–75; Arquivo Cotegipe, 75/42, Ambrósio Wanderley to Cotegipe, Jan. 10, 1857, on marrying off sisters; Morley, *Diary*, pp. 97, 159, 251–53, 276; [Wanderley] Pinho, *Cotegipe*, p. 623n; Arquivo Cotegipe, 56/122, Araujo Pinho to Cotegipe (ca. 1888), on concerns about a girl's future.

53. Von Binzer, *Meus romanos*; Santos Filho, *Comunidade rural*, pp. 57–61; advertisements for boarding schools in Cachoeira newspapers such as *A Formiga*, May 27, 1871, *O Americano* Feb. 19 and July 19, 1870; Arquivo Cotegipe, 56/109, Araujo Pinho to Cotegipe (ca. 1885) and 56/121 (ca. 1888).

54. Santos Filho, *Comunidade rural*, pp. 57–61. Just as they used the city for schooling, landlord families of the backlands sent women to the city to give birth with access to medical attention (interviews, Sr. Maria Teresa [Mariana da Costa Pinto Dantas] and Hilda Noronha, 1981). See [Bittencourt] Cabral, "Prefácio," p. 31, on a mother moving to Salvador for three years so that her twelve-year-old son could study the preparatory courses. For a view of households set up in Salvador for schooling in the 1850's, see Bittencourt, "Memórias," pp. 60, 118. See also Nogueira, *Caminhos*, pp. 7–14, on the Ginásio Carneiro Ribeiro; Santos Filho, *Comunidade rural*, p. 63, on the role of merchant *correspondentes* as guardians of students in the capital.

55. As long as hygienic standards of ventilation and cleanliness were maintained, the Brazilian medical literature approved of boarding schools. [Freire] Costa, *Ordem médica*, pp. 171–75, 179–91, points out that some medical theo-

rists were hostile to the family and hoped that boarding schools would separate children from the pernicious influences of their homes. See, too, Fletcher and Kidder, *Brazil and the Brazilians*, pp. 163–66; Cássia, *Memórias de Veridiana*, pp. 25–31; Freyre, *Mansions and the Shanties*, pp. 62–63; Lins, "Discurso." *Estatutos do Collégio Archiepiscopal Patrocínio* outlines the regulations, curriculum, and expenses of a boarding school for boys founded in 1897. And see Raul Pompéia, *O Ateneu* (1888); Rêgo, *Doidinho*; [Abílio Cesar] Borges, *Vinte annos de propaganda*; [Hermes] Lima, *Travessia*, p. 12, on Jesuits and Anísio Teixeira in the 1920's.

56. Sant'Ana, *Outros bambangas*, pp. 37–39; Cássia, *Memórias de Veridiana*, pp. 25–28; interview, Sr. Maria Teresa (Mariana da Costa Pinto Dantas), 1981.

57. Arquivo Cotegipe, 5/87, Pedro Moniz to Cotegipe, Mar. 16, [1888], on impending abolition; Morley, *Diary*, pp. 35–36, 67, 111, 176, 263; Bittencourt, "Memórias," pp. 14, 17.

58. APEB, Notas, 1330, pp. 192–93, Mar. 5, 1927, Testamento, Cel. Rufino [Correia] Caldas; 1292, p. 78, Aug. 18, 1920, viscount of Oliveira; [Wanderley] Pinho, *Política e políticos*, p. 11; [Pedro] Calmon, *História da Casa da Torre*, pp. 157–64.

59. [Mário] Torres, "Morgados do 'Sodré'"; Bittencourt, "Memórias," pp. 6, 19; [Bittencourt] Cabral, "Prefácio," p. 12.

60. [Pondé de] Sena, *Itapicurú*, pp. 191–92, recounts the case of a woman who was taken in by her widowed cousin and later married him; Santos Filho, *Comunidade*, pp. 149–78; [Graciliano] Ramos, *Infância*, 16th ed., pp. 158–65.

61. [Costa Pinto] Victória, "Família Costa Pinto," p. 64; interview, Sr. Maria Teresa (Mariana da Costa Pinto Dantas), 1981; Bittencourt, "Memórias," pp. 61–73.

62. Bittencourt, "Memórias," pp. 109–10.

63. Lloyd, *Impressões do Brazil*; Westphalen, *Bach*; Pang, *Bahia*, pp. 42–55, 126, 151–53; Needell, *Tropical Belle Epoque*; Needell, "Making the Carioca Belle Epoque Concrete"; Teixeira et al., "Memória fotográfica," pp. xi-2 to xi-13.

64. Wildberger, *Meu pai*, p. 30; Mattoso, *Bahia*, p. 196; [José Francisco da Silva] Lima, "Bahia," pp. 96–99, 115; [Mário Augusto da Silva] Santos, *Caixeiros*, p. 53; Gomes, *Mundo da minha infância*, pp. 63–68. Lugar, "Merchant Community," pp. 212–13, documents a shift of residences from Lower City to Upper City between 1754 and 1817, but from at least 1894, the unmarried German clerks of Westphalen, Bach—and perhaps of other firms—lived in pensions near Victória and the Barra district (*Westphalen, Bach*, pp. 41, 59–60). On Rio in the early nineteenth century, cf. Martinho, "Organização do trabalho," pp. 46–47.

65. Teixeira et al., "Memória fotográfica," pp. xi-12, xi-17 to xi-22; Mattoso, *Bahia*, pp. 170–88. Wetherell, *Stray Notes*, p. 110, says foreigners began the movement there to be able to see ships arrive. "Another reason is the congregational feeling there is in a small community." Germans crowded in, rents doubled, and a small house in Victória cost the price of a mansion elsewhere. See also [Carlos Alberto Caroso] Soares, "Expedientes de vida," on prostitution zoning of the Maciel District.

66. Dantas Júnior, "Gonçalves Tourinho," p. 33; Cássia, *Memórias de Veri-*

diana, p. 27, on the *casa cheia* ideal among the middle class; interview, Stella Calmon Wanderley Pinho, 1981.

67. APEB, Seção Judiciária, Autos Cíveis da Capital, auto 4, maço 6650, 1903, p. 201; [José] Silveira, *Vela acesa*, pp. 50–52; [Madureira de] Pinho, *Carrossel*, p. 5 ("She was brown, she must have been about seventy, but she ate at table with the family, knew everything and told nothing"); APEB, Testamentos, Inventário de Francisca de Piedade Marinho, condessa de Pereira Marinho, 1897–98; Morley, *Diary*, pp. 37–38, 259. *Agregadas* were mentioned in legacies in testaments: APEB, Notas, 1330, pp. 135–36, Oct. 23, 1926; p. 187, Feb. 12, 1927. There is notice of the custom of criação in deeds in which, occasionally, a couple would legally adopt a filho de criação: APEB, Notas, 1238, pp. 136–39, June 4, 1926, revoking a previous adoption for ingratitude; APEB, Notas, 405, p. 44, May 16, 1870, adoption of a child taken from an orphanage.

68. Freyre, *Order and Progress*, pp. 141–44. APEB, Seção Judiciária, Autos Cíveis da Capital, auto 4, maço 6650, 1903, and Arquivo da Cúria de Salvador, Divórcios, maço 39, 1878–84, describe households.

69. See articles concerned about effects of the Law of the Free Womb, calling for a passbook system, *Jornal de Notícias*, Dec. 7, 10, 12, 13, 1883; and after abolition, calling for a servants' passbook, ibid., Feb. 16, 1897, noted in "Revista dos Jornaes," *Diário da Bahia*, Feb. 18, 1897; see also [Sandra] Graham, *House and Street*.

70. [Viana] Bandeira, *Lado a lado*, pp. 6, 25–26, 62–63. Wetherell, *Stray Notes*, pp. 66–67, remarked in 1853 on black nurses carrying white children on their backs or hip: "It is astonishing how very fond they become of the black women, who appear to have quite a knack of managing children."

71. Von Binzer, *Meus romanos*; Arquivo Cotegipe, 75/46, Antonia [Wanderley] to Cotegipe, Dec. 17, [1871], on governess; [Viana] Bandeira, *Lado a lado*, pp. 62–63; ACRB, Adelaide Dobbert, letter to Maria Luiza Viana Bandeira, Bahia, Feb. 28, [?], on friends bringing a governess from Rio; interview, Stella Calmon Wanderley Pinho, 1980.

72. Morton, "Conservative Revolution," pp. 28–29, on Recôncavo residence patterns.

73. APEB, Seção Judiciária, Autos Cíveis da Capital, auto 4, maço 6650, 1903; interview, Berenice Noronha Diniz Gonçalves, 1981; Miller, "Middle-Class Kinship Networks," pp. 110–42, on contemporary compounds.

74. Wetherell, *Stray Notes*, p. 105; Fletcher and Kidder, *Brazil and the Brazilians*, pp. 166, 173; Santos Filho, *Comunidade rural*, p. 62, on rural rising early, meals at ten and four.

75. Teixeira et al., "Memória fotográfica," p. xi-16, streetcars; p. xi-18, Hotel Bon Sejour. In 1897 the newly opened Cafe Amazonas in the business district boasted of its nickel and glass chairs, rose marble and bronze tables, pumps for champagne and beer, and electric lighters for cigars (*Diário da Bahia*, Apr. 24, 1897, p. 1); cf. the notice of the reopening of the Armazem Mattos off the Rua Chile, renamed El Dourado and boasting ices, drinks, "intense electric illumination, billiards, special seating, art nouveau moulding; a thing worthy to be visited" (*Diário da Bahia*, January 24, 1905). Wetherell observes that "shops are frequent

places for gossiping" (*Stray Notes* p. 148). In the 1910's the Palace Club cabaret, next to the Diário da Bahia building, was different from nightclubs of the 1970's "because the only family types there were men" ([Hermes] Lima, *Travessia*, pp. 30–31). See also [José] Silveira, *Neto de Dona Sinhá*, pp. 94–100, on brothels.

76. [Wanderley] Pinho, *Salões*, pp. 47–62, on salons in turn-of-the-century Salvador; *Westphalen, Bach*, p. 40; Marques, *O feiticeiro*, pp. 55–59; [Cardoso de] Oliveira, *Dois metros e cinco*, pp. 86–89.

77. ACRB, Maria Luisa Viana Ferreira Bandeira, letter, Bahia, May 20, 1882, Maria Luisa to Maria Augusta Barbosa, on hiring a seamstress; letter, Friburgo, June 29, 1887, Rui Barbosa to Maria Luisa, on payments to servants; letter, Bahia, Feb. 27, 1882, Maria Luisa to Maria Augusta Barbosa, on firing a servant because "she's too much of an aristocrat."

78. Interviews, Stella Calmon Wanderley Pinho and Maria dos Prazeres Calmon de Sá, 1980; *Goes Calmon*, p. 26. Caricatures of worldly routines are found in "Meios de acção: Exemplo das ligas congêneres," p. 26; Peixoto, "Nem com uma flor." On rural confinement, see Arquivo Cotegipe, 75/45, Antonia Teresa Wanderley to Cotegipe, T.G., Mar. 10, 1862: "You give me permission for outings [but] you know very well I can't go out[;] much less do I have anywhere to go."

79. In the 1920's the Rua Chile became the symbol of luxury and illusion in Bahia's modernist poems, like the prostitute's "mask of rouge" (Chevalier, "Elegâncias"). On shopping, see [Hildegardes] Vianna, *A Bahia já foi assim*, pp. 46–49, 74–86; Wetherell, *Stray Notes*, pp. 14, 15; Mattoso, *Bahia*, pp. 171–73; Teixeira et al., "Memória fotográfica," pp. xi-5, 6.

80. Dantas Júnior, "Gonçalves Tourinho," p. 34, on families in Itapagipe organizing a neighborhood Christmas crèche; [Antonio] Vianna, *Casos e coisas*, on festive cycle; interviews, Innocêncio Marques de Goes Calmon and Stella Calmon Wanderley Pinho, 1980; [Madureira de] Pinho, *Carrossel*, pp. 24–29, 45–48; Requião, *Itapagipe*, pp. 45–54, 79.

81. Interview, Stella Calmon Wanderley Pinho, 1980; Arquivo Municipal de Salvador, Registro de Casamento Civil, Sant'Anna, livro 18.3–21, p. 101, Mar. 19, 1897, civil marriage of Francisco Marques de Goes Calmon and Maria Julieta de Couto Maia in the home of the baron of Desterro. Even the civil ceremony of a politician's son would bring together the elite (ACRB, Rui Barbosa, Documentos Pessoais, João Rui Barbosa, Certidão de Casamento, June 29, 1915). A wedding toast would appear in the newspapers (ACRB, Rui Barbosa, Documentos Pessoais, Maria Adélia Rui Barbosa Batista Pereira, copy of wedding speech published July 16, 1908, in three newspapers).

82. *Diário da Bahia*, Apr. 6, 1897, p. 2, describes the funeral cortege for Innocêncio Marques de Araujo Goes Filho in 1897: 20 carriages accompanying the coffin, many on foot. *Goes Calmon*, pp. 130–31, describes the funeral of Francisco Marques de Goes Calmon, former governor of Bahia, in 1931: 10 streetcars and 80 automobiles, three salvos from the state police. See also obituaries and memorials mourning the young lawyer Dr. Flávio Araujo, the "hope" of a prominent family, in *Diário da Bahia*, Apr. 11, 12, and June 10, 1897; "Loja Masónica Udo Schleusner," *Diário da Bahia*, June 22, 1897; interview, Stella Calmon Wanderley Pinho, 1981; Valladares, *Arte e sociedade nos cemitérios*, pp. 590–91, 1314–25, on

tombs. Photographs and postcards in APEB, Arquivo Goes Calmon, document the publicity of family gatherings. See also ACRB, Rui Barbosa, Documentos Pessoais, Francisca Ruy Barbosa Airosa, bookmark souvenir of a first communion, 1939. See *Diário de Notícias*, Jan. 2, 10, 11, 1906, on union leaders meeting their "illustrious countryman" Miguel Calmon at the docks upon his return from a commission to Ceylon.

83. Interviews, Stella Calmon Wanderley Pinho and Maria dos Prazeres Calmon de Sá, 1980. The home is now the Museu do Estado da Bahia, Salvador. See Sales, *Dados biográficos*, a fictional "memoir" of an aristocratic home; [Madureira de] Pinho, *Carrossel*, pp. 54–55. The Arquivo Público holds many uncatalogued floor plans from building permits.

84. [Targínio] Martinez, "Ordens terceiras," pp. 87–93; Valladares, *Arte e sociedade nos cemitérios*, pp. 302–4. On the Euterpe club: interview, Stella Calmon Wanderley Pinho, 1980; "Revista dos Jornaes," *Diário da Bahia*, Mar. 17, 1897: "E, então, na Euterpe onde se reune o que há de chic entre nós!" On regattas, Club de Tênis: Gama, "Sports," pp. 319–21; [Mário Augusto da Silva] Santos, *Comércio português*, pp. 141–77; and cf. Requião, *Itapagipe*, pp. 85–90, and [Madureira de] Pinho, *Carrossel*, pp. 49–50.

85. Interview, Paulo Sérgio Freire de Carvalho, 1980. His maternal great-grandfather sent all his grandchildren to Europe. Some studied there, but the "readaptation to the [Brazilian] milieu was difficult for them." Mariani, "Análise," pp. 3–5; Levi, "Prado Family"; Wildberger, *Meu pai*, pp. 21–22; *Goes Calmon*.

86. Dantas Júnior, "Gonçalves Tourinho," p. 33: "a woman who came to this world only to do good"; a couple defined by "understanding, solidarity, and reciprocal cooperation."

87. [Maria] Graham, *Journal*, p. 134. On women's roles, see *Goes Calmon*, pp. 11, 25–26; Hahner, *Mulher brasileira*, pp. 40–42; interviews, Stella Calmon Wanderley Pinho and Maria dos Prazeres Calmon de Sá, 1980. Conversations are described in Wetherell, *Stray Notes*, p. 135, on the 1850's; and Fletcher and Kidder, *Brazil and the Brazilians*, p. 163, on the 1860's: ladies "chatter pleasantly but have no knowledge."

88. For the ideal of the elite man around the turn of the century, see Needell, *Tropical Belle Epoque; Goes Calmon*, pp. 9–10, 15–26, and passim; Sales, *Dados biográficos*; [Hermes] Lima, *Travessia*, pp. 21, 28; [Francisco] Mangabeira, *João Mangabeira*, p. 14, on the "science of friendship"; Valladares, *Arte e sociedade nos cemitérios*, pp. 940–41, 1313, calls the late nineteenth and early twentieth centuries the "época dos comendadores," when men adopted the pose of the philanthropist in the effigies on their tombs; [Mário Augusto da Silva] Santos, *Caixeiros*, pp. 75–79; [José Francisco da Silva] Lima, "Bahia"; cf. Rogério, "Reminiscências de Couto Maia," p. 94.

89. [Viana] Bandeira, *Lado a lado*, pp. 6–7, 12–13: "When he was present, with what solemnity family life was conducted! His speech was sweet to his wife, affable with his mother-in-law, soft with me, and smooth with the servants" (p. 6). Interviews, Luis Raimundo Tourinho Dantas and Stella Calmon Wanderley Pinho, 1980, on grandmothers rather than grandfathers arranging marriage; Caminho, *Educação*; Wetherell, *Stray Notes*, p. 119, documents the old patrician customs;

interviews, Stella Calmon Wanderley Pinho, 1980, and Hildegardes Vianna, 1981, on men's formal dress in the home by the 1920's and 1930's.

90. Interview, Stella Calmon Wanderley Pinho, 1980.

91. Interviews, Paulo Sérgio Freire de Carvalho, Stella Calmon Wanderley Pinho, and Clemente Mariani Ribeiro Bittencourt, 1980; Mariani, "Análise."

92. Bulcão, *Colégio Antônio Vieira*; [Hermes] Lima, *Travessia*; [Madureira de] Pinho, *Carrossel*, pp. 32–34; [Gastão] Sampaio, *Nazaré das Farinhas*, pp. 104–13.

93. The metaphors of monarchical and republican government were often used to describe authority in the family in the late nineteenth and early twentieth centuries: "[Ruizinho] needs a slightly more severe and despotic government. Mama is far too constitutional for such an advanced child" (ACRB, Fernando Gustavo Dobbert, letter, Dobbert to Rui Barbosa, Bahia, Mar. 29, 1882). Cf. *In memoriam Dra. Francisca Praguer Frões*, pp. 50, 55, 59, on the home "where there often reigns the absolutism of a negligent and despotic chieftain."

94. [José] Silveira, *Vela acesa*, pp. 147–70; Dantas Júnior, "João Gonçalves Tourinho," pp. 22–26, and [Cardoso de] Oliveira, *Dois metros e cinco*, pp. 1–45, on Recife, 1880's; [Hermes] Lima, *Travessia*, p. 17; [Herman] Lima, *Poeira*, pp. 270–79; ACRB, Brites Barbosa de Oliveira Lopes, letter, Bahia, May 31, 1869, Brites to Rui Barbosa, teasing him about the "good life of a student." Contrasting student "republics" to store-clerk "republics," see [Mário Augusto da Silva] Santos, *Caixeiros*, pp. 82–83.

95. Freyre, *Mansions and the Shanties*, pp. 69–71; id., *Order and Progress*, pp. 367, 374; Requião, *Itapagipe*, pp. 37, 85; Gama, "Sports."

96. ACRB, Documentos Pessoais, João Rui Barbosa, Ação de divórcio, June 16, 1926, p. 4, letter, Aug. 4, 1925; Pierson, *Negroes in Brazil*, pp. 327–28; Rogério, "Reminiscências de Couto Maia."

97. Cova, *Esposa*, pp. 51–56, criticizing public religiosity; [Marieta] Alves, "Henriqueta Martins Catharino," on women's social work; Levi, *Prados of São Paulo*, pp. 45–47, 215–16, on a scandalous separation in São Paulo.

98. This vicarious identification extended beyond the middle class: the industrialist Luis Tarquínio complained that he couldn't get whites to work in a factory if they were related to fidalgos or could "point out as a relative someone who attended an academy and got a diploma"; they would rather starve than "give themselves up to occupations that they only consider fitting for blacks, for plebeians, or for someone who never had a rich or educated relative" (Luis Tarquínio, *Preceitos moraes e cívicos* [1901], cited in [José Luis Pamponet] Sampaio, "Evolução de uma empresa," pp. 124–25).

99. [Thales de] Azevedo, "Discurso," p. 40; the Pereira family was one of the notable instances of integration into the middle class and the elite. [Ordival Cassiano] Gomes, *Manuel Victorino Pereira*, pp. 11–22; Passos, *Manuel Victorino*, p. 216.

100. Viana Filho, *Vida de Rui*, pp. 3–64; [Ordival Cassiano] Gomes, *Pai de Rui*; [Viana] Bandiera, *Lado a lado*, pp. 3–8, 182–85.

101. Middle-class men and women were indeed patrons as well as clients. A man who managed his brother-in-law's shoe factory might also be the honorary president of a philharmonic society (Requião, *Itapagipe*, p. 45). See [Herundino

da Costa] Leal, *Santo Amaro*, pp. 1–20, 37–47, on his father's career as a political sub-chieftain in Santo Amaro around 1900, and pp. 20, 74, on the banquet his father gave on his birthday. See [Mário Augusto da Silva] Santos, *Caixeiros*, pp. 92–105, on the Associação dos Empregados no Comércio and other clerks' associations, and pp. 112–41 on the political activities of clerks. On the title "Major," see Requião, *Itapagipe*, p. 125, profiling the famous defender of the poor, Major Cosme de Farias; [Xavier] Marques, *O feiticeiro*, p. 12; cf. ACRB, Maria Augusta Barbosa, Certidão de Casamento, Nov. 23, 1876, describing her father, head clerk in a Treasury office, with the title of "Major."

102. [Hermes] Lima, *Travessia*, p. 6, pp. 5–9, 12; Lins, *Médio São Francisco*, pp. 157–58, argues that petty merchants and public employees in small towns followed in their fathers' footsteps partly for lack of opportunity; [Herundino da Costa] Leal, *Santo Amaro*, pp. 20, 26, 37–47; [Heitor de] Araujo, *Vinte anos de sertão*, pp. 113–15.

103. Discussions of rent and moves in ACRB, Maria Luisa Viana Ferreira Bandeira, Bahia, Jan. 2, 1882, letter to Maria Augusta Barbosa on getting a house for 50$ a month, with her son-in-law as co-signer, and moving expenses; [Viana] Bandeira, *Lado a lado*, pp. 11–12; concern with rent for widows and spinsters in APEB, Notas, 1330, p. 184, Feb. 3, 1927, and p. 185, Feb. 7, 1927; Sylvínio Júnior, *Dona de casa*, pp. 101–22, on learning budgeting to live with inflation. After the 1890's, commentary on the cost of living was common: Juvenal, "Cavaqueemos," *Diário da Bahia*, Jan. 27, 1897: "I rented a garret, neighbor to a multitude of bats and facing a lugubrious bell that always tolls for the dead," but rent increased from 20$000 to 60$000; Paul Kline, "Cavaqueemos," *Diário da Bahia*, Feb. 2, 1897; Pancrácio, "Cavaqueemos," *Diário da Bahia*, Mar. 31, 1897; Tupinambá, "Cavaqueemos," *Diário da Bahia*, Apr. 18, 1897; [Mário Augusto da Silva] Santos, *Caixeiros*, pp. 61–74, 141, 162.

104. [Hildegardes] Vianna, *A Bahia já foi assim*, pp. 4, 11–16; [Hermes] Lima, *Travessia*, p. 22.

105. Wetherell, *Stray Notes*, p. 118, on piano; Bittencourt, "Memórias," p. 50; ACRB, Brites Barbosa de Oliveira Lopes, letter (n.d., ca. 1867), Brites to Rui Barbosa; letter, Apr. 28, 1868, Brites to Rui Barbosa, on the "big expense" of piano lessons; letters, May 2, 1870, and June 1, 1870, on gift of a portrait of Gottschalk; Rui Barbosa, Cartas de Noivo, June 30, 1876, recommending piano lessons; Requião, *Itapagipe*, p. 28.

106. Requião, *Itapagipe*, p. 37; [Hildegardes] Vianna, *A Bahia já foi assim*, pp. 31–33; Morley, *Diary*, pp. 46, 224; C. Mager, "A Pedido," *Diário da Bahia*, Apr. 30, 1897. The relationship could turn into a familial one: see the testament of an illiterate spinster leaving her house and furniture to a young man whom she had brought up "from two years of age," who was now an employee in trade and paying for treatment of her illness in APEB, Notas, 1032, p. 45, May 18, 1900.

107. [Mário Augusto da Silva] Santos, *Caixeiros*, pp. 61–63, 90–91, Anexo I-1, I-3a, I-3b, I-4. In the 1920's the firm of Westphalen, Bach maintained a *"república de rapazes"* for its twelve bachelor German clerks, but "naturally" the firm's three married employees had their own houses (*Westphalen, Bach*, pp. 58–60).

108. ACRB, Adelaide Dobbert, letter, to Maria Luisa Viana Ferreira Bandeira,

Bahia, June 27, 1884; letter, Maria Luisa Viana Ferreira Bandeira to Adelaide Dobbert, Bahia, July 29, 1884; ACRB, Cartas de Noivo, Oct. 19, 1876, Rui Barbosa, stating that "the idea of constituting a family under a roof shared with others, even though these might be my closest relatives—brothers or parents—always repelled me invincibly," but conceding the necessity of doing so; ACRB, Cartas, Adelaide Dobbert to Maria Luiza Vianna Bandeira, June 27, [1884], and reply, July 29, 1884; cf. Adelaide Dobbert to Maria Augusta Barbosa (n.d.) implying some break between the families.

109. The number of civil marriages by clerks in Salvador declined after 1908 but then rose in 1912–13 to an average of 102 a year. Marriages fell 14 percent (to an average of 88 a year) from 1914 to 1917, the first years of World War I, then increased 22 percent (to an average of 107 a year) from 1918 to 1920. This decline in marriages may reflect a crisis in salaries. The war years were a time of relatively high export earnings, and 1919 recorded the highest export earnings in Bahia during the Old Republic. But there was a corresponding inflation crisis during the war (between 1914 and 1919, food prices increased by 53 percent) that may have cancelled out the effects of the boom for employees in the commercial sector. Between 1914 and 1917, there were 10 percent fewer marriages in Salvador overall than in the 1912–13 period, and the number of marriages increased 5 percent during the 1918–21 period. The 65 percent drop in the number of clerks marrying after 1928— from an average of 108 a year in 1925–27 to an average of 38 a year in 1928–30— was much more dramatic and strongly suggests the repercussions of a commercial crisis. The number of marriages in the city of Salvador overall fell in 1928–30, but only slightly, by 6 percent. Figures derived from [Mário Augusto da Silva] Santos, *Caixeiros*, Anexo I-1, recording numbers of marriages by clerks (*caixeiros*) as declared in the civil registry, Arquivo Municipal de Cidade de Salvador, Registro de Casamento Civil (1890–1910), and Salvador, Forum Rui Barbosa, Cartório da 5ª Vara de Família (1910–30).

110. [Viana] Bandeira, *Lado a lado*, pp. 34–35. "Society among brothers" was regulated in the *Código Philippino*, 4: 792–831, livro. 4, título 44.

111. ACRB, Cartas de Noivo, Aug. 15, 1876, on adjoining residences in Rio de Janeiro; Lemos, *Cozinhas*, pp. 157–66, esp. p. 158 n. 1; Miller, "Middle Class," pp. 110–42. In Salvador in 1981 at least three separate sets of kin occupied parts of a 20-story condominium with 80 large apartments.

112. ACRB, Brites Barbosa de Oliveira Lopes, letter, April 3, 1869, Brites to Rui Barbosa; Teixeira et al., "Memória fotográfica," p. xi-7 illustrates São Bento; ACRB, Cartas de Noivo, Oct. 8, 1876; ACRB, Maria Luisa Viana Ferreira Bandeira, letter, Rio, Nov. 5, 1880, Rui Barbosa to Maria Luisa; Requião, *Itapagipe*, p. 38, on sea-baths and bathing suits of the 1910's and 1920's; interview, Hilda Noronha, 1981, on the "first two-piece bathing suit in Bahia." Teixeira et al., "Memória fotográfica," pp. xi-20, xi-22, illustrates the Barra beach and bathing in the early twentieth century.

113. Viana Filho, *Vida de Rui*, p. 8; Cássia, *Memórias de Veridiana*, pp. 16–18, 25–26; [Mário Augusto da Silva] Santos, *Caixeiros*, pp. 61–62; [Hildegardes] Vianna, *A Bahia já foi assim*, pp. 202–7, on schoolteachers, pp. 34–36 on kitchens.

114. But fathers were often wary of their families, even children, participating

in folk processions traditionally conducted by the poor in front of the homes of their patrons; Requião, *Itapagipe*, p. 79: "When my father heard that the children's Three Kings troupe was going out on the street, he frowned and put his foot down. He wouldn't allow it. My mother . . . as always, overcame the 'old man's' resistance." [Antônio] Vianna, *Casos e coisas*; Requião, *Itapagipe*, pp. 29–36. [Manuel] Bandeira, "Evocação do Recife," makes São João in Recife a symbol of neighborhood solidarity.

115. [Herundino da Costa] Leal, *Santo Amaro*, pp. 80–86, 95–96; cf. Requião, *Itapagipe*, p. 77; "Festa de Reis," *Diário da Bahia*, Jan. 8, 1897.

116. Requião, *Itapagipe*, pp. 99–101.

117. Bulcão, *Colégio*, pp. 17–18; [Madureira de] Pinho, *Carrossel*, pp. 64–67; interview, Maria dos Prazeres Calmon de Sá, 1980; Sylvínio Júnior, *Dona da casa*, pp. 129–36; Lemos, *Cozinhas*, pp. 151–55, on home life in São Paulo in the 1920's and 1930's.

118. Silveira, "Discurso," p. 137; [Madureira de] Pinho, *Carrossel*, pp. 22–23. See Cássia, *Memórias de Veridiana*, p. 22; and see also the moralizing etiquette books on women's roles: Sylvínio Júnior, *Dona da casa* (1903), Caminha, *Educação* (1913), [Guimarães] Cova, *Esposa* (1914), available or printed in Bahia; [Júlia Lopes de] Almeida, *Livro das noivas*; d'Avila, *Boas maneiras*; also see Susan Besse, "Freedom and Bondage"; [Eugênio] Gomes, *Mundo*, pp. 126–31.

119. Amado, *Gabriela, Clove and Cinnamon* and *Dona Flor*; Da Matta, "*Dona Flor*: A Relational Novel," pp. 30–32.

120. Sylvínio Júnior, *Dona da casa*, p. 19; ACRB, Cartas, Maria Luiza Viana Ferreira Bandeira to Maria Augusta Barbosa, Oct. 15, 1879, on choosing a wet nurse; [Alberto] Silva, "Elógio da Antônio Vianna"; [Thales de] Azevedo, "Discurso," pp. 43–44; Requião, *Itapagipe*, pp. 55–62; [Walter da] Silveira, "Discurso," pp. 137–42, and *História do cinema vista da província*, pp. 19–20.

121. [Isaías] Alves, "Proteção à criança," in *Educação e brasildade*, p. 58. The Bahian categorization may have been a retention of nineteenth-century categories. Early nineteenth-century population surveys call children under seven *crianças* and children aged seven to fourteen *rapazes, moças*, or *raparigas* ([Menezes] Martinho, "Organização do trabalho," p. 54).

122. [José Francisco da Silva] Lima, "Bahia"; [Ordival Cassiano] Gomes, *Manuel Victorino Pereira*, pp. 16–20; Chastinet, "Mancos Chastinet," pp. 1–23, on Alexandre Borges dos Reis.

123. [Madureira de] Pinho, *Carrossel*, pp. 52–53, 57; Sant'Ana, *Bambanga*, pp. 61–62; [Thales de] Azevedo, "Discurso no centenário do Dr. João de Sousa Pondé," pp. 158–60.

124. Interview, Luis Raimundo Tourinho Dantas, 1980: "parecia ameaça [quando diziam] 'se não trabalhar vou lhe botar no comércio.'"

125. Ribeiro, "Sociologia pedagógica," p. 210; [Silva] Campos, "Chrónicas bahianas," p. 323 and passim, describes theatrical factions of the *classe caixeiral* and the *classe académica* that pitted the Lower City against the Upper City; [Mário Augusto da Silva] Santos, *Caixeiros*, pp. 41–42, 90–91, 160–61, estimates that at most one in five caixeiros advanced up the hierarchy of their firms to become partners; among 263 directors of the Associação Commercial da Bahia, however, one

clerk recognized 120 who had been caixeiros at some point in their careers (some of them caixeiros of their fathers). Most agreed that the likeliest way to become a partner was to marry a partner's daughter.

126. Interview, Hildegardes Vianna, 1981 ("o Doutor dos Relógios"). In the 1860's Fletcher and Kidder observed: "The young Brazilian likes nothing ignoble: he prefers to have a gold lace around his cap and a starving salary to the cares and toils of the counting-room" (*Brazil and the Brazilians*, p. 180). Wetherell noted that lower-class whites in Bahia were envious of the Portuguese: "They refuse to place themselves in a similar *degrading* position, namely that of making money. . . . They accept small, underpaid Government situations, . . . or starve from day to day" (*Stray Notes*, p. 75).

127. They complained that schools were located not where most convenient to pupils but where rents were lowest ("Actualidades: Educação Popular," *Diário da Bahia*, Mar. 6, 1897, p. 1).

128. Lins, "Discurso," p. 148: "Divided between the marvelous world sprung from the talk of the gunmen [on my father's fazenda] and games based on back-lands battles, and the boring world of Felisberto de Carvalho and Trajano, my spirit deadened." Later, at the Ginásio Carneiro Ribeiro in Salvador, he was a poor student.

129. Tupinambá, "Cavaqueemos," *Diário da Bahia*, Mar. 28, 1897, on decline of corporal punishment; [Graciliano] Ramos, *Infância*, pp. 110–25; Requião, *Itapagipe*, pp. 17–21; [Abílio Cesar] Borges, *Vinte annos de propaganda*, p. iii: "castigos corporaes que até para os escravos começam a ser abandonados."

130. Nogueira, *Caminhos de um magistrado*, p. 5, "rigor"; Requião, *Itapagipe*, p. 17, "the terror"; [Herundino da Costa] Leal, *Santo Amaro*, pp. 32–36, "tenderness."

131. Sant'Ana, *Outros bambangas*, p. 130; [Aragão] Bulcão, *Colégio*; [Hermes] Lima, *Travessia*, pp. 14, 16, on Antônio Vieira.

132. Ribeiro, "Estudantes," pp. 168–71, on the honor of status of *estudantes*, the disgrace of the 1932 rebellion at the Faculdade de Medicina: "It was unthinkable that a student should be a prisoner in jail, like a nun in a candomblé." See, too, Sant'Ana, *Bambanga*, p. 155; Morley, *Diary*, pp. 260–61; APEB, Arquivo Goes Calmon, letter, João Martins to Goes Calmon, Sept. 5, 1924, pointing out that his son, a fourth-year student at the medical school, had not been promoted as a proofreader on the *Diário Oficial*, and asking that he be given a post as intern in the Hospital João de Deus. José Silveira had a proofreading job on the *Diário Oficial* arranged for him while he was a secondary school student in 1921 (*Vela acesa*, p. 62). Lima Barreto's novel *Isaías Caminha* (1909) centers on the hero's aspiration to a patronage job that will support him while he is studying in Rio. Also, interview, Orlando Moscoso Barretto de Araujo, 1980, on his small-town uncles pooling funds to educate their youngest brother, his father; interview, Hildegardes Vianna, 1981, on "graduating" others; [Walter da] Silveira, "Discurso," p. 139, on the 1930's: "In the Ginásio, the uniform leveled the students. In the Law School, clothes marked the differences"; cf. [Hildegardes] Vianna, *A Bahia já foi assim*, pp. 194–97, on wardrobe.

133. Cabussú et al., *Memória sobre o ensino secundário*, p. 48; Campos, "Cró-

nicas bahianas," p. 361, on the irony of a beggar boasting, "My children are all raised and employed"; and see APEB, Seção Judiciária, Autos Cíveis da Capital, Tribunal de Relações, Ação de Desquite, 1910–13, no. 1718, Travessa v. Travessa, pp. 3, 16, 58, on the *colocação* in midst of family strife.

134. ACRB, Brites Barbosa de Oliveira Lopes, letter, Bahia, June 29, 1867, Brites to Rui Barbosa: "I who was accustomed always to be near her, who never was separated from her . . ."; and Rio de Janeiro, Aug. 14, 1867, Brites to Rui Barbosa: she will try to "take the place of our Mother. It is a very difficult task, my Brother; it seems almost impossible to me, but I will do what I can, and I hope that my Mother there in Heaven will ask God for me to substitute for her, that I can be virtuous as she was, and you, too, my Brother, ask her for that." Interview, Hildegardes Vianna, Dec. 1981; Requião, *Itapagipe*, pp. 91–99, on the Bomfim footing in the 1920's, says a girl who "*tirava linha*" (flirted) "would hardly ever manage to get engaged." The piano teacher was a necessary adjunct to a girl's development, but a danger as a possible seducer. Brites Barbosa was making arrangements to come in to town to take lessons "at some family's house" in 1868 (ACRB, Brites Barbosa de Oliveira Lopes, letter, April 28, 1868); the topic was treated as a cliché in Andrade, "Menina de ôlho no fundo" (1925) in *Os contos de Belazarte*. On girls' education, Morley, *Diary*, pp. 233–41; ACRB, Adelaide Dobbert, letter, Adelaide Dobbert to Maria Luisa Viana Ferreira Bandeira, Hamburg, June 9, [ca. 1880].

135. Amélia Rodrigues, "Que rico sermão!"; Requião, *Itapagipe*, pp. 55–62, on the craze for movie stars in the 1920's; Amélia Rodrigues, "O 'defeitinho' de Carmita," pp. 61–73; [Carmelita] Hutchinson, "Notas preliminares," p. 269, on the 1950's.

136. Requião, *Itapagipe*, p. 65, on "little servants or loose girls" in the 1920's; APEB, Seção Judiciária, Autos Cíveis, Tribunal de Appellação, maço 6650, auto 6, 1911, p. 6; [Herman] Lima, *Poeira*, pp. 277–79.

137. Interview, Hildegardes Vianna, 1981; id., *A Bahia já foi assim*, pp. 37–40.

138. See Marques, *O feiticeiro*, p. 73, using the phrase *famílias e populacho* (families and rabble); "Festa de Reis," *Diário da Bahia*, Jan. 8, 1897, p. 2; *Diário da Bahia*, Jan. 9, 1897, "groups of *populares* who address insolent remarks to passersby . . . in such a manner as to make the transit of families along that street almost impossible"; Rodrigues, *Mestra e mãe*, p. 43, describing a festivity with girls, boys, musicians, and "the povo, the good povo, anonymous and carefree"; Teixeira et al., "Memória fotográfica," pp. xi-15, 16, illustrating families in crowds. Families might be contrasted to their servants as "the families who are the order of society" (*Jornal de Notícias*, Dec. 10, 1883, p. 1). Another distinction made within the upper classes was that between *famílias* as mixed company and crowds that were all male, [Wanderley] Pinho, *Salões*, p. 38, citing Maria Graham on the theater: families in the boxes and men only in the orchestra. On language in the streets, see Vilhena, *Bahia*; Paul Kline, "Cavaqueemos," *Diário da Bahia*, May 26, 1897. The distinction between genteel home and indecent street is emphasized in [Sandra] Graham, *House and Street*.

139. Athayde, "Ville de Salvador," pp. 164–71.

140. Of 73 men marrying in the optional civil register for the district of Santana, 1877–80, 27 percent were of high status: liberal professionals, military officers,

merchants and capitalists, and students; 43 percent of middle status: public employees, craftsmen, and merchants; and 28 percent of low or indeterminate status: artisans and workers, "doing business," and undeclared (Arquivo Municipal de Salvador, Registro de Casamento Civil, Santana, livro 18.1, 1–19, 1877–83; and cf. [Mário Augusto da Silva] Santos, *Caixeiros*, Anexo I–1). Of a total of 1,075 men marrying in urban and suburban districts of Salvador in 1898, 1900, and 1901, 12.9 percent (139) were liberal professionals and public employees. In the 1920 census, about twenty years later, 8.2 percent of the men over 21 in Salvador were professionals and public employees, so that these occupational groups were probably significantly overrepresented among men marrying in 1898–1901. Workers, artisans, soldiers, and sailors were 46 percent of the work force and 48 percent (520) of those marrying, so that they were very slightly overrepresented. Farmers were 12.5 percent of the work force and 3.2 percent (35) of men marrying, and domestic servants were 1.8 percent of the work force and .74 percent (8) of those marrying, and so both were underrepresented ([Eudóxio de] Oliveira, "Demografia sanitária," 1899, 1901, 1902; *Recenseamento de 1920, profissões*, pp. 110–11). Of 839 men marrying in Salvador in 1926, professionals and public employees were 15 percent (130); workers, artisans, soldiers, and sailors, 44 percent (369); and farmers, 4.6 percent (39) ([Goes] Calmon, *Mensagem . . . 1927*, p. 159). See also Nascimento, *Dez freguesias*, p. 126, table 22, comparing race of heads of households of legitimate and illegitimate families in the incomplete 1855 household survey.

141. [Heitor de] Araujo, *Vinte anos de sertão*, pp. 116–17, on fathers concerned to "succour their daughters."

142. Requião, *Itapagipe*, pp. 117–23. He goes on to say that the rules seem rigorous, but they were appropriate to the times, and because of them, "it was rare for a girl to leave home [be deflowered]."

143. Fernandes, *Negro*, pp. 117–20; Fausto, *Crime e cotidiano*.

144. The rules for families of millworkers in the paternalistic workers' village of Luis Tarquínio's Empório Industrial do Norte recognized the difficulties of maintaining proper families; see Requião, *Itapagipe*, pp. 116ff.

145. Mattoso, "Au nouveau monde," pp. 257 (42.2 percent of households in inventories and an 1855 survey had female heads); and see also id., "Slave, Free, and Freed Family Structures."

146. Frazier, "Negro Family"; [Levy] Cruz, "Aspectos"; Athayde, "Ville de Salvador," points out that white families were more likely to abandon infants for reasons of "honor."

147. Mattoso, "Au nouveau monde," pp. 239–41, speculates that African women in Bahia might have found female-headed households a liberation from African patriarchalism; Landes, *City of Women*; [Hildegardes] Vianna, *A Bahia já foi assim*, pp. 144–46; [Vivaldo da Costa] Lima, "Família-de-santo."

148. Cândido, "Brazilian Family," pp. 291–312; and see also id., "Dialética da malandragem."

149. Cândido, *Parceiros do Rio Bonito*.

150. Mintz and Price, *Anthropological Approach to the Afro-American Past*; cf. [João José] Reis, *Rebelião escrava*.

151. Mattoso, "Au nouveau monde," pp. 241–42; id., "Slave, Free, and Freed Family Structures," p. 75 n. 13.

152. Amado, *Two Deaths of Quincas Wateryell.*

153. Morse, *Espejo de Próspero*, esp. pp. 213–16.

Chapter 3

1. Mortality statistics by disease for the city of Salvador for the years 1897–1925 are collected in Bahia, Directoria do Serviço de Estatística, *Anuário estatístico: 1924*, pp. 650–59. Of the mortality that statistics attribute to contagious diseases (which was never as much as half of total mortality), tuberculosis and malaria accounted for about 80 percent in nonepidemic years, but that would fall to 35–50 percent at the time of major epidemics. The most serious epidemic diseases were smallpox (epidemics in 1897, 1908–10, and 1919), yellow fever (1899, 1909, 1913–14, 1919, 1923), and typhoid (1897–99, 1924). There were also significant outbreaks of measles (1905, 1914, 1920), diphtheria (1912–14, 1918–19, 1925), "dysentery" (1908–9, 1913, 1920–21, 1923–25), plague (1904–7, 1909–10, 1913–14, 1920), and "grippe," or influenza (1907, 1918, 1922–24). In Salvador, the smallpox epidemic of 1919 was much greater in magnitude than the flu epidemic.

2. Arquivo Cotegipe, 5/38, Moniz to Cotegipe, Bahia, Sept. 16, 1855; Arquivo Cotegipe, 7/1, Argolo to Cotegipe, Matoim, Dec. 28, 1855. Cf. the lament over cholera deaths in an inventory of 1857 or 1858, translated in [Henry] Hutchinson, *Village and Plantation Life*, p. 40. ACRB, Fernando Gustavo Dobbert, letter, Dobbert to Rui Barbosa, Aug. 5, 1882, on vaccination; Adelaide Dobbert, letter, Adelaide Dobbert to Maria Luisa Viana Bandeira (n.d.) mentioning fear of smallpox in the city; ACRB, Maria Luisa Viana Ferreira Bandeira, letter, Bahia, Sept. 27, 1880, Maria Luisa to Maria Augusta Barbosa; letter, Friburgo, June 26, 1887, Rui Barbosa to Maria Luisa, wanting children vaccinated; also Maria Luisa Viana Ferreira Bandeira, letter, Rio de Janeiro, June 28, 1887, Rui Barbosa to Maria Luisa. See Cássia, *Memórias de Veridiana*, pp. 35–40, 76–78, on 1919 epidemic.

3. Arquivo Cotegipe, 56/128, Maria Luisa Wanderley [Pinho] to Cotegipe, Bomfim, Feb. 26, 1872; ACRB, Maria Luisa Viana Ferreira Bandeira, letter, Bahia, Jan. 2, 1882, Maria Luisa to Maria Augusta Barbosa; Arquivo Cotegipe, 56/96, Araujo Pinho to Cotegipe, Oct. 27, 1885, "a chill." Gouvéia, *Puericultura social* (1947), is the best work on infant mortality. He argues that so many births were unregistered (30 percent) that infant mortality rates derived from vital statistics are barely usable; even applying a correction, the rates for deaths at age 0 to 1 in Hora, *Mortalidade infantil . . . 1904–1918* (1922), p. 27, would be high, usually between 30 and 40 percent. Mattoso, "Au nouveau monde," p. 215, finds declarations of deaths of children consistent with these rates. ACRB, Documentos Pessoais, Maria Augusta Rui Barbosa, bill, June 28, 1893, from the Santa Casa da Misericórdia Empreza Funerária, for burial of an "*anjo.*" Arquivo Cotegipe, 6/110, Argolo to Cotegipe, Bahia, Aug. 4, 1883, on weakness after birth; and 56/122, Araujo Pinho to Cotegipe, Santo Amaro, Nov. 4, [1888], on almost losing a son, twisted in his umbilical cord.

4. Bittencourt, "Memórias," pp. 40–42, 74–77, 118, 127, on lung and eye ail-

ments; [Bittencourt] Cabral, "Prefácio," p. 30, on diabetes; for a satire of contemporary manners surrounding illness, see Kelleman, *Brasil para principiantes*, pp. 45–49.

5. ACRB, Maria Luisa Viana Ferreira Bandeira, letter, Bahia, Jan. 2, 1882, Maria Luisa to Maria Augusta Barbosa, on expenses. ACRB, Brites Barbosa de Oliveira Lopes, letter, Mar. 17, 1878, Brites to Rui Barbosa, on Eva. But paternalism had its limits. In the cholera epidemic of 1855, masters had to be charged with paying for the treatment of slaves who collapsed in the street; see ACRB, João José Barbosa de Oliveira, Sept. 4, 1855.

6. ACRB, Adelaide Dobbert, letter, Adelaide Dobbert to Maria Luisa Viana Ferreira Bandeira, Bahia, July 4 [ca. 1884], on "poverty"; ACRB, Brites Barbosa de Oliveira Lopes, letter, Brites to Rui Barbosa, Rio de Janeiro (n.d., but ca. July 1867).

7. Santos Filho, *História geral da medicina brasileira*, pp. 59–67; Russell-Wood, *Fidalgos and Philanthropists*, pp. 260–94; Santos Filho, *História da medicina no Brasil*, 1: 315; cf. Shryock, *American Medicine in Transition*.

8. [Thales de] Azevedo, *Ciências sociais*, pp. 39–44. A law school was founded in Bahia in 1891, and a polytechnical institute in 1897, but they were relatively precarious institutions for their first decades.

9. [José] Silveira, *Vela acesa*, is in great measure an indictment of the education in the 1920's, written by an alumnus who felt himself an outsider; cf. the milder Sant'Ana, *Outros bambangas*. Official criticism is found in "A propósito das Memórias Históricas," and Moniz, *Memória histórica de 1924*. And see Santos Filho, *História da medicina no Brasil*, 1:225–38, on deficiencies and their reforms; [Nancy] Stepan, *Beginnings of Brazilian Science*, p. 50, reports that few students managed to graduate from the Rio faculty in its first decades.

10. [José] Silveira, *Vela acesa*, pp. 86–89; Sant'Ana, *Outros bambangas*, pp. 141–42.

11. [Nancy] Stepan, *Beginnings of Brazilian Science*; Coni, *Escola tropicalista*, pp. 66–73; Corrêa, "Ilusões da liberdade."

12. Shryock, *Development of Modern Medicine*, pp. 206–40; Rosen, *From Medical Police to Social Medicine*.

13. [Nancy] Stepan, *Beginnings of Brazilian Science*; the thesis of Jambeiro, *A hereditariedade da tuberculose* (1885), reports the arguments of Araujo Goes.

14. Shryock, *Development of Modern Medicine*, pp. 206–40; Rosen, *From Medical Police to Social Medicine*; Machado et al., *Danação da norma*, pp. 166–70. The reception came mainly through France. Even classic English and German texts were read in French translations in the library of the medical school; on the general cultural influence of France in Brazil, see Needell, *Tropical Belle Epoque*.

15. Léonard, *Vie quotidienne du médecin de province*.

16. [Freire] Costa, *Ordem médica*, pp. 33, 121; the Bahian Luiz Anselmo de Fonseca's *A escravidão, o clero, e o abolicionismo* (1887) was an exception; but politicians formed by the Bahian Medical School, such as the deputy Jerônimo Sodré, were prominent in the abolitionist movement; see Toplin, *Abolition*, pp. 60–61; [Dinorah Berbert de] Castro, "Idéias filosóficas," pp. 276–77.

17. Domingos Guedes Cabral, *Funções do cérebro* (Tese de doutoramento, Faculdade de Medicina da Bahia, 1875), cited in [Dinorah Berbert de] Castro, "Idéias filosóficas," pp. 339–47.

18. [Freire] Costa, *Ordem médica*, p. 30. See also Shryock, *Development of Modern Medicine*, pp. 78–106; Rosen, *From Medical Police to Social Medicine*, pp. 120–58; Donzelot, *Policing of Families*, pp. 6–7. In extending their attention to these areas, Brazilian doctors drew new conclusions and conflicted with established customs and traditions. Although they seldom confronted other institutions head on, one dispute over jurisdiction is illuminating. After the cholera pandemic of the 1830's, governments throughout the world moved to prohibit burial inside buildings and churches and to require burial in special ground. Miasmas from decomposing corpses trapped in enclosed spaces were identified by doctors as a cause of the disease. In Bahia there were riots in 1835, allegedly instigated by the Franciscan brotherhoods, over transferring the public concession for burials to private parties. In 1855, after the cholera epidemic struck Bahia, a law forbade burial in churches, requiring burial outdoors, which had previously been the fate only of slaves, criminals, and non-Catholics (Valladares, *Arte e sociedade nos cemitérios*, pp. 279–85). Thus, at one stroke, the jurisdiction of medicine prevailed over that of the church with regard to the proper manner of burial, though it did not intervene in church rites and customs such as the wake, which might seem equally unhygienic. The victory was not complete. In 1897 an article complained vehemently of rumors that a foreign nun had died of infectious disease in a Salvador convent and been buried within its walls despite the law and good common sense to the contrary ("Prática abusiva," *Diário da Bahia*, May 19, 1897).

19. Freyre's portrait of the patriarchal woman in *Sobrados e mucambos*, pp. 114–18, derives much from such medical analyses. [Freire] Costa, *Ordem médica*, pp. 115–19, transcribes some of these statements. Bittencourt, "Memórias," p. 66, describes a physician uncle speaking out against women's confinement in the cells of a convent in the 1850's.

20. ACRB, Cartas de Noivo, June 18, 1876; and discussing "hygienic outings," July 13, 1876.

21. Many institutions work partly to regulate others. Law relates to market commerce, criticism to art, and the novel to the bourgeois individual in different ways and varying degrees, much as medicine hoped to relate to the family: with varying formality and authority over their subjects, they are all institutions that give other institutions cues as to how to operate, that set limits, and that reward and punish. Lasch, *Haven*, pp. 14–19 and passim, argues that social welfare and educational agencies in the United States between 1900 and 1930 used the analogy of the therapeutic relationship between doctor and patient to justify establishing their authority over the family. Here I consider a different endeavor, the attempt to legitimate medical authority itself in a far less organized society. Donzelot, *Policing*, pp. 9–26, provides suggestive cues in his reference to the medical origins of state policy toward the family in France in the early nineteenth century. But he, too, is primarily concerned with contemporary social welfare institutions.

22. Freyre, *Sobrados e mucambos*, pp. 120, 122, 123. The translation is mine, drawing on *Mansions and the Shanties*. Freyre argues that even reforms within

the church itself contributed to a decline in patriarchal power. For example, the church required that mass be held only in chapels located with access to the public roads rather than on private estates.

23. [Manoel Fernandes da] Silveira, *Estudo clínico do rachitismo* (1890), p. 1, "mantle"; [Joaquim Telesphoro Ferreira Lopes] Vianna, *Breves considerações* (1855), p. 5, "edifice"; [Freire] Costa, *Ordem médica*, pp. 171–75.

24. Santos Filho, *Comunidade*, pp. 191–200, esp. p. 199; cf. Nava, *Baú*, pp. 231–32; Bittencourt, "Memórias," p. 14; [Bittencourt] Cabral, "Prefácio," p. 24.

25. [Joaquim Telesphoro Ferreira Lopes] Vianna, *Breves considerações* (1855), p. 24, "Africans"; Sant'Anna and Gonzaga, *Escola de mães*, p. 35. On midwives, see Cerqueira, *Prophylaxia alimentar* (1903), p. 18. Although one twentieth-century doctor, Almeida Gouvéia, was able to assemble strong evidence of the perniciousness of the old ways, in most cases in the nineteenth century, the attack did not rest on such clear empirical evidence. Almeida Gouvéia's well-documented thesis traced infant tetanus mortality to home births on certain streets, and ulti-mately to the unlicensed midwives (*aparadeiras*) living on those streets, who prob-ably applied the traditional plasters of spiderweb powder, dung, and tobacco dust to the umbilicus (Gouvéia, *Puericultura social*, p. 207).

26. "Variedades: A mulher médica," *Gazeta Médica da Bahia* 3, 54 (Oct. 31, 1868): 70–72 (reprinted from the Portuguese journal *Escholiaste Médico*); see also a humorous article lampooning women's careers, "Variedades: Cousas da terra," *O Monitor*, Dec. 7, 1878; [Alberto] Silva, *Primeira médica*; Fernand Mazade, "A propósito de mulheres médicas," *Diário da Bahia*, Mar. 21, 1897.

27. ACRB, Cartas de Noivo, Sept. 18, 1876; ACRB, Cartas de Noivo, Sept. 15, 1876; urging outings, cf. Arquivo Cotegipe, 75/45, Antônia Teresa Wanderley to Cotegipe, T.G., Mar. 10, 1862.

28. ACRB, Cartas de Noivo, Oct. 8, 1876; [Ordival Cassiano] Gomes, *Pai de Rui*; [Rui] Barbosa, *Correspondência: Primeiros tempos*, p. 117, letter, João José Barbosa to Rui Barbosa, May 6, 1870, and p. 122, letter, João José Barbosa to Rui Barbosa, May 29, 1870, contain medical advice from father to son, warning against the dangers of sexual excess.

29. [Alfredo Ferreira] Magalhães, "Educação eugénica," describes his extensive propagandizing, lecturing, and journalism since 1899; and see *Paladina* 2, 10 (Oct. 1910). To date the beginning or to measure the stages in the diffusion of the idea of medical authority is difficult. Machado et al., *Danação da norma*, pp. 153–59, argues that medicine did not begin to propose a *consistent* health policy until the first two decades of the nineteenth century. [Freire] Costa, *Ordem médica*, takes most of its examples from medical theses defended at Rio de Janeiro between 1836 and 1850.

30. Warren, "Healing Art," demonstrates the pervasive appeal of homeopathic and spiritualist medicine. Chernoviz's *Diccionário* (first published in 1842) and *Formulário e guia médico* (first published in 1841) were probably the most wide-spread sources of medical doctrine in Brazil, particularly in the countryside. Orga-nized by alphabetical entries as a practical layman's guide, the *Diccionário* says little about hygiene. The *Formulário* includes an entry on onanism that condemns the practice and enjoins marriage, repeating a commonplace of European medical

doctrine rarely echoed by Brazilian writers (p. 1088). Bittencourt, "Memórias," tells of her father's pessimistic self-diagnosis using Chernoviz in the mid nineteenth century. Santos Filho, *História da medicina no Brasil*, 1:156–60, mentions other popular medical manuals.

31. Sant'Ana, *Bambanga*, pp. 71, 108–10; [Gilberto] Amado, *História da minha infância*, p. 35.

32. [Freire] Costa, *Ordem médica*, pp. 162–63.

33. Ibid., pp. 171–75, 179–91.

34. [José Leite de Mello] Pereira, *Breves considerações* (1853), pp. 18, 20–21; Carteado, *Cultura d'alma* (1913), p. 79.

35. Freyre, *Sobrados e mucambos*, pp. 67–69; Rosen, *From Medical Police to Social Medicine*, pp. 120–41; Flandrin, *Families in Former Times*, pp. 212–13, on contraception in France. The census of 1940 for Bahia showed that married mothers (excluding widows) born 1891–1900 had completed families in 1940 of an average size of 7.8 children; other age cohorts showed a similar fertility (IBGE, *Características demográficas*, p. 244). The median completed family size among the upper classes declined earlier, to about 5 after 1900; see Chapter 7.

36. [Freire] Costa, *Ordem médica*, p. 226; Süssekind, *Tal Brasil*.

37. The selection of topics was not absolutely free at the Bahia medical school. During part of the nineteenth century, students had to choose to address one of a list of questions (*pontos*). When choices were free, students often preferred to discharge the obligation of writing a thesis by going over the orthodox doctrine on some issue. Most theses have value precisely as samples of boilerplate; others have value as original social speculation. A few combine speculation with some social observation. All were published, at the expense of the student, and most probably circulated to family and patrons.

38. Bahiense, *Da alimentação* (1898), p. 22; Albernaz, *Primeira infância* (1898), pp. 24, 48–53. The most cited text of the early nineteenth century was the medical manual of J. B. A. Imbert, *Guia médica das mães de família* (1843), excerpted in Conrad, *Children of God's Fire*, pp. 135–36; and cited in Freyre, *Masters and the Slaves*, pp. 378–83. As early as 1870, the *Gazeta Médica da Bahia* reported the conclusions of a French commission that recommended a *bain-marie* for children's milk ("Projecto de instrucção," pp. 130–32).

39. Freyre, *Masters and the Slaves*, pp. 278–79; [Sandra] Graham, *House and Street*, p. 115, plate 11, photograph of a wet nurse and her former charge, ca. 1860. See also APEB, Inventários, Capital, 02/99/145/01, Francisco de Souza Paraiso, 1843–60, in which the cost of hiring a wet nurse for a one-and-a-half year old girl was charged to the husband's estate by Rosa da Cruz Paraiso, the widow; Charles Expilly, 1863, quoted in Conrad, *Children of God's Fire*, pp. 139–40.

40. ACRB, Maria Luisa Viana Ferreira Bandeira, letters, Bahia, Oct. 2, 1879, Maria Luisa Viana Ferreira Bandeira to Rui Barbosa; Rio de Janeiro, June 29, 1880, Rui Barbosa to Maria Luisa Viana Ferreira Bandeira; and Bahia, Oct. 15, 1879, Maria Luisa Viana Ferreira Bandeira to Maria Augusta Barbosa. ACRB, Alfredo Rui Barbosa, letter, Alfredo to Rui Barbosa, Rio de Janeiro, Mar. 26, 1911.

41. Ariès, *Centuries of Childhood*, pp. 374–75; Flandrin, *Families in Former*

Times, pp. 203–9; [José Leite de Mello] Pereira, *Breves considerações* (1853), p. 3; Goulart, *Hygiene alimentar* (1900), p. 27, said greater rural nursing was observed in Rio Grande do Sul; Borba Júnior, *Aleitamento materno* (1913), p. 24, on infant mortality.

42. Bahiense, *Da alimentação* (1898), p. 58, noted a large-scale trend among the poor in Bahia of using imported condensed milk, and many remarked that poor Bahians traditionally weaned infants to paps much earlier than upper-class mothers; Adeodato Filho, *Parto em domicílio* (1949), for example, studies a state social program to provide medical assistance for home births.

43. [Joaquim Telesphoro Ferreira Lopes] Vianna, *Breves considerações* (1855), p. 9.

44. [Calmon de] Siqueira, *Infância* (1858), p. 6.

45. [Joaquim Telesphoro Ferreira Lopes] Vianna, *Breves considerações* (1855), p. 24.

46. [Cabral] Netto, *Da alimentação* (1912), p. 100; [Manuel José da] França, *Syphilis e amamentação* (1918), p. 54.

47. For a different interpretation emphasizing the anxiety of the upper classes about controlling the servant class before and after abolition, see [Sandra] Graham, *House and Street*, pp. 117–20, 123–25, 130–31.

48. [José Leite de Mello] Pereira, *Breves considerações* (1853), p. 14; Bahiense, *Da alimentação* (1898), p. 22; [Armando Vieira] Lima, *Pediátrica médica* (1918), p. 93. The distinction between contagious and hereditary transmission of disease was fuzzy. Nineteenth-century medical theories often allowed a broad range of "hereditary" influences, including transmission of characteristics in early infancy (Rosenberg, "Bitter Fruit," pp. 25–53). On turn-of-the-century French theory about heredity, see Nye, *Crime, Madness, and Politics*.

49. [Joaquim Telesphoro Ferreira Lopes] Vianna, *Breves considerações* (1855), pp. 14–16, also expressed it as "inscribing, in the Koran of the married couple, phrases from the novel of single persons."

50. [Cacilda Vieira dos] Reis, *Ligeira contribuição* (1927), p. 9, contrasts the "futile pretexts" of wealthy mothers to the "necessity" of poor mothers. On "fatigues," see Albernaz, *Primeira infância* (1898), p. 40.

51. Certainly, preventing disease was highest among those motivations. And the stereotypes had at least a grain of truth: one Bahian woman interviewed in 1981, describing her father's family, mentioned family tradition that he had contracted syphilis as an infant from his wet nurse; cf. Freyre, *Masters and the Slaves*, p. 325.

52. [Freire] Costa, *Ordem médica*, p. 226; of course, this theme came from Christian morality. What was different was the instrumental legitimation of it.

53. [A. Ferreira] Guimarães, *Deve ser regulamentada* (1899), p. 36, on "consequences"; [Angelo Godinho] Santos, *Influência da prostituição* (1909), pp. 15–17, "orgies."

54. [Viveiros de] Castro, *Attentados ao pudor*, pp. xi–xii.

55. Brandão, *Do casamento* (1905), pp. 78–84; [A. Ferreira] Guimarães, *Deve ser regulamentada* (1899), p. 4. On devout lay opinion favorable to clerical marriage, see Bittencourt, "Memórias." The sexual frustration of girls was a favorite

theme of naturalist literature (e.g., Süssekind, *Tal Brasil*). A girl with a heart condition might be given advice not to marry because the stress of sexual intercourse could be deadly ("Questão Braga," *O Monitor*, Feb. 5, 1879).

56. As well as being a libertine, the "celibate" bachelor might be an onanist or a homosexual. Homosexuality fell so far outside the pale that hygienists alluded to it only in passing until the late nineteenth century. The first Brazilian doctor to address the topic, Domingos Firmino Pinheiro, met resistance to his research in Salvador and protected himself by camouflaging his prose in circumlocutions and Latin; he argued that homosexuals were victims of "sexual psycho-neurosis," but at the same time spoke of their "guilt" (Pinheiro, *Androphilismo*, pp. 184, 166). [Viveiros de] Castro had treated homosexuality briefly in his 1895 work, *Attentados ao pudor*.

57. Brandão, *Do casamento* (1905), pp. 34, 12–13, 21–25, 28; see also Nazzari, "Dowry in São Paulo," pp. 384–87.

58. Chamberlain and Gilman, *Degeneration*; Nye, *Crime, Madness and Politics*; Skidmore, *Black into White*; Kehl, "Eugenics Abroad"; Trounson, "Literature Reviewed." [Nancy] Stepan, "Eugenesia," is a broad history of Brazilian eugenics.

59. Bittencourt, "Memórias," p. 124.

60. [Gonçalo] Moniz, *A consanguineidade e o código civil*, pp. 7, 196, 17, 198.

61. [Freire] Costa, *Ordem médica*, p. 232, argues that doctors belonged to an upwardly mobile group that wished to open up the restricted endogamous marriage market of the planter caste. This interpretation of their motives is rather shallow and is contradicted by the fact that many doctors in Bahia were actually sons of the "planter caste." It seems obvious that a main concern of medical thought on the practice of consanguineous marriage was to address its social repercussions.

62. [Francisco Cavalcante] Mangabeira, *Impedimentos* (1900), pp. 37–38.

63. I draw on the suggestion in Douglas, *Purity and Danger*, that codes of purity and pollution use the body as a metaphor for social boundaries.

64. [Francisco Cavalcante] Mangabeira, *Impedimentos*, p. 38.

65. I do not argue that medicine somehow *accomplished* the transformation of society; but see [Freire] Costa, *Ordem médica*, p. 139, for this view.

66. Lemos, *Cozinhas, etc.*; [Hildegardes] Vianna, *A Bahia já foi assim*, pp. 28–36; Sylvínio Júnior, *Dona de casa*, p. 47, criticizing the management of kitchens by slaves.

67. One descendant of a prominent family claimed to have made over five contos a year (about U.S.$2,750) in his first two years of clinical practice in Santo Amaro in 1880 (Rodrigo Brandão, *Carta*). Faculty salaries in the medical school were between 2:000$ and 1:200$ in 1840; an equivalent salary (that of professor in the official secondary school) was 3:000$ (U.S. $1,650) by 1889 (APEB, Colonia e Província, Histórico, Instrucção Pública Superior, Faculdade de Medicina, maço 4046-1, 1832–49). See, too, Mattoso, "Au nouveau monde," p. 424; Sant'Ana, *Bambanga*, p. 48; Nava, *Baú*, pp. 231–32. Bulcão Sobrinho, "Família Bulcão," pp. 81–175, describes whole branches of his family that transplanted themselves to Rio Grande do Sul and Minas Gerais in army service. See also discussion of a patronage appointment as doctor of the Colónia D. Isabel in Rio Grande do

Sul "with a good salary" in 1877 (Arquivo Cotegipe, 5/53, Moniz to Cotegipe, Engenho, Mar. 7, 1877).

68. Indeed, doctors were probably far less dependent on state prebends than *bacharéis* or priests; Santos Filho, *História da medicina no Brasil*, 1: 79, points out that more doctors made independent careers in the nineteenth century than in the colonial period.

69. Freyre, *Sobrados e mucambos*; Pang and Seckinger, "Mandarins"; Barman and Barman, "Role of the Law Graduate"; [Murilo de] Carvalho, *Construção da ordem* and "Elite and State-Building in Imperial Brazil."

70. Machado et al., *Danação da norma*, pp. 18, 143ff.; [Freire] Costa, *Ordem médica*, pp. 211–14.

71. Peixoto, *Medicina legal*; Corrêa, "Ilusões da liberdade."

72. Vasconcellos, *Do defloramento* (1935), pp. 31–45. For a discussion of the law regarding defloration after 1890, see Fausto, *Crime e cotidiano*.

73. [Euphrasio José] Rodrigues, *Defloramentos e seus erros* (1895), p. 26.

74. Nava, *Baú*, pp. 100–101, provides a succinct account of the Braga affair. See also Peixoto, *Medicina legal*, p. 55; [Euphrasio José] Rodrigues, *Defloramentos e seus errores* (1895), pp. 11 and 46–48 (referring to another scandal, the Questão Rosa Benedetti, in 1888).

75. Peixoto, *Medicina legal*, pp. 28–30.

76. Quoted in Vasconcellos, *Do defloramento*, pp. 28–30.

77. Ibid., pp. 48–49, 126–28, 135, 85.

78. Freire Costa and Machado make a dichotomized case for the distinct nature of modern hygiene, for its characteristic preference for establishing norms rather than setting laws (Machado et al., *Danação da norma*; [Freire] Costa, *Ordem médica*, pp. 49–52); in this they follow Foucault, *History of Sexuality*, vol. 1.

79. [Sandra] Graham, *House and Street*, ch. 5 passim.

80. Eisenberg, *Sugar Industry*, esp. pp. 210–12, describes alternatives in the province adjacent to Bahia. See also [Célia] Azevedo, *Onda negra*; Conrad, *Destruction*; Toplin, *Abolition*; Lopes, *Espelho*; Conrad, "Chinese Immigration."

81. [Nancy] Stepan, "Eugenesia"; [Dain] Borges, "Reverso fatal"; [Célia] Azevedo, *Onda negra*; Morse, *Espejo de Próspero*, on Euclides da Cunha's vision of race as a response to the problem of nation-building; Lenharo, *Sacralização da política*; cf. Frederickson, *Black Image*, pp. 265, 321. Skidmore, *Black into White*, charts debates over race and the nation.

82. Shryock, *Development of Modern Medicine*, pp. 265–81; [Nancy] Stepan, *Beginnings of Brazilian Science*; Needell, *Tropical Belle Epoque*; Needell, "Revolta Contra Vacina," pp. 233–70; [Murilo de] Carvalho, *Bestializados*.

83. Pereira cited in Martins, *História da inteligência*, 7: 117; Penna, *Saneamento do Brasil*, p. iv; Lobato, "Urupês," p. 254, and see also prefaces, pp. vii–x, and cf. id., "Jeca Tatú: A ressurreição"; Castro-Santos, "Public Health in Brazil," pp. 230–35.

84. The law allowed parents to require a prenuptial exam of suitors; *Casamento Civil*, dec. 181 of Jan. 24, 1890, arts. 20, 21. The civil code of 1916 dropped this measure.

85. Brandão, *Do casamento* (1905), pp. 96–98, 99; [Antônio Raposo] Pinto, *Traz o casamento consanguíneo a degeneração da raça?* (1905), pp. 33, 35.

86. [Freire] Costa, *História da psiquiatria*; [Nancy] Stepan, "Eugenesia." There was at least one Bahian thesis favorably citing German race laws and pro-maternity policies: Lages, *Contribuição ao estudo da mortalidade infantil* (1940), pp. 69–76.

87. Founded in 1903, the Instituto de Proteção e Assistência à Infância began to function in 1904 as a dispensary and expanded its activities after 1907. See [Alfredo Ferreira] Magalhães, "Educação eugênica"; Gouvéia, *Puericultura social*, pp. 32–38. Cf. Donzelot, *Policing*, esp. pp. 88–92.

88. Needell, "Revolta Contra Vacina"; [Murilo de] Carvalho, *Bestializados*; [Nancy] Stepan, *Beginnings of Brazilian Science*; [Nina] Rodrigues, "Loucura epidémica"; id., "A loucura das multidões," pp. 131–32; Corrêa, "Ilusões da liberdade." Rebutting racism, see Querino, *Raça africana*. Amado's novel *Tent of Miracles* confronts characters modeled on Querino and Nina Rodrigues to represent the dilemma of Bahian racial identity. [Thales de] Azevedo, *Ciências*, pp. 47–51, describes the difference between Nina Rodrigues's work and that of less sympathetic intellectuals also working within the premises of criminology.

Chapter 4

1. Alves and Barsted, "Legislação sobre família." In contemporary Brazilian social analysis, one of the most influential visions of the distinction between law and social practice derives from the definition of power by Michel Foucault in works such as *History of Sexuality*, 1: 92–102; cf. Cardoso, *Political Regime*.

2. Law did acknowledge the godparent relationship in definitions of legal conflict of interest, along with other forms of kinship.

3. Glendon, *State, Law and Family*, pp. 308–15; Goody, *Development of the Family*; Glendon, *Transformation of Family Law*; [Nizza da] Silva, *Sistema de casamento*. The *Constituições primeiras do arcebispado da Bahia* (1707) established exceptional Brazilian institutions such as special provisions for slave catechism.

4. *Constituições primeiras*, livro 1, título 64, art. 267.

5. Ibid., livro 1, títulos 62–73, esp. arts. 285/4 and 285/11 (marriage). By canon law, collateral kinship is reckoned by the greatest number of generations from a common ancestor; therefore, an uncle is kin in the second canonical degree, a first cousin is also kin in the second degree, and a third cousin is kin in the fourth degree (Metz, *Canon Law*, pp. 144–46). And see *Constituicões*, livro 1, título 72, arts. 305–6 (dissolution); 310–17 (separation); [Nizza da] Silva, *Sistema de casamento*, pp. 126–31, 243–49.

6. *Código Philippino ou Ordenações e Leis do Reino do Portugal*, livro 4, título 46, para. 5/2; livro 4, título 92. In nineteenth-century Brazilian legal argument, the Philippine Code was most often cited as Ordenações do Reino.

7. Goody, Thirsk, and Thompson, eds., *Family and Inheritance*; Glendon, *State, Law and Family*.

8. Nazzari, "Dowry in São Paulo," p. 402. Russell-Wood, *Fidalgos and Philanthropists*, pp. 173–200, discusses colonial dowry. Inventories and wills imply that gifts to married couples had generally entered their community property; for ex-

ample, APEB, Inventários, Maragogipe, 2388/08, Manuel João de Souza Barreto, 1881; 2388/04, Francisco Rodrigues Lima, 1881; 2305/05, Caetano Moreira de Jesus and Ana Josefa de Souza; APEB, Notas, 178, p. 38, Sept. 7, 1813.

9. APEB, Notas, 160, p. 81, Sept. 6, 1808; 393, p. 87, Nov. 30, 1867, a gift by an uncle to his sister's daughter of a *creoulinha*, "who from a tender age was brought up [*criada e educada*] by his aforesaid sister Dona Francisca"; 186, p. 27, Nov. 11, 1815.

10. *Código Philippino*, 4: 832, and livro 4, título 47 (*arrhas*, or dower), 96 (dowry property), 97 (calculation of dowry in inheritance).

11. APEB, Notas, 425, p. 9, July 29, 1873 (Pereira de Aguiar family). It was, of course, highly likely that gifts of real estate would be subdivided from a larger family holding and hence bounded by the property of other family members. See also, e.g., APEB, Notas, 186, p. 27, Nov. 11, 1815; 238, p. 60, Apr. 11, 1832; 425, pp. 25–26, Aug. 22–23, 1873 (three deeds of houses by a man to his wife's nieces); 885, n.p., July 13, 1891 (Gomes de Oliveira and Oliveira Porto); 787, p. 46, Sept. 24, 1887.

12. APEB, Notas, 178, p. 38, Sept. 7, 1813; 178, p. 124, Nov. 25, 1813 (cousins marrying, she with no property); 712, p. 24, Dec. 1, 1882 (Italian merchant marrying Brazilian woman); 1268, p. 28, Mar. 19, 1915; 1443, p. 7, Mar. 9, 1939; 324, p. 39, Sept. 4, 1855; 324, p. 45, Oct. 3, 1855; 334, p. 77, Sept. 11, 1857; 712, p. 24, Dec. 1, 1882.

13. APEB, Notas, 787, p. 79, May 24, 1888; 1244, p. 80, Dec. 20, 1912; 1375, p. 23, Oct. 14, 1932; 1408, p. 33, Feb. 11, 1936; *Código Civil*, arts. 263/7, 264, 276.

14. *Código Philippino*, livro 4, títulos 44, 46, 47, 80–87, 92–97, 100–101.

15. Ibid., títulos 99, 105. For examples of remarriage with a prenuptial contract, see APEB, Notas, 425, p. 4, July 18, 1873 (a complex arrangement separating the property of a couple who had previously had a common illegitimate child, isolating the inheritance rights of another illegitimate child that she had previously by another man) and 426, pp. 9–10, June 20, 1873 (a widow remarrying and in two deeds donating property to children, and marrying by a regime of separate property).

16. I have found few similar references in Bahia, with exceptions: APEB, Notas, 161, p. 20, July 6, 1809 ("as she is the first to be married").

17. Metcalf, "Fathers and Sons," esp. pp. 469–73; see also id., "Families of Planters"; cf. [Nizza da] Silva, *Sistema de casamento*, pp. 106–8. Probably similar evasion of the principle of partible inheritance prevailed in Portugal. In the course of the reforms of the 1760's, the Crown claimed that huge dowries were ruining the male lines of noble families and forbade families to give their daughters dowries or even to pay for a wedding reception. See *Código Philippino*, Law of Aug. 17, 1761, p. 1031; Alvará (charter) of Aug. 17, 1761, p. 1033; Alvará of Feb. 4, 1765, p. 1034; Law of June 25, 1766, p. 1054; Law of Sept. 9, 1769, p. 1057; and, rescinding most of their provisions, Decree of July 17, 1778, p. 1036, coming shortly after the downfall of Pombal. Cf. Russell-Wood, *Fidalgos and Philanthropists*, pp. 183–84, speculating on special reasons for Brazilians to prefer transmitting property through female lines.

18. A survey of inventories and testaments in the Arquivo Público do Estado

da Bahia suggests that dowered daughters sometimes paid back, in the probate deduction, or *colação*, a prenuptial gift that was greater than their equal share. Bert Barickman, personal communication, 1987, regarding research in progress on lavradores in the Recôncavo.

19. *Código Philippino*, livro 4, título 88, para. 3; Law of June 19, 1775, p. 4: 1051; Law of Nov. 29, 1775, p. 4: 1051; Law of Oct. 6, 1784, p. 4: 1030. In other parts of Europe in the late eighteenth century, regalist governments tried to require paternal consent to marriage, in policies such as the British Matrimonial Act and French enforcements of older legislation on marriage (Traer, *Marriage and the Family*).

20. [Murilo de] Carvalho, *Construção da ordem*, pp. 51–91, esp. p. 59, on the legal training of the Brazilian elite; Maxwell, *Conflicts and Conspiracies*; Morton, "Conservative Revolution"; Glendon, *State, Law and Family*; Traer, *Marriage and the Family*.

21. Armitage, *History of Brazil*, 1: 8; Mattoso, "Au nouveau monde," pp. 196–97; Morton, "Conservative Revolution," pp. 25–28; [Wanderley] Pinho, *Engenho*, p. 342; Schwartz, *Sugar Plantations*, pp. 292–94; [Mário] Torres, "Morgados do 'Sodré'."

22. Armitage, *History of Brazil*, 2: 14, 49–51; [Rui Vieira da] Cunha, *Parlamento e a nobreza*; Law of Oct. 6, 1835, in Brazil, *Colleção das leis*.

23. Pang, *In Pursuit of Honor and Power*; [Rui Vieira da] Cunha, *Parlamento e a nobreza*; Katz, "Republicanism and the Law of Inheritance."

24. Brazil, *Colleção das leis*, Decree of Aug. 11, 1831; Decree No. 463 of Sept. 2, 1847.

25. The Philippine Code had allowed the illegitimate children of "plebeians" (*peões*), but not those of "nobles," to inherit intestate (*Código Philippino*, livro 4, título 46, para. 5/2, livro 4, título 92; see also [Rui Vieira da] Cunha, *Parlamento e a nobreza*). There was no provision in Brazilian law for women's adulterous children; maternal legitimacy could not be questioned.

26. APEB, Seção Judiciária, Livros de Notas da Capital (cited as APEB, Notas), holds notarial books for the city of Salvador recording deeds of *perfilhação*, formal recognition of "natural" illegitimate children according to the Law of Sept. 2, 1847. The archive holds approximately 900 books from Salvador notaries between 1870 and 1930, not all of which contain deeds of legitimation. After promulgation of the civil code of 1917, paternal recognition could be declared in the registry of birth, and notarial deeds of recognition became less common. A sampling of 10 Salvador notaries' books from the years 1870 and 1880, and 13 books from years between 1895 and 1934, yielded 116 deeds of legitimation. Of the fathers recognizing paternity, 25 percent declared occupations suggesting high and middle status (military officer, coronel, merchant or capitalist, professional); 16 percent were of low status (artisan, worker, farmer) and 59 percent of indeterminate and probably low status (*negociante* and undeclared). Overall 84 percent of the men declared that they were single. Only 7 percent of them legitimated children by more than one mother in one deed. Among the 116 deeds of recognition and an additional 4 notarial testaments that included legitimations, 40 percent legitimated more than one child by the same father, which suggests that many informal unions in Salvador were last-

ing consensual unions. The remaining 60 percent legitimated a single child on that occasion (which does not exclude the possibility that these men legitimated other children on other occasions). Perhaps out of consideration of women's need for honor, men may have been more inclined to recognize their daughters than their sons; 48 percent of the deeds included daughters alone, 23 percent both daughters and sons, and 28 percent sons alone.

27. The Bahian population geneticist Eliane de Azevedo has found a strong statistical correlation between the index of "religious" surnames in a population and the index of genetic or phenotypical markers of descent from an African population ([Eliane de] Azevedo, "Family Names in Bahia").

28. [Mário Augusto da Silva] Santos, *Caixeiros*, pp. 61–62; Nascimento, *Dez frequesias*, p. 125; APEB, Notas, 408, 1870–71, passim.

29. Men did not necessarily assume responsibility toward the mother of their children. Many legitimations took place after the death of the mother.

30. In 1909, for example, Coronel Jacintho Febrônio de Oliveira, a public employee, came forward after the death of his wife fifteen months earlier to recognize his illegitimate daughter (now 33 years old), who "was always brought up by him" (APEB, Notas, 1189, p. 19, Sept. 11, 1909). Cf. APEB, Notas, 639, July 1, 1880; APEB, Notas, 965, p. 16, Jan. 15, 1896. This practice also existed among the povo (APEB, Notas, 1032, pp. 46–47, May 21, 1900); on the elite, see APEB, Inventários, Capital, 02/99/145/01, Francisco de Souza Paraiso, 1843–60, esp. pp. 122–24.

31. [Wanderley] Pinho, *Engenho*, pp. 177–86; see another case in [Pedro] Calmon, *História da Casa da Torre*, pp. 157–64.

32. See discussion of this case in Chapter 7 below.

33. The civil code of 1916 allowed paternal recognition of an illegitimate child in the act of registering the birth, a procedural reform that may have made paternal recognition more common. Cautious fathers still used the notarial register to assure rights.

34. Brazil, *Colleção das leis*, Law of Dec. 16, 1830 [*Código Criminal*]; Flory, *Judge and Jury*, pp. 108–11.

35. *Código Criminal*, arts. 16, 5, 7; Freyre, *Sobrados e mucambos*, pp. 69–70; Araripe, "Pater-Famílias," pp. 15–23.

36. *Código Criminal*, arts. 247, 248.

37. *Código Criminal*, arts. 250–53. Fausto, *Criminalidade e cotidiano*, pp. 177–78, points out that men's and women's adultery was made equivalent in the 1940 criminal code. He suggests that this was perhaps because the fantasy of a wife introducing a bastard into the lineage had diminished.

38. *Código Criminal*, arts. 250–53, 254; Athayde, "Ville de Salvador," pp. 181–82, says that 2.5 percent of all baptisms in Salvador from 1830 to 1859 were of foundlings. About 45 percent were called white; the census of 1872 classified 35 percent of the population of Salvador as white. See also Russell-Wood, *Fidalgos and Philanthropists*, pp. 295–319, on the foundling wheel.

39. *Código Criminal*, arts. 227, 219. Fausto, *Criminalidade e cotidiano*, pp. 176, 188–89, 195–96, 199, 203, discusses marriage to avoid penalties for defloration in São Paulo between 1880 and 1920; Ramos, *Infância*, pp. 163–65; Martínez Alier, *Marriage, Class and Colour in . . . Cuba*, on elopement as a custom in Cuba;

Freyre, *Sobrados e mucambos*, pp. 129–30; Mattoso, "Au nouveau monde," pp. 296–303. In Bahia, elopement became commonplace among the lower class; in the 1920's, 150 to 200 complaints of defloration were filed every year, at a time when Salvador saw about 700 marriages a year (Vasconcellos, *Do defloramento*, p. 85). Bahia, Directoria do Serviço de Estatística, *Anuário estatístico: 1924*, p. 648, gives 732 civil marriages for Salvador in 1924, and [Gonçalo] Moniz, *Memória histó-rica . . . 1924*, pp. 206–7, reports statistics of the Serviço Médico-Legal do Estado da Bahia for 1924 recording 158 complaints of defloramento, 26 white, 93 brown, and 39 black, with a finding of 110 positive and 48 negative. Pedro José da Silva Lima, "A Pedido," *Diário da Bahia*, Mar. 11, 1897, p. 3, accuses an ex-sergeant of the fire brigade of deflowering a servant in his home. For one feud, see Santos Filho, *Comunidade*, pp. 149–78.

40. For figures on upper-class marriages, see Chapter 7, Table 2; for figures on consanguineous marriages in Salvador, Johildo Athayde, personal communication, based upon ecclesiastical registers; Lewin, "Historical Implications"; Freire-Maia, "Consanguineous Marriages"; Goody, *Development of the Family*, p. 45.

41. See the list of *impedimentos dirimentes* in *Constituições primeiras*, livro 1, título 67; cf. [Nizza da] Silva, *Sistema de casamento*, pp. 129–31.

42. [Nizza da] Silva, *Cultura no Brasil*, pp. 18–26. In *Breves* of 1848 and 1859, the Vatican again gave Brazilian bishops limited authority to grant dispensations.

43. Arquivo da Cúria, Dispensas series (*Dispensas de impedimentos, Dispensas de parentesco, Dispensas matrimoniaes*); [Nizza da] Silva, *Sistema de casamento*, p. 133.

44. Arquivo da Cúria, *Dispensas de parentesco, 1859–1863*, Dec. 28, 1861, Joazeiro, Chrispim Francisco de Oliveira and Maria Joanna de Oliveira.

45. Arquivo da Cúria, *Dispensas de impedimentos, 1859–1885*, Mar. 2, 1870, Hilário José Barbosa and Maria Magdalena de Jesus; *Dispensas matrimoniaes, 1889–1897*, Oct. 1894, Oliver and Moniz de Aragão; *Dispensas de impedimentos, 1859–1885*, Jan. 23, Feb. 25, 1885, Deocleciano Pires Teixeira.

46. Extant petitions for dispensation in the Arquivo da Cúria in Salvador show that both well-to-do and poor Brazilians in the backlands petitioned for dispensations; in the late nineteenth century the fees for a dispensation ranged from 12$ to 72$, roughly equivalent to the price of a horse; Arquivo da Cúria, *Dispensas matrimoniaes, 1864–1872*, pasta no. 28, Apr. 7, 1865, Souza and de Jesus. But fees might be waived for poor petitioners: see *Dispensas de parentesco, 1859–1863*, Sept. 3, 1861, Ferreira and das Virgens, a couple told to confess, take communion, say seven rosaries, and hold three fasts; Santos Filho, *Comunidade*, pp. 188–89, lists marriage and dispensation expenses.

47. For example, Arquivo da Cúria, *Dispensas de impedimentos, 1859–1885*, Feb. 13, 1885, da Silva and Encarnação: "So far, nothing is spoken or little is known; but it won't be long for this to become common knowledge, since the petitioner will turn up pregnant."

48. Arquivo da Cúria, *Dispensas de impedimentos, 1859–1885*, Feb. 28, 1865, Manuel Felippe dos Santos and Feliciana Maria da Conceição.

49. Arquivo da Cúria, *Dispensas de parentesco, [1859–1863]*, Antônio Mariano

Homem d'El Rei and Camilla Pinto Ferreira de Sá, Jan. 28, 1862. Godparents and co-parents were supposed to avoid sexual relations with their godchildren.

50. Arquivo da Cúria, *Dispensas de impedimentos, 1859–1885*, Jan. 23–Feb. 25, 1885, Dr. Deocleciano Pires Teixeira and Anna de Souza Spínola; *Dispensas de parentesco, [1859–1863]*, Guilherme José de Andrade and Guilhermina Maria da Silveira, Apr. 18, 1863; interview, Nelson Spínola Teixeira, 1981; [Hermes] Lima, *Anísio Teixeira*, pp. 22–27.

51. [Renato Berbert de] Castro, *Junqueira Freire*; [Nizza da] Silva, *Sistema de casamento*, pp. 209–52. Nascimento, "Divórcio por sentença."

52. Rosenn, "Jeito."

53. See discussion in Chapter 7.

54. Gerson, *Regalismo brasileiro*, pp. 74–78, 122. Haring, *Empire*, p. 114.

55. Nabuco, *Estadista do Império*, 1: 293–98.

56. Ibid., pp. 299–303.

57. Brazil, *Colleção das leis*, Decree 1114 of Sept. 11, 1861; Gerson, *Regalismo*, pp. 131–32, 271–72; Brazil, *Colleção das leis*, Law 1829 of Sept. 9, 1870, Decree 5604 of Apr. 25, 1874, Decree 3316 of June 11, 1887, Law 3349 of Oct. 20, 1887, Decree 9886 of Mar. 7, 1888, Decree 10044 of Sept. 22, 1888, Decree 10354 of Sept. 14, 1889; Brazil, Senado Federal, *Parlamento*, 5: 162–64. The Arquivo Municipal de Salvador, Seção Administrativa, Registro de Casamento Civil, holds civil registries beginning in 1877.

58. Arquivo da Cúria, *Dispensas de impedimentos, 1859–1885*, July 18, 1859, Adolfo Becke and Anna Gracinda Caldas Leal. *Dispensas matrimoniaes, 1889–1897*, pasta no. 4: on July 8, 1889, James Smith, a Protestant, got a recommendation from his bride's parish priest, who pointed out that she was "destitute." *Dispensas matrimoniaes, 1889–1897*, Mar. 23, 1890, Emil Wildberger and Adélia Urpia. Oct. 22, 1890, Augusto Benzaquem and Maria Augusta dos Reis Araujo Goes (the religion of Benzaquem was unspecified). *Dispensas matrimoniaes, 1889–1897*, Oct. 1894, George Brown Oliver and Joanna Moniz de Aragão; cf. Bulcão Sobrinho, *Famílias bahianas*, 3: 125, 129–31, which indicates that she (like another of her sisters) married only months after the death of her father, the 3d baron of Rio das Contas. Cf. Arquivo da Cúria, *Dispensas matrimoniaes, 1889–1897*, pasta no. 2: on Dec. 20, 1889, a longtime German immigrant requesting dispensation from banns because of need to marry a young Brazilian woman "in haste" apparently had his marriage denied when his parish priest noted that he was a Protestant.

59. Nabuco, *Estadista do Império*, 2: 377.

60. Brazil, Senado Federal, *Parlamento*, 5: 157, citing Saldanha Marinho on Feb. 12, 1879.

61. Brazil, Senado Federal, *Parlamento*, 5: 171, 173.

62. Gerson, *Regalismo*, pp. 271–73, mentions two attempts, by Conselheiro Lafayette in 1883, and by Deputy Mata Machado in 1887, both tabled by changes in government.

63. *Casamento Civil*, Decree no. 181 of Jan. 24, 1890, and Decree no. 521 of June 26, 1890.

64. Glendon, *State, Law and Family*; Pope Leo XIII, *Arcanum*, and *Dum Multa*, pp. 517–18, addressed to the bishops of Ecuador.

65. U.S. National Archives, Dispatches from Consuls, Roll 6, David N. Burke to Department of State, no. 99, Bahia, June 12, 1890, mentions concerns of "better" Catholics and the reports of 130 Catholic weddings in Salvador in the three days before the civil marriage decree took effect. See also ibid., [no. 101,] Bahia, July 17, 1890, and no. 140, Bahia, Jan. 29, 1891. For continuing debate, see Paraizo, "A pedido," *Diário da Bahia*, Mar. 6, 1897, p. 3, replying to an article attacking civil marriage in the Catholic newspaper, *Cidade do Salvador*; also Paraizo, "A pedido," *Diário da Bahia*, Mar. 17, 1897, and Apr. 8, 1897, denying that children born to civil marriages are illegitimate.

66. Lewin, *Paraíba*, p. 231 n. 5. Defense of inheritance rights was a concern of upper-class Bahians who boycotted civil marriage. For a recently widowed retired judge securing the rights of his children, see APEB, Notas, 1330, p. 124, Oct. 8, 1926; and for another "widower, religiously speaking," see APEB, Notas, 1189, pp. 65–66, Nov. 26, 1909.

67. See the verses denouncing civil marriage as "the law of the Hound [Satan]" in [Euclides da] Cunha, *Rebellion*, pp. 163–64.

68. "A pedido: O sacrílego Antônio Gomes Leite," *Diário da Bahia*, May 19, 1897, p. 3, is one of a series of attacks on a supposedly anti-Brazilian Portuguese merchant, accusing him of marrying only by civil ceremony, being a "pretended Voltairean" whose only religion is money. The series ran Apr. 21, 1897 to June 2, 1897.

69. [Silva, Dom Jerônimo Thomé da,] "Appendice à Terceira Pastoral Collectiva," p. 64. In later publications, Dom Jerônimo emphasized that the religious ceremony should precede the civil ceremony; see, e.g., id., "Precedência obrigatória," p. 64.

70. Bahia, Directoria do Serviço de Estatística, *Anuário estatístico: 1924*, pp. 213–20, 648, counted 12,717 Catholic marriages and 6,453 civil marriages in the interior of the state, 381 Catholic marriages and 732 civil marriages in Salvador. The figures are incomplete and only indicate the relative incidence of religious and civil marriage. Many couples underwent both civil marriage and religious marriage. Baptisms exceeded registered births by a ratio of 4.57 to 1. It is interesting that some of the newer regions of the state, such as the cacao frontier town of Ilhéus, had relatively high rates of civil marriage in 1923. Perhaps the index of civil marriage could be taken as an indicator of traditional religiosity. Levy Cruz, "Rio Rico."

71. Meira, *Teixeira de Freitas*; [Teixeira de] Freitas, *Consolidação das leis civis*.

72. Calasans, *Faculdade Livre de Direito*; Wirth, *Minas Gerais*, pp. 86–88; [Hermes] Lima, *Travessia*; Nogueira, *Caminhos*; [Thales de] Azevedo, *Ciências sociais*, pp. 48–55, 62–67, describes some of the major works from the Faculdade.

73. Beviláqua, *Direito da família*, p. 58; "Projecto de Código Civil Brasileiro organisado pelo Dr. Clovis Beviláqua . . . e revisto pela commissão . . . ," *Diário Oficial dos Estados Unidos do Brasil* 314, supplement (Nov. 24, 1901): 1–88.

74. Brazil, Ministério de Justiça, *Atas da commissão revisora*; for accounts of the saga of the civil code, see Borchard, *Guide to the Law and Legal Literature*

of Argentina, Brazil and Chile, pp. 238–44; Câmara, *História do direito pátrio,* 3: 132–70, 4: 147–98; Meira, *Teixeira de Freitas.* On the symbolic importance of the code, cf. J. Carlos, "O analfabeto," in Fiorentino, *Utopia,* p. 42.

75. Glendon, *Transformation of Family Law,* pp. 33–34, 66–75. In 1937 and 1941, the Brazilian government passed laws allowing the priest celebrating a religious marriage also to read the act of civil marriage; Azevedo, "Family, Marriage, and Divorce," p. 303.

76. Beviláqua, "Linhas gerais," p. 89.

77. *Código Civil,* arts. 231, 233, 235, 242/2, 248–56, 384.

78. Arquivo da Cúria, *Dispensas matrimoniaes, 1889–1897,* May 2, 1890, Agostinho Dias Lima Sobrinho, "para livrar-se do casamento civil"; June 1, 1891, Farmacêutico Honório Tibúrcio de Moura and Dalila Costa Lima, "tendo casado no civil em Maranhão." For the testimony of a backlands priest who despised his parishioners, see Araujo, *Vinte anos de sertão,* pp. 117–18.

79. For example, Arquivo Municipal, Registro de Casamento Civil, livro 18.2–12, Santana (Jan. 1889–Jan. 1895), Aug. 17, 1893: Antônio José Ferreira Gaia, a Portuguese, aged 54, married the Bahian Maria das Neves de Jesus, aged 46, on July 24 at 11 A.M., thus legitimating their four children aged 23 to 13, and died at 2 P.M. the same day.

80. Mattoso and Athayde, "Epidemias e flutuações de preços," p. 195; Arquivo Municipal de Salvador, Registro de Casamento Civil, livro 18.1, 1–19, Santana (Apr. 1877–Dec. 1883), Apr. 7, 1877: Roberto Ayres dos Santos, *liberto,* age 54, and Bemvinda Maria da Conceição, on deathbed, legitimating two children; June 4, 1878: Martinho José Coutinho, *africano liberto,* 50, marrying Maria Ritta Vieira, *africana liberta,* 50, on deathbed.

81. *Casamento Civil,* arts. 56–60; *Código Civil,* arts. 256–314.

82. In other provisions, the marriage law seemed concerned to prevent conspiracies to connive to promote marriages of interest. It forbade a family court judge (*juiz de orfãos*) or a guardian, or any member of his immediate family, to marry anyone under his tutelage; *Casamento Civil,* arts. 24, 25 (doors be open), 7/6 (abduction), 7/11–12 (guardians); *Código Civil,* arts. 193, 183/10, 183/15–16; *Casamento Civil,* arts. 58, 59; *Código Civil,* art. 258 (separate property). Separate property was required for a man marrying over the age of 60. The code no longer required separate property for double cousins, but it entirely forbade marriage between kin in the third degree (art. 183/4).

83. *Casamento Civil,* arts. 7/1–4 (nullity), 71, 72 (annulment); *Código Civil,* arts. 183, 207–19.

84. *Casamento Civil,* arts. 7/7, 7/10–18; *Código Civil,* arts. 185–88. The code of 1916 withdrew the right of a woman's father to demand a certificate of good behavior or a health certificate.

85. Canon law counted degrees of consanguinity between collateral kin by the greatest number of generations to a common ancestor. Thus siblings were kin in the first degree, first cousins kin in the second degree, first cousins once removed kin in the third degree. Portuguese and Brazilian civil law counted degrees of consanguinity by the Roman system: the number of generations up to the common ancestor and back down. Siblings were kin in the second degree, uncles were

kin in the third degree, first cousins kin in the fourth degree, and first cousins once removed kin in the fifth degree; *Casamento Civil*, art. 7; *Código Civil*, arts. 183/4, 190.

86. Athayde, "Ville de Salvador," p. 335, age at marriage; *Casamento Civil*, arts. 7/7, 18 (consent), art. 7/9–12 (widows), arts. 12–15 (family can invoke); *Código Civil*, arts. 189–90.

87. [Xavier] Marques, *Boa madrasta*, p. 9.

88. [Maria Amélia Ferreira de] Almeida, "Feminismo na Bahia," pp. 33–34. See interview with Francisca Praguer Fróes, *A Tarde*, Apr. 2, 1931, ambivalent on divorce; and "Mulheres na política," "Voto feminino," in *In memoriam Dra. Francisca Praguer Fróes*, pp. 41, 50, 56–57.

89. Bulhões, *Leopoldo de Bulhões*; Wirth, *Minas Gerais*, pp. 90–93, 125–29; "Congresso Catholico: Moção contra o divórcio," *Mensageiro da Fé* 6, no. 21 (Nov. 1, 1908), p. 85.

90. From the 1890's through the early twentieth century, the word *divórcio* was most often used to refer to permanent legal separation without remarriage (also *separação perpetua*), just as it had been used in canon law, until *desquite* became the preferred term in the twentieth century. In contemporary Brazil, *divórcio* is used to mean divorce with the possibility of remarriage, as opposed to *desquite*; *Casamento Civil*, arts. 82/1–3 (grounds), 88 (effects); *Código Civil*, art. 317; cf. *Constituições primeiras*, livro 1, título 72, art. 310–17.

91. Nascimento, "Divórcio por sentença"; [Nizza da] Silva, "Divórcio," pp. 151–94 and *Sistema de casamento*; Arquivo da Cúria, Divórcios, Moraes Barboza v. Azevedo, Nov. 19, 1856, Apellação, Mar. 2 1861; *Casamento Civil*, art. 82/4, arts. 85–87, *Código Civil*, art. 318 (mutual consent).

92. APEB, Seção Judiciária, Autos Cíveis da Capital, 6650/7 (1914), Tribunal de Appellações no. 1946; 6650/1 (1891); 6650/2 (1896); 6650/3 (1901); 8153/15 (1906). Another case, 8125/5 (1904), began as a contested divorce, but ended as a divorce by mutual consent. These six cases represented a third of the sample of eighteen found. Five of the eighteen cases were formally contested, twelve were effectively uncontested. Only eighteen cases of divorce in ibid., 1890 to 1915, were catalogued and accessible, but recently larger numbers of uncatalogued cases have become available; the Arquivo da Cúria de Salvador, Divórcios, holds records of a greater number for the nineteenth century through 1890.

93. Ibid., 6679/3 (1909–10), pp. 69–70. She was in despair, ill, "skipping payments on her house, grocery, doctor, etc." Cf. 1718 (1910), pp. 2, 10–30, on expenses; 6650/4 (1903), pp. 28–30, on a man's obligation to be a gentleman; 6650/6 (1911–12), accusing the husband's party of destroying the records of proceedings.

94. Ibid., 7739/7 (1895), 1718 (1910), 6679/3 (1909–14), 6650/4 (1903); and cf. Fausto, *Criminalidade e cotidiano*, pp. 107–17, on the idealized models of husbands (mild, good provider) and wives (hardworking, staying at home) in homicide trials in São Paulo.

95. APEB, Seção Judiciária, Autos Cíveis da Capital, 8145/1 (1901), n.p.: ("left path of honor"), and p. 13: "[The witness] understands that the accused does not live virtuously (*honestamente*), so much so that she had two children after she

left her husband's company"; 7696/11 (1895), (prostituted, child). See also ibid., 7702/8 (1902); 7711/2 (1905), p. 3, "In January of 1901, his wife abandoned the conjugal home, to which she never again returned, and she has lived from prostitution"; 7739/9 (1895), p. 3: "She resides with a citizen who she says is her uncle, but whom the plaintiff does not know; and with such behavior she becomes ineligible to return to the conjugal domicile"; 7722/3 (1895–1908), p. [3]: his wife, "adultering herself," had three illegitimate children baptized in the parish of Sé, and for the last used a changed name. Only one case was filed by a man for cruelty, and that against a wife who was portrayed as violent-tempered, if not insane: 7686/6 (1894).

96. Ibid., 7711/2 (1905), pp. 34–39; Fausto, *Criminalidade e cotidiano*; Corrêa, *Crimes da paixão*.

97. For character witnesses, see APEB, Seção Judiciária, Tribunal de Relações, Juiz de Direito da Vara de Orfãos, 1718 (1910), p. 9, including a petition signed by 21 physicians at the hospital where the woman found work. Finding another home was also a critical problem in ecclesiastical divorces: see, e.g., Arquivo da Cúria, Divórcios, Tavares v. Tavares, Mar. 5, 1874.

98. APEB, Seção Judiciária, Tribunal de Relações, 6650/4 (1903), p. 218: "Ouviu dizer . . . pelos creados do Reu e da mãe da autora que a dita mãe da autora era o *diabo* naquela casa"; see also 6679/3 (1909–14), p. 13.

99. The contemporary civil marriage register, Arquivo do Foro Rui Barbosa, Registro Civil de Casamentos, might furnish a fuller count of divorces granted, as procedure called for the registration of a final sentence of divorce in the margin of the entry for the marriage in the registry book. The older, archived registers contain some *desquite* annotations; see, e.g., Arquivo Municipal de Salvador, Registro de Casamento Civil, livro 18.2–12, Santana (Jan. 1889–Jan. 1895): July 20, 1894, Manoel Augusto de Athayde, noting divorce sentence on Aug. 7, 1900.

100. [Thales de] Azevedo, "Family, Marriage, and Divorce."

101. Beviláqua, "Evolução do direito," p. 90; [Emílio] Guimarães, *Brasil-acordãos*, reports decisions by appeals courts in Rio de Janeiro and São Paulo in the 1910's and 1920's both upholding and denying petitions for annulment on such grounds; see also Susan Besse, "Freedom and Bondage."

102. Wildberger, *Meu pai*, pp. 74–77; Neeser, "Família Urpia," p. 44; [Thales de] Azevedo, *Social Change*, pp. 27–31.

103. [Alfred] Stepan, *State and Society*; Mainwaring, *Church and Politics*, pp. 25–28; Freyre, *Order and Progress*, pp. 322–27, on Catholic church farms and factory paternalism.

104. Dean, *Industrialization*, p. 151; Love, *São Paulo*, pp. 87–89; Stein, *Vassouras*; Saffioti, *Mulher*; Fausto, *Trabalho urbano*, p. 116. On the industrialization of the Bahian labor force, cf. the censuses of 1872 and 1920; on child labor of caixeiros, see [Mário Augusto da Silva] Santos, *Caixeiros*, pp. 40–44; and for a semidocumentary novel denouncing the conditions of workers in Salvador, see Amado, *Suor* (1934).

105. São Paulo had a number of model factory towns, such as the isolated Votorantim factory community outside rural Sorocaba and Jorge Street's factory

village in São Paulo. See Dean, *Industrialization*, pp. 155–56, 226, making an interesting distinction between sentimental paternalism and calculated "behaviorism"; Rago, *Do cabaré ao lar*; Fausto, *Trabalho urbano*, p. 117. And see Freyre, *Order and Progress*, p. 325.

106. [Péricles Madureira de] Pinho, *São assim*, pp. 84–86, 90–99; Requião, *Itapagipe*, pp. 117–22, on physician, child labor; Sampaio, "Evolução de uma empresa," pp. 108, 99, notes that the work force in 1896 was primarily female, with 171 men and 526 women; pay was 20$000 a week, about U.S.$3, of which one quarter was deducted for rent and eventually amortization of workers' houses. "Empório Industrial do Norte," *Diário da Bahia*, Apr. 27, 1897, p. 1; *Diário Oficial do Centenário*. "Villa Operária," *Diário da Bahia*, May 17, 1897, p. 1, advertising a dance, and Luiz Tarquínio, "A pedido," *Diário da Bahia*, May 19, 1897, p. 1, limiting it to invited guests. In the 1850's, the Valença textile factory, which recruited from local orphanages, was compared to Lowell, Massachusetts (Fletcher and Kidder, *Brazil and the Brazilians*, p. 498).

107. [José Luis Pamponet] Sampaio, "Evolução de uma empresa," pp. 108–23, says Tarquínio rationalized his paternalism by the need to keep good workers and lower absenteeism.

108. APEB, Arquivo Wanderley Pinho, circular, [R. P. Magalhães] to employees of Usina São Bento, Santo Amaro, Apr. 12, 1919: "Vote for whom you wish: vote for Rui Barbosa!"; and letter, José Muniz Souza Sobrinho to Pedro Lago, Valença, Dec. 6, 1919; [Rafael de Albuquerque] Uchoa, *Odysséa de um revolucionário*. See Sampaio, "Evolução de uma empresa," Anexo, letter, Leopoldo José da Silva and Luis Tarquínio to shareholders, May 24, 1902, on a maternal paternalism: "It is necessary, finally, that the worker of the Companhia Empório Industrial do Norte see in it a grateful and caring mother on whom they can count in hard times, and that because of this they must love her, demonstrating their love through dedicated and willing work, the only truly productive and profitable work." Cf. the nostalgic memoir of plantation life by a slave's son in [Teodoro] Sampaio, "Engenho de assucar"; [Castro] Gomes, *Burguesia e trabalho*, pp. 32, 49, on dependency of poor; Timotheo, "Revista da Semana," *Diário da Bahia*, May 30, 1897, p. 1, describing the factory as a temple, and as a machine that assembles the worker's life.

109. Teixeira, "Batistas na Bahia," pp. 216, 225–42, describes the puritanical moralism of early Protestant working-class converts; Freyre, *Order and Progress*, p. 184.

110. APEB, Presidência Provincial, Sociedades, maços 1571–79; for example, 1575/66, relating to organizations such as the Sociedade Protectora e Beneficente dos Artifices Carpinteiros e Calafates, 1861; Braga, "Sociedade Protetora dos Desvalidos," discusses the 1874 *estatutos* of the society, founded in 1832 as a credit union for slaves to buy their freedom; *Diário Oficial do Centenário*, pp. 494, 397, 351; [Mário Augusto da Silva] Santos, *Caixeiros*, pp. 92–105; Fausto, *Trabalho urbano*, pp. 72–74.

111. Fausto, *Trabalho urbano*, pp. 84–90; Rago, *Cabaré*; [Freire] Costa, *História da psiquiatria*. Ironically, like the Catholic moralists, they condemned Carnival, but on quite opposed grounds: it brought workers' children and wives into a cor-

rupt milieu full of "ruffians, priests, and policemen" (Fausto, *Trabalho urbano*, p. 90).

112. Pang, *Bahia*, pp. 116–21; cf. Dulles, *Anarchists and Communists in Brazil*, pp. 95–96; [Mário Augusto da Silva] Santos, *Caixeiros*, pp. 52–59, 92–99.

113. These were the notoriously "popular" politicians; some of them were more populistic (the young Seabra and Mangabeira), and others were more clientelistic (Antônio Calmon). See Pang, *Bahia*; Oliveira, *Octávio Mangabeira*. Major Cosme de Farias was probably the most representative "popular" politician of Salvador; see Requião, *Itapagipe*, for a portrait.

114. Fausto, *Trabalho urbano*, pp. 225–30. The "question for the police" aphorism is attributed to Washington Luis in 1920; Love, *São Paulo*, p. 246; [Castro] Gomes, *Burguesia e trabalho*.

115. Fausto, *Trabalho urbano*, pp. 234–35; [Castro] Gomes, *Burguesia e trabalho*, passim, esp. pp. 87–89.

116. See [Mário Augusto da Silva] Santos, *Caixeiros*, pp. 42–44, on Salvador's Postura Municipal 50a, October 1911. [Castro] Gomes, *Burguesia e trabalho*, pp. 182–84, 188–94. Code of Minors, Decree no. 5083 of Dec. 1, 1926; initially in São Paulo, the law was applied only to minors working in the "immoral" entertainment industry; only after it was implemented by a second decree, no. 17943a of Dec. 12, 1927, did it apply theoretically to factories; Dean, *Industrialization*, pp. 161–62.

117. APEB, Sociedades, 1575/90, "Mappa de Sociedades de Socorros Mútuos" (n.d., probably ca. 1871), counted 2,429 members of twelve associations; over half of those belonged to a single association, the Real Sociedade Portuguesa de Beneficência 16 de Setembro. Bahia, Directoria do Serviço de Estatística, *Anuário estatístico: 1924*, pp. 190–91, counted 11,833 members of twenty associations in 1924; *Diário Oficial do Centenário*, pp. 475, 480, 494–96. Bittencourt, "Memórias," pp. 22, 60, on pensions. Cf. Conniff, "Voluntary Associations"; [Castro] Gomes, *Burguesia e trabalho*, pp. 16–17, 94–96, 226, on Caixas de Aposentadoria laws.

118. As James Malloy puts it, the Brazilian and other Latin American governments wrote laws, promulgated constitutions, and set precedents that "committed them to becoming social-service states, if not welfare states" (*Politics of Social Security*, p. 154, and see pp. 68, 102). By 1939 the basic system insured 1.8 million active insured and 81,000 passive insured persons (not counting military personnel and civil servants covered under other pension plans).

119. [Thales de] Azevedo, "Family, Marriage, Divorce"; Malloy, *Politics of Social Security*.

120. Corrêa, "Ilusões da liberdade," pp. 183–93, on the rise of medical ideology of juvenile delinquency, and the figure of the "minor"; Todaro, "Pastors, Prophets and Politicians," pp. 30–34, on Padre Júlio Maria, pp. 186–88, 208, 430–46; Mainwaring, *Church and Politics*.

121. [Juracy] Magalhães, *Minhas memórias provisórias*; Pang, *Bahia*, p. 201.

122. Lowenstein, *Brazil Under Vargas*, pp. 20–26: "What strikes the foreign observer is the strong reflection of the socializing Weimar constitution" (p. 24); cf. [Castro] Gomes, *Burguesia e trabalho*, p. 14.

123. Todaro, "Pastors," pp. 273–80, 326–44.

124. The constitution's preamble makes clear its concern with the security threat posed by communist insurrection, and it was never fully implemented, as Vargas governed by a decree of emergency.

125. On the health of children, also art. 16, item 27; on the principle of protection of women, mothers, and children under eighteen in work, see art. 137, items K, L; translations from Brazil, Departamento de Imprensa e Propaganda, *Constitution of the United States of Brazil*.

126. [Isaías] Alves, *Educação e saude*; [Juracy] Magalhães, *Minhas memórias provisórias*, pp. 81, 87–88; cf. Seabra, *Esfola de um mentiroso*, pp. 76–77, claiming that Magalhães's program increased the number of teachers greatly (from 1,964 in 1930 to 2,640 in 1933), while enrollment and attendance at schools dropped; and cf. [Juracy] Magalhães, *Mensagem . . . 1936*, pp. 46–49, 174. The Departamento da Criança was created in 1935, changed to Inspetoria de Higiene Prenatal e Infantil in 1938, and lowered to a Seção de Higiene Prenatal e Infantil in 1946; Gouvéia, *Puericultura social*, pp. 32–38.

127. [Isaías] Alves, *Educação e brasildade*, pp. 34–47, 49; id., *Educação e saude*.

128. Amado, *Suor* and *Cacau*; [Hermes] Lima, *Anísio Teixeira*, pp. 35–68, passim; Geribello, *Anísio Teixeira*, pp. 17–32; Pang, *Bahia*, pp. 202–5.

129. [Goes] Calmon, *Mensagem . . . 1925*, pp. 41, 55; [Dias] Tavares, *Duas reformas da educação*, pp. 51–54; [Vital] Soares, *Mensagem . . . 1930*; [Goes] Calmon, *Mensagem . . . 1927*, pp. 41–43, cf. [Renato Pinto] Aleixo, *Relatório . . . 1943* (1945), p. 66.

Chapter 5

1. Freyre, *Sobrados e mucambos*, pp. 122–24; Hoornaert, *Formação do catolicismo*, pp. 66–91.

2. Russell-Wood, *Fidalgos and Philanthropists*.

3. Hoornaert, *Formação do catolicismo*, pp. 13–21; Novinsky, *Cristãos novos*. Vilhena, *Bahia*, 2: 440–78, is the best contemporary description of the establishments and finances of the Bahian church at the turn of the nineteenth century.

4. See Dornas Filho, *Padroado*; Cardozo, "Holy See," on relations of church and state. The Registros Ecclesiásticos de Terras land survey of 1856–58 in the Arquivo Público, undertaken by parish priests, is an example of the church's public functions. See also Mattoso, "Au nouveau monde," pp. 438–43.

5. See the slave catechism from the *Constituições primeiras* translated in Conrad, *Children of God's Fire*, pp. 154–59; Ortega y Gassett, *España invertebrada*, p. 69.

6. Hoornaert et al., *História da igreja . . . Primeira época*.

7. Maximiliano de Habsburgo [Archduke Ferdinand Maximilian], *Bahia 1860*, pp. 128–33.

8. [Thales de] Azevedo, *Social Change*, pp. 72–74, argues that participation in baptism in Brazil had become a customary, rather than spiritual, observance by the 1950's, but was the most important sacrament to nominal Catholics in the lower classes who may have done without marriage; see also Souza, *Compadrio*.

9. [Hildegardes] Vianna, *A Bahia já foi assim*, pp. 61–73; [Herundino da Costa] Leal, *Santo Amaro*, p. 99.

10. Von Binzer, *Meus romanos,* pp. 49–51; [Bittencourt] Cabral, "Prefácio," p. 34; Bittencourt, "Memórias," pp. 18–22; Santos Filho, *Comunidade,* p. 187.

11. Arquivo Cotegipe, 59/91, Araujo Pinho to Cotegipe, Agoa Boa, Nov. 26, 1882.

12. [Herundino da Costa] Leal, *Santo Amaro,* pp. 92–95.

13. Fry, "Negros e brancos no Carnaval"; cf. the middle-class "family Carnival" that focused on costume parties for children; Sant'Ana, *Mais bambangas,* p. 42; [Herundino da Costa] Leal, *Santo Amaro,* pp. 89–92; [Costa e] Silva, *Roteiro da vida e da morte,* p. 71, on denunciation of a defloration in 1923.

14. Bittencourt, "Memórias," pp. 61–70; Freyre, *Sobrados e mucambos,* pp. 68, 89n.

15. *Estatutos das Senhoras da Caridade;* "Amparo religioso à infância e à juventude," *Diário Oficial do Centenário,* pp. 442–43.

16. ACRB, Brites Barbosa de Oliveira Lopes, letter, Aug. 7, 1876, Brites to Rui Barbosa.

17. "Expedição a Canudos," *Diário da Bahia,* Mar. 11, 1897, p. 1. In 1900 in Santo Amaro there were still caponas in the street ([Herundino da Costa] Leal, *Santo Amaro,* p. 107).

18. Freyre, *Sobrados e mucambos,* pp. 93–94; cf. *In memoriam Dra. Francisca Praguer Frões,* pp. 56–57; see [Aluísio de] Azevedo, *Mulato* (1880) and [Machado de] Assis, *Dom Casmurro* (1900) for priests as characters; Bittencourt, "Memórias."

19. Müller, *Religião na Bahia,* pp. 146–47; Nascimento, "Divórcio," pp. 265–69.

20. Soeiro, "Feminine Orders"; Bittencourt, "Memórias," pp. 41, 53–54; [Wanderley] Pinho, *Salões,* p. 30.

21. [Thales de] Azevedo, *Social Change,* p. 68.

22. "Maria, nossa Mãe," *Mensageiro da Fé* 7, no. 8 (Apr. 25, 1909): 30–31, comparing Mary to earthly mothers in her self-sacrifice; ACRB, Maria Augusta Rui Barbosa, a small collection of early twentieth-century lithographed images; Azzi, *Catolicismo popular,* pp. 25–27; [Thales de] Azevedo, *Social Change,* p. 71.

23. Bittencourt, "Memórias," p. 3, on her namesake, Santa Anna; [João Camilo de Oliveira] Torres, *História das idéias religiosas,* pp. 99–100; [Silva] Campos, "Apontamentos folclóricos," p. 153; [Alvares do] Amaral, *Resumo chronológico,* pp. 30–31; both Amaral, in 1880, and his editor Barros, in 1917, felt that the festivities of São Gonçalo's day were less observed than in the past.

24. Bittencourt, "Memórias," p. 142.

25. [Amélia] Rodrigues, *Verdadeira missão social;* [Machado de] Assis's "Caso da vara" (1891) presents a drama of slavery in which a mistress beats a tubercular slave girl rented out as a lacemaker; the memoir of Ina von Binzer, *Meus romanos,* p. 20 and passim, portrays women as harsh, if not cruel, mistresses.

25. Dom Macedo Costa, "Resumo do que há de fazer um cristão para se santificar e salvar" (1875), cited in Azzi, "Família e valores," pp. 88–89; [Amélia] Rodrigues, *Mestra e mãe,* pp. 285–88, 293–96.

27. João Baptista Cingoli, "Sermões para as missões A.D. 1900," cited in [Costa e] Silva, *Roteiro,* p. 44. On medical views of celibacy, see Chapter 3 above.

[Amélia] Rodrigues, *Mestra e mãe*, p. 202, "moral disinfectant." On divorce: Pope Leo XIII, *Arcanum*; Pope Pius XII, *Sertium laetitae.*

28. Arquivo da Cúria, *Dispensas de impedimentos, 1859–1885*, Oct. 10, 1883, Mascarenhas and Mascarenhas. [Alfredo Ferreira] Magalhães, "Pro eugenismo," pp. 4–5 ("The physician is an important associate of the priest"); Padre Mello Lula, "A castidade e a medicina," *Mensageiro da Fé* 17, no. 7 (Apr. 6, 1919): 52.

29. [Hildegardes] Vianna, *A Bahia já foi assim*, p. 65; Jean Baptiste Debret's famous engraving of a bourgeois paterfamilias leading his household out to mass in single file—daughters, wife, and jewel-bedecked slave girl—shows the man at his finest hour (from Debret, *Voyage pittoresque et historique au Brésil* [1834–39], reproduced in [Sandra] Graham, *House and Street*, p. 11, plate 1).

30. See the theory of Brazilian social space in Roberto Da Matta, "Ethic of Umbanda"; id., *A casa & a rua*, pp. 31–71.

31. Mattoso, "Au nouveau monde," p. 562 n. 40.

32. Valladares, *Arte e sociedade nos cemitérios*, pp. 304, 318; Conniff, "Voluntary Associations"; [Mário Augusto da Silva] Santos, *Comércio português*; Santos Filho, *Comunidade*, pp. 145–78; "Lojas maçonicas," *Diário Oficial do Centenário*, pp. 455–56.

33. Toplin, *Abolition*; Hauck, et al., *História da igreja . . . Segunda época*, pp. 257–95; *Constituições primeiras*, livro 1, arts. 50–58, livro 1, título 71, arts. 303–4; Antônio Vieira, "Children of God's Fire," in Conrad, *Children of God's Fire*, pp. 163–73.

34. Bastide, *African Religions of Brazil*; [João José] Reis, *Rebelião escrava*; [Nina] Rodrigues, *Africanos no Brasil.*

35. Teixeira, "Batistas," pp. 227–29, 235.

36. *Westphalen, Bach*, p. 57, citing the recollections of a traveling salesman in the sertão: "Menina, si teu pai te quer casar com um rapaz sómente no civil, nega-te, mas não caia neste pecado!"; [Costa e] Silva, *Roteiro*, pp. 33–55, esp. p. 41; Bittencourt, "Memórias," pp. 42–46, on a mission to Catú; [Hermes] Lima, *Travessia.*

37. Mattoso, "Au nouveau monde," p. 566.

38. Della Cava, *Miracle at Joaseiro*; [Heitor de] Araujo, *Vinte anos de sertão.*

39. Da Matta, *A casa & a rua*, pp. 31–72; Fry, "Two Religious Movements."

40. [Thales de] Azevedo, *Social Change*, pp. 73–74.

41. [Machado de] Assis, *Dom Casmurro*, ch. 27, "In the Gateway." Schwarz, "Misplaced Ideas," provides an introduction to the analysis of the function of favor in Brazilian social practice, which he develops at greater length in an analysis of Machado's early works in *Ao vencedor as batatas*. In "Caso da vara," Machado has another reluctant seminarian faced with a dilemma: either abet the whipping of a pathetic slave girl or lose the patronage of a woman who can achieve his freedom from the seminary.

42. Other life-passage rituals also offered an opportunity to choose godparents. The rite of confirmation allowed a girl or boy to take an additional godparent, and a couple at marriage chose godparents. But baptismal godparents were the most important.

43. The civil registry was resisted by people in the countryside in Bahia. In 1923,

only 18,330 infants were recorded in the civil registry, but 83,878 were baptized (Bahia, Directoria do Serviço de Estatística, *Anuário estatístico: 1924*, p. 216). In 1987 the archive of baptismal records in the Arquivo da Cúria in Salvador was still consulted as a registry of vital records. By contrast, civil registry witnesses evidently sometimes included the godfather, but at other times the signatures seem to have been merely those of courthouse loafers.

44. Valladares, *Arte e sociedade nos cemitérios*, pp. 302–8; Pang, *Bahia*, pp. 37, 113–14, 129; see also Pang, "Changing Roles of Priests."

45. Bruneau, *Church in Brazil*, pp. 15–17; Müller, *Religião na Bahia*, pp. 87–96; Mattoso, "Au nouveau monde," pp. 483–84.

46. Hoornaert, *Formação do catolicismo*, pp. 79–81. For Brazil, see Bruneau, *Political Transformation*, pp. 23, 25, citing figures from Padre Júlio Maria's 1900 estimate of the number of priests; also Boehrer, "Church in the Second Reign," pp. 113–40, on the many vacant parishes. For Bahia, see *Recenseamento de 1872*, p. 515; [Costa e] Silva, *Roteiro*, pp. 1–32, on the growth of a sertão parish; Mattoso, "Au nouveau monde," pp. 483–90; Santos Filho, *Comunidade*, pp. 186–87; [Ana Mariani Bittencourt] Cabral, "Prefácio," p. 34; Bittencourt, "Memórias," p. 18.

47. Boehrer, "Church in the Second Reign," pp. 121, 124–26; Bruneau, *Transformation*, p. 74; Müller, *Religião na Bahia*, pp. 87–96. There were scandals in the 1830's and 1840's, and in 1882 a Portuguese provincial trying to reform abuses in the order was murdered by slaves on one of the Calced Carmelites' plantations.

48. Fletcher and Kidder, *Brazil and the Brazilians*, p. 142; Wetherell, *Stray Notes*, p. 99. Wetherell's conclusion is borne out by the decline of irmandades in Salvador, and also by attempts by landlords to get rid of capella endowments on their plantations. On a capella stuck in a plantation "like a bone in my throat," see Arquivo Cotegipe, Argolo to Cotegipe, Engenho São Paulo, Nov. 18, [ca. 1861–67]; and 7/4, Cotegipe to Argolo, Nov. 20, responding. Even priests left more to their families than to the church (Mattoso, "Au nouveau monde," pp. 519–24) and this continued through the twentieth century (APEB, Notas, 1395, p. 92, Feb. 4, 1935, Mons. João Gonçalves da Cruz, leaving some property to church establishments but most to nephews and nieces).

49. Mattoso, "Au nouveau monde," pp. 493–98, reviewing testaments and inventories, found that 51 percent of the priests dying between 1851 and 1889 left children; furthermore, they had families as large as most legal families. See also Boehrer, "Church in the Second Reign," pp. 124–26. Bittencourt, "Memórias," pp. 6–9, 41, 53, provides an unusually close look at such a family. Many prominent Brazilians were illegitimate sons of priests, some of them acknowledged, such as the jurist Clovis Beviláqua; [João Camilo de Oliveira] Torres, *História das idéias religiosas*, pp. 144–45; Cardozo, "Holy See"; Dornas Filho, *Padroado*, pp. 53–106.

50. Nabuco, *Estadista do Império*, 1:304–16; Mattoso, "Au nouveau monde," pp. 529–40.

51. Nóbrega, "Dióceses," pp. 179–85; [Costa e] Silva and Azzi, *Dois estudos*; Mattoso, "Au nouveau monde," pp. 500–506.

52. Boehrer, "Church in the Second Reign," pp. 121–23; but speaking around 1844, the new bishop of Mariana, Dom Viçoso, complained that he had to pro-

mote one immoral priest because none of the others was any better ([João Camilo de Oliveira]) Torres, *Historia das idéias religiosas*, pp. 144–45). Mattoso, "Au nouveau monde," p. 498, pp. 511–26 passim, says that Bellarmino Sylvestre Torres was one of the few priests reprimanded by Dom Romualdo in Bahia. And see Azzi, "Antônio Joaquim de Melo"; Communications, CEPEHIB Conference, História da igreja no Brasil, Salvador, Bahia, July 21, 1981; Nobrega, "Dióceses," pp. 194–96.

53. The incident began when, perhaps encouraged by the pope, Dom Vital indicated that he intended to insist in the condemnation of Masonry. This had appeared in Pius IX's 1864 "Syllabus of Errors," but was not officially church doctrine in Brazil because Pedro II had denied his placet to the papal bull, *Quanta cura*, to which it was appended. Many Brazilian Catholics were Masons, including Pedro II, and some of the Catholic brotherhoods were virtually merged with Masonic lodges. Masons in Olinda took up the challenge by provocatively advertising a mass commissioned for the anniversary of a Masonic lodge. When Dom Vital ordered that the mass not be celebrated, the Masons retaliated by publishing a list of laymen and priests who were both Masons and members of the Catholic brotherhoods. Dom Vital ordered that all the clergy abjure Masonry and that the brotherhoods expel any lay members who did not follow suit. At this point, the Trindade brotherhood appealed. For refusing to obey the order to lift the interdict, Dom Vital and Dom Macedo Costa of Pará were put on trial. A Brazilian emissary had negotiated a papal rebuke to the bishops in return for restoration of the status quo, but they were jailed before it could be agreed upon. See Dornas Filho, *Padroado*, pp. 107–281.

54. Mattoso, "Au nouveau monde," p. 579. Manuel Victorino's mother, supposedly the daughter of Portuguese immigrants, was very religious, read her children passages from scripture, taught them catechism, and led family prayers. One of his brothers, José Basílio, became a priest. See [Ordival Cassiano] Gomes, *Manuel Victorino Pereira*, pp. 12–16; [Afonso] Costa, "Manuel Victorino Pereira," pp. 30–43.

55. Toplin, *Abolition*; Mattoso, "Au nouveau monde," p. 471, on early antislavery arguments in church periodicals in 1871; Hauck et al., *História da igreja . . . Segunda época*, pp. 257–95.

56. ACRB, Cartas de Noivo, Rui Barbosa to Maria Augusta Viana Bandeira, Oct. 30 and Nov. 3, 1876.

57. Boehrer, "Church in the Second Reign," pp. 128–30. This practice, which had begun as early as 1855, continued through the rest of the Empire; Mattoso, "Au nouveau monde," p. 510.

58. Maria, *A igreja e a república*, esp. p. 85; Bruneau, *Transformation*, pp. 29–32.

59. Müller, *Religião na Bahia*, pp. 81–109, 141.

60. Ibid., pp. 98–108, and passim.

61. Ibid., pp. 59–61, 135–36, 143–44; ACRB, João Rui Barbosa, Programa, Collégio Anchieta, 1904; cf. Needell, *Tropical Belle Epoque*, pp. 52–63, contrasting the educational ethics of the secular Colégio Pedro Segundo and the religious

Colégio Sion in Rio de Janeiro; Bulcão, *Colégio Antônio Vieira*; [Hermes] Lima, *Travessia*, pp. 11–16 and *Anísio Teixeira*, pp. 16–19.

62. *Recenseamento de 1920, profissões*, pp. 18–21, 108–11, 198–201. Foreigners had constituted 12 percent of the Brazilian clergy in 1872.

63. Müller, *Religião na Bahia*, pp. 36–52; "Visita," *Mensageiro da Fé* 5, no. 2 (Jan. 20, 1907): 1, on a visit to the sertão; Nóbrega, "Dióceses," pp. 257–58. Dom Jerônimo's successor, Dom Augusto, also traveled, going on a mission to the sertão in 1934 ([Costa e] Silva, *Roteiro*, pp. 54–55). On priests becoming the heads of widows' families, see [José] Silveira, *Vela acesa*; Cássia, *Memórias de Veridiana*.

64. [Thales de] Azevedo, "Discurso," p. 40; Bittencourt, "Memórias," p. 142, describes spiritist experimentation among her family around 1899; Della Cava, "Catholicism and Society"; *Mensageiro da Fé* 7, no. 5 (Mar. 7, 1909): 19, advertising the *Manual das mães cristans*, a guide to the practices of the Confraria das Mães Christans, including a "summary of the lives of the principal saints who were mothers," for 3$.

65. [Pondé de] Sena, *Itapicurú*, analyzing inventories of the property of landlord and small-town families through 1889; collection in ACRB, Maria Augusta Rui Barbosa; there is another, similar collection in ACRB, Francisca Rui Barbosa Airosa; and in Bahia, APEB, Arquivo Wanderley Pinho, Postais, Seção de Cartografia Postal, a mix of tourist (no. 30), genre (no. 47), and religious (no. 114) postcards, dated 1905–15.

66. [Amélia] Rodrigues, *Mestra e mãe*, p. 13, on Saint Joseph; ibid., pp. 200–203, on Mês de Maria; Mattoso, "Au nouveau monde," pp. 568–69.

67. APEB, Notas, 1330, p. 135, Oct. 23, 1926, Inventário.

68. Dom Macedo Costa, "Resumo," quoted in Azzi, "Família e valores," p. 88; Pope Benedict XV, *Sacra propediem*, p. 210, encouraging women in the Third Order of St. Francis to set an example, to combat indecency of clothing as well as luxury in clothing; *Mensageiro da Fé* 5, no. 15 (Sept. 22, 1907): 70, on Filhas de Maria in São Paulo boycotting immoral magazines, even dress patterns; "Luxo e moda," on luxury ruining families; Rodrigues, "Vida intensa"; *Legionários das Missões* 7, no. 2 (Sept. 15, 1926): 67; [João] Bahiano, "As modas," pp. 177–78, reproducing a pastoral by the archbishop of Toledo; [Maria Luiza] Alves, "Se todos fazem . . . ," pp. 73–74; Zeca, "Pedacinhos," p. 79, claiming that Paris fashions were designed in "Jewish agencies, *outside* Paris"; Pierson, *Negroes in Brazil*, pp. 13–14. Modesty was a major theme of the Baptists in Bahia as well; they urged women to wear simple dress and, in 1918, not to cut their hair ([Marli Geralda] Teixeira, "Batistas," p. 235 and passim).

69. See Chapter 6 below on the changes in women's roles; on feminism, see *In memoriam Dra. Francisca Praguer Fróes*; [Maria Amélia Ferreira de] Almeida, "Feminismo na Bahia."

70. [Thales de] Azevedo, *Social Change*, p. 26, interprets the divorce statistics to indicate that there was a falling rate of divorce from 1890 to 1950; Bruneau, *Transformation*, p. 34.

71. Rodrigues, "Escándalo! Escándalo!" p. 250, quoting the Spanish Padre Dueso; Minas Gerais bishops hoped for a Catholic humor magazine to combat the

popular *O Malho* and *Tico-Tico*; the Bahian church opened the Cinema Theatro S. Jeronymo, in the Rua do Arcebispado, on Sept. 29, 1922; the theater belonged to the Obra Social Cathólica, which had been exhibiting films since 1917 (Boccanera Júnior, "Theatro na Bahia").

72. *Almanach do Mensageiro da Fé para o anno de 1917*, p. 110; [Costa e] Silva, *Roteiro*, p. 41. The newspaper *Mensageiro da Fé* itself claimed a circulation of approximately 28,000 in 1913 (Rodrigues, *Do meu archivo*, p. 250).

73. *Almanach . . . 1917*, frontispiece, p. 101. Firmo Antonio, "Meu ideal de amor," *Almanak . . . 1923*, p. 109.

74. Amaral, "Pingos," p. 6. On the roles of mothers, see "Preces e exemplos da mãe christã"; "A mãe," *Paladina* 2, no. 6 (June 1911); and the illustrations of *Leituras Cathólicas* (1906, 1917), in Arquivo Amélia Rodrigues.

75. [Amélia] Rodrigues, "Acção social cathólica feminina," pp. 78–88. See also *Mensageiro da Fé* 7, no. 21 (Nov. 7, 1909): 84, on inauguration of the Liga.

76. The Liga also opened a bookstore, Casa Santa Cruz, in 1916 (*Mensageiro da Fé* 14, no. 9 [May 7, 1916]: 72, 88).

77. Amélia's father, Felix Rodrigues, is described as a small farmer (lavrador) and also *escrivão de paz*, clerk of the justice of the peace (perhaps in her birthplace, the parish of Oliveira dos Campinhos of Santo Amaro); her brother, Seraphim Rodrigues, was an employee in the Caixa Econômica do Estado, and had six children, one or two of whom she raised (Maria Cristina Fraga Tanajura, "Amélia Augusta do Sacramento Rodrigues: A educadora" [MS, 1961, Arquivo Amélia Rodrigues], p. 3). A colleague said that the baron of Vila-Viçosa had patronized her career as a schoolteacher ("Amélia Rodrigues," *A Tarde para Domingo*, May 27–28, 1961, pp. 6–7). See, too, [Marieta] Alves, "Amélia Rodrigues"; [Aloysio Guilherme da] Silva, *Amélia Rodrigues*; Machado Neto, "Bahia Intelectual."

78. [Amélia] Rodrigues, *Mestra e mãe*, p. 11.

79. Ibid., p. 33.

80. Ibid., pp. 252–53, 277.

81. Ibid., pp. 202, 294, 169.

82. Ibid., p. 316.

83. [Amélia] Rodrigues, *Verdadeira missão social*.

84. [Amélia] Rodrigues, "Limpeza nos corréios."

85. [Amélia] Rodrigues, *Carnaval*, pp. 5, 8–9. Criticism of Carnival was a common theme of Catholic moralists. Levine, *Pernambuco*, p. 66, tells of the Congregação Mariana in Recife promoting retreats for youth during Carnival. "O Carnaval," *Mensageiro da Fé*, 12, no. 4 (Feb. 15, 1914): 27, called for honest diversions. "Carnavalescos," *A Voz* 6, 11 (Feb. 1918), reprinted an article by Lacerda de Almeida in *A União*, criticizing contemporary Carnival in Rio de Janeiro, comparing it to the Carnival in Rio Grande do Sul in the 1880's, "as innocent as English literature." And see Sant'Ana, *Mais bambangas*, pp. 42–43. Rodrigues's indignation was apparently really occasioned by some unusually sacrilegious antics that year: one group paraded a satirical effigy of the city's patron, Our Lord of Bomfim, and another group of boys appeared in First Communion dresses (Arquivo Amélia Rodrigues, letter, Enock Torres to Marieta Alves, Apr. 17,

1961). Enock Torres explained that his brothers, cousins, and friends had dressed up as girls of the catechism class of the "Colégio Dona Pombinha," which allegedly was a front for procuring adolescent girls for gentlemen of high society. Attacked in sermons and an article in the *Mensageiro da Fé*, they sent a letter of explanation and a photo to Amélia Rodrigues, who replied calling herself a crotchety old lady and pardoning them, but asking that they play in such a way as not to "hurt the Catholic feelings of their mothers" (copy, letter, Amélia Rodrigues to Enock Torres, Mar. 7, 1915).

86. [Amélia] Rodrigues, "Acção social cathólica feminina," p. 83, and "Mulher quebra as cadéias."

87. [Amélia] Rodrigues, "Progresso feminino."

88. [Maria Luiza] Alves, "Sou feminista."

89. B.P., "Aos homens," *Mensageiro da Fé* 12, no. 9 (May 3, 1914): 71. The article goes on to say that the reason for the preponderance of women at mass is that men have not been instructed properly. And see "Uma obrigação grave," *Mensageiro da Fé* 6, no. 12 (June 21, 1908): 48, on men's activities on Sunday. [Henry] Hutchinson, *Village and Plantation Life*, p. 166, shows that women attended church more than men in one Recôncavo community in 1950–51, but not quite in such disproportionate numbers.

90. Rogério, "Reminiscências de Couto Maia," pp. 98–99; [Carlos] Torres, *Gonçalo Moniz*, pp. 66, 70–72, 89–92.

91. See "O que nos falta," *Mensageiro da Fé* 11, no. 7 (Apr. 6, 1913): 49, on lack of the "principle of chastity" among young men; *Mensageiro da Fé* 11, no. 13 (July 16, 1913): 104, on the founding of the Congregação Mariana in the Convent of São Francisco with 50 members, in 1912; [Thales de] Azevedo, "Discurso," p. 40; notice on founding of the "Liga para a Restauração dos Ideaes" among the youth of the Antônio Vieira and N.S. da Victória schools, in *Legionários das Missões* 7, no. 2 (Sept. 15, 1926): 68–69. On Magalhães and Salesians, see [Amélia] Rodrigues, *Do meu archivo*, pp. 33–44; *Almanach do Mensageiro da Fé . . . 1917*, p. 102.

92. Initially named the Casa São Vicente, the institute was renamed Instituto Feminino da Bahia in 1929, and moved to its present site in the 1930's (Alves, "Henriqueta Martins Catharino," p. 38). On friction between the hierarchy and Rodrigues, see Arquivo Amélia Rodrigues, letter, Dom Joaquim Silvério de Sousa, archbishop of Diamantina to Maria Salomé de Queiroga Brandão, Jan. 17, 1916, in which he reviewed some circulars of the Liga Cathólica das Senhoras Brasileiras branch in Minas Gerais, approved them, but crossed out a phrase calling Amélia Rodrigues the "sponsoring Apostle of the League" (*Apóstola promotora da Liga*). Arquivo Amélia Rodrigues, letter, Rodrigues to Alda [Leal], Bahia, June 10, 1918, on the "hostility" of the league's advisor.

93. Mainwaring, *Church and Politics*, p. 25, citing Leme's "Carta Pastoral a Olinda," written when Leme was bishop of Olinda; Todaro, "Pastors, Prophets, and Politicians," pp. 30–59.

94. *A Ordem* was founded in 1921; the Centro Dom Vital in 1922. Alceu Amoroso Lima converted and became head of the Centro in 1928. See Todaro,

"Pastors, Prophets," esp. pp. 74–94, 106. Antoine, *Integrismo brasileiro*, traces some latter-day sequels to the Catholic Right of the 1920's. And see Lenharo, *Sacralização da política*.

95. [Alceu Amoroso] Lima, *Idade*, pp. 181–83, 201–3, esp. p. 203.

96. Todaro, "Pastors, Prophets," pp. 341–42, discusses the activities of Padre Franca around the Centro.

97. The Catholic press was full of notices on campaigns and petitions against divorce, e.g., "Congresso Cathólico: Moção contra o divórcio," *Mensageiro da Fé* 6, no. 21 (Nov. 1, 1908): 85; "União Popular," *Mensageiro da Fé* 7, no. 22 (Nov. 14, 1909): 88, on Minas organization against divorce.

98. [Macário] Pinto, "Divórcio," pp. 46–47, against a bill introduced by Deputy Floriano de Brito; "No enxurro do divórcio," *Mensageiro da Fé* 6, no. 2 (Jan. 19, 1908): 8; "Olhemos para a França . . . athea," *Mensageiro da Fé* 5, no. 21 (Nov. 3, 1907): 84.

99. See, e.g., Bulhões, "Parecer sobre o divórcio," pp. 317–20, urging limited concession of divorce in extreme cases.

100. Fausto, *Trabalho urbano*.

101. Wirth, *Minas Gerais*, esp. pp. 90–93, 123–25; Azzi, "Restauração católica."

102. [Thales de] Azevedo, *Social Change*, pp. 68–71; Müller, *Religião na Bahia*.

103. Todaro, "Pastors, Prophets," pp. 273–344; Bruneau, *Political Transformation*, pp. 38, 42; Lenharo, *Sacralização da política*.

104. Mainwaring, *Church and Politics*, discusses the awareness of "religious ignorance" in the 1940's and 1950's. On Protestantism in Bahia, see [Marli Geralda] Teixeira, "Batistas"; Mattoso, "Au nouveau monde," p. 569.

105. Müller, *Religião na Bahia*, pp. 231–47.

106. [João Camilo de Oliveira] Torres, *Historia das idéias religiosas*, p. 88; João do Norte, "Mês de Maria," *Mensageiro da Fé* 14, no. 9 (May 7, 1916): 66; Requião, *Itapagipe*, pp. 23–36; Hoornaert, *Formação do catolicismo*, p. 83; [Antônio] Vianna, *Casos e coisas*, pp. 72–76; [Herundino da Costa] Leal, *Santo Amaro*, pp. 89–92.

Chapter 6

1. Laclau, *Politics and Ideology*, pp. 158–76.

2. I use the term *common sense* more loosely than Geertz, "Common Sense as a Cultural System," which proposes it.

3. Lewin, *Paraíba*, pp. 148–49.

4. See Table 1.

5. Russell-Wood, *Fidalgos and Philanthropists*, pp. 173–99; *Código Philippino*, livro 4, títulos 88–89, and Law of June 19, 1775, Law of Nov. 29, 1775, Law of Oct. 6, 1784, pp. 1030, 1051; *Código Civil*, arts. 185–88.

6. [Estácio de] Lima, "Ciumes," interprets the proverb in Freudian terms as alluding to the conflict between mothers and daughters-in-law; but cf. Banfield, *Moral Basis*, suggesting that in a patriarchal family, sons must break with their family of origin in order to establish autonomy. Metcalf, "Families of Planters," pp.

106–9, 93–131, on São Paulo; see also [Wanderley] Pinho, *Cotegipe*, and *Engenho*, pp. 321–40, for evidence of this pattern in the mid and late nineteenth century.

7. This may have been the case of João Ferreira de Araujo Pinho, whose second marriage in 1885 to the daughter of his political boss, the baron of Cotegipe, cemented his political succession (Arquivo Araujo Pinho, 548/74, Cotegipe to Araujo Pinho, Sept. 22, 1885).

8. Paternity was questionable, or implicitly questioned, in the recognition of illegitimate children. In 1870 one man revoked his recognition of the earlier of two sets of natural children, claiming that he had recognized two children of Maria Senhorinha do Espirito Santo, "this for the simple fact of having at one or another time had copulation with this Senhorinha, in the fountain, or river, where he found her," and that she had later declared publicly, and eventually sworn, that the children were not his (APEB, Notas, 403, p. 74, Mar. 6, 1870; cf. ibid., 404, p. 25, Dec. 18, 1869).

9. There had been opposition to this view of marriage at the Council of Trent, and particularly lobbying for requirements of parental consent for marriage (Glendon, *State, Law and Family*, p. 314; *Constituições primeiras*, arts. 259–94).

10. Traer, *Marriage and the Family; Código Philippino*, Law of June 19, 1775, art. 5, Law of Nov. 29, 1775, Law of Oct. 6, 1784, arts. 4, 6, Law of Sept. 22, 1828, pp. 1029–52; [Teixeira de] Freitas, *Consolidação*, pp. 93–96. And see Chapter 4 above.

11. Schwarz, "Misplaced Ideas" and *Ao vencedor as batatas*; Bittencourt, "Memorias," pp. 68–69, on a mother forcing her children into the church; Camino, *Educação*, p. 178, using the metaphor of women as slaves.

12. [Maria] Graham, *Journal*, pp. 305–6. One of the greatest nineteenth-century Brazilian jurists, Teixeira de Freitas, maintained that children, even past the age of majority, remained *filhosfamílias* as long as they were supported in the household of their parents, and as such required paternal consent for marriage (Freitas, *Consolidação*, arts. 8–10, pp. 6–10; arts. 201–6).

13. Freyre, *Sobrados e mucambos*, pp. 129–32. Kátia Mattoso suggests that the documents in question may simply reflect more rigorous reporting of abduction by the church ("Au nouveau monde," pp. 296–303).

14. [Barbosa de] Oliveira, *Memórias de um magistrado*, pp. 168–70; Pang, *Engenho Central*, pp. 196, 205–7; [Wanderley] Pinho, *Cotegipe*, p. 623n; [Costa Pinto] Victória, "Família Costa Pinto," pp. 38–40, 86–87; Morley, *Diary*, pp. 97, 159, 197, 251–53, 276; "Helena Morley" was the pseudonym of Alice Dayrell Brant.

15. [Bittencourt] Cabral, "Prefácio," p. 27; Bittencourt, "Memórias," pp. 123–32. Anna's earlier secret understanding with her cousin Pedro da Trindade had been approved by her mother without the father's knowledge.

16. Bittencourt, "Memórias," pp. 73, 93–112.

17. Rêgo, *Meus verdes anos*, pp. 178–84.

18. [José] Silveira, *Vela acesa*, pp. 189–91.

19. See [Thales de] Azevedo, *Namoro à antiga*, "Fazer a corte," and "Namoro à antiga."

20. [Hildegardes] Vianna, *A Bahia já foi assim*, pp. 40–42, 208–13; [Machado

de] Assis, *Esau and Jacob*, pp. 235–38. The propensity of women in Salvador to linger at their windows was noted by the anthropologist Donald Pierson in the 1930's; indeed, he took advantage of it to develop an off-the-cuff survey of the racial composition of neighboring households (Pierson, *Negroes in Brazil*, p. 23).

21. Arquivo Amélia Rodrigues, Amélia Rodrigues, "Vida intensa: Comedia" (typescript, n.d. [1932]). Between 1908 and 1922 the number of telephones rose from 363 to 3,025, and they became common in the "family" homes of Salvador (Costa, "Corréios, telégrafos, e telephones").

22. Requião, *Itapagipe*, p. 71.

23. [Cardoso de] Oliveira, *Dois metros e cinco*, p. 104.

24. Interview, Hilda Noronha, 1981.

25. Interview, Berenice Noronha Diniz Gonçalves, 1981; see Andrade, *Belazarte*, and Amado, *Dona Flor*, pp. 89–112, for satire of namoro de rua in the early twentieth century.

26. This is certainly the implication of the satire of contrasting courtships in [Machado de] Assis's *Esau and Jacob*, pp. 235–38, 249–55.

27. Arquivo Cotegipe, 7/2, Argolo to Cotegipe, Matoim, [May] 28, 1856.

28. See a *carta de pedido* of 1891, from Rui Barbosa in Rio to his wife's mother's sister Escholástica in Bahia, asking for the hand of her daughter Guilhermina, on behalf of his young brother-in-law, Carlos Viana Bandeira. The letter is ceremonious and tentative, speaking of Carlos's character and earning power, and of the girl's fine character. Interestingly, there is no mention whatsoever of their being cousins (Viana Bandeira, *Lado a lado*, pp. 33–34). On discussing and accepting a pedido in 1885, see Arquivo Araujo Pinho, 548/74, Cotegipe to Araujo Pinho, Sept. 22, 1885.

29. As yet we have no study of the reasons for the decline of dowry in Bahia, though Nazzari, "Women, the Family, and Property," dates its definite decline to around 1870 in São Paulo. Dowries were apparently almost universal in Bahia through the eighteenth century, according to Russell-Wood, *Fidalgos and Philanthropists*, pp. 173–200. By the late nineteenth century, a sampling of formal, separate property dowries registered in notarial deeds shows that they were most common in marriages between Brazilians and foreigners, especially Portuguese; see, e.g., APEB, Notas, 632, p. 32, Apr. 30, 1880; or Notas, 1050, p. 1, Aug. 29, 1900, separate property established as dowry for a wealthy orphan girl by her guardians. For mention of dowry property during an inheritance, see APEB, Notas, 400, p. 82, 1869, Partilha, and APEB, Inventários, Maragogipe, 2388/4, Francisco Rodrigues Lima, Mar. 1, 1882. In the countryside, property and marriage were still strongly associated in the 1920's: people would say, "a poor girl doesn't marry" ("moça pobre não se casa"; [Amélia] Rodrigues, "Desastre feliz," p. 29; cf. id., *Mestra e mãe* [1898], p. 314).

30. Arquivo Cotegipe, 7/3, Francisco Antônio Rocha Pita Argolo to Cotegipe, Bahia, July 3, 1856; I have translated "Que me embaraça!" as "What do I care!"

31. It is not clear whether the old Portuguese law requiring parents to disinherit a daughter who married without consent remained in effect in Brazil after independence; see *Código Philippino*, 4: 927–35, with commentary on livro 4, títulos 88–89. The 1890 law of civil marriage required consent for persons in the power or

under administration of another, presumably including minors and filhosfamílias (*Casamento Civil*, arts. 7/7, 14, 20–21; elopement, art. 7/6). The 1916 civil code required children under the age of 21 (*Código Civil*, arts. 185–88, 384/3) and all those under *pátrio poder* (art. 183/11) to obtain paternal consent for marriage; see Beviláqua, *Direito da família*, pp. 79–87.

32. Arquivo Cotegipe, 75/60, Cotegipe to João Maurício Wanderley, Sept. 24, [1885]; Bittencourt, "Memórias," pp. 93–97; *Casamento Civil*, arts. 20–21; this provision was little more than a charter for fathers to harass unwelcome suitors, and the civil code of 1916 dropped it.

33. APEB, Notas, 1332, pp. 163–64, Mar. 18, 1927.

34. "I married off [*Já casei*] our sister Rita, and did for her what I could, though it wasn't much to my liking" (Arquivo Cotegipe, 75/42, Ambrósio Wanderley to Cotegipe, Utinga, Jan. 10, 1857). And see Freyre, "Social Life in Brazil," p. 618; Cova, *Esposa*, pp. 1–18; cf. on coercion of women, Morley, *Diary*, pp. 251–53, and Besse, "Freedom and Bondage."

35. [Carmen] d'Avila, *Boas maneiras*, p. 264 and passim; ACRB, Brites Barbosa de Oliveira Lopes, letter, Brites to Rui Barbosa, May 2, 1870; cf. Arquivo Araujo Pinho, 549/10, Maria Luiza Wanderley de Araujo Pinho to Maria de Araujo Pinho, Roçado, Dec. 14, 1903; Rui Barbosa, Cartas de Noivo, Oct. 27, 1876.

36. Viana Filho, *Vida de Rui*, pp. 65–78; ACRB, Cartas de Noivo, esp. May 25, May 31, June 8, 1876, on establishing relations with his fiancée's family; eventually the engagement was truncated by a hasty marriage.

37. Goode, "Love"; Augel, *Visitantes estrangeiros*, pp. 218–30.

38. ACRB, Brites Barbosa de Oliveira Lopes, letter, Brites to Rui Barbosa, May 2, 1870.

39. ACRB, Cartas de Noivo, letters to Maria Augusta Viana Bandeira: July 1, July 15, July 19, Aug. 15, 1876; Viana Filho, *Vida de Rui*, pp. 40–41; [Rui] Barbosa, *Mocidade e exílio*, pp. 68–69; Silveira, *Vela*, pp. 189–91; Marques's *O feiticeiro* (1922) dramatizes anxieties about breaking an "understanding" in courtship.

40. About 22 percent of the marriages of men born into Bahian upper-class families of the Recôncavo between 1860 and 1889, and thus marrying roughly between 1880 and 1915, were to cousins, aunts, nieces, or sisters-in-law; see Table 2. And see [José Francisco da Silva] Lima, "Bahia," p. 106; Wetherell, *Stray Notes*, p. 94; Dantas Júnior, "João Gonçalves Tourinho," p. 33; cf. discussions of courting in rural circles, Arquivo Cotegipe, 7/1, Argolo to Cotegipe, Matoim, Dec. 28, 1855; 7/2, Matoim, [May] 28, 1856.

41. "Primos e pombos é que sujam nossas casas" (Azevedo, "Namoro," p. 245); this proverb was also collected in 1879–80 by [Vale] Cabral (*Achegas*, p. 97). And see Bittencourt, "Memórias," p. 121; [José] Silveira, *Vela acesa*, p. 190; Rêgo, *Meus verdes anos*, p. 178; [Pondé de] Sena, *Itapicurú*, pp. 191–92; ACRB, letter, Adelaide Dobbert to Maria Luiza Viana Ferreira Bandeira, Bahia, June 27, 1884, on the inconvenience of an extended visit by an adolescent uncle to a household with young women: "I have two grown daughters and he too is a young man, I am wary of having upsets and vexations [*zangas e contrariedades*], don't you think[?]" Between 1850 and 1870, successful petitions to the archdiocese of Bahia for dispensation of marital impediments often declared that co-residence had led to intimacy,

love, and embarrassing pregnancies (Arquivo da Cúria, Dispensas Matrimoniais, Diversos). Cf. Anderson, "Cousin Marriage in Victorian England."

42. Querino, *Raça africana*, pp. 152–62, provides a list of prominent black and mulatto Bahians; see also [Thales de] Azevedo, *Elites de couleur*. And see, for example, the physical descriptions of family members in Antônio Ribeiro de Carvalho, "Traços biográficos da família Frões ou propriamente Ribeiro de Araujo, descendentes do Portuguez Luis Felix do Bomfim e Francisca Maria da Conceição, oriundos da Fazenda [Pinuim]" (MS, 1931, Frões Papers, original in the collection of Consuelo Pondé de Sena) p. 9, passim. See also ACRB, Maria Luisa Viana Ferreira Bandeira, letter, Friburgo, June 27, 1887, Maria Augusta Barbosa to Maria Luisa: ". . . they are two darling children, they look like Germans!"

43. ACRB, Brites Barbosa de Oliveira Lopes, letter, June 1, 1870, Brites to Rui Barbosa; [Rui] Barbosa, *Correspondência: Primeiros tempos*, p. 93, letter, João José Barbosa to Rui Barbosa, Sept. 27, 1869; and cf. ACRB, Brites Barbosa de Oliveira Lopes, letter, Brites to Rui Barbosa, May 2, 1870, about other marriages in this circle. Doggerel in "Piparotes," *A Formiga* (Cachoeira), Aug. 20, 1870: "Me diga porque razão / Quer namorar moça branca? / Não seja tolo meu moço / Empregue o tempo na banca."

44. Arquivo Cotegipe, 7/2, Francisco Antônio Rocha Pita Argolo to Cotegipe, May 28, 1856; [Prisco] Paraiso Neto, *Descendência*, p. 3. Nascimento, *Dez freguesias*, p. 122; Athayde, "Ville de Salvador," pp. 308–18, and Pierson, *Negroes in Brazil*, pp. 147–48, point out that documents from 1850–74, and 1933–34 show little interracial marriage. See Russell-Wood, *Fidalgos and Philanthropists*, pp. 180–81, on colonial period.

45. Arquivo Cotegipe, 56/122, Araujo Pinho to Cotegipe, Nov. 4, [1888].

46. See testaments such as APEB, Inventários, Francisca da Piedade Marinho, countess of Pereira Marinho, 1897–98, distributing many legacies to young women. A *monsenhor* bequeathed income from bonds to 24 kinspeople and charged a young "*doutor*" to watch out for his aunt and cousins, "so that they aren't exploited giving powers of attorney to strangers to receive their shares from this small inheritance" (APEB, Notas, 1330, p. 112, Oct. 11, 1926). And see marriage contract, APEB, Notas, 405, p. 6, Dec. 18, 1869.

47. APEB, Notas, 405, p. 50, n.d. (ca. 1870). There were many gifts and legacies of this sort: see, e.g., APEB, Notas, 1330, p. 112, Oct. 11, 1926; APEB, Notas, 1330, p. 135, Oct. 23, 1926.

48. Rêgo, *Meus verdes anos*; [Pedro] Calmon, *História da Casa da Torre*, p. 163; [Wanderley] Pinho, *Engenho*, pp. 103–4. On convents, see Russell-Wood, *Fidalgos and Philanthropists*, pp. 177–79; Soeiro, "Social and Economic Role of the Convent."

49. Cova, *Esposa*, p. 19; Camino, *Educação*, p. 178; cf. Francisca Praguer Frões, "Em prol do voto feminino" (1917), in *In memoriam Dra. Francisca Praguer Frões*, pp. 56–57, a feminist indictment of bad marriages; and [Amélia] Rodrigues, *Mestra e mãe* (1898), pp. 285–88, 293–96, on future husbands.

50. Wetherell, *Stray Notes*, p. 94.

51. [Thales de] Azevedo, "Namoro à antiga" pp. 227–29, 258–63, and esp.

reproductions of cartoon satire of love "in the century of velocity" from the fashionable magazine *A Luva* (1925); Teixeira et al., "Memória fotográfica," pp. xi-5, 6; Chevalier, "Elegâncias."

52. Requião, *Itapagipe*, p. 63; cf. Eskelund, *Drums in Bahia*, p. 39, which describes "footing" in the late 1950's in "the plaza [in Salvador] where young couples strolled arm in arm. From the benches, mothers and old aunts kept them under strict surveillance. In Rio, lovers kiss and embrace openly in the streets and along the beaches, but Bahia is more old-fashioned."

53. Bittencourt, "Memórias," p. 94.

54. [José] Silveira, *Vela acesa*, pp. 180–91.

55. Peristiany, ed., *Honour and Shame*; Campbell, *Honour, Family and Patronage*; Pitt-Rivers, *People of the Sierra*.

56. Franco, *Homens livres*; cf. Fausto, *Crime e cotidiano*, pp. 119–23, on the contexts of homicide in urban São Paulo, 1880–1924.

57. On passing a counterfeit lottery ticket, for example, see APEB, Tribunal de Relações, Autos Cíveis, auto 4, maço 6650, Ação de Desquite, 1903, Correia, p. 177. On practical jokes of students, see [José] Silveira, *Vela acesa*, pp. 149–53. See Morse, "Claims of Tradition," pp. 480–94, for reflections on status and violence in Brazil and the United States.

58. Vilhena, *Bahia no século XVIII*, p. 52, "a duke"; Wetherell, *Stray Notes*, pp. 108–9, "graves." See also Bulcão Sobrinho, "Ascendência do governador da Bahia," denying any "intuito de hostilidade" in his task; cf. "A Pedidos: Ilheos," in *Diário da Bahia*, Jan. 12, 1897, a scathing debunking of a fake pedigree. On purity of blood, Russell-Wood, *Fidalgos and Philanthropists*, p. 177.

59. Patterson, *Slavery and Social Death*; Martínez Alier, *Marriage, Class and Colour in . . . Cuba*.

60. Pierson, *Negroes in Brazil*, p. 227, translates and attributes this verse to João Varella. Luz, "Bahia renovada," p. 52, presents a version that preserves the punning allusion to prostitution: "Do pae, a quem nunca viu / Tem o retrato na sala; / Mais da . . . preta que o pariu, / Não tem retrato nem fala." See also Eskelund, *Drums in Bahia*.

61. Francisco de Assis Oliveira, "A Pedido," *Diário da Bahia*, Mar. 5, 1897, p. 1.

62. [Costa] Pinto, *Lutas de famílias*; Santos Filho, *Comunidade rural*, pp. 149–78; Chandler, *Feitosas*; Lewin, *Paraíba*, pp. 59–62.

63. Pang, *Bahia*, pp. 114–55; the tensions in the ethic of urbane *doutores* and crude cacao *coronéis* were a favorite theme of Amado's, in, e.g., *Terras do sem fim* (1942) and *Gabriela, Clove and Cinnamon* (1958).

64. [Pedro] Calmon, *História da Casa da Torre*, p. 102. On a decadent martial ethic, see Santos Filho, *Comunidade*, pp. 144–45: in old age, the senile Coronel Exupério Pinheiro Cangaçu, veteran of feuds of the 1840's, would be handed a musket loaded with powder to fire off, to soothe his delusions that the fazenda was under attack. Cf. [Wilson] Lins, *Médio São Francisco*.

65. Aufderheide, "Order and Violence"; [Teodoro] Sampaio, "Engenho de assucar," pp. 22–24, on granting sanctuary, and on entourages.

66. [Machado de] Assis, "Galeria posthuma."

67. Corrêa, *Crimes de paixão*; Amado, *Gabriela, Clove and Cinnamon*, p. 426; Pitt-Rivers, *People of the Sierra*, pp. 113–21; *Casamento Civil*, arts. 82–84; *Código Civil*, arts. 317, 319.

68. ACRB, Brites Barbosa de Oliveira Lopes, letter, Nova Friburgo, Dec. 8, 1876, Rui Barbosa to Brites: "uma menina tão pura quanto tú, e tão virtuosa quanto a mais virtuosa deste mundo. Minha Mãe não o era mais."

69. [Sandra] Graham, *House and Street*, ch. 1, passim; Da Matta, "Virgindade."

70. Freyre, *Mansions and the Shanties*, pp. 33–36, 273–77; [Antônio Moniz de] Souza, "Viagems e observações"; Morley, *Diary*, pp. 83–85, 197, 256; Bittencourt, "Memórias"; Santos Filho, *Comunidade rural*, p. 61.

71. Wetherell, *Stray Notes*, p. 149; Freyre, *Mansions and the Shanties*, pp. 288–89; Julius Naeher, *Land und Leute in der brasilianischen Provinz Bahia* (1881), reproduced in Augel, *Visitantes*, p. 234.

72. [José Francisco da Silva] Lima, "Bahia," passim.

73. The incident is reported, and perhaps embroidered, in Nava, *Baú*, pp. 100–101; [Kátia Maria de Carvalho] Silva, *Diário da Bahia e o século XIX*, pp. 149–52. Newspaper articles of the time were reprinted in pamphlets collected in the library of the Instituto Geográfico e Histórico da Bahia: [Manuel Alves] Ferreira, ed., *Questão de honra*; *Terceiro livro do monstruoso drama nupcial*; *Transcripções do "Diário da Bahia"*; and *Questão Braga*.

74. [Manuel Alves] Ferreira, *Questão de honra*, p. 49.

75. *Questão Braga*, p. 165.

76. "Questão Braga," *O Monitor*, Feb. 11, 14, 1879; they were sons-in-law of Cândida's godfather.

77. *Terceiro livro do monstruoso drama nupcial*, pp. 4–6.

78. It is perhaps more than a coincidence that Rui Barbosa, editor of the *Diário da Bahia*, had prosecuted Godinho; see Viana Filho, *Vida de Rui*, pp. 40, 45 n.9; ACRB, Discursos, pastas 20–21, clippings from *O Alabama*, Mar. 5, 1872, and *O Alabama*, ser. 92, no. 912, Mar. 8, 1872. Rui's estranged Barbosa de Almeida kin directed *O Monitor*.

79. *Transcripções do "Diario da Bahia*," p. 9; "O Sr. Dr. Antônio Eusébio Gonsalves de Almeida," *O Monitor*, Feb. 18, 1879.

80. *Transcripções do "Diario da Bahia*," p. 24.

81. Nava, *Baú*, p. 101.

82. Arquivo da Cúria, Dispensas Matrimoniais, holds records of cases of defloration and breach of promise, e.g., Arquivo da Cúria, *Dispensas de impedimentos, 1859–1885*: Joaquina Leopoldina de Napoles Massa, Mar. 3, 1859; José da Silva Torres, Nov. 24, 1855; Firmino Dias de Affonseca, Oct. 10, 1867. See Russell-Wood, *Fidalgos and Philanthropists*, pp. 295–319, esp. pp. 311–15; Athayde, "Ville de Salvador," pp. 176–86, on the foundling wheel in Salvador; [Gonçalo] Moniz, *Memória historica*, pp. 206–7.

83. [Mário] Torres, "Lino Coutinho": "Tua razão é bastante, / Para emfim te fazer ver, / que não pode uma plantinha, / De nossas vidas saber."

84. Fausto, *Crime e cotidiano*, pp. 182–223, esp. pp. 203–5, on São Paulo.

85. Arquivo da Cúria, *Dispensas de impedimentos, 1859–1885*, Aug. 21, 1869–Mar. 29, 1870–Apr. 4, 1871, Joaquim Lopes Moutinho. See letter, Nov. 10, 1867;

testimony, Oct. 23, 1869, about events of July 1868; letters, May 13, 1869, May 14, 1869. Cônego Emílio Lobo conceded that there had not legally been any formal promise to marry, and denied the impediment, but ruled that "in the tribunal of his conscience and *coram seo*, he should seriously weigh the gravity of the step that he is going to take."

86. "That she had been in his company *com guarda de ventre* [literally, 'with custody over her womb'], and that he consequently recognizes the child as his" (APEB, Notas, 400, p. 115, Dec. 18, 1869); ibid., 1198, pp. 15–16, Mar. 30, 1910, "under his roof."

87. "Manteve relações de amizade com a segunda outorgante . . . resultando dessas relações o ter tido della uma filha" (APEB, Notas, 632, p. 15, Jan. 29, 1870).

88. Ibid., 400, p. 111, Dec. 9, 1869; 1330, p. 184, Feb. 3, 1927, and p. 185, Feb. 7, 1927; 1395, p. 21, Sept. 30, 1934.

89. Ibid., 1198, p. 50, May 14, 1910. Priests: ibid., 650, p. 18, Dec. 4, 1880; 1189, p. 78, Dec. 20, 1909; 1200, p. 92, Nov. 4, 1910.

90. There were certainly exceptions, notably slaves and freedmen, particularly Africans, in the 1870's and 1880's, who clearly used the deeds as a way to legitimate children conceived in long-term consensual unions; see APEB, Notas, 406, p. 1, May 21, 1870; 639, Sept. 14, 1880; 632, p. 9, Apr. 1, 1880; and cf. 1198, pp. 15–16, Mar. 30, 1910, cited above.

91. Amado, *Gabriela, Clove and Cinnamon*, pp. 55, 372.

92. Bittencourt, "Memórias," pp. 68–69; [Amélia] Rodrigues, "Carnaval," glossing conventional church doctrine on marriage, such as Pope Leo XIII's 1880 encyclical *Arcanum*; Camino, *Educação*, p. 178; ACRB, Adelaide Dobbert, letter, Adelaide Dobbert to Maria Augusta Barbosa, Lisbon, Feb. 21, [1894]: "uma verdadeira vida de Freiras, estamos todos os dias sós em caza"; and cf. [Viana] Bandeira, *Lado a lado*, pp. 45–56; ACRB, Adelaide Dobbert, letter, Adelaide to Maria Luiza Viana Bandeira (n.d., ca. 1880–82): "e não sei quando poderei sahir d'esta prizão."

93. Arquivo Cotegipe, 56/127, Maria Luiza Wanderley [Pinho] to Cotegipe, Pindobas, Oct. 17, 1871; [Antônio Moniz de] Souza, "Viagems e observações"; Bittencourt, "Memórias," p. 17.

94. ACRB, Adelaide Dobbert, letter, Adelaide Dobbert to Maria Luisa Ferreira Viana Bandeira, Bahia, Mar. 26, [ca. 1880's], referring to "Maricota," possibly Maria Constância Viana, daughter of Miguel Luis Viana; cf. Arquivo Cotegipe, 56/62, Araujo Pinho to Cotegipe, (n.d., ca. 1880–88), on widows as the objects of men's marriage ambitions.

95. Hahner, "Women and Work," pp. 91, 114–16; Saffioti, *Mulher*, esp. pp. 32–66, 233–54. Although women's literacy lagged behind that of men in the nation as a whole, in big cities it was more or less the same; the literacy of women in the city of Salvador was 26 percent in 1872, 21 percent in 1890, and 53 percent in 1920. The literacy of men in Salvador was 36 percent in 1872, 27 percent in 1890, and 60 percent in 1920. See *Recenseamento de 1920, instrucção*, p. 15; *Recenseamento de 1872*, p. 515.

96. In 1870 the baron of São Lourenço pointed out that the women's boarding section had been more successful than the men's, "as it does not go against the

nature of the habits of the naturally cloistered sex" ([Alípio] França, *Escola Normal*, pp. 37, 76). It may be that opportunities for women increased at the expense of opportunities for black and mulatto men. Through the late 1870's in Salvador, and later in the interior of the state, educated black men constituted a notable part of the ranks of schoolmasters. See [Albino José Barbosa de] Oliveira, *Memórias de um magistrado*, p. 55; Querino, *Raça africana*, pp. 161–62.

97. [Alberto] Silva, *Primeira médica do Brasil*, pp. 51–52, 215–26; Hahner, "Women and Work," pp. 97–99; "Faculdade de Direito da Bahia," in *Diário Oficial do Centenário*, p. 360; Almeida, "Feminismo na Bahia," pp. 41–48.

98. Figures on schoolteachers may be found in Masson, ed., *Almanak* (1862), pp. 269–77; [Braz do] Amaral, *História da Bahia*, pp. 253–54, 291; *Recenseamento de 1872*; Brazil, Centro Brasileiro de Pesquisas Educacionais, *Fontes*, pp. 72, 391, 397; [Borges dos] Reis, *Almanak . . . para 1902*; *Recenseamento de 1920, profissões*, pp. 20–21, 110–11; [Goes] Calmon, *Mensagem . . . 1925*, pp. 75–79; IBGE, *Educação no estado da Bahia*, p. 40. The proportion of female schoolteachers in the province of Bahia was roughly equivalent to that in Rio de Janeiro and São Paulo (Hahner, "Women and Work," p. 94, table 4).

99. [Egas] Moniz, "Evolução pedagógica." In 1897 a critic exemplified the pinch in teachers' salaries by pointing out that they could rarely any longer afford domestic service (C. Mager, "A pedido," *Diário da Bahia*, Apr. 30, 1897). In 1902 the stated salary of a state schoolteacher was 2:000$ a year (approximately U.S. $468), lower than that of a fourth class clerk, but higher than that of a seaman or a laborer ([Borges dos] Reis, ed., *Almanak . . . para 1902*, pp. 173–75).

100. Hahner, "Women and Work," p. 100; *Recenseamento de 1920, profissões*, pp. 20–21. In 1905 it was not at all usual for young women in Bahia to be working behind store counters. What most impressed a Bahian visiting Hamburg was the great number of young women working in stores (Arquivo do Instituto Geográfico e Histórico da Bahia, Gonçalo Moniz, pasta 36, doc. 9, letter, Miguel de Teive e Argollo to [Gonçalo Moniz], Hamburg, Aug. 29, 1905).

101. "Variedades: Cousas da terra," *O Monitor*, Dec. 7, 1878.

102. [Hildegardes] Vianna, *A Bahia já foi assim*, pp. 194–201, primarily on the 1930's.

103. [Maria Luiza] Alves, "Sou feminista," p. 120, satirizing the boldness of "feminists."

104. On Bahian provincialism compared to Rio de Janeiro or Lisbon, see ACRB, Adelaide Dobbert, letter to Maria Luisa Viana Ferreira Bandeira, Graça, May 15, [ca. 1880]: "I don't feel like wearing anything pretty in insipid Bahia"; letter to Bandeira, São Nicolau, Aug. 31, [?]: "Bahia is a neglected pigsty, these days it is impossible to live in such a village." And see Juvenal, "Cavaqueemos," *Diário da Bahia*, Feb. 21, 1897, p. 1; interview, Hilda Noronha, 1981.

105. *Diário da Bahia*, Mar. 27, 1897; *Diário de Notícias*, Jan. 2, 1906, p. 2; Jan. 9, p. 3. Ticket prices were 10$ a box, 1$ general admission. There is a photograph of the entrance to the Cinema Guaraní in the Praça Castro Alves in Teixeira et al. "Memória fotográfica," p. xi-6.

106. [Amélia] Rodrigues, "Limpeza nos corréios" (1910) and "Acção social"

(1915). For a sample of rather innocent—yet symbolically cosmopolitan—postcards from 1905 to 1910, see APEB, Arquivo Wanderley Pinho, Seção de Cartografia Postal.

107. Carrie Chapman Catt, quoted in Hahner, "Women and Work," p. 100.

108. "Numa época em que só desciam o Plano Inclinado quatro moças" (Nair Alves in [Maria Amélia Ferreira de] Almeida, "Feminismo na Bahia," p. 68).

109. Besse, "Freedom and Bondage"; "Cousas da terra," *O Monitor*, Dec. 7, 1878; [Amélia] Rodrigues, *Mestra e mãe*, pp. 168–69: "Just as the father of a family has the duty to defend the house to the extent he can against any external danger, so the mother of a family is obliged to watch over the health and lives of those who are under her roof, paying full attention to domestic hygiene."

110. Saffioti, *Mulher*, pp. 255–83; Hahner, *Mulher brasileira*.

111. [Maria Amélia Ferreira de] Almeida, "Feminismo na Bahia," pp. 25–32, 56–57, 63; [Nelson de Souza] Sampaio, *Diálogo democrático*, pp. 100–101; Abreu, "Federação Bahiana." The principal political work of the federation was voter registration.

112. [Amélia] Rodrigues, "Progresso feminino," pp. 67–87.

113. APEB, Arquivo Wanderley Pinho, mother to son [José Wanderley Araujo Pinho], [1921]; Pang, *Bahia*; [Madureira de] Pinho, *Carrossel*, pp. 56–57.

114. Hahner, *Mulher brasileira*, p. 121; [Maria Amélia Ferreira de] Almeida, "Feminismo na Bahia," pp. 63, 34.

115. Maria Lícia Costa de Souza in [Maria Amélia Ferreira de] Almeida, "Feminismo na Bahia," pp. 66–68.

116. Praguer Frões, "Hygiene e maternidade," in *In memoriam Dra. Francisca Praguer Frões*, pp. 27–38; see also pp. 7–26.

117. Ibid., pp. 39–44.

118. The tendency to conceive of political and social change as a matter of pacing Brazilian adaptation to cosmopolitan evolution may be found in discussions of the pro-slavery and gradualist positions in the abolition debate, such as Toplin, *Abolition*, esp. pp. 130–44, passim; in discussions of labor legislation in [Castro] Gomes, *Burguesia e trabalho*, pp. 171–72, 188; and in Morse, "Some Themes of Brazilian History." Finally, consider this advice from João José Barbosa to his son Rui in 1870 over Rui's radical positions: "I don't want you to be a hypocrite, . . . but I want you to be prudent. You're a boy, a protected son [*filho família*], you weren't ever in the thick of political scheming—why reveal, and with the ardor of aggressive enthusiasm, opinions that still haven't ripened among us [Brazilians], and that will appear later, more authorized?" ([Rui] Barbosa, *Correspondência: Primeiros tempos*, p. 122, letter, João José Barbosa to Rui Barbosa, May 29, 1870).

119. [Braz do] Amaral, *Recordações históricas*, p. 271; Harris, *Town and Country*, pp. 173–74.

120. [Buarque de] Holanda, *Raízes*.

121. Freyre, *Mansions and the Shanties*, pp. 30, 45, 52, 107–9; Da Matta, *Carnavais*, pp. 67–78 and *A casa & a rua*. Da Matta's third coordinate of Brazilian social space is the other world, the realm of the supernatural.

122. In an interview in 1954, Cardoso de Oliveira said that he based the novel

Dois metros e cinco on his experiences as prosecutor in Vila Brejo Grande, Ituassú, and as municipal judge in Barra do Rio Grande ([Epaminondas Berbert de] Castro, "Dois metros e cinco").

123. See the discussion of the "dialectic of roguery" from Cândido, "Dialética da malandragem," above in Chapter 2.

124. Oliveira, *Dois metros e cinco*, p. 163.

125. Marques, *O feiticeiro* (1922) was a revised version of a novel first published as *Bôto & Cia* in 1897.

126. Lewin, *Paraíba*, pp. 17, 131–33, points out that Brazilian kin groups were not clans in the technical sense of the word, and recommends using the word *parentela*; but *clan* is closer to *clã*, a word occasionally used by contemporary polemicists such as Sílvio Romero, *Brasil social* (1907), p. 13. *Parentela* was also used by contemporaries (Magalhães Júnior, *Rui*, p. 383).

127. [Carmelita] Hutchinson, "Notas preliminares," p. 265.

128. Lewin, "Historical Implications of Kinship Organization," hints that a daughter might deliberately be married off to an opposition family, in Machiavellian anticipation of extraordinary circumstances in which the rest of the family might need to appeal to them through a weak kinship link.

129. *Constituições primeiras do arcebispado da Bahia*, 10/33, 18/64–65. To be precise, no kinship was established between the two godparents, or between the godparents and the officiating priest. See Mintz and Wolf, "Compadrazgo," p. 8; [Itamar de] Souza, *Compadrio*; Wagley, "Luso-Brazilian Kinship," pp. 174–89.

130. Stein, *Vassouras*, pp. 147–49; Slenes and Carvalho de Mello, "Paternalism and Social Control," p. 18; cf. Gudeman and Schwartz, "Cleansing Original Sin," and Schwartz, *Sugar Plantations*, pp. 406–12; Cândido, "Brazilian Family"; and see Wagley, "Luso-Brazilian Kinship."

131. Wildberger, "Pereira de Aguiar"; poor Bahians would also choose relatives for their children's godparents, as in APEB, Notas, 1390, p. [73], July 28, 1934. APEB, Inventários da Capital, Francisca da Piedade Marinho, countess of Pereira Marinho, 1897–98, pp. 2–4, 169–207, 318–26, 406–88, 702–27, 760–93, 991–1047; APEB, Notas, 1330, p. 135, Oct. 23, 1926. [Itamar de] Souza, *Compadrio*, pp. 37–43, 56, on Natal; Wagley, "Luso-Brazilian Kinship."

132. Bittencourt, "Memórias," p. 26; *Constituições primeiras do arcebispado da Bahia*, 18/65; [Nizza da] Silva, *Cultura*, pp. 18–20; [Henry] Hutchinson, *Village and Plantation Life*, p. 147. But requests for marriage dispensations indicated that when widows or widowers married close kin, they were almost inevitably marrying compadres; for example, Antônio Mariano Homem d'El Rei and Camilla Pinto Ferreira de Sá were cousins; he had been married to her deceased sister, and she was godmother to two of his six children (Arquivo da Cúria, *Dispensas de parentesco, 1859–1863*, Jan. 28, 1862). On blessings, see Leal, *Santo Amaro*, p. 107; d'Avila, *Boas maneiras*, pp. 244–46.

133. ACRB, Maria Luisa Viana Ferreira Bandeira, letter, Bahia, July 15, 1880, to Maria Augusta Barbosa; Maria Luisa mentioned the godmother in the context of finding her son Cazuza a patronage job; letter, Rio de Janeiro, Jan. 11, 1881, Rui Barbosa to Maria Luisa, indicates that Cazuza did indeed get a job. See also letter, Bahia, Sept. 27, 1880, Maria Luisa to Maria Augusta Barbosa, inquiring about the

girl's godfather. See also [Rui] Barbosa, *Correspondência: Primeiros tempos*, pp. 71–74, letters from Rui to João Ferreira de Moura, on confirmation godfatherhood, 1868, 1869; *Constituições primeiras do arcebispado da Bahia*, 21/76–80, regulating godparenthood at confirmation; ACRB, Cartas de Noivo, Oct. 23, 1876, on selecting godparents for a wedding; Viana Filho, *Vida de Rui*, n. 8, pp. 327–28, reproduces a letter inviting a godfather to a wedding, 1908.

134. Mattoso, "Au nouveau monde," p. 264. Arquivo Cotegipe, letters, Moniz to Cotegipe, 5/43, Aug. 13, 1875, 5/45, Oct. 14, 1875, 5/48, Dec. 7, 1875, recruiting Cotegipe as patron and co-parent.

135. Lewin, *Paraíba*, p. 149.

136. This is implied in Russell-Wood, "Women and Society in Colonial Brazil," p. 28; and Metcalf, "Fathers and Sons." Cf. Lomnitz and Lizaur, "History of a Mexican Urban Family," pp. 399–400, 404, for a suggestive interpretation of a twentieth-century Mexican upper-class kindred whose social exchanges are maintained through "centralizing women."

137. ACRB, letter, Adelaide Dobbert to Mãe [Maria Luiza Viana Ferreira Bandeira], Bahia, Jan. 8, [ca. 1880–84]; Arquivo Cotegipe, 6/114, Antônio Rocha Martins Argolo to Cotegipe, June 4, 1888.

138. Marques, *O feiticeiro*, p. 15. This was a commonplace in Brazilian literature, as in Machado de Assis's "Almas agradecidas," p. 14: "Oliveira put into play his feminine resources. Two ladies of his acquaintance went in person to speak to the minister in favor of the lucky candidate."

139. Men did this as well, of course. See, e.g., APEB, Arquivo Wanderley Pinho, letter, João Ferreira de Araujo Pinho Júnior to Wanderley Pinho, Santo Amaro, Nov. 9, 1927, with request for collars and cigarettes from town.

140. ACRB, Adelaide Dobbert, letter to her mother [Maria Luisa Ferreira Viana Bandeira], Bahia, Mar. 21, [?]: "Peço-te de ajuntares o teu pedido a Cota para ella pedir em meu pequeno nome a Ruy o favor d'elle pedir por este moço filho da Baroneza de Rio Vermelho vai o pedido por escrito e Voce dizer a Ruy que me escreva respondendo." ACRB, Maria Luisa Viana Ferreira Bandeira, letter, Bahia, Feb. 27, 1882, Maria Luisa to Cota, "not demanding." See also Arquivo Araujo Pinho, 549/10, letter, Maria Luiza Wanderley Araujo Pinho to Enteada [Maria de Araujo Pinho], Roçado, Feb. 23, 1905, passing on, but not endorsing, the request of her godchild, a schoolteacher, to be transferred to the capital.

141. See the discussion of [Raphael de Albuquerque] Uchoa's *Odysséa de um revolucionário*; and cf. [José] Silveira, *Vela acesa*, pp. 59–62, on a patroness who reneged on a promise made to his grandmother and mother.

142. ACRB, João José Barbosa de Oliveira, copy, letter, Francisco Gonçalves Martins to Sr. Honório, Bahia, Feb. 16, 1844; Arquivo Cotegipe, 75/143, Maria Clara Wanderley, Rita de Cassia Wanderley, Ana Joaquina Wanderley, and Francisca Antonia Wanderley Borges to Cotegipe, Barra do Rio Grande, Apr. 29, 1876. APEB, Arquivo Goes Calmon, letters, Madre Maria Francisca Calmon to Goes Calmon, Santo Amaro, Jan. 27, 1926, and n.d. On moradores, APEB, Arquivo Wanderley Pinho, letter, Flávia Costa Pinto to José Wanderley Pinho, Conceição, Santo Amaro, Dec. 1, 1920 (a nice contrast of lady's notecard trimmed with green flowers and wardheeling advice "from a cousin who esteems you"). ACRB, Ade-

laide Dobbert, letter to Maria Luisa Viana Ferreira Bandeira, Bahia, March 19, [?]: "Tito dizia, só quem foi vé, é que credita." Servants were often literal and symbolic proxies of family members. Angry that his sister had not attended his wedding, Rui Barbosa pointed out that she had not, the day after, congratulated him "by one line, or by any means, even through a slave" (ACRB, Brites Barbosa de Oliveira Lopes, letter, Rui Barbosa to Brites, Dec. 8, 1876).

143. Schwartz, *Sovereignty and Society*, pp. 315, 326.

144. [Wanderley] Pinho, *Cotegipe*, pp. 556–58, on electoral circles crisis. I was not able to consult Richard Graham, *Patronage and Politics*, now the standard account of nineteenth-century patronage.

145. Arquivo Cotegipe, 56/63, Araujo Pinho to Cotegipe (n.d.); 56/83, July 26, [1879].

146. Pang, *Bahia*, pp. 42–46; Lewin, *Paraíba*, pp. 230–31, points out that in Paraíba in the late Empire, the Liberal and Conservative parties each had a dominant and a dissident faction, or "current." In order for a party to win elections, it would make deals with dissidents of the other party while trying to hold on to the loyalty of the dissident wing of its own party; cf. Love, *Rio Grande do Sul*, pp. 22, 21–28 passim.

147. Arquivo Cotegipe, 56/113, Araujo Pinho to Cotegipe, Oct. 27, [1887].

148. This strategy often allowed the rise of "men of talent"—that is to say, men without an obvious electoral base—into ministerial positions; see, e.g., [Mário Ferreira] Barboza, *Dr. Goes Calmon*, passim, on appointment of young aides; [Hermes] Lima, *Anísio Teixeira*, pp. 36–42, and *Travessia*, pp. 32–33. On Bahian parties during the Republic, see Pang, *Bahia*; and [Consuelo Novais] Sampaio, *Partidos políticos*.

149. Um indignado, "Abuso e traição," *Diário da Bahia*, Feb. 21, 1897, pp. 2–3, "entranhas"; Arquivo Cotegipe, 5/35, Pedro Moniz to Cotegipe, Oct. 24, [1885]; [Wanderley] Pinho, *Cotegipe*, pp. 562–64, on Dantas. Splits within the diffuse Dantas kindred continued through the Empire; while most were Liberals, Cícero Dantas Martins, baron of Geremoabo, was a leading Conservative (Pang, *Bahia*, p. 49). Luis Antônio Barbosa de Almeida, "Notícias Diversas," *O Monitor*, Aug. 13, 1878, in ACRB, Artigos de Jornais, pasta 96; and see [Rui] Barbosa, "Appéndice II: Resposta a Pereira Franco / Undécimo distrito da Bahia / O Conselheiro Rui Barbosa," in *Obras completas*, vol. 13, part 2, *1886 Trabalhos diversos*, pp. 337–38; Viana Filho, *Vida de Rui*, pp. 84–85.

150. Magalhães Júnior, *Rui*; [Ordival Cassiano] Gomes, *Pai de Rui*; Viana Filho, *Vida de Rui*, pp. 18–19, 84–85.

151. [Rui] Barbosa, *Correspondência, Manuel P. de Souza Dantas and Rodolfo E. de Sousa Dantas*; Viana Filho, *Vida de Rui*, pp. 56–65.

152. Pang, *Bahia*, p. 166; Needell, *Tropical Belle Epoque*, pp. 83–86 and passim, provides context for Rui's movement from provincial bases into elite circles in Rio de Janeiro; ACRB, Alfredo Rui Barbosa, letters, Alfredo to Rui, March 12, 1911, discuss loss of political supremacy to J. J. Seabra's faction; cf. Pang, *Bahia*, pp. 102–3, on the 1915 confirmation of Seabra's control.

153. ACRB, Adelaide Dobbert to Maria Luiza Viana Ferreira Bandeira, June 27, 1884; [Viana] Bandeira, *Lado a lado*, pp. 5, 184; Magalhães Júnior, *Rui*, pp. 382–83, 391–98, and 382–411 passim.

154. Colson, "Destruction of a Revolution Polity," discusses electoral laws and power; cf. Lewin, *Paraíba*, pp. 199–200, on districting in Paraíba. Criticizing the Saraiva law, Magalhães Júnior, *Rui*, pp. 24–40; and Love, "Political Participation."

155. Pang, *Bahia*, p. 208, table 2; cf. Love, *Rio Grande do Sul*, pp. 137–38, which argues that inflated Bahian votes reported in federal elections were significantly reduced by a skeptical Congress, and generally on voting in the Old Republic, pp. 24–25, 44, 115–19; Love, "Political Participation."

156. Love, *Rio Grande do Sul*, pp. 118–21; Pang, *Bahia*, pp. 34–36, and p. 17: "In short, the outcome of elections under the First Republic was a collaborative product of those who controlled the municípios (the coronéis) and those who controlled the legislatures (presidents and governors)"; Lewin, *Paraíba*, pp. 261–63.

157. Angelo Pitú, "Cavaqueemos," *Diário da Bahia*, May 8, 1897; portraying violence at the polls in the election of 1878, see Marques, *O feiticeiro*, pp. 77–82; Pang, *Bahia*, pp. 15–18.

158. See Pang, *Bahia*; Lins, "Um baiano como os outros," pp. 144–45; Magalhães Júnior, *Como você se chama?* p. 159; interview, Stella Calmon Wanderley Pinho, 1980.

159. In the Santo Amaro area around 1919–1921, votes went for 15$ to 30$, approximately U.S.$3–6, a good week's wage; see APEB, Arquivo Wanderley Pinho, invoice from Loja ao Bello Sexo, Santo Amaro, May 15, 1919; letter, Eduardo Pinto to José Wanderley de Araujo Pinho, Santo Amaro, Sept. 11, 1937, requesting 8$ for medicine. The Arquivo Wanderley Pinho records the tactics of campaigns from 1919 through the 1950's; cf. Pang, *Bahia*, pp. 16–17.

160. According to Pang, *Bahia*, table 2, p. 208, the total voting electorate in Bahia grew from about 73,000 in 1905, to 99,935 in 1910, to 153,000 in 1934, but Love, *Rio Grande do Sul*, pp. 137–38 argues that in response to congressional pressure, the claimed Bahian vote declined from 103,000 in the presidential election of 1898 to 61,000 in the election of 1910. See, too, Pang, *Bahia*, p. 150, on parties; APEB, Arquivo Wanderley Pinho, letter, Ursulino José Nascimento to José Wanderley de Araujo Pinho, Santo Amaro, Dec. 22, 1920, on paying train fares for voters; letter, A. Soveral to José Wanderley de Araujo Pinho, Usina Colônia, Feb. 20, 1921, on relative skills of competing campaign workers.

161. Pang, "Revolt of the Bahian *Coronéis*"; Pang, *Bahia*, pp. 86–88, 94, 196–204; Levine, *Pernambuco*, pp. 81–82, 93; Wirth, *Minas Gerais*, pp. 118–19, comparing Minas and Bahia; [Juracy] Magalhães, *Minhas memórias provisorias*, pp. 81–83.

162. Pang, *Bahia*, pp. 117–19; [Mário Augusto da Silva] Santos, *Caixeiros*, pp. 121, 133–38; Wirth, *Minas Gerais*, pp. 134–39, 196 (on the early secret ballot in that state in 1927). Coronelismo did not end because it was no longer possible to double-check the obedience of clients, but the secret vote limited its efficiency ([Nelson de Souza] Sampaio, *Diálogo democrático*; Pang, *Bahia*, pp. 202–4).

163. APEB, Arquivo Wanderley Pinho, [Rómulo] Moraes to Wanderley Pinho, Apr. 1, 1919.

164. APEB, Arquivo Wanderley Pinho, viscount of Oliveira to Wanderley Pinho, Outeiro, Dec. 22, 1919; for the context of this election, see [Consuelo Novais] Sampaio, *Partidos políticos*, pp. 107–8.

165. APEB, Arquivo Wanderley Pinho, Antônio Theophilo Moreira to José Wanderley Pinho, Lustosa, Oct. 16, 1934: "As to Porphyrio, I can't confirm his stand because the vote is secret"; see [Nelson de Souza] Sampaio, *Diálogo democrático.*

166. Arquivo Cotegipe, 6/115, Antônio Rocha Martins Argolo to Cotegipe, Dec. 10, 1888. Mattoso, "Au nouveau monde," pp. 8–9, makes a distinction, identifying the vice as *ingratitude* on the part of clients, *indifference* on the part of patrons: "Ele não da mais bola para mim" ("He doesn't throw me the ball anymore").

167. [Mary Garcia] Castro, "Mudança, mobilidade e valores," pp. 84–87, describes the defeat of a landlord in 1967 mayoral elections in São Francisco by a former clerk in the sugar mill, following which the landlord said he had been "betrayed by the povo of the town." [Bittencourt] Cabral, "Prefácio, p. 36, describes abolition and freedmen who "abandoned" their labor.

168. [Raphael de Albuquerque] Uchoa, *Odysséa de un revolucionário*, pp. 25, 27–28, 29.

169. Ibid., pp. 29, 30–38. Uchoa's patroness, identified as Sra. Teive e Argolo, was probably Joviana de Almeida Crissiuma, the mother-in-law of Antônio Moniz Sodré de Aragão, a federal deputy at the time, but later federal senator; Moniz Sodré was the cousin and brother-in-law of Antônio Ferrao Moniz de Aragão, then governor of Bahia; see Bulcão Sobrinho, *Famílias bahianas*, pp. 101–3.

170. Marques, *O feiticeiro*, p. 229. Of course, the context is sightseeing at the pilgrimage to the most powerful saint of the city.

171. Cf. Schwarz, *Ao vencedor as batatas*, on Alencar and Machado de Assis; and Cândido, "Dialética da malandragem."

172. Süssekind, *Tal Brasil*, discusses Amado and northeastern regionalists such as José Lins do Rêgo as successors to the naturalist aesthetic of the 1880's. Xavier Marques's work belongs to a transitional phase between the biologistic naturalism of Aluísio de Azevedo and the economistic naturalism of the regionalists; see Salles, *Ficcionista Xavier Marques.*

173. [Wanderley Guilherme dos] Santos, "Praxis liberal," esp. pp. 93–97; Needell, "Oliveira Vianna."

174. [Oliveira] Vianna, *Populações meridionais*, p. 163; Freyre, *Masters and the Slaves*, pp. 26–27, 83, 74–77, and *Mansions and the Shanties*, p. 24; [Buarque de] Holanda, *Raízes*, pp. 53, 101–7.

175. Duarte, *Ordem privada*; [Costa] Pinto, *Lutas de famílias*; [Oliveira] Vianna, *Instituições políticas brasileiras*; [Victor Nunes] Leal, *Coronelismo.*

176. [Sílvio] Romero's *Brasil social* (1907) offers only a superficial treatment of the family, but its recognition of regional and ecological variation in family types makes it more similar in spirit to contemporary family history and sociology than to the literature of the 1940's.

Chapter 7

1. Bourdieu, "Marriage Strategies"; Cole and Wolf, *Hidden Frontier*; Davis, "Ghosts, Kin, and Progeny."

2. Perhaps collating fortune with Machiavellian *virtù*, or talent, rather than with

Aristotelian *habitus*, or disposition, would explain their strategies; but cf. Morse, "The Lima of Joaquín Capelo," esp. pp. 108–10, for another twist.

3. Wetherell, *Stray Notes*, pp. 139–40.

4. Median family size was four children in families established between 1750 and 1875 ($n = 108$), declining to three children for families established between 1875 and 1925 ($n = 134$). These figures, and some of the discussion following in this chapter, draw on analysis of what I call the Traditional Families Sample, 2,025 cases (about 3,000 individuals) with vital statistics (birth, death, marriage), derived from the genealogies of Bulcão Sobrinho, *Famílias bahianas*, including genealogies of descent of the Bulcão, Pires de Carvalho, Vicente Viana, Bandeira, Brandão, Gonçalves da Costa, Moniz, Cavalcante e Albuquerque, and Machado Velho families, which I cite as Traditional Families Sample. The genealogies begin, in some cases, in the seventeenth century, and continue through the 1940's, so that relevant subsamples are usually smaller than the larger sample. I added details on the Bulcão family found in Bulcão Sobrinho, "Família Bulcão," and I incorporated portions of Wildberger, "Pereira de Aguiar." Discussions of demographic analysis using genealogies are found in Hollingsworth, *Demography of the British Peerage* and id., *Historical Demography*, pp. 201–12. See the Appendix for additional discussion of the sample.

5. Schwartz, "Patterns of Slaveholding," esp. pp. 62–71; Luna and da Costa, "Posse de escravos"; Mattoso, *Bahia*, pp. 39–46, on Santiago de Iguape landholdings.

6. [Wanderley] Pinho, *Engenho*; Wirth, *Minas Gerais*, pp. 65–75, esp. p. 72.

7. Soeiro, "Social and Economic Role," esp. pp. 214–18; and see Table 1 for proportion of women who never married in the nineteenth century.

8. See Russell-Wood, *Fidalgos and Philanthropists*, p. 177, on an arrangement in 1718. [Graciliano] Ramos, *Infância*, pp. 158–65, analyzes the calculations of a marriage settlement on a small scale around 1900. Soeiro, "Social and Economic Role," p. 223, says convent dowries were not a lump sum. And see APEB, Inventários, Capital, 02/99/145/01, Francisco de Souza Paraiso, 1843–60, on a husband suing the estate to deliver his wife's overdue share of the inheritance. There are very few deeds of dotal property, and few prenuptial contracts of any sort, registered in the notarial records in the APEB, Seção Judiciária, Notas, 1800–1930. Nazzari, "Women, the Family and Property," p. 402, says that the dotal property was little used in São Paulo.

9. Soeiro, "Feminine Orders"; Bittencourt, "Memórias," pp. 41, 53–54; Soeiro, "Social and Economic Role," p. 223; [Wanderley] Pinho, *Salões*; Russell-Wood, *Fidalgos and Philanthropists*, pp. 177–79, 320–36. Deeds establishing a priest's "patrimony" in the nineteenth century can be found in APEB, Notas.

10. Freyre, *Sobrados e mucambos*, pp. 122–24; Mattoso, "Au nouveau monde," pp. 511–24.

11. [Pondé de] Sena, *Itapicurú*, pp. 112, 146, 154–55; Santos Filho, *Comunidade*, p. 189; Mattoso, "Para uma história social," esp. pp. 169–98; Arquivo Cotegipe, 7/4, letter, Francisco Antônio Rocha Pitta Argollo to Cotegipe, Nov. 18, [1861] and reply Nov. 20, [1861] on responsibility to maintain a perpetual endowment.

12. Wetherell, *Stray Notes*; [Maria] Graham, *Journal*, p. 226; Freire-Maia, "Consanguineous Marriages."

13. But cousin marriage alone would be an insignificant tactic in comparison with the further strategy of willing the third of free disposition, the *terça*, to a grandchild. Assume that two grandparents reserve 33 percent of their property and that the remaining 66 percent is divided into four equal mandatory shares (*legítimas*) of 16.5 percent apiece. Each of the eight grandchildren would receive a mandatory share of 8.25 percent. The two cousins marrying would reunite their portions, to 16.5 percent and add to that the 33 percent that their grandparents could will freely, to make 49.5 percent. This abstract case of course assumes that no property is gained or spent between generations, and that the children do not marry spouses with property of their own. If their grandparents died intestate and the property was divided evenly, the couple of first cousins would inherit only 25 percent, and each of their six cousins, 12.5 percent.

14. This is the case in nineteenth- and twentieth-century inventories for Salvador that I have reviewed, but further research would be needed to establish the fact.

15. [Prisco] Paraiso Neto, *Descendência*, p. 3; [Nizza] da Silva, *Cultura*, pp. 22–25; Arquivo da Cúria, *Dispensas de impedimentos, 1859–1885*, Jan. 23, 1885, Teixeira and Spinola; [Oliveira] Vianna, *Instituições políticas*, 1: 258–62 argues that the location of families on neighboring fazendas led to endogamy; [Nizza da] Silva, *Sistema de casamento*; Arquivo Cotegipe, 7/1, Rocha Pita to Cotegipe, Dec. 28, 1855.

16. [Maria] Graham, *Journal*, pp. 224–26; these are standard arguments of the Catholic church against endogamous marriage; cf. Goody, *Development of the Family and Marriage*, p. 57 and passim.

17. [Prisco] Paraiso Neto, *Descendência*; [Henry] Hutchinson, *Village and Plantation Life*.

18. Mattoso, "Au nouveau monde," pp. 271–91, esp. pp. 286–87; Pang, *Engenho Central*, pp. 196–207; cf. [Wanderley] Pinho, *Cotegipe*, p. 623.

19. Yet contrast Hall, "Family Structure," and "Marital Selection," arguing that merchants in mercantilist economies needed similar family strategies to ensure continuity of capital in the family firm after the death of a partner.

20. Lugar, "Merchant Community," pp. 226–34, 241–47. On the twentieth century, see [Mário Augusto da Silva] Santos, *Caixeiros*. And see Metcalf, "Families of Planters, Peasants, and Slaves"; Freyre, *Mansions and the Shanties*, pp. 177–79; Flory, "Bahian Society," pp. 230–32; Flory and Smith, "Bahian Merchants," pp. 576–77.

21. For a nineteenth-century Portuguese artisan-commercial family, the Pereiras, see [Ordival Cassiano] Gomes, *Manuel Victorino Pereira*, pp. 11–15; [Afonso] Costa, "Manuel Victorino Pereira"; [Manuel] Pereira and Sá Menezes, "Família Pereira." On the colonial period, see [Rae] Flory, "Bahian Society," pp. 231–34, 302–6. Morton, "Conservative Revolution," pp. 29, 51, suggests that marriage between merchants and planter families was not common; cf. Flory and Smith, "Bahian Merchants"; Lugar, "Merchant Community," pp. 235–40.

22. Bulcão Sobrinho, *Famílias bahianas*, "Vicente Viana," pp. 98–127.

23. Lugar, "Merchant Community," pp. 256–305; *Westphalen, Bach*; Wetherell, *Stray Notes*, pp. 105, 110, 116; Ridings, "Bahian Commercial Association," pp. 23–34. For the late nineteenth century, see Fletcher and Kidder, *Brazil and the Bra-*

zilians, p. 484. A somewhat similar development may be observed in the position of officers in the regular army. Even before independence, the Bahian officer corps was virtually a caste; officers' families intermarried and officers' sons rose through the ranks fastest. This tendency toward endogamy continued after independence, and regular army officers became even less of a factor in the marriage schemes of landlord families (Morton, "Military and Society"; Kennedy, "Bahian Elites").

24. Morton, "Conservative Revolution," passim; [Wanderley] Pinho, *Engenho*; sugar rose as a proportion of Bahian exports from 1818 until in 1845 it represented 76 percent of their value (Lugar, "Merchant Community," pp. 113–20).

25. Colson, "Destruction," pp. 50–54; [Wanderley] Pinho, *Cotegipe*, pp. 22–25; Schwartz, *Sovereignty and Society*, on marriages between Crown judges and planters in the colonial period.

26. Morton, "Conservative Revolution"; Colson, "Destruction," esp. pp. 20–30, 57–62; for a view opposing, cf. [Oliveira] Vianna, *Instituições*, 1: 258–62. On coffee, see Stanley Stein, *Vassouras*.

27. Arquivo Cotegipe, 6/111, Antônio Rocha Martins Argolo to Cotegipe, Cajahiba, Feb. 27, 1885; and 6/114, Cajahiba, June 4, 1888. Mattoso, "Au nouveau monde," p. 905, table vi, p. 919, and pp. 933–39, 960ff, on decline in land values.

28. [Consuelo Novais] Sampaio, *Formação do regionalismo*, states the problem of economic decline. See also [Murilo de] Carvalho, *Construção da ordem*, pp. 168–71, on São Paulo's lack of representation.

29. [Barbosa de] Oliveira, *Memórias de um magistrado*, pp. 168–69; the match was made in 1847. See Needell, *Tropical Belle Epoque*, pp. 116–24, on the Rio de Janeiro marriage market, esp. Joaquim Nabuco. As Freyre portrays it in *The Mansions and the Shanties*, the shift manifested itself in the early nineteenth century as a conflict between generations, between the earthbound, unlettered, backwoods lords and their cosmopolitan, educated, town-dwelling sons and sons-in-law. Whereas the old planters represented the patriarchal tradition of localism, the young law graduates represented the modern, urban, and European institutions that supplanted patriarchal power. Freyre plays up the contrast between the old and the new forms of the family. I stress the continuity between the older family strategies and the renewed ones that emerged in the nineteenth century. See Freyre, *Sobrados e mucambos*, 1: 3–23, 67–88, 2: 573–632.

30. Soeiro, "Social and Economic Role."

31. Of the descendants of elite Bahian families (male and female) who married between 1750 and 1869 ($n = 142$), 33 percent made kin marriages; of those married between 1870 and 1899 ($n = 64$), 23 percent made kin marriages; of those married between 1900 and 1944 ($n = 301$), 12 percent made kin marriages (Traditional Families Sample). The rate of endogamous marriage among traditional elite families in Salvador and the province of Bahia was much higher than that among the population of Salvador as a whole in the nineteenth century. Johildo Athayde (research in progress) has studied the ecclesiastical marriage registers of the São Pedro, Santana, and Sé parishes of Salvador for the periods 1835–54 and 1871–90. In none of these parishes did the proportion of consanguineous marriages at any time exceed 8 percent. Cousin marriages seem to have been declining: they constituted 7.6 percent of marriages in São Pedro in 1835–44, 5.8 percent in 1881–90;

6.7 percent in Santana in 1845–54, 3.4 percent in 1871–80.

32. Lewin, "Historical Implications," following [Oliveira] Vianna, *Instituições*, suggests that in Paraíba, endogamous marriage was a function of localism, and that when families sought province-wide connections they discarded kin marriage.

33. Traditional Families Sample.

34. Interview, Stella Calmon Wanderley Pinho, 1981; obviously, the legend had been embroidered with hindsight; cf. Menezes, "Família Calmon," pp. 155–56.

35. In Paraíba, Linda Lewin found a preference for patrilateral parallel cousin marriage—that is, for marriages among the father's brothers' children (Lewin, *Paraíba*, pp. 147–58).

36. Freyre, *Sobrados e mucambos*, 1: 3–23, 67–88, 2: 573–632; Nazzari, "Women, the Family and Property," pp. 384–90; and cf. Chapter 4 above.

37. The idiom is archaic. See Russell-Wood, *Fidalgos and Philanthropists*, p. 194.

38. Nabuco, *Estadista do Império*, 1: 304–16; [Braz do] Amaral, *História da Bahia*, pp. 197–198n; cf. Bittencourt, "Memórias," pp. 68–69; interview, Sr. Maria Teresa [Mariana da Costa Pinto Dantas], 1981.

39. *Casamento Civil*, art. 58/3; *Código Civil* (1916), art. 183/4.

40. Bittencourt, "Memórias," p. 124; this was only one of the pretexts that he offered for rejecting the pedido from a kinsman of his wife's family.

41. For a lay argument against the medical consequences of cousin marriage, see Heriberto Filho, "Primos."

42. "Revista dos Jornaes," *Diário da Bahia*, Feb. 4, 1897.

43. [Hermes] Lima, *Travessia*, pp. 21–22; [José] Silveira, *Vela acesa*, pp. 186–90.

44. See Meireles, *Acontecimentos*, p. 29 and Ribeiro, "Estudantes," for two versions of the *almofadinha* anecdote. And see Harris, *Town and Country*, pp. 173–74; [Hildegardes] Vianna, *A Bahia já foi assim*, pp. 202–7.

45. The sorts of unique dynastic considerations that would have gone into planning cousin marriages could hardly be instilled into children as a set of principles. But cf. Lewin, *Paraíba*, pp. 147–49, 200–203, a persuasive argument that "cousin marriage" was a logical way for men to bond with some of their "cousins" as brothers-in-law.

46. Bittencourt, "Memórias"; and Rêgo, *Meus verdes anos*, pp. 178–84, describe family councils on marriage.

47. Traditional Families Sample; the mean completed family size for Bahian-born members of traditional Bahian families declined from 4.14 ($n = 108$) for those marrying between 1750 and 1874 to 3.70 for those marrying between 1875 and 1924 ($n = 134$); the standard deviations are broad enough that the difference in means may not be statistically significant. The decline in size was largely a matter of the decline in large families. In the pre-1875 sample, the median was 4 and the third quartile 6. In the post-1875 sample, the median was 3 and the third quartile 5. The mean completed family size was 3.07 ($n = 13$) for branches that had migrated to the south of Brazil. Genealogies are likely to miss some births of children who did not survive, so these figures should be treated as low estimates.

48. Hora, *Mortalidade infantil . . . 1904–1918*. Gouvéia, *Puericultura social*, p. 52, argues that rates based on Bahian vital statistics are useless for tracing trends,

as his sample study from 1940 to 1946 showed that 30 percent of the births in Salvador were never registered, and 36 percent of the births registered were registered upon the death of the infant. The lack of registration is confirmed in [IBGE], *Características demográficas*, pp. 285–86. However, these statistics can indicate an order of magnitude. Such high rates of infant mortality (20–30 percent, or one in five to one in three infants) are comparable with the highest rates in the British North American colonies in the seventeenth century.

49. For example, more children born to married women, whose social status was higher than that of single mothers, survived. Compare the proportion of children surviving at the date of the census for married and never-married women in the state of Bahia in 1940. In the cohort of women born between 1880 and 1890, the rate of child survival for unmarried mothers was 57.5 percent, the rate for widows 62.8 percent, and the rate for married women 68.9 percent. In the younger cohort of women born between 1904 and 1910, the proportion of children still alive was 69.2 percent for unmarried mothers, 65.6 percent for widows, and 75.7 percent for married women. See IBGE, *Características demográficas*, pp. 249–51.

50. Hajnal, "European Marriage Patterns"; Van de Walle, "Marital Fertility."

51. If we assume that, in the 15–19 age group, the number of single women with children had the same relation to the total number of single women at risk of pregnancy as the number of married women with children did to the total number of married women (.54), then we may estimate that the ratio of single women in unions to married women was higher in the 15–19 age group (.37 of the number of married women) than it was in older age groups such as the 50–59 years cohort (.20 of the number of married women). This suggests that, between 1930 and 1940, Bahian women who entered free unions were likely to begin them at a younger age than women who married. See IBGE, *Características demográficas*, pp. 249–52.

52. Many marriages in Bahia were those of mature parents legitimating their children after years of consensual union, further distorting the significance of mean age at marriage as an indicator of fertility control in the population. See IBGE, *Características demográficas*, pp. 249–50.

53. In the Sé parish between 1830 and 1874, 33.5 percent of free "white" infants were illegitimate, and 62.3 percent of all free infants were illegitimate. Whereas "whites" constituted 35 percent of the population in 1872, "white" infants were 45 percent of the foundlings in the 1852–61 period. Athayde, "Ville de Salvador," pp. 167, 182.

54. The age of marriage for their cousins born in the south of Brazil (primarily Rio and São Paulo) may have remained about the same; among a small sample of 10 women descended from emigrated Bahian families, born in the south of Brazil and marrying between 1875 and 1925, the median age at marriage remained low (about 20.5). The median age at marriage of 95 Bahian-born women rose from 20 to 23 for those marrying after 1875.

55. I found no mention whatsoever of contraception in the *Gazeta Médica da Bahia* (1860's through 1960's, with interruptions) and only rare references in catalogued theses of the Faculdade de Medicina da Bahia, ca. 1850 to ca. 1945; see, e.g., Brandão, *Do casamento*, pp. 64–68. Stepan, "Eugenesia," pp. 378–79, found some eugenicist discussion of contraception in the 1930's. Albuquerque, *Educação*

sexual, pp. 158–63, endorsed contraception, but referred couples to their physicians for details. On abortion, see Souza, *Aborto*; Garnier, *Matrimônio*, p. 362; Chernoviz, *Diccionário*.

56. *Diário da Bahia*, Jan. 11, 1897; cf. Sant'Ana, *Outros bambangas*, pp. 57–58.

57. IBGE, *Características demográficas*, p. 250. Married women in the state of Bahia born between 1880 and 1895, and thus marrying roughly between 1900 and 1925, reported an average of 7.6 live births. Completed families in the Traditional Families Sample averaged 3.7 births, 1875–1925 (*n* = 134). It may be misleading to compare these figures, as the genealogies almost certainly underreported children who died young; it is better to use the Traditional Families Sample data for discussion of trends within these families. Yet there does seem to be a higher proportion of couples with no children among the Traditional Families Sample cohort born between 1865 and 1889 (14 percent) than among married women of the Bahian population cohort born between 1881 and 1890 (10 percent); more among the Traditional Families cohort born between 1890 and 1914 (18 percent) than the population cohort of 1891–95 (9 percent). Cf. Mattoso, "Au nouveau monde," p. 226, table XII, and p. 214, table VII: 7 of 41 legal families in the Salvador household surveys of 1855 (17 percent) had no children under the age of twenty in the household; 155 of a sample of 421 individuals inventoried in the nineteenth century (36.8 percent) had no surviving children. See Saunders, *Differential Fertility*, pp. 14–16.

58. Stone, "Rise of the Nuclear Family"; and *Family, Sex, and Marriage*.

59. Cândido, "Brazilian Family," pp. 291–312; *Código Civil*, arts. 337–46, 364.

60. APEB, Notas, 1189, p. 19, Sept. 11, 1909, and 1201, p. 28, Sept. 20, 1910, are cases in which widowers waited until after the deaths of their legal wives to recognize illegitimate children born before their marriages; ibid., 965, p. 16, Jan. 15, 1896, is a prenuptial agreement ratifying the man's earlier recognition of two illegitimate children.

61. Ibid., 1332, p. 196, July 11, 1927, testament of a merchant securing the rights of his daughter by a religious marriage; and 1332, pp. 182–83, Apr. 22, 1927, testament of an illiterate man owning a few small houses, leaving property to his current mistress and a son by another woman; 1935, a rural landlord, aged 76, leaving half his estate to three male children of a single woman, "whom he raised like his own children" (though he does not recognize them), and half to his sister-in-law and godchild; 1395, p. 4, Sept. 2, 1935.

62. This was not the only option: in 1925, a planter put his legitimate sons into schools, while giving his illegitimate son a placement as a store clerk in the commercial district ([Mário Augusto da Silva] Santos, *Caixeiros*, p. 160). And see *Código Civil*, arts. 1177, 248/4, 178/7, on transfers to concubines.

63. By the law of Aug. 11, 1831, Souza Paraiso could have left a legacy to Francisco Joaquim, but the inventory makes no mention of a will.

64. APEB, Inventários, Francisco de Souza Paraiso, 1843–60, esp. pp. 122–24; APEB, Notas, 639, p. 53, Nov. 2, 1880.

65. Caio Moura was born before the death of his father's second wife, Maria Luisa de Costa Pinto, in 1891. There is no record of a deed of recognition, but legally it would not have been possible to recognize an adulterine child as an heir,

and, in some interpretations, even to leave one a legacy. See [Costa Pinto] Victória, "Família Costa Pinto," pp. 32–33; Pang, *Engenho*, pp. 187–93; [José] Silveira, *Vela acesa*, pp. 122–23.

66. Torres, "Morgados do 'Sodré,'" pp. 23, 103; Carvalho, *Successão de morgado*; [Antônio Euzébio de] Almeida, *Successão de morgado extincto*. [Mário] Torres, "Sodrés," p. 103, says that Alagoinhas was the son of Anna de Menezes; Mattoso, "Au nouveau monde," pp. 193–96, esp. n. 41, says that Alagoinhas was the natural son of Mariana Rita de Menezes Brandão. Francisco Maria Sodré Pereira's personal estate was only 67 contos, by no means a great fortune among the Recôncavo senhores de engenho. Large sugar mill estates around that time could be worth as much as 392 contos ([Wanderley] Pinho, *Engenho*, pp. 119–25) or even 570 contos (Pang, *Engenho Central*, pp. 186, 190, and Dantas Júnior, "Lopes de Santo Amaro," pp. 29–38). The share of each of Sodré Pereira's five heirs of the personal property was only 13:518$ (about U.S. $7,500). The entailed portion of Sodré Pereira's estate was never fully appraised, but it was reputed to be worth over 70 contos, including a sugar mill and urban properties in Salvador and Portugal ([Carvalho], *Successão de morgado extincto*, pp. 16, 39).

67. In 1911 Cora Moniz Sodré de Aragão (1875–?) married her mother's brother's son, Coronel Jerônimo Sodré Pereira Sobrinho (1875–1943), a landlord and later state deputy (Bulcão Sobrinho, *Famílias bahianas*, pp. 98–99).

68. [Carlos] Torres, *Gonçalo Moniz*.

69. Maria da Purificação was the daughter of Gonçalo's father's half-sister. Her mother, Maria José Coutinho da França (1834–98), was the one daughter of Lino Coutinho's brief marriage to Maria Adelaide Sodré Pereira. Her first husband, the magistrate Tranquilino Leovigildo Torres (1859–96), was one of several illegitimate children of the Conservative politician-priest, Belarmino Silvestre Torres (1829–96) and the widow Umbelina Emília dos Santos (1824–87). See [Mário] Torres, "Torres," esp. pp. 31–34, 40–49.

70. Ibid. omits a wedding date. APEB, Notas, 1198, p. 50, May 14, 1910. [José] Silveira, *Vela acesa*, pp. 50–52. A strong reason not to marry was the law of guardianship that took power over the children's affairs and property away from a widow who remarried.

71. Mattoso, "Au nouveau monde," p. 193; cf. poem decrying hostility to illegitimate kin, 1850, quoted in Bulcão Sobrinho, *Famílias bahianas*, 1: 53.

72. APEB, Notas, 405, p. 44, May 16, 1870, adopting a girl taken from the Santa Casa da Misericórdia orphanage; 1395, p. 97, Feb. 14, 1935, dividing a sizeable estate among legitimate children and filhos de criação; 1330, pp. 192–93, Mar. 5, 1927, legacy to an illegitimate nephew, "for good services, for more than ten years, living in his company."

73. Cf. Bourdieu, "Marriage Strategies."

74. "Salada de Fructas," *Diário da Bahia*, 1897; [Wanderley] Pinho, *Engenho*, pp. 315–27, and *Salões*, p. 48; Wetherell, *Stray Notes*, p. 74; *Código Civil*, arts. 459–62; interview, Inocêncio Marques de Goes Calmon, 1980, courtesy of Harry Makler; Inocêncio and other children of the Goes Calmon family reported that Francisco Marques de Goes Calmon had been ruined by expenses incurred personally while governor.

75. See Goode, *World Revolution*, pp. 12–14.

76. Nabuco, *Abolicionismo*, pp. 156–64, esp. p. 163.

77. Wetherell, *Stray Notes*, pp. 140, 75; Wetherell himself was a placeseeker who started as a merchant and honorary consul and eventually tried to secure a post as a paid consul.

78. [Barbosa de] Oliveira, *Memórias de um magistrado*; [Mario de Lima] Barbosa, "Antepassados de Ruy Barbosa"; ACRB, Rui Barbosa, Documentos Pessoais, Brites Barbosa de Oliveira Lopes, Enxoval de Brites, Mar. 16, 1876; the total cost of the trousseau was 911$; ACRB, Cartas de Noivo, letters, Rui Barbosa to Maria Augusta Viana Bandeira, June 9, 1876, July 19, 1876; [Ordival Cassiano] Gomes, *Pai de Rui*; Magalhães Júnior, *Rui*, pp. 1–4, 48–91; Viana Filho, *Vida de Rui*, pp. 48–55, 65–78.

79. Levi, *Prado Family*; Dean, *Industrialization*.

80. [Bertram] Hutchinson, *Mobilidade e trabalho*; in Hutchinson's terminology, São Paulo exhibited much "structural mobility," brought about by a change in the structure of occupational positions, and little "exchange mobility," brought about by an exchange of members between one position and another. See also Love, *São Paulo*, pp. 19–20, 84–86, 100; Wirth, *Minas Gerais*, pp. 72–75.

81. Tupinambá, "Cavaqueemos," *Diário da Bahia*, Apr. 6, 1897, p. 1.

82. Mattoso, "Au nouveau monde"; Jancso, "Exportações da Bahia," p. 337, esp. n. 4; Arquivo Cotegipe, 56/126, Araujo Pinho to Cotegipe, Santo Amaro, Jan. 20, 1889; at prices of 450$ (1880) to 400$ (1888) each, according to Mattoso (*To Be a Slave*, p. 79, table 7), 300 slaves could have been a loss of 120–135 contos; Arquivo Cotegipe, 6/105, Antônio Rocha Martins Argolo to Cotegipe, [Engenho] São Paulo, July 29, 1878; 6/113, Bahia, Feb. 19, 1888; 6/114, Cajahiba, June 4, 1888; Coleção Araujo Pinho, 549/20, Antônio Rocha Martins Argolo to Mariquinhas [Maria Luiza Wanderley Araujo Pinho], Bahia, July 15, 1897 and Maria Luiza Wanderley Araujo Pinho to Argolo, Santo Amaro, June 18, 1897.

83. Arquivo Cotegipe, letters, Pedro Moniz to Cotegipe, 5/39, Oct. 3, 1855; 5/63, Sept. 10, 1885; 5/87, Mar. 16, [1888].

84. Arquivo Cotegipe, 56/123, Araujo Pinho to Cotegipe, Nov. 12, [1888].

85. Jancso, "Exportações," p. 339 and passim.

86. *Westphalen, Bach*; Lloyd, *Impressões do Brasil*; [Mário Augusto da Silva] Santos, *Comércio português*; [Wildberger], *Wildberger & Cia*. The figures for Wildberger's cacao trade are estimates derived from collating those given by Wildberger, *Meu pai*, pp. 32, 38, 47, and Jancso, "Exportações," p. 350, table 3.

87. [Péricles Madureira de] Pinho, *São assim*, pp. 35–116; [Mário Augusto da Silva] Santos, *Comércio português*; [Célia Maria Leal] Braga, "Espanhóis." The new wave of Spanish immigrants specialized in retail shops and bakeries.

88. Pang, *Engenho*; on a bankruptcy, [Walter da] Silveira, "Discurso." Cardoso, *Empresário industrial*, pp. 143–44, describes the speculator-entrepreneur type in São Paulo.

89. Garcez, "Propriedade cacaueira" and *Instituto de Cacau*. Wright, "Market, Land and Class." Cf. Mattoso, "Au nouveau monde," p. 285 n. 67, arguing that in the Recôncavo, endogamy was a strategy to ward off decline in the nineteenth century, and that arriviste families had tended to follow exogamous marriage strate-

gies to build alliances. And cf., in the 1950's, the ethos of cacao farmers studied by Anthony Leeds ("Economic Cycles") and the sugar planters studied by Henry Hutchinson (*Village and Plantation Life*).

90. [Hermes] Lima, *Travessia*, p. 12, quoting Pe. Cabral, geography professor at Colégio Antônio Vieira; Juvenal, "Cavaqueemos," *Diário da Bahia*, Feb. 12, 1897, p. 1, on sons of the Mulata Velha; and Juvenal, "Cavaqueemos," *Diário da Bahia*, Feb. 21, 1897, p. 1.

91. Traditional Families Sample: for 1865–89, out of 154 descendants of Bahian traditional families, 1 percent were born in the center-south of Brazil (Rio de Janeiro and São Paulo), 8 percent elsewhere outside Bahia; for 1890–1914, out of 223, 31 percent were born in the center-south, 6 percent elsewhere outside Bahia; for 1915–50, out of 591, 51 percent were born in the center-south, 4 percent elsewhere outside Bahia. Clearly, "Bahian" genealogies could be biased toward selecting families that remained in place during the nineteenth century; nonetheless, the trend suggests that there was an exodus among the upper and middle classes.

92. [Francisco] Mangabeira, *João Mangabeira*; [Octávio] Mangabeira, "Cinqüentanário do falecimento de Francisco Mangabeira"; [Yves de] Oliveira, *Octávio Mangabeira*; Pang, *Bahia*, pp. 150–53.

93. Cássia, *Memórias de Veridiana*.

94. Bulcão, *Colégio Antônio Vieira*, pp. 17–18; [José] Silveira, *Vela acesa*; interview, Orlando Moscoso Barretto de Araujo, 1980; [Joaquim Barretto de] Araujo, *Reminiscências*; Sant'Ana, *Outros bambangas*; [Gastão] Sampaio, *Nazaré das Farinhas*.

95. For criticism of this superficial education, [Maria Luiza] Alves, "Se todos fazem," pp. 73–74; Bahiano, "Casamento e arte doméstica."

96. ACRB, Cartas, Adelaide Dobbert to Maria Luiza Viana, Hamburg, June 9, [ca. 1880]. The language was often piteous; in 1926, when Francisco Marques de Goes Calmon was governor, his cousin, a nun in Santo Amaro, wrote him pleading for a teaching position for a widowed girl who was the "daughter of a godson of my late father" (APEB, Arquivo Goes Calmon, letter, Maria Francisca Calmon to Goes Calmon, Santo Amaro, Aug. 8, 1926). See also Morley, *Diary*, pp. 233–35, 241; Russell-Wood, *Fidalgos and Philanthropists*, pp. 185–87.

97. Russell-Wood, *Fidalgos and Philanthropists*; Mattoso, *Bahia*, pp. 218–27.

98. [Thales de] Azevedo, *Social Change*, p. 17.

99. See Chapter 2 above on Anna Ribeiro de Goes Bittencourt and her son, Pedro Ribeiro.

100. Bulcão Sobrinho, *Famílias bahianas*, 1: 32–36; Bulcão Sobrinho, "Família Bulcão," 13: 73; in the first genealogy Bulcão Sobrinho gave his own birthdate as 1894 and no date for his parents' marriage. In the second genealogy, he gave his parents' marriage date as Mar. 20, 1897, and his own birthdate as Jan. 4, 1898.

101. Bulcão Sobrinho, "Família Bulcão," 13: 48–49, 73–76, passim; Silva, *À barra*, pp. 34–36; see Wirth, *Minas Gerais*, pp. 70–71, on the "multicareer" pattern among the political elite.

102. See Lewin, *Paraíba*, pp. 200–207, on "sibling axes" and "brother bonding" in marriage strategies among the Paraíba oligarchy.

103. Wildberger, *Meu pai*; Neeser, "Família Urpia"; interview, Arnold Wildberger, 1981.

104. [Carmelita] Hutchinson, "Notas preliminares"; Dean, *Industrialization*; Morse, *From Community to Metropolis*.

105. Leeds, "Brazilian Careers," describes the panelinha.

106. Lewin, *Paraíba*, pp. 200–207; id., "Historical Implications"; and cf. Hall, "Marital Selection."

107. There were others, of course. For politics, the newspaper became the arena in which older men let young men display their rhetorical talent. See also Mattoso, *Bahia*, pp. 201–24, on religious brotherhoods. On school ties versus kinship, see Maxwell, *Conflicts and Conspiracies*; Morton, "Conservative Revolution."

108. "Folhetim," *O Monitor* Mar. 23, 1879: "E pena não tenhamos, meu visinho / Essa felicidade / De um egual parentesco! / Mesmo que fosse alguma affinidade, / Um pobre compadresco! . . . / Diabo! si eu não fosse baptisado / Ou pudesse crismar-me duas vezes, / Como o nosso Barreto de Menezes / Podia ser do Dantas afilhado!"

109. Lewin, *Paraíba*, argues that kin networks dominated Paraíba political associations, but her history of Epitácio Pessoa's political clique documents friendship as much or more than kinship ties.

110. Pang, *Bahia*.

111. On coronelismo, see Pang, *Bahia*; and [Nunes] Leal, *Coronelismo*. See [Xavier] Marques, "Caderno," on the sanctions for breaking loyalty.

112. Pang, *Bahia*, pp. 189–201.

113. APEB, Arquivo Wanderley Pinho, documents the change in tactics from the rigged "penstroke" elections of the 1920's to the mass elections of the 1950's. See also [Nelson de Souza] Sampaio, *Diálogo democrático*, and Pang, *Bahia*, pp. 202–5, on the residues of coronelismo.

114. Interview, Inocêncio Marques de Goes Calmon, 1980; Sá Menezes, "Família Calmon"; Pang, *Bahia*, pp. 150–52, 166; interview, Stella Calmon Wanderley Pinho, 1980.

115. Perhaps a bias in the memoir literature tends to exaggerate the importance of rural-urban migration; [Hermes] Lima, *Travessia*; Nogueira, *Caminhos de um magistrado*; cf. Miceli, *Intelectuais e classe dirigente*.

116. Nabuco, *Abolicionismo*, p. 164.

Bibliography

Archives and Documents

Arquivo da Casa de Rui Barbosa [ACRB], Rio de Janeiro.
  Rui Barbosa, Correspondência.
  Rui Barbosa, Correspondência, Cartas de Noivo.
  Rui Barbosa, Documentos Pessoais.
Arquivo da Cúria de Salvador, Salvador [Arquivo da Cúria].
  Divórcios Ecclesiais.
  Dispensas.
Arquivo do Foro Rui Barbosa, Salvador, Bahia.
  Registro Civil de Casamentos.
Arquivo do Instituto Geográfico e Histórico da Bahia, Salvador.
  Sampaio, Teodoro. "O engenho de assucar no recôncavo de Santo Amaro." MS.
  Seção Theodoro Sampaio, pasta 2, documento 8.
  Coleção Gonçalo Moniz.
  Recenseamento de 1920.
Arquivo do Instituto Histórico e Geográfico Brasileiro, Rio de Janeiro.
  Arquivo do Barão de Cotegipe, João Maurício Wanderley [Arquivo Cotegipe].
  Coleção Araujo Pinho [Arquivo Araujo Pinho].
  Coleção Araujo Goes [Arquivo Araujo Goes].
Arquivo Municipal da Cidade de Salvador, Salvador.
  Seção Administrativa, Registro de Casamento Civil.
Arquivo Público do Estado da Bahia [APEB], Salvador.
  Seção Judiciária, Livros de Notas da Capital.
  Seção Judiciária, Autos Cíveis da Capital.
  Seção Judiciária, Inventários.
  Seção Histórica, Coleção Francisco Marques de Goes Calmon [Arquivo Goes Calmon].
  Seção Histórica, Coleção Wanderley Pinho [Arquivo Wanderley Pinho].
  Presidência da Província, Sociedades e Associações.
  Presidência da Província, Governo, Qualificações, Listas Eleitorais.
  Presidência da Província, Viação, Registros Ecclesiásticos de Terras, 1856–58.

Frões Papers, Salvador.
Forum Rui Barbosa, Salvador.
    Registro de Casamento Civil.
Instituto Feminino da Bahia, Salvador.
    Coleção Amélia Rodrigues [Arquivo Amélia Rodrigues].
Ribeiro Papers, Salvador.
    Bittencourt, Anna Ribeiro de Goes. "Memórias de D. Anna Ribeiro de Goes
    Bittencourt." Typescript. N.d. (ca. 1920–30).
United States National Archives.
    Dispatches from U.S. consuls in Bahia, 1850–1906. Vol. 6, May 6, 1890–
    December 15, 1894 (Microcopy T331, Roll 6).

Interviews

Orlando Moscoso Barretto de Araujo, Salvador, July 1980.
Inocêncio Marques de Goes Calmon, Salvador, July 1980.
Paulo Sérgio Freire de Carvalho, Salvador, July 1980.
Luis Raimundo Tourinho Dantas, Salvador, July 1980.
Berenice Diniz Gonçalves, Salvador, July 1980.
Clemente Mariani, Salvador, July 1980.
Hilda Noronha, Salvador, June 1981, June 1987.
Sister Maria Teresa, Mariana da Costa Pinto Dantas, Salvador, May 1981.
Stella Calmon Wanderley Pinho, Salvador, July 1980.
Maria dos Prazeres Calmon de Sá, Salvador, July 1980.
Consuelo Pondé de Sena, Salvador, June 1987.
Nelson Spínola Teixeira, Rio de Janeiro, August 1981.
Hildegardes Vianna, Salvador, December 1981.
Arnold Wildberger, Salvador, November 1981.

Printed Sources

"A propósito das Memórias Históricas das Faculdades de Medicina da Bahia e do
    Rio de Janeiro." *Gazeta Médica da Bahia* 3, 51 (September 15, 1868): 25–26.
Abreu, Edith Mendes da Gama e. "A Federação Bahiana pelo Progresso Femi-
    nino, fator de elevação social." In *IV Colóquio Internacional de Estudos Luso-
    Brasileiros, Bahia, agosto de 1959*, pp. 20–21. Bahia, n.d.
Adeodato Filho, José. *Parto em domicílio: Aspectos clínicos e sociaes*. Tese de
    concurso, Cátedra Obstétrica, Faculdade de Medicina da Bahia. Salvador, 1949.
Albernaz, Pedro de Barros. *Primeira infância (Hygiene e aleitamento)*. Tese de
    doutoramento, Faculdade de Medicina da Bahia. Salvador, 1898.
Albuquerque, José de. *Catecismo da educação sexual para uso de educandos e
    educadores*. Rio de Janeiro, 1940.
Aleixo, Renato Onofre Pinto. *Relatório do exercício de 1943 . . . pelo General
    Renato Onofre Pinto Aleixo, interventor federal no Estado da Bahia*. Salva-
    dor, 1944.
Almanach do Mensageiro da Fé para o anno de 1917. Salvador, 1917.
Almanak do Mensageiro da Fé para o anno de 1923. Salvador, 1923.
Almeida, Antônio Euzébio de. *Successão de morgado extincto / Apellação na acção*

proposta aos filhos naturaes reconhecidos do finado Major Jeronimo Sodré Pereira por D. Maria Clementina Sodré de Carvalho e outros . . . irman e sobrinhos d'aquelle major. Salvador, 1883.

Almeida, Júlia Lopes de. *Livro das noivas.* 3d ed. Rio de Janeiro, 1896.

Almeida, Lacerda de. "Carnavalescos." *A Voz* 6, 11 (February 1918): 161–63.

Almeida, Maria Amélia Ferreira de. "Feminismo na Bahia, 1930–1950." Dissertação de mestrado em Ciências Humanas, Universidade Federal da Bahia, 1986.

Almeida, Rômulo. *Traços da história econômica da Bahia no último século e meio.* Salvador, 1951.

Alves, Branca Moreira, and Leila de Andrade Linhares Barsted. "Permanência ou mudança: A legislação sobre família no Brasil." In *Sociedade brasileira contemporânea: Família e valores,* edited by Ivete Ribeiro, pp. 165–88. São Paulo, 1987.

Alves, Isaías. *Educação e brasildade (Idéias forças do Estado Novo).* Rio de Janeiro, 1939.

———. *Educação e saude na Bahia na Interventoria Landulpho Alves (Abril 1938–Junho 1939).* Salvador, 1939.

Alves, Maria Luiza de Souza. "Se todos fazem . . . ." *Mensageiro da Fé* 23, 10 (May 17, 1925): 73–74.

———. "Sou feminista: Monologo." In *Almanak do Mensageiro da Fé para o anno de 1923,* pp. 119–23. Salvador, 1923.

Alves, Marieta. "Amélia Rodrigues como a conheci." *A Tarde para Domingo,* May 27–28, 1961, pp. 6–7.

———. "Henriqueta Martins Catharino: Sua vida e sua obra." *Revista do Instituto Genealógico da Bahia* 18 (1972): 38–51.

Amado, Gilberto. *História da minha infância.* Rio de Janeiro, 1966.

Amado, Jorge. *Cacau.* 1933. 34th ed. Rio de Janeiro, 1980.

———. *Dona Flor and Her Two Husbands.* 1966. Translated by Harriet de Onís. New York, 1969.

———. *Gabriela, Clove and Cinnamon.* 1958. Translated by James L. Taylor and William Grossman. New York, 1962.

———. *Suor.* 1934. 31st ed. Rio de Janeiro, 1978.

———. *Tent of Miracles.* 1969. Translated by Barbara Shelby. New York, 1978.

———. *Terras do sem fim.* 1942. 42d ed. Rio de Janeiro, 1980.

———. *The Two Deaths of Quincas Wateryell.* 1961. Translated by Barbara Shelby. New York, 1965.

[Amaral, Braz do]. "Discurso do Dr. Braz do Amaral em 3 de maio de 1910 (sócios fallecidos)." *Revista do Instituto Geográfico e Histórico da Bahia* 17, 36 (1910): 124.

———. *História da Bahia do Império à República.* Salvador, 1923.

———. "Quadros de Goya." *Revista da Academia de Letras da Bahia* 5–7, 8–10 (June 1934–December 1936): 52–66.

———. *Recordações históricas.* Porto, 1921.

Amaral, José Alvares do. *Resumo chronologico e noticioso da Provincia da Bahia desde o seu descobrimento em 1500.* 1881. 2d ed. Revised by J. Teixeira Barros. Salvador, 1922.

Amaral, Luiz. "Pingos." *Lar Catholico* (September 9, 1923): 6.

Anderson, Nancy Fix. "Cousin Marriage in Victorian England." *Journal of Family History* 11, 3 (1986): 285–301.

Andrade, Mário de. *Os contos de Belazarte.* 1934. 7th ed. Belo Horizonte, 1980.

Andrews, C. C. *Brazil: Its Conditions and Prospects.* New York, 1887.

Antoine, Charles. *O integrismo brasileiro.* Rio de Janeiro, 1980.

Araripe, Tristão de Alencar. "Pater-Famílias no Brazil nos tempos coloniais." *Revista Trimensal do Instituto Histórico e Geográfico Brasileiro* 55, 2 (1893): 15–23.

Araujo, Heitor de. *Vinte anos de sertão.* Salvador, 1953.

Araujo, Joaquim Barretto de. *Reminiscências.* Salvador, 1979.

Ariès, Philippe. *Centuries of Childhood: A Social History of Family Life.* New York, 1962.

Armitage, John. *The History of Brazil, from the Period of the Arrival of the Braganza Family in 1808 to the Abdication of Don Pedro the First in 1831.* 2 vols. London, 1836.

Assis, Joaquim Maria Machado de. "Almas agradecidas." In *Contos.* São Paulo, 1979.

———. "O caso da vara." 1891. Translated by Helen Caldwell as "Rod of Justice" in *The Psychiatrist and Other Stories.* Berkeley, 1963.

———. *Dom Casmurro.* 1900. Translated by Helen Caldwell. Berkeley, 1966.

———. *Esau and Jacob.* 1904. Translated by Helen Caldwell. Berkeley, 1966.

———. "Galeria posthuma." In *Histórias sem data,* pp. 85–101. 1st ed. 1884. Rio de Janeiro, 1938.

Athayde, Johildo Lopes de. "La ville de Salvador au XIXe siècle: Aspects démographiques (D'apres les registres paroissaux)." Ph.D. diss., Université de Paris-X, 1975.

Aufderheide, Patricia. "Order and Violence: Social Deviance and Social Control in Brazil, 1780–1840." Ph.D. diss., University of Minnesota, 1976.

Augel, Moema Parente. *Visitantes estrangeiros na Bahia oitocentista.* São Paulo, 1980.

Azevedo, Aluísio de. *O homem.* 1887. São Paulo, 1970

———. *O mulato.* 1881. 3d ed. Rio de Janeiro, 1981.

Azevedo, Célia Maria Marinho de. *Onda negra, medo branco: O negro no imaginário das elites, século XIX.* Rio de Janeiro, 1987.

Azevedo, Eliane de. "The Anthropological and Cultural Meaning of Family Names in Bahia, Brazil." *Current Anthropology* 21, 3 (June 1980): 360–63.

Azevedo, José Sérgio Gabrielli de. "Industrialização e incentivos fiscais na Bahia: Uma tentativa de interpretação histórica." Tese de mestrado, Universidade Federal da Bahia, 1975.

Azevedo, Thales de. *As ciências sociais na Bahia: Notas para sua história.* Salvador, 1964.

———. "Discurso." *Revista da Academia de Letras da Bahia* 21 (1962–70): 37–44.

———. "Discurso no centenário do Dr. João de Sousa Pondé." *Revista do Instituto Genealógico da Bahia* 20 (1975): 137–62.

———. *Les Élites de couleur dans une ville brésilienne.* Paris, 1953.

———. "Family, Marriage, and Divorce in Brazil." In *Contemporary Cultures and*

Societies of Latin America, edited by Dwight B. Heath and Richard N. Adams, pp. 288–310. New York, 1965.

——. "Fazer a corte, no Brasil: O namoro e a paquera." *Caravelle: Cahiers du Monde Hispanique et Luso-Brésilien* 30 (1978): 117–26.

——. "Introdução." In Anna Ribeiro de Goes Bittencourt, "Memórias." Typescript. 1981.

——. *Namoro à antiga: Tradição e mudança.* Salvador, 1975.

——. "Namoro à antiga: Tradição e mudança." In *Família, psicologia e sociedade*, edited by Gilberto Velho and Sérvulo A. Figueira, pp. 219–75. Rio de Janeiro, 1981.

——. *Social Change in Brazil.* Latin American Monographs, No. 22. Gainesville, Fla., 1963.

Azzi, Riolando. *O catolicismo popular no Brasil.* Petrópolis, 1978.

——. "Dom Antônio Joaquim de Melo, bispo de São Paulo (1851–1861), e o movimento de reforma católica no seculo XIX." *Revista Eclesiástica Brasileira* 35, 140 (December 1975): 902–22.

——. "Família e valores no pensamento brasileiro (1870–1950): Um enfoque histórico." In *Sociedade brasileira contemporânea: Família e valores*, edited by Ivete Ribeiro, pp. 85–120. São Paulo, 1987.

——. "O início da restauração católica em Minas Gerais: 1920–1930." *Síntese Política Econômica Social* 14 (1978): 65–92.

Bacelar, Jeferson Afonso. *A família da prostituta.* São Paulo, 1982.

Bahia. Directoria do Serviço de Estatística do Estado da Bahia. *Anuário estatístico: Anno de 1924.* Vol. 1, *Território e população.* Salvador, 1926.

——. *O desenvolvimento progressivo da vida econômica da Bahia.* Salvador, 1925.

Bahia. Directoria Geral de Estatística e do Bem Estar Público da Bahia. *Anuário estatístico: Annos de 1926–1927.* Salvador, 1930.

——. *Anuário estatístico da Bahia: 1929–1930.* Salvador, 1930.

Bahia. Secretaria do Planejamento, Ciência e Tecnologia [SEPLANTEC]. Fundação de Pesquisas, CPE. *Bibliografia baiana.* 2 vols. Salvador, 1977.

Bahiano, João. "As modas." *Mensageiro da Fé* 17, 23 (December 7, 1919): 177–78.

——. "Casamento e arte doméstica." *Mensageiro da Fé* 20, 20 (October 15, 1922): 153–54.

Bahiense, Laura Amália de Souza. *Da alimentação das crianças na primeira infância.* Tese de doutoramento, Faculdade de Medicina da Bahia. Salvador, 1898.

"Baianos ilustres: Conselheiro Francisco Sodré Pereira." *Revista do Instituto Geográphico e Histórico da Bahia* 13, 32 (1906): 54–56.

Balmori, Diana, Stuart F. Voss, and Miles Wortman. *Notable Family Networks in Latin America.* Chicago, 1984.

Bandeira, Carlos Viana. *Lado a lado de Rui (1876–1923).* Rio de Janeiro, 1960.

Bandeira, Manuel. "Evocação do Recife." In *Estrela da vida inteira*, pp. 104–6. Rio de Janeiro, 1976.

Banfield, Edward. *The Moral Basis of a Backward Society.* Glencoe, Ill., 1958.

Barbosa, Mario de Lima. "Os antepassados de Ruy Barbosa." *Revista do Instituto Genealógico da Bahia* 5 (1950): 85–90.

Barbosa, Rui. *Correspondência de Rodolfo E. de Sousa Dantas*. Edited by Américo Jacobina Lacombe. Rio de Janeiro, 1973.

————. *Correspondência do Conselheiro Manuel P. de Souza Dantas*. Edited by Américo Jacobina Lacombe. Rio de Janeiro, 1962.

————. *Correspondência: Primeiros tempos. Curso jurídico. Colegas e parentes.* Edited by Américo Jacobina Lacombe. Rio de Janeiro, 1973.

————. *Mocidade e exílio: Cartas ao Conselheiro Albino José Barbosa de Oliveira e ao Dr. Antônio d'Araujo Ferreira Jacobina*. Edited by Américo Jacobina Lacombe. São Paulo, 1940.

————. *Obras completas* (1886), vol. 13, part 2, *Trabalhos diversos*. Rio de Janeiro, 1962.

Barboza, Mário Ferreira. *Dr. Goes Calmon: A sua vida e o seu governo*. Salvador, 1933.

Barman, Roderick, and Jean Barman. "The Role of the Law Graduate in the Political Elite of Imperial Brazil." *Journal of Interamerican Studies and World Affairs* 18, 4 (November 1976): 423–50.

Barreto, [Afonso Henriques de] Lima. *Recordações do escrivão Isaías Caminha*. 1909. 6th ed. São Paulo, 1976.

Barreto, Francisco Ferreira. *Obras religiosas e profanas*. Edited by Antônio Joaquim de Mello. 2 vols. Recife, 1874.

Barreto, Francisco Moniz. *Ao prematuro e chorado passamento da Excellentissima Senhora D. Antônia Thereza de Sá Pitta Argollo Wanderley, Baroneza de Cotegipe, Nênia recitada depois da missa do séptimo dia*. Salvador, 1864.

Bastide, Roger. *The African Religions of Brazil: Toward a Sociology of the Interpenetration of Civilizations*. Baltimore, 1978.

Benedict XV. "*Sacra propediem*: Encyclical on the Third Order of Saint Francis, January 6, 1921." In *The Papal Encyclicals*, edited by Claudia Carlen, vol. 3, *1903–1939*, pp. 207–10. Raleigh, N.C., 1981.

Besse, Susan. "Freedom and Bondage: The Impact of Capitalism on Women in São Paulo, Brazil, 1917–1937." Ph.D. diss., Yale University, 1983.

Beviláqua, Clovis. *Direito da família*. 1896. 5th rev. ed. Rio de Janeiro, 1933.

————. "Linhas gerais da evolução do direito constitucional, da família, e da propriedade." In *Linhas e perfis jurídicos*. Rio de Janeiro, 1930.

Binzer, Ina von. *Os meus romanos: Alegrias e tristezas de uma educadora alemã no Brasil*. 1887. Translated by Alice Rossi and Luisita da Gama Cerqueira. Rio de Janeiro, 1980.

Bittencourt, Anna Ribeiro de Goes. "Memórias de D. Anna Ribeiro de Goes Bittencourt." Typescript. N.d.

————. *Contos*. Prefácio de Anna Mariani Bittencourt Cabral. Salvador, 1980.

Boccanera Júnior, Sílio. "O theatro na Bahia." In *Diário Oficial do Estado da Bahia: Edição Especial do Centenário*, pp. 65–69. Salvador, 1923.

Boehrer, George. "The Brazilian Republican Revolution: Old and New Views." *Luso-Brazilian Review* 3, 2 (December 1966): 43–57.

————. "The Church in the Second Reign, 1840–1889." In *Conflict and Continuity in Brazilian Society*, edited by Henry H. Keith and S. F. Edwards, pp. 113–40. Columbia, S.C., 1969.

Borba Júnior, Antônio de Azevedo. *O aleitamento materno sob o ponto de vista médico-social.* Tese de doutoramento, Faculdade de Medicina da Bahia. Salvador, 1913.

Borchard, Edwin M. [and U.S. Library of Congress, Law Library]. *Guide to the Law and Legal Literature of Argentina, Brazil and Chile.* Washington, D.C., 1917.

Borges, Abílio Cesar. *Vinte annos de propaganda contra o emprego da palmatória e outros meios aviltantes no ensino da mocidade.* Brussels, 1880.

Borges, Dain. "El reverso fatal de los acontecimientos: Dos momentos de la degeneración en la literatura brasileña." In *La voluntad de humanismo: Homenaje a Juan Marichal,* edited by Biruté Ciplijauskaité and Christopher Mauer, pp. 121–33. Barcelona, 1990.

Bourdieu, Pierre. "Marriage Strategies as Strategies of Social Reproduction." In *Family and Society, Selections from the Annales,* edited by Robert Forster and Orest Ranum, pp. 117–44. Baltimore, 1976.

Brading, David. *Miners and Merchants in Bourbon Mexico, 1763–1810.* London, 1971.

Braga, Célia Maria Leal. "Os espanhóis em Salvador: Análise sociológica das possibilidades de assimilação de um grupo de imigrantes." Tese de concurso para profesor assistente em sociologia, Universidade Federal da Bahia, 1972.

Braga, Júlio Santana. "Sociedade Protetora dos Desvalidos: Uma agência de prestígio." Tese de mestrado, Universidade Federal da Bahia, 1975.

Brandão, Octávio de Sousa. *Do casamento e sua regulamentação.* Tese de doutoramento, Faculdade de Medicina da Bahia. Salvador, 1905.

Brandão, Rodrigo. *Carta do Dr. Rodrigo Brandão.* Salvador, 1900.

Brant, Alice Dayrell. *See* Morley, Helena.

Braudel, Fernand. "In Bahia, Brazil: The Present Explains the Past." In *On History,* pp. 165–76. Chicago, 1980.

Brazil. Centro Brasileiro de Pesquisas Educacionais. *Fontes para o estudo da educação no Brasil.* Vol. 1, *Bahia, fontes oficiais.* Rio de Janeiro, 1959.

Brazil. *Código civil dos Estados Unidos do Brasil* [Law 3071 of January 1, 1916]. Edited by Clovis Bevilaqua. 6 vols. Rio de Janeiro, 1938–45.

––––––. *Colleção das leis do Império do Brasil.* Rio de Janeiro, 1875.

Brazil. Departamento de Imprensa e Propaganda. *Constitution of the United States of Brazil with the Constitutional Laws Nos. 1, 2, 3 and 4.* Constitution of November 10, 1937. Rio de Janeiro, 1941.

Brazil. Directoria Geral de Estatística. *Annuaire statistique du Brésil: 1ère année: (1908–1912).* Vol. 1, *Territoire et population.* [Rio de Janeiro], 1916.

––––––. *Annuário estatístico do Brasil: Anno I (1908–1912).* Vol. 3, *Economia e finanças.* Rio de Janeiro, 1917.

––––––. [*Recenseamento da população do Imperio do Brazil a que se procedeu no dia 1º de agosto de 1872.*] *Quadros geraes do recenseamento de 1872.* [Rio de Janeiro, 1873–76].

––––––. *Synopse do recenseamento realizado em 1 de setembro 1920. População do Brazil. Resumo do censo demographico segundo as profissões, a nacionalidade, o sexo e a idade.* Rio de Janeiro, 1926.

————. *Synopse do recenseamento realizado em 1 de setembro 1920. População do Brasil. Resumo do censo demographico segundo o gráo de instrucção, a idade, o sexo e a nacionalidade.* Rio de Janeiro, 1925.

Brazil. Instituto Brasileiro de Geografia e Estatística [IBGE]. *Características demográficas do Estado da Bahia. Edição comemorativa do IV centenário da Cidade do Salvador.* 2d ed. Rio de Janeiro, 1949.

————. Conselho Nacional de Estatística. *A educação no Estado da Bahia. Repertório estatístico comemorativo do IV centenário da Cidade do Salvador.* Rio de Janeiro, 1949.

Brazil. Ministério de Justiça. Commissão Especial do Código Civil. *Atas da commissão revisora do projecto de código civil brazileiro elaborado pelo Dr. Clovis Beviláqua.* Rio de Janeiro, 1900.

Brazil. Senado Federal. *O parlamento e a evolução nacional, 1871–1889.* Edited by Fábio Vieira Bruno. 5 vols. Brasília, 1980.

Bruneau, Thomas. *The Church in Brazil.* Austin, 1982.

————. *The Political Transformation of the Brazilian Catholic Church.* London, 1975.

Bulcão, Octávio de Aragão. *O Colégio Antônio Vieira do meu tempo—1927/1933.* Salvador, 1977.

Bulcão Sobrinho, Antônio de Araujo de Aragão. "A ascendência do governador da Bahia, Dr. Luiz Regis Pacheco Pereira." *Revista do Instituto Genealógico da Bahia* 7 (1952): 45–52.

————. "Chefes de polícia da Bahia no Império, 1822–1889." *Revista do Instituto Histórico e Geográfico Brasileiro* 253 (October–December 1961): 13–33.

————. *Famílias bahianas.* 3 vols. Salvador, 1945–46.

————. "Famílias bahianas: Família Bulcão." *Revista do Instituto Genealógico da Bahia* 13 (1961): 1–83, and 14 (1962): 81–175.

————. "Representantes da Bahia na Câmara Federal da Primeira República." *Revista do Instituto Histórico e Geográfico Brasileiro* 263 (April–June 1964): 55–86.

————. "Titulares bahianos." *Revista do Instituto Genealógico da Bahia* 2 (1946): 26–40.

Bulhões, Leopoldo de. *Leopoldo de Bulhões: Discursos parlamentares.* Edited by Wagner Estelita Campos. Brasília, 1979.

Cabral, Alfredo do Vale. *Achegas ao estudo do folclore brasileiro.* Edited by José Calasans Brandão da Silva. Rio de Janeiro, 1978.

Cabral, Ana Mariani Bittencourt. "Prefácio." In Anna Ribeiro de Goes Bittencourt, *Contos.* Salvador, 1980.

Cabussú, Alfredo Cesar, Glycerio José Velloso da Silva, Joaquim Climerio Dantas Bião, Cyrdião Durval, and Dionizio Gonçalves Martins; Lyceu Rui Barbosa. *Memória sobre o ensino secundário e seo necessário desenvolvimento no Estado da Bahia.* Salvador, 1894.

Calasans, José. *A Faculdade Livre de Direito da Bahia (Subsídios para sua história).* Salvador, 1984.

Calmon, Francisco Marques de Goes. *Mensagem apresentada pelo Exmo. Snr.*

Dr. Francisco Marques de Goes Calmon governador do Estado da Bahia . . . em 7 de abril de 1925. Salvador, 1925.

———. *Mensagem apresentada pelo Exmo. Snr. Dr. Francisco Marques de Goes Calmon governador do Estado da Bahia . . . em 7 de abril de 1927.* Salvador, 1927.

———. *Vida econômico-financieira da Bahia: Elementos para a história de 1808 a 1899.* Salvador, 1982.

Calmon, Pedro. *História da Casa da Torre: Uma dinastia de pioneiros.* 2d ed. Rio de Janeiro, 1958.

Câmara, José Gomes B. *Subsídios para a história do direito pátrio.* 4 vols. Rio de Janeiro, 1964–67.

Camino, Luiz da. *Educação: Livro dos bons costumes.* Salvador, 1913.

Campbell, J. K. *Honour, Family and Patronage: A Study of Institutions and Moral Values in a Greek Mountain Community.* Oxford, 1964.

Campos, João da Silva. "Apontamentos folclóricos." *Revista da Academia de Letras da Bahia* 5–7, 8–10 (June 1934–December 1936): 153.

———. "Crônicas bahianas do século XIX." *Annaes do Archivo Público da Bahia* 25 (1937): 295–365.

Cândido [de Mello e Souza], Antônio. "The Brazilian Family." In *Brazil: Portrait of Half a Continent,* edited by T. Lynn Smith and Alexander Marchant, pp. 291–312. New York, 1951.

———. "Dialética da malandragem (Caracterização das *Memórias de um sargento de milícias*)." *Revista do Instituto de Estudos Brasileiros* 8 (1970): 67–89.

———. "Literatura e cultura de 1900 a 1945 (Panorama para estrangeiros)." In *Literatura e sociedade: Estudos de teoria e história literária,* pp. 109–38. 5th ed. São Paulo, 1976.

———. *Os parceiros do Rio Bonito: Estudo sobre o caipira paulista e a transformação dos seus meios de vida.* 4th ed. São Paulo, 1977.

Cardoso, Ciro Flamarion de. "The Peasant Breach in the Slave System: New Developments in Brazil." *Luso-Brazilian Review* 25, 1 (Summer 1988): 49–58.

Cardoso, Fernando Henrique. *Empresário industrial e desenvolvimento econômico.* São Paulo, 1964.

———. *Political Regime and Social Change: Some Reflections Concerning the Brazilian Case.* Stanford-Berkeley Occasional Papers in Latin American Studies, No. 3. Stanford, 1981.

Cardozo, Manoel. "The Holy See and the Question of the Bishop-Elect of Rio, 1833–1839." *The Americas* 10 (1953–54): 3–74.

Carneiro, Júlio Cesar de Morais. *See* Maria, Júlio.

Carteado, Enoch. *Da cultura d'alma na infância.* Tese de doutoramento, Faculdade de Medicina da Bahia. Salvador, 1913.

Carvalho, José Murilo de. *Os bestializados: O Rio de Janeiro e a República que não foi.* São Paulo, 1987.

———. *A construção da ordem: A elite política imperial.* Rio de Janeiro, 1980.

———. "Elite and State-Building in Imperial Brazil." Ph.D. diss., Stanford University, 1975.

[Carvalho, Sebastião Pinto de]. *Successão de morgado extincto / Libello e allegações finais / Acção proposta pelos herdeiros legítimos da linha do instituidor contra os filhos naturaes do último administrador.* Salvador, 1882.

Casamento civil: Recapitulação em ordem alphabética do Decreto n. 181 de 24 de janeiro de 1890 e dos demais que se seguiram. Compiled by Manuel André da Rocha. Rio de Janeiro, 1890.

Cássia, Rita de. *Memórias de Veridiana, 1869–1969.* Salvador, 1970.

Castro, Dinorah D'Araujo Berbert de. "Idéias filosóficas nas teses inaugurais da Faculdade de Medicina da Bahia (1838–1889)." Tese de mestrado, Universidade Federal da Bahia, 1973.

Castro, Epaminondas Berbert de. "Dois metros e cinco." *Revista da Academia de Letras da Bahia* 16 (1955): 16–26.

Castro, Mary Garcia. "Mundança, mobilidade e valores (Uma experiência no Recôncavo baiano: São Francisco do Conde)." Dissertação de mestrado em Ciências Humanas, Universidade Federal da Bahia, 1971.

Castro, Renato Berbert de. *Em torno da vida de Junqueira Freire.* Salvador, 1980.

———. *Os vice-presidentes da Província da Bahia.* Salvador, 1978.

Castro, Viveiros de. *Attentados ao pudor (Estudo sobre as aberrações do instincto sexual).* Rio de Janeiro, 1895.

Castro-Santos, Luiz Antonio de. "Power, Ideology, and Public Health in Brazil, 1889–1930." Ph.D. diss., Harvard University, 1987.

Cerqueira, Mário Cardoso de. *Prophylaxia alimentar da primeira infância.* Tese de doutoramento, Faculdade de Medicina da Bahia. Salvador, 1903.

Chamberlain, J. Edward, and Sander L. Gilman, eds. *Degeneration: The Dark Side of Progress.* New York, 1985.

Chandler, Billy Jaynes. *The Feitosas and the Sertão dos Inhamuns: The History of a Family and a Community in Northeast Brazil, 1700–1930.* Gainesville, Fla., 1972.

Chastinet, Mancos. "Discurso de posse do Acadêmico Mancos Chastinet." *Revista da Academia de Letras da Bahia* 3, 4–5 (June–December 1932): 1–23.

Chernoviz, Pedro Luiz Napoleão. *Diccionário de medicina popular e das sciências accessórias.* 2 vols. 4th ed. Paris, 1870.

———. *Formulário e guia médico.* 13th ed. Paris, 1888.

Chevalier, Ramayana de. "Elegâncias." *Arco & Flexa* 4–5 (1929): 29. Facsimile edition. Salvador, 1978.

The Civil Code of Brazil, Being Law No. 3071 of January 1, 1916. Translated by Joseph Wheless. St. Louis, 1920.

Coatsworth, John. "Obstacles to Economic Growth in Nineteenth-Century Mexico." *American Historical Review* 83, 1 (February 1978): 80–100.

Código Philippino ou Ordenações e leis do reino do Portugal. Edited by Cândido Mendes de Almeida. 14th ed. Rio de Janeiro, 1870.

Cole, John, and Eric Wolf. *The Hidden Frontier: Ecology and Ethnicity in an Alpine Valley.* New York, 1974.

Colson, Roger Frank. "The Destruction of a Revolution: Polity, Economy and Society in Brazil, 1750–1895." Ph.D. diss., Princeton University, 1979.

————. "On Expectations—Perspectives on the Crisis of 1889 in Brazil." *Journal of Latin American Studies* 13, 2 (1981): 265–92.

Coni, Antônio Caldas. *A escola tropicalista bahiana: Paterson, Wucherer, Silva Lima*. Salvador, 1952.

Conniff, Michael. "Voluntary Associations in Rio, 1870–1945: A New Approach to Urban Social Dynamics." *Journal of Inter-American Studies and World Affairs* 17, 1 (February 1975): 64–82.

Conrad, Robert. *Children of God's Fire: A Documentary History of Black Slavery in Brazil*. Princeton, 1983.

————. *The Destruction of Brazilian Slavery, 1850–1888*. Berkeley, 1972.

————. "The Planter Class and the Debate over Chinese Immigration to Brazil, 1850–1893." *International Migrations Review* 9, 1 (Spring 1975): 41–55.

Constituições primeiras do arcebispado da Bahia feitas, e ordenadas pelo Illustrissimo e Reverendissimo Senhor D. Sebastião Monteiro da Vide, 5° arcebispo do dito arcebispado, e do conselho de Sua Magestade: Propostas, e aceitas em o synodo diocesano, que o dito senhor celebrou em 12 de junho do anno de 1707. São Paulo, 1853.

Corrêa, Mariza. *Os crimes de paixão*. São Paulo, 1981.

————. "As ilusões da liberdade: A Escola Nina Rodrigues e a antropologia no Brasil." Ph.D. diss., Faculdade de Filosofia, Letras e Ciências Humanas da Universidade de São Paulo, 1982.

Costa, Afonso. "Manuel Victorino Pereira." *Revista da Academia de Letras da Bahia* 15 (1954): 30–43.

Costa, Emília Viotti da. *Da monarquia à república: Momentos decisivos*. 2d ed. São Paulo, 1979.

————. "The Myth of Racial Democracy." In *The Brazilian Empire: Myths and Histories*. Chicago, 1985.

Costa, José Antonio. "Corréios, telégrafos, e telephones na Bahia." In *Diário Oficial do Estado da Bahia: Edição especial do centenário*, pp. 56–64. Salvador, 1923.

Costa, Jurandir Freire. *História da psiquiatria no Brasil*. Rio de Janeiro, 1976.

————. *Ordem médica e norma familiar*. Rio de Janeiro, 1979.

Cova, [João Macário de] Guimarães. *A esposa: Livro doutrinário e moralista para as noivas e mães de família*. 2d ed. Salvador, 1914.

Cruz, Levy. "Aspectos da formação e desintegração da família em Rio Rico." *Sociologia* 16, 4 (October 1954): 390–412.

Cunha, Euclides da. *Rebellion in the Backlands*. 1902. Translated by Samuel Putnam. Chicago, 1944.

Cunha, Rui Vieira da. *O parlamento e a nobreza brasileira*. Brasília, 1979.

Da Matta, Roberto. *Carnavais, malandros e heróis: Para uma sociologia do dilema brasileiro*. Rio de Janeiro, 1979.

————. *A casa & a rua: Espaço, cidadania, mulher e morte no Brasil*. Rio de Janeiro, 1987.

————. "*Dona Flor e seus dois maridos*: A Relational Novel." *Social Science Information* 21, 1 (1982): 19–46.

————. "The Ethic of Umbanda and the Spirit of Messianism: Reflections on the Brazilian Model." In *Authoritarian Capitalism: Brazil's Contemporary Economic and Political Development*, edited by Thomas Bruneau and Philippe Faucher, pp. 237–65. Boulder, Colo., 1981.

————. "Virgindade: O tabú sobrevive em 1984?" In *Explorações: Ensaios de sociologia interpretativa*, pp. 129–32. Rio de Janeiro, 1986.

Dantas Júnior [João da Costa Pinto]. "Algumas famílias bahianas: Lopes de Santo Amaro." *Revista do Instituto Genealógico da Bahia* 12 (1960): 29–38.

————. "Capitão-Mor João D'Antas dos Imperiais Itapicurú." *Revista do Instituto Genealógico da Bahia* 15 (1967): 15–222.

————. "Desembargador Pedro Ribeiro de Araujo Bittencourt," *Revista do Instituto Genealógico da Bahia* 16 (1968): 117–18.

d'Avila, Carmen. *Boas maneiras*. Rio de Janeiro, 1942.

Davis, Natalie. "Ghosts, Kin, and Progeny: Some Features of Family Life in Early Modern France." *Dædalus* 106, 2 (Spring 1977): 87–114.

Dean, Warren. "Latifundio and Land Policy in Nineteenth-Century Brazil." *Hispanic American Historical Review* 51, 4 (September 1971): 606–26.

————. *The Industrialization of São Paulo, 1880–1945*. Austin, 1969.

Degler, Carl. *Neither Black nor White: Slavery and Race Relations in Brazil and the United States*. New York, 1971.

Della Cava, Ralph. "Brazilian Messianism and National Institutions: A Reappraisal of Canudos and Joaseiro." *Hispanic American Historical Review* 48 (August 1968): 402–20.

————. "Catholicism and Society in Twentieth-Century Brazil." *Latin American Research Review* 11, 2 (1976): 7–50.

————. *Miracle at Joaseiro*. New York, 1970.

Diamantino, Pedro. *Juàzeiro de minha infância: Memórias*. Rio de Janeiro, 1959.

Diário Oficial do Estado da Bahia: Edição especial do centenário. July 2, 1923. Salvador, 1923.

Donzelot, Jacques. *The Policing of Families*. New York, 1979.

Dornas Filho, João. *O Padroado e a igreja brasileira*. São Paulo, 1938.

Douglas, Mary. *Purity and Danger: An Analysis of the Concepts of Pollution and Taboo*. London, 1966.

Duarte, Nestor. *A ordem privada e a organização política nacional (Contribuição à sociologia política brasileira)*. 1939. 2d ed. São Paulo, 1966.

Dulles, John. *Anarchists and Communists in Brazil, 1900–1935*. Austin, 1973.

Eisenberg, Peter. *The Sugar Industry in Pernambuco: Modernization Without Change, 1840–1910*. Berkeley, 1974.

Ellis Júnior, Alfredo. *Raça de gigantes*. 1926. 2d ed. *Os primeiros troncos paulistas*. São Paulo, 1976.

Eskelund, Karl. *Drums in Bahia: Travels in Brazil*. London, 1960.

Estatutos da Confraria das Senhoras da Caridade. Salvador, 1908.

Estatutos do Collégio Archiepiscopal Patrocínio em São José das Tres Ilhas. Juiz de Fora, 1923.

Evans, Peter. *Dependent Development: The Alliance of Multinational, State, and Local Capital in Brazil*. Princeton, 1979.

"Faculdade de Direito da Bahia." In *Diário Oficial do Estado da Bahia: Edição especial do centenário*, p. 360. Salvador, 1923.

Faculdade de Filosofia e Ciencias Humanas, Universidade Federal da Bahia, 1941–1981. Salvador, 1981.

Fausto, Boris. "As crises dos anos vinte e a revolução de 1930." In *Historia geral da civilização brasileira*, part 3, O Brasil republicano, vol. 2, *Sociedade e instituicoes (1889–1930)*, pp. 401–26. São Paulo, 1977.

———. *Crime e cotidiano: A criminalidade em São Paulo (1880–1924)*. São Paulo, 1984.

———. *A revolução de 1930: História e historiografia*. São Paulo, 1970.

———. *Trabalho urbano e conflito social (1890–1920)*. São Paulo, 1976.

Fernandes, Florestan. *The Negro in Brazilian Society*. New York, 1969.

Ferreira, Manuel Alves, ed. *Questão de honra: Colleção dos escriptos do Alabama*. Salvador, 1878.

Fiorentino, Teresinha Aparecida Del. *Utopia e realidade: O Brasil no começo do século XX*. São Paulo, 1979.

Flandrin, Jean-Louis. *Families in Former Times: Kinship, Household, and Sexuality*. London, 1979.

Fletcher, James C., and Daniel P. Kidder. *Brazil and the Brazilians*. 6th rev. ed. London, 1866.

Flory, Rae. "Bahian Society in the Mid-Colonial Period: The Sugar Planters, Tobacco Growers, Merchants and Artisans of Salvador and the Recôncavo, 1680–1725." Ph.D. diss., University of Texas at Austin, 1978.

Flory, Rae, and David Grant Smith. "Bahian Merchants and Planters in the Seventeenth and Early Eighteenth Centuries." *Hispanic American Historical Review* 58, 4 (1978): 571–94.

Flory, Thomas. *Judge and Jury in Imperial Brazil, 1808–1871: Social Control and Political Stability in the New State*. Austin, 1981.

———. "Race and Social Control in Independent Brazil." *Journal of Latin American Studies* 9, 2 (November 1977): 199–224.

Foucault, Michel. *The History of Sexuality*. Vol. 1, *An Introduction*. New York, 1980.

França, Alípio. *Escola Normal da Bahia: Memória histórica, 1836 a 1936*. Salvador, 1936.

Franca, Leonel. *O divórcio*. 7th ed. Rio de Janeiro, 1952.

França, Manoel José da. *Syphilis e amamentação*. Tese de doutoramento, Faculdade de Medicina da Bahia. Salvador, 1918.

Franco, Maria Sylvia de Carvalho. *Homens livres na ordem escravocrata*. 2d ed. São Paulo, 1976.

Frazier, E. Franklin. "The Negro Family in Bahia, Brazil." *American Sociological Review* 7, 4 (August 1942): 465–78.

Frederickson, George M. *The Black Image in the White Mind: The Debate on Afro-American Character and Destiny, 1817–1914*. New York, 1971.

Freire-Maia, Newton. "Consanguineous Marriages and Inbreeding Load." In *The Ongoing Evolution of Latin American Populations*, edited by Francisco M. Salzano, pp. 189–220. Springfield, Ill., 1971.

Freitas, [Augusto] Teixeira de. *Consolidação das leis civis*. 1858. 5th ed. Annotated by Martinho Garcez. Rio de Janeiro, 1915.

Freyre, Gilberto. *Casa-grande e senzala (Formação da família brasileira sob o regime de economia patriarcal)*. 1933. 4th ed. Rio de Janeiro, 1943.

———. *Manifesto regionalista*. 1926. 4th ed. Recife, 1967.

———. *The Mansions and the Shanties: The Making of Modern Brazil*. A translation by Harriet de Onís of *Sobrados e mucambos* (1936). Berkeley, 1986.

———. *The Masters and the Slaves: A Study in the Development of Brazilian Civilization*. A translation by Samuel Putnam of *Casa-grande e senzala* (1933). Berkeley, 1986.

———. *Ordem e progresso: Processo de desintegração das sociedades patriarcal e semipatriarcal no Brasil sob o regime do trabalho livre: Aspectos de um quase méio século de transição do trabalho escravo para o trabalho livre; e da monarquia para a república*. 2 vols. Rio de Janeiro, 1959.

———. *Order and Progress: Brazil from Monarchy to Republic*. Edited and translated by Rod W. Horton. New York, 1970.

———. *Sobrados e mucambos: Decadência do patriarcado rural e desenvolvimento do urbano*. 1936. 6th ed. 2 vols. Rio de Janeiro, 1981.

———. "Social Life in Brazil in the Middle of the Nineteenth Century." *Hispanic American Historical Review* 2 (1922): 597–630.

Frões, João A. Garcez. "O Barão de Villa Viçosa, homem de letras." *Revista da Academia de Letras da Bahia* 18 (1957): 184.

Fry, Peter. "Two Religious Movements: Protestantism and Umbanda." In *Manchester and São Paulo: Problems of Rapid Urban Growth*, edited by John Wirth and Robert Jones, pp. 177–202. Stanford, 1978.

Fry, Peter, Sérgio Carrara, and Ana Luiza Martins-Costa. "Negros e brancos no Carnaval da Velha República." In *Escravidão e invenção da liberdade: Estudos sobre o negro no Brasil*, edited by João José Reis, pp. 232–63. São Paulo, 1988.

Galloway, J. H. "The Last Years of Slavery on the Sugar Plantations of Northeastern Brazil." *Hispanic American Historical Review* 51, 4 (November 1971): 586–605.

Gama, Mário. "Como os 'sports' se iniciaram e progrediram na Bahia." In *Diário Oficial do Estado da Bahia: Edição especial do centenário*, pp. 319–21. Salvador, 1923.

Garcez, Angelina Nobre Rolim. *Associação Commercial da Bahia, 175 anos: Trajetoria e perspectivas*. Rio de Janeiro, 1987.

———. *Instituto de Cacau da Bahia, meio século de história*. Salvador, 1981.

———. *Joaquim Inácio Tosta Filho: Biografia*. Salvador, 1986.

———. "Mecanismos de formação da propriedade cacaueira no eixo Itabuna-Ilhéus 1890–1930 (Um estudo de História Agrária)." Tese de mestrado em Ciências Sociais, Universidade Federal da Bahia.

Garcez, Angelina Nobre Rolim, and Antonio Fernando Guerreiro de Freitas. *Bahia cacaueira: Um estudo de história recente*. Salvador, 1979.

Garnier, P. *O matrimônio considerado nos seus deveres, relações e effeitos conjugaes sob o ponto de vista legal, hygiênico, physiológico e moral*. Paris, n.d.

Geertz, Clifford. "Common Sense as a Cultural System." *Antioch Review* 33, 1 (Spring 1975): 5–26.

Geribello, Wanda Pompeu. *Anísio Teixeira: Análise e sistematização de sua obra*. São Paulo, 1977.

Gerson, Brasil. *O regalismo brasileiro*. Rio de Janeiro, 1978.

Glendon, Mary Ann. *The New Family and the New Property*. Toronto, 1981.

———. *State, Law and Family: Family Law in Transition in the United States and Western Europe*. Amsterdam, 1977.

———. *The Transformation of Family Law: State, Law, and Family in the United States and Western Europe*. Chicago, 1989.

Goes Calmon: In memoriam. Rio de Janeiro, 1933.

Gomes, Angela Maria de Castro. *Burguesia e trabalho: Política e legislação social no Brasil, 1917–1937*. Rio de Janeiro, 1979.

Gomes, Eugênio. *O mundo da minha infância: Memórias*. Rio de Janeiro, 1969.

Gomes, Ordival Cassiano. *Manuel Victorino Pereira: Médico e cirurgião*. Rio de Janeiro, 1957.

———. *O pai de Rui: Dr. João José Barbosa de Oliveira*. Rio de Janeiro, 1949.

Goode, William. "The Theoretical Importance of Love." *American Sociological Review* 24 (1959): 38–47.

———. *World Revolution and Family Patterns*. Rev. ed. New York, 1970.

Goody, Jack. *The Development of the Family and Marriage in Europe*. Cambridge, 1983.

Gordilho, Walter Veloso. "O sítio urbano—seu desenvolvimento." In *A grande Salvador: Posse e uso da terra*, edited by Cydelmo Teixeira, ch. 10. Salvador, 1978.

Goulart, Octaviano de Abreu. *Hygiene alimentar da primeira infância*. Tese de doutoramento, Faculdade de Medicina da Bahia. Salvador, 1900.

Gouvéia, [Raymundo Nonato de] Almeida. *Puericultura social: Natimortalidade—mortalidade neonatal: Salvador Bahia 1940–6*. Tese de docência livre de Clínica Pediátrica Médica e Higiene Infantil, Faculdade de Medicina da Bahia. Salvador, 1947.

Graham, Lawrence S. *Civil Service Reform in Brazil: Principles Versus Practice*. Austin, 1968.

Graham, Maria. *Journal of a Voyage to Brazil, and Residence There, During Part of the Years 1821, 1822, 1823*. London, 1824.

Graham, Richard. *Patronage and Politics in Nineteenth-Century Brazil*. Stanford, 1990.

Graham, Sandra Lauderdale. *House and Street: The Domestic World of Masters and Servants in Nineteenth-Century Rio de Janeiro*. Cambridge, Engl., 1986.

Grupo Ceres [Branca Moreira Alves, Jacqueline Pitanguy, Leila Linhares Barsted, Mariska Ribeiro, and Sandra Boschi]. *Espelho de Vênus: Identidade social e sexual da mulher*. São Paulo, 1981.

Gudeman, Stephen, and Stuart Schwartz. "Cleansing Original Sin: Godparenthood and the Baptism of Slaves in Eighteenth-Century Bahia." In *Kinship Ideology and Practice in Latin America*, edited by Raymond T. Smith, pp. 35–58. Chapel Hill, N.C., 1984.

Guimarães, A. Ferreira. *Deve ser regulamentada a prostituição?* Tese de doutoramento, Faculdade de Medicina da Bahia. Salvador, 1899.

Guimarães, Emílio. *Brasil-acordãos (Repertório de jurisprudência dos tribunais brasileiros).* Rio de Janeiro, 1935.

Haberly, David. "Abolitionism in Brazil: Anti-Slavery and Anti-Slave." *Luso-Brazilian Review* 9, 2 (December 1972): 30–46.

Hahner, June. "Women and Work in Brazil, 1850–1920: A Preliminary Investigation." In *Essays Concerning the Socioeconomic History of Brazil and Portuguese India,* edited by Dauril Alden and Warren Dean, pp. 87–117. Gainesville, Fla., 1977.

———. *A mulher brasileira e suas lutas sociais e políticas, 1850–1937.* São Paulo, 1981.

Hajnal, J[ohn]. "European Marriage Patterns in Perspective." In *Population in History: Essays in Historical Demography,* edited by D. V. Glass and D. E. C. Eversley, pp. 101–46. London, 1965.

Hall, Peter Dobkin. "Family Structure and Economic Organization: Massachusetts Merchants, 1700–1850." In *Family and Kin in Urban Communities, 1700–1930,* edited by Tamara Hareven, pp. 38–61. New York, 1977.

———. "Marital Selection and Business in Massachusetts Merchant Families, 1700–1900." In *The American Family in Social-Historical Perspective,* edited by Michael Gordon, pp. 101–14. 2d ed. New York, 1978.

Harris, Marvin. *Town and Country in Brazil.* New York, 1956.

Hauck, João Fagundes, Hugo Fragoso, José Oscar Beozzo, Klaus van der Grijp, and Benno Brod. *História da igreja no Brasil: Ensaio de interperetação a partir do povo.* Vol. 2, *Segunda época: A igreja no Brasil no século XIX.* História Geral da Igreja na América Latina, Part 2. Petrópolis, 1980.

Heriberto Filho, P. B. "Os primos e o casamento." *Mensageiro da Fé* 23, 10 (May 17, 1925): 79.

Holanda, Sérgio Buarque de. *História geral da civilização brasileira,* part 2, *O Brasil monárquico,* vol. 5, *Do Império à República.* São Paulo, 1977.

———. *Raízes do Brasil.* 1936. 14th ed. Rio de Janeiro, 1981.

Hollingsworth, T. H. *The Demography of the British Peerage.* Supplement to *Population Studies* 14, 2 (1964): i–108.

———. *Historical Demography.* Ithaca, N.Y., 1969.

Homenagem de amigos e admiradores do Exmo. Sr. Dr. Miguel Calmon du Pin e Almeida. Salvador, 1911.

Hoornaert, Eduardo. *Formação do catolicismo brasileiro, 1550–1800: Ensaio de interpretação a partir de oprimidos.* Petrópolis, 1974.

Hoornaert, Eduardo, Riolando Azzi, Klaus van der Grijp, and Benno Brod. *História da igreja no Brasil: Ensaio de interpretação a partir do povo.* Vol. 1, *Primeira época.* História Geral da Igreja na América Latina, Part 2. Petrópolis, 1979.

Hora, Lauro Dantas. *Mortalidade infantil na Bahia (capital), 1904–1918.* Tese de doutoramento, Faculdade de Medicina da Bahia. Salvador, 1922.

Hutchinson, Bertram. *Mobilidade e trabalho: Um estudo na cidade de São Paulo.* Rio de Janeiro, 1960.

Hutchinson, Carmelita Junqueira Ayres. "Notas preliminares ao estudo da família no Brasil." In *Anais da II Reunião Brasileira de Antropologia, Bahia, Julho de 1955*, pp. 261–74. Salvador, 1957.

Hutchinson, Henry William. *Village and Plantation Life in Northeastern Brazil.* Seattle, 1957.

In memoriam Dra. Francisca Praguer Frões. Edited by Anísio Circundes. Salvador, 1932.

Jambeiro, Raphael José. *A hereditariedade da tuberculose pulmonar deve-se [sustentar] deante da etiologia parasitária?* Tese de doutoramento, Faculdade de Medicina da Bahia. Salvador, 1885.

Jancso, Istvan. "As exportações da Bahia durante a República Velha (1889–1930), considerações preliminares." In *Colloque international sur l'histoire quantitative du Brésil de 1800 a 1930, Paris, 1971*, edited by Frederic Mauro, pp. 335–59. Paris, 1973.

Katz, Stanley N. "Republicanism and the Law of Inheritance in the American Revolutionary Era." *Michigan Law Review* 76 (1977–78): 1–29.

Kehl, Renato. "Eugenics Abroad, III: In Brazil." *Eugenics Review* 23, 3 (October 1931): 234–36.

Kelleman, Peter. *Brasil para principiantes: Venturas e desventuras de um brasileiro naturalizado.* Rio de Janeiro, 1960.

Kennedy, John Norman. "Bahian Elites, 1750–1822." *Hispanic American Historical Review* 53, 3 (August 1973): 415–39.

Kuznesof, Elizabeth. *Household Economy and Urban Development: São Paulo, 1765–1836.* Boulder, Colo., 1986.

Laclau, Ernesto. *Politics and Ideology in Marxist Theory.* London, 1979.

Lages, Waldemar. *Contribuição ao estudo da mortalidade infantil na Cidade do Salvador.* Tese de docência livre para cadeira de Pediatria Médica e Hygiene Infantil, Faculdade de Medicina da Bahia. Salvador, 1940.

Landes, Ruth. *The City of Women.* New York, 1947.

Lasch, Christopher. "The Freudian Left and Cultural Revolution." *New Left Review* 129 (September–October 1981): 23–34.

———. *Haven in a Heartless World: The Family Besieged.* New York, 1979.

Leal, Herundino da Costa. *Vida e passado de Santo Amaro.* Salvador, 1950.

Leal, Victor Nunes. *Coronelismo: The Municipality and Representative Government in Brazil.* 1949. Translated by June Henfrey. Cambridge, Engl., 1977.

Leeds, Anthony. "Brazilian Careers and Social Structure: A Case History and Model." In *Contemporary Cultures and Societies of Latin America*, edited by Dwight Heath and Richard N. Adams, pp. 379–404. New York, 1965.

———. "Economic Cycles in Brazil: The Persistence of a Total Culture Pattern: Cacao and Other Cases." Ph.D. diss., Columbia University, 1957.

Leff, Nathaniel. "Economic Development and Regional Inequality: Origins of the Brazilian Case." *Quarterly Journal of Economics* 86, 2 (May 1972): 243–62.

———. *Underdevelopment and Development in Brazil.* Vol. 1, *Economic Structure and Change, 1822–1947*; vol. 2, *Reassessing the Obstacles to Economic Development.* London, 1982.

Lemos, A. C. *Cozinhas, etc.* São Paulo, 1972.

Lenharo, Alcir. *Sacralização da política.* Campinas, 1986.

Leo XIII. "*Arcanum*: Encyclical of Pope Leo XIII on Christian Marriage, February 10, 1880." In *The Papal Encyclicals*, edited by Claudia Carlen. Vol. 2, *1878–1903*, pp. 29–40. Raleigh, N.C., 1981.

——. "*Dum multa*: Encyclical of Pope Leo XIII on Marriage Legislation, December 24, 1902." In *The Papal Encyclicals*, edited by Claudia Carlen. Vol. 2, *1878–1903*, pp. 517–18. Raleigh, N.C., 1981.

Léonard, Jacques. *La Vie quotidienne du médecin de province au XIXe siècle*. Paris, 1979.

Lerner, Gerda. *The Creation of Patriarchy*. New York, 1986.

Levi, Darrell. "The Prado Family, European Culture, and the Rediscovery of Brazil, 1860–1930." *Revista de História* 104 (1975): 803–23.

——. *The Prados of São Paulo, Brazil: An Elite Family and Social Change, 1840–1930*. Athens, Ga., 1987.

Levine, Robert. "Mud-Hut Jerusalem: Canudos Revisited." *Hispanic American Historical Review* 68, 3 (August 1988): 525–72.

——. *Pernambuco in the Brazilian Federation, 1889–1937*. Stanford, 1979.

Lewin, Linda. *Politics and Parentela in Paraíba: A Case Study of Family-Based Oligarchy in Brazil*. Princeton, 1987.

——. "Some Historical Implications of Kinship Organization for Family-Based Politics in the Brazilian Northeast." *Comparative Studies in Society and History* 21, 2 (April 1979): 262–92.

Lima, Alceu Amoroso. *Idade, sexo e tempo: Três aspectos da psicologia humana*. 3d ed. Rio de Janeiro, 1940.

Lima, Armando Vieira. *Pediátrica médica e hygiene infantil*. Tese de doutoramento, Faculdade de Medicina da Bahia. Salvador, 1918.

Lima, Estácio de. "Ciumes." *Revista da Academia de Letras da Bahia* 15 (1954): 131–40.

Lima, Herman. *Poeira do tempo: Memórias*. Rio de Janeiro, 1974.

Lima, Hermes. *Anísio Teixeira: Estadista da educação*. Rio de Janeiro, 1978.

——. *Travessia: Memórias*. Rio de Janeiro, 1974.

Lima, José Francisco da Silva [Senex, pseud.]. "A Bahia de há 66 anos (Reminiscências de um contemporâneo)." *Revista do Instituto Geográfico e Histórico da Bahia* 34 (1909): 93–117.

Lima, Vivaldo da Costa. "O conceito de 'nação' nos candomblés da Bahia." *Afro-Asia* 12 (June 1976): 65–90.

——. "A família-de-santo nos candomblés Jejé-Nagôs da Bahia: Um estudo de relações intra-grupais." Tese de pos-graduação em Ciências Humanas, Universidade Federal da Bahia, 1977.

Lins, Wilson. "Um baiano como os outros." In *Um praticante da democracia: Octávio Mangabeira*. Salvador, 1980.

——. "Discurso." *Revista da Academia de Letras da Bahia* 21 (1962–70): 147–61.

——. *O Médio São Francisco: Uma sociedade de pastores e guerreiros*. Salvador, 1952.

Lloyd, Reginald, W. Feldwick, L. T. Delaney, and J. Eulalio, eds. *Impressões do*

Brasil no século vinte: Sua história, seo povo, commércio, indústrias e recursos. London, 1913.

Lobato, Monteiro. "Jeca Tatú: A ressurreição." In *Obras completas.* Vol. 8, *Mr. Slang e o Brasil* and *O problema vital.* São Paulo, 1948.

———. "Urupês." In *Urupês.* 9th ed. São Paulo, 1923.

Lomnitz, Larissa, and Marisol Pérez Lizaur. "The History of a Mexican Urban Family." *Journal of Family History* 3, 4 (Winter 1978): 392–409.

Lopes, Luis Carlos. *O espelho e a imagem: O escravo na historiografia brasileira (1808–1920).* Rio de Janeiro, 1987.

Love, Joseph. "Political Participation in Brazil, 1881–1969." *Luso-Brazilian Review* 7, 2 (December 1970): 2–24.

———. *Rio Grande do Sul and Brazilian Regionalism, 1882–1930.* Stanford, 1971.

———. *São Paulo in the Brazilian Federation, 1889–1937.* Stanford, 1980.

Lowenstein, Karl. *Brazil Under Vargas.* New York, 1942.

Ludwig, Armin K. *Brazil: A Handbook of Historical Statistics.* Boston, 1985.

Lugar, Catherine. "The Merchant Community of Salvador, Bahia, 1780–1830." Ph.D. diss., State University of New York at Stonybrook, 1980.

———. "The Portuguese Tobacco Trade and Tobacco Growers of Bahia in the Late Colonial Period." In *Essays Concerning the Socioeconomic History of Brazil and Portuguese India*, edited by Dauril Alden and Warren Dean, pp. 26–70. Gainesville, Fla., 1977.

Luna, Francisco Vidal, and Irací del Nero da Costa. "Posse de escravos em São Paulo no início do século XIX." *Estudos Econômicos* 13, 1 (January–April 1983): 1–11.

———. "Sinopse de alguns trabalhos de demografia histórica referentes a Minas Gerais." Paper presented at the 3d Encontro Nacional de Estudos Populacionais da Associação Brasileira de Estudos Populacionais, Vitória, Espíritu Santo, October 1982.

"Luxo e moda." *Mensageiro da Fé* 12, 21 (November 1, 1914): 178–79.

Luz, Fábio. "Bahia renovada." *Revista da Academia de Letras da Bahia* 4, 6–7 (June–December 1933): 40–53.

Machado, [José de] Alcântara. *Vida e morte do bandeirante.* São Paulo, 1930.

Machado, Roberto, Angela Loureiro, Rogério Luz, and Kátia Muricy. *Danação da norma: Medicina social e constituição da psiquiatria no Brasil.* Rio de Janeiro, 1978.

Machado Neto, Antônio Luis. "A Bahia Intelectual (1900–1930)." *Universitas* 12–13 (1972): 261–306.

Magalhães, Alfredo Ferreira. "Educação eugênica em geral, consciência da responsabilidade eugênica na família, nas escolas, na universidade." *Gazeta Médica da Bahia* 60, 12 (June 1930): 532.

———. "Pro eugenismo." *Mensageiro da Fé* 11, 1 (January 5, 1913): 4–5.

Magalhães, Juracy. *Mensagem . . . pelo Sr. Governador Juracy Montenegro Magalhães em 2 de julho de 1936.* Salvador, 1936.

———. *Minhas memórias provisórias: Depoimento prestado ao CPDOC.* Rio de Janeiro, 1982.

Magalhães Júnior, R. *Como você se chama? Estudo sócio-psicológico de prenomes e cognomes*. Rio de Janeiro, 1974.

———. *Rui: O homem e o mito*. Rio de Janeiro, 1965.

Mainwaring, Scott. *The Catholic Church and Politics in Brazil, 1916–1985*. Stanford, 1986.

Malloy, James. *The Politics of Social Security in Brazil*. Pittsburgh, 1979.

Mangabeira, Francisco. *João Mangabeira: República e socialismo no Brasil*. Rio de Janeiro, 1979.

Mangabeira, Francisco Cavalcante. *Impedimentos do casamento relativos ao parentesco*. Tese de doutoramento, Faculdade de Medicina da Bahia. Salvador, 1900.

Mangabeira, Octávio. "Cinqüentanário do falecimento de Francisco Mangabeira." *Revista da Academia de Letras da Bahia* 15 (1954): 100–128.

———. *Mensagem apresentada à Assembléia Legislativa pelo Sr. Governador do Estado da Bahia Octávio Mangabeira . . . em 7 de abril de 1948*. Salvador, 1948.

Marcílio, Maria Luiza. *A cidade de São Paulo: Povoamento e população, 1750–1850*. São Paulo, 1974.

Maria, Júlio [pseud. Júlio Cesar de Morais Carneiro]. "Memória sobre a religião no Brasil." 1900. Reprinted as *A igreja e a república*. Brasília, 1981.

Mariani, Clemente. "Análise do problema econômico baiano." *Observador Econômico e Financeiro* 267 (May 1958): 1–27.

Marques, A. H. de Oliveira. *The History of Portugal*. 2 vols. New York, 1972.

Marques, [Francisco] Xavier [Ferreira]. *A boa madrasta*. Rio de Janeiro, 1919.

———. "Caderno de pensamentos e lembranças." *Revista da Academia de Letras da Bahia* 6, 11–12 (1937–39): 1–7.

———. *O feiticeiro*. 1922. Revised version of *Boto & Cia.* (1897). 3d ed. São Paulo, 1975.

Martinez, Socorro Targínio. "Ordens Terceiras: Ideologia e Arquitetura." Dissertação de mestrado, Universidade Federal da Bahia, 1969.

Martínez Alier, Verena. *Marriage, Class and Colour in Nineteenth-Century Cuba: A Study of Racial Attitudes and Sexual Values in a Slave Society*. New York, 1974.

Martínez Estrada, Ezequiel. *X-Ray of the Pampa*. Austin, 1971.

Martinho, Lenira Menezes. "Organização do trabalho e relações sociais nas firmas comerciais do Rio de Janeiro (Primeira metade do século XIX)." *Revista do Instituto de Estudos Brasileiros* 18 (1976): 41–62.

Martins, Wilson. *História da inteligência brasileira*. Vol. 6, *1915–1933*. São Paulo, 1978.

Masson, Camilo de Lellis, ed. *Almanak administrativo, mercantil e industrial da Bahia, 1862*. Salvador, 1862.

Mattoso, K[átia] M. de Queirós. "Au nouveau monde: Une Province d'un nouvel empire: Bahia au XIXe siècle." Thèse pour le doctorat d'état, Université de Paris Sorbonne (Paris IV), 1986. Portions of this thesis have been published as *Família e sociedade na Bahia do século XIX*. São Paulo, 1988.

———. *Bahia: A Cidade do Salvador e seu mercado no século XIX*. São Paulo, 1977.

————. *Família e sociedade na Bahia do século XIX*. Translated by James Amado. São Paulo, 1988.

————. "Para uma história social da Cidade do Salvador no século XIX: Os testamentos e inventários como fonte de estudo da estrutura social e de mentalidade." *Anais do Arquivo do Estado da Bahia* 42 (1976): 147–98.

————. "Slave, Free, and Freed Family Structures in Nineteenth-Century Salvador, Bahia." *Luso-Brazilian Review* 25, 1 (Summer 1988): 69–84.

————. *To Be a Slave in Brazil, 1550–1888*. New Brunswick, N.J., 1986.

Mattoso, Kátia de Queirós, and Johildo de Athayde. "Epidemias e flutuações de preços na Bahia no século XIX." In *Colloque international sur l'histoire quantitative du Brésil de 1800 a 1930, Paris, 1971*, edited by Frederic Mauro, pp. 183–202. Paris, 1973.

Maximiliano de Habsburgo [Archduke Ferdinand Maximilian]. *Bahia 1860: Esboço de viagem*. Rio de Janeiro, 1982.

Maxwell, Kenneth. *Conflicts and Conspiracies: Brazil and Portugal, 1750–1808*. Cambridge, Engl., 1973.

"Meios de acção: Exemplo das Ligas congeneres." *Voz da Liga Catholica das Senhoras Bahianas* 1, 3 (March 1913): 26–28.

Meira, Sílvio. *Teixeira de Freitas: O jurisconsulto do Império*. Rio de Janeiro, 1979.

Meireles, Edison de Palma. *Acontecimentos*. Salvador, 1976.

Menezes, Jayme de Sá. "Família Calmon." *Revista do Instituto Genealógico da Bahia* 16 (1968): 125–68.

Metcalf, Alida. "Families of Planters, Peasants, and Slaves: Strategies for Survival in Santana de Parnaiba, Brazil, 1720–1820." Ph.D. diss., University of Texas at Austin, 1982.

————. "Fathers and Sons: The Politics of Inheritance in a Colonial Brazilian Township." *Hispanic American Historical Review* 66, 3 (August 1986): 455–84.

————. "Inheritance, Marriage, Family and Structure in Eighteenth-Century Brazil: Strategies for Survival in a Changing Society." Paper presented at American Historical Association Convention, December 27–32, 1982.

Metz, René. *What is Canon Law?* Twentieth Century Encyclopedia of Catholicism, vol. 80. New York, 1960.

Miceli, Sérgio. *Intelectuais e classe dirigente no Brasil (1920–1945)*. São Paulo, 1979.

Miller, Charlotte. "Middle-Class Kinship Networks in Belo Horizonte, Minas Gerais, Brazil: The Functions of the Urban Parentela." Ph.D. diss., University of Florida, 1976.

Mintz, Sidney, and Richard Price. *An Anthropological Approach to the Afro-American Past: A Caribbean Perspective*. Philadelphia, 1976.

Mintz, Sidney, and Eric Wolf. "An Analysis of Ritual Co-Parenthood (Compadrazgo)." In *Friends, Followers and Factions: A Reader in Political Clientelism*, edited by Steffen W. Schmidt, James C. Scott, Carl Lande, and Laura Guasti, pp. 1–15. Berkeley, 1977.

Moniz, Egas. "A evolução pedagógica na Bahia." In *Diário Oficial do Estado da Bahia: Edição especial do centenário*, pp. 48–55. Salvador, 1923.

Moniz [Sodré de Aragão], Gonçalo. *A consanguineidade e o código civil brasileiro.* Rio de Janeiro, 1925.

——. "Dr. Egas Carlos Moniz Sodré de Aragão." *Revista da Academia de Letras da Bahia* 4, 6–7 (June–December 1933): 152–57.

——. *Memória histórica da Faculdade de Medicina da Bahia relativa ao anno de 1924.* 2d ed. Rio de Janeiro, 1940.

Moraes, Walfrido. *Jagunços e heróis: A civilização do diamante nas Lavras da Bahia.* Brasília, 1984.

Morgan, Edmund. *The Puritan Family: Religion and Domestic Relations in Seventeenth-Century New England.* Rev. ed. New York, 1966.

Morley, Helena [pseud. Alice Dayrell Brant]. *The Diary of Helena Morley.* New York, 1957.

Morse, Richard. "Brazil's Urban Development: Colony and Empire." In *From Colony to Nation: Essays on the Independence of Brazil,* edited by A. J. R. Russell-Wood, pp. 155–81. Baltimore, 1975.

——. "Cities and Society in Nineteenth-Century Latin America: The Illustrative Case of Brazil." In *Urbanization in the Americas from Its Beginnings to the Present,* edited by Richard Schaedel, Jorge Hardoy, and Nora Scott Kinzer, pp. 282–302. The Hague, 1978.

——. "The Claims of Tradition in Urban Latin America." In *Contemporary Cultures and Societies of Latin America: A Reader in the Social Anthropology of Middle and South America,* edited by Dwight B. Heath, pp. 480–94. 2d rev. ed. New York, 1974.

——. "Erecting a Boomstone." Paper presented at "The Rise of the New Latin American Narrative" symposium, Wilson Center, Washington, D.C., October 18–20, 1979.

——. *El espejo de Próspero: Un estudio de la dialéctica del Nuevo Mundo.* Mexico City, 1982.

——. *From Community to Metropolis: A Biography of São Paulo, Brazil.* Gainesville, Fla., 1958.

——. "The Lima of Joaquín Capelo: A Latin-American Archetype." *Journal of Contemporary History* 4, 3 (July 1969): 95–110.

——. "Some Themes of Brazilian History." *South Atlantic Quarterly* 61, 2 (Spring 1962): 159–82.

Morton, F. W. O. "The Conservative Revolution of Independence: Economy, Society and Politics in Bahia, 1790–1840." Ph.D. diss., Oxford University, 1974.

——. "The Military and Society in Bahia, 1800–1821." *Journal of Latin American Studies* 7, 2 (1975): 249–69.

Müller, Christiano. *Memória histórica sobre a religião na Bahia, 1823–1923.* Salvador, 1923.

Nabuco, Joaquim. *O abolicionismo.* Petrópolis, 1977.

——. *Um estadista do Império.* 3 vols. Rio de Janeiro, 1897.

Nascimento, Anna Amália Vieira. *Dez freguesias da Cidade do Salvador: Aspectos sociais e urbanos do século XIX.* Salvador, 1986.

——. " 'Divórcio' por sentença." *Anais do Arquivo do Estado da Bahia* 44 (1979): 261–71.

Nava, Pedro. *Baú de ossos: Memórias.* Rio de Janeiro, 1974.

Nazzari, Muriel Smith. "Women, the Family and Property: The Decline of the Dowry in São Paulo, Brazil (1600–1870)." Ph.D. diss., Yale University, 1986.

Needell, Jeffrey. "Making the Carioca Belle Epoque Concrete: The Urban Reforms of Rio de Janeiro Under Pereira Passos." *Journal of Urban History* 10, 4 (August 1984): 382–422.

———. "Oliveira Vianna and the Conservative Reinterpretation of Modern Brazil." Paper presented at the 15th International Congress of the Latin American Studies Association, Miami, December 4–6, 1989.

———. "A Revolta Contra Vacina." *Hispanic American Historical Review* 67, 2 (May 1987): pp. 233–70.

———. *A Tropical Belle Epoque: Elite Culture and Society in Turn-of-the-Century Rio de Janeiro.* Cambridge, Engl., 1987.

Neeser, Hermann. "A família Urpia." *Revista do Instituto Genealógico da Bahia* 2 (1946): 41–71.

Netto, Alcebiades Cabral. *Da alimentação nas primeiras idades.* Tese de doutoramento, Faculdade de Medicina da Bahia. Salvador, 1912.

Nóbrega, Apolônio. "Dióceses e bispos do Brasil." *Revista do Instituto Histórico e Geográfico Brasileiro* 222 (1954): 1–318.

Nogueira, Adalício Coelho. *Caminhos de um magistrado.* Rio de Janeiro, 1978.

Novinsky, Anita. *Cristãos novos na Bahia, 1624–1654.* São Paulo, 1972.

Nunberg, Barbara. "State Intervention in the Sugar Sector in Brazil: A Study of the Institute of Sugar and Alcohol." Ph.D. diss., Stanford University, 1979.

———. "Structural Change and State Policy: The Politics of Sugar in Brazil Since 1964." *Latin American Research Review* 21, 2 (1986): 53–92.

Nye, Robert A. *Crime, Madness, and Politics in Modern France: The Medical Concept of National Decline.* Princeton, 1984.

Oliveira, Albino José Barbosa de. *Memórias de um magistrado do império.* Edited by Américo Jacobina Lacombe. São Paulo, 1943.

Oliveira, Cardoso de. *Dois metros e cinco.* Rio de Janeiro, 1905.

Oliveira, Eudóxio de. "Demografia sanitária." *Gazeta Médica da Bahia* 30, 2 (April 1899): 470–75.

———. "Demografia sanitária." *Gazeta Médica da Bahia* 32, 11 (May 1901): 546.

———. "Demografia sanitária." *Gazeta Médica da Bahia* 33, 9 (March 1902): 427–29.

Oliveira, Yves de. *Octávio Mangabeira: Alma e voz da República.* Rio de Janeiro, 1971.

Ortega y Gassett, José. *España invertebrada.* 1921. Madrid, 1971.

Ott, Carlos. *Formação e evolução étnica da Cidade do Salvador.* 2 vols. Rio de Janeiro, 1955.

Pang, Eul-Soo. *Bahia in the First Brazilian Republic: Coronelismo and Oligarchies, 1889–1934.* Gainesville, Fla., 1977.

———. "The Changing Roles of Priests in the Politics of Northeast Brazil, 1889–1964." *The Americas* 30 (January 1974): 341–72.

———. *O Engenho Central do Bom Jardim na economia baiana: Alguns aspectos de sua história, 1875–1891.* Rio de Janeiro, 1979.

———. *In Pursuit of Honor and Power: Brazil's Noblemen of the Southern Cross.* Tuscaloosa, Ala., 1988.

———. "The Revolt of the Bahian *Coronéis* and the Federal Intervention of 1920." *Luso-Brazilian Review* 8, 2 (December 1971): 3–25.

Pang, Eul-Soo, and Ronald Seckinger. "The Mandarins of Imperial Brazil." *Comparative Studies in Society and History* 14 (March 1972): 215–44.

Paraiso Neto, J[oão] F[rancisco] Prisco. *Descendência de José Vicente Gonçalves Tourinho (1801–1888).* Salvador, 1977.

Patterson, Orlando. *Slavery and Social Death.* Cambridge, Mass., 1982.

Peixoto, Afrânio. *Medicina legal.* 2 vols. Rio de Janeiro, 1931.

———. "Nem com uma flor." *Revista da Academia de Letras da Bahia* 3, 4–5 (June–December 1932): 81–86.

Penna, Belisário. *Saneamento do Brasil.* Rio de Janeiro, 1918.

Pereira, José Leite de Mello. *Breves considerações sobre a educação physica e moral dos meninos.* Tese de doutoramento, Faculdade de Medicina da Bahia. Salvador, 1853.

Pereira, Manuel, and Jayme de Sá Menezes. "A família Pereira (Manuel Vitorino, irmãos, e descendentes)." *Revista do Instituto Genealógico da Bahia* 20 (1975): 69–102.

Peristiany, J. G., ed. *Honour and Shame: The Values of Mediterranean Society.* Chicago, 1966.

Pierson, Donald. *Negroes in Brazil: A Study of Race Contact at Bahia.* 1942. Rev. ed. Carbondale, Ill., 1967.

Pinheiro, Domingos Firmino. *O androphilismo.* Tese de doutoramento, Faculdade de Medicina da Bahia. Salvador, 1898.

Pinho, Demósthenes Madureira de. *Carrossel da vida (páginas de memórias).* Rio de Janeiro, 1974.

Pinho, J[oão] F[erreira] de Araujo. *O Barão de Cotegipe no Rio da Prata & O grande estadista na intimidade.* Salvador, 1916.

Pinho, Joaquim Wanderley de Araujo. "A viação na Bahia." *Diário Oficial do Estado da Bahia: Edição especial do centenário,* pp. 132–43. Salvador, 1923.

Pinho, [José] Wanderley [de Araujo]. *Cotegipe e seu tempo: Primeira phase, 1815–1867.* São Paulo, 1937.

———. *História de um engenho do Recôncavo: Matoim-Novo Caboto-Freguesia, 1552–1944.* Rio de Janeiro, 1946.

———. *Política e políticos no Império.* Rio de Janeiro, 1930.

———. *Salões e damas do segundo reinado.* 3d ed. São Paulo, 1959.

Pinho, Péricles Madureira de. *São assim os baianos.* Rio de Janeiro, 1960.

Pinto, Antônio Raposo. *Traz o casamento consanguineo a degeneração da raça?* Tese de doutoramento, Faculdade de Medicina da Bahia. Salvador, 1905.

Pinto, Luiz de Aguiar Costa. *Lutas de famílias no Brasil (Introdução ao seu estudo).* 1946. 2d ed. São Paulo, 1980.

Pinto, Macário. "O divórcio." *Mensageiro da Fé* 11, 6 (March 16, 1913): 46–47.

Pitt-Rivers, Julian A. *The People of the Sierra.* 2d ed. Chicago, 1971.

Pius XI. "*Casti connubii*: Encyclical of Pope Pius XI on Christian Marriage,

December 31, 1930." In *The Papal Encyclicals*, edited by Claudia Carlen. Vol. 3, *1903–1939*, pp. 391–414. Raleigh, N.C., 1981.

Pius XII. "*Sertium laetitae*: Encyclical of Pope Pius XII on the Church in the United States, November 1, 1939." In *The Papal Encyclicals*, edited by Claudia Carlen. Vol. 4, *1939–1958*, p. 27. Raleigh, N.C., 1981.

Pompéia, Raul. *O Ateneu: Crônica de saudades*. 1st ed. 1888. 2d rev. ed. 1905. 3d ed. São Paulo, 1976.

Poppino, Rollie. *Feira de Santana*. Salvador, 1968.

Prado Júnior, Caio. *The Colonial Background of Modern Brazil*. Berkeley, 1971.

Prandi, José Reginaldo. *Catolicismo e família: Transformação de uma ideologia*. São Paulo, 1975.

"Preces e exemplos da mãe christã." *A Voz* 6, 11 (February 1918): 171.

"Projecto de instrucção sobre a hygiene dos recem-nascidos." *Gazeta Médica da Bahia* 4, 83 (January 15, 1870): 130–32.

Querino, Manoel. "O africano como colonisador." In *A raça africana e os seus costumes*, pp. 121–52. Salvador, 1955.

———. *A raça africana e os seus costumes*. Salvador, 1955.

Questão Braga: Discussão do exame médico-legal do dia [title page damaged] de dezembro de 1878. Salvador, 1879.

Rago, Margareth. *Do cabaré ao lar: A utopia da cidade disciplinar, Brasil, 1890– 1930*. Rio de Janeiro, 1985.

Ramos, Donald. "City and Country: The Family in Minas Gerais, 1804–1838." In *The Family in Latin America*, special issue of *Journal of Family History* 3, 4 (Winter 1978): 361–75.

———. "Marriage and the Family in Colonial Vila Rica." *Hispanic American Historical Review* 55, 2 (May 1975): 200–225.

Ramos, Graciliano. *Infância*. 1945. 16th ed. Rio de Janeiro, 1980.

Ramos, Samuel. *Profile of Man and Culture in Mexico*. Austin, 1962.

Rêgo, José Lins do. *Doidinho*. 1932. 19th ed. Rio de Janeiro, 1979.

———. *Meus verdes anos (Memórias)*. 1956. Rio de Janeiro, n.d.

Reis, Antônio Alexandre Borges dos, ed. *Almanak administrativo, indicador, noticioso, commercial e litterário do Estado da Bahia para 1902*. Salvador, 1902.

Reis, Cacilda Vieira dos. *Ligeira contribuição ao estudo da sub-alimentação dos lactentes*. Tese de doutoramento, Faculdade de Medicina da Bahia. Salvador, 1927.

Reis, João José. "A elite baiana face os movimentos sociais, Bahia, 1824–1840." *Revista de História* 108 (1976): 341–84.

———. *Rebelião escrava no Brasil: A história do levante dos malês*. São Paulo, 1987.

———. "Slave Rebellion in Brazil: The African Muslim Uprising in Bahia, 1835." Ph.D. diss., University of Minnesota, 1982.

Requião, Hermano. *Itapagipe (Minha infância na Bahia)*. Rio de Janeiro, 1949.

Ribeiro, Carlos. "Estudantes." *Revista da Academia de Letras da Bahia* 5–7, 8–10 (June 1934–December 1936): 168–71.

———. "Sociologia Pedagógica." *Revista da Academia de Letras da Bahia* 2, 2–3 (June–December 1931): 206–16.

Ridings, Eugene. "The Bahian Commercial Association, 1840–1889: A Pressure Group in an Underdeveloped Area." Ph.D. diss., University of Florida, 1970.

──── . "Elite Conflict and Cooperation in the Brazilian Empire: The Case of Bahia's Businessmen and Planters." *Luso-Brazilian Review* 12, 1 (Summer 1975): 80–99.

──── . "The Merchant Elite and the Development of Brazil: The Case of Bahia During the Empire." *Journal of Inter-American Studies and World Affairs* 15, 3 (August 1973): 335–53.

Rodrigues, Amélia. "A acção social cathólica feminina." *A Voz: Orgam da Liga Cathólica das Senhoras Brasileiras* 3, 31 (October 1915): 78–88.

──── . "Amparo religioso à infância e à juventude." In *Do meu archivo*, p. 250.

──── . *O carnaval.* N.p., 1915. Reprinted in *Apostolado das Filhas de Maria no Brasil* 13, 8 (March 1916): 5.

──── . "O 'defeitinho' de Carmita." In *Do meu archivo*, pp. 61–73.

──── . "Desastre feliz." In *Do meu archivo*, pp. 30–31.

──── . *Do meu archivo.* 2d ed. Salvador, 1929.

──── . "Escándalo! Escándalo!" In *Do meu archivo*, p. 249.

──── . "Limpeza nos correios." *Paladina* 1, 6 (June 1910): 3–6.

──── . *Mestra e mãe: Quarto livro de leitura.* Salvador, 1898.

──── . "A mulher quebra as cadéias." *A Noite* (Rio de Janeiro), October 21, 1919.

──── . "Progresso feminino, comédia infantil em um acto." In *Almanak do Mensageiro da Fé para o anno de 1924*, pp. 67–87. Salvador, 1924.

──── . "Que rico sermão!" Manuscript. Ca. 1910.

──── . *Verdadeira missão social da mulher: Discurso inaugural da Associação das Damas de Maria Auxiliadora em 4 de agosto de 1907.* Salvador, 1907.

──── . "Vida intensa: Comédia." Typescript. 1932.

Rodrigues, Euphrasio José. *Defloramentos e seus erros de diagnóstico.* Tese de doutoramento, Faculdade de Medicina da Bahia. Salvador, 1895.

Rodrigues, Raimundo Nina. *Os africanos no Brasil.* Edited by Homero Pires. São Paulo, 1976.

──── . *O animismo fetichista dos negros bahianos.* São Paulo, 1935.

──── . "A loucura das multidões: Nova contribuição ao estudo das loucuras epidémicas no Brasil." In *As collectividades anormaes*, edited by Arthur Ramos, pp. 78–153. Rio de Janeiro, 1939.

──── . "A loucura epidémica de Canudos: Antonio Conselheiro e os jagunços." In *As collectividades anormaes*, edited by Arthur Ramos, pp. 50–77. Rio de Janeiro, 1939.

Rogério [de Souza], Luiz. "Reminiscências de Couto Maia." *Revista de Cultura da Bahia* 11 (1976): 93–99.

Romero, Sylvio. *O Brasil social (Vistas synthéticas obtidas pelos processos de Le Play).* Rio de Janeiro, 1907.

Rosen, George. *From Medical Police to Social Medicine: Essays on the History of Health Care.* New York, 1974.

Rosenberg, Charles. "The Bitter Fruit: Heredity, Disease, and Social Thought." In *No Other Gods: On Science and American Social Thought*, pp. 25–53. Baltimore, 1976.

Rosenn, Keith. "The Jeito, Brazil's Institutionalized Bypass of the Formal Legal System and Its Developmental Implications." *American Journal of Comparative Law* 19 (1971): 514–49.

Russell-Wood, A. J. R. *The Black Man in Slavery and Freedom in Colonial Brazil.* New York, 1982.

———. *Fidalgos and Philanthropists: The Santa Casa da Misericórdia of Bahia, 1550–1755.* Berkeley, 1968.

———. "Women and Society in Colonial Brazil." *Journal of Latin American Studies* 9, 1 (1977): 1–34.

Saes, Décio. *Classe média e política na Primeira República brasileira (1889–1930).* Petrópolis, 1975.

Saffioti, Heleieth Iara Bongiovani. *A mulher na sociedade de classes: Mito e realidade.* 2d ed. Petrópolis, 1979.

Sales, Herberto. *Dados biográficos do finado Marcellino.* 2d ed. Rio de Janeiro, 1974.

Salles, David. *O ficcionista Xavier Marques: Um estudo da "transição" ornamental.* Rio de Janeiro, 1977.

Samara, Eni de Mesquita. *A família brasileira.* São Paulo, 1985.

Sampaio, Consuelo Novais. *Formação do regionalismo no Brasil: Bahia e São Paulo no século XIX.* Salvador, 1977.

———. *Os partidos políticos da Bahia na Primeira República: Uma política de acomodação.* Salvador, 1978.

Sampaio, Consuelo, and Mário Augusto da Silva Santos. "Trabalho urbano na Bahia." Panel presented at the 33d Reunião da Sociedade Brasileira para o Progresso da Ciência, Salvador, July 8–15, 1981.

Sampaio, Gastão. *Nazaré das Farinhas.* Salvador, n.d.

Sampaio, José Luis Pamponet. "Evolução de uma empresa no contexto da industrialização brasileira. A companhia Empório Industrial do Norte, 1891–1973." Tese de mestrado, Universidade Federal da Bahia, 1975.

Sampaio, Nelson de Souza. *O diálogo democrático na Bahia.* Belo Horizonte, 1960.

Sampaio, Teodoro. "O engenho de assucar." *See* Arquivo do Instituto Geográfico e Histórico da Bahia.

Sampaio Neto, José Augusto Vaz, Magaly de Barros Maia Serrão, Maria Lúcia Horta Ludolf de Mello, and Vanda Maria Bravo Ururahy. *Canudos: Subsídios para a sua reavaliação histórica.* Rio de Janeiro, 1986.

Sant'Ana, José Lemos de. *Ainda bambangas (4° volume de memórias).* Salvador, 1980.

———. *Bambanga (Memórias).* Salvador, 1978.

———. *Mais bambangas (3° volume de memórias).* 2d ed. Salvador, 1981.

———. *Outros bambangas (2° volume de memórias).* Petrópolis, 1980.

Sant'Anna, Jorge, and Leonel Gonzaga. *Escola de mães, saude de filhos.* Rio de Janeiro, 1926.

Santos, Angelo de Lima Godinho. *Influência da prostituição sobre a sociedade actual.* Tese de doutoramento, Faculdade de Medicina da Bahia. Salvador, 1909.

Santos, Mário Augusto da Silva. *Os caixeiros da Bahia: Seu papel conservador na Primeira República.* Salvador, 1974.

———. *Comércio português na Bahia, 1870–1930: Centenário de Manoel Joaquim de Carvalho & Cia. Ltda.* Salvador, 1977.

Santos, Ruy. "Discurso de posse." *Revista da Academia de Letras da Bahia* 8 (1957): 126–42.

Santos, Wanderley Guilherme dos. *Cidadania e justiça: A política social na ordem brasileira.* Rio de Janeiro, 1979.

———. "A praxis liberal no Brasil: Propostas para reflexão e pesquisa." In *Ordem burguesa e liberalismo político*, pp. 65–118. São Paulo, 1978.

Santos Filho, Lycurgo [de Castro]. *História da medicina no Brasil (Do século XVI ao século XIX).* 2 vols. São Paulo, 1947.

———. *História geral da medicina brasileira.* Vol. 1. São Paulo, 1977.

———. *Uma comunidade rural do Brasil antigo: Aspectos da vida patriarcal no sertão da Bahia nos séculos XVIII e XIX.* São Paulo, 1956.

Saunders, John Van Dyke. *Differential Fertility in Brazil.* Gainesville, Fla., 1958.

Schwartz, Stuart. "Elite Politics and the Growth of a Peasantry in Late Colonial Brazil." In *From Colony to Nation: Essays on the Independence of Brazil*, edited by A. J. R. Russell-Wood, pp. 133–54. Baltimore, 1975.

———. "Free Labor in a Slave Economy: The *Lavradores de Cana* of Colonial Bahia." In *Colonial Roots of Modern Brazil*, edited by Dauril Alden, pp. 147–98. Berkeley, 1973.

———. "Patterns of Slaveholding in the Americas: New Evidence from Brazil." *American Historical Review* 87 (1982): 55–86.

———. "Recent Trends in the Study of Slavery in Brazil." *Luso-Brazilian Review* 25, 1 (Summer 1988): 1–26.

———. "Resistance and Accommodation in Eighteenth-Century Brazil: The Slaves' View of Slavery." *Hispanic American Historical Review* 57 (1977): 69–81.

———. *Sovereignty and Society in Colonial Brazil: The High Court of Bahia and Its Judges, 1609–1751.* Berkeley, 1973.

———. *Sugar Plantations in the Formation of Brazilian Society: Bahia, 1550–1835.* Cambridge, Engl., 1985.

Schwarz, Roberto. *Ao vencedor as batatas: Forma literária e processo social nos inícios do romance brasileiro.* São Paulo, 1977.

———. "Misplaced Ideas: Literature and Society in Late Nineteenth-Century Brazil." *Comparative Civilizations Review* 5 (Fall 1980): 33–51.

Seabra, J. J. *Esfola de um mentiroso.* Rio de Janeiro, 1936.

Sena, Consuelo Pondé de. *Introdução ao estudo de uma comunidade do agreste baiano: Itapicurú, 1830–1892.* Salvador, 1979.

Senex. *See* Lima, José Francisco da Silva.

Shryock, Richard. *American Medicine in Transition, 1660–1860.* New York, 1960.

———. *The Development of Modern Medicine: An Interpretation of the Social and Scientific Factors Involved.* Philadelphia, 1936.

Silva, Alberto. "Elógio de Antônio Vianna." *Revista da Academia de Letras da Bahia* 14 (1953): 31–43.

————. *A primeira médica do Brasil.* Rio de Janeiro, 1954.

Silva, Alvaro Augusto da. *À barra do tribunal verificador.* Salvador, 1924.

Silva, Aloysio Guilherme da. *Amélia Rodrigues: Evocação.* Rio de Janeiro, 1963.

Silva, Cândido da Costa e. *Roteiro da vida e da morte (Um estudo do catolicismo no sertão da Bahia).* São Paulo, 1982.

Silva, Cândido da Costa e, and Riolando Azzi. *Dois estudos sobre Dom Romualdo Antonio de Seixas, arcebispo da Bahia.* Salvador, 1982.

[Silva, Dom Jerônimo Thomé da]. "Appendice à Terceira Pastoral Collectiva do Episcopado da Província Ecclesiástica de São Salvador da Bahia . . . : Matrimônio." *Mensageiro da Fé* 6, 16 (August 15, 1908): 64.

————. "A precedência obrigatória do casamento civil." *Mensageiro da Fé* 12, 8 (April 12, 1914): 64.

Silva, Kátia Maria de Carvalho. *O Diário da Bahia e o século XIX.* Rio de Janeiro, 1979.

Silva, Maria Beatriz Nizza da. *Cultura no Brasil colônia.* Petrópolis, 1981.

————. "O divórcio na Capitania de São Paulo." In *Vivência: História, sexualidade e imagens femininas,* edited by Maria Cristina A. Bruschini and Fúlvia Rosemberg, pp. 151–94. São Paulo, 1980.

————. *Sistema de casamento no Brasil colonial.* São Paulo, 1984.

Silveira, José. *O neto de Dona Sinhá.* Rio de Janeiro, 1985.

————. *Vela acesa: Memórias.* Rio de Janeiro, 1980.

Silveira, Manoel Fernandes da. *Estudo clínico do rachitismo.* Tese de doutoramento, Faculdade de Medicina da Bahia. Salvador, 1890.

Silveira, Walter da. "Discurso." *Revista da Academia de Letras da Bahia* 21 (1962–70): 131–42.

————. *A história do cinema vista da província.* Salvador, 1978.

Simões Filho, Américo. "Evolução urbana da cidade do Salvador." In *A grande Salvador: Posse e uso da terra,* edited by Cydelmo Teixeira, ch. 9. Salvador, 1978.

Siqueira, Augusto Calmon de. *Infância.* Tese de doutoramento, Faculdade de Medicina da Bahia. Salvador, 1858.

Skidmore, Thomas. *Black into White: Race and Nationality in Brazilian Thought.* New York, 1970.

————. "Gilberto Freyre and the Early Brazilian Republic: Some Notes on Methodology." *Comparative Studies in Society and History* 6, 4 (July 1964): 490–505.

Slenes, Robert, and Pedro Carvalho de Mello. "Paternalism and Social Control in a Slave Society: The Coffee Regions of Brazil, 1850–1888." Paper presented at the 9th World Congress of Sociology, Uppsala, Sweden, August 1978.

Soares, Carlos Alberto Caroso. "Expedientes de vida: Um ensaio de antropologia urbana." Tese de pos-graduação em Ciências Sociais, Universidade Federal da Bahia, 1979.

Soares, Vital Henriques Baptista. *Mensagem apresentada pelo Exmo. Sr. Dr. Vital Henriques Baptista Soares governador do Estado da Bahia . . . em 2 de julho de 1930.* Salvador, 1930.

Socolow, Susan. *The Merchants of Buenos Aires, 1778–1810: Family and Commerce.* Cambridge, Engl., 1978.

Soeiro, Susan. "The Feminine Orders in Colonial Bahia, Brazil: Economic, Social, and Demographic Implications, 1677–1800." In *Latin American Women: Historical Perspectives*, edited by Asunción Lavrin, pp. 173–97. Westport, Conn., 1978.

————. "The Social and Economic Role of the Convent: Women and Nuns in Colonial Bahia, 1677–1800." *Hispanic American Historical Review* 54, 2 (May 1974): 209–32.

Souza, Antônio Moniz de. "Viagems e observações de hum brasileiro." *Revista do Instituto Geográfico e Histórico da Bahia* 72 (1945): 100–104.

Souza, Guaraci Adeodato Alves de. "Urbanização e fluxos migratórios para Salvador." In *Bahia de todos os pobres*, edited by Guaraci Adeodato Alves de Souza and Vilmar Faria, pp. 103–28. Petrópolis, 1980.

Souza, Guaraci Adeodato Alves de, and Vilmar Faria, eds. *Bahia de todos os pobres*. Petrópolis, 1980.

Souza, Itamar de. *O compadrio: Da política ao sexo*. Petrópolis, 1981.

Stein, Stanley. *The Brazilian Cotton Manufacture: Textile Enterprise in an Underdeveloped Area, 1850–1920*. Cambridge, Mass., 1957.

————. "The Historiography of Brazil, 1808–1889." *Hispanic American Historical Review* 40, 2 (May 1960): 234–78.

————. *Vassouras: A Brazilian Coffee County*. New York, 1976.

Stepan, Alfred. *The State and Society: Peru in Comparative Perspective*. Princeton, 1978.

Stepan, Nancy. *The Beginnings of Brazilian Science: Oswaldo Cruz, Medical Research and Policy, 1890–1920*. New York, 1976.

————. "Eugenesia, genética y salud pública: El movimiento eugenésico brasileño y mundial." *Quipu: Revista Latinoamericana de Historia de las Ciencias y la Tecnología* 2, 3 (September–December 1985): 351–84.

Stone, Lawrence. *The Family, Sex and Marriage in England, 1500–1800*. New York, 1977.

————. "The Rise of the Nuclear Family in Early Modern England." In *The Family in History*, edited by Charles E. Rosenberg, pp. 13–58. Philadelphia, 1975.

Süssekind, Flora. *Tal Brasil, qual romance? Uma ideologia estética e sua história: O naturalismo*. Rio de Janeiro, 1984.

Sylvínio Júnior. *A dona de casa: A mais util publicação em portuguez*. 1894. 2d ed. Rio de Janeiro, 1903.

Tate, Allen. *On the Limits of Poetry: Selected Essays, 1928–1945*. New York, 1948.

Tavares, Luis Henrique Dias. *Duas reformas da educação na Bahia, 1895–1925*. Salvador, 1968.

————. *O problema da involução industrial da Bahia*. Salvador, 1965.

Teixeira, Cid, Cydelmo Teixeira, and Rino Marconi. "Memória fotográfica." In *A grande Salvador: Posse e uso da terra*, edited by Cydelmo Teixeira, ch. 11. Salvador, 1978.

Teixeira, Marli Geralda. "Os Batistas na Bahia, 1882–1925: Um estudo de história social." Dissertação de mestrado em Ciências Humanas, Universidade Federal da Bahia, 1975.

Terceiro livro do monstruoso drama nupcial de que é protagonista o médico e lente da Faculdade de Medicina Doutor José Pedro de Souza Braga. Salvador, 1879.

Todaro, Margaret. "Pastors, Prophets, and Politicians: A Study of the Brazilian Catholic Church, 1916–1945." Ph.D. diss., Columbia University, 1971.

Toplin, Robert Brent. *The Abolition of Slavery in Brazil.* New York, 1972.

Torres, Carlos. *Gonçalo Moniz Sodré de Aragão (Esboço biográfico).* Salvador, 1960.

Torres, João Camilo de Oliveira. *História das idéias religiosas no Brasil (A igreja e a sociedade brasileira).* São Paulo, 1968.

Torres, Mário. "Commemoração do centenário de Lino Coutinho." *Revista do Instituto Geográfico e Histórico da Bahia* 62 (1936): 493–505.

——— . "Os morgados do 'Sodré.' " *Revista do Instituto Genealógico da Bahia* 6 (1951): 9–34.

——— . "Os Sodrés." *Revista do Instituto Genealógico da Bahia* 7 (1952): 89–148.

——— . "Os Torres." *Revista do Instituto Genealógico da Bahia* 1 (1945): 23–67.

Torres, Octávio. "Discurso do Prof. Octávio Torres ao ser recebido pelo Prof. Heitor Praguer Frões na Academia de Letras da Bahia." *Revista da Academia de Letras da Bahia* 6, 11–13 (1937–39): 77–104.

Traer, James F. *Marriage and the Family in Eighteenth-Century France.* Ithaca, N.Y., 1980.

Transcripções do "Diário da Bahia." N.p., n.d.

Trounson, K. E. "The Literature Reviewed." *Eugenics Review* 23, 3 (October 1931): 236–37.

Uchoa, Raphael de Albuquerque. *A odysséa de um revolucionário.* Salvador, 1931.

United States. Bureau of the Census. *Historical Statistics of the United States, Colonial Times to 1957: A Statistical Abstract Supplement.* Washington, D.C., 1960.

Valladares, Clarival do Prado. *Arte e sociedade nos cemitérios brasileiros.* 2 vols. Rio de Janeiro, 1972.

Van de Walle, Etienne. "Marriage and Marital Fertility." *Historical Population Studies* issue of *Dædalus* 97, 2 (Spring 1968): 486–501.

"Variedades: A mulher médica." *Gazeta Médica da Bahia* 3, 54 (October 31, 1868): 70–72.

Vasconcellos, Ademar Almeida. *Do defloramento.* Tese de doutoramento, Faculdade de Medicina da Bahia. Salvador, 1935.

Verger, Pierre. *Trade Relations Between the Bight of Benin and Bahia from the 17th to 19th Century.* Ibadan, 1976.

Viana Filho, Luís. *A vida de Rui Barbosa.* Rio de Janeiro, 1977.

Vianna, António. *Casos e coisas da Bahia.* Salvador, 1950.

——— . "Evocação." *Revista da Academia de Letras da Bahia* 5–7, 8–10 (June 1934–December 1936): 1–21.

Vianna, [Francisco José] Oliveira. *Evolução do povo brasileiro.* 1922. 2d ed. São Paulo, 1933.

——— . *Instituições políticas brasileiras.* 2 vols. Rio de Janeiro, 1949.

——— . *Populações meridionais do Brasil.* 1920. 2 vols. 4th ed. São Paulo, 1938.

Vianna, Francisco Vicente. *Memoir of the State of Bahia.* Salvador, 1893.

Vianna, Hildegardes. *A Bahia já foi assim (Crônicas de costumes).* Salvador, 1973.
Vianna, Joaquim Telesphoro Ferreira Lopes. *Breves considerações sobre o aleitamento.* Tese de doutoramento, Faculdade de Medicina da Bahia. Salvador, 1855.
Victória, João da Costa Pinto. "Família Costa Pinto." *Revista do Instituto Genealógico da Bahia* 11 (1959): 17–110.
Vilhena, Luis dos Santos. *A Bahia no século XVIII.* Original title *Cartas de Vilhena: Recopilação de notícias soteropolitanas e brasílicas contidas em XX cartas* (1922). 3 vols. Edited by Braz do Amaral. Salvador, 1969.
Wagley, Charles. "Luso-Brazilian Kinship Patterns: The Persistence of a Cultural Tradition." In *Politics of Change in Latin America*, edited by Joseph Maier and Richard W. Weatherhead, pp. 174–89. New York, 1964.
————, ed., *Race and Class in Rural Brazil.* New York, 1952.
Warren, Donald. "The Healing Art in the Urban Setting, 1880–1930." Paper presented to the Symposium on Popular Dimensions of Brazil, University of California, Los Angeles, February 1–2, 1979.
Weber, Max. *Economy and Society.* 2 vols. Berkeley, 1978.
Westphalen, Bach & Krohn / Bahia, 1828–1928. N.p., 1928.
Wetherell, James. *Brazil. Stray Notes from Bahia: Being Extracts from Letters, &c., During a Residence of Fifteen Years.* Edited by William Hadfield. Liverpool, 1860.
Wildberger, Arnold. "O Marechal de Campo Francisco Pereira de Aguiar." *Revista do Instituto Genealógico da Bahia* 9 (1954): 17–112.
————. *Meu pai, Emil Wildberger, 1871–1946: Um suiço a serviço da Bahia.* Salvador, 1979.
————. *Notícia histórica de Wildberger & Cia., 1829–1942.* Salvador, 1942.
————. *Os presidentes da província da Bahia, efetivos e interinos, 1824–1889.* Salvador, 1949.
Willems, Emílio. "On Portuguese Family Structure." *International Journal of Comparative Sociology* 3, 2 (December 1962): 65–79.
————. "The Structure of the Brazilian Family." *Social Forces* 31, 4 (May 1953): 339–45.
Williams, Raymond. *Keywords: A Vocabulary of Culture and Society.* New York, 1976.
Wirth, John. *The Politics of Brazilian Development, 1930–1954.* Stanford, 1970.
————. *Minas Gerais in the Brazilian Federation, 1889–1937.* Stanford, 1977.
Wright, Angus Lindsay. "Market, Land and Class: Southern Bahia, Brazil, 1890–1942." Ph.D. diss., University of Michigan, 1976.
Zeca. "Pedacinhos." *Mensageiro da Fé* 23, 10 (May 17, 1925): 79.

Index

In this index an "f" after a number indicates a separate reference on the next page, and an "ff" indicates separate references on the next two pages. A continuous discussion over two or more pages is indicated by a span of page numbers, e.g., "57–59." *Passim* is used for a cluster of references in close but not consecutive sequence.

Library of Congress Cataloging-in-Publication Data

Borges, Dain Edward.
    The family in Bahia, Brazil, 1870–1945 / Dain Borges.
        p.   cm.
    Includes bibliographical references and index.
    ISBN 0-8047-1921-7
        1. Family—Brazil—Bahia (State)—History—19th century.
    2. Family—Brazil—Bahia (State)—History—20th century.
    3. Upper classes—Brazil—Bahia (State)—History—19th
    century.   4. Upper classes—Brazil—Bahia (State)—
    History—20th century.   5. Elite (Social sciences)—
    Brazil—Bahia (State)   6. Bahia (Brazil : State)—
    Social conditions.   I. Title.
    HQ594.15.B34B67   1992
    306.85'0981'42—dc20   91-44471
                                                        CIP